Wuest's Word Studies

VOLUME THREE

Wuest's Word Studies

From the Greek New Testament

FOR THE ENGLISH READER

Volume Three

GOLDEN NUGGETS
BYPATHS — TREASURES
UNTRANSLATABLE RICHES
STUDIES IN THE VOCABULARY
GREAT TRUTHS TO LIVE BY

by

Kenneth S. Wuest

Wm. B. Eerdmans Publishing Company
Grand Rapids, Michigan 49502

GOLDEN NUGGETS
From the Greek New Testament

To My Wife

JEANNETTE IRENE WUEST

My Companion and Co-Laborer in the
Gospel

Foreword

Among the gifts which the glorified Christ has bestowed upon His body, the Church, is that of "teachers" (Eph. 4:11). How grateful we should be that it is so, and how deeply indebted we are to those Spirit-filled men and women who have brought to our minds and hearts, by word of mouth and the printed page, precious truths from God's holy Word.

The author of this book possesses the gift of teaching to an unusual degree, and his faithful exercise of this gift, in the classrooms of The Moody Bible Institute of Chicago, on the public platform, as well as over the radio, combined with a humble dependence upon the energy of the Holy Spirit, has made his ministry of untold value to multitudes of believers.

The material in these pages has been broadcast over the Institute station, WMBI, Chicago, and has proved to be so helpful, that Mr. Wuest was asked to send it forth in printed form. The studies are brief and to the point, thoroughly scriptural in every respect, and so carefully worded that they may be clearly understood by the reader who has no knowledge of the Greek New Testament, and at the same time will furnish seed thoughts to the seasoned Bible student, teacher and preacher which will lead out into the refreshing streams of deep truth.

So far as we know, this book is unique in the field of Bible exposition, being the first of its kind to appear. We predict that it will be enthusiastically received, more enthusiastically read, and most enthusiastically reread. May God be pleased to richly bless its author and readers.

WENDELL P. LOVELESS

Director, Radio Department,
The Moody Bible Institute of Chicago.

Preface

The purpose of this book is to make available to the Bible student who is not familiar with the original text, the added richness and light which a study of the Greek Scriptures brings.

The reliable English versions give the meaning of the Greek in a translation which is held down to the fewest possible words which will best convey to the reader the thought of the original. However, no translation is able to bring out all that is in the Greek. There are delicate shades of meaning, vivid word pictures, language idioms, that no standard version can handle. These we will seek to bring out.

Then again, some English words have changed their meaning, and we must substitute a word in use today that will better express the meaning of the Greek word. Finally we have come in these latter years to a better knowldge of the Greek language, and therefore in some instances can offer a clearer translation.

But we must not let these facts disturb our confidence in and dependence upon our reliable translations. We are concerned here with minor details, not with the great outstanding eternal doctrines and facts in God's Word. Most men have been saved and have grown in grace through faith in the Word in its translated form. The Holy Spirit owns and quickens the translated Word, and has done so from the beginning. Therefore, as we seek to bring out from the Greek text aspects of truth that the translations do not handle, let us thank God for these translations which He has given us, and receive with gratefulness any added light which the labors of Bible students have been able to gather from the original text.

K.S.W.

The Moody Bible Institute,
Chicago, Illinois.

CONTENTS

CONTENTS—Continued

1

The Peculiar People of God

❡ THE WORD "peculiar" is found in Titus 2:14. Christians are the peculiar people of God. We use the word sometimes when we speak of something odd or strange. But that is not its use here. The word is translated from a Greek word which is made up of two words, one which means "around," as a circle, and the other which means "to be." It can be charted by a dot within a circle. This will help us to understand the meaning of the combined word. As the circle is around the dot, so God is around each one of His saints. The circle monopolizes the dot, has the dot all to itself. So God has His own all to Himself. They are His own private unique possession. He has reserved them for Himself. The expression in I Thessalonians 1:1, "The church of the Thessalonians in God," has in it the same idea, for the Greek case is locative of sphere. That is, it is in the sphere of God, circumscribed by God, surrounded by Him.

This is a place of high privilege. In I Peter 2:7, the Greek has it, "Unto you who believe, is the preciousness." That is, the preciousness of Jesus is imputed to us. He becomes our preciousness in the eyes of the Father as He becomes our righteousness before the law. The Son dwells in the bosom of the Father, closest to the Father's

15

affections. Marvellous grace, that we sinners saved by grace are brought into that favored place closest to the Father's affections. The Father loves us as much as He loves His only begotten Son. What a pillow on which to rest our weary hearts when going through a testing time.

This is also a place of protection. Place a dot outside of the circle, and draw an arrow from that dot to the dot inside the circle. Label that dot a temptation. As the arrow cannot reach the dot except it go through the circle, so no temptation can reach us except it go through the permissive will of God first. As we walk in the center of God's will, He will not permit the Devil to confront us with a temptation too great for us, but will provide us with the necessary faith and spiritual strength to overcome it. Victory over sin is a guaranteed fact when we are in the center of God's will. Put another dot outside the circle. Run an arrow to the dot inside. Label the outside dot "a trial or testing time." As the arrow cannot reach the dot inside unless it goes through the circle, so no time of testing, no sorrow, can reach the child of God who dwells in the center of His will, unless it comes through the permissive will of God, and when it reaches us, God sees to it that all needed grace is given to bear that trial. He is the God of all grace who comforts us in all our afflictions. And this is what Paul means in I Corinthians 10:13 when he says, "There hath no temptation taken you but such as is common to man: but God is faithful, who will not suffer you to be tempted above that ye are able; but will with the temptation also make a way of escape, that ye may be able to bear it." The

Greek word translated "temptation" has two meanings, first, "a time of testing or trial," second, "a solicitation to do evil." We are the peculiar people of God, all His own, closest to His affections, under His protecting care, the recipients of all needed comfort and grace.

God in His wisdom plans the test, and limits the temptation. God in His love sends the test, and permits the temptation. God in His grace meets the test, and overcomes the temptation. In His wisdom He plans and limits. The purpose of Christian suffering is that it is a means whereby sin is put out of our lives and likeness to Jesus produced. "We must be ground between the millstones of suffering before we can become bread for the hungry multitudes." In His love He sends and permits. Christian suffering shows God's love for that saint. God wants him more to Himself. In His grace He meets and overcomes. The grace of God is sufficient to surmount every difficulty, comfort any sorrow, overcome any temptation.

2

The Christian and Trench Warfare

❡ THERE ARE some interesting word studies in Galations 5:16-17. Those we will study are "walk, Spirit, lusteth, against, contrary, cannot."

The Christian is exhorted to walk in the Spirit. The word "walk" is used in an early Greek manuscript in the sentence, "I am going about in a disgraceful state." The writer of this sentence was commenting upon the kind of life he was living, how he was conducting himself. The form in the Greek shows that it is a command to be constantly obeyed. "Be constantly conducting yourselves in the Spirit." The word "Spirit," referring here to the Holy Spirit, is in the locative of sphere, and could be charted by a dot within a circle. The dot is ensphered within the circle. The exhortation therefore is, "Be constantly conducting yourselves in the sphere of the Spirit." That is, determine every thought, word, and deed by the leading of the Spirit through the Word, and think every thought, speak every word, and do every deed, in an attitude of entire dependence upon the Holy Spirit's empowering energy, "Bringing into captivity every thought to the obedience of Christ" (II Cor. 10:5).

"If we do this, we have God's guarantee and promise that we shall not fulfill the lust of the flesh. The word "flesh" refers here to the fallen depraved nature with which we were born, but whose power was broken when we were saved. The word "lust" has changed its meaning. Today it refers to an immoral desire. When the Authorized Version was translated, it meant what the Greek word means from which it is translated, simply a desire. The desire may be a good one or a bad one, according to the context. The word in the Greek has in this verse a preposition prefixed which intensifies its meaning. It is not only a desire, it is a craving. But as we determine our conduct by what the Spirit leads us to do, and yield to Him for the divine energy with which to do it, we have

God's promise that we will not; there is a double negative in the Greek which strengthens the negation, we will absolutely not fulfill the cravings of the fallen nature.

The explanation of how we are delivered from those cravings and the actions which would satisfy those cravings, is found in verse seventeen. The fallen nature lusts against the Holy Spirit. The same word for "lust" is used as in the previous verse. The flesh has a strong desire again the Spirit. The word "against" is from a Greek preposition which literally means "down." The idea is one of defeat, suppression. One could render the sentence, "The flesh has constantly a strong desire to suppress the Spirit." The work of the Holy Spirit in the believer is two-fold, namely, to put sin out of the life and to produce His own fruit. The fallen nature has a strong desire to suppress the Holy Spirit in the work of His office. But the Holy Spirit has a strong desire likewise to suppress the fallen nature in its attempt to cause the believer to obey its behests. They are contrary to one another. The words "one another" are a reciprocal pronoun in the Greek. The Spirit and the flesh reciprocate the antagonism each has for the other. The word "contrary," speaks of a permanent attitude of opposition toward each other on the part of both the flesh and the Spirit. The picture in the Greek word is that of two opposing armies, each digging a system of trenches for the purpose of holding the land they have and conducting a trench warfare. They have dug themselves in for a long drawn-out contest.

This contest is going on all the time in the heart of every child of God. It continues until the death of the believer. The Holy Spirit is the divine provision for victory over sin, "so that ye may not do the things that ye would desire to do." The part the Christian must play in this trench warfare is found in our previous verse, namely, to be constantly determining his every thought, word, and deed by the leading of the Spirit, yielding to Him for the energy to act in the premises. The entire translation could read, "But I say, be constantly conducting yourselves within the sphere of the Spirit, and ye shall not fulfill the cravings of the flesh. For the flesh has constantly a strong desire to suppress the Spirit, and the Spirit has as constantly a strong desire to suppress the flesh, and these are entrenched in a permanent attitude of opposition to one another, so that ye may not do the things that ye would desire to do."

3
The "Falling Away" of Hebrews VI

¶ THERE IS but one sin spoken of in the Book of Hebrews, namely, the act of a first century Jew who has left Judaism and has identified himself with the visible Christian church, who having made a profession of Christ now is in danger under stress of persecution, of renouncing that faith and going back to the abrogated ritual of the Levitical system.

It is described in chapter 2:1 as a "slipping away from the New Testament truth," a "hardening of the heart against the Holy Spirit" (3:7, 8), a "falling away," and a "crucifying the Son of God afresh" (6:6), a "wilful sin" consisting of three-fold sin against the Triune God, "treading under foot the Son of God," a sin against the Father who sent the Son, "counting Jesus' blood as common blood," a sin against the Son who shed His blood, and "doing despite to the Holy Ghost," a sin against the Holy Ghost who led them to the place of repentance (10:26, 29).

The words "falling away" are from a Greek word which literally means "to fall beside a person or thing, to slip away, to deviate from the right path, to turn aside." From early manuscripts we have two illustrations of its use: "if the terms of the contract be broken," and where it is used of a person who falls back to his earlier interpretation.

These two uses fit exactly into the historical background of the book, and the context in which the word is found. Here is the case of Jews who professed faith in Christ, who going along with the Holy Spirit in His pre-salvation work, had been brought into the place of repentance, to the very threshold of salvation. They had made a contract so to speak with the Spirit, willingly being led along by Him. Now, should they refuse the proffered faith and return to Judaism, they would be breaking their contract which they made with the Spirit.

Again, at one time they had adhered to the sacrificial system of the First Testament. Then they had left it to embrace the New Testament truth. Now, should they return to the temple sacrifices, they would be reverting to their former opinion regarding the same.

These words "falling away," can only refer to the one sin spoken of in this book. It could only be committed in the first century and by a Jew, or a Gentile proselyte to Judaism, and for the reason that conditions since A. D. 70 have been such as to make impossible the committing of that sin. The temple at Jerusalem was destroyed on that date. There are no Jewish sacrifices to leave nor to return to. This was apostasy, a most serious sin. These Jews had been made partakers, "partners," see Luke 5:7, same Greek word, of the Holy Ghost, going along with Him in His pre-salvation work. Now, to reject His further ministrations, was a most serious thing from which act there was no recovery.

4

Does He Feel at Home?

❡ PAUL PRAYS (Eph. 3:17) that Christ may dwell in the hearts of the saints. The word "dwell" is from a Greek word made up of two words, one meaning "to live in a home," and the other, literally meaning "down." Paul prays that our Lord might live in our hearts as His home. He is already in us, therefore Paul's thought must be that He feel at home in our hearts. The tense speaks of finality, the word for "down" speaking of permanency. The full translation is, "That Christ may finally settle down and feel completely at home in your hearts."

It is one thing to be in a person's home, another thing to feel completely at home there. Our Lord condescends to live in the heart of a sinner saved by grace. What an honor to have such a guest in our hearts. Do we make Him feel at home? Does He have free access to all parts of our heart life, or is He shut out from this thing or that? Is He our constant companion or are we occupied at times with persons or things that we feel are not consistent with our fellowship with Him? Is He Lord of our lives, the invited guest to occupy the throne room of our hearts? Many have tried to make Jesus Lord of their lives, and have failed because they have tried in their own strength. No man calls Jesus Lord except by the Holy Spirit. That is why Paul prays that we might be strengthened with might by His Spirit in order that Christ might finally settle down and feel completely at home in our hearts. The secret of the Lordship of Jesus, is a desire that the Holy Spirit make Him Lord of our lives, and a trust in the Spirit to accomplish that for us.

5

Dislocated Saints

℄ WE HAVE the case (Gal. 6:1) of a child of God overtaken in a fault, the Greek word for "overtaken" carrying the idea here of a Christian surprised by the fault itself. He was hurried into sin. He sinned before he knew it. That person needs to be restored. Sin in a Chris-

tian's life that is known and cherished, causes the fellowship between the saint and God to be broken. That which
restores fellowship in confession of that sin (I John 1:9).
This restoration is an act of God.

But sometimes God uses another Christian as a channel
through which He can work to bring the sinning saint to
the place where he will confess the sin. Our verse speaks
of this. The word "restore" is from a Greek word which
means "to reconcile factions, to set broken bones, to set a
dislocation, to mend nets, to equip or prepare." What the
particular meaning is in this instance will be determined
by the context. Paul is speaking of a child of God, a born-
again blood-cleansed believer in the Lord Jesus Christ.
As a believer, that person is a member of the Body of
which Christ is the Head (Eph. 1:22, 23; 5:23, 30), the
figure being that of a human body and a human head, the
saints of this Age of Grace as members of the Body and
thus composing it, and our Lord as the Head of the Body.

The saint with sin in his life is not in correct relationship to his Head and to the rest of the Body, just as an
arm out of joint is not in correct relationship to the body
and the head. But the saint still is a member of the Body
as the dislocated arm is a member of the human body.
Again, the life of the Head still abides in the saint as the
life in the human head still flows through the arm. Once
more, as a dislocated arm is useless to the body and head
and will obey neither, so a saint out of fellowship with his
Lord is useless to both the Body and the Head, and will
obey neither. As a dislocated arm is a hindrance to the

body and head, so is a saint with sin in his life a hindrance to the Church and its Head. As an arm out of joint is a source of pain to both body and head, so is a Christian with sin in his life, a source of heart pain to his fellow saints and his Lord. As a dislocated arm is extremely painful in itself, so a child of God with sin in his life, is a miserable Christian. The longer an arm is out of joint, the more painful it becomes, and the harder it is to put back. The longer a child of God remains in sin, the more miserable he becomes, and the harder it is to restore him to fellowship again. But thank God, he can be restored.

Restoration to fellowship from the standpoint of cleansing from the defilement of sin, is the work of our Lord as Advocate (I John 2:1-2). The restoration spoken of in Galatians is the work of bringing that saint to the place where he will confess that sin. Here God is pleased often to use one of His children. Putting an arm back in joint is a delicate piece of work that should be undertaken only by a doctor, who with utmost gentleness and careful handling skilfully restores the dislocated arm. There is a gentle way and a rough way. The Christian worker must be spiritual to do this work. That is, he must be a Spirit-filled saint. As such, God works through him, gently, tactfully, lovingly, wooing the saint away from his sin and to the place of confession. As the saint prays for his fellow saint and speaks with him, the work is done, done by the Holy Spirit. A Christian worker must do this work in a humble, meek, gentle way, remembering that he himself is subject to temptation and possible sin in his life.

6

Transfigured Saints

❡ WE READ in Matthew 17:2 that our Lord "was transfigured before them: and his face did shine as the sun, and his raiment was white as the light." The word "transfigured" is from a Greek word made up of two words, one word referring to the outward expression one gives to his inmost true nature, the other, signifying a change of activity. We could translate, "His mode of expression was changed before them."

Our Lord's usual mode of expression while on earth in His humiliation, was that of a servant. He came (Mark 10:45) "not to be ministered unto, but to minister, and to give his life a ransom for many." But now, that usual mode of expression was changed. Our Lord now gave expression to the glory of His deity. The word "transfigured" here means that He changed His outward form of expression, namely, from that of a servant to that of Deity.

We have in II Corinthians 11:13-15 another Greek word of the direct opposite meaning, namely, the act of changing the outward expression of that which inwardly remains the same, that outward expression not being representative of that person's inmost nature. Satan, his false apostles and ministers assume an outward expression which does not correspond to their true natures. Before masquerading, and that is what the Greek word means, as an angel of light, Satan gave outward expression to his inmost nature. But in order to mislead the human race and gain followers, he had to pose as an angel of light. He changed that outward expression which was expressive of his inmost nature, and assumed another, which did not correspond to it. Satan masquerades as an angel of light, whereas he is all the while an angel of darkness.

In Romans 12:2, we have both words used. Paul exhorts the saints not to be conformed to this world. Here he uses the word found in our Corinthian passage. Christians must not change their outward expression from that of a true expression of their inmost natures, to an assumed expression not true of their new regenerated inmost being, that assumed expression patterned after the world. He exhorts them instead to be transformed, and here we have the same Greek word which is used in the Matthew passage and translated "transfigured." Saints are to change their outward expression from that which was true of them before salvation, when they gave expression to what was in their indwelling sinful nature, to an expression of their inmost regenerated being. Then they would be transfigured saints.

Thus Paul exhorts the saints not to assume as an outward expression the fashions, habits, speech expressions, and artificiality of this evil age, thus hiding that expression of themselves which should come from what they are intrinsically as children of God. How saints sometimes like to have just a dash of the world about them so as not to appear too unworldly. How a coat of worldliness can cover up the Christ within. But instead, saints are to be transformed, that is, give expression of what they really are, partakers of the divine nature, indwelt by the Spirit. They are to do so by having their inward life renewed by the Holy Spirit so that the Lord Jesus may be seen. Thus they will be transfigured saints. And as our Lord was seen by the disciples, shining resplendent in the glory of His deity, so the saints will shine with a heavenly radiance pervading their thoughts, words, and deeds even on their earthly pilgrimage, lighting many a lost wanderer home amid the darkening shadows of this age.

7

Everlasting Watchfulness

¶ IN LUKE 4:13 we read, "And when the devil had ended all the temptation, he departed from him for a season." The English words "for a season," could imply that there are times when the saint is free from the temptations of Satan, and thus he might relax his vigilance. But the Greek words do not permit of such a thought. The thought in the original text is that Satan departed from our Lord until a more opportune, propitious, or favorable time, when our Lord would be more susceptible to temptation, when Satan could work more effectively. The word "departed" is from a Greek word which literally means "to stand off from." Thus Satan never leaves the saint. alone. If he ceases his activities, it is only that he might stand off from him and wait for a time when the saint is more susceptible to temptation. Therefore, the price of victory over Satan is in everlasting watchfulness, "lest Satan should get an advantage of us, for we are not ignorant of his devices" (II Cor. 2:11).

8
The Needle's Eye

℃ THE RICH young ruler loved his riches so much that they kept him from accepting eternal life from the Son of God. In speaking of the impossibility of such entering the kingdom of God, Jesus uses the illustration of the impossibility of a camel going through the eye of a needle. Some have taught that the needle's eye referred to a gate in the wall of Jerusalem through which by means of much pulling and pushing a camel could finally be taken.

The Greek of Matthew 19:24 and Mark 10:25 speaks of a needle that is used with thread, and Luke 18:25 uses the medical term for the needle used in surgical operations. It is evident that the gate is not meant, but the tiny eye of a sewing needle. This was probably a current proverb for the impossible. The Talmud twice speaks of an elephant passing through the eye of a needle as being impossible. It is therefore impossible for anyone whose love for wealth keeps him from trusting Jesus Christ as Saviour, to be saved.

In answer to the disciples' question, "Who then can be saved?" Jesus says, "The things that are impossible with

men, are possible with God." The word "with" in the
Greek means litterally "beside." Take your stand beside
man on the question of riches and it is impossible to be
saved. But take your stand beside God on the matter, and
the formerly impossible becomes possible.

9

Our Lord's Prayer for Resurrection

❧ FREQUENTLY the fine shades of meaning in the
Greek bring out wonderful truth. In Hebrews 5:7 our
Lord is referred to as the One "who in the days of his
flesh when he had offered up prayers and supplications
with strong cryings and tears unto him that was able to
save him *from* death." The preposition "from" in the
Greek is the key to the understanding of this passage.
There are two prepositions which mean "from," one,
"from the edge of," the other, "out from within." The
first one could be used when one goes from the building,
having stood outside against its wall. The other would be
used when one is inside of a building and goes out from
it. The second is used here.

Our Lord prayed to be saved from the Cross if there
was such a possibility and it was within the will of God.
Not that He was unwilling to suffer for lost sinners, but

His holy soul shrank very properly and naturally from the terrible ordeal of being made sin and of having His Father turn away His face. It was the revulsion of His holy soul from that awful thing called sin, and the natural yearning of His heart for unbroken fellowship with the Father that wrung from His lips that prayer. There in Gethsemane He prayed to be saved from all of this. The first Greek preposition could be used in this case.

But the second one appears in the Greek text. This reference is not to the Gethsemane prayer. Here He prayed to be saved not from the edge of death, but out of death. Here He expected to die, and He prayed to be saved out from under the dominion of death. That meant that He prayed to be raised from the dead. We find His prayer recorded in Psalm 22, a Messianic Psalm which many believe our Lord uttered in its entirety while on the Cross. "But be not thou far from me, O God. O my strength, haste thee to help me. Deliver my soul from the sword; my darling from the power of the dog. Save me from the lion's mouth." This is His prayer for resurrection.

He praises God for answered prayer in the words, "for thou hast heard me from the horns of the unicorns. I will declare thy name unto my brethren." Our Lord's earthly life was saturated with prayer. As the Man Christ Jesus, He prayed His way through His ministry even to the very end. What a lesson to us. Let us live prayer-saturated lives.

10

God's University for Angels

⟨ IN Ephesians (3:10) we read that one of the purposes of Paul's ministry was "that now unto the principalities and powers in heavenly places might be known by the church the manifold wisdom of God." The word "by" is from a Greek preposition which speaks of intermediate agency. It is through the agency of the Church, that the holy angels are learning the manifold wisdom of God. The angels were created before this universe was brought into existence through the creative act of God, for they shouted for joy at the beauty of the original creation (Job. 38:7). The universe is very old, millions of years, as shown by the science of astronomy. The angels have been contemplating the majesty and the glory of the Godhead all those years, and yet have not learned some things regarding their Creator which the Church can teach them. Peter in his first epistle (1:12) tells us what those things are which "the angels passionately desire to bend low and look into." The angels never had a conception of the love, the grace, the humility, the self-sacrifice of God until they saw it in the Church. There they see Calvary where the Creator died, the Just for the unjust. There they see the incarnation where the Creator took to Himself the form and limitation of a created being. There they see the power of God in transforming a sinful human being into the image of God's dear Son, manifestation of power far greater than that which operated in the creation of the universe. God spoke a universe into being by uttering a word. It took Calvary to make possible the Church. Thus, the Church provides a university course for angels. How they watch us. How they wonder at us. Beings lower than angels in the scale of creation, raised in Christ to beings higher than angels, into the family of God.

The translation is as follows, "In order that the variegated wisdom of God might be known to the principalities and authorities in the heavenlies through the intermediate agency of the Church."

11

The Fullness of the Spirit

❧ THERE ARE four grammatical rules in the Greek language which lead us to four truths relative to this great subject. The words in Ephesians 5:18 are, "Be filled with the Spirit." First, the verb is in the imperative mode. That is, it is imperative that we be filled with the Spirit, first, because God commands it, second, because the fullness of the spirit is the divine enablement in the life of a Christian which results in a Christ-like life. Failure to be filled with the Spirit is sin and results in failure to live a life honoring to God.

Second, the tense of the verb is present, and this tense in the imperative mode always represents action going on. We learn from this that the mechanics of a Spirit-filled life do not provide for a spasmodic filling, that is, the Christian is not filled only when doing service such as preaching or teaching. But the Christian living a normal life of moment by moment yieldedness to God, experiences a moment by moment fullness of the Spirit. No Christian can do with less and at the same time live a victorious life.

Third, the verb is in the plural number, which teaches us that this command is addressed, not only to the preacher and the deacon, and the teacher in the Sunday School, but to every Christian, to the business man, the laborer, the housewife. It is the responsibility of every Christian to be always filled with the Holy Spirit.

Fourth, the verb is in the passive voice. This grammatical classification represents the subject of the verb as inactive but being acted upon. This teaches us that the filling with the Spirit is not a work of man but of God. We cannot work ourselves up to that condition by any amount of tarrying, praying, or agonizing. A simple desire for that fullness and a trust in the Lord Jesus for that fullness will result in that fullness (John 7:37-39).

But what is meant by the fullness of the Holy Spirit? We find the answer in James 4:5, "Do ye think that the Scripture saith in vain, 'The Spirit that dwelleth in us lusteth to envy'?" The word "lust" is an obsolete English word meaning "to earnestly desire." The translation reads, "The Spirit who has taken up his permanent abode in us constantly and earnestly desires to the point of envy."

Now, what does He desire even to the point of a divine envy? In Galatians 5:17 we read, "For the flesh has a strong desire to suppress the Spirit, and the Spirit has a strong desire to suppress the flesh, and these are firmly settled in an attitude of opposition to one another that you may not do the things which you constantly desire to do." The constant desire of the fallen nature is to sin. The Holy Spirit is the divine provision against sin in the life of a Christian. The evil nature wishes to use the faculties of the believer for sinful purposes. The Holy Spirit desires to use them for God's glory. The choice is with the Christian. He chooses which of the two will control his faculties. Thus the passage in James reads in paraphrase, "The Spirit who has taken up his final abode in us, jealously desires the whole of us." Yieldedness to and dependence upon the Holy Spirit results in the Spirit putting down the evil nature in defeat and producing in the believer a life pleasing to God. Thus, the fullness of the Spirit refers to His control over the believer. The translation of our text is, "Be ye being constantly filled with the Spirit."

12

The Saint's Individual Responsibility

❡ PUNCTUATION in neither the present Greek nor the English texts is inspired. The earliest manuscripts of the New Testament which we possess have no punctuation. The punctuation of Ephesians 4:12, A.V., works havoc with God's plan of operation in the Church, namely, that each saint is expected to be engaged in some form of Christian service as God may lead, for it puts the entire responsibility of proclaiming the Word upon the shoulders of the gifted men who are God's gift to the Church, and requires nothing of the saints to whom they minister.

The men to whom God has given special gifts for ministering in the Word as given in verse eleven are, apostles, prophets, evangelists, and teaching pastors. The construction in the Greek does not allow us to speak of pastors and teachers as two individuals here. The two designations refer to a pastor who has also the gift of teaching. The two gifts go together in the divine economy, and it therefore follows that a God-called pastor is to exercise a didactic ministry. That is, his chief business will be to teach the Word of God. His is a ministry of explaining in simple terms what the Word of God means. The word "pastor" is from a Greek word which means "a shepherd." The illustration is evident. The pastor is to bear the same relationship to the people to whom he ministers, that a shepherd does to his flock of sheep.

Turning to verse twelve, we find that the word "perfecting" is not from the Greek word which refers to spiritual maturity, but from one that has the idea of equipping someone or something so that it might serve the purpose or do the work for which it was brought into being. The English word "ministry" has changed its meaning. Today when we speak of the ministry, we usually have in mind the regularly ordained clergymen of the church. The word has no such meaning here. The Greek word from which it is translated comes by transliteration into our language in the word "deacon," and translated, it means "one who serves." The full translation is as follows: "And he himself gave the apostles, and the prophets, and the evangelists, and the teaching pastors, for the equipping of the saints for ministering work, resulting in the building up of the Body of Christ."

From this translation we see that the pastor of a church, for instance, is a specialist. His work is to teach the Word to the saints, and to train them in the art of winning souls and of teaching and preaching the Word. Each church should be a miniature Bible Institute, a training station from which saints go out to spread the gospel. The pastor thus multiplies himself. He has a ministry to the unsaved, that of preaching the gospel to them, and of winning them to a saving knowledge of the Lord Jesus. But his chief work is to equip the saints to do that work. Since the pastor must specialize in the work of training the saints, it follows that he cannot spend his time and energy upon a thousand and one things in the work of the church which should be done by its members. It is a wise pastor that puts people to work and holds himself to a life of prayer and the ministry of the Word.

Each of us is to engage in some form of Christian service as the Lord leads. It may be a ministry of prayer, or of tract distribution, or of personal work or of teaching the Word, or of song. Thus each saint has his own responsibility in the service of our Lord.

13

The Greek Word for Faith

¶ THE USAGE in early secular documents throws light upon its meaning. In the sentence "whom no one would trust, even if they were willing to work," we see its meaning of confidence in the person's character and motives. The sentence "I have trusted no one to take it to her," speaks of a person's lack of confidence in the ability of another to perform a certain task. From the standpoint of the one trusted we have "I am no longer trusted, unless I behave fairly." Paul uses the word in I Thessalonians 2:4; Galatians 2:7; I Corinthians 9:17; and I Timothy 1:11 "I was put in trust with the gospel, the gospel . . . was committed unto me, the gospel . . . which was committed to my trust." This is the verb usage.

When we come to the noun, we have the meaning of "faith and confidence, fidelity and faithfulness." The adjective gives us "faithful and trustworthy." Paul uses the word in his directions to the Philippean jailer, "Believe on the Lord Jesus Christ, and thou shalt be saved, and thy house" (Acts 16:31). He exhorts him to consider the Lord Jesus worthy of trust as to His character and motives. He exhorts him to place his confidence in His ability to do just what He says He will do. He exhorts him to entrust the salvation of his soul into the hands of the Lord Jesus. He exhorts him to commit the work of saving his soul to the care of the Lord. That means a definite taking of one's self out of one's own keeping and entrusting one's self into the keeping of the Lord Jesus. That is what is meant by believing in the Lord Jesus Christ.

14
About Tents

❡ PAUL WAS a tentmaker. He like every Jewish boy learned some manual trade in addition to his chosen profession. The great scholar made tents for a living while preaching Christ (Acts 18:3). Writing to the Philippians (1:23), he tells them of his conflicting desires, to depart and be with Christ, or to remain with them for their benefit. The words "to depart" are from a military word meaning "to take down one's tent and be off." Paul wrote this in a military camp. Paul's human body was the tent in which he was living. Abraham, Isaac and Jacob (Heb. 11:9), lived in tents. A tent speaks of a pilgrim journey. They were looking for a permanent place of abode. "The Word became flesh and dwelt among us" (John 1:14). The word "dwelt" in the Greek is not the ordinary word which means "to abide," but a verb whose root is our word "tent." Literally, "the Word took up his residence in a tent among us." Out from the ivory palaces, the King of Glory came to live in a tent among a people who lived in tents. What condescension. But that is not all. In Revelation 21:3 we read, literally, "The tent of God is with men, and he will live in a tent in company with them." This tent is the same human body in which our Lord lived while on earth, glorified. Wonder of wonders. The King condescends to live in a tent all through eternity with His Bride. If His Bride lives in a tent, He will. He chose Her for Himself notwithstanding the tent.

15

A Contradiction Cleared Up by the Greek

❡ LUKE WHO wrote the Book of Acts, records for us under the superintendence of the Holy Spirit, Paul's experience on the road to Damascus, as he heard it from the lips of Paul himself (Acts 9). Luke also records Paul's speech of defense to the Jews (Acts 22) as he heard it from Paul. In 9:7 the statement is made that the men with Paul heard the voice of the One speaking to him, and in 22:9, that they did not hear the voice. Here we have a real contradiction in the English translation.

We believe in an infallible inspired text. We claim verbal inspiration for the original Hebrew and Greek manuscripts, and for our present day manuscripts where textual criticism assures us of a correct text, which is in the case of the New Testament, 999 words out of every one thousand. We do not claim verbal inspiration for any translation. Therefore, the Greek text is the final court of appeal.

In the Greek of Acts 9:7, the word "voice" is in the genitive case, and in 22:9, it is in the accusative case. The grammar rule here states that in the first instance, the voice is heard only as a sound. The meaning of the words are not understood. The men with Paul heard the sound but did not understand the words which our Lord spoke to Paul. It states in the second instance, that not only is the voice heard, but the words are understood. Thus the men with Paul did not hear the voice so as to understand the words.

The contradiction is not a contradiction in the Greek text. Child of God, trust your Bible. It is the very Word of God, given by revelation and written down by inspiration.

16

The Husband of One Wife

❡ "A BISHOP then must be . . . the husband of one wife" (I Tim. 3:2). The nouns are without the definite article, indicating that character is stressed. The teaching is that a bishop can only marry once. Expositors Greek Testament says: The better to ensure that the bishop be *without reproach*, his leading characteristic must be self-control. He must have a high conception of the sexes, a married man who, if his wife dies, does not marry again. Men whose position is less open to criticism may do this without discredit. But the bishop must hold up high ideals. Alford says that the words do not mean that the bishop should have only one wife at a time, since polygamy was unknown in the early Church, also, how far such a prohibition is binding today, now that the Christian life has entered into another and totally different phase, is an open question. The Revised Standard Version has, "married only once."

17

Contact

❮ IN MARK 6:48 we read of our Lord "walking upon the sea." The preposition in the Greek is used with a certain case which means that the idea of actual contact is in mind. Our Lord was not in any mysterious way moving over the general surface of the water, but was walking upon it, His feet contacting the surface of the water just as naturally and really as our feet have contact with the hard surface of the pavement.

In Revelation 5:10, the Church is seen in heaven after the Rapture. Its song includes the words "We shall reign on the earth." The same preposition and case is used as in Mark 6:48, which means that the Church saints, associated with our Lord in reigning over this earth, will have contact with this earth in the Millennium. That means that millions of glorified saints will be visible object lessons of what God's grace can do for a poor lost sinner.

God will use us in His last great attempt to save the lost of the human race, in that last great harvest of souls (Acts 15:17) before the final judgment at The Great White Throne.

18

Why Worry?

❡ IN PHILIPPIANS 4:6 we are exhorted to be careful for nothing. We have here a word that has changed its meaning. Today it means to exercise caution. When our translation was made it meant to be full of anxious care. The Greek word is used in a second century sentence, "I am writing in haste to prevent your being anxious, for I will see that you are not worried." The word therefore is a synonym for the word "worry." The force of the word in the Greek is that of forbidding the continuance of an action already going on. Thus the translation is, "Stop perpetually worrying about even one thing." The same Greek word is found in Matthew 6:25 and is translated, "Take no thought." We have the same force of the Greek here. "Stop perpetually worrying." This recognizes the habitual attitude of the unsaved human heart toward the problems and difficulties of life. God commands us to "Stop perpetually worrying about even one thing." We commit sin when we worry. We do not trust God when we worry. We do not receive answers to prayer when we worry, because we are not trusting.

But this command not to worry is founded upon a reasonable basis. That is, there is a reason why we need not worry. In I Peter 5:7 we have, "Casting all your care upon him, for he careth for you." The word "care" is from the same Greek word. We are commanded to cast all our worry upon Him. The word "cast" is not the ordinary word in Greek which means "to throw," but one which signifies a definite act of the will in committing to Him our worries, giving them up to Him. That means that we are through worrying about the matter. We will let God assume the responsibility for our welfare in the premises. And that is just what He desires to do. We are to commit to Him all our worries, or the things that would worry us if we assumed the responsibility, because He cares for us. But the word "careth" is not the word for "worry" in the Greek. The expression in the original means literally, "it is a care to him concerning you." That is, your welfare is His concern. He in bringing you in salvation into His family, has undertaken the responsibility of caring for your welfare. Therefore, if that is true, why worry?

There is on record in an early Greek manuscript, the name of a man called Titedios Amerimnos. The first name is a proper name. The second name is made up of the word which means "to worry," with the Greek letter Alpha prefixed to it which makes the word mean the opposite of what it formerly meant. It is thought that this man was a pagan Greek who perpetually worried, but who after being saved, stopped worrying. So he was called, "Titedios, the Man who Never Worries." Can we write our name and add to it, "The One Who Never Worries"?

19

Bondslaves

❡ IN ROMANS˙ 6:16-18, the word "servants" is from a Greek word that has its derivation in a word which means "to bind." Thus the word in Romans refers to one who is bound to another, a slave. There are two words in Greek referring to a person in slavery. One speaks of a slave taken in war. The other refers to a person born into slavery. The latter is the one used in Romans.

It presents the slave in various aspects. He is one bound to his master. We who believe in the Lord Jesus as our Saviour, were once bound to Satan in the bonds of sin. We were his bondslaves. Now we are bound to our Lord Jesus by the bonds of an eternal life. Again, this slave is in a permanent relationship to his master which only death can break. We were in permanent relationship to Satan until by our identification with Christ in His death, those bonds were broken. Now we are in permanent relationship to Jesus Christ, a relationship which only death could break. But praise God, because He lives, we live, and since He never dies, we will never die. We are His bondslaves forever. And yet again, this slave is one born into slavery. We were born into slavery to Satan by our first birth. We are born by our second birth into slavery to Jesus Christ, into a glorious free, blessed, condition in which we are His loving bondslaves forever. In addition to that, the word refers to one whose will is swallowed up in the will of another. Before we were saved, our wills were swallowed up in the will of Satan. We walked according to the prince of the power of the air. Now our wills as we yield to the Holy Spirit's fullness, are swallowed up in the will of Another, our blessed Lord. "Have thine own way Lord," is the song of our hearts. The word also refers to a slave who is devoted to the interests of his master to the extent that he disregards his own interests. While we were Satan's slaves, we served him to the disregard of our own best interests, for the wages we received from him was death. We recklessly served him, no matter how dearly we paid for it. And now, are we as bondslaves of Jesus Christ, serving Him to the disregard of our own interests? Are we serving Him just to the point where it starts costing us something, and we are stopping there? Or are we in utter abandonment of self serving Him, not counting the cost, not counting our lives dear to ourselves?

What an example we have in the apostle Paul. His favorite designation of himself is that of a bondslave of Jesus Christ. His apostleship comes next. He counts all things but loss for the excellency of the knowledge of his Lord.

20

Intense Christianity

❡ IN PHILIPPIANS 1:20, the apostle Paul has an earnest expectation and hope that Christ shall be magnified in his body whether it be by life or by death. He was awaiting trial before Nero, the Roman emperor. The intensity of Paul's Christianity is seen in the words "earnest expectation." They are one word in the Greek which in turn is made up of three words meaning respectively, "away, the head, to watch." They together speak of a watching with the head erect or outstretched, hence a waiting in suspense, the first word meaning "away" or "from," implying abstraction, the attention turned from other objects. The word is used in the Greek classics of the watchman awaiting the beacon which is to announce the capture of Troy.

With such intensity of purpose Paul desired that Christ be magnified in his body, whether in a life of continued service for the Lord Jesus, or by a martyr's death. The word "magnified" is from a Greek word made up of a verb meaning to "unloose or set free," and an adjective meaning "great." The English word "magnify" which is used to translate this word means to take something small in size and make it appear large by means of a magnifying glass. But the Greek word literally means "to greatly unloose or set free," in this context, "to display in a way so that Christ may be seen in all His glory." The word is used in an early secular document in the sense of "get glory and praise." Paul's intense desire is that the Lord Jesus indwelling His heart may be allowed freedom of action in Paul so that being greatly unloosed or set free, that is, not hindered in His manifestation of Himself through the Holy Spirit by anything which Paul might do, He might get glory and praise to Himself whose right it is to be glorified, and that, either in Paul's life or by his death. That is, Paul's thought is that nothing really matters except that his Lord is glorified. His own circumstances and wishes do not come in for consideration. Oh, for such an intensity of purpose in our Christian lives today.

21

The Natural and the Spiritual Body

❡ PAUL SAYS in I Corinthians 15:44, "It is sown a natural body, it is raised a spiritual body." The first expression refers to the human body as it comes into the world. The second expression refers to that same body raised from the dead. We will study the two words, "natural" and "spiritual."

The word "natural" is from the word which the Greeks used to designate the soul of man. The word "spiritual" is from a word which speaks of the spirit of man. A human being is composed of three parts. With his physical body he has world consciousness. His five senses located in this body receive sense impressions from the outside world. With his soul he has self-consciousness. He knows that he is a personality. With his spirit, he has God-consciousness. He is enabled to know that there is a God, and to worship that God when that spirit, dead because of sin, is made alive by the operation of the Holy Spirit.

The body as it exists before death is a natural or "soulicle" body. That is, it is so constituted that most of its activities are concerned with the individual's experience on earth, in his adjustments to his fellow man, his work, his play, himself. The human spirit functions at the same time, enabling man to adjust himself to the religious environment which surrounds him. If he is a pagan, he worships idols and participates in the ceremonies of the idol's temple. If his human spirit is quickened by the Holy Spirit as part of the saving work of God, he is enabled to worship God and participate in the service of the Lord Jesus. But this constitutes a lesser part of his life than that occupied by the activities of the soul. But it is the determining factor. The type of spiritual life determines the quality of the soul life. Thus the body we have now is a natural body, one in which the spiritual life is not absent, but where it occupies not a lesser place but less of one's time and energy, and where the soul life is most prominent in the sense of the latter two specifications.

The resurrection body will be a spiritual body. By that we do not mean that it will be composed of some intangible, vapory, illusive substance. It will be a body in which the spiritual life of man will predominate. That is, the individual will be occupied for the most part with the things of God, His worship, His fellowship, His service, while to a far less degree will one be occupied with the soul life. In other words, the tables will be turned. As the song goes, "Eternity's too short to sing Thy praise." This body dominated by the spirit, will be the same body as to identity which we have now, but changed as to composition and life principle. It will be a body of flesh and bones that can be felt by the physical sense of touch as

we have that sense today, for the disciples handled our
Lord's resurrection body with a view to investigating as
to whether or not it was a body of flesh and bones as He
claimed to have (Luke 24:39; I John 1:1). This body
will have no blood, and since the life of the body today is
in the blood, it follows that a new life principle must ani-
mate that body. Our resurrection bodies will be like our
Lord's (Phil 3:20, 21).

22

The Word of God

❡ JOHN USES it as a name for our Lord (1:1).
There are three words in the Greek language for "word,"
one referring to the mere articulate sound of the voice,
another speaking of that sound as the manifestation of
a mental state, and still another, the one used by John, and
whose meaning will be discussed.

The word is Logos. It comes from the verb which
means literally "to pick out or select," thus "to pick
words in order to express one's thoughts," thus "to
speak." It speaks of a word uttered by the human voice
which embodies a conception or idea. It refers not merely to a part of speech but to a concept or idea. Greek
philosophers, in attempting to understand the relationship
between God and the universe, spoke of an unknown
mediator between God and the universe, naming this mediator, "Logos." John tells them that this mediator un-

known to them is our Lord, and he uses the same name "Logos." Our Lord is the Logos of God in the sense that He is the total concept of God, Deity speaking through the Son of God, not in parts of speech as in a sentence composed of words, but in the human life of a divine Person. Our Lord said, "He that hath seen me hath seen the Father," Paul says that (Heb. 1:1-2) whereas in times past God spoke to Israel using the prophets as mouthpieces, He now has spoken in the Person of His Son. Our Lord is therefore the Word of God in that He is Deity told out.

The definite article appears before "Word." He is not merely a concept of God among many others, for the heathen have many concepts of God. He is THE concept of God, the only true one, the unique one. He was in existence when things started to come into being through the creative act of God. He existed before all created things. Therefore, He is uncreated, and therefore eternal in His being, and therefore God.

The Word was with God. The word "with" is from a preposition meaning literally "facing." Thus the Word is a Person facing God the Father. The article appears before the word "God" in the Greek, which indicates that the First Person of the Trinity is meant. Thus, John is speaking of the fellowship between the Word, Jesus Christ, and the Father, a fellowship that existed from all eternity and will exist to all eternity, and which was never broken except at that dark mysterious moment at Calvary when the Son cried, "My God, my God, why hast thou forsaken me?"

The Word was God. Here the word "God" is without the article in the original. When it is used in that way, it refers to divine essence. Emphasis is upon quality or character. Thus, John teaches us here that our Lord is essentially Deity. He possesses the same essence as God the Father, is one with Him in nature and attributes. Jesus of Nazareth, the carpenter, the teacher, is Very God.

"In the beginning was the Word (total concept of God), and the Word was in constant fellowship with God (the Father), and the Word was (as to His essence or nature) God."

23

Luke, the Greek Historian

❧ LUKE WAS a Greek, educated in the Greek schools, prepared for the medical practice which was held in high regard as a profession, and among the Greeks had attained to a place of eminence among the nations of the world. Greek doctors of medicine were in attendance upon many of the royal families of other nations.

The Greeks were by nature and training, a race of creative thinkers who pursued their studies in a scientific manner. Their sense of what really constituted scientific accuracy and method in the recording of history was well developed. The writings of Luke, both his Gospel and The Acts, demonstrates Luke's training as an historian.

He writes his Gospel to a Gentile friend, Theophilus. The name means "a god-lover," or "god-beloved," and may have been given him when he became a Christian.

The words "most excellent" according to Ramsay, were a title like "Your Excellency," and show that he held office, perhaps was a Knight. Luke wrote the Gospel for Theophilus to use as a standard whereby to judge the accuracy of the many uninspired accounts of our Lord's life which were written in the first century. The facts he records were most surely believed by the first century church. Luke arranges the facts of our Lord's life in historical order as they occurred. The other Gospels do not claim to do that. The arrangement of events was dictated by the purpose which each author had in writing his account.

The sources of Luke's information were oral and written, from eye-witnesses of the events recorded. He as a trained historian would carefully check over these accounts, investigating and verifying every fact. And this is what he has reference to when he uses the words "having had perfect understanding of all things from the very first." The words "having had perfect understanding" are literally, "having closely traced." The verb means "to follow along a thing in the mind." The word was used for the investigation of symptoms. Thus it speaks of a careful investigation of all sources, oral and written, which purport to be accounts of our Lord's life.

Luke had the historian's mind, a thing native to the educated Greek. Herodotus, the father of Greek history, exhibited the Greek determination to get at the truth no matter how much work it required, when he travelled to central Africa to verify the account of the annual rise and fall of the Nile River. In those days this was a long and difficult journey. Sir William Ramsey said, "I regard

Luke as the greatest historian who has ever lived, save only Thucydides." Thus we have no doubt but that Luke made a personal investigation of all the facts he had recorded. He interviewed every witness, visited every locality. If Mary was still alive, he, a doctor of medicine investigated the story of the virgin birth by hearing it from Mary's own lips. And as Professor John A. Scott, a great Greek scholar has said, "You could not fool Doctor Luke."

But Luke was not dependent alone upon his personal investigations for the accuracy of his record. He says that he closely traced all things *from above*. The words "from above" are from a Greek word translated "from the very first," in the Authorized Version. The word occurs in John 3:31; 19:11; James 1:17; 3:15, 17, and is in every instance translated "from above." It is used often in contrast to a word which means "from beneath." Paul had doubtless heard the account of the institution of the Lord's Supper from the eleven, but he also had it by revelation from the Lord (I Cor. 11:23). He had received his gospel by direct revelation in Arabia, and this was his check upon the gospel he heard at Jerusalem from the apostles.

So Luke claims to have closely investigated the facts he had received, and to have done so through the inspiration of the Holy Spirit, which fact guarantees the absolute accuracy of the record (Luke 1:1-4).

24

The Indestructibility of the Church

❡ PETER HAD just given his testimony to the fact that Jesus Christ is God. That was his estimation of his Lord. Now Peter's Lord gives His estimation of Peter. Peter's original name was Simon. Our Lord adds the name Cephas, which in Aramaic means "a stone" (John 1:42), as a descriptive name that will show the character of Simon in the days when the Holy Spirit should fill him. Our Lord in Matthew 16:18 reminds Peter of his future character by the same designation, Matthew however reporting the name by the Greek word which means "a little rock," from which word we obtain the English name "Peter."

Having finished his appraisal of Peter which answered to Peter's appraisal of his Lord, Jesus uses Peter's estimation of Him as a basis for a further declaration. He declares that His deity is the rock upon which He will build His Church. The second word "rock" is from a different form of the word than that which is translated by the name "Peter." It refers to a large massive rock like Gibraltar. Thus Peter is not the rock foundation of the Church. The deity of Jesus Christ is the foundation.

Because the foundation of the Church is the deity of Jesus Christ, the church is indestructible. The declaration of our Lord is that the gates of hell shall not prevail against it. We will study the three words, "prevail," "hell," and "gates." The word "prevail" is from a Greek word which means "to overpower, to be strong to another's detriment." Thus the indestructibility of the

Church is in view here. The word "hell" is from a Greek word which is brought over into our English language in the word "Hades." This is not the translation of the word, but its transliteration. In the former we bring over the meaning of a word into another language, in the latter, its spelling. The pagan Greeks designated the world of departed human beings by the name "Hades." It had two compartments, one for the evil doers, Tartarus, and one for those who were good, Elysium. These were the permanent abodes of the dead. Likewise, the word "Hades" is used in Christian terminology to designate the place of departed human beings, it being divided into a place for the unrighteous dead, and one for the righteous. The former is still occupied and the place where the unsaved go, but the latter is empty, for the righteous dead which occupied that place before the resurrection of our Lord are now in heaven, and believers since that great event go at once to be with their Lord.

The question comes, then, as to who in Hades would have the power to wage war against the Church. Surely the unsaved dead are powerless in the premises. The saints there at the time our Lord uttered these words would have no such desire. It follows therefore that Hades cannot be referred to here. We turn from the transliteration of the Greek word to its translation. The word is made up of one word which means "to see," and the Greek letter Alpha, which when prefixed to a word causes it to have the opposite meaning to that which it originally had. The word means therefore "not to see," and in its noun form, "the unseen." It refers to the unseen world, that world of personalities that is unseen. The unseen world of the Christian system includes the place called Hades, and also the kingdom of Satan and his demons in the air. Hades is eliminated as a possible enemy of the Church. The logical enemy therefore in view here is Satan and his kingdom.

Now as to the word "gates." The idea of literal gates is out of the question here, for the unseen world has no boundaries. When the term is not used to refer to literal gates, it is used in its oriental sense, that of referring to a council or ruling body whose meeting place in ancient times was the gates of the city. Lot sat in the gate of Sodom (Gen. 19:1), that is, he was one of the officials of the council ruling the city. Boaz took care of a legal matter at the gate of Bethlehem (Ruth 4). Our Lord suffered outside of the gate (Heb. 13:12), not of Jerusalem here, although that was true, but outside of the jurisdiction of the First Testament. The word therefore refers here to a council. The councils of the Unseen will not overcome the Church, that is, the councils of Satan and his demons, for it is founded upon a Rock, even our God and Saviour Jesus Christ.

25

Entree

¶ IN ROMANS 5:2, Paul speaks of the fact that we have access through our Lord into the grace in which we stand. The word "access" is from a Greek word which refers to the act of one who secures for another an interview with a sovereign.

In the first place, the person thus acting must be close to the king himself. Our Lord dwells in the bosom of the Father. He occupies the place closest to the Father's affections. He is therefore fitted for His task. In the second place, the one for whom this entree has been gained, and the French word most happily gives the meaning of the Greek, must be rendered acceptable to the king. This our Lord did through the blood of His Cross whereby He put away the guilt and penalty of our sin and bestowed upon us a righteousness, even His own standing before the Throne, and thus we are "accepted in the Beloved." As I Peter 2:7 says, "Unto you therefore that believe is the preciousness." The preciousness of Jesus in the eyes of God the Father has been imputed to us, as His righteous standing has been imputed. God therefore looks upon us with all the favor with which He looks upon His own well-beloved Son. Then again, the one presented at the High Court of Heaven must be correctly attired. Our Lord clothes us with His own beauty, for He is made unto us sanctification, Paul says. The Father sees us in His Son, not apart from Him. And the glorious radiance of the One Altogether Lovely shines upon us. Finally, when we have been brought by Him into the place where we have entree into the presence of God, we find that we are standing in His unlimited favor, in unlimited grace. No demand made upon that grace can exhaust it. For time and eternity we are the objects of the Father's supreme affection, the recipients of His boundless mercies, the favored ones of His matchless grace. Hallelujah! Praise the Lord "by whom we have our permanent entree by faith into this grace in which we stand."

26
Concerning Fellowship With Jesus

❦ I JOHN is the epistle of fellowship. It is a family letter written to the children of God. This fellowship is therefore only between the saved person and God, not the unsaved.

The word "walk" (1:7), is from a Greek word which appears in a second century manuscript in the sentence, "I am going about in a disgraceful state," the words "going about" being its translation. The word refers to conduct. Our conduct consists of our thoughts, words, and deeds. The action in the word is continuous, "If we are constantly walking in the light." The normal experience of a Christian should be just that, a life constantly lived according to the Word of God.

The word "fellowship" is from a Greek word which means "to have in common with." The basis of human fellowship is a common nature. An artist and a ditch-digger have no fellowship because they have no common nature, but two artists do, for their natures are the same. So with man's fellowship with God. If a man is to have fellowship with God he must have a common nature. Man has a nature subject to wrath (Eph. 2:3). But in answer to faith in the Lord Jesus as Saviour, a believing sinner is made a partaker of the divine nature (II Peter 1:4), thus having a common nature with God. As a result he has common likes and dislikes. The Christian who loves what Jesus loves and hates what Jesus hates has fellowhip with Him. The person who loves what Jesus hates, namely, sin, does not have fellowship with Him.

The fellowship here is not between Christian and Christian, but between the Christian and God, for the theme of the Book (1:3) "The Believer's Fellowship with God," and the analysis of the section in which this verse is found, "A Condition of Fellowship with God, Walking in the Light," requires the second meaning.

Again, the words, "one with another" are from a reciprocal pronoun in Greek. That speaks of reciprocity, the act of two individuals returning to each other mutual love. This fellowship is not only on the part of the saint with Jesus, but on the part of the Lord Jesus with the saint.

The word "cleanseth" speaks in the Greek of action in progress. The blood of Jesus keeps continually cleansing us from sins of ignorance.

The fuller translation is, "If we are constantly walking in the light as he himself is in the light, we are having constant fellowship with one another, and the blood of Jesus Christ his Son keeps continually cleansing us from all sin."

27

"Agapao" Love

¶ "AGAPAO" speaks of a love which is awakened by a sense of value in an object which causes one to prize it. It springs from an apprehension of the preciousness of an object. It is a love of esteem and approbation. The quality of this love is determined by the character of the one who loves, and that of the object loved.

Agapao is used in John 3:16. God's love for a sinful and lost race springs from His heart in response to the high value He places upon each human soul. Every sinner is exceedingly precious in His sight.

"Phileo," which is another word for love, a love which is the response of the human spirit to what appeals to it as pleasurable, will not do here, for there is nothing in a lost sinner that the heart of God can find pleasure in, but on the contrary, everything that His holiness rebels against. But each sinner is most precious to God, first, because he bears the image of his Creator even though that image be marred by sin, and second, because through redemption, that sinner can be conformed into the very image of God's dear Son. This preciousness of each member of the human race to the heart of God is the constituent element of the love that gave His Son to die on the Cross. The degree of the preciousness is measured by the infinite sacrifice which God made. The love in John 3:16 therefore is a love whose essence is that of self-sacrifice for the benefit of the one loved, this love based upon an evaluation of the preciousness of the one loved. This use of "agapao" is seen also in Ephesians 5:25; Romans 5:5, 8; John 15:9-13; 14:28, 31; I John 4:7-5:3; Matthew 5:43-44. The word is also used in I Corinthians 13, where its content is defined by Paul, the idea of self-sacrifice, of self-abnegation, being found in all its constituent elements in some way.

The word is used in I John 2:15. Here saints are forbidden to set a high value upon the world, namely the

world system of evil, to consider it as precious and thus
have a love for it. Here the love is of the wrong kind, a
sinful love.

28

"Phileo" Love

❡ "PHILEO" is a love which consists of the glow of
the heart kindled by the perception of that in the object
which affords us pleasure. It is the response of the human
spirit to what appeals to it as pleasurable. The Greeks
made much of friendship. The word was used to speak
of a friendly affection. It is a love called out of one in
response to a feeling of pleasure or delight which one
experiences from an apprehension of qualities in another
that furnish such pleasure or delight. "Agapao" on the
other hand, speaks of a love which is awakened by a
sense of value in the object loved, an apprehension of its
preciousness. "Phileo" is found in Revelation 22:15;
Matthew 6:5; 10:37; 23:6; Luke 20:46; John 11:3,36; I
Corinthians 16:22. Those who find pleasure in a lie and
thus love it, will go to a lost eternity. Hypocrites find
pleasure in ostentatious prayer and thus love it. Those
that take more delight in father or mother than in God,
love them better and for that reason. Our Lord found
delight in the response of the heart of Lazarus to His
own and thus loved him. God has a love of delight in
those whose love for Jesus is based upon their delight in

Him. "Phileo" like "agapao" has its quality determined by the character of the one who loves and of the object loved.

"Agapao" is a love springing from a sense of the preciousness of the object loved, while "phileo" arises from a sense of pleasure found in the object loved. When used in a good meaning, both are legitimate, but the first is the nobler word.

In John 21: our Lord uses "apapao" in verses 15 and 16, "phileo" in 17. Peter uses "phileo" three times. Our Lord uses the noblest word in the Greek language the first two times and changes to Peter's word the third time, but assures Peter that his coming martyrdom speaks of the fact that his future love for his Lord will be based not only upon his delight in his Lord but upon his apprehension of His preciousness.

"Phileo" is used in John 16:27. The saints have a love for the Lord Jesus which springs from their joy in Him, a love of delight. The Father has a love of delight in the saints, for He finds in each saint the One in whom He takes delight, the Lord Jesus, and because the saints find their delight in Him also.

29

The Monkey Wrench in the Machinery

❡ PAUL SAYS in Romans 7:15, "That which I do, I allow not." He is describing his experience as a saved person, but one ignorant of the way of living the victorious life. The things he desires to do, namely, good things, he does not do. Things he does not want to do, namely, sinful things, he does do. The power of sin in his life has been broken, and the divine nature implanted. But the correct adjustment to these facts, Paul does not know. Hence the evil nature is still the master. Paul says that this experience he does not "allow." The word "allow" is from a Greek word which means "to know by experience." Paul says in effect, "What I carry out I do not recognize in its true nature, as a slave who ignorantly performs his master's behest without knowing its tendency or result." Paul does not recognize his experience in its true nature. He is acting blindly at the dictates of another, like a slave who does not have the liberty to determine the details of his life for himself because he is governed by another. He is somewhat of an automaton, not quite a machine, but yet a human being without self-determination in his spiritual life. He has the desire to do good but no power to put that desire into practice. He rebels against doing evil, but does not have the power to keep from sinning. He fights as one that blindly beats the air. He is in a spiritual fog. He does not understand his experience, for he is acting involuntarily.

Romans can be likened to a great factory. The sixth chapter takes us to the floors where the machinery is located. There we have the mechanics of the Spirit-filled life, namely, the power of sin broken and the divine nature implanted. The eighth ushers us into the basement where the power to operate that machinery is generated. There we have the dynamics of the Spirit-filled life, the power of the Holy Spirit. Chapters twelve to sixteen take us to the upper floors of the factory where the finished product is on display. Chapter seven is the monkey wrench which, if it falls into the machinery, interferes with its working and thus prevents the production of the finished product. That monkey wrench in the Christian life is self-dependence. All the resources of the Holy Spirit are there to put down sin and produce a Christ-like life, but they are not appropriated because the believer is depending upon self.

Paul never finds the way to a victorious life until he cries out "Who" with a question mark after it. The minute he says that word, he despairs of himself, and despairing of himself, he turns to the Holy Spirit, whom the Lord Jesus has made available to the saint. Instead of self effort, his reliance is upon what God has done for him as recorded in Romans six and upon what the Holy Spirit is doing for him moment by moment as stated in Romans eight.

30

Citizens of Heaven

❡ THE GREEK word translated "conversation" in Phil. 1:27 is found in an early manuscript in the sentence, "I live the life of a member of a citizen body," that is, the writer was fulfilling the duties expected of a citizen of a commonwealth. Indeed, our English word "politics," is a transliteration of this Greek word. Paul exhorts them, "Only be constantly performing your duties as citizens, worthy of the gospel of Christ." In Philippians 3:20 we have the noun, "Our citizenship is in heaven."

Philippi was a Greek city far from Rome, but in the Roman Empire, and a colony of Rome in the sense that its citizens possessed Roman citizenship. The inhabitants of Philippi recognized the emperor of Rome as their sovereign and were obligated to conduct themselves as Roman citizens, just as if they were residents of Rome itself.

Paul was teaching the Philippian saints that just as they constituted a colony of Rome so far as their earthly connections were concerned, so they were also a colony of heaven so far as their heavenly relationships were concerned. They were far from their home country, far from their Sovereign, the Lord Jesus, just a little colony of citizens of heaven in the midst of a godless and perverse generation, among which they were to shine as luminaries, that is the word in the Greek. They were a heavenly people with a heavenly origin, a heavenly citizenship, a heavenly destiny, to live heavenly lives in a foreign land, telling others of a heavenly Father who offered them salvation through faith in His Son. What was true of the Philippian saints then is true of all the saints. We are a heavenly people with the obligation and privilege of living a heavenly life on earth. Some day our Sovereign (Phil. 3:20, 21) will come back for us and take us to our native land, changing this body of our humiliation, fashioning it like to the body of His glory. The word "vile" is obsolete English for our word "humiliation." The physical body has been humiliated by the curse of sin. It will be freed from that curse at the coming of the Lord for His Bride. In the meanwhile, we are to live on earth the same holy life that we would were we walking the streets of heaven.

31

Apostolic Memory

❡ THE Apostle John writing about A. D. 90, says in his first epistle (1:1-3), "That which we have heard, that which we have seen with our eyes, that which we have looked upon and our hands have handled concerning the Word of life . . . declare we unto you." The things he refers to, of course, are recorded in the Gospel which he wrote somewhere between A.D. 85-90. A lapse of 50 to 60 years is quite a long time for one to accurately report the happenings in our Lord's life. Yet John claims to remember them as if they happened but yesterday.

The words "we have heard" are in the perfect tense in the Greek. This tense speaks of an action which was completed in past time whose results still exist in present time. The full translation reads "that which we have heard in times past and which we still retain in our memory." Likewise, the words "we have seen" are in the same tense and are fully rendered, "that which we have seen in times past and which we still have in our mind's eye." John therefore claims that the things which he heard and saw, were still fresh in his mind after all those years. But in the word for "seen" he refers to more than the physical act of seeing, for he uses a word which speaks of discerning sight. The apostles understood the things they saw, and thus could be accurate witnesses and hand down to us a correct account of His life. The translation could read, "that which we discerningly saw with our eyes, and which we still have in our mind's eye."

The next word translated "looked upon" also means "to see," but is a different word. It means literally "to view attentively, to contemplate." No wonder that, after the apostles saw our Lord with discerning eyes, they watched His wonderful life with attention and contemplation. Their question must often have been, "What manner of Man is this?" This verb is not in the perfect tense but in the aorist, the tense used most naturally when the Greek writer does not want to go into detail. John had already informed his reader of his fitness to report what he saw and heard in our Lord's life, and he did not feel the need of repeating that fact.

Then he says, "our hands handled." The verb referred to the act of handling something in order to investigate the nature of that thing. The same word is used in Luke 24:39, where our Lord says, "Handle me and see; for a spirit hath not flesh and bones as ye see me have." One of the evidences of the fact that our Lord was raised out of death in the same body in which He died is that the disciples felt of that body after the resurrection, investigating the claim of Jesus that it was a true physical body of flesh and bones.

Thus, the apostle John when writing his account of our Lord's life had clearly in mind the things he saw our Lord do and heard Him say approximately sixty years before. But how can a man remember so much for so long a time, and with such accuracy? There are two answers, one from the human side, one from the divine. In the first century, there were few books, and consequently people were forced to retain in their memory much more than we do today when we have many books. In fact, many ancient peoples have been known to hand down from generation to generation, large quantities of poetry and prose by committing it to memory. So John remembered much of what he had seen. He may have had access to some written records also. In addition to this, he had the promise of our Lord in John 14:26 that the Holy Spirit would bring all the things Jesus said, to the remembrance of the apostles. We have therefore the answer as to how John could have written the Gospel attributed to him, so many years after the events took place.

32

Working Out Your Own Salvation

¶ BEFORE attempting to explain this passage (Phil. 2:12-13), we must be clear as to what it does not teach. There is no idea here of an unsaved person doing good works to earn salvation, and for two reasons, first, because those addressed were already saved, and second, because the Bible is clear in its teaching that "not by works of righteousness which we have done, but according to his mercy he saved us" (Titus 3:5). Again, the passage does not mean that a Christian should work out an inworked salvation. There is no such idea in the Greek.

The English translation is good, if one uses the words "work out" as one does when referring to the working out of a problem in mathematics, that is, carrying it to its ultimate goal or conclusion. The Greek word here means just this.

The words "your own salvation," are to be taken in
their context. The working out of the Philippians' salvation was affected in some way by the presence of Paul
with them and his absence from them. When Paul was
with them, his teaching instructed them, his example inspired them, his encouragement urged them on in their
growth in grace. Now in his absence they were thrown
upon their own initiative. They must learn to paddle
their own canoe. Thus Paul sets before them their human
responsibility in their growth in grace, for sanctification
is in the apostle's mind. They have their justification.
Their glorification will be theirs in eternity. Their growth
in Christ-likeness is the salvation concerning which Paul
is speaking. Thus, the saints are exhorted to carry their
growth in grace to its ultimate goal, Christ-likeness.
I John 3:2 speaks of the saint's future conformation to
the image of Christ, and (3:3) says, "And every man that
hath this hope set on him purifieth himself even as he is
pure."

The salvation spoken of in verse twelve is defined for
us in verse thirteen, namely, the definite act of willing to
do God's good pleasure and the doing of it. That is the
saint's responsibility from the human standpoint. But
the saint is not left without resources with which to do
both, for God the Holy Spirit indwelling him produces in
him both the willingness and the power to do His will.
The saint avails himself of both of these by fulfilling the
requirements laid down by our Lord in John 7:37, 38,
namely, a thirst or desire for the fullness of the Spirit,
and a trust in the Lord Jesus for that fullness. The literal
translation is as follows: "Wherefore, my beloved, as

ye have always obeyed, not as in my presence only, but now much more in my absence, carry to its ultimate goal your own salvation with fear and trembling, for God is the One who is constantly supplying you the impulse, giving you both the power to resolve and the strength to perform his good pleasure." In verse twelve we have human responsibility, and in verse thirteen, divine enablement.

33

About Saints

⟨ EPHESIANS 1:1 reads, "Paul...to the saints... and to the faithful in Christ Jesus." The word translated "faithful" has the idea here, not of faithfulness in the Christian life, but of the act of believing. But why the double characterization, "saints and believers in Christ Jesus"? Surely, every saint is a believer in the Lord Jesus Christ. The Greek word for "and" can also be translated "even." From a consideration of the historical background of this epistle this is the better translation. Paul was writing to the saints in Ephesus, namely, those saints who were believers in Christ Jesus. Indeed, Paul finds it necessary to define the word "saint" every time he uses it as a term of address in his epistles. In Romans, it is "saints beloved of God," in First and Second Corinthians, "saints sanctified in Christ Jesus," and in Colossians, "saints, even believing brethren in Christ."

In the pagan religions of Greece, we find a word for the act of setting apart a building, an altar, an offering for religious purposes. The object set apart was thus declared sacred, holy, devoted to religious purposes. It applied also to the worshippers. They were set apart persons, thus religious devotees of the temple. The pagan Greek worshippers would therefore in our English language be called saints, for this word coming from the Latin means "holy." The pagan Greeks were holy, not in the sense of our word "holy" which has a certain content of meaning, namely, pure, righteous, free from sin, but holy in the sense of their set-apartness for the worship of their deities. When they acquired the characteristics of their gods, they were saints in conduct as well as in position. Of course, their saintliness consisted of the most degraded forms of sin.

But Paul was not writing to the set apart ones in the pagan mystery religions. Those to whom this letter was addressed were set apart ones in Christ Jesus, set apart by God the Holy Spirit to obedience and sprinkling of the blood of Jesus Christ (I Peter 1:2). They were saints of the Most High God. The word "sanctification" is from the same Greek word and has the same idea, that of setting apart. As set apart ones by God in His worship and service, they gradually acquired through the sanctifying (setting apart) work of the Spirit, more of His characteristics in their experience. Thus their lives became holy, and they were saints in experience as well as in position. The words "sanctify, sanctification, saint, and holy," are all from the same Greek root and have basically the same meaning, namely, "set apart," to be translated and interpreted according to their context. There is positional sanctification, the act of God the Holy Spirit setting believing sinners apart in Christ Jesus. This is an act resulting in a position. There is progressive sanctification, the work of the Holy Spirit producing in the lives of believers, a set apart life consistent with their new position. This is a process, resulting finally in conformity to the image of Christ in glorification.

34

Regarding Peter's Denial of His Lord

❡ MARK 14:71 reports Peter as cursing and swearing when denying his Lord. Some have imagined that Peter was a man given to profanity, for these English words are sometimes used in that connection. The Greek helps us here. The word translated "curse" is the same word which Paul uses in Galatians 1:9, but different from the word translated "curse" in Galatians 3:10. The word in Mark 14:71 and Galatians 1:9 means "to declare anathema or cursed, to declare one's self liable to the severest divine penalties." Thus Peter was calling down upon himself the severest divine penalties if his words were not true.

The word translated "swear" is from the same word in Hebrews 6:13 which means "to take an oath." Thus Peter in denying any connection with Jesus, attempted to convince his accusers of the truthfulness of his words by taking an oath upon that statement. This explanation

does not lessen Peter's guilt in the matter, but clears him
of the charge of profanity, while it also gives one the
correct meaning of the words.

35

The Personality of the Life

❡   THAT ETERNAL life which is given to the believing sinner is not a mere abstraction, not some spiritual energy or dynamic, but a Person, the Lord Jesus.
Paul speaks of "Christ, our life" (Col. 3:4). John speaks
of "the Word of the life" (I John 1:1). The life here is
eternal life. It has the definite article in the Greek,
pointing out the particular life which the Scriptures reveal, not here the Greek word speaking of the necessities
of physical life, such as food, clothing and shelter, but the
word referring to the principle of life. The word "Word"
is in the Greek, not the usual word speaking of a part of
speech, that is, a word in a sentence, but one which
means a word as setting forth a concept, an idea in its
complete presentation. This is the use of the word in
John 1:1, where our Lord is the Word in the sense that
He in His incarnation presents to humanity the picture
or concept of God, God revealed in the Person of His Son
who is Very God Himself. John uses the phrase, "concerning the Word of the life." That is, our Lord is both

the life itself and the embodiment or concept of that life in His incarnation.

This life, John says, was with the Father. The word "with" is from a Greek word whose root meaning is "facing." The life was facing the Father, referring to the pre-incarnate fellowship between the Father and the Son. Fellowship demands personality. Therefore, that eternal life which is ours is a Person, Jesus Christ. Christianity is a Person, Jesus Christ living in and through a believer. The part of the Christian in the plan of salvation, is to allow Him to act freely in him, so that He can manifest Himself through that saint. The secret of this is in yielding to the ministry of the Holy Spirit, trusting Him to enthrone Jesus in his heart.

36

Our Lord's Proclamation in Tartarus

❡ I PETER 3:19 says, "By which also he went and preached unto the spirits in prison." Who were these spirits, what did our Lord preach, and what was this prison? In verse eighteen we offer the translation "being put to death as to the flesh, but being quickened as to the spirit." The word "spirit" in the Greek does not begin with a capital letter in the best texts. The word "flesh" refers to our Lord's human body. He died as to His human body. Then the contrast is maintained. He was quickened, made alive, in spiritual life as to His human spirit. Our Lord, very God, in His incarnation added to Himself a human body, soul, and spirit. It was in this human spirit as quickened by the Holy Spirit, that the Man Christ Jesus preached to the spirits in prison, between His death on the Cross and His resurrection from the tomb.

Now, God is spirit (John 4:24), not a spirit. The indefinite article appears in the A.V., but should not be there. There is no indefinite article in the Greek language. The English indefinite article should only be included in the translation when the original in its context demands it. A spirit is a created intelligence. But God is not created. The absence of the definite article in Greek emphasizes character or quality. The translation could read, "God in His essence is spirit." That is, He is Personality without a body. Human beings have spirits (Heb. 12:23). Angels are spirits (Heb. 1:7).

Our Lord preached to angels in prison. The name of this prison is given us in II Peter 2:4, where the word "hell" is translated from the Greek word "Tartarus," which is distinct from hell, namely, the Lake of Fire, being the prison house of the wicked angels. In both passages Peter connects these angels with the time of the flood, speaking of their disobedience and their sin. They are today in Tartarus awaiting the judgment of the Great White Throne, from where they will be cast into the Lake of Fire. These are the angels whom the saints of the church age will judge (I Cor. 6:3). Their sin consisted of cohabiting with sinful women of the human race and of producing a composite being, part **angel**, part man, the giants in the earth at that time (Gen. 6:6). This seems to have been the work of Satan, attempting to dehumanize the human race, thoroughly impregnate it with angelic nature, and so prevent the incarnation, and therefore the Cross, and therefore his defeat. The flood was God's answer, wiping out the human race which seems to have been more or less permeated by this evil, those in the ark being saved.

What our Lord preached to them is not explicitly revealed, but it was not the gospel, and for several reasons. First, the Greek word which means to preach the gospel is not used, but a word which means merely to proclaim something. It was used of heralds who made an official proclamation of some kind. The word translated "preached" here does not convey within itself the content or nature of the message. It needs a qualifying word as in Acts 8:5, "Philip preached Christ unto them." Second, there is no provision in the atonement for the salvation of angels, for our Lord as the great High Priest did not reach a helping hand to angels, but to the seed of Abraham (Heb. 2:16), for He assumed human, not angelic nature for His substitutionary work on the Cross. Some have surmised that He proclaimed His victory over the fallen angels which He procured at the Cross, the angelic apostasy having for its purpose the defeat of God's plans through the Cross. This portion of the Word does not therefore teach a second chance after death given to the wicked dead to believe the gospel and be saved. "It is appointed unto men once to die, but after this the judgment" (Heb. 9:27).

37

The Lord's Day

❡ JOHN IN REV. 1:10 refers to the fact that he was in the Spirit on the Lord's Day. Opinion is divided as to the meaning of the phrase "on the Lord's Day." Some think that it refers to the Day of the Lord, an expression referring to the Great Tribulation period when the judgment of God will fall upon the earth, and that John was projected ahead in the control of the Holy Spirit to see the things that would take place at that time as recorded in chapters six to nineteen of this book. But the expression, "the Lord's Day," was a technical expression used in the first century, which had a certain content of meaning that requires us to put another interpretation upon it.

In the first place, the expression, "the day of the Lord" is a technical expression with a uniform grammatical arrangement. The phrase, "the Lord's Day," has a different grammatical order, and is found only here. Why, if the inspired writer meant the Great Tribulation, would he change the grammatical form here, in the climax of all the revelations referring to this time? These references are uniform throughout the Bible, and to present a different grammatical form here, would tend to mislead the reader.

In the second place, the expression in the Revelation has a counterpart in first century documents. This form of the word "Lord" was in common use for the sense "imperial," as "imperial finance" and "imperial treasury."

There was an expression, "'Augustus' Day," which was the first day of the month, Emperor's Day, on which money payments were made. It was natural for the Christians to take this term already in use and apply it to the first day of the week in honor of the Lord's resurrection on that day. Thus, the designation, "The Lord's Day," is the scriptural name for the day which is commonly called Sunday, or, by some, the Sabbath.

38

The Mote, the Beam, and The Hypocrite

❡ THE GREEK word translated "mote" (Matthew 7:3-5) was found on a tombstone of the first century in the sentence, "He was not a whit injured," the words "a whit" being the translation of the word. That is, he was not injured in the slightest degree. The word in other connections refers to a straw, or a piece of chaff, a very small particle.

The word for "beam" is found in the early inscriptions referring to logs used for heating the bath, or heavy beams on which a temple was to be built.

A log of that size would distort one's vision regarding a small particle in the eye of another. Our obligation is to put out of our lives those glaring faults that prevent us from properly appraising the character of another, before we seek to deal with the tiny faults of someone else.

The person with a log in his own eye who attempts to deal with the tiny fault of another is a hypocrite. The

Greek word here was used in ancient times to refer to one who judges under a mask. That is the composition of the word. It referred also to the person who played a part on the stage, to an actor, one who pretends to be what he is not. Here the person judging another from back of the mask of his self-righteousness, plays the part of an actor, giving out that he is something which he is not. Therefore, our Lord says, "Stop constantly judging, in order that ye be not judged."

39

Superabundant Grace

❡ IN ROMANS 5:20 the Word tells us, "But where sin abounded, grace did much more abound." The word "grace" is one of the most precious words in Scripture. Archbishop Trench says of this word in the Greek language, "It is hardly too much to say that the Greek mind has in no word uttered itself and all that was in its heart more distinctly than in this." The Greeks were lovers of beauty, in nature, in their architecture, their statuary, their poetry, their drama. Anything which called out of the heart wonder, admiration, pleasure, or joy, was designated by this word. The word came also to signify the doing of a favor graciously, spontaneously, a favor done without expectation of return but arising only out of the generosity of the giver.

When we take the Greek word for grace over into the New Testament, we can apply Trench's words as well: "It is hardly too much to say that God has in no word uttered Himself and all that is in His heart more distinctly than in this." God's grace is that matchless, wonderful, marvelous, act on His part when He out of the spontaneous infinite love of His heart steps down from His judgment throne in heaven to take upon Himself the guilt of our sin and the penalty which is justly ours, doing this not for His friends but for His enemies. Here the word "grace" goes infinitely beyond its meaning in pagan Greece.

The word "abounded," is from a different Greek word than that which is translated "abound." The word means "to exist in abundance." But the second word which meaning also "to exist in abundance," carries with it the added idea that that abundance is more than enough. The thing exists in superfluity. A cognate of the word is used in a letter of A.D. 108, "More than enough has been written," or in one of A.D. 117, "I count it superfluous to write at greater length." In addition to that, Paul prefixes a preposition to the word which means "to be over and above." Thus the translation reads, "Where sin existed in abundance, grace was in superabundance, and then some more added on top of that."

God created the sun to give light and heat to the earth upon which we live. But only a very small fraction of that light and heat ever reaches our globe. The rest is lost in space. We need never be concerned that the light and heat of the sun will fail us. God has made an oversize reservoir to serve us.

There is enough grace in God's heart of love to save and keep saved for time and eternity, every sinner that ever has or ever will live, and then enough left over to save a million more universes full of sinners, were there such, and then some more. There is enough grace available to give every saint constant victory over sin, and then some more. There is enough grace to meet and cope with all the sorrows, heartaches, difficulties, temptations, testings, and trials of human existence, and more added to that. God's salvation is an oversize salvation. It is shock proof, strain proof, unbreakable, all sufficient. It is equal to every emergency, for it flows from the heart of an infinite God freely bestowed and righteously given through the all-sufficient sacrifice of our Lord on the Cross. Salvation is all of grace. Trust God's grace. It is superabounding grace.

40

Jesus of Nazareth, Who Is He?

❡ PAUL IN Colossians 1:15 speaks of Him as "the image of the invisible God, the firstborn of every creature." We will study the words "image" and "firstborn." The word "image" has the obvious idea of likeness. But the Greek word does not refer to an accidental likeness, as one egg is like another. It implies an original of which the image is a copy. But the image in this case is not the result of direct imitation as the head of a king on a coin, but is derived, like the features of the parent in the child. In John 3:16 our Lord is the only begotten Son of God. John 1:18 refers to Him as the only begotten God, the word "God" appearing in the best manuscripts. It is a tremendous thought. The word "only begotten" does not only mean that our Lord was the only Son of God, but that He as God the Son is alone of His kind, unique, begotten of God through eternal generation. He is the image of God in the sense that He is a derived representation of God the Father, co-existent eternally with Him, possessing the same essence, Deity Himself. Being the representative of God, He is also therefore the manifestation of God. He said to Philip, "He that hath seen me hath seen the Father" (John 14:9).

Our Lord is also the firstborn of every creature. The word "firstborn" is from a Greek word that had a certain technical use in the first century. It is difficult to bring out all its content of meaning in a translation. It implied priority to all creation. Our Lord was not the first created thing to be brought into existence. The word declares the absolute pre-existence of the Son. He existed before any created thing was brought into existence. Therefore He is not created, and being uncreated, He is eternal. Paul in the next verse says, "For by him were all things created." Instead of being the first in order of created things, He is their Creator. That is what our Lord has reference to in Revelation 3:14 when He speaks of Himself as "the beginning of the creation of God."

The word "beginning" in the Greek has two meanings, "the first in a series," and "the originator" of something. Our Lord was the originator of the created universe in that He was its Creator. Thus the Greek word translated "firstborn" implies here "priority to all creation."

It speaks also of sovereignty over all creation. The first born is the natural ruler, the acknowledged head. He is also ruler by right of the fact that He is the Creator. The words "every creature" are more properly translated "all creation." Jesus of Nazareth, the Galilean peasant, the carpenter, the friend of publicans and sinners, is the image of God, a derived copy by eternal generation of God the Father, the Creator of the universe and its sovereign Lord.

He is also the One who made peace through the blood of His Cross. That is, through His substitutionary death He satisfied completely all the claims which the law of God had against us. We as lost sinners violated that law. The justice of God demanded that the penalty, death, be paid. But God in His love desired to save those who would come to Him in faith to appropriate salvation. So He in the Person of His Son, Jesus of Nazareth, stepped down from His judgment throne to take upon Himself at Calvary your sin and mine, your penalty and mine. God's law being satisfied, He is now free to righteously bestow mercy. If you have never definitely placed your trust in the Lord Jesus as your personal Saviour, will you not just now do so? Settle the matter of your eternal salvation once for all. Do not put it off. Delay is dangerous. "Believe on the Lord Jesus Christ, and thou shalt be saved, and thy house" (Acts 16:31).

41

The Exegesis of God

❡ IN JOHN 1:18 we read in a literal translation and paraphrase, "God in his invisible essence no one has ever yet seen. The only begotten God who is constantly in the bosom of the Father, that one has fully explained him." The words "only begotten God" are in the best manuscripts. What a tremendous thought. To think that the eternal God and Saviour Jesus Christ, the One who has no beginning, the Ancient of Days, yet was begotten. He proceeds by eternal generation from the Father as the Son, and because eternal, that birth never took place, it always was. Our Lord never started to be God's only begotten Son. He always was His Son. He possesses the same essence as God the Father, and therefore He can in His incarnation fully explain God. The word "declared" in our English version is from a Greek word which means "to lead out." God the Son in His incarnation led the Father out from behind the curtain of His invisibility into full view. The Greek word here comes into the English language in the word "exegesis." Exegesis is the method of Bible study in which we fully explain every detail of the text. Jesus Christ has in His incarnation, fully explained in finite terms so far as finite minds can grasp, all the details of the Person of God the Father. He said, "He that hath seen me hath seen the Father." Thus Jesus Christ is the exegesis of God.

42

Two Obsolete Words

❡ THE WORD "prevent" in I Thessalonians 4:15 means today "to so order or control circumstances that a certain proposed act will not take place." But when the Authorized Version was translated in A.D. 1611, it meant what the Greek word from which it is translated means. The word means "to precede, to get the start of." The teaching is that the saints who are alive when our Lord comes, will not precede the saints who died previous to the Rapture, in receiving their glorified bodies, for the dead in Christ shall take the precedence, being glorified first.

The other word is "letteth," in II Thessalonians 2:7. The word today means "to allow," but when the Authorized Version was made, it meant what the Greek word from which it is translated means, namely, "to hold down," thus "to restrain." It is spoken of the Holy Spirit who through the Church is restraining evil on earth. The words "taken home" are from a word which literally means, "to become." The Holy Spirit will restrain evil until He "become out of the midst," that is, go out of the midst of humanity. And when He goes back to heaven, the saints will go with Him, for He has taken up His permanent abode in them.

43

Praying Without Ceasing

❡ THE GREEK language can say more in one word through the grammatical rules that pertain to it, than the English language can in half a dozen words. In the imperative mode, the Greek tenses are very definite in their distinctions. We have the imperative mode in the exhortations in Matthew 7:7-8 as well as the indicative mode, both used in the present tense, the former always speaking of continuous action, the latter usually, as the context allows it. We have the word "knock" in verse 7. There are two words for "knock" in Greek, one which refers to an unceremonious pounding, the other to a polite knock. The latter is used here.

Thus we have the translation: "Keep on asking, and it shall be given you: keep on seeking and ye shall find, keep on reverently knocking, and it shall be opened unto you: for everyone that keeps on asking, keeps on receiving; and he that keeps on seeking, keeps on finding, and to him that keeps on reverently knocking, it shall be opened."

The lessons we learn from this fuller translation are as follows: First we learn that the Scriptures teach that if we do not receive answers to prayers at once, we should persevere in prayer until we do, or until God shows us that the petition is not according to His will. Second, we are taught that in the case of some prayers, it takes God time to answer the petition. It takes God time to grow a beautiful rose. Likewise, it takes Him time to bring the granite-like heart of a sinner to bow in submissive faith to the Lord Jesus. Third, this text teaches that while we keep on praying, God keeps on working in our behalf. Many a meagre Christian experience is due to a meagre prayer life. Fourth, we learn that we have no right to demand of God that He answer our prayer, but we may keep on reverently knocking with the hand of faith. Perhaps this brief study may be the means of solving some of our problems relating to the prayer life.

44

The Road to Heaven

❡ IN ROMANS 3:23 we read, "All have sinned and come short of the glory of God." The Greek word translated "sin" is a word which among the pagan Greeks meant "to be without a share in," thus, "to miss the mark, to fail of doing." The Greek athletes aiming at a target would sometimes miss the mark. Thus, the human race has missed the mark, namely, a life lived to the glory of God.

Our Lord in John 14:6 says, "I am the way, the truth, and the life.' The word "way" is from a Greek word which has two uses, a literal and a metaphorical. It was used to speak of a road and also to refer to a method or manner of accomplishing something. These uses are closely intertwined and cannot be disassociated. The road leading to a certain place is the method of getting there. Our Lord is the literal road which a sinner must take if he is to reach heaven, and Jesus thus becomes the method by which he is saved. Missing the glory of God is evidence of the fact that the sinner has not gone in the right direction, and that shows that he has not been on the right road. He has missed the road. To reach heaven, the sinner must put himself on the road to heaven. Jesus is that road.

But, that Jesus is not that road as a teacher or an example, is clear, for Paul in Heb. 10:19-20 says, "Having therefore, brethren, boldness to enter into the holiest by the blood of Jesus, by a new and living way, which he hath consecrated for us through the veil, that is to say, his flesh." The writer to the Hebrews is inviting Jews to receive Jesus Christ as Saviour, and is using Old Testament typology in an effort to make himself clear to them. The word "way" is again this road which is the method whereby one reaches heaven. The word "new" is from a word which is used in the Greek translation of the Old Testament to refer to the slaying of sacrificial victims. A Greek preposition prefixed to the word makes the composite word mean "freshly slain." The road is a freshly slain road. That reminds us of the road in the Holy of Holies which led to the Mercy Seat, sprinkled with the blood of the sacrificial animals. It was the road which led into the presence of God through a substitutionary sacrifice which put away sin. But that road was only typical of another road, this freshly slain road which is actual and living, an effective way to God, namely Jesus Christ who is that road by virtue of His outpoured blood on Calvary's Cross. Are you on that road? There is no other that leads to heaven.

45

The Other Comforter

❡ OUR LORD was about to return to heaven. The disciples were troubled because the One who had been their Guardian, Helper, Adviser, Strength-giver, was now leaving them. They thought that Jesus would leave them alone. But He told them that "another Comforter" would come to their aid, even the Holy Spirit (John 14:16, 17).

The word "comforter" is from a Greek word which means literally "to call alongside." It was used in the first century of one called in to support another or give him aid. It was a technical term to describe a lawyer in the Greek law courts, one who was called in to aid the accused.

But in this case, we do not have to do with the law, for a Christian is not under the law but under grace. Therefore, the word here merely means "one called in to help another." The word "comforter" is a good translation if rightly understood. It comes from the Latin and means "one who comes with strength." To comfort in the sense of consoling one, is just one of the many ministries of the Holy Spirit to the believer. His many-sided work can be summed up in the phrase "one called in to stand by and give aid." The idea "to stand by" comes from the preposition which is part of this Greek word.

The word "another" is significant. There are two words in Greek which mean "another," one referring to another of a different kind, and the other meaning "another of the same kind." Jesus uses the latter word. The Holy Spirit is a Helper of the same kind as Jesus. The Holy Spirit is a divine Person just like our Lord and has the same attributes and qualities.

Paul says in I Corinthians 6:19, "What? know ye not that your body is an inner sanctuary of the Holy Spirit who is in you, whom ye have from God, and that ye are not your own?" There are two words in Greek translated "temple," one referring to the temple in its entirety, the other speaking of the inner sanctuary. The latter is used here. The physical body of each saint is an inner sanctuary in which the Holy Spirit has come to take up His permanent abode. The truth of the fact that the Holy Spirit resides permanently in the body of the believer is from the word translated "dwelleth" in James 4:5. Thus our great Helper, the One Jesus called to the aid of the believer when He left this earth, has taken up His permanent residence in our hearts to stand by, ready to render instant help at any time.

But He comes to the help of the saint when that saint expresses a desire for that help and trusts Him to render that help. Our Lord says (John 7:37-38), "If any man thirst, let him come unto me and drink. He that believeth on me, as the Scripture hath said, out from his inmost being shall flow rivers of living water." John says that the living water refers to the Holy Spirit. Our Lord sent the Holy Spirit to come to our aid. Now He lays down the necessary procedure for the believer to follow in order to avail himself of that aid.

The Christian life is not a life of self-effort but of dependence upon the Holy Spirit to put sin out of the life and to produce His fruit in us. He does that as we desire Him to do that and trust Him to do that. As we fulfill these two requirements, we are filled with the Spirit. The Holy Spirit is constantly working in and for the believer who is filled with the Spirit. Only in that way can He give us aid. The Holy Spirit is God's provision for living a life pleasing to Him.

46

A Parable

⁋ ONE OF our Lord's favorite methods of teaching was that of using parables (Matt. 13:3). The English word "parable" is from a Greek word which means "to throw alongside." Thus, a parable is an illustration thrown alongside of a truth in order to explain it. Someone has said, "A pound of illustration is worth a ton of explanation." It was a gracious act of mercy to those whose hearts were darkened by sin, to have the truth brought to them so simply.

47
Defending the Faith

❡ IT IS every saint's obligation (I Peter 3:15). In days of apostasy, every believer needs divine protection against false teaching. The best protection is found in obeying Peter's words, "Sanctify Christ as Lord in your hearts." The word "sanctify" is from a Greek word whose root meaning is "to set apart." The Greeks sanctified their temples and their gods in the sense that they set them apart for religious purposes, thus declaring them non-secular, that is, holy. Then they set themselves apart as worshippers of these gods, and as those who attended the temple worship. Thus they acquired the character of the deities worshipped.

This use of the word holds good in the Christian life. We who are saved in the precious bood of Jesus Christ are also indwelt by Him. We are to set Him apart in our hearts as the alone object of worship. He is to occupy the throne of our lives. We set ourselves apart to His worship and obedience. Thus we acquire a character like His. This results in a holy separated Christ-like Spirit-filled life. This is the best protection of the saints against becoming entangled in false teaching.

As thus living close to the Lord Jesus, we must "be ready always to give an answer to every man that asks us a reason for the hope" that is in us, Peter states. The words "give an answer" are from a Greek word which means literally "to talk one's self off from a charge preferred against one." It was a technical word in the Greek law courts used to designate the work of a lawyer, one

who presented a verbal defense for his client, proving
that the charge preferred against his client was not true.

The Bible today is being charged with being a man-
made book, full of inaccuracies, a mass of myths and
fairy tales. Christians are exhorted to present a verbal
defense for the Bible, proving that that charge is not
true. Fulfilled prophecy, the proof that the miracles of
the Gospels actually took place, the transformed lives of
believers, all constitute proof of that fact. We are to
contend for the Faith once for all delivered to the saints.

48
Two Kinds of Power

¶ THERE ARE two Greek words translated by the
word "power," one in John 1:12, the other in Romans
1:16. "To as many as received him, to them gave he the
power to become the sons of God." The word here is
from a Greek word which was used in the first century
to refer to a legal right, that is, a person was given the
legal right to do or be something. A sinner who appropriates Jesus Christ as Saviour, is given the legal right to
become a child of God. He becomes a child of God
through regeneration. But his legal right to regeneration
is procured by his action of trusting the Lord Jesus as
Saviour.

In regeneration, God is extending mercy to a sinner
who has violated His laws. Violation of laws incurs a
penalty. Justice demands that the penalty be paid. Until

the penalty is paid, no mercy can be given. But if one bears the penalty himself, no mercy can be shown. Therefore Jesus Christ paid the penalty of the broken law in the sinner's stead. Justice is satisfied. If the sinner desires mercy from God, he must recognize the payment of the penalty by Jesus Christ before he can be a recipient of that mercy. When he does that, he has the legal right to accept that mercy. Therefore, regeneration must first be preceded by justification, not in point of time, but in the divine economy. Therefore, "To as many as received him, to them gave he the legal right to become children of God." The word in the Greek translated "sons" is from a word whose root comes from a verb which means "to give birth to." Thus the word means, "born ones." The new birth is in view here. The word "receive" here implies an active appropriation, not a passive acceptance. It is used synonymously for the word "believe" which in a context like this one refers to a definite act of the will entrusting one's self into the keeping of another. The same word for "believe" is used in John 2:24, where Jesus did not commit Himself or entrust Himself to men. The whole translation can read, "To as many as appropriated him, to them gave he the legal right to become born ones of God, to them that are trusting in his name."

The other word for "power" is in Romans 1:16, "I am not ashamed of the gospel, for it is the power of God unto salvation to every one that believeth." The word in the Greek means "power," in the sense of that which overcomes resistance. Our English word "dynamite," comes from this Greek word. The gospel is God's spiritual dynamite which breaks the granite-like heart of the sinner into rock dust, pulverizing it so that it becomes rich soil in which the seed of the Word finds root and grows. The gospel is the most powerful thing in all the world. When it is unloosed in the Spirit-empowering preaching of the Word, souls are saved.

The word "gospel" is from a Greek word which means "good news." The good news is that God has wrought out a salvation through the blood of the Cross for needy sinners who may by pure faith without the addition of good works, appropriate that salvation as a free unmerited gift. Anything else than that is not gospel, for it is not good news.

49

Since or When Ye Believed?

❡ THE TRANSLATION in Acts 19:2, "Have ye received the Holy Ghost since ye believed," has been a basis for the unscriptural teaching to the effect that the Holy Spirit does not come to indwell the believer at the moment he believes, but that that believer must come to some certain degree of holiness in his life as a Christian before the Spirit is given. Greek authorities agree on the translation, "Did ye receive the Holy Spirit when ye believed?" Or it could be rendered, "Did ye receive the Holy Spirit, having believed?" The tense of the participle and verb point to a simultaneous act. That is, the reception of the Holy Spirit occurs at the same instant as the act of believing in the Lord Jesus as Saviour. This is what the Greek grammar here teaches.

Indeed, Paul's words, "Unto what then were ye baptized?" indicate that the reception of the Spirit is connected with the act of believing, not with anything which might take place after that act. It developed that these individuals were disciples of John the Baptist, who announced a coming Messiah, rather than converts of Paul, who preached a crucified risen Saviour who sent the Holy Spirit at Pentecost.

Furthermore, when the converts of John extended their faith to take in a Saviour who had already died for them, they received the Holy Spirit. Therefore, the coming of the Spirit to indwell a believer is always in this age in response to that person's faith in the Lord Jesus as Saviour. When Peter was preaching to the Gentiles in the house of Cornelius, the Spirit came upon the hearers while Peter was preaching. Paul says (Rom. 8:9), "If any man have not the Spirit of Christ, he is none of his." That is, the person in whom the Spirit does not dwell, is not a Christian. Again, in I Corinthians 6:19, he says, "What? know ye not that your body is an inner sanctuary of the Holy Ghost who is in you?"

This teaching that the Holy Spirit does not indwell a believer until he comes to a certain state of holiness, is most harmful. It deprives that Christian of the help of the Holy Spirit in his life. It is a most ridiculous teaching, for how can a believer come to that state of holy living except through the sanctifying work of the Holy Spirit?

50

The Spirit's Ministry in Prayer

❡ THE INFIRMITIES in Romans 8:26-27 have to do with certain weaknesses in our prayer life. The Holy Spirit, Paul says, helps them. The Greek word translated "helpeth," literally means "to lend a hand together with, and at the same time with one." Martha used the same word when appealing to our Lord to bid Mary help her with the preparation of the meal (Luke 10:40). The Holy Spirit lends a hand together with us as we are praying. It is not that He helps us bear our weaknesses, but He helps our weaknesses.

The weaknesses spoken of here are two, what we should pray for, the matter of prayer, and how we should pray, the form and manner of our prayer. The word "what" has an article before it in the Greek. Literally, we do not know "the what" to pray for. That is, we do not know the particular definite thing to pray for. As to the general subjects for prayer, the salvation of the lost, the sanctification of the saints, our daily needs, these we know of. But to be specific in our praying involves a knowledge of God's will in particular instances, and of that we are naturally ignorant. It is right here that the Spirit comes to our aid.

The word "pray" is from a Greek word made up of a word which means "to pray," with a prefixed preposition which means literally "toward." The composite word refers to prayer directed to God, a conscious definite commitment to Him of our needs, our desires, our petitions. The Holy Spirit thus energizes the saint along the line of prayer for particular things which are according to the will of God, prayer directed consciously to Him.

The word translated "know," is not the Greek word which means "knowledge gained by experience," but "knowledge that is intuitive, natural to one's being and constitution." We do not have intuitive knowledge of the particular thing to pray for. The word "ought" is the same word used in John 3:7 in the word "must." Literally it means, "it is necessary in the nature of the case." The necessity in the nature of the case is found in the fact that God brings His plans to fruition through the prayers of the saints, and in order for us to pray according to the will of God, we must be so yielded to the control of the Spirit that He can bring into our prayer ministry, the things which God is planning to accomplish. It is clear, therefore, that in order to pray aright, we must be filled with the Spirit.

The Spirit Himself, not "itself," should be the translation here. The word "spirit" in the Greek language is in the neuter gender, and consequently its pronoun is neuter. But the Holy Spirit is a Person, and should not be referred to as "it." The translation should be according to sense here, not grammar.

He makes intercession. This word comes from a Greek word which is most picturesque. It is used of one who happens upon one who is in trouble and pleads in that one's behalf. As Alford says, "The Holy Spirit of God dwelling in us, knowing our wants better than we, Himself pleads in our prayers, raising us to higher and holier desires than we can express in words, which can only find utterance in sighings and aspirations."

God the Father who searches the hearts of His saints for their prayers, uttered and unexpressed, interprets those inarticulate sighings of the Spirit in us by reason of the fact that the Spirit pleads for us and in us and through us according to the will of God.

The lesson for us here is that if we expect to have an intelligent, powerful, rich prayer life, we must live Spirit controlled lives.

51

God's Emancipation Proclamation

❡ A LITERAL translation of Romans 6:12-14 is as follows: "Therefore, stop letting sin rule constantly as king in your bodies which are subject to death, resulting in your habitual obedience to its cravings. Neither keep on habitually putting your members at the service of sin as weapons of unrighteousness. But put yourselves once for all at the service of God, as those who are living ones out from among the dead, and put your members once for all at the service of God as weapons of righteousness, for sin shall not have dominion over you, for you are not under law but under grace."

The word studies are as follows: In verse twelve, the Greek construction in the exhortation forbids the continuance of a habit already going on. Those believers before salvation had been constantly allowing sin to reign over their bodies. The word "reign" is from a word which refers to a king reigning. The prepositional phrase could show either purpose or result. This preposition often means the latter, and we have so translated it. The word "lust" has changed its meaning since the Authorized Version was made. It refers today to an immoral desire. The Greek word refers simply to a desire, and has a preposition prefixed which intensifies the meaning, thus, a craving. The context rules as to whether it is an evil or a good desire.

In verse thirteen, the first exhortation is in the same construction as in verse twelve, forbidding the continuance of an action already going on. The word "yield" is from a word which means "to put at the service of," as a volunteer placing himself at the service of this government or an individual at the service of a master. The word "instruments" is from a Greek word which means, "tools or instruments, a ship's tackle, implements of war." It is used in John 18:3 in the last sense. Our members, namely, our eyes, hands, feet, mind, are weapons which either Satan or God may use. This at once brings to mind the conception of two armies, Satan's and God's. When a saint puts his members at the service of Satan, he fights against God and His army, which is a serious thing. The second exhortation in verse thirteen is in a construction which exhorts to a once-for-all act. We are to put ourselves and our members at the service of God once for all. Having done that we must keep hands off. We are bought with a price, and we are not our own. We must daily, yes, hourly, count ourselves as having thus put ourselves into the hands of God for His service.

In verse fourteen we have the promise, that having done this, sin shall no longer have lordship over us. This is God's emancipation proclamation. The definite article before the word "law,' does not appear in the Greek. The absence of the article gives the idea that Christians are not under the law as a method of divine dealing. That is, we are not unsaved persons upon whom the law makes demands that no unsaved person can ever meet, for the law commands to obedience but gives neither the desire nor the power to obey. But we are under grace as a method of divine dealing, for grace sweetly exhorts to a life of obedience and provides both the desire and the power to obey (Phil. 2:12-13).

52

Divine Wood Cutters

℘ PAUL IS IN prison in Rome, writing to his beloved Philippians. He is assuring them that the circumstances in which he finds himself, are contributing to, rather than hindering, the advance of the gospel. He says in Philippians 1:12 that the things that have happened to him have fallen out rather to the furtherance of the gospel. The word "furtherance" is from a Greek word which is thought to have been used in the first century to refer to a company of wood cutters preceding the progress of an army, cutting a road through the forest so that it might advance. Paul says that his circumstances are divine wood cutters, cutting a way through the opposition so that the gospel might be advanced. What were these circumstances? His liberty was gone. He was chained to a Roman soldier night and day. God had built a fence around the apostle. He had put limitations about him. He had placed handicaps upon him. But Paul says that they are God's wood cutters making a road for the advancement of the gospel.

The gospel was now being proclaimed from the pulpit of the Roman empire. The Praetorium guard of 10,000 picked Roman soldiers was hearing it from the soldiers chained to Paul. The jealous brethren in Rome were announcing Christ more energetically, out of envy of course, but yet announcing Him. The friendly brethren out of love for Paul were more zealous in their preaching.

And so it is in every Christian's life. The things that hedge us in, the things that handicap us, the tests that we go through and the temptations that assail us, are all divinely appointed wood cutters used by God to hew out a path for our preaching of the gospel. It may be that our fondest hopes are not realized. We are in difficult circumstances. Illness may be our lot. Yet if we are in the center of God's will, all these are contributing to the progress of the gospel. They draw us closer to the Lord so that the testimony of our lives will count more for God, and thus we become more efficient in proclaiming the gospel. Thank God for the handicaps and the testings. They are blessings in disguise. When we have limitations imposed upon us we do our best work for the Lord, for then we are most dependent upon Him. Paul said, "Most gladly therefore will 1 rather glory in my infirmities, that the power of Christ may rest upon me" (II Cor. 12:9). Paul knew then, for he had plenty of them.

53

The Devil and His Demons

⁋ THERE ARE two different Greek words translated by the one English word "devil" in the Authorized Version which fact leads to some confusion in our thinking. One word is "diabolos," which in its literal meaning refers to one who falsely accuses another or slanders him. The word comes from another word which literally means "to throw through." Thus it means "to riddle one with accusations." This title is coupled with the word "Satan" in Revelation 20:2, the latter being a transliteration of a Hebrew word which means "adversary." These two names are used to refer to the angel Lucifer who as regent of God fell from his high position through sin and today is god of this world.

The other word is "daimonion," quite a different word. It was used in pagan Greek writings to refer to an inferior race of divine beings, lower than the Greek gods, but more powerful than men. The Bible uses the term to refer to the evil spirits who are servants of the Devil. They are the principalities and powers of Ephesians 6:12, the kingdoms of the Devil located in the atmosphere surrounding this earth. There is one Devil and many demons. We must be careful to distinguish between them.

The rule for the English reader to follow as he seeks to correctly interpret the passages in which these two Greek words are found, is as follows: First, where the word is found in the plural, as "devils," always translate by the word "demons," for the word "daimonion" is in the Greek. Second, where you have the word "devil" in a passage that speaks of a person possessed with a devil, as for instance Matthew 9:32, or a person having a devil as in Luke 7:33, always translate by the word "demon." Third, where the king of the demons is in view, that awful personality known as Satan, as in Luke 4:2; I Peter 5:8; Revelation 20:2, translate by the word "Devil." In John 6:70 Judas is called a devil by our Lord, the word here being "diabolos."

54

Fellowship With Jesus

⊄ THERE are two Greek words translated "wash" that appear in John 13:5-10. The one which means "to wash part of the body" appears in verses five, six, nine, and in verse ten the second time the word is used. The other word, meaning "to perform a complete ablution," is used in verse ten in the word "washed." These two words in their usage here point to two truths of the standing of a believer in Christ, and his experience. The first remains the same for time and eternity. The latter changes from time to time during this life. Someone has said, "Union with Jesus is so strong, that nothing can break it. Communion with Jesus is so fragile that the slightest sin can break it."

To understand the conversation between our Lord and Peter, and the spiritual lesson in it, we must understand something of the habits of the citizen of that time. Rome established public baths in the cities of the empire. A

Roman would bathe completely at the public bath, and upon reaching his home needed to wash his feet, for although cleansed at the time, they contracted defilement by reason of the insufficient covering which his sandals afforded. Peter refuses to allow the Lord to wash his feet, but upon being told that if he does not permit the Lord to do that for him, he will have no fellowship with Jesus, he asks that the Lord wash his hands and his head. Our Lord answers, "He that is bathed all over stays bathed and needs not except to wash his feet, but is clean every whit." The spiritual lesson we have from this is as follows. Every believer has been cleansed completely from his sins in the precious blood of Jesus once and for all at Calvary. This is his standing before God, guiltless, sinless, righteous. That position is permanent, as changeless as our unchanging Lord. If sin comes into the life, it does not affect that standing, for that standing is Jesus Christ who is accepted by God and we in Him. Thus, if a believer sins, he does not need to go back to Calvary to be saved all over again, any more than the Roman needed to go back to the public baths for a complete bath just because his feet became dusty on the way home.

Feet stand for a person's walk, his experience. As we are on our way home to heaven, sin sometimes enters our lives. No saint wants to sin. It is his nature to hate sin. But when sin does enter, our walk is defiled and needs to be cleansed. Our Lord said to Peter, "If I wash thee not, thou hast no part with me." That is, if we are not cleansed from sin in our experience, we have no fellowship with our Lord. Known sin in the life that is held to and cherished, breaks our fellowship with Him. The only way to regain that blessed privilege of fellowship is to confess our sins (I John 1:9), and God will cleanse us and restore to us that communion with our Lord which we enjoyed before. The word "confess" is from two Greek words joined together to make one word in the original. One means "to speak," the other "the same." The word means "to speak the same thing." Thus, if we speak the same thing about our sin to God that He does to us, that is confession. That includes sorrow for sin because it is evil, hatred of the sin, and the putting away of the same with the determination never to do that thing again. Our experience is then cleansed from sin's defilement and we are restored to fellowship with our Lord.

55

About Trances

⟪ JOHN IN Revelation 1:10 states that he was in the Spirit on the Lord's Day. The word translated "was" is not from the simple verb of being in the Greek, but from a word which means "to become." The experience John had that Lord's Day was not the usual moment by moment experience he enjoyed, namely, that of being filled with the Holy Spirit. He literally "became in the Spirit." That is, he entered into a new kind of experience relative to the Spirit's control over him.

Peter in Acts 10:10 had the same kind of experience. The translators called it a trance. The word "trance" here is from a Greek word which literally means "to stand out of," and is brought over into our language in the word "ecstasy." The experience which both of these apostles went through was that of being so absolutely controlled by the Holy Spirit, that their physical senses of sight, hearing, feeling, were not registered so far as any recognized impressions were concerned. It was as if they were temporarily outside of their bodies. The control of the Holy Spirit over their faculties was such that He could give them the visions they had, Peter, the vision of the sheet let down from heaven, John, the prophetic visions of the Revelation.

A word of warning is in order here. The revelation to the saints closed with the last book in the Bible. All that God has for us is included in the books from Genesis to the Revelation. No further revelations are being made. The Holy Spirit now illuminates the sacred page of Scripture for our understanding.

Since such visions were for that time only, it follows that a trance such as these men had is a thing of the past also. Satan in these last days is counterfeiting these Holy Spirit given trances with disastrous results to those who lend themselves unwittingly to his control. Those who are not properly taught regarding their relationship to the third Person of the Triune God, fall a prey to Satan.

The safeguard against this is found in the words of Sir Robert Anderson, "In proportion therefore as mind and heart are fixed on Christ, we may count on the Spirit's presence and power; but if we make the Holy Ghost Himself the object of our aspirations and worship, some false spirit may counterfeit the true and take us for a prey."

56

Unfeigned Love

❡ IN ROMANS 12:9 we have the exhortation, "Let love be without dissimulation." The word "love" is from the same Greek word for "love" that we have in John 3:16; Romans 5:5; and I Corinthians 13. It is in its essence a self-sacrificial love, a love that puts self aside in an effort to help and bless others, yes, a love that goes to the point of suffering if that is necessary in order to bless others. And for the highest kind of blessing, suffering is necessary, for "we must bleed if we would bless." This is the love *of* God, not love for God, but the love which God is and which He provides through the operation of the Holy Spirit as the believer depends upon His ministry, a love that will flow like rivers of water out from the Christian who is filled with the Spirit, refreshing the dry parched lives around him and making a desert-heart blossom like a rose. This is the love which God says should be without dissimulation.

The word "dissimulation" is from a Greek word which is made up of three parts, a verb which means "to judge," a preposition which means "under," and the Greek letter Alpha which when prefixed to a word gives it a meaning directly opposite to that which it had before. The preposition and verb together mean literally, "to judge under," and had reference to one who gave off his judgment from under a mask or a cloak, thus appearing to be what he was not. This word comes over into our language in the word "hypocrite," one who plays the part of a character which he is not, and does it to deceive. The word means "hypocrisy." The Alpha prefixed gives us the translation "without hypocrisy." "Let love be without hypocrisy." That is, do not try to counterfeit this love by seeming to love a Christian brother and yet not be willing to put that love into action. The same word is used in II Corinthians 6:6 and I Peter 1:22, where it is translated "unfeigned." The world wears a mask. The love which it shows on the face is only external. That is feigned love. Ours should be unfeigned. If a saint does not have a love which is unfeigned, the trouble is with his adjustment to the Holy Spirit who is the One to provide that saint with that love. The Spirit-filled saint does not have to play the hypocrite in the matter of love, for love shines right out of his eyes. It is on his face, in his actions.

57

Base Things

❧ PAUL TELLS us in I Corinthians 1:28 that God has chosen the base things of the world to bring to naught the things that are. That is, the great majority of sinners He saves are base. Of course, all sinners are totally depraved, yet some are base and others are not base. In verse twenty-six Paul tells us that God does not call many noble unto salvation. The word "noble" here does not refer to nobility of character, but to nobility of birth.

The word "base" is the same word in the Greek that is used for "nobility" except that instead of it being compounded of the words "well" and "born" it is made up of the word "born" and the letter Alpha, which together mean here, "not well born." Indeed, Shakespearean English uses the expression "base born," when it refers to one who is not of the titled nobility. The idea therefore is that the great majority of those who are saved come from that section of the human race called "the common people." Abraham Lincoln said, "God must have loved the common people. He made so many of them." And yet, the great heart of God pulsates with infinite love for the nobility also. It is still true that "whosoever will, let him take the water of life freely" (Rev. 22:17).

58

The Names, Christ and Jesus

¶ ACTS 9:20 reads, "And straightway he preached Christ in the synagogues that he is the Son of God." Paul's synagogue audiences were amazed at Paul's theology. But surely, a Jewish audience would find nothing surprising in the fact that Christ is the Son of God, for that was clearly taught in the Old Testament and believed by an orthodox Jew. What is more, they wanted to kill Paul, we read, for having made that statement. The word "Christ" is a transliteration of a Greek word which means "anointed." By transliteration we mean the act of bringing a word from one language into another in its spelling, whereas by translation we refer to the meaning of the word being taken over into the second language.

The Greek word "anointed," is a translation from a Hebrew word which means "the Anointed" and which latter is brought over into English by transliteration in the word "Messiah." The Messiah of Israel is the Anointed of God. Thus when the name Christ is found in connection with Israel, either in the Old or New Testament, it refers to Israel's Messiah.

Now, if Paul had preached that in the synagogue in Damascus, the Jews would have welcomed him with open arms. The solution to our problem is in the fact that the best Greek texts have the word "Jesus" not "Christ." To announce Jesus of Nazareth, the One whom the highest court of Israel condemned as a blasphemer, as the Son of God, therefore Messiah, was quite another thing. No wonder that the hatred and antagonism of the Jews was aroused, and that they were amazed at the fact that one who had so recently persecuted those who were preaching the same message which he was presenting, should have turned so suddenly. Paul was announcing Jesus of Nazareth as Deity. The Jews had tried to stone our Lord for claiming to be the unique Son of God. "Therefore the Jews sought the more to kill him, because he not only had broken the sabbath, but said also that God was his Father, making himself equal with God" (John 5:18). The key to the interpretation of this passage is in the Greek word translated "his." Had our Lord used the ordinary pronoun showing possession, the Jews would have taken no exception to His words. But He used a word which in the Greek speaks of uniqueness. Our Lord was the Son of God in a way different from that of any other person. A believer is a son of God like all other believers. But our

Lord's sonship was unique. It was not only different from
that of others, but it was the only one of its kind. The
Jews at once recognized it as a claim to joint participation
in the divine essence of the Father. Thus, Jesus of Nazareth is the Messiah of Israel.

The name Jesus is also a transliteration from the Hebrew. The angel said to Mary (Matt. 1:21), "Thou shalt
call his name Jesus, for he shall save his people from
their sins." Matthew reports the angel's words in Greek.
Being a Jew, Matthew of course knew Hebrew and transliterated the Hebrew word which means "Saviour," into
Greek, from which language we brought the name over
into English in the name Jesus. The Hebrew word is in
English "Yeshua." Thus the name "Jesus" speaks of our
Lord as the Saviour, the One who shed His precious blood
on Calvary's Cross for lost sinners, while the name
"Christ" speaks of Him in a context of Israel, as Israel's
Messiah. Where the two names appear together they
refer to Him as the Anointed of God, the Saviour. The
name "Lord," refers to Him in His relation to the Church,
its Head.

59

A Castaway

⁋ PAUL IN a figurative sense beats his body black
and blue, and brings it into bondage to himself, lest after
having preached to others, he himself should be a castaway (1 Cor. 9:27). Some have interpreted this as mean-

ing that Paul feared that if he did not properly fulfill his apostolic office, he would be cast away by God into an eternity of suffering in the Lake of Fire. But there are three things that forbid this meaning. First, the context is not one of salvation, but of service and rewards. Salvation is a free gift with no strings tied to it. It was made possible by the infinite price that was paid at the Cross. Rewards are earned by service

Second, the words of Paul's Saviour are pertinent here, "Him that cometh unto me, I will in no wise cast out" (John 6:37). The word "castaway" in our Corinthian passage is an entirely different word from the two Greek words translated "cast out," the latter being literally "cast out into the outside." The words "in no wise" are from a double negative in the Greek which does not make a positive assertion but means a most emphatic "NOT."

Third, the word "castaway" is from a word compounded of two parts of speech, a word meaning "to put one's approval upon after one has tested something," and the Greek letter Alpha, which when prefixed to a word makes the word mean the opposite to that which it originally meant. The word means "disapproval after having failed to meet the requirements." Paul was speaking of his apostolic service. He was careful lest that should not meet the requirements of His Lord and that therefore he be disapproved, not as a Christian, for salvation is not in view here, but as an apostle, for his service was the thing that was being weighed in God's balances. Before Paul could be disapproved as to his standing in Christ, namely, as to his salvation, his Lord would have to be disapproved. But He is God Himself, in His holy character unchangeable.

Paul was running a race.   To win a crown, his service must be acceptable. Greek runners would compete for a prize, a crown of oak leaves. If they broke training, they would be disqualified, forbidden to race. The Greek word translated "castaway" is this word "disqualified," disapproved after having failed to meet the requirements. Paul served his Lord with an intense earnestness lest he be disqualified, forbidden to exercise his ministry. Let us who are serving the Lord do our very best to please Him lest we be set aside and someone else put in our place.

60

The Grace of Giving

℅ PAUL SAYS in Gal. 6:6, "Let him that is taught in the word communicate unto him that teacheth in all good things." The word "communicate" is from a Greek word which means "to share with another." In this context it means to share with another in his necessities by making those necessities one's own. Those who are instructed in the Word, have the responsibility of making the teacher's needs his own. That is, in the case of a God-called servant of the Lord who devotes his full time to the Lord's work, those who regularly are recipients of his ministry are to make it their business to see that he is properly taken care of financially, so that he might be able to give of his best to the Lord's work. The same Greek word is used in Philippians 4:15 where Paul says that only the Philippian church recognized their obligation to make Paul's necessities their own.

In Philippians 1:3-6 Paul says, "I thank my God . . . for your fellowship in the gospel from the first day until now." The word "fellowship" is from the same Greek word that he used in the Galatian and Philippian passages, except that the preposition is not prefixed. Here the word has a slightly different shade of meaning, namely, "joint participation." But this joint participation does not refer to their fellowship with Paul over the Word or their companionship with him. The word "in" is in the Greek a preposition of motion. Paul thanks God for their joint participation in the progress of the gospel. The occasion for the writing of this book was a gift which the Philippians sent to Paul while he was in prison in Rome (4:10-12). It is clear that this consisted of financial support. He thanks them in so many words as he closes his letter. But in 1:3-6 he with Pauline delicacy indicates his gratitude without mentioning the specific gift. He does not want to appear as if in thanking them he is looking for another gift. So he thanks God for their joint participation in the progress of the gospel from the first day when Lydia, the purple dye seller, opened her home as a meeting place where Paul could preach the Word until that present moment. In the Greek the definite article appears before the adverb "now." Paul says, "From the first day until the now." That article is a delicate finger pointing to that present moment as characterized by the receipt of the gift.

Then Paul adds that he is confident that God who has begun in them this good work of giving liberally to the support of the work of the gospel, will continue to impart grace to continue that same liberality until the Philippian saints stand before the Judgment Seat of Christ. Paul speaks of the liberality of the Macedonian churches as the grace of giving (II Cor. 8:1-7). It is a spiritual grace produced in the saint by the Holy Spirit. Thus, the grace of giving is one of the necessary ingredients of Christian character, if that character is to be a well rounded complete one. And then Paul has this promise from God for the liberal giver, "My God shall supply all your need according to his riches in glory by Christ Jesus." I am persuaded that this promise is for the one who is generous with God. God cannot afford to lavish his gifts upon the stingy Christian, for he would only squander them upon his own selfish desires. And then Paul in our Galatian passage tells the saint that if he is liberal with God, he will reap spiritual blessings, but if he uses his money for his own selfish purposes, that money and what it will buy, will breed corruption in his life.

61

The Intense Life

❡ PAUL WRITES to Timothy (II Tim. 2:15), "Study to show thyself approved unto God, a workman that needeth not to be ashamed, rightly dividing the word of truth." The word "study" has changed its meaning somewhat in the 300 years since the Authorized Version was made. Today the word refers to the mental effort put forth in an attempt to add to one's store of knowledge and one's ability to use that knowledge in an effective way. When we use the word "study," we think of school,

the class room, the teacher, and books. But the word is
not so used here.

The following are some examples of its usage in the
early centuries which should determine its translation today. "I wish to know that you are hurrying on the making of it." "Make haste therefore and put our little slave
Artemidorus under pledge." "In accordance with the
king's desire." "That he may . . . do his best until it is
effected." "Take care that Onnophris buys me what
Irene's mother told him." The ideas of making haste,
being eager, and giving diligence, with the added idea of
effort put forth, are in the Greek usage of the word.

The context of this exhortation includes both Christian
character and service. Timothy is exhorted to study to
show himself approved to God in both respects. The exhortation is addressed to every Christian. The Christian
life is a matter of reckoning ourselves dead to sin and
alive to God, of presenting our members as instruments
of warfare to God. It is a life of dependence upon God,
of allowing God the Holy Spirit to produce in and
through us a Christlike life. The Christian life is a rest
in God, a trust in Him to impart both the desire and the
power to do His will (Phil. 2:13).

But there is another side to the living of a Christian
life. It is not merely a rest in God, it is a constant battle
on the part of the believer. Paul says, "Fight the good
fight of faith" (I Tim. 6:12). There must be an eager,
active, intense determination to live a life pleasing to God.
We must not only yield to the Holy Spirit's fullness, trusting Him to produce in us that love that God is, but we
must definitely will to be loving and try to be loving. In-

tensity in the living of a Christian life is the total concept of this word translated "study." The Greek word implies haste, desire, the doing of one's best, the act of carefully attending to a duty. The living of a Christian life is an urgent matter. One must with intensity of desire will to live the highest type of Christian life. The Christian must do his best to live a life pleasing to his Lord. One must attend carefully to that matter. Thus, the word "study" has in it all of these meanings.

62

A Perfect Salvation

❧ THE PERFECT tense in Greek is very expressive. It speaks of an action that took place in the past, which was completed in past time, and the existence of its finished results. For instance: "I have closed the door," speaks of a past completed action. But the implication is that as a result the door is still closed. Thus, the entire meaning is, "I have closed the door and it is closed at present."

In John 19:30 our Lord cries from the Cross, "It is finished," referring to His work of procuring for lost sinners a salvation from sin through the blood of His Cross. The entire sense is, "It was finished and as a result it is forever done." "It stands finished" would be a good translation. The priests in the tabernacle always stood when ministering in the sacrifices. But our great High Priest is seated. His work is finished. He need never arise and offer another sacrifice.

In Matthew 4:4, our Lord answers Satan, "It is written." The perfect tense is used. He quoted from Deuteronomy. The words had been written by Moses 1500 years before, but are still on record. David said, "Forever, O Lord, thy word is settled in heaven." A good translation reads, "It stands written." It is the eternal word of God.

In Ephesians 2:8 we have, "For by the grace are ye saved." The definite article appears in the Greek. God's salvation does not merely issue from a gracious attitude on His part. It proceeds from that particular gracious act of God the Son in dying upon the Cross to pay man's penalty incurred by him through sin. It is the particular grace that issues from Calvary that saves sinners.

The words, "ye are saved," are in the perfect tense in Greek. That is, a Christian was given a perfect salvation in past time when he believed, and as a result of that past completed work of Jesus Christ on the Cross and his past acceptance of the same, he at present is a saved person. His present possession of salvation is based upon one thing only, what Jesus did on the Cross for him and his past acceptance of that work. That means that the works of an individual, past or present, do not enter into his acceptance or retertion of salvation. Salvation is the alone work of Christ. The believer is the recipient. That means that the believer is saved and saved forever, for as he reads this text, the present results of the perfect tense are always present with the reader. And to strengthen the assertion, Paul adds another word in the present tense to show not only the existence but the persistence of the results. The full translation is, "By the grace ye were saved and as a result are in a saved state at the present time."

INDEX TO SCRIPTURE REFERENCES

BYPATHS
In the Greek New Testament

To my mother, who, like Hannah
of old, gave her son to the Lord
"all the days of his life."

Foreword

The author of this book has already introduced himself to the reading public through his helpful volume, *Golden Nuggets from the Greek New Testament for the English Reader*. He is well known to thousands of friends of the Moody Bible Institute, and is held in admiration and affection by hundreds of present and former students.

The Greek New Testament is to Mr. Wuest a real mine, with gold and diamonds to be found by the diligent miner. His work in this book arouses the desire to do some mining for one's self, and will induce many ministers to make larger use of their Greek. At the same time the book gives stirring information for readers who may know nothing of Greek.

Preachers, Sunday School teachers, and other Christian workers will find the book packed with valuable material they can use in preaching and teaching. And the ordinary reader will find his heart warmed and his faith strengthened through the perusal of these pages. May God bless this good book and give it a wide ministry.

WILL H. HOUGHTON
President, Moody Bible Institute

Preface

A. T. Robertson in his book, *The Minister and His Greek New Testament,* says, "The Greek New Testament has a message for each mind. Some of the truth in it has never yet been seen by anyone else. It is waiting like a virgin forest to be explored."

We have called this small volume which follows *Golden Nuggets from the Greek New Testament for the English Reader*: *Bypaths in the Greek New Testament for the English reader*. It is the author's constant delight to explore this virgin forest, and to come upon precious truths that do not appear in the English translation, but which are hidden away in secluded nooks in the Greek text. It is a fresh delight to lead the English reader along the same paths, pointing out those precious truths to which only a Greek student has access.

The plan of this book has been to treat only those things which the English reader cannot find for himself. While the book can be read as a series of separate articles, it should also be useful as a reference work. When the English reader is studying a portion of the New Testament, he can consult the "Index to Scripture References," and if the passage is commented upon, obtain help from the Greek text presented in a simple non-technical way. Or, should one be looking for a germ-thought which will lead out into a fresh bit of truth, he will find the word studies helpful.

The English words treated are from the Authorized Version. The author's justification in sometimes offering a fuller or a slightly different translation is found in the fact that no single translation is able to bring out all the delicate shades of meaning, all the expressions peculiar to the Greek language, and for the reason that the standard translations are held down to a minimum of words which would best express the thought of the Greek, and rightly so. Then there are a limited number of English words that have changed their meaning in the last three hundred years since the Authorized Version was made. Since the majority of Bible students still use this version, it is necessary to take care of these words.

But we must not allow these facts to disturb our confidence in and dependence upon our reliable translations. We are concerned here with minor details, not with the great outstanding doctrines and facts in God's Word. Most men have been saved and have grown in grace through faith in the Word in its translated form. The Holy Spirit owns and quickens the translated Word, and has always done so. Therefore, as we seek to bring out from the Greek text aspects of truth that the translations do not handle, let us thank God for these translations which He has given us, and receive with gratefulness any added light which the labors of Bible students have been able to gather from the Greek text.

K. S. W.
The Moody Bible Institute,
Chicago, Illinois.

Contents

The Romance of the Inscriptions

¶ IN RECENT years there has been unearthed in the Bible lands a great deal of rich material which throws a flood of light upon certain details of first-century life and which gives one a new and clearer insight into certain portions of the New Testament. This material is in the form of inscriptions dating from Alexander the Great, 332 B.C., to Constantine the Great, A.D. 313, and has been found on the sites of ancient civilizations all over the Graeco-Roman world, from the Rhine to the upper reaches of the Nile, and from the Euphrates to Britain. It consists of non-literary inscriptions from governmental or religious sources, or from the under-privileged classes of society. They are written on various materials, stone, metal, wax tablets, or are in the form of scribblings found on walls, and inscriptions on bronze, lead, or gold tablets.

A great number are found written on papyrus, the ancient form of paper. This was manufactured from the inner pith of the papyrus plant which was cut into thin strips, laid side by side perpendicularly, in length and number sufficient to form a sheet. Upon these another layer was laid horizontally. The two layers were glued

together with adhesive, pressed, sun-dried, and then made
smooth by polishing. A great quantity of these papyri
was found in Egypt where the dry climate has preserved
them for thousands of years. The oldest papyrus sheet
dates from about 2600 B.C. Many of these have been
dug up from the rubbish heaps of buried cities. There
they were thrown, old discarded office-records, worn-out
books, legal documents, leases, bills and receipts, marriage
contracts, bills of divorce, wills, decrees issued by authority, denunciations, suings for the punishment of wrong-
doers, minutes of judicial proceedings, and tax-papers in
great numbers. There are letters and notes, schoolboy's
exercise-books, magical texts, diaries and horoscopes,
letters of consolation, letters of prodigal sons writing
home. These furnish a vivid cross-section of contemporary
life as it was lived during the time when Christianity was
gaining a foothold in the eastern world. There is a freshness, warmth, and sincerity about them that one does not
find in the literary productions of the same age. These
show us the people, their characters, and the inner recesses
of their hearts. Since Christianity procured most of its
converts from the under-privileged classes, these papyrus
sheets throw a flood of light upon the New Testament.
Another thing that makes these records so valuable is that
most of them are dated, and the place of writing noted.

Another rich source of information is the ostraca.
These are broken pieces of pottery upon which something
has been written. Papyrus was the rich man's writing
material, the ostraca, the poor man's. The man of humble

means would search the rubbish heaps in his neighborhood for the discarded fragments of a broken piece of pottery. New Testament manuscripts were costly and few, so the poor would copy Scripture portions on these pieces of pottery. On these ostraca are found receipts, letters, contracts, bills, decrees, even extracts from classical authors. The great majority are, however, tax-receipts.

The Greek found on these inscriptions is known as the Koine Greek and is the same as that found in the New Testament. This Greek was the international language of the Roman world. It numbered more speakers than Latin with its millions. Just before the beginning of the Christian era, the conquests of Alexander the Great spread the Greek language throughout the then-known world, and thus made possible the rapid spread of the gospel through the medium of an international language, Greek. This Greek is called Koine or "common" Greek, because after the conquests of Alexander, men did not speak the local dialects of Greece any more, but a Greek tongue common to all. Thus, the fact that both the inscriptions and the New Testament are written in the same international Greek, and because the inscriptions provide a vivid picture of contemporary life, we have in this material uncovered by the spade of the archæologist, a source of information which helps us to better understand the historical background, local customs, and certain details with reference to the New Testament manuscripts which otherwise would be somewhat obscure to a western mind. Instances of some of these are found in certain chapters in this book.

II

The Title Deed to Answered Prayer

¶ "FAITH is the substance of things hoped for" (Heb. 11:1). The Greek word translated "substance" had a technical meaning in the business world of the first century. It referred to one's property or effects. It was used in such expressions as "Out of this *estate* I declare that my husband owes me," or, "more land than I actually *possess*," the italicized words being the translation of the word. It was also used to refer to "the whole body of documents bearing on the ownership of a person's property, deposited in the archives, and forming the evidence of ownership."

Moulton and Milligan in their "Vocabulary of the Greek Testament" say of these uses, "These varied uses are at first sight somewhat perplexing, but in all the cases there is the same central idea of something that underlies visible conditions and guarantees a future possession." Thus they translate "Faith is the title deed of things hoped for."

To substantiate this usage, there is in "Living Yesterdays," a delightful brochure by H. R. Minn, the story of a woman named Dionysia. She is described as "a woman of set jaw and grim determination." It seems that she had lost a case in a local court over a piece of land to which she laid claim. Not satisfied with the decision of a lower court, she determined to take her case to a higher

court in Alexandria. She sent her slave to that city, with
the legal documents safely encased in a stone box.
On the way, the slave lost his life in a fire which destroyed
the inn where he had put up for the night. For 2,000
years the sands of the desert covered the ruins of the inn,
the charred bones of the slave, and the stone box.
Archæologists have recently uncovered these remains. In
the box they found the legal documents. They read the
note which this woman had sent to the judge in Alexandria, "In order that my lord the judge may know that
my appeal is just, I attach my *hypostasis*." That which was
attached to this note, she designated by the Greek word
translated "substance" in Heb. 11:1. The attached document was translated and found to be the title deed to the
piece of land which she claimed as her own possession,
the evidence of her ownership.

What a flood of light is thrown upon this teaching
regarding faith. The act of exercising true faith as one
prays, or as one leans on the resources of God, is itself
the title deed or evidence of the sure answer to our prayer
or the unfailing source of the divine supply. It is God's
guarantee in advance that we already possess the things
asked for. They may still be in His hands, awaiting the
proper time for their delivery, but they are ours. If the
answers to our prayers are not forthcoming at once, let us
rest content with the title deed which God has given us,
namely, a Holy Spirit energized act of faith. We may be
absolutely certain that our God will honor this title deed
at the right moment.

III

The Imperialism of Christianity

¶ CHRISTIANITY came into a world dominated by the Cult of the Cæsar, a religious system in which the Roman emperor was worshipped as a god. The empire, made up of many widely different peoples with their own distinctive languages, customs, and religions, was held together not merely by one central ruling power at Rome which was supported by the military power of its legions, but also and probably more efficiently so, by the universal religion of Emperor-worship. Political and military ties are strong, but religious ties are stronger. Rome knew this and guarded jealously its Cult of the Cæsar. Its policy was to allow its subjects to retain their own religions as long as they accepted Emperor-worship in addition to their own system of belief. But Rome would not countenance a religion that set itself up as unique and as taking that place in the hearts of men which was occupied by the Cult of the Cæsar. Into this atmosphere Christianity came with its unique and imperialistic claims. It was inevitable that there would be a clash between these two imperialisms, that of Heaven and that of Rome. It came in the form of the bloody persecutions hurled against the Christian Church by Rome during the first three hundred years of its existence. What an unanswerable proof of the divine origin of Christianity do we have in the fact that by A.D. 316, Christianity had displaced Emperor-worship as the predominating system of belief in the Roman world and that the Emperor Constantine at that time made it the state religion.

The inscriptions which archæologists have unearthed give us some information regarding the Cult of the Cæsar which throws an abundance of light upon some passages in the New Testament. They reveal a parallelism between Christianity and the imperial cult with reference to the position of the Lord Jesus in the system called Christianity and that of the Roman emperor in the system called the Cult of Cæsar, and the official titles held by each.

For instance, the term *kurios* meaning "Lord" was used as a divine title of the emperor. It was also an official title of our Lord Jesus. This Greek word *kurios* is the translation in the Septuagint of the august title of God in the Old Testament, "Jehovah." The term "Lord" was understood to be a title which included within its meaning of "master" the idea of divinity. It was a divine title. These facts throw a flood of light on Paul's assertion (I Corinthians 8:5, 6), "For though there be that are called gods, whether in heaven or in earth, (as there be gods many, and lords many,) but to us there is but one God, the Father, of whom are all things, and we in him; and one Lord Jesus Christ, by whom are all things, and we by him." These words are set in a context in which Paul is pleading for separation from the pagan Greek mystery religions. He cites the example of the Christian's separation from the Cult of Cæsar, arguing that if the Corinthian Christians have thrown off their allegiance to the Cæsar so far as worshipping him is concerned, they ought also to separate themselves from any participation in the Greek religious practices. Here the chief exponent of Christianity is throwing out into the arena of the imperialistic contest the imperialistic challenge of Christianity, namely, that while the Greeks may people the heavens with deities, and the Romans may worship the emperor on earth, yet so far as Christians are concerned, they do not recognize these, for they are monotheists, worshipping the absolute God, and His Son Jesus Christ who Himself is God.

Our Lord referred to this practice of the deification of the emperor when He said (Luke 22:25), "The kings of the Gentiles exercise lordship over them." The meaning of the word "lordship" here is not merely that the emperor rules as an absolute autocrat, but that he rules as an emperor-god. In answer to the question of the Herodians (Matt. 22:15-22), "Is it lawful to pay taxes to Cæsar, or not?" He said, "Render therefore to Cæsar the things that are Cæsar's." The question was fully answered. The words, "and unto God the things that are God's," is a protest against Emperor-worship. Taxes should be paid to Cæsar, but no worship should be accorded him. To be worshipped is the prerogative of God alone.

"There went out a decree from Cæsar Augustus that the whole inhabited earth" i.e., the Roman Empire, "should be enrolled" (Luke 2:1). The Greek word is not "taxed" but "enrolled." Taxation was probably one of the purposes of this enrollment, but it was the imperial census that was being taken. The inscriptions furnish instances of other enrollments, showing that such a thing was neither unreasonable nor impossible, the destructive critics notwithstanding. Joseph and Mary in obedience to the imperial decree go to Bethlehem where the prophecy of Micah (5:2) is fulfilled. Now comes the imperialistic announcement, brought by an angel from heaven (Luke 2:10, 11), "Fear not; for, behold, I bring you good tidings of great joy, which shall be all people. For unto you is born this day in the city of David a Saviour which is Christ the Lord." Here was heaven's King coming to dispute the claims and position of the Cæsar who arrogated to himself the title of "lord," and who was worshipped as a god. No wonder that Herod and the Jews were agitated at this news (Matt. 2:1-8), the former because of the imperialistic challenge which would present new problems of administration to him in addition to the ones he already had in connection with troublesome Israel, the latter because, entrenched in their ecclesiastical sin, they did not want to be deprived of their lucrative positions. But while heaven's King came in humiliation the first time and did not displace the world empire of the ruling Cæsar but only found a place in a few hearts, He will some day come in exaltation to dethrone Antichrist, the then ruling Cæsar, and, occupying the throne of David, rule over a world-empire as King of kings, and Lord of lords.

It was Thomas who exclaimed (John 20:27), "My Lord and my God." This was enough to involve him in serious trouble with the Roman authorities had they known of it, for he was acknowledging Jesus of Nazareth as his Lord and his God instead of Cæsar. Polycarp, who lived A.D. 156, was confronted with the question by the Roman official, "What is the harm in saying 'lord Cæsar'?" And because he refused to acknowledge Cæsar as lord, he was martyred. Festus (Acts 25:26) said regarding Paul, "Of whom I have no certain thing to write unto my lord." His lord was Cæsar, "lord" in the sense that

Festus recognized Nero, who was then Cæsar, as the emperor-god to whom worship was due.

But see the imperialistic challenge of Christianity in the words of the apostle Paul (Phil. 2:9-11), "Wherefore God also hath highly exalted Him, and given Him the Name which is above every name, that at the Name of Jesus every knee should bow, of things in heaven, and things in earth, and things under the earth; and that every tongue should confess that Jesus Christ is Lord, to the glory of God the Father."

The terms *theos,* "god," and *huios theou,* "son of god," were both used in the Cult of the Cæsar and were titles of the emperor. Our Lord claimed oneness in essence with the Father (John 10:30). He said (John 8:58), "Before Abraham came into existence, I am." He claimed to be the Son of God (John 9:35-38) and accepted worship as the Son of God, thus demonstrating the fact that His position as Son of God made Him a co-participant in the essence of Deity. All this was in startling contrast to the claims of the then ruling emperc., and our blessed Lord knew it. Luke 22:25 shows His accurate knowledge of the customs, political practices, and happenings of His day, when He speaks of those who exercise authority over the people as being called "benefactors." The term "benefactor" was an honorable title given to princes and other eminent men for valuable services rendered to the State.

The emperor was also given the title "overseer." He was the "overseer" of his subjects in that he was charged with the responsibility of caring for their welfare. The same term "overseer" is given God the Father in I Peter

2:25 where the word meaning "overseer" is translated "bishop." Peter, in writing his epistle, must have been conscious of the imperialistic challenge of Christianity when presenting the God of Christians as the Overseer of their souls, refusing to acknowledge the overseeing care of the emperor-god.

Another title given the emperor was *basileus,* "king." Some monarchs used the title "king of kings." Our Lord claimed this title in relation to His distinctive position as the Messiah of Israel. The Jews recognized this as directly opposed to the imperial position of Cæsar as king. Not that there were no kings in the empire ruling under the authority of the world-Cæsar. But the Jewish leaders understood Old Testament truth well enough to know that our Lord's claim to the position of king over Israel involved world-dominion, which at once struck at the throne of Cæsar. They tried to use this as a means of involving Him in difficulties with Rome, for they said to Pilate (John 19:12), "If thou let this man go, thou art not Cæsar's friend: whosoever maketh himself a king speaketh against Cæsar." They had accused Him of forbidding them to pay taxes to Cæsar, which was a lie, and of claiming to be the Anointed of God, which was the truth (Luke 23:2). Upon our Lord's acknowledging the fact that He was a king, Pilate turned to the Jews and said, "I find no fault in this man" (Luke 23:3, 4). One look at Jesus was enough to convince Pilate that he was not a dangerous character, and he dismissed from his mind any disposition to treat our Lord's claim seriously. Had Pilate taken our Lord's claims at their face value, his position as a representative of Cæsar would have demanded that he deal with the case before him in no hesitant manner. When Pilate said to them (John 19:14, 15), "Behold your king," the Jews who hated and despised the Roman yoke and the emperor who ruled them, cried in a false patriotism, "We have no king but Cæsar."

Paul, after he had faced Nero as the prisoner of the Roman empire and had been liberated, wrote the following to Timothy (First epistle 1:17, 6:15), "Now unto the King eternal, immortal, invisible, the only wise God, be glory and honor for ever and ever. Amen." "Which in his times he shall show, who is the blessed and only Potentate, the King of kings and Lord of lords, who only hath immortality, dwelling in the light which no man can approach unto; whom no man hath seen, nor can see: to whom be honor and power everlasting. Amen." Again the great apostle, having been snatched from the jaws of death at the hands of Rome, puts himself within reach of the long arm of the empire when he denies the supremacy of the emperor in things spiritual.

But not only did the emperor have the titles of lord, son of god, god, overseer, and king, all of which were titles of our Lord also, but he was given the title *soter,* "saviour."

At least eight of the emperors carried the title "saviour of the world." They were hailed as the saviours of the people. For the most part, the Roman world was well governed and policed, Roman law was administered in equity, the Roman roads caused travel and commerce to flourish, and the Roman peace made living conditions bearable and in some instances pleasant. Thus the emper-

ors were the world-saviours. Now comes Christianity
with its imperialistic announcement (Luke 2:11), "For
unto you is born this day in the city of David a Saviour,
which is Christ the Lord." But this Saviour's name was
Jesus, one who would save them from the sins which they
loved and from which they did not want to be separated.
What motive would they have in transferring their allegiance from a world-saviour who gave them the comforts
of life and at the same time allowed them to go on in their
sin, to the Lord Jesus, especially when allegiance to this
new Saviour could very well result in their crucifixion by
Rome? And yet for the first three hundred years of the
Church's history, tens of thousands willingly embraced this
new Saviour and went to a horrible death. How explain
this? The only answer is that the supernatural power of
God was operative in their hearts. The Samaritans said
(John 4:42), "We have heard him ourselves, and know
that this is indeed the Christ, the Saviour of the world."
It took grace to say that, for they realized that should this
come to the ears of Rome, they would be charged with
treason.

In I Timothy 1:1, Paul refers to "the commandment
of our God and Saviour Jesus Christ," coupling the titles
"God" and "Saviour" together as they are in the Cult of
the Cæsar. In the same epistle (4:10), he speaks of God
as the Saviour of all men. The context, which brings in
the idea of faith, seems to indicate that the idea of salvation from sin and the impartation of eternal life is the
function here of God as Saviour. He is Saviour of all
men in the sense that our Lord is "the Saviour of the
world" (John 4:42). He is the actual Saviour of those

who believe, and the potential Saviour of the unbeliever in the sense that He has provided a salvation at the Cross for the sinner, and stands ready to save that sinner when the latter places his faith in the Lord Jesus. The Emperor was the Saviour of the world. No wonder that Rome recognized in Christianity a formidable rival. No wonder the Roman writer Tacitus says of Christianity, "This destructive superstition, repressed for awhile, again broke out, and spread not only through Judæa where it originated, but reached this city also (Rome), into which flow all things that are vile and abominable, and where they are encouraged." Paul uses the words "God our Saviour" in Titus 1:3, here the Saviour of believers in a spiritual sense. Peter applies the title "Saviour" to our Lord in his second epistle (1:11), adding the title "Lord," which also was claimed by the emperor. Jude closes his book with the words, "to the only wise God our Saviour," again a conscious assertion of the preeminence of God over all the claims of earthly sovereigns.

Another term found in the Christian system and which was used by Roman emperors was *archiereus,* "high priest." The emperors were called "Pontifex Maximus" in the east, the name being the Latin translation of the Greek *archiereus.* In contrast to the arrogancy, cruelty, and wickedness of the Roman emperor who was recognized not only as lord, son of god, god, saviour, but also as high priest, we have the words of Paul, "Seeing then that we have a great high priest, that is passed through the heavens, Jesus the Son of God, let us hold fast our profession, for we have not an high priest which cannot be touched with the feeling of our infirmities: but was in all points tempted like as we are, yet without sin. Let us therefore come boldly unto the throne of grace, that we may obtain mercy, and find grace to help in time of need" (Heb. 4:14-16). The primary contrast here is undoubtedly between the Aaronic high priest and our Lord as High Priest, but the background of Roman imperialism seems to be in the picture also. The Roman emperor was Pontifex Maximus, a high priest upon the throne of the Cæsars. But our Lord Jesus is a high priest who, now seated upon a throne of grace, will some day as High Priest in the Messianic Kingdom occupy the throne of David in Jerusalem, as Zechariah says, "He shall be a priest upon his throne" (Zech. 6:13).

Turning now to words used in a technical sense in the Cult of the Cæsar with reference to the people instead of the emperor, we have the expression, "friend (*philos*) of the emperor," which was an official title in the imperial period. What a flood of light this throws upon our Lord's words, "Ye are my friends, if ye do whatsoever I command you. Henceforth I call you not bondslaves, for a bondslave knoweth not what his lord doeth: but I have called you friends" (John 15:14, 15). As our Lord knew of the Roman custom of calling a servant of the State a Benefactor (Luke 22:25), so He knew of this custom of certain ones being called "friends of the emperor." There was real point to His words and they were not lost upon His disciples. Think of what faith this involved on His part and theirs. The King of kings was on His way from the upper room where they had celebrated the Passover together for the last time, to His crucifixion and death, the rejected King of Israel. Yet in all the dignity of His royal position as King of the Jews in the Davidic dynasty, He said, "I have called you friends." Yes, they were friends of the Emperor who would be raised from the dead, ascend to heaven, and some day come back to this earth to reign as King of kings and Lord of lords.

Another official title was "bondslave (*doulos*) of the emperor." There were imperial slaves all over the Roman world. There was an honor in even being a bondslave of Cæsar. Paul must have been conscious of the analogy when he wrote, "Paul, a bondslave of Christ Jesus" (Rom. 1:1). If it was an honor in the Roman world to be a bondslave of the emperor, what an exalted privilege it was to be a bondslave of the King of kings.

In II Corinthians 5:20, Paul calls himself (editorial "we") an ambassador for Christ. The Greek word is *presbeuo,* a technical term used of the emperor's legate, namely, the one who speaks for the emperor. Paul was a spokesman on behalf of Christ. The word is used also in Ephesians 6:20 and in Luke 14:32, in the latter text appearing in the translation as "ambassage." The word clearly refers to the imperial service of Cæsar, and in the Scriptures to the imperial service of Christ in which the saints are engaged. Thus did Christianity parallel the imperialism of Rome.

The imperial secretary used the technical expression *pepisteumai* which meant "I am entrusted," the qualifying word being added which would designate the matter with which he was entrusted. Paul as an imperial secretary of the Lord Jesus entrusted with the writings of the epistles which bear his name, uses the same technical phrase current in the Roman world at that time. The word is used in Galatians 2:7, "committed;" in I Corinthians 9:17, "committed;" in I Thessalonians 2:4, "put in trust;" I Timothy 1:11, "committed to my trust;" and in Titus 1:3, "committed."

The correspondence of the imperial secretary was designated by the technical expression, *hiera grammata,* "sacred writings." It was used of imperial letters and decrees. The expression *theia grammata,* "divine writings" was used of imperial letters. Imperial ordinances were referred to as "divine commandments." This shows clearly how completely the religious or ecclesiastical position of the emperor made its influence felt throughout the affairs of state. Alongside of all this we have Paul using the same expression, *hiera grammata,* in II Timothy 3:15 in the words "holy scriptures." Here the writings of the Old Testament are put over against the imperial decrees of Cæsar, which latter had not only governmental but also religious significance. New Testament writings were looked upon by the early Christians in the same way.

Finally, the word *euaggelion* "good news" or "good tidings" was used in a profane sense of any piece of good news. But it also had a sacred connection as when it was used to refer to the good news of the birthday of the emperor-god. At the accession of a Cæsar to the throne, the account of this event was spoken of as *euaggelion* "good tidings."

See the parallel in the imperialistic announcement by the angels, "Fear not: for, behold, I bring you good tidings of great joy, which shall be to all people. For unto you is born this day in the city of David a Saviour, which is Christ the Lord" (Luke 2:10, 11). How all this gives further point to Paul's words "I am ready to preach the good news to you that are at Rome also. For I am not ashamed of the good news: for it is the power of God resulting in salvation to every one that believeth." Paul was expecting to come to Rome where the "good news" of the emperor found its reality, that emperor who was called lord, son of God, god, king, saviour, and high priest, and he was to announce the true Lord from heaven who was the Son of the eternal God, yes, very God Himself, coming King of kings, Saviour of the believer, and High Priest who by His atoning death on Calvary's Cross paid for sin and put it away. He was to announce this good news, this gospel, for that is what the word "gospel" means, right in the stronghold of Emperor-worship. But he was not afraid to do so, for he knew that it was of divine and supernatural origin and would accomplish that whereunto it was sent.

Dear reader, what do you think of the Lord Jesus? Have you taken him as your personal Saviour? Are you trusting in His precious blood for your salvation from sin? If you have not yet received the gift of salvation by faith from the hands of a God eager to save you, will you not just now do so? "For God so loved the world, that he gave his only begotten Son, that whosoever believeth in him should not perish, but have everlasting life" (John 3:16).

IV

About Royal Visits

¶ THE GREEK inscriptions throw a flood of light upon the New Testament. One of the current expressions in the first century was the word *parousia,* used in the east as a technical expression for the *royal visit of a king or emperor.* The word means literally "the being beside," thus, "the personal presence." The *parousia* of the king must have been well known to the people, for there were special payments and taxes to defray the cost of the festivities on that occasion. All over the world, advent-coins were struck after a *parousia* of the emperor. Advent-sacrifices were offered at these *parousiai.* A papyrus manuscript speaks of contributions given for a crown of gold to be presented to the king at his *parousia.* A papyrus found among the wrappings of the mummy of a sacred crocodile, speaks of the requisition of corn to help defray the expenses of the *parousia* of a king, which was being collected from the peasants by the village headman and the elders.

These *parousiai* were noted for their special brilliance. New eras in the history of mankind were proclaimed at the *parousia* of a sovereign. Advent coins, the word "advent" being the Latin equivalent of the Greek for *parousia,* were struck and became official coinage of the empire. Solemn sacrifices were offered in the king's presence. Monuments were erected. The day of the visit was designated "a holy day." As the pagan world designated the *parousiai* of its sovereigns by their number, so the Christian system has its three *parousiai* of the Kings of kings and Lord of lords, twice to the earth, and once between these events, into the air.

This word *parousia* is translated "coming" in our English text, in relation to the coming of our Lord into the air to catch out His Bride the Church, the coming of our Lord to the earth to Israel to set up His Millennial kingdom, and the coming of Antichrist to establish his worldwide kingdom during the Tribulation (II Thess. 2:1, 8, 9).

The Christians of the first century felt the parallelism between the *parousia* of the reigning emperor and the *parousia* of Christ. In the case of the Rapture, it will be the royal visit of the Bridegroom into the atmosphere of this earth to receive His Bride the Church to Himself and to take her with Him to heaven. In the case of the return of the Lord to this earth, it will be the royal visit of the King of kings and Lord of lords who comes from the royal line of David, who will dethrone Antichrist and set up the throne of David. In the case of Antichrist, it will be the coming of the Wild Beast (Greek) of Revelation 13:1-8 as a king, to assume absolute authority as world dictator, occupying Satan's throne for a brief space of seven years.

Note again if you will the parallelism which exists. As the royal visit of a Roman emperor was marked by elaborate and brilliant festivities, so our blessed Lord's *parousia*, both when He comes *for* His Bride, and when He comes to the earth *with* His Bride to reign as King of kings, will be accompanied by a heavenly splendor that will far outshine the displays of earthly sovereigns. As the *parousia* of a Roman emperor brought in a new era, so the first advent of our Lord ushered in a new era, both dispensationally, and for the world at large. As advent coins were struck at the *parousia* of a Roman emperor, so our money is dated according to our Lord's first advent. But note the contrast. Solemn sacrifices were offered before earthly sovereigns who were worshipped as gods, whereas our Lord in His first advent was Himself the sacrifice that paid for sin.

Other scriptures where the word occurs and in which it has the meaning of the royal visit of a sovereign are, I Corinthians 1:7, 15:23; I Thessalonians 2:19, 3:13, 4:15, 5:23; James 5:7; II Peter 1:16, 3:4, 12; and I John 2:28. Such was the imperialism of Christianity in the first century that it clearly saw the parallel between the *parousia* of an earthly sovereign and the *parousia* of the Lord Jesus, and at the same time, the rival claims of each. These Christians were not afraid to give allegiance to the lowly carpenter from Nazareth, the travel-worn itinerant teacher who was rejected by His own people and nailed to a Roman cross. They were convinced that He was what He claimed to be, God the Son, incarnate in humanity. They were not intrigued by the Roman purple, the armies of the empire, the far-flung colonies. Their hearts responded to the unique beauty of the meek and lowly Jesus, and to the fragrance of His Person. He was the King of Glory, and they would rejoice in His *parousia*.

V

The Power of a Christlike Life

"Dearly beloved, I beseech you as strangers and pilgrims, abstain from fleshly lusts which war against the soul; having your conversation honest among the Gentiles: that, whereas they speak against you as evildoers, they may by your good works, glorify God in the day of visitation" (I Peter 2:11, 12).

Word Studies

¶ THE WORDS "dearly beloved" are from a Greek word which speaks of God's love as seen in John 3:16 and Romans 5:5 where the same word is used, referring to that love expressed at Calvary in the giving of His Son and shed abroad in the heart of the believer by the Holy Spirit. Peter is reminding the believers to whom he is writing that they are divinely loved ones, divinely loved by God. What a comfort that is to the sorely tempted heart. The word "beseech" is from a Greek word which was used in the sense of "I ask, beseech, exhort, urge, I beg of you, please." Think of the infinite condescension of God who when asking something of His blood-bought children, does not command but instead says, "I beg of you, please." The word "strangers" refers to a person living alongside of someone else. It speaks of a temporary home. The word "pilgrims" is the translation of a word literally meaning, "to live alongside of the natives in a foreign land." Christians are living in the midst of unsaved people in territory ruled over by Satan, for he is the god of this age. The believer's home is in heaven. He sings, "I am a stranger here within a foreign land; My home is far away upon a golden strand; Ambassador to be of realms beyond the sea, I'm here on business for my king."

Living in the midst of a foreign population, representing our Sovereign, the Lord Jesus, we are exhorted by God to abstain from fleshly lusts. "Abstain" is literally "hold yourselves back from." "Lusts" is confined today in its meaning almost entirely to an immoral desire. The Greek word means simply "a strong desire," and in our context it refers to a strong desire coming from the evil nature. "Which" is literally "which are of such a nature." The character of these cravings is emphasized. "War" is from a Greek word which was used in various ways, "to lead a military expedition, to lead soldiers to war or battle, to carry on a campaign." These evil cravings are carrying on a campaign against the Christian. The word "against" is from a Greek word whose root meaning is "down." We get a picture of these evil cravings hurling themselves down upon our souls in a campaign designed to cause their downfall.

"Conversation" today refers to the interchange of words between two or more persons. When the Authorized Version was made, it meant what the Greek word means from which it is translated, namely, "behaviour," or "manner of life." "Having" in the Greek emphasizes action going on steadily, and so we translate by the word "holding." "Honest" is from a Greek word meaning "good." There are two words in Greek meaning "good," one, "inner intrinsic goodness," the other, "outer goodness," namely the expression of this inner goodness as seen by the eye. Our Lord used the second word when he said (John 10:11) "I am the good shepherd." A sheep knows its shepherd, not by what is in the shepherd's heart, but by what it can see of the shepherd. So it is the beautiful fragrance of our Lord's Person that attracts His sheep, and by which they know Him. Peter uses the same word. It is the beauty and fragrance of the Christian's life which the unsaved see, not what is in his heart. The Bible they read is our lives.

The word "whereas" is literally "in which," and refers to the Christ-like life the believer is exhorted to live. The unsaved speak evil of the goodness of a Christian, defaming him as an evil worker. But the Christian is exhorted to hold his manner of life steadily beautiful in its goodness, so that even though the world may defame that beautiful life, many lost sinners beholding it, that is, viewing it carefully, might be led to a saving knowledge of the Lord Jesus, having been attracted to Him by the Christ-like life of the believer.

The word "visitation" is translated from the same Greek word rendered "overseer" in Acts 20:28, "bishop" in I Tim. 3:1, "visitest" in Heb. 2:6, and refers to the act of overseeing the spiritual welfare of another. It refers here to the time when God shall become the spiritual overseer of their souls, and that will be when the unsaved person appropriates the Lord Jesus as Saviour. God's Word testifies to the power of a Christlike life, for it is able to lead an unsaved person to the place where he has the desire to know the Lord Jesus, and the simple gospel story will tell him how he can be saved. Someone has said that the greatest power in the universe next to the power

of God, is the power of a life definitely subject to the
Holy Spirit, exhibiting the beauty of the Lord Jesus.
And so God exhorts us, "Divinely loved ones, I beg of you
as those who are living in the midst of a foreign population as strangers and pilgrims, I beg of you to hold yourselves back from the fleshly cravings, cravings of such a
nature that, like an army waging an offensive warfare,
they are hurling themselves down upon your soul; holding
your manner of life among the nations steadily beautiful
in its goodness, in order that in that thing in which they
defame you as those who do evil, because of your works
beautiful in their goodness which they are carefully viewing, they might glorify God in the day of His overseeing
care."

VI

Three Steps in a Sinner's Salvation

Peter, an ambassador of Jesus Christ with a commission to selected-out ones who are sojourners in a foreign
land, those scattered throughout Pontus, Galatia, Cappa-
docia, Asia, and Bithynia, selected out ones by the foreordination of God the Father to be recipients of the setting-apart work of the Spirit which results in obedience
(of faith) and sprinkling of the blood of Jesus Christ.
Grace to you (for daily living) and (heart) peace be mul-
tiplied (I Peter 1:1, 2).

Word Studies in Authorized Version

¶ THE FIRST step is the sinner's election according to the foreknowledge of God the Father. "Elect" is from a word which means "to pick out" or "select." It refers here to the act of God in sovereign grace choosing individuals to salvation. The same word is translated "chosen" in Ephesians 1:4, and is literally "chosen out," that is, the choice is made out of a number. God chose us out before the foundation of the world. In the eternity before the universe came into existence, yes, always, God had us in His heart for salvation.

This election was according to the foreknowledge of God the Father. The word translated "foreknowledge" is from a Greek word which in a connection like this means more than mere previous knowledge. It is used in Acts 2:23, "delivered by the determinate counsel and foreknowledge of God," the words "counsel" and "foreknowledge" being in a construction in the Greek text which makes the latter word refer to the same thing to which the word "counsel" refers, and makes it a further description of that thing. The word "determinate" is the translation of a Greek word which in the form in which it is used here means "that which has been appointed or decreed." The word "counsel" refers to an interchange of opinions, a mutual advising, the exchange of deliberative judgment. Thus the word "foreknowledge" refers to that counsel of God in which after deliberative judgment certain among mankind were designated to a certain position, that position being defined by the context. The same Greek word translated "foreknowledge" in verse two is

translated by the word "foreordained" in verse twenty.
Therefore the election of the saints was determined in the
counsel of God which consisted of a judgment which was
the outgrowth of deliberation, that judgment having for
its purpose the designating of certain ones to a position
defined in the context. The words "according to" are from
a preposition which implies domination or control over
something. Mere foreknowledge does not have within it
any compelling necessities which would require the election of certain individuals. The fact that the saints were
elected, was part of God's previous knowledge. The election or choice of the saints was therefore in accordance
with or determined by the counsel of God the Father.
That is the first step in our salvation.

The second step is found in the words, "through sanctification of the Spirit unto obedience." The Greek word
translated "sanctification" means literally "to set apart" or
"to consecrate." We must not confuse the act of dedica-
tion with that of consecration. A saint may dedicate himself and all he possesses to God. God consecrates a saint
to a certain position, that is, He sets him apart. Here we
have the act of God the Holy Spirit setting the individual
apart, consequent upon his being selected out by God the
Father. The idea in the Greek is that God the Father
chose the saint to a certain thing, and that was, to be set
apart by the Holy Spirit. Thus we have the Holy Spirit
taking hold of the one chosen, for the purpose of bringing
that lost sinner to the act of faith in the Lord Jesus and
His precious blood. The obedience here is not that of the
saint as engendered in the heart by the Holy Spirit, but
the obedience of the *sinner* to the faith, as in Acts 6:7,

where "a great company of the priests were obedient to the faith." Peter refers here to the act of placing faith in the Lord Jesus as the One who shed His precious blood on Calvary's Cross to atone for man's sin. The act of God the Spirit in setting apart the individual, is His work of bringing that lost sinner to the place where he puts his faith in the Saviour. There is nothing in the sin-darkened heart of a sinner which would reach out and appropriate the Lord Jesus as Saviour. The hand of faith must be energized or motivated by the Holy Spirit. He supplies the faith necessary. Salvation is a work of God from start to finish. And yet it is true that each lost sinner must by an act of his will place his faith in the Saviour. He has that responsibility. "Ye have not chosen me, but I have chosen you" (John 15:16), is sublimely true. But "whosoever will, let him take the water of life freely" (Rev. 22:17), is also true. We cannot reconcile or understand these things, but we can trust God for them and believe them.

The third step in our salvation is expressed by the words, "and sprinkling of the blood of Jesus Christ." The divine order is first, obedience, then the sprinkling of the blood. The latter expression is taken by Peter from Old Testament usage, the blood of sprinkling referring there to animal blood typical of the cleansing blood of our Lord.

This act of faith results in the individual's cleansing by the precious blood of Christ, the work of God the Son. This is justification, the removal of the guilt and penalty of sin and the imputation of a righteousness, Christ Himself, in whom the believer stands complete forever.

Thus each believer is elected or chosen out, this choice determined by the deliberative counsel of God the Father. The individual chosen is set apart or consecrated by the Holy Spirit, this being the work of God the Spirit in imparting faith to him. This faith is answered by God the Son, who through His precious blood cleanses the believer and brings him unto salvation. God the Father chooses the individual, God the Spirit brings him to the act of faith, and God the Son cleanses him from sin.

Put your faith in the Lord Jesus as your personal Saviour, and you will find that God the Father chose you to salvation, God the Holy Spirit brought you to the act of faith, and God the Son cleansed you from sin in His precious blood.

VII

Not With Wisdom of Words

❡ BUSINESS, government, warfare, athletics, labor, — Paul the scholar draws from them all as he seeks to make clear the message of God. In business it may be a title deed, the credit and debit side of a ledger, the forfeiture of what was thought to be a gain, the earnest-money paid down in the transference of property, the receipt "paid in full," a last will or testament, a broken contract.

In warfare, it is the soldier, his weapons, his armor, his shield, his wages. In government, the commonwealth, its citizens, their responsibilities and privileges, appear in the apostle's writings. In the world of labor, the slave and the skilled artisan, the finished product, the possibility that a piece of work may be returned by the employer, rejected because of failure to meet specifications, all become illustrations which Paul uses.

In athletics, the race course down which the runners speed, the crown of oak leaves that graces the brow of the winner, the desperate agonizing efforts of two wrestlers, the concerted team work of one group of athletes against another group, the Greek stadium with the watchers intent upon the outcome, the judge's stand, all become for Paul illustrations familiar to the public of the Roman world, and because familiar, an ideal medium by which to preach the gospel. Paul, the scholar, the man of books, trained in the Greek schools, yet spoke and wrote the language of the average man when he preached the Word of God.

Writing to the Corinthians he says in his first epistle (2:1-5), "And I having come to you, brethren, came, not having my message dominated by transcendent rhetorical display or by philosophical subtlety when I was announcing authoritatively to you the testimony of God, for after weighing the issues, I did not decide to know anything among you except Jesus Christ and Him crucified. And when I faced you, I fell into a state of weakness and fear and much trembling. And my message and my preaching were not couched in specious words of philosophy, but were dependent for their efficacy upon a demonstration of the Spirit and of power, in order that your faith should not be resting in human philosophy but in God's power."

The words, "I did not decide," are a literal rendering from the Greek, possibly a bit cumbersome in English, but nevertheless a true representation of what Paul wrote. The tendency in the first century was that of the blending of religions. If someone embraced a new faith, his desire would be to bring over into its system some of the elements of the old. We see that in the case of Judaism. Another tendency was that of the new convert explaining his new found faith in terms of the old, or harmonizing the new with the old. This we observe in instances where Greeks embraced Christianity.

Paul was faced with this situation when he was saved, and with respect to both Judaism and the Greek Philosophies, for he was well trained in both. Consequently when he said, "I did not decide to know anything among you except Jesus Christ and Him crucified," he meant that he, after weighing the issues, after reflecting on the matter of presenting the gospel to the Greeks in terms of their philosophy (for he said he wanted to become all things to all men, that is, adapt himself and his methods to their needs), decided not to do so, but to preach Christ, not "with wisdom of words" (I Cor. 1:17), that is, not in specious words of a false philosophy, but in the everyday language of the people. Thus we see him drawing from contemporary life, from the Greek games, the Roman armies, the language of government, the business world, and the life of the laboring classes.

He uses a business term when he speaks of faith as the title deed of things hoped for (Heb. 11:1), the word "substance" being translated from a Greek word used in legal practice for a title deed. When he warns the

Hebrews against the act of renouncing their professed faith in Messiah and going back to the Old Testament sacrifices after having been led along by the Holy Spirit in His pre-salvation work up to and including repentance, he says that that renunciation would be like the act of a man breaking a contract which he had made (Heb. 6:6), for they would be breaking the contract which they had made with the Holy Spirit in allowing Him to lead them on towards Christ, the words "fall away" being the ones referred to here.

When he desires to explain the necessity of the death of Christ in order that the New Testament might become effective, he uses the illustration of a will not being effective until the death of the testator (Heb. 9:16, 17). When he tells us (Rom. 8:17) that as heirs of God, we are also joint-heirs with Christ, he draws from Roman law which made all children, including adopted ones, equal heirs. Think of it, equal heirs with Jesus Christ! Should he wish to assure believers that they will receive their glorification, he uses the business term "earnest" a down-payment in kind, guaranteeing the full payment of the rest (Eph. 1:14). The Spirit is the down-payment in kind, His indwelling being part of our salvation.

He explains to the Philippians (3:8) that when he trusted Christ as his Saviour, he "suffered the loss of all things." He uses a business term which meant "to punish by exacting a forfeit." The verb is in the passive voice, and should be rendered, "I have been caused to forfeit." Paul took punishment in the business sense when he put his trust in Christ. It meant the forfeiture of all that he counted dear. That meant crucifixion of self, and self dies hard. He thanks the Philippians (4:15) for the gift which they had sent, and reminds them that when he left Macedonia, no church but theirs "communicated," that is, "had partnership" with him "as concerning giving and receiving." After the words "had partnership," the Greek has "with respect to an account of giving and receiving," the ledger with a credit and debit page. The Philippians kept a ledger in which they recorded the good things received from Paul on the credit page, and the debt they owed Paul on the debit side. He acknowledged the receipt of their gift in the words, "I have all," using a business term meaning, "I have received in full" (4:18). The word "abound" in 4:17, is taken from the money market. It was used of the accumulation of interest. The word "account" is used here much as we would use the term "bank-account." The fruit concerning which Paul is speaking is the reward accumulating on the bank-account of the Philippian saints in the bank of Heaven, reward given for the generosity of these believers in their support of Paul the missionary.

When he desired a word that would give to the ordinary reader of the first century, what the Christian system of teaching included with respect to the individual believer's relation to his Lord as a servant, he searched the vocabulary of the laboring man for the proper term. He had a choice of six words, all speaking of one who serves. One referred to a person captured in war or kidnapped, and sold as a slave. Another spoke of a household servant, as in Romans 14:4 and I Peter 2:18. Another was used as a designation of a servant in official capacity, with emphasis upon his activity in service, as in John 2:5, 12:26;

Romans 13:4, 15:8, 16:1; I Corinthians 3:5; Philippians
1:1 (deacon). Still another referred to servants who
were court officers, as in Matthew 26:58. Yet another
word (Heb. 3:5) spoke of a servant who was an attend
ant upon someone, the emphasis being upon the fact that
his services are voluntary, whether as a freeman or as a
slave. But he chose none of these. The word which the
Holy Spirit led him to use is found in Philemon 16.
Onesimus was the slave of Philemon, one bound to him,
one born into slavery, one bound to his master in a permanent relationship which only death could break, one
whose will is swallowed up in the will of his master, one
who is devoted to his master even to the disregard of his
own interests. Onesimus did not before his salvation live
up to the last two specifications, but the Greek word which
Paul used to speak of the place he occupied among the
various classes of slaves in the Roman world, included the
above details. This was the word known to the average
man of the first century, whose content of meaning as
given above, would exactly fit Paul's teaching regarding
the believer's relationship to the Lord Jesus, and the
unbeliever's relationship to Satan as well. The word was
used as the exact opposite of the world for "freeman,"
thus emphasizing the fact that the Christian is not his
own, but is bought with a price. Again, the servile
relationship is emphasized. These two conceptions were
part of that "offence of the Cross" which confronted the
first century sinner. The word meant "a slave." Other
words for the idea of one who serves were more noble and
tender. But this one just referred to a common slave.
This was the word Paul chose. To translate this word by

"servant" in such passages as Romans 1:1 or 6:16-17, is just to miss the point in Paul's teaching. The word should be rendered either by "slave" or "bondman." Of course, to be a slave of a pagan master, with all that that implied of misery, cruelty, abject servitude, was one thing. To be a slave of the Lord Jesus, with all that that implies of wonderful fellowship with one's Master, and the high privilege of serving the Lord of glory, is quite another. Nevertheless, the term "slave" or "bondman" is the idea presented. The first century world so understood Paul's use of the word. And that is the way in which we of the twentieth century should use it.

Again, Paul speaks to the laboring classes in his use of the Greek word which means, "to labor to the point of exhaustion," which experience was a very common thing among the down-trodden masses of the Roman world. He speaks of a certain Mary "who was of such a nature as to have labored to the point of exhaustion with reference to many things for us" (Rom. 16:6). He speaks of himself in the words, "I labored more abundantly than they all" (I Cor. 15:10). Thus they understood Paul's language. He spoke and wrote the tongue of the working man. He kept in mind that "Not many wise men after the flesh, not many mighty, not many noble, are called, but God hath chosen the foolish things of the world . . . the weak things of the world . . . and base things, and things that are not" (I Cor. 1:26-28).

Paul also borrows from the language of the soldier and of war. The instruments we are to put at the service of God in Romans 6:13 are referred to by the Greek word as weapons. The word was used of implements of war, either offensive or defensive, harness, armor, the heavy shield used by the Greek foot-soldiers. Its use here gives one the idea of two armies, Satan's and God's with the believer in God's army. The word "wages" in 6:23 is from a Greek word which means "cooked meat." At Athens it meant "fish." It came to mean the "provision-money" which Rome gave its soldiers. The same word is used in I Corinthians 9:7, "Who goeth a warfare any time at his own charges?"

As the Roman soldier received provision-money with which to sustain life so that he could fight and die for Caesar, so the unsaved receive provision-money from sin, spiritual death, so that they can serve it, then physical death, and final banishment from the presence of God for all eternity. Neither receives wages, only enough sustenance to enable him to serve his master.

In Ephesians 6 we have accoutrements of warfare, armor, breastplate, shield, arrows, illustrations which Paul took from the marching legions of Rome. See his reference to the expected endurance of a soldier in II Timothy 2:3, and to the man in verse 4, who raises an army for military purposes. In II Corinthians 2:14 in the words "causeth us to triumph," and in Colossians 2:15, in the word "triumphing" we have another instance where Paul draws from first century life. The translation should read, "leadeth us in triumph" and "leading them in triumph." The word referred to a victorious general, home from the wars, leading a triumphal procession through the streets of Rome. The captives and spoils of war would precede him, and he would follow in a chariot, a slave holding over his head a jewelled crown. Then would come the victorious army. Paul's readers were conversant with all this. They would understand his illustrations as well. In II Corinthians 2:14, it is God who leads Paul in a triumphal procession as His captive, by means of whom the knowledge and fame of the Victor is made manifest. He rejoices that he has been so used of God. In Colossians 2:15, our Lord through His victory over the hosts of evil is enabled to lead them in a triumphal procession as His captives. In II Corinthians 10:4, Paul again uses the illustration of war, and of a fortress.

As to his use of terms taken from the language of government, we have Philippians 1:27, and 3:20. In the first passage, the words "let your conversation be," are from a word which refers to the duty of citizens to the commonwealth in which they live, and in the second, "conversation" is translated from a Greek word meaning "commonwealth." The illustration is taken from the fact that the city of Philippi was a Roman colony, its citizens possessing Roman citizenship with its privleges and responsibilities. So the Philippian saints are citizens of heaven, to live a heavenly life in that colony of heaven far from their commonwealth itself. Translate, "only conduct yourselves as citizens as it becometh the gospel of Christ," "for the commonwealth of which we are citizens has its fixed abode in heaven."

The frequency with which Paul refers to the Greek athletic games far surpasses his illustrations from any other single department of first century life. The Greeks were an athletic-minded people. Paul himself, though a son of Hebrew parents who maintained their Jewish separation even to the point of refusing to read their Scrip-

tures in the Septuagint translation (Acts 6:1, Phil. 3:5),
yet did not wash his hands of his Hellenistic training before his fellow-countrymen when he admitted that he
was a native of the Greek city of Tarsus, for he used the
milder of two Greek adversatives (Acts 22:3). He was
influenced greatly by his Greek training, and he could not
deny it. Part of that Greek culture included a familiarity
with and interest in athletics. It is significant that when
writing to the Romans, he uses terms borrowed from warfare, but his epistles to the Corinthians and Philippians,
which were to churches composed of Greek Christians,
and those to Timothy, whose father was a Greek (Acts
16:1), abound with illustrations from the Greek games.
The great apostle was chosen by God for his Greek background as well as for his Jewish training. Truly, he was
the apostle to the Gentiles. And his Greek training played
no little part in his ministry to them. As to his references
to the Greek athletic games so well known even in the
Roman period, having such a background of history in the
time when Greece was at the height of its glory, we have
the following. Both the Christian life (Phil. 3:7-16),
and Christian service (I Cor. 9:24-27) are illustrated by
the stadium games and the desperate agonizing efforts
put forth by the Greek athletes in their endeavor to win.
He visualizes the stadium crowds intently watching the
contest. He speaks of the garland or crown of oak leaves
placed upon the winner's brow.

One of the classic passages in which Paul refers to the
Greek games is I Corinthians 9:24-27. The isthmus of
Corinth was the scene of the Isthmian games, one of the
four great national festivals of the Greeks. During the

period of the writing of the Pauline epistles, these games were still being celebrated. He was familiar with similar scenes in Tarsus and in all of the great cities of Asia Minor, especially at Ephesus. The word "race" in this passage is from a Greek word which comes over into our language in the word "stadium" and "stade." The stade was a race course 606¾ feet long, and the word came to mean a "race" because the track at Olympia was exactly that number of feet in length. Here Paul uses the figure of a race to illustrate the life of Christian service. "Striveth for the masteries" is from a Greek word which refers to an athlete contending or striving in the games. "Temperate" is from a word occurring only here and in I Corinthians 7:9. Here it refers to the ten months preparatory training, and the practice in the gymnasium immediately before the games under the direction of the judges who had themselves been instructed for ten months in the details of the games. The training was largely dietary. Epictetus says, "Thou must be orderly, living on spare food; abstain from confections; make a point of exercising at the appointed time, in heat and in cold; nor drink cold water or wine at hazard." Horace says, "The youth who would win in the race hath borne and done much, he hath sweat and hath been cold: he hath abstained from love and wine." Tertullian, commending the example of athletes to the persecuted Christians, says, "They are constrained, harassed, wearied" (Vincent).

If an athlete goes through ten months of rigorous training which involves rigid self-denial and much hardship in order that he might compete in a contest that may last a few minutes or a few hours at the most, and for a prize, a chaplet of oak leaves, should not a Christian be willing to subject himself to just as rigid a discipline and self-denial in order that he might serve the Lord Jesus in an acceptable manner? What soft flabby lives we Christians live. How little of stern soul-discipline do we know. The training period of a Greek athlete was a time of separation for him, separation from things which might in their place be perfectly proper but which would prevent him from running his best race, and separation most certainly from things that were of a harmful nature. If we Christians would exercise as much care and self-denial, and rigidly hold to a life of separation as did the Greek athlete, what powerful, successful, God-glorifying lives we would live. Illustrations such as these were not lost upon Paul's Greek readers.

Paul uses the chaplet or crown of oak leaves which fades, as an illustration of the unfading victor's crown which the Christian will wear some day, given him for the service he rendered in the power of the Holy Spirit. He speaks of the Greek runner who speeds down the race course not uncertainly, but straight as an arrow for the goal. So should a Christian run his race, refusing to allow anyone or anything to turn him from the consuming desire that the Lord Jesus be preeminent in his life.

In Philippians 3:13, 14, we catch a glimpse of Paul's knowledge of racing technique. He uses the illustration of a runner "pressing toward the mark for the prize," that is, literally, "pursuing down toward the mark for the prize." See him flashing down the race course. He forgets the things which are behind. The word is a strong one, "completely forgetting." Paul knew that the moment a Greek runner would think of the men behind him, the thud thud of their pounding feet, his speed would be slackened. So he presses home the lesson that when a child of God thinks of his past failures, the things he should have done and failed to do, the things he did which he should not have done, his onward progress in the Christian life is hindered. When a Christian has made things right with God and his fellow-man, the proper technique is to completely forget them.

A similar idea is presented in Hebrews 12:1, 2, where Paul visualizes the stadium crowds, and the runners settling themselves for a race which they know will be a long grind and a real test of endurance. But they run entirely oblivious of the thousands of onlookers, their attention diverted from every consideration except that of running the best possible race. We get that from the words "looking unto." The word, "looking" has a prefixed preposition which implies abstraction. That is, the person's attention is concentrated upon one thing to the total exclusion of everything else, It is, "looking off or away to Jesus," as the Greek runner looks away from everything else and with eyes fixed upon the goal sees not the cheering crowds or even his own opponents. To turn his head ever so slightly toward the tiers upon tiers of spectators, means that his speed will be lessened, and he himself will be just that much behind.

What a lesson for the Christian. The minute we turn our eyes toward our fellow-men and take them from our Lord, our pace is slackened. Pride, discouragement, envy, the desire for praise, these and other evils incapacitate the Christian runner as he looks at men instead of keeping his eyes fixed upon Jesus. The word "fight" (I Cor. 9:26, 27) is from a Greek word which means "to fight with the fists." He speaks of the Greek boxer who beats the air, that is, practices without an adversary. This is called shadow-boxing. Or, he might purposely strike into the air in order to spare his adversary, or the adversary might evade his blow, and thus cause him to spend his strength on the air. But Paul says that he is not like the Greek boxer in these respects. In his conflict with evil, he strikes straight and does not spare.

The words "keep under" are from a word which means "to strike under the eye," or "to give one a black eye." When we think that the Greek boxer wore a pair of fur-lined gloves covered with cowhide which was loaded with lead and iron, one can imagine the punishment to which the recipient of the blows is subjected. If a Christian would be as energetic against and unsparing of evil in his life as the Greek boxer was of his opponent, and would strike with the same devastating force, sin would soon be cleared out of his life and would stay out. What "softies" we Christians are with regard to sin in our lives. How we sometimes cherish it, pamper it, play with it, instead of striking it with the mailed fist of a Holy-Spirit inspired hatred of sin and a refusal to allow it to reign as king in our lives. As we consider this illustration of a boxer which Paul uses, we must remember that boxing among the Greeks was not the degraded form of pugilism such as we have today with all its attendant evils and associations, but was part of the great program of the stadium athletic games which included foot races, discus throwing, wrestling, and other forms of athletics, engaged in by athletes of splendid physique, expending their last ounce of energy, not for a money prize, but for a simple garland of oak leaves which would fade in a few days. Thus, this form of athletic competition while extremely brutal among the Greeks, and therefore to be condemned as a sin against the human body, yet was devoid of much which is associated with pugilism today.

Finally, the word "castaway" is from a technical word used in the Greek games, referring to the disqualifying of a runner because he broke the training rules. He was barred from competing for the prize. Paul was apprehensive, that, if he did not live a life of separation from the world, if he did not live a victorious life over sin, God would disqualify him, that is, take away from him his position as apostle to the Gentiles. A Christian sometimes wonders, after years of fruitful service, why he should so suddenly see his usefulness gone, and his life powerless and without the joy of the Lord. The answer lies in the words, "disqualified, broke training rules." Paul refers to this same matter of obeying training rules in I Timothy 4:7, 8 and II Timothy 2:5, where he says that if a Greek athlete is to be awarded the victor's garland he must strive lawfully, that is, live up to the requirements prescribed for the preparation which the athlete makes and the life which he lives while engaged in athletic competition. He warns Timothy regarding this, and then in II Timothy 4:8, uses the illustration borrowed from the act of the judges at the goal awarding the victor's crown to the winning athlete. So will Timothy some day, like Paul, receive a crown of righteousness from the Lord Jesus.

Then, there are passages where the background of the Greek games is not so evident in the English translation. For instance, in Philippians 1:27 "striving together," and Philippians 4:3, "labored with" are from a Greek word used of athletes contending in concert with one another against the opposition, for the prize offered at the athletic games. The root of the word comes into English in our word "athlete." In Romans 15:30 "strive together," is from a Greek word which refers to the concerted action of a group of athletes working in harmony against opposition. The root of the word comes into our language in the word "agony." What a plea this is for unity among the saints and the expenditure of agonizing effort in concert against evil rather than the use of that energy in contention against one another. In Philippians 1:30, "conflict," Colossians 2:1, "conflict," I Thessalonians 2:2, "contention," II Timothy 4:7, "fight," and Hebrews 12:1, "race" are all from the noun whose root gives us the word "agony," referring in the Greek to the contests in the Greek athletic games. In Colossians 1:29, "striving," 4:12, "laboring," I Timothy 6:12 "fight," II Timothy 4:7, "fought," are all from the verb whose root comes into English in the word "agony," and the meaning of which is "to contend in the Greek games for a prize." Here we have instances where first-century Christians were striving in concert for the faith of the gospel; where some had labored with Paul in the extension of the gospel; where others were exhorted to strive in concert with Paul in prayer; where still others were having conflict, that is, were enduring persecution; and the case of Paul, where he fought the good fight; all these varied activities of the Christian life being referred to by the two Greek words used of an athlete engaged in the intense competition of the games even to the point of physical agony. What a commentary this is upon first-century Christianity. What intense lives these early Christians must have lived. With what desperate earnestness they must have worked for the Lord. What fervor and intensity there must have been in their prayers.

These Christians did not have a long line of Christian ancestry back of them, nor centuries of Christian practice and tradition to encourage them. They were saved out of paganism. Yet they lived their Christian lives with an intensity of purpose which puts us of the twentieth century to shame. The secret of all this is in the fulness of the Holy Spirit, which results in a conscience sensitive to the slightest sin, the enthronement of Jesus as Lord of the life, and a love for Him that finds expression in a life of intense and purposeful service in His name. If there were more believers filled moment by moment with the Holy Spirit, controlled by Him in thought, word, and deed, there would be more first-century Christianity in the present day church. The secret of that fullness is in a desire for His control and a trust in the Lord Jesus for the same (John 7:37, 38).

Paul, who seeks to become all things to all men that he might by all means save some, sets aside the language of the schools, the highly polished rhetoric, the philosophical subtleties which he learned in the Greek schools at Tarsus, and instead uses the every day words of the common people. He neither wrote above the understanding nor talked above the heads of those to whom he ministered. What an admonition this is to us who have the high privilege and great responsibility of ministering the Word. With us let utter simplicity be the watchword, "not with wisdom of words, lest the cross of Christ be made of none effect."

VIII

About Crowns

¶ IT SURPRISES one to see how much of the life and speech-expressions of the first century is reflected in the statements found in the Greek manuscripts of the New Testament. The writers under the guidance of the Holy Spirit (I Cor. 2:13) constantly draw from contemporary life as they seek to bring to man the message of God. To understand something of first century life and its use of words, is to have a clearer understanding of the message they bring. That is why a knowledge of the Greek language, and a study of the early secular manuscripts, is of great help in the explanation of the New Testament.

The one English word "crown" is used to translate two Greek words, each of which speaks of a different kind of crown, both of them being in common use in the first century in connection with the daily life of the people. To understand their difference and significance as they are related to the local customs, is to come into a fuller, clearer appreciation of those passages in the New Testament which contain them.

One of the words is *stephanos*. It was the crown given to the victor in the Greek athletic games, the runner who first crossed the goal, the athlete who hurled the discus farthest, the wrestler who pinned his opponent to the mat. It was given to the servant of the State whose work deserved to be honored. It was worn at marriage feasts. A *stephanos* was therefore a symbol of victory, of deserved honor, and of festal gladness. The crown was woven of oak leaves, of ivy, of parsley, of myrtle, of olive, of violets, of roses.

The inscriptions give us concrete instances of its use. The emperor Claudius acknowledges the golden *stephanos* sent him by the Worshipful Gymnastic Club of Nomads on the occasion of his victory over the Britons. An inscription of A.D. 138-161 may refer to this club, where "allowances" are made to an athlete on account of his "athletic *stephanos*."

The word was used in the sense of a reward other than a crown. An inscription of 2 B.C., speaks of Peteuris, who promises a reward (*stephanos*) of five talents of copper, on account of some special service. The verb form of the noun *stephanos* is found in a manuscript of 257 B.C., in which a certain Hierokles writes to Zenon regarding a boy who is Zenon's nominee in the athletic games, "I hope that you will be crowned (i.e., be victorious) through him."

To us today, a crown is just a crown. The English word usually brings to our minds the picture of a large golden crown set with jewels, such as is or was worn by the crowned heads of Europe. But to impose this conception upon the passages in the New Testament where the word *stephanos* is found, is to misconstrue and at the same time lose some precious truth. But when the first century reader found that word in the holy Scriptures, he recognized it as a word familiar to him by reason of its association in the ordinary secular life by which he was always surrounded. Thus he understood the full implication of this secular word brought over into the sacred text of the new Faith that was sweeping the Roman empire. And this ability to understand a word like this was not confined merely to the native Greek speaking population of the empire, for the Roman world was as to its culture, predominantly Grecian. The Greek language was the international language. There was more Greek spoken than Latin.

The other word translated "crown" is *diadema,* from which we get our word "diadem." This Greek word is derived from a verb meaning "to bind around." It referred to a blue band of ribbon marked with white which the Persian kings used to bind on a turban or tiara. It was the kingly ornament for the head, and signified royalty. A *stephanos* is therefore a victor's crown, whereas a *diadema* is a royal crown. We will study those passages in which each one is found.

Paul in I Corinthians 9:24-27 is speaking of Christian service in a context of Christian service that takes in the entire chapter. In verse 24, he is using the foot races held in the Greek athletic games as an illustration of the activity of a Christian in his work for the Lord. He uses the same illustration borrowed from contemporary life in Philippians 3:7-14, where he speaks, not of Christian service but of progress in the living of a Christlike life. He says that the Greek athletes run a race in order to obtain a corruptible *stephanos* of oak leaves that soon will wither and fade. But he speaks of a *stephanos* which a Christian receives as a reward for his services, as an incorruptible crown. Then he tells us that he buffets his body and makes it his slave in order that after preaching to others he might not be a castaway. The word "castaway" comes from a Greek word which means, "to be put to the test and after being tested, to be rejected because of not meeting that test." Paul draws this word from the Greek games where it was a technical expression meaning "to disqualify a runner from competing for the *stephanos* because he broke the training rules." If Paul did not practice what he preached, he would be disqualified, not allowed to compete for the crown given to those who rendered Christian service. He was afraid his apostleship would be taken away and given to another. The first century reader, having the historical background of the Greek games in his mind, would interpret this passage correctly. He would understand that Paul is not speaking of his eternal salvation here, for rewards are in view, and salvation is a gift. The same can be said of Philippians 3:7-14, where sanctification is referred to, not justification. It is the victor's crown won through Christian service which Paul wants to win.

In Philippians 4:1, Paul calls the Philippian saints his crown. As oak leaves were woven together to form a *stephanos,* a chaplet or garland of victory or of civic worth, so Paul says in effect, "You Philippians are woven together into my crown of victory, an eternal symbol of my victory over the hosts of Satan at Philippi, and my reward for service in that place." He speaks of the Thessalonian saints whom he also won to the Lord as his *stephanos* of rejoicing. He will wear a victor's crown at the coming of the Lord Jesus for the saints, his converts composing a more beautiful festal garland than ever graced the brow of a Greek athlete, even though that *stephanos* were made of roses or violets (I Thes. 2:19).

In II Timothy 4:8 we have the crown of righteousness. The imagery is again that of the Greek games. "I have fought" not "a good fight," but "the good fight." The indefinite article would indicate egotism on the part of the apostle. The definite article is used in the Greek, pointing to the good fight which each Christian is expected to wage. The picture here is taken from the Greek stadium where the huge crowd of spectators is keenly watching two Greek athletes as they engage perhaps in a wrestling contest. Here is not a race, but a tremendous contest of strength competing with strength. The words "fought" and "fight" come from the same Greek root. We get our word "agony" from this word. It refers to a contest in which the participants exert their strength to the point of agony. What for? For a *stephanos* of oak leaves that will shortly fade away, and for the plaudits of a fickle crowd that may the next moment turn thumbs down. How this should convict us of laziness, indolence, laxness in Christian service. The word "good" is from the Greek word meaning "goodness as seen from the outside by a spectator," in contrast to another word which speaks of internal intrinsic goodness. The Greek spectators would say, "That was a beautiful display of skill and strength." Paul says that the Christian life as it is related to the antagonism of the powers of evil, should display a beauty of skill and spiritual strength that will glorify the Lord Jesus. Such a battle he waged. Notice in passing, if you will, the composition of that word, "antagonism," from our word "agony," and "anti" which comes from the Greek, meaning "against." That is, an antagonist is one who fights against one to the point of agony.

But Paul also says, "I have finished my course." The word "course" is from the Greek word meaning "a race-course," here used in connection with foot races. It is the "cinder-path" of college athletic fields. The word "finished" means "to come to the end." It is in the perfect tense in the Greek which speaks of a past completed action with present existing results. Paul, awaiting martyrdom in Rome, looks back upon his life as a runner who, having won his race, is resting at the goal and is looking back down the cinder path over which he sped to victory, and sees the race as over, and its result, the *stephanos* of righteousness awaiting him.

The crowds leave the Greek stadium after the games are over, and the victors crowned with a garland of oak-leaves, are carried on the shoulders of rejoicing friends. So some day, the saints will leave the stadium of this life's battles, and in heaven will rejoice with each other over the crowns they have won through the wonderful grace of God.

In James 1:12 we have the *stephanos* of life. "Blessed" is literally in this context, "spiritually prosperous." "Temptation" is from a Greek word which has two meanings, to be used according to the context in which the word may

be found. It means either "to put one to a test" as in
Genesis 22:1 where God tempted Abraham, that is, tested
him to see whether he would be obedient in relation to the
request that he sacrifice his son (Septuagint, Greek translation of Old Testament), or "to solicit one to do evil,"
as in our context in James.

The word "endureth" is literally "to remain under,"
and must be interpreted in its context, namely, the word
"tried." The word "tried" is from a technical Greek expression found in an early manuscript, where it referred
to the action of an examining board putting its approval
upon those who had successfully passed the examinations
for the degree of Doctor of Medicine. The verb means
"to test for the purpose of approving," the noun, "the
approved character of the one who has successfully met
the test."

Here is a child of God who has been solicited to do
evil. He has successfully met the test by refusing to sin.
That is what James means by "enduring temptation." The
"stephanos of the life" is his reward. This is not eternal
life. He has that already, or he could not have overcome
temptation. Furthermore, this is a reward given in recognition of what the believer has done, whereas salvation is
a free gift given in view of what Christ has done on the
Cross. The article in the Greek before "life," points to a
particular kind of life, here to that eternal life which is in
Christ Jesus which enabled the believer to overcome temptation. Thus, this crown is a *stephanos* given in recognition of the believer's victory over sin, that victory having

been procured by means of the eternal life he has, and which energizes his being.

When we come to Peter's use of *stephanos* in his first epistle (5:4), we have another illustration of how Greek culture had stamped itself upon the life of the Roman world. Peter knew Greek, but he had not lived in a Greek city such as Tarsus, the home of the apostle Paul. He was not schooled in Greek learning as was Paul. Yet this fisherman, reared in a Jewish environment, engaged in the fishing trade around the Sea of Galilee, was conversant enough with the life about and beyond his little world, that he used a typical illustration from a phase of first century life of which he as a Jew was not a part. The same can be said of John, and also of James the brother of our Lord, for they also use *stephanos*.

John, writing from the island of Patmos in the Aegean Sea to the church at Smyrna, a city which was in a region where Greek culture predominated, exhorts the Christians there who were undergoing severe persecutions, "Be thou faithful unto death, and I will give thee the *stephanos* of the life." The word "unto" does not mean "until." The same Greek word is used in Philippians 2:8, where our Lord was obedient "up to the point" or "to the extent" of death. This Smyrna church represents the "Martyr Period" of church history, from A.D. 100-316 when ten bloody persecutions were hurled at the Christian church by Rome. This is the victor's crown given to those who are martyrs to the Faith once for all delivered to the saints. The word "martyr" comes from the Greek word meaning "to bear witness to." These Christians bore witness to the Christian faith by death (Rev. 2:10). It is touching to know that the name of the first recorded Christian martyr was Stephen, which comes from *stephanos*.

The Philadelphian church saints are exhorted to hold fast the little spiritual strength which they have (Rev. 3:11), lest they lose their *stephanos*, namely, their victor's crown, a reward for service. The elders (Rev. 4:4, 10) representing the redeemed in heaven, are seen, each with a golden *stephanos* on their heads. Sometimes a *stephanos* of gold, made in the form of an oak leaf garland for instance, was used in the first century. We saw that in the case of the golden *stephanos* given to the emperor Claudias. Here the glorified saints wear such a victor's crown, but not for long, for, overcome with gratitude, they cast their victor's crowns at the feet of the One who through His victory at Calvary gave them the grace to overcome in their own lives.

There are two riders on white horses in the Revelation, one in chapter 6:2, Antichrist, and the other, chapter 19:11, Jesus Christ. To Antichrist there is given a *stephanos*, the victor's crown. He goes forth conquering and to conquer. The superhuman beings of Revelation 9:7 have victor's crowns on their heads. The woman clothed with the sun, representing Israel, has a *stephanos* made of stars, indicative of Israel's final victory over Satan and persecuting Antichrist when Jesus Christ comes to its rescue. Then in Revelation 14:14, we have the Lord Jesus with a victor's crown on His head, coming in His second Advent to conquer Antichrist and set up His kingdom.

The verb form of the noun *stephanos* is used in II Timothy 2:5. Paul uses the illustrations of a soldier in verses

3 and 4, of an athlete in verse 5, and of a farmer in verse 6. In verse 5 the words "strive for masteries" is from a word which comes into our language in the word "athlete." It means "to exert one's self in a contest as an athlete, for a prize or reward." "Is crowned" is from our word "stephanos," "is crowned with a victor's crown." The same verb is used in Hebrews 2:7, 9, where we see the Son of Man, made for a little time lower than the angels, now in His glorified state, crowned with the garland of victory.

What shall we say when we come to the *stephanos* of thorns which the soldiers placed on the head of our Lord (Matt. 27:29; Mark 15:17; John 19:2, 5)? While there is an instance where the word *stephanos* is used to signify royalty, as in "the crown-tax," yet its predominant usage was that of a victor's crown. The other word *diadema* which refers to a royal crown, could hardly be used here, for it referred to a narrow ribbon-like band worn around the head. The crown of thorns was of inter-woven material like the *stephanos* of oak leaves or ivy, and this word was probably chosen for that reason. But what the soldiers meant in mockery for a royal crown, became for our Lord in the hour of seeming defeat, the victor's crown, for Paul could write (I Cor. 15:55) "Where, O death is your victory? Where, O death* is your sting?" The victor's crown was placed on His brow before the victory was complete. So sure was the victory of the Cross. So sure will be the victory procured at the Cross for you and for me who are trusting in the Saviour's precious

---

*The best texts read "death" not "grave."

blood poured out at Calvary as the God-appointed substitutionary atonement for sin.

The other word translated "crown" is *diadema*. It comes from a verb which means "to bind around." It referred to the narrow blue band of ribbon marked with white which the Persian kings used to bind on a turban or tiara. It was the kingly ornament for the head. Sometimes more than one *diadema* was worn at the same time. When Ptolemy, king of Egypt entered Antioch in triumph, he set two crowns on his head, the *diadema* showing his sovereignty over Asia, and the *diadema* speaking of his kingly authority over Egypt (I Maccabees, XI 13).

Satan (Rev. 12:3) has seven *diadema* on his head, showing his close connection with and supremacy over the seven Roman emperors of Revelation 17:10. These are royal crowns, indicating imperial authority over the Revived Roman empire. Antichrist (Rev. 13:1) has ten kingly crowns upon his head, showing his sovereignty over the ten kings and their kingdoms in the Revived Roman empire (Rev. 17:12, 13). The Lord Jesus (Rev. 19:12), when He comes to bring in the Messianic Kingdom which will be world-wide, will wear many crowns. To one whose conception of a crown is limited to that of a large golden crown studded with jewels, this statement is unintelligible. But when one understands that these crowns consist of narrow bands of ribbon encircling the head at the forehead, one can appreciate the description. These *diadema* represent all the kingdoms and other political units over which the Lord Jesus will rule as supreme Sovereign. He will truly be King of kings and Lord of lords.

IX

The Crucible of Christian Suffering

¶ "BELOVED, think it not strange concerning the fiery trial which is to try you, as though some strange thing happened unto you: But rejoice, inasmuch as ye are partakers of Christ's sufferings; that, when his glory shall be revealed, ye may be glad also with exceeding joy. If ye be reproached for the name of Christ, happy are ye; for the spirit of glory and of God resteth upon you: on their part he is evil spoken of, but on your part he is glorified" (I Peter 4:12-14).

The word "beloved" is from a Greek word which speaks of the love of God. It is the same Greek word for "love" which is used in John 3:16; I Corinthians 13; I John 4:8, and Romans 5:5. It speaks of a love which is called out of one's heart by the preciousness of the person loved, a love that is self-sacrificial in its essence, yes, the love that God is in His own essence. The word is an adjective in the plural number. While there may be in it a reflection of Peter's love for these saints to whom he is writing, yet the full glow of the word in this context seems to come from the idea that these saints are divinely loved by God. Peter says "Divinely loved ones." These saints were undergoing severe suffering in the form of persecution by the world because of their testimony by life and word to the Lord Jesus. What a comfort it is when undergoing testing times, to know that each one of God's saints is divinely loved by Him. It is a sweet pillow upon which to rest our weary heads and sorely tried hearts. God's Word says

(I John 4:18), "There is no fear in love; but perfect love casteth out fear, because fear hath torment." This perfect love is God's love for us, not our love for Him, which latter is always most imperfect. To realize that God loves His own with a perfect love, is to know assuredly that He will in His love for us not allow anything to come to us that would work us harm, and that whatever comes of pain or sorrow, of loss or cross, is only for our good. Therefore, "Divinely loved ones."

The words "think it not strange" are in a construction in the Greek text which forbids the continuance of an action already going on. These saints were thinking it strange that they as Christians were going through such trials, as if the Christian life procured for them an immunity from suffering. Peter says, "stop thinking it strange." The Greek word translated "strange" means more than "unusual." It means "alien" or "foreign." Not only did these saints think it a thing unusual that they should be suffering, but they thought it a thing alien or foreign to them, a thing in which they as Christians were not to be at home. They thought that the Christian life was of such a character that suffering was not one of its natural constituent elements. These were first-century saints, people who had been saved out of paganism, who had had no background of a long line of Christian ancestors, and who had not learned as yet that suffering for righteousness' sake was a natural result of a Christlike life, for the world hates the Lord Jesus and therefore hates the Christian in whose life the Lord Jesus is seen.

The words "fiery trial" are from a Greek word which literally means "a burning." The word occurs in the Septuagint translation of the Old Testament (Proverbs 27:21) in the phrase, "As the fining pot for silver, and the furnace for gold." It is the word "furnace." The word occurs also in Psalm 66:10, "For thou, O God, hast proved us: thou hast tried us, as silver is tried." One translator renders it, "thou hast smelted us as silver is smelted." Thus we could translate instead of "fiery trial," "smelting process." Peter says that suffering for righteousness' sake is a smelting process.

The illustration is that of the ancient goldsmith who refines the crude gold ore in his crucible. The pure metal is mixed with much foreign material from which it must be separated. The only way to bring about this separation is to reduce the ore to liquid form. The impurities rise to the surface and are then skimmed off. But intense heat is needed to liquefy this ore. So the goldsmith puts his crucible in the fire, reduces the ore to a liquid state and skims off the impurities. When he can see the reflection of his face clearly mirrored in the surface of the liquid, he knows that the contents are pure gold. The smelting process has done its work.

Christian suffering, whether it be in the form of persecution because of a Christlike life, or whether it comes to us in the form of the trials and testings which are the natural accompaniment of a Christlike life, such as illness, sorrow, or financial losses, is always used by a God of love to refine our lives. It burns out the dross, makes for humility, purifies and increases our faith, and enriches our lives. And like the goldsmith of old, God keeps us in the smelting furnace until He can see the reflection of the face of the Lord Jesus in our lives. God is not so much interest-

ed in how much work we do for Him, as He is in how much
we resemble His Son. Sometimes we think that if God
would remove the present affliction or handicap which to us
seems to put a limitation upon our usefulness to Him, we
could do far more efficient work for Him. Our first answer to that would be that God knows what He is doing,
and it is not for us to question His dealings with us. Our
second answer is that all things being equal, we might be
able to do more work for Him. But God is not interested
in the quantity of work but in the quality. We may not
be able to turn out as much work for the Lord Jesus as
some other saint, but if the furnace of affliction has produced in us a more Christlike character, the service we do
render, is of far more value than the service rendered by
the saint who does not have so much of the Lord Jesus in
his life. The third answer is that God is building Christian personality for eternity, which is far more important
to Him than the amount of service one might render in
this brief life.

The word "happened" is literally "happened by chance."
Nothing happens by chance in the Christian life. Nothing
is allowed to come to a saint which does not come through
the permissive will of God. God built a fence around Job,
and Satan could not touch him until God opened the gate.
And then when Satan did come in, he was still acting under the limitations imposed upon him by God. Therefore
Peter says "Divinely loved ones, stop entertaining the
thought that the smelting process which is operated among
you and which is for the purpose of testing you, is a thing
alien to you, as if an alien thing were falling by chance
upon you."

Instead of thinking that suffering is a thing alien to them, the saints are exhorted to rejoice that such is their lot. But this rejoicing has its limitations. They are to rejoice in the fact of this suffering only in as far as these sufferings are a natural consequence or a natural accompaniment of a Christlike life. The word "inasmuch" is from a Greek word which means "in as far." They are not to rejoice when they suffer for evil doing, but there is good cause for them to rejoice when suffering as a Christian, for then they are co-participants of the sufferings of Christ. He suffered for righteousness' sake, and the saints experience the same kind of suffering. Not that we can be co-participant with Him in His expiatory sufferings which He endured on the Cross, but in His sufferings endured during His ministry on earth during which He suffered the abuse and persecution of sinners against Himself. This is what Paul refers to when he says (Col. 1:24), "And fill up that which is behind of the afflictions of Christ in my flesh for his body's sake which is the church." It was the expiatory sufferings of Christ by which He purchased the Church with His own blood (Acts 20:28). It is the suffering for righteousness' sake which is the natural accompaniment of the efforts of our Lord and His apostles and all the Christian witnesses down the centuries which had for their purpose the bringing of lost sinners to a saving knowledge of the Lamb of God who poured out His blood that sinners might be saved. Therefore, saints are to rejoice in the fact that they are co-participants of the sufferings of Christ.

This persecution took the form sometimes of bitter ridicule and invective. The words, "if ye be reproached for the name of Christ" are in the Greek, "if, as is the case, ye are having cast in your teeth, reproach because of the name of Christ." The word "reproach" in the Greek text is the same word translated "revile" in Matthew 5:11. The word "if" here represents a fulfilled condition. These saints were being reviled by their former pagan associates because they were now living such holy lives. Peter says that if that is the case, they are happy. The word "happy" is from a Greek word which literally means "prosperous." The idea is that the fact that these saints were being persecuted, was an indication that they were in a happy or prosperous condition spiritually. John writes to Gaius in his third epistle that he wishes above all things that his financial and physical condition might be as prosperous as the prosperity of his soul. Thus persecution by the world is an evidence of a good, healthy, spiritual state.

But suffering for righteousness sake is also an indication, Peter tells us, that the spirit of glory and of God is resting upon us. The construction in the Greek indicates that it is the same spirit that is meant, namely, the Holy Spirit of God. He is the Spirit of the glory and at the same time the Spirit of God. As the Spirit of the glory, He is the reality of which the Shekinah Glory was the type. As the Spirit of God, He is the third Person of the Triune God. The word "resteth" is from a Greek word which is found in a manuscript of B.C. 103 as a technical term used in agriculture. It spoke of a farmer resting his land by sowing light crops upon it. The farmer thus relieved the land of the burden of producing a heavy crop that season, which gave the land an opportunity to recuperate and thus gain strength. The same word is used in

Matthew 11:28-30, where it is translated from a verb form in verse 28 in the words "I will give rest," and in verse 29 from the noun form in the word "rest." Our Lord said, "I will rest you." He takes the load and thus rests us.

The word in both the Matthew and Peter passages means "to cause or permit one to cease from any movement or labor in order to recover and collect one's strength." In Matthew, the Lord Jesus causes the believer to cease from his own efforts at carrying the load of sin, taking it upon Himself at Calvary, allowing the believer in his new life power imparted, to function in the Christian life. In Peter, the Holy Spirit rests and refreshes the believer by Himself putting out sin in the life, keeping it out, and producing His own fruit. This in the life of the Christian is the target of the reproach of the world. The word "resteth" does not indicate a position of rest which the Holy Spirit has taken upon the Christian, for the Spirit does not come upon saints in this dispensation as He did in the dispensation of law. He comes into their hearts to make the saint His permanent residence, (James 4:5) "Do you think the scripture saith in vain, 'The Spirit who has been caused to take up His permanent residence in us has a passionate longing to the point of envy?'" The word "resteth" refers to the sanctifying work of the Holy Spirit in the saint who is subjected to His control, and this will result in persecution by the world, for the Spirit glorifies the Lord Jesus in the life of the believer, and the world hates the Lord of glory. Therefore Peter says, "In view of the fact that you have cast in your teeth as it were, reproach because of the name of Christ, consider yourselves as being in a spiritually prosperous condition, because that is an indication that the Spirit of the glory, even the Spirit of God is resting with refreshing power upon you." The Holy Spirit in His ministry produces that spiritually prosperous condition.

Peter agains refers to Christian suffering as a smelting process in chapter one, verse seven, in the words, "That the trial of your faith, being much more precious than of gold that perisheth, though it be tried with fire, might be found unto praise and honor and glory at the appearing of Jesus Christ" (1:7). These saints had been put to grief in the experiencing of many kinds of temptations, the word "temptations" in the Greek, referring to trials, testings, and solicitations to do evil. These, Peter speaks of, as "the trial of your faith." That is, these trials, testings, and solicitations to do evil constituted the trial of their faith. The word "trial" used here in connection with "faith" is from a different word than that translated "temptations." It means "to test something for the purpose of approving it." The word was used in secular documents of the testing of candidates for the degree of Doctor of Medicine, this test being given them for the purpose of approving them. It is in contrast to the word translated "temptations" in verse six which means "to try or tempt in order to put to the proof to discover what good or evil is in a person." From the fact that such a scrutiny often develops the existence and energy of evil, the word acquired a predominant sense of putting to the proof with the design or hope of breaking down the subject undergoing the test. Hence, Satan is called the "tempter," this Greek word being used as a proper noun.

God allows these testing times, trials, and solicitations to do evil to come to us in order that while Satan may try to discover what evil there is in us and try to bring it out in our experience, He might test our faith and approve it as a living God-given faith because by His grace we have exercised it in gaining victory over the very things which Satan desired to use in an effort at bringing about our downfall. Thus our faith is shown to be an approved faith. In addition to our faith being approved in the smelting process, it is also being purified. The self-dependence and unbelief to which saints are so prone, is burned away, and our faith strengthened. Thus it is the approval of our faith to which Peter refers in the words "the trial of your faith."

Then Peter brings in the illustration of the goldsmith as he refines the gold. He says that this approval of our faith is much more precious than perishable gold, even though that gold be approved by fire-testing. That is, the process of refining and purifying gold is compared with God's process of purifying our faith. Purified and approved gold may be of value for a time, but our faith purified of all of its attendant unbelief and self-dependence is of eternal value. This faith will be found to result in praise and glory and honor at the revelation of Jesus Christ. A fuller translation of this verse is as follows, "In order that the approval of your faith, which faith was examined by testing, that approval being much more precious than perishable gold even though that gold be approved by fire-testing, might be found to result in praise and glory and honor at the revelation of Jesus Christ."

Thus, Christian suffering, whether it be in the form of persecution by the world, trials and testings in the form of hardships, privation, illness, or any other kind of suffering that is a natural accompaniment of the Christian life, yes, temptations which Satan puts before us, are a potent means in the hands of God of purging the dross out of our lives, of purifying and strengthening our faith, and of conforming us to the image of His dear Son. Christian suffering is the crucible into which God places us, and in which He keeps us until He can see a reflection of the face of Jesus Christ in our lives. It is a mark of God's especial favor towards and confidence in that saint who is exercised thereby.

X

The Self-Emptied Life

¶ A QUARREL between two saints in the church at Philippi (Phil. 4:2), and other minor dissensions, gave rise to one of the greatest Christological passages in the New Testament. The apostle is exhorting to humility among the believers in 2:3-4, and now in 2:5-8 presents our blessed Lord as the example. Humility of life is therefore our analytical key which will unlock the treasures of these wonderful verses.

The words. "Let this mind be in you which was also in Christ Jesus," could be variously translated: "Be thinking this in yourselves which was also in Christ Jesus." "Be having this mind in you which was also in Christ Jesus." "Reflect in your own mind that which was also in Christ Jesus." "Let the same purpose inspire you as was in Christ Jesus" (Way). Putting all these together, we have what the apostle means. He describes the mind of Christ in verses 5-8, presenting the controlling factor, humility, that made His mind what it was.

The word "form" comes from a Greek word which refers to the outward expression one gives of his inner being. It is used here as one would use it in the sentence, "The tennis-player's form was excellent." We mean that the expression he gave in action of his ability to play tennis was excellent. The word has no idea of physical form or shape. Here the word refers to that expression of the glory and majesty of His deity which our Lord gave to the angels before He came to earth in incarnation. This expression was through a spiritual medium, discernible only to the spiritual faculties of the angels. The same Greek word is found in Matthew 17:2 with a preposition prefixed which when in composition signifies a change. It is translated there, "transfigured," but the sentence could be rendered, "His mode of expression was changed before them." That is, our Lord's usual mode of expression in His days of humiliation on earth was that of a servant (bond-slave [Greek], same word translated "servant" in Romans 1:1). That was an expression which came from His innermost being as the One who "came not to be ministered unto but to minister." But now for a moment, the mode of His expression was changed. He gave expression to the essence of deity in which He is a co-participant with God the Father and God the Holy Spirit. The splendor and majesty of His deity shone through the clay walls of His humanity, and by means of a medium discernible to the physical eyesight of the spectators. But the Philippian passage speaks of an expression of glory not discernible to our physical vision, but only to the spiritual capacities of angels. However, this expression of glory which the angels saw, will be discernible to the saints when they receive their glorified bodies, for then they will be spiritual intelligences with spiritual capacities like the angels. This is what John had in mind when he wrote (I John 3:2), "When He shall appear, we shall be like Him, for we shall see Him just as He is." But in the meanwhile, it is (I Peter 1:8), "Of whom not having had a glimpse, yet whom we love." Thus our Lord in His preincarnate state manifested the glory of His deity to the holy angels in an outward mode of expression discernible to these spiritual intelligences. This is what is meant by the phrase, "Being in the form of God."

The word "being" is not from the usual verb of "being" in Greek, but from a word which refers to an antecedent condition which is protracted into the present. That is, our Lord's being in the form of God was true of Him before He became Man and was true of Him at the time of the writing of this epistle, which tells us that in taking upon Himself humanity with its limitations yet without its sin, He lost nothing of His intrinsic deity, its attributes or its prerogatives. We could translate, "Who subsisting, being constitutionally, being by nature, in that mode of existence in which He gave outward expression of the essence of His deity." The word "God" does not have the article, quality or essence being stressed.

The word "thought" in the original, refers to a judgment based upon facts. The word "robbery" is from a Greek word which has two meanings, "a thing unlawfully seized," and "a prize or treasure to be retained at all hazards." The context decides which meaning is to be used here. If our Lord considered that equality with God in the expression of the divine essence was not a thing to be unlawfully seized, then He would be asserting His rights to the expression of Deity, for He would be claiming this as His rightful prerogative. But to assert one's rights does not partake of humility. But if He did not consider this expression of His deity a prize or treasure to be retained at all hazards, He would be showing a willingness to relinquish His divine rights, which is the essence of humility. Paul is setting forth our Lord as an example of humility. Therefore, the second meaning is the one to be taken here.

That is, when He was marked out as the Lamb for sacrifice in the eternal ages before the universe was created, and when He was exercising His divine prerogative of giving expression to the glory of His deity, He did not at that time consider that equality with God such a treasure that its exercise would keep Him from setting aside that activity for the time being, so as to change His mode of expression from that of the glory of Deity to the humiliation of Deity incarnate in humanity. It was the King of Glory willing to step down to the place of a bondslave.

But, instead of asserting His prerogative of giving expression to His deity, He "made Himself of no reputation." The word in the Greek means either "to empty" or "make void." Of what did He empty Himself? What did He make void? He emptied Himself of self, which is the essence of humility. He made self void, which is again the essence of humility. He set self aside when He set His legitimate desires aside. His rightful natural desire as Deity was to be glorified, to give expression of His glory to the angels. But to go to the Cross, He had to set that desire aside. Setting that desire aside, He set self aside, He emptied Himself of self, He made self void, the very Person who had the right to assert self, which is the prerogative of Deity alone. Here is the supreme example of the self-emptied life.

The word "took" is an instrumental participle in the Greek, indicating the means by which the action in the main verb is accomplished. Our Lord set Himself aside by taking upon Himself the form of a servant. The word "form" has the same content of meaning as the word "form" in verse six. The word "servant" is literally "bondslave." He changed His mode of expression from that of the glory of Deity to that of the humiliation of a bondslave, and in doing that, He set His legitimate desire of being glorified aside, thus setting self aside to express Himself as a bondslave, receiving instead of the worship of the angels, the curses and hatred of mankind.

It was the Lord of Glory at the Passover feast (John 13) who laid aside His outer garments to wrap a towel about Himself and perform the duties of a slave. Those garments speak of the expression of glory given to the angels in His preincarnate state. That towel, symbol of His position as a bondslave, speaks of the humility with which He clothed Himself. One had to be laid aside if the other was to be taken up. While He was kneeling on the floor washing the disciples' feet, He was still the Lord of Glory although He looked like a bondslave. The travel-stained, weary, homeless, itinerant preacher of Galilee looked like a man, yet He was the Lord from heaven. When He had finished the duties of a bondslave in an oriental household, He laid aside the towel and took His robes again. When He had finished His work of salvation wrought out on Calvary's Cross, He took His robes of Glory again, resuming the expression of the glory of Deity to the angels.

He "was made in the likeness of men." The Greek for "likeness" refers to "that which has been made after the likeness of something else." Our Lord's humanity was a real likeness, not a mere phantom. But this likeness did not express the whole of Christ's nature. His mode of manifestation resembled what men are. But His human-ity was not all that there was of Him. He was not a man, but the Son of God manifest in the flesh and nature of man.

He was "found in fashion as a man." The Greek word for "fashion" refers to that which is purely outward and appeals to the senses. The contrast here is between what He was in Himself, God, and what He appeared in the eyes of man. "Likeness" states the fact of His real re-semblance to men in mode of existence. "Fashion" de-fines the outward mode and expression. While on earth,

He did not give expression to the glory of His deity except on the Mount of Transfiguration. He appeared as the Man Christ Jesus to the world around Him. He was in His humiliation.

In this lowly estate He humbled Himself. The Greek word translated "humbled" is used in an early document, of the Nile River at its low stage, in the sentence, "It runs low," a good description of the humility of our Lord, who said of Himself, "I am meek and lowly of heart." He became obedient, not to death, but obedient to the Father up to the point of death, even the death of a cross.

The translation reads: "This mind be ye constantly having in you which also was in Christ Jesus, who has always been and at present still continues to be by nature in that mode of being in which He gives outward expression of His inmost nature, that of Deity, and who did not after weighing the facts, consider it a treasure to be clutched and retained at all hazards, to be equal with God (in the expression of His essential nature), but emptied Himself, having taken upon Himself that mode of being in which He gave outward expression of Himself as a bondslave, doing this by entering into a new state of existence, that of likeness to mankind. And being found to be in outward guise as a man, He brought Himself to a lowly place by having become obedient to the extent of death, even the death of a cross" (2:5-8). This is the self-emptied life, ever an example and a challenge to us as servants of the One who came not to be ministered unto but to minister, and to give His life a ransom for many.

XI

Forsaken

¶ OUR blessed Lord cried on the Cross, "My God, my God, why hast thou forsaken me?" (Matt. 27:46). The Greek word "forsaken" is a composite of three words, "to leave," "down," and "in." The first has the idea of forsaking one. The second suggests rejection, defeat, helplessness. The third refers to some place or circumstance. The total meaning of the word is that of forsaking someone in a state of defeat or helplessness in the midst of hostile circumstances. The word means "to abandon, desert, to leave in straits, to leave helpless, to leave destitute, to leave in the lurch, to let one down." All these meanings were included in that awful cry that came from the lips of the Son of God as He was about to die for lost humanity.

Many believe, and with good reason, that our Lord uttered Psalm 22 in its entirety while hanging on the Cross, verses one to six speaking of His abandonment by Deity, verses seven to thirteen telling of the ridicule to which He was subjected, verses fourteen to eighteen describing His physical sufferings, verses nineteen to twenty-one being His prayer for resurrection, and verses twenty-two to thirty-one constituting His praise for answered prayer even before the prayer for resurrection was actually answered.

The Septuagint, the Greek translation of the Old Testament, uses the same Greek word for "forsaken." The word remained constant in meaning for three hundred years, and when Matthew wrote, was chosen by the Holy

Spirit as the one that would adequately convey to the reader the content of the word uttered by our Lord in His native tongue.

When our Lord uttered that cry, He was speaking as the Man Christ Jesus, Very God, yet true man, and therefore when recognizing God as His God, speaking in the capacity of His humanity. The cry was addressed to God the Father, God the Son, and God the Holy Spirit. The possessive pronoun "my," tells us that while our Lord was bearing the sin of humanity, while He was charged by the High Court of Heaven with those sins just as if He had committed them, He yet had the consciousness that that indissoluble union between Father and Son in the God-head was still a fact, that He still partook of the same essence of Deity as God the Father, and that He in His intrinsic purity and righteousness was still that spotless Lamb of God.

But the fact still remains that He was abandoned and deserted by God the Father, and for the reason that God "appointed Him to be sin for us who knew no sin; that we might become the righteousness of God in Him" (II Cor. 5:21). A fellowship had been broken that had always existed, a fellowship that had continued all during our Lord's earthly life. But now the Father's smiling face was turned away. Understand the "how" of it we cannot. Feel the awfulness of it, we may not. Believe the fact of it, we must. Our Lord said His God had abandoned Him, deserted Him.

No words come from the skies in answer to the prayer of our Lord. He answers it Himself in Psalm 22:3 when He says that God abandoned Him because He was holy.

whereas the Son was laden with the sin of mankind. This unanswered prayer of our Lord was predicted in type in Leviticus 5:11, where an offerer too poor to bring two turtledoves or two pigeons for a sin-offering, could bring the tenth part of an ephah of fine flour, just enough to bake one day's supply of bread, the giving up of the flour typifying the giving up of life, thus pointing to our Lord's death. But he was forbidden to include frankincense with the flour. Frankincense is a type of answered prayer. Flour without frankincense speaks of our Lord's death and His unanswered prayer. These words, "Why hast thou abandoned Me" were addressed to God the Father. God the Father abandoned Him.

Our Lord cried, "My God, My God, why hast thou left Me helpless, destitute, in the lurch, why hast thou let Me down," These words were addressed to God the Holy Spirit. All through our Lord's life on earth, as the Man Christ Jesus, He lived in dependence upon the Holy Spirit. That was part of His humiliation. To be God, and yet to live as a man in dependence upon God, that was His normal life on earth. The words, "Jesus being full of the Holy Ghost returned from Jordan, and was led by the Spirit into the wilderness" (Luke 4:1), are characteristic of our Lord's entire life. No prayer our Lord ever uttered, but was energized by the Spirit. No temptation He ever overcame, but He did so in the power of the Spirit. No miracle He ever performed, but it was done through dependence upon the Holy Spirit. No thought ever passed through His mind, no word ever left His lips, but it was originated by the Spirit.

But now, when He needed the help of the Holy Spirit most, in the moment of His direst need, the Holy Spirit left Him helpless, destitute. He left Him in the lurch. He let Him down in a set of circumstances that were antagonistic, frightful, terrible. He was abandoned by Heaven, spurned by earth, laden with man's sin, suffering the excruciating anguish of crucifixion. He suffered all alone. The same sin offering that forbade the inclusion of frankincense, forbade the provision of oil. Oil is a type of the Holy Spirit. No oil in the flour, speaks of the withdrawal of the Holy Spirit's sustaining presence at the Cross. The Holy Spirit left our Lord. This fact will help us to understand I Peter 3:18, where our Lord is spoken of as being put to death with respect to the flesh, but quickened or made alive with respect to the spirit, His human spirit, from which the Holy Spirit had departed when He left our Lord helpless on the Cross. That is, our Lord died with respect to His human body, but in His human spirit, made alive again by the Holy Spirit after He had abandoned our Lord, He proceeded and made a proclamation to the fallen angels in Tartarus, (I Peter 3:18; II Peter 2:4; Jude 6; Gen. 6:1-4).

Not only did God the Father and God the Holy Spirit abandon the Man Christ Jesus on the Cross, but God the Son now turns against Himself. It was as if a man of high ideals who had lived an exemplary life, should at its close be guilty of a loathsome deed. From the exalted position of his high idealism, he looks down upon himself, loathes and repudiates himself. Our Lord as the Son of God, holy, spotless, repudiated His own humanity now laden with sin not His own. "The moral sense of His own deity revolted against His own humanity as the representative of sin." Hear His words, "But I am a worm" (Psalm 22:6). "Mine iniquities have taken hold upon me, so I am not able to look up; they are more than the hairs of mine head: therefore my heart faileth me" (Psalm 40:12). In Him as He hung on the Cross, was the fullness of Deity. He was forsaken of the fullness of Deity. That is the meaning of that terrible cry, "My God, my God, why hast thou forsaken me?"

Unsaved reader, have you some small conception now of what the Lord Jesus suffered for you? He would have endured it all for you alone, if you were the only lost soul in the universe. Does such love touch your heart, Do you see your own sinfulness and lost condition in view of all this? Will you not just now say to the Lord Jesus, "I trust Thee right now as my own personal Saviour, the One who died and poured out His precious blood for me as a sinner"?

XII

A Portrait of the Suffering Servant of Jehovah

¶ HOUSEHOLD slaves, put yourselves in constant subjection with every fear to your absolute lords and masters, not only to those who are good at heart and reasonable, but also to those who are against you. For this subjection to those who are against you is something which is beyond the ordinary course of what might be expected,

and is therefore commendable, namely, when a person because of the conscious sense of his relation to God bears
up under pain, suffering unjustly. For what sort of fame
would be yours if when ye fall short of the mark and are
pummeled with the fist, ye endure this patiently. But
when ye are in the habit of doing good and then suffer
constantly for it, if this ye patiently endure, this is an
unusual and not-to-be-expected action, and therefore commendable in the sight of God. For to this very thing were
ye called, namely, to patient endurance in the case of unjust punishment, remembering that Christ also suffered
on our behalf, leaving behind for you a model for you to
imitate, in order that by close application you might follow in His footprints, who never in a single instance committed a sin, and in whose mouth, after careful scrutiny,
there was not even found craftiness; who when His heart
was being wounded with an accursed sting, and when He
was being made the object of harsh rebuke and biting,
never retaliated, and who while suffering never threat-
ened, but rather, constantly committed *all* to the One who
judges righteously; who Himself carried up to the cross
our sins in His own body and offered Himself there as on
an altar, doing this in order that we, having ceased to
exist with respect to sins, might live with respect to righteousness, by means of whose bleeding stripes ye were
healed. For ye were straying like sheep, but ye have
turned back to the Shepherd and Overseer of your souls
(I Peter 2:18-25).

Word Studies in Authorized Version

Verse 18 "Servants" is from the Greek word referring
to household slaves. Many of these were won to Christi-

anity in the first century, and occupied positions of servitude in heathen households. These are exhorted literally, "Put yourselves in subjection to your masters." "Masters" is from a word which means "an absolute owner," and which comes into our language in the word "despot." There are two classes of these "despots," the good and kind, and the froward. The word "good" in the Greek refers to intrinsic goodness, namely, good at heart. "Gentle" is from a word meaning "mild, yielding, indulgent." It comes in its derivation from a word meaning "not being unduly rigorous." Alford describes the master, "Where not strictness of legal right, but consideration for another, is the rule of practice." The idea can be summed up in the word "reasonable," a reasonable man. "Froward" is from a word which literally means "crooked." The English word "froward" comes from the Anglo-Saxon "from-ward," namely, "averse." It describes a master whose face is averse to the slave, whose whole attitude is one of averseness to him. Household slaves are exhorted to put themselves in subjection to both classes.

Verse 19 The word "this" refers to the phrase immediately preceding. "This thing," it is in the Greek, namely, that of being obedient to masters whose faces are set against their slaves. "Thankworthy" is from the same word in Greek that is translated "grace" when referring to the grace of God as in Romans 5:20. The word when used in connection with a human being, refers to the doing of something which is out of or beyond the ordinary course of what might be expected, and is therefore commendable. What God did at Calvary is surely out of or beyond the ordinary course of what might be expected.

All the human race could rightfully expect was divine wrath because of its sin. But it is offered grace instead. So Peter exhorts slaves to put themselves in subjection to these masters whose faces are set against them, and so do that which is out of or beyond the ordinary course of what might be expected, namely, a surly obedience, and instead, offer them a willing subjection. This is grace, provided by God, and produced in the heart of the believer by the God of all grace. One can see what effect such an attitude would have upon many masters, leading them to the Lord Jesus. The words "conscience toward God" are interesting. The idea in the Greek is not that of conscientiousness in the ordinary sense, but of the conscious sense of one's relation to God, a realization of God's presence and one's relationship to Him. Thus the slave is exhorted to perform his duties to his master "not with eyeservice as menpleasers" (Eph. 6:6), but with the consciousness that he is working under the all-seeing eye of God. "Endure" is from a Greek word which literally means "to be under a burden and to carry it." Vincent says, "Suffering here is not because of a conscientious sense of duty, but because of a realization of one's relation to God as a son, which involves suffering with Him no less than being glorified with Him." "Wrongfully" is from the Greek word which means "justly," with the Greek letter Alpha prefixed, making the word mean "unjustly." That is, as the Just One suffered for the unjust on the cross, and suffered unjustly before the law which we broke, so slaves are exhorted to suffer unjustly if they are called upon to do so.

Verse 20 "Glory" is not from the Greek word which is translated "glory" in other places in the New Testament, where it refers to the glory of God in each case. The word Peter uses is found only here in the New Testament. It was used in secular documents to refer to glory in the sense of "fame." Peter says that a man will never become famous by patiently enduring punishment which is rightfully inflicted. "Buffeted" is from a Greek word which means "to strike with the fist." The same word is used in Matthew 26:67, where the angry mob struck our Lord with their fists. The result of those brutal blows is referred to in Isaiah's prophecy (52:14), "His visage was so marred more than any man, and his form more than the sons of men." That is, the brutalities inflicted upon our Lord marred His face so that it did not look human any more. Peter was there and saw it all. This passage bears the marks of his memories of that terrible night. So he says to the household slaves to whom he is writing, "What fame will come to you if when you are struck with the fist for your faults, ye take it patiently?" These slaves knew what it was to be beaten unjustly by the hard fists of their masters. Peter reminds them of their Saviour and Lord who was struck with the hard fists of an infuriated mob, not for His own sins, for He had none, but because He, the spotless Lamb of God, was going to the cross for our sins. The word "patiently" in this context speaks, not of the dull reluctance of a criminal who cannot avoid his punishment, but of a patient endurance, whether the suffering is endured justly or unjustly. The words "acceptable with God" are most precious. "Acceptable" is from the Greek word which means "grace," and is the same word used when the Bible speaks of the grace of God. The same word is translated "thankworthy" in verse nineteen.

The word, as we saw, refers to an action that is far above
the usually expected thing, something worthy of meritorious mention. Peter says that patient endurance in suffering by the innocent is meritorious, is something worthy of
commendation in the sight of God. The great example of
that is our Lord. A bondslave is not greater than his Lord
(John 15:20). If the Saviour thus suffered, so should
each one of His saints be willing if necessary to patiently
endure unjust suffering.

Verse 21 "Hereunto" means literally, "unto this," that
is, "unto this circumscribed state," that of suffering
wrongfully. That is, Christian suffering is one of the very
definite parts of the saint's experience. The word "also,"
Alford says, puts the wrongful suffering of a Christian
slave on a new plane, for Christ suffered in the same way,
and we participate with Him in those sufferings. The
word "for" is from the preposition of substitution, referring to the act of one person taking the place of another.
Christ took our place on the cross. He became sin who
knew no sin. He paid the penalty which was justly ours.
His sufferings were expiatory, ours are not. They are
alike only in that both are examples of unjust suffering.
The word "leaving" is literally "leaving behind." "Example" is from a Greek word referring to a writing copy
for one to imitate. It was used of the copy-head at the top
of a child's exercise book for him to imitate, and included
all the letters of the alphabet. How that reminds one of
our Lord's words, "I am the Alpha and the Omega, the
first and the last" (Rev. 1:8). "Follow" is from a word
which means "to follow closely upon," and denotes close
application. As a child follows closely the shape of the

letters and by close application reproduces them for the teacher, so saints should follow closely "the writing copy" given us to imitate, the picture of our Lord in the sacred pages of Scripture. The copied character bears a closer likeness to the original when the student applies himself to his task. So the more closely a saint applies himself to the practice of imitating his Lord, the clearer the likeness will be in his life of the One Altogether Lovely.

Verse 22 The word "guile" in the Greek refers to craftiness or trickery. Our Lord said, "I am the truth" (John 14:6). "Truth" comes from a Greek word meaning "not to hide," or "that which is not hidden." Our Lord's words and actions were always out in the open. Nothing was covered. He employed no crafty or tricky methods in His ministry. His was a life open to the gaze of everyone. So should our behaviour be open and aboveboard. The words "was found," indicate in the original something stronger than would be expressed by the simple verb of being. They indicate a guilelessness which stood the test of scrutiny (Matt. 26:60, John 18:38, 19:4, 6). Again, the words "did no sin" are from a tense that causes us to translate, "who never in a single instance committed sin."

Verse 23 "Revileth" is a strong word. The same word is used in I Corinthians 4:12. It refers to a harsh railing which not only rebukes a man, but also sharply bites him, and stamps him with open contumely. It is to wound a man with an accursed sting. Thus was our Lord reviled, and His servant Paul likewise. In that manner were the household slaves treated, to whom Peter refers. When undergoing such treatment, a Christian should not resent it. When our Lord suffered, He did not keep on threatening. The word "but" in the original can be translated "yea, rather." It removes the thing previously negatived altogether out of our field of view and substitutes something totally different. Instead of threatening, He kept on committing Himself and all these insults and injuries to God the Father, the One who judges righteously.

Verse 24 "Bare" is a word in Scripture that belongs to the idea of sacrifice and is not to be disassociated from it. He "bore up to the cross as to an altar and offered Himself there." The word "tree" here refers not to a literal tree nor merely to a piece of wood, but to something fashioned out of wood, in this case, a cross. The words "being dead," come from a compound word which literally means "having become off," that is, having ceased to exist with regard to sin. The idea is one of separation from the power of the sinful nature. Not only is the power of indwelling sin broken in the believer, but the divine nature is implanted in order that we should live with respect to righteousness. This is the result of our Lord's work on the cross for us, which lays upon us an obligation to become free with respect to sin, to be done with sin, and to live a righteous life. The word "stripes" in the Greek, refers to a bloody wale which is found to issue from under a blow. Peter remembered the body of the Lord Jesus Christ after the scourging, the flesh so dreadfully mangled that the disfigured form appeared in his eyes like one single bruise. How often were these household slaves beaten by their masters, and frequently unjustly. Then they could remember the sufferings of their Lord and be comforted.

Verse 25 They were sheep who had wandered away, but now had returned to the Shepherd and the Overseer of their souls. The word "bishop" in the Greek means literally, "one who oversees."

XIII

The Divine Sculptor's Masterpiece

¶ "WHOM HE did foreknow, he also did predestinate to be conformed to the image of his Son, that he might be the first born among many brethren. Moreover whom he did predestinate, them he also called: and whom he called, them he also justified: and whom he justified, them he also glorified" (Rom. 8:29, 30). The glorious story is told in five words, "foreknow, predestinate, called, justified, glorified."

The first step in the salvation of a believer is God's foreknowledge of him. The word is used seven times in the New Testament. In two instances it means simply "to know previously" (Acts 26:5, and II Peter 3:17). In the other five cases, it has a deeper broader meaning. In Acts 2:23 we have, "Him being delivered by the determinate counsel and foreknowledge of God." These words are in a construction in the Greek text which shows that the word "foreknowledge" refers to the same thing to which the word "counsel" refers. The Greek word for "foreknowledge" is translated in I Peter 1:20 by the word "foreordained," and means "to designate before" to a position or function.

The word "counsel" is from a Greek word which like
the English word refers to the interchange of opinions,
to deliberation together, to the exercise of deliberative
judgment. The two verbs in Greek which have the same
root have the following implications. The one refers to
the exercise of the will but with premeditation, and is illustrated in the sentence from the papyri, the latter term referring to the non-literary manuscripts of the early centuries of the Christian era which afford abundant illustrations of the usage of New Testament Greek words, "I
wish to begin to practice the trade of a river-worker." The
other refers to an intention which is the result of reflection, and is used in the sentence "I have formed this intention."

The word "determinate" which describes "counsel" is
from a word which literally means "to draw a boundary
around," thus "to divide or separate from," and is used in
the clause, "Since the boundaries of a piece of land are to
be fixed." It comes finally to mean, "to fix a limit" or "to
set apart."

The words "counsel" and "foreknowledge" refer to the
same act of God when as the result of the exercise of deliberative judgment, that judgment having been for the
purpose of fixing a limit upon something, He designated
the believer to the position of a saved person before this
universe was created. The word "chosen" in Ephesians
1:4 speaks of the same act. The word "foreknow" in
Romans 8:29, 11:2; I Peter 1:2, and Acts 2:23 means "to
designate to a certain position or function, this act of
designating being dictated by judgment that had found
its basis in deliberation."

The sculptor had a wonderful son. He had many statues in his art gallery which he had cut out of rough granite in the course of his lifetime. But now he has come to the decision that he would like a group of statues all made in the very image of that son. So he goes to the stone quarry, and after some deliberation selects some large blocks of granite which the quarrymen have blasted out of the mountainside. One might wonder at his selection, for they appear to be the least promising of all those from which he had to choose. There they were, scarred by the weather, discolored, cracked.

In the eternity before this universe was created, the Divine Sculptor had it in His heart to make some images of His Son, the Lord Jesus, not carved out of granite, but moulded from living personalities. He passed by fallen angels (Heb. 2:16 "Not of angels doth He take hold, but He taketh hold of the seed of Abraham"), and chose inferior material, lost human beings, creatures full of sin, rebellious toward Him, scarred and seamed with the deadly result of evil-doing. He chose the most unlikely material He could find. He gets more glory to Himself by choosing red clay into which He has breathed the breath of lives (Gen. 2:7) and conforming that inferior material into the very image of His Son than if He had taken hold of angels for salvation. In perfect justice and righteousness He passed by fallen angels and in infinite mercy chose fallen human beings.

After the sculptor had selected the blocks of granite, he placed a tag upon each of them. On the tag was written, "to be conformed to the image of my son." This sculptor had many blocks of granite coming from that quarry, some to be used for one purpose and others for another. But these which were labelled, "to be conformed to the image of my son," were to be kept separate. They were labelled for this one destiny.

So the Divine Sculptor, after designating certain out of lost humanity to be conformed to the image of His Son, predestinated them to this wonderful destiny. The word "predestinated" comes from a Greek word which means "to fix the limit to, to fix a boundary beforehand." It was used in the sentence "Since the boundaries of a piece of land are to be fixed." After God foreknew the sinner, He put a tag upon him, "to be conformed to the image of my Son." The sinner was to be kept for just that purpose and no other. This is the meaning of the Greek word translated "predestinated." It is the same Greek word translated "determinate" in Acts 2:23.

After the sculptor had selected his blocks of granite at the quarry, and had put a label upon each one, "to be conformed to the image of my son," he returned to his home and sent his men with the large stone wagon and derrick to haul the granite to his studios. Just so, after He foreknew us, that is, after He had chosen us to a certain destiny, and after He had predestinated us, that is, after He had put a label on us "to be conformed to the image of my Son," which label answered to the specifications of the foreknowledge, the Divine Sculptor called us. This Greek word was used in the first century as a technical word in legal practice, and meant "an official summons," as in the case of the summoning of a witness to court. The word means here more than a mere invitation. It is a divine summons. The one summoned is constituted willing to obey this summons, not against but with his free will and consent. It is an effectual call. The one called always responds. "By the grace are ye saved," namely, that particular grace made possible of bestowal and thus operative at Calvary, "and that not of yourselves, it is the gift of God," the word "that" in the Greek text referring not to the word "faith," but to the idea of salvation which dominates the context. Salvation is all of grace. The faith we exercise in our appropriation of the Saviour is given by God, and is included in the salvation provided. Thus the call of the Divine Sculptor is a divine summons which is always answered by the one summoned (Eph. 2:8).

After the sculptor has his chosen blocks of granite in his studios, he starts work on them. There they are, scarred, irregular, rough, cracked, discolored. A visitor comes in. "What, do you mean to tell me that you are using that poor looking material for the statues of your son?" "Yes," replies the sculptor, "I receive far more satisfaction and fame from using inferior material and turning out a superior piece of work. And, after all, you are directing your criticism against these rough hewn blocks of granite. I do not see these when I work. I have in mind the finished product, and that will be perfect. You are not touching the statue of my son with your criticism, but rather, these rough blocks of granite. I stand here in their justification, for I see them as perfect, conformed already to the image of my son. In my reputation as a sculptor, I have assumed the responsibility for choosing such inferior granite. If my reputation is being maligned as a result, I cannot help it. I am doing it for the sake of the finished product and the increased fame which will finally come to me."

And so Satan enters the studios of the Divine Sculptor and prefers charges against the saints. How imperfect they are, how weak, how unfaithful, how prone to sin. But he is only looking at the unfinished product. His charges fall short of the mark, for the Divine Sculptor answers, "Your charges may all be true, but I am not looking at the material upon which I am working, but at the finished product. I took upon myself at Calvary all their sins. I made myself of no reputation (Phil. 2:7). Their sins have been paid for and put away on the basis of divine justice. I see each saint right now, perfect, sinless, shining with all the beauty of my only begotten Son." So God justifies us. His Son is our righteousness, our beauty, our adornment.

The sculptor goes on, day after day with his work of cutting the granite. Rough corners are hewn off, discolorations disappear. Jagged surfaces are made smooth. The block of granite begins to assume the shape and contour of the sculptor's son. But the sculptor does not see the unfinished block of granite before him. He sees the image of his son as he looks right through the rough edges, the weather scarred surface.

God foreknew us, predestinated us, called us, justified us, and glorified us. We are already glorified in His eyes. The Divine Sculptor sees the finished product while He through the process of sanctification, namely, the work of the Holy Spirit, gradually conforms us to the image of His Son. We are already glorified in His eyes. Some day

we will be in actuality what the Divine Sculptor sees us to
be now as He works upon us. In the twinkling of an eye,
at the last trump, we shall be changed, the miracle of glorification completing the work which the process of sanctification began (I Cor. 15:52), and then "we shall be like
Him, for we shall see Him just as He is" (I John 3:2).
A sinner, saved by grace, conformed to the image of the
wonderful Son of God, that is the Divine Sculptor's mas-
terpiece.

XIV

The Soul-Winner's Adornment

¶ IN I PETER 3:1-5 we have the case of Christian
women of the first century seeking to win their unsaved
husbands to the Lord Jesus as Saviour. These husbands
are of that non-persuasible type that will not listen to
reason. Obstinacy, stubbornness, inflexibility are here per-
sonified. We see this in the use of the words "obey not"
which come from a Greek word literally meaning, "non-
persuasible." The word "if" represents a fulfilled condition. There were such cases in those days, as there are
such instances today.

The Christian wife is exhorted to be in subjection to her
unsaved husband, in order that he might without *a* word,
not *the* Word, be won by the behaviour of the wife. "Behaviour" is from the Greek word rendered "conversation,"
the latter having changed its meaning since the A.V. was
translated. There is no definite article before the second

use of the word "word." No one has ever been won to the
Lord Jesus apart from the Word of God. Peter is exhorting these wives who have given the gospel to their husbands time after time, to stop talking about it lest they
start nagging, and instead, live the gospel before them.
If the husband is so obstinate as to refuse to listen to her,
well then, the next best thing is to keep quiet and let the
gospel speak through a Christlike life. He may refuse to
listen to her words, but he cannot but see the Lord Jesus
in her life.

But as the Christian wife thus seeks to live before her
husband, the apostle warns her that she must not depend
upon outward adornment in her effort to win her husband
to the Lord. Her adornment must come from within,
from a heart pervaded with the beauty and fragrance of
Christ. Thus it is the presence of the Lord Jesus in the
life of the soul-winner which the Holy Spirit uses to at-
tract sinners to Jesus, not the adornment one puts on.
This is the principle which Peter brings before us in verses
three and four.

The word "adornment" is from the Greek word *kosmos*.
It means literally "an ordered system." It speaks of that
which is congruous, fitting. A Christian worker's clothing
should be in keeping with the simplicity, purity, and beauty
of the Lord Jesus. What one wears on the outside of the
body should be an expression of what is in the heart.

Then the Spirit of God speaks of the three parts of a
Christian woman's adornment, the way she wears her
hair, the jewelry she puts on, and the apparel she selects.

First, she is not to depend upon the plaiting of the hair in her effort to win her husband to the Lord. Reference is made here to the extravagant and costly excesses to which women of the first century went in hair ornament. Quoting from an early manuscript we have this: "The attendants will vote on the dressing of the hair as if a question of reputation or of life were at stake, so great is the trouble she takes in quest of beauty; with so many tiers does she load, with so many continuous stories does she build up on high her head. She is as tall as Andromache in front, behind she is shorter. You would think her another person" (Vincent). Thus, extravagant excesses and intricate artificiality of hairdress are forbidden the Christian woman as adornment.

Second, the wearing of gold is forbidden. The word "wearing" is from a Greek word which means literally "to hang around," as one hangs ornaments around a Christmas tree. The wearing of jewelry is not forbidden here, but the gaudy, conspicuous, extravagant, obtrusive display of the same as adornment.

Third, dependence upon apparel is forbidden. The purpose of clothing is for the protection of the body. The purpose of apparel is for the ornamentation of the person. That which is forbidden is the donning of apparel for the purpose of making ourselves pleasing in the eyes of the unsaved so that we may win them to a saving faith in the Lord Jesus.

Why does not dependence upon outward adornment help us to win souls to the Lord Jesus? First, it is because the Holy Spirit does not use the styles of the world in winning a soul to the Lord, as He seeks to work through the believer. Second, it is because such an elaborate display satisfies the lust or desire of the eyes of the unsaved one whom we are seeking to win. When a Christian worker thus appeals to the fallen nature of the sinner, she cannot at the same time appeal to him to trust in the Lord Jesus. Third, it is because such a display destroys the personal testimony of the soul winner. We may be *fundamental* in our doctrine, and yet defeat the power of the Word we give out by the *modernism* of our appearance. The unsaved person will say, "What you appear to be on the outside speaks so loudly I cannot hear what you are saying." For these reasons, no dependence must be placed upon outward adornment as we seek to win the lost.

Instead of this, we are to depend upon the hidden man of the heart. The expression refers to the inner heart life of the Christian in which the Lord Jesus reigns supreme When we depend upon that for our adornment, then the Lord Jesus is seen in the life, His beauty, His sweetness, His simplicity. This the Holy Spirit uses as He gently woos a soul to the Saviour. The more of the Lord Jesus which the sinner sees in the believer's life, the more powerful is the latter's testimony, the more usable her words, usable to the Holy Spirit. Alas, as someone has said, "What cheap perfume we sometimes use."

This brings us to certain principles regarding adornment. If a personality is to be seen at its best, it must be seen alone, not merged with another personality. Either the Lord Jesus is seen in all His beauty, or the personality of the believer is seen and her adornment. The Holy Spirit attracts sinners to the Lord Jesus, not by displaying the latest styles in dress, but by exhibiting the Lord Jesus. If the sinner is attracted by the modernism of the believer's adornment, the fundamentalism of the believer's doctrine will be neutralized. When a Christian woman depends upon the Lord Jesus for her adornment, the manner of wearing the hair, the kind and amount of ornament she wears, and the kind of clothing she puts on, will all be in keeping with the purity, simplicity, and beauty of the Lord Jesus. All will be attractive without attracting from the Lord Jesus. All will be beautiful without detracting from Him. All will have character without attracting one to the person herself. Then the sinner will see the Lord Jesus in the heart and life of the believer, and in her adornment as well. Then will the Holy Spirit be able to work through the soul winner, attracting sinners to the Saviour.

XV

The Words for "Love" in the Greek New Testament

¶ THERE ARE four words in the Greek language for "love." *Stergein* is a love that has its basis in one's own nature. It speaks of the constitutional efflux of natural affection. *Eran* is a love that has its basis in passion, and its expression takes the form of a blind impulse produced by passion. *Philein* is a love that has its basis in pleasurableness, and is the glow of the heart kindled the perception of that in the object loved which affords one pleasure. *Agapan* is a love that has its basis in preciousness, a love called out of one's heart by an awakened sense of value in the object loved that causes one to prize it.

Stergein is used in the New Testament in its noun form, with the letter "Alpha" prefixed which negates the word, that is, makes it mean the opposite to what it meant in itself. It occurs in Romans 1:31 and II Timothy 3:3, and is translated in both instances by the words "without natural affection." The word appears also in Romans 12:10 with the word philos, "love", compounded with it, and is translated, "kindly affectioned." *Stergein* designates "the quiet and abiding feeling within us, which, resting on an object as near to us, recognizes that we are closely bound up with it and takes satisfaction in its recognition." It is a love that is "a natural movement of the soul," "something almost like gravitation or some other force of blind nature." It is the love of parents for children and children for parents, of husband for wife and wife for husband, of close relations one for another. It is found in the animal world in the love which the animal has for its offspring. It is a love of obligatoriness, the term being used here not in its moral sense, but in a natural sense. It is a necessity under the circumstances. This kind of love is the binding factor by which any natural or social unit is held together.

The word *astorgos* (Rom. 1:31; II Tim. 3:3) which denotes the absence of this kind of love, designates "the unfeeling and hard, whose heart is warmed by no noble sentiment; it is applied particularly to inhuman parents, but also to animals who do not love their young." It is used in pagan writings, of women who have many love affairs and as a result do not have that nobler love for their husbands which they should have.

Eran is a word that is not found in the New Testament. The word "passion" describes it. It is passion seeking satisfaction. It is not intrinsically a base word. In its use it is found at the two extremes of low and high. It was used in pagan Greek writings of sex love. It was used in Christian writings of divine love. It was used of the love of children to their mother. This love is "an over-mastering passion seizing upon and absorbing into itself the whole mind."

Philein is used forty-five times in its various forms of verb and noun. This is an unimpassioned love, a friendly love. It is a love that is called out of one's heart as a re-sponse to the pleasure one takes in a person or object. It is based upon an inner community between the person lov-ing and the person or object loved. That is, both have things in common with one another. The one loving finds a reflection of his own nature in the person or thing loved. It is a love of liking, an affection for someone or some-thing that is the outgoing of one's heart in delight to that which affords pleasure. The Greeks made much of friend-ship, and this word was used by them to designate this form of mutual attraction. "Whatever in an object that is adapted to give pleasure, tends to call out this affection." It is connected with the sense of the agreeable in the ob-ject loved. The words which best express this kind of love are "fondness, affection, liking." "It shows the inclina-tion which springs out of commerce with a person or is called out by qualities in an object which are agreeable to us." As an outgrowth of its meaning of fondness, it sometimes carries that sentiment over into an outward expression of the same, that of kissing.

Agapan is used in its verb, noun, and adjective forms about three hundred and twenty times in the New Testament. It is a love called out of a person's heart by "an awakened sense of value in an object which causes one to prize it." It expresses a love of approbation and esteem. Its impulse comes from the idea of prizing. It is a love that recognizes the worthiness of the object loved. Thus, this love consists of the soul's sense of the value and preciousness of its object, and its response to its recognized worth in admiring affection."

In contrasting *philein* and *agapan*, we might say that the former is a love of pleasure, the latter a love of preciousness; the former a love of delight, the latter a love of esteem; the former a love called out of the heart by the apprehension of pleasurable qualities in the object loved, the latter a love called out of the heart by the apprehension of valuable qualities in the object loved; the former takes pleasure in, the latter ascribes value to; the former is a love of liking, the latter a love of prizing.

As to the reason why *philein* occurs only forty-five times in the New Testament in all forms, while *agapan* is found three hundred and twenty times in its various forms, the following can be said. The principal reason for the more frequent use of *agapan* in the New Testament as over against the infrequent use of *philein* is that *philein* was a commonly used word for "love" in the classics, and *agapan* was used most infrequently, and when Attic Greek was spread over the world by the conquering armies of Alexander the Great, and remained in its simplified and modified form as the international language of the period between Alexander and Constantine, *agapan* suddenly sprang into the ascendancy. Because it was the common word for "love" during these centuries, the New Testament writers naturally found it not only desirable but necessary to use it. It became the general word for love in the New Testament.

But this does not mean that both words are used indiscriminately, the one for the other, without any conscious sense of the differences between them. Whenever *philein* is used, it means that the writer goes out of his way to use a word that was not in common use, and because he desired to convey a thought which *agapan* did not contain. There was always a reason for such a selection although we may not always be able to see it. The writers (I Cor. 2:13) claim that their choice of words was taught them by the Holy Spirit. This being the case, we have an infallible use of the Greek words in their content of meaning and general usage in the Roman world at that period. The Holy Spirit used *agapan* and *philein* advisedly in the places where they occur, and it is for us to find His reason and the truth He wishes us to have from His use of the terms.

But there is another reason why *agapan* is used so frequently. *Agapan* never was a common word in classical literature, although it was in use from the beginning and occupied a distinctive place of its own. In Homer it is used only ten times, in Euripedes but three. Its noun form *agapesis* is rare. The form *agape,* so frequently found in the New Testament, does not occur at all. Its first appearance is in the Greek translation of the Old Testament. It conveyed the ideas of astonishment, wonder, admiration, and approbation when connected with the word *agamai* which meant "to wonder at or admire." It was used in classical literature in the same sentence with *philein* and had its distinctive sense of "a love of prizing" as contrasted to *philein,* "a love of liking." But owing to the very infrequency of its use, it was an admirable word which could be put to use to convey the new and higher conception of divine love which the New Testament presents. Its relative emptiness, so far as the general knowledge of the person was concerned who spoke Greek as his second language, made it the ideal receptacle into which the new moral and ethical content of Christianity could be poured.

The pagan Greeks knew nothing of the love of self-sacrifice for one's enemy which was exhibited at Calvary. Therefore they had no word for that kind of love. They knew nothing about the divine analysis of this love which Paul gives us in I Corinthians 13. So the New Testament writers seized upon this word as one that would express these exalted conceptions. Therefore, the word *agapan* in the New Testament is to be understood in its meaning as given above, but also in the added meaning which has been poured into it by its use in the New Testament, the context of such passages as John 3:16; I Corinthians 13; I John 4:16, and Romans 5:5 giving us an adequate conception of its New Testament content of meaning.

The English reader can see from this study the importance of knowing what Greek word lies back of the English word "love." While the English student is able to come to a good understanding of the passages in which the words occur, yet a full-orbed view of the scripture under consideration is only possible when one knows what the distinctive Greek word for "love" is. It is to help the student who does not have access to the Greek New Testament, that this study has been written. It is impossible within the brief compass of this chapter to comment upon all of the passages, but a representative list will be treated, leaving the student the delightful task of studying the others for himself. It should be kept in mind, however, that all the shades of meaning in each word will not be applicable on each occasion of its use. A study of the context will guide one in ascertaining just what distinctive meaning the word will have in each passage. For this groundwork in the study of the Greek words for "love," I am indebted to Benjamin B. Warfield's excellent articles, "The Terminology of Love in the New Testament," which appeared in The Princeton Theological Review of January and April of 1918.

Agapan occurs in John 3:16. The love exhibited at Calvary was called out of the heart of God because of the preciousness of each lost soul, precious to God because He sees in lost humanity His own image even though that image be marred by sin, precious to God because made of material which through redemption can be transformed into the very image of His dear Son. While it is a love based upon the estimation of the preciousness of the object loved, this from its classical usage, it is also a love of self-sacrifice, complete self-sacrifice to the point of death to self, and that for one who bitterly hates the one who loves. This latter is its added New Testament meaning. Include in that the constitutent elements as analyzed by Paul in I Corinthians 13 where "charity" should be translated "love," and we have the full content of this love which should always be kept in mind when interpreting passages in the New Testament in which this word occurs, and where the love is shown either by God to man, or by the Christian to others.

For instance, in interpreting "Husbands, love your wives" (Eph. 5:25), the love of John 3:16 and I Corinthians 13 is meant. They already have a *stergein* and *philein* love for them. These latter should be saturated and thus elevated, purified, and ennobled by *agapan*. But these Christian husbands are not left helpless in an attempt to obey this exhortation, for this very love is shed abroad in their hearts by the Holy Spirit (Rom. 5:5) and is one of His fruits (Gal. 5:22). When saints are exhorted to love one another (I John 4:11) it is with this kind of love.

When we come to "men loved darkness rather than light" (John 3:19), and "love not the world" (I John 2:15), we come to some isolated instances where the classical meaning which has been brought over into the New Testament, can only be applied. Here it is no love of self-sacrifice for the benefit of the object loved. It is a love for sin and for the world system of evil that is called out of the sinful heart because of the estimation which that person puts upon the preciousness of the object loved. The saints are exhorted not to set a high value upon the world and thus love it. Aside from such exceptional cases like these, *agapan* is to be given its full-orbed New Testament meaning.

In order that the reader can make a study of *agapan* in the New Testament, we append the following list containing the places where its verb occurs, and where the word "love" is in the translation. Matthew 5:43, 44, 46, 6:24, 19:19, 22:37, 39; Mark 10:21, 12:30, 31, 33; Luke 6:27, 32, 35, 7:5, 42, 47, 10:27, 11:43, 16:13; John 3:16, 19, 35, 8:42, 10:17, 11:5, 12:43, 13:1, 23, 13:34, 14:15, 21, 23, 24, 28, 31, 15:9, 12, 17, 17:23, 24, 26, 19:26, 21:7, 15, 16, (first occurrences only in verses 15 and 16), 20; Romans 8:28, 37, 9:13, 25, 13:8, 9; I Corinthians 2:9, 8:3; II Corinthians 9:7, 11:11, 12:15; Galatians 2:20, 5:14; Ephesians 1:6, 2:4, 5:2, 25, 28, 33, 6:24; Colossians 3:12, 19; I Thessalonians 1:4, 4:9; II Thessalonians 2:13, 16; II Timothy 4:8, 10; Hebrews 1:9, 12:6; James 1:12, 2:5, 8; I Peter 1:8, 22 (second occurrence only), 2:17, 3:10; II Peter 2:15; I John 2:10, 15, 3:10, 11, 14, 3:18, 23, 4:7, 8, 10, 11, 12, 19, 20, 21, 5:1, 2; II John 1, 5; III John 1; Revelation 1:5, 3:9, 12:11, 20:9

The noun form *agape* occurs in the following places where it is translated either by "love" or "charity." Where the word "charity" appears, the translation should read "love." There is no good reason for the change to "charity." Matthew 24:12; Luke 11:42; John 5:42, 13:35, 15:9, 10, 13, 17:26; Romans 5:5, 8, 8:35, 39, 12:9, 13:10, 14:15, 15:30; I Corinthians 4:21, 8:1, 13:1, 2, 3, 4, 8, 13, 14:1, 16:14, 24; II Corinthians 2:4, 8, 5:14, 6:6, 8:7,

8, 24, 13:11, 14; Galatians 5:6, 13, 22; Ephesians 1:4, 15, 2:4, 3:17, 19, 4:2, 15, 16, 5:2, 6:23; Philippians 1:9, 17, 2:1, 2; Colossians 1:4, 8, 13, 2:2, 3:14; I Thessalonians 1:3, 3:6, 12, 5:8, 13; II Thessalonians 1:3, 2:10, 3:5; I Timothy 1:5, 14, 2:15, 4:12, 6:11; II Timothy 1:7, 13, 2:22, 3:10; Titus 2:2; Philemon 5, 7, 9; Hebrews 6:10, 10:24; I Peter 4:8, 5:14; II Peter 1:7; I John 2:5, 15, 3:1, 16, 17, 4:7, 8, 9, 10, 12, 16, 17, 18, 5:3; II John 3, 6; III John 6; Jude 2, 12, 21; Revelation 2:4, 19.

The adjective form *agapetos,* translated "beloved" is found in Matthew 3:17, 12:18, 17:5; Mark 1:11, 9:7, 12:6; Luke 3:22, 9:35, 20:13; Acts 15:25; Romans 1:7, 11:28, 12:19, 16:5, 8, 9, 12; I Corinthians 4:14, 17, 10:14, 15:58; II Corinthians 7:1, 12:19; Ephesians 5:1, 6:21; Philippians 2:12, 4:1; Colossians 1:7, 4:7, 9, 14; I Thessalonians 2:8; I Timothy 6:2; II Timothy 1:2; Philemon 1, 2, 16; Hebrews 6:9; James 1:16, 19, 2:5; I Peter 2:11, 4:12; II Peter 1:17, 3:1, 8, 14, 15, 17; I John 3:2, 21, 4:1, 7, 11; III John 1, 2, 5, 11; Jude 3, 17, 20.

We come now to a consideration of *philein* in the New Testament. We will examine a few representative passages. The hypocrites love to pray standing in the synagogues and in the corners of the streets (Matt. 6:5). *Philein* is used here rather than *agapan* because the inspired writer wishes to show that they take pleasure in that sort of thing, that it is part of their nature to desire to be seen of men. They love to do it. "Everyone that loveth and maketh a lie" (Rev. 22:15) uses *philein* in order to show that there is "a personal affinity with the false, inward kinship with it, leading to its outward practice." *Philein* is a love of liking. One likes someone because that person is like himself. The one loving in this way finds in the object loved a reflection of himself. Thus the one who loves a lie, loves it because he finds in a lie that which is reflected in his own bosom. "He that loveth his life shall lose it" (John 12:25). It is a love that finds such pleasure in life that it becomes a fixed attitude in one's outlook, and nothing else comes into consideration in comparison with it. "If the world hateth you, ye know that it hath hated me first; if ye were of the world, the world would love its own" (John 15:19). *Philein* is most appropriate here. The words "the world would love its own," speak of an inner affinity. They speak of a community of nature between the world and its own. *Philein* is a love of liking, and we like that which is like us. But the world finds no community of nature in itself and the Christian, for the latter has been made a partaker of the divine nature (II Peter 1:4), and for that reason the world hates the Christian.

Philein is used of Jesus' love for Lazarus (John 11:3, 36), the emphasis being upon the love of friendship which existed between the Man Christ Jesus and His friend Lazarus. It is the human heart of Jesus which we see here. *Philein* shows the personal intimacy of the affection existing between them. How wonderful, that, included in the self-humbling of God the Son in the incarnation, there should be this capacity for human friendship. Of course, our Lord loved Lazarus with an *agapan* love also, for He died for him on the Cross. But here the inspired writer wishes to present this particular kind of love. It fits the context. The appeal of the sisters was upon the basis of the mutual friendship existing between our Lord and Lazarus. When John speaks of Jesus' love for Martha, and Mary, and Lazarus, he uses *agapan,* the general term for love. They were precious to Him. The non-use of *philein* is a good commentary upon the reserve which our Lord maintained toward womanhood.

In the conversation between our Lord and Peter (John 21:15-19), our Lord uses *agapan* twice and *philein* the third time, while Peter uses *philein* three times. Of the use of these two words for love in this passage, Warfield says, "That anyone should doubt that the words are used here in distinctive senses would seem incredible prior to experience." He quotes Moulton and Milligan as saying that it is "supremely hard in so severely simple a writer as John, to reconcile ourselves to a meaningless use of synonyms, where the point would seem to lie in the identity of the word employed."

Our Lord said to Peter twice, "Simon, son of Jonas, dost thou have a love for Me that is called out of thine heart because I am precious to thee, a love of deep devotion that is sacrificial in its essence, a love that would make thee willing to die for Me?" Three times Peter said, "Yea, Lord, thou knowest that I am fond of Thee, thou knowest that I have an affection for Thee that is called out of my heart because of the pleasure I take in Thee."

Jesus asked for a love of complete devotion. Peter offers Him a love of personal heart emotion. Jesus asked for a love of surrendering obedience. Peter offers Him a love of personal attachment.

Peter at the crucifixion had denied his Lord even in the face of his statements, "Though all men should be offended because of thee, yet will I never be offended." "Though I should die with thee, yet will I not deny thee" (Matt. 26:33, 35). Peter had compared himself with the other disciples. Now our Lord asks, "Peter, dost thou have a personal devotion to Me to the point of self-sacrifice which is stronger than the personal devotion of these your fellow-disciples?" Peter answers in deep humility, remembering his denial of his Lord, and without comparing his love for Jesus with that of the other disciples. In our Lord's second question the comparison is omitted, and Peter has the opportunity to tell of his personal devotion for Jesus without comparing it with that of the other disciples. But he only speaks of his personal friendly affection for Him.

The third time Jesus questions Peter He uses *philein,* and asks with sharp directness and brevity whether Peter has any real affection for Him at all. Peter was grieved because Jesus used *philein,* yet he only asserts his fondness and friendly affection for his Master.

Then Jesus tells Peter that some day he will exhibit an *agapan* love for Him in that he will die a martyr's death for Him, for He tells him that he will die by crucifixion for his testimony to his Saviour.

Philein is used in John 16:27 where God the Father takes pleasure in and loves those believers who take pleasure in His Son and therefore love Him. It is a love of friendly affection. The Father finds the same kind of love for the Son in the hearts of the saints that is in His own heart for His Son, a love called out of the heart because of the pleasure one takes in the object loved. This is a natural love of complacency as *agapan* in John 3:16 is a love of pity (John 16:27, 5:20). These instances of the use of *philein* will suffice as illustrations to guide the Bible student in his study of those places where *philein* occurs.

Philein in its verb form occurs in Matthew 6:5, 10:37, 23:6, 26:48; Mark 14:44; Luke 20:46, 22:47; John 5:20, 11:3, 36, 12:25, 15:19, 16:27, 20:2, 21:15, 16, 17; I Corinthians 16:22; Titus 3:15; Revelation 3:19, 22:15, and is translated by the words "love" or "kiss."

Its noun form *philos* is found in Matthew 11:19; Luke 7:6, 34, 11:5, 6, 8, 12:4, 14:10, 12, 15:6, 9, 29, 16:9, 21:16, 23:12; John 3:29, 11:11, 15:13, 14, 15, 19:12; Acts 10:24, 19:31, 27:3; James 2:23, 4:4; III John 14, where it is translated by the word "friend." Interpret these passages in the light of the meaning of *philein*.

In II Timothy 3:4, III John 9, "love" is from *philein*. In James 4:4, "friendship" is from *philein*. "Hospitality" (Rom. 12:13), "entertain strangers" (Heb. 13:2), "given to hospitality" (I Tim. 3:2), "lover of hospitality" (Titus 1:8), "use hospitality" (I Peter 4:9) are from a word made up of the word *philein* and "stranger," thus, "showing one's self friendly to those who do not belong in our own home." "Philosophy" (Col. 2:8) and "philosopher" (Acts 17:18) are from a word made up of *philein* and "wisdom," thus "a love of" and "a lover of wisdom." "Be kindly affectioned" (Rom. 12:10) is from *philein* and a form of *stergein*, speaking of that natural friendliness which should be shown by the saints toward one another. "Love their husbands and their children" (Titus 2:4) uses *philein*.

"A lover of good men," better, "a lover of that which is good" (Titus 1:8), is from *philein* and the word for "intrinsic inner goodness." "Brotherly love" and brotherly kindness" are from *philein* and the Greek word for "brother" which latter literally means "from the same womb" (Rom. 12:10; I Thess. 4:9; Heb. 13:1; I Peter 1:22; "love of the brethren;" II Peter 1:7, I Peter 3:8, "love as brethren,"). "Kindness" (Acts 28:2), "love toward man" (Titus 3:4), "courteously" (Acts 27:3) are from *philein* and the word for "man," the Greek word for "man" here being the racial term for man, really, "love for mankind." Our word "philanthropy" is a transliteration of this Greek word. "Lovers of their own selves" (II Tim. 3:2) is from *philein* and the pronoun "himself." "Love of money" (I Tim. 6:10) and "covetous" (Luke 16:14, II Tim. 3:2) are from *philein* and the word "money."

"So have strived" (Rom. 15:20), "labor" (II Cor. 5:9), and "study" (I Thess. 4:11) are from a verb which is made up of *philein* and *time*, "honor," literally meaning, "to be fond of honor, to be actuated by a love of honor." In later Greek it came to mean "to strive earnestly, to make it one's aim," which latter two meanings we must understand for the three passages quoted above. But because Paul in other places uses terms taken from the world of athletics when he is speaking of intense effort, we conclude that in the background of his mind there is that thought of the maintenance of his honor and his testimony as an apostle of the Lord Jesus, and that was one of the motivating factors in his service for his Lord, as it should be of ours.

"Courteously" (Acts 28:7) and "courteous" (I Peter 3:8) are from a word made up of *philein* and a Greek word speaking of "the faculty of perceiving and judging." The courtesy spoken of here is that rare and beautiful combination of friendliness and tactful and delicate sense of perception and judgment which should be a part of every Christian's spiritual equipment.

We have in this section listed every occurrence of both *agapan* and *philein* in the New Testament in all their forms and where they appear in composition with other words. The Bible student who is not conversant with Greek can thus know just what Greek word for "love" lies back of the English word, and can therefore interpret the passage more accurately.

Note: The Scripture locations listed in this chapter do not appear in the "Index to Scripture References." For the word "love" as it appears in the New Testament, please consult the lists in this section.

INDEX OF SCRIPTURE REFERENCES

INDEX OF SCRIPTURE REFERENCES

Continued

INDEX OF SCRIPTURE REFERENCES

Continued

TREASURES
from the
Greek New Testament

DEDICATED

To My Students in Greek
at the
Moody Bible Institute —
Lovers of the Greek New Testament

PREFACE

A. T. Robertson in his book, *The Minister and His Greek New Testament,* says with reference to certain translations of the New Testament which he mentions: "We shall have many more. They will all have special merit, and they will all fail to bring out all that is in the Greek. One needs to read these translations; the more the better. But when he has read them all, there will remain a large and rich untranslatable element that the preacher ought to know. . . . It is not possible to reproduce the delicate turns of thought, the nuances of language, in translation. The freshness of the strawberry cannot be preserved in any extract."

It is the purpose of this book to bring to the Bible student who does not have access to the Greek, some of the untranslatable richness of the greatest book in all the world, the Greek New Testament. We have called this small volume which follows *Golden Nuggets from the Greek New Testament for the English Reader,* and *Bypaths in the Greek New Testament for the English Reader*: *Treasures from the Greek New Testament for the English Reader.* It follows the plan of its predecessors in treating only those things which the student of the English Bible cannot obtain for himself, and in presenting that material in such a simple, non-technical way that the average Christian, even though he has had no formal training in Bible study, can easily follow the author's thought.

While the book can be read as a series of articles, it should also prove useful as a reference work when light from the Greek text is desired upon any verse commented upon in the book. For this, the "Index to Scripture References" will be helpful. Or, when one is looking for some fresh bit of truth for a message, the material from the Greek text will be found rich in suggestiveness.

The English words treated are from the Authorized Version. The author's justification in sometimes offering a fuller or a slightly different translation is found in the fact that no single translation is able to bring out all the delicate shades of meaning, all the expressions peculiar to the Greek language, and for the reason that the standard translations are held down to a minimum of words which would best express the thought of the Greek, and rightly so. Then there are a limited number of English words that have changed their meaning in the last three hundred years since the Authorized Version was made. Since the majority of Bible students still use this version, it is necessary to take care of these words.

But we must not allow these facts to disturb our confidence in and dependence upon our reliable translations. We are concerned here with minor details, not with the great outstanding doctrines and facts in God's Word. Most men have been saved and have grown in grace through faith in the Word in its translated form. The Holy Spirit owns and quickens the translated Word, and has always done so. Therefore, as we seek to bring out from the Greek text aspects of truth that the translations do not handle, let us thank God for these translations which He has given us, and receive with gratefulness any added light which the labors of Bible students have been able to gather from the Greek text.

K. S. W.

The Moody Bible Institute,
Chicago, Illinois.

CONTENTS

TREASURES
from the
Greek New Testament

I.

The Word "GRACE" in the New Testament

ARCHBISHOP TRENCH in his *Synonyms of the New Testament* says of this word, "It is hardly too much to say that the Greek mind has in no word uttered itself and all that was at its heart more distinctly than in this." This was his comment regarding the word "grace" as it was used in the language of pagan Greece. In the case of the use of the same word in the Greek New Testament, we can repeat this Greek scholar's words, substituting the word "God" for the word "Greek." *It is hardly too much to say that the mind of God has in no word uttered itself and all that was in His heart more distinctly than in this.*

We will look first at the way the word was used in pagan Greece, Greece with its philosophy, its athletics, its poetry and drama, its wonderful architecture and statuary, its blue skies and rugged mountains, its love of the beautiful. The word itself is a beautiful word, *charis*. It is pronounced as follows: *ch* as in Scotch lo*ch*, or as in our word *ch*asm, *a* as in f*a*ther, *i* as in pol*i*ce, and the *s* as in cer*i*se. The voice is stressed on the first syllable. The Christian poet wrote "Grace! 'tis a charming sound, Harmonious to the ear; Heav'n with the echo shall resound, And all the earth shall hear. Saved by grace alone! This is all my plea: Jesus died for all mankind, And Jesus died for me." But of the latter, the Greeks of the pre-Christian era knew nothing.

15

Charis referred first of all to "that property in a thing which causes it to give joy to the hearers or beholders of it. . . . After awhile it came to signify not necessarily the grace or beauty of a thing, as a quality appertaining to it; but the gracious or beautiful thing, act, thought, speech, or person it might be, itself — the grace embodying and uttering itself, where there was room or call for this, in gracious outcomings toward such as might be its objects . . . There is a further sense which the word obtained, namely, the thankfulness which the favor calls out in return. . . . In the ethical terminology of the Greek schools *charis* implied ever a favor freely done, without claim or expectation of return. . . . Thus Aristotle, defining *charis,* 'lays the whole stress on this very point, that it is conferred freely, with no expectation of return, and finding its only motive in the bounty and free-heartedness of the giver'."* Charis was also used to describe an act that was beyond the ordinary course of what might be expected, and was therefore commend-able.

This word the inspired writers take over into the New Testament. In a few instances it has its distinctively classical meaning, but in the other places where it is used, it takes an infinite step forward to a deeper, richer, more wonderful content of meaning. Luke uses it in its purely classical meaning when he says (4:22), "And all bare him witness, and wondered at the gracious words which proceeded out of his mouth." Here the word has its classical meaning of that property in our Lord's words which caused them to give joy to the hearers. How wonderful it must have been to hear the Lord Jesus speak in human speech and human tones. Not only was the content of His words gracious and beautiful, but the tones of His voice must have reflected all the depth of His personality, the intensity of His convictions (John 2:17), the fervor of His desire to

*Trench

serve (Matt. 20:28), the pathos and tenderness of His sorrow (Matt. 23:37-39). It was the infinite God speaking with human lips and in human tones.

Both Luke (17:9) and Paul in Romans 6:17 and II Corinthians 8:16 use *charis* in its classical meaning of "thankfulness." Peter uses the word in its meaning of "that which is beyond the ordinary course of what might be expected, and is therefore commendable," in his first epistle (2:19, 20), where the words "thankworthy" and "acceptable" are the translations of *charis* which appears in the Greek text. Surely, for a slave to manifest a spirit of patient submission toward a master who mistreats him, is an action beyond the ordinary course of what might be expected and is therefore commendable. The usual reaction on the part of a slave who is mistreated is to rebel against his master.

But how this purely classical meaning of the word describes what took place at Calvary. All the human race could expect in view of its sin, was the righteous wrath of a holy God, that and eternal banishment from His glorious presence. But instead, that holy God stepped down from His judgment seat and took upon Himself at Calvary's Cross, the guilt and penalty of human sin, thus satisfying His justice and making possible the bestowal of His mercy. And this He did, not for those who were His friends, but His bitter enemies, unlovely creatures saturated with sin. *Charis* in classical Greek referred to a favor conferred freely, with no expectation of return, and finding its only motive in the bounty and free-heartedness of the giver. This favor was always done to a friend, never to an enemy. Right here *charis* leaps forward an infinite distance, for the Lord Jesus died for His enemies (Rom. 5:8-10), a thing unheard of in the human race. Surely this was beyond the ordinary course of what might be expected and is therefore commendable. This is what John is speaking of in his first epistle (3:1) when he says, "Behold, what manner of love the Father has bestowed on us, that we should be called the children of God." The words "what manner of" are from a Greek word which means "what foreign kind of." That is, the love shown by God at the Cross is foreign to the human race. Man simply does not act that way (Rom. 5:7, 8, 10). That is why God's action at the Cross in dying for lost humanity is an action beyond the ordinary course of what might be expected and is therefore commendable. Here is one of the strongest proofs of the divine source of the Bible. The substitutionary atonement never came from the philosophies of man but from the heart of God.

Thus, the word *charis* comes to its highest and most exalted content of meaning in the New Testament. It refers to God's offer of salvation with all that that implies, which salvation was procured at Calvary's Cross with all the personal sacrifice which that included, offered to one who is His bitter enemy and who is not only undeserving of that salvation but deserves condign punishment for his sins, offered without any expectation of return, but given out of the bounty and free-heartedness of the giver. This means that there is no room for good works on the part of the sinner as a means whereby he could earn his salvation, or after salvation whereby he might retain that salvation. Paul sets grace over against works as things directly in opposition to one another so far as the means of salvation is concerned (Rom. 4:4-5, 11:6). But Paul is very careful to make plain that good works naturally issue from and are required by grace (Titus 2:11-12).

Furthermore, he shows that this grace is unlimited in its resources. In Romans 5:20 he says, "Where sin abounded, grace did much more abound." The word "abound" is from a different Greek word than that which is translated "abounded." It is a compound word made up of a verb which means "to exist in superabundance," and a prefixed preposition which means "above." The translation could read "grace existed in superabundance and then more grace added to this superabundance."

Thus, salvation is a gift, to be received by the open hand of faith, not something to be earned. Dear reader, if you have been attempting to find acceptance with God by your good works, if you have been depending in the least upon any personal merit, will you not now cast aside all this, and accept the free grace of God by faith in Jesus Christ as your personal Saviour, the One who died on the Cross for you, pouring out His precious blood as the God-appointed sacrifice for sins? "For God so loved the world that He gave His Son, the only begotten One, that whosoever believeth in Him might not perish but have everlasting life" (John 3:16).

II.

Christian Optimism and a Carefree Mind

"BLESSED be the God and Father of our Lord Jesus Christ, which according to his abundant mercy hath begotten us again unto a lively hope by the resurrection of Jesus Christ from the dead. . . . Wherefore gird up the loins of your mind, be sober, and hope to the end for the grace that is to be brought unto you at the revelation of Jesus Christ" (I Peter 1:3, 13).

The English word "blessed" is the translation of two totally different Greek words in the New Testament. In Matthew 5:1-12 it is the rendering of a Greek word which means "prosperous." Here the context limits its meaning to spiritual prosperity. That is, "spiritually prosperous are the poor in spirit: for theirs is the kingdom of heaven." Heaven's blessings flood the soul of those saints who have a contrite and humble heart. Their prosperity consists of heaven's blessings. Their spiritual condition is prosperous. The word "blessed" in the text under consideration is from a Greek word which means "to speak well of." The word comes into our language in the words "eulogy" and "eulogize." The idea is that of "praising." However, there is another word in Greek which means "praise." We could translate, "Let the God and Father of our Lord Jesus Christ be well spoken of."

The words "according to" are from a Greek word which literally means "down." The idea is not "according to the measure or extent of His mercy," but "impelled by His mercy." God's merciful heart impelled Him to do what He did at the Cross, die for a race of lost sinners. We were begotten again, the translation tells us. The word "again" is from a Greek word which has two meanings, "again," and "from above," the meaning to be used being determined by the context. Our Lord in John 3:3 uses it in its meaning "again," since Nicodemus understands Him to speak of a second birth as he says, "How can a man be born when he is old? can he enter the second time into his mother's womb, and be born?" There are two words in Greek meaning "again," one refers to the mere repetition of an action, the other, to the repetition of an action, the repeated action having the same source as the first act. The latter is used here. The second birth has its source in the Spirit. The first act was the impartation of divine life to Adam.

One result of being born from above is that the believer has a lively hope. The word "lively" is from the Greek word which speaks of the life principle. It is the word used when the inspired writers speak of eternal life. The word "lively" in the Greek text is not an adjective but a participle. A participle is a verbal adjective, having the action of a verb and the descriptive powers of an adjective. The word "hope" is described by an action. The word "lively" is an excellent translation. The margin gives "living." But it is more than a hope that is alive. It is actively alive. This hope is an energizing principle, a spontaneous, overflowing, buoyant thing. It is a hopefulness, a spirit of optimism, a looking ever upon the bright side of things, a looking forward to only that which is good, an expectancy of continued blessing and joy. It is the opposite of that fear of the future which grips so many hearts. This Christian optimism, this exuberant hopefulness, leaves no room for worry. This lively hope should be the normal atmosphere of every Christian heart.

How may we have it? By yielding to the One whose ministry it is to produce this hopefulness in our hearts, the Holy Spirit. This Christian optimism is a heaven-born thing, something supernatural. The secret of enjoying it is in the fullness of the Holy Spirit. The secret of the fullness of the Spirit is in a moment by moment desire for that fullness, and a moment by moment trust in the Lord Jesus for the same (John 7:37, 38). And so Peter says, "Praised be the God and Father of our Lord Jesus Christ who, impelled by His great mercy, begot us from above, so that we have a spontaneous, buoyant, exultant spirit of hopefulness, this begetting having been accomplished through the intermediate instrumentality of the resurrection of Jesus Christ out from among those who are dead."

In connection with and in view of this Christian optimism, Peter exhorts us to have a carefree mind. He says, "Gird up the loins of your mind." The words "gird up" are from a construction in the Greek which is literally, "having girded up," the God-expected duty of every saint. We have here an oriental expression which must be explained. The people to whom Peter addressed this letter wore long, flowing, loose, outer garments. Preparatory to engaging in physical exertion such as running, they would gather these garments about their loins so that they would not impede the free action of the limbs. Peter tells us that we are pilgrims on our way home to heaven, and as such, must ever be ready to be on the move, that is, in a spiritual sense. The exhortation therefore is to put out of the way all that disturbs our minds, things that would impede the free exercise of our spiritual faculties. We know how worry, fretfulness, fear, anger, and their related mental attitudes all freeze up the mind and make it unfit for the best kind of work and the highest type of Christian life. In view of the fact that the Holy Spirit is producing in the Christian's heart that buoyant spirit of hopefulness, it is the responsibility of that Christian to put out of his mind everything that would disturb that Christian optimism which always hopes for the best and always looks on the bright side of things. The believer can do that by the same power of the Holy Spirit which produces this lively hope. This is what we mean by a carefree mind.

It is not a mind which does not recognize the responsibilities of life, but a mind free from care, for Peter says, "Wherefore, having put out of the way all that disturbs your mind (thus allowing that buoyant Christian hopefulness to predominate), being mentally self-controlled and calm, set your hope perfectly, wholly, unchangeably, and without doubt and despondency upon the grace which is being brought to you upon the occasion of the revelation of Jesus Christ." The words "be sober" in our translation refer to a mental self-control and calmness. The words "hope to the end" do not refer to the length of time this hope is held, but to the quality of this hope, a hope that is a perfect, unchangeable one. The hope in verse three is a subjective one, being an inner hopefulness, the normal Christian attitude towards life, whereas the hope of verse thirteen is an objective hope, resting itself upon some future happening, here the glorification of the believer at the return of the Lord into the air. This is the grace which is being brought to the believer. The word "brought" is not future in the Greek, but present. Our glorification is not looked upon as a future event which is isolated from the two other parts of our salvation, namely, our justification and our sanctification. It is part of our salvation. It is on the Divine Menu. When we sit down to a sumptuous repast, we are never concerned as to whether there will be dessert or not. We know it is on the menu. So why be in doubt as to whether you as a true believer in the Lord Jesus as your personal Saviour, will reach heaven and all that goes with the glories of that blessed place? It is all on the Divine Menu placed before us in God's holy Word.

The normal Christian life lived in the fullness of the Holy Spirit is a life in which a supernaturally produced Christian optimism and a carefreeness of mind make possible the most efficient use of our spiritual faculties, used to the glory of God. Do not allow Satan to rob you of this precious heritage.

III.

"Golden Nugget" Promises

THE first one is, "He hath said, 'I will never leave thee, nor forsake thee'" (Heb. 13:5). The translation says, "He hath said." But it is intensive in the Greek. "He Himself hath said." That is, the Lord Jesus Himself personally made this promise. The word "leave" is not from the usual Greek word which means "to leave," but from a word which means "to uphold" or "sustain." In the Greek there are two negatives before the word "leave," presenting a very strong negation. The promise is, "I will not, I will not cease to uphold or sustain thee." Thus Paul can say "I am strong for all things through the One who infuses strength in me" (Phil. 4:13). We are assured therefore of the sustaining grace of God as we go through trials and testing times.

The word "forsake" is a composite of three words, "to leave," "down," and "in." The first has the idea of forsaking one. The second suggests rejection, defeat, helplessness. The third refers to some place or circumstance in which a person may find himself helpless, forsaken. The meaning of the word is that of forsaking someone in a state of defeat or helplessness in the midst of hostile circumstances. The word means in its totality, "to abandon, to desert, to leave in straits, to leave helpless, to leave destitute, to leave in the lurch, to let one down." There are three negatives before this word, making the promise one of triple assurance. It is, "I will not, I will not, I will not forsake thee." Not only do we have the assurance of God's all-sufficient sustaining power to hold us true to Him and in perfect peace as we go through testing times, but we have His promise that He will never abandon us, never desert us, never leave us in straits but will come to our help, never leave us destitute but will supply all our need, never leave us in the lurch but will see to it that we are rescued from the difficulties in which we sometimes find ourselves. *He will never let us down.*

The second promise is, "Him that cometh to me I will in no wise cast out" (John 6:37). Here again we have two negatives before the verb: "I will not, I will not cast out." The words "cast out" are from one word made up of two words, the word "to throw" and a preposition meaning "out from within." That is, our Lord is speaking of those who are in salvation, in the Father's house. He gives us a double-strength promise that He will not throw us out of that house. But there is another word in the Greek which does not appear in the English, the word "outside." Literally, the promise reads, "The one who comes to Me, I will not, I will not throw out into the outside." Imagine a heavenly Father throwing His own child out. That is exactly what the Greek word means. This word "outside" is found in Revelation 22:15, where it is translated "without." The New Jerusalem is spoken of in the previous verse, but "without," that is, "outside, are dogs, and sorcerers, and whoremongers, and murderers, and idolaters, and whosoever loveth and maketh a lie." We have the solemn promise of our Lord that the Christian will never be ejected from the Father's house and thrown into the outside where those are who have rejected His grace.

The third is, "If ye abide in me, and my words abide in you" (John 15:7). The words, "ye shall ask," are in the you, ye shall ask what ye will, and it shall be done unto imperative mood, which makes them a command, and are to be taken in the sense of "I command you to ask." "Abiding" implies fellowship with the Lord, "nothing between myself and my Saviour," and dependence upon Him. To those who thus abide, God issues the gracious command, "ask whatever ye desire." It is more than a command. It is a challenge. It is as if God said, "You meet the conditions, and I challenge you to ask, and then see how faithful and able I am to answer your prayer." The word "desire" implies a desire that proceeds, not from deliberate forethought, but from inclination. This is a perfectly safe command and promise, because when we live in close fellowship with Jesus, our desires and our inclinations are His desires and His inclinations. The word "ask" is in the middle voice which speaks of the subject of the verb acting in its own interest. Therefore we translate, "ask for yourselves." But as we live in intimate fellowship with Jesus, those things which we ask for ourselves, we ask, not for the purpose of gratifying a selfish desire, but for the purpose of glorifying Him. Prayers of that kind are answered.

The word "done" is not from the Greek word which means to do something in the sense of making something. That would imply taking something in existence and fashioning it to suit our needs. The word is from the Greek word meaning "to become, to come into existence." God will if necessary bring into existence that for which we asked. The word "ask" is in the aorist tense which when used in a command means, "do at once what is commanded." Thus as we are abiding in Jesus, we are commanded not to hesitate, but to ask at once. The translation reads, "If ye abide in Me, and my words abide in you, I command you to ask at once and for yourselves whatever ye desire, and it shall be yours."

The fourth promise is, "My sheep hear my voice, and I know them, and they follow me, and I give unto them eternal life; and they shall never perish, neither shall any man pluck them out of my hand. My Father which gave them me, is greater than all; and no man is able to pluck them out of my Father's hand. I and my Father are one" (John 10:27-30). The expression, "they shall never perish" is a very strong one in the Greek. There are two negatives before the word "perish." "They shall not, they shall not perish." In addition to the double negative, there are three words which follow the word "perish," which are translated by the one word "never." The phrase is found in John 6:51, where it is translated "forever." The Greek papyri give an instance where the crowd in a public meeting cries repeatedly, "the emperors forever,"* using the Greek phrase found in this verse. The noun in the phrase means "eternal," and has the same root as the adjective "eternal" in the words "eternal life" in verse 28. The English language creaks and groans in its effort to translate the Greek here. "They shall not, they shall not perish, no, not eternally." The word "eternal" gives an infinite reach to the two negatives.

The word "man" is in italics, which means that it is not in the Greek text, and is supplied by the translators to complete the sense. There are two words in the Greek language meaning "a man," but neither is used here. The word "any" is an indefinite pronoun in the Greek, and the word "one" would complete its meaning better than the word "man." The translation "anyone" is truer to the sense of the original. That includes Satan. The word "pluck" is literally "snatch," and is often used in a bad sense as when death snatches its victim or where someone carries something off by force. When we consider the size of God's hand,

*Moulton and Milligan.

large enough to hold all of the oceans on earth, wide enough
to stretch from where the east begins and where the west
ends (Isaiah 40:12), we can understand why no one, including Satan himself, is able to snatch the believer out of its
protecting care.

The word "gave" in verse 29 is in the perfect tense in
Greek, which tense refers to a past completed action having
present results. The aorist tense is the customary tense to
use in Greek when the writer merely wishes to speak of the
fact of the action. Whenever a writer uses another tense,
he goes out of his way to do so, which means that he has
some special information to convey to the reader. The perfect tense here is like a carpenter who drives a nail through
a board, and then to assure himself that it is there to stay,
he clinches it on the other side. The Father gave believers
to the Lord Jesus as a permanent gift to be retained permanently by Him. And then, not only are we in the clasp
of the hand of our Lord, but we are safely resting in the
hand of God the Father. Two hands of infinite proportions are holding us in salvation. And the owners of these
hands are one in essence, two Persons of the Triune God.

The fifth promise is, "Whosoever drinketh of this water
shall thirst again: but whosoever drinketh of the water that
I shall give him shall never thirst; but the water that I shall
give him shall be in him a well of water springing up into
everlasting life" (John 4:13, 14).

The first occurrence of the word "drinketh" is in a construction in the Greek which refers to continuous action,
and the second use of the word in the original presents the
mere fact of the action without reference to the progress of
the action. The fuller translation therefore reads, "Every
one who keeps on constantly drinking of this water shall
thirst again. But whosoever takes a drink of the water
which I shall give him shall never thirst." The words

"shall never thirst" are from a construction in the Greek in which there are two negatives before the verb, and a phrase which means "forever," which comes after the verb. The idea is, "shall not, shall not thirst, ever." A double negative in the Greek does not make a positive statement but only strengthens the negation. The word "forever" gives an infinite reach to the two negatives.

In the Greek text, John reports the Samaritan woman as speaking of a well of water, and our Lord as speaking of a spring of water, while both words are translated by the one English word "well." The person who keeps on drinking of the wells of the world, lifeless, dull, brackish, polluted, stale, will thirst again. The world with all its sin does not satisfy, never can. But the person who takes one drink of the spring of eternal life never thirsts again.

The reason why one drink satisfies is that when the sinner takes one drink of eternal life, that one drink becomes in him a spring of water leaping up into a fountain of eternal life. The word "be" is in the Greek literally "become," and the word "well" is from the Greek word meaning a "spring." The one drink is itself a spring that ever keeps bubbling up, ever refreshing and satisfying the one who takes a drink of the water of life. This spring becomes a river of living water (John 7:37, 38), and this living water is just a symbol of the indwelling Holy Spirit who constantly ministers the Lord Jesus to the believer. And because Jesus completely satisfies, the person who takes one drink of this living water, never thirsts again. Have you experienced the truth of this promise?

IV.

Greek Grammar and the Deity of Jesus Christ

THE New Testament in its English translation plainly teaches that Jesus Christ is the second Person of the Triune God, possessing the same essence as God the Father. It is interesting to know that a rule of Greek grammar brings out the same truth.

The rule is as follows: When two nouns in the same case are connected by the Greek word "and," and the first noun is preceded by the article "the," and the second noun is not preceded by the article, the second noun refers to the same person or thing to which the first noun refers, and is a farther description of it. For instance, the words "pastors" and "teachers" in Eph. 4:11 are in the same case and are connected by the word "and." The word "pastors," is preceded by the article "the," whereas the word "teachers" is not. This construction requires us to understand that the words "pastors" and "teachers" refer to the same individual, and that the word "teacher" is a farther description of the individual called a "pastor." The expression therefore refers to pastors who are also teachers, "teaching-pastors."

This rule also applies to the following passages where the names "God" and "Father" are in the same case and are connected by the Greek word "and," while the word "God" is preceded by the article, and the word "Father" is not. The Greek word "and" can be translated by any of the following words, "and, even, also," depending upon the context in which it is found. In the passages under discussion, it is translated by "and" or "even." These passages are Romans 15:6; I Corinthians 15:24; II Corinthians 1:3, 11:31; Galatians 1:4; Ephesians 5:20; Philippians 4:20; I Thessalonians 1:3, 3:11, 13, where God and the Father are not two persons but one and the same, and the word "Father" is a farther description of the Person called "God."

In II Peter 1:11, 2:20, and 3:18, we have the phrase, "Lord and Saviour Jesus Christ." Here we find the same construction in the Greek text. The same rule of grammar applies. The Lord and the Saviour are the same person, the word "Saviour" being a farther description of the Person described as "Lord." This speaks of the deity of Jesus Christ, because the Greek word translated "Lord" was used as a name of Deity. The translators of the Septuagint version of the Old Testament (285-150 B.C.) used it to translate the august title of God, "Jehovah." The word was used in the Roman empire as a name for the ruling Caesar who was worshipped as a god. Christianity challenged the imperialism of the Caesars by announcing that there was born "in the city of David a Saviour, which is Christ the Lord" (Luke 2:11). The word "Lord" was an accepted title of Deity in the terminology of Israel, the Roman empire, and Christianity. Thus, a simple rule of Greek grammar teaches the deity of Jesus Christ.

But to make the case still stronger, we find in II Peter 1:1 the expression, "God and our Saviour Jesus Christ," where the same construction occurs, and the same rule of grammar applies. Solid ground for correct translation and interpretation is found in a careful application of the rules of Greek grammar. The inspired writers of the New Testament held to the grammar of the international Greek spoken throughout the Roman world. Only in that way could they expect to be correctly understood. Thus Greek grammar testifies that Jesus Christ is Lord, the Jehovah of the Old Testament, and Deity, the God of the New Testament. The apostles uniformly testify that Jesus Christ is God, and this is just another example of their statements challenging the Imperial Cult of the Caesar. The translation should read, "through the righteousness of our God and Saviour, Jesus Christ." The Roman emperor was recognized by his subjects as their god and their saviour. Peter tells us that Jesus Christ is the God and the Saviour of Christians.

In Titus 2:13 we have "the great God and our Saviour Jesus Christ." We find the same construction in the Greek, and the same rule of grammar requires us to interpret the phrase as teaching that Jesus Christ is the great God. Since the Greek word for "and" should be translated by the word "even" where the context demands such a meaning, we are justified in rendering this phrase "the great God, even our Saviour Jesus Christ," for the grammatical construction demands that the two expressions, "the great God," and "Saviour Jesus Christ," refer to one individual. The word "even" brings out this meaning. The translation could also read, "our great God and Saviour, Jesus Christ." Thus the rules of Greek grammar teach the deity of Jesus Christ.

V.

Is Future Punishment Everlasting?

THE Church has always held tenaciously to the teaching that the punishment of those who enter eternity unsaved, is unending. There is abundant evidence in the apocryphal literature of Israel to show that that nation believed and taught the same thing. Of late, however, the assertion is being made that this punishment is for a limited time only, this contention being based upon the statement that the two Greek words used to describe this punishment, refer to a limited period of time. These two words are, the noun, *aion,* and the adjective, *aionios.*

We submit Moulton and Milligan in their *Vocabulary of the Greek Testament* as our first authority. The work of these scholars is recognized as the latest advance in New Testament research, since it is based upon the study of the Greek secular documents known as "The Papyri." These latter are the last court of appeal on the usage of Greek words in the first century. They give two uses for *aion.* In a phrase from one of these early manuscripts, "For the rest of your life," *aion* refers to a limited period of time. A public meeting at Oxyrhynchus was punctuated with cries of "The Emperors forever," where *aion* has the meaning of "unending."

They have this to say about *aionios.* "Without pronouncing any opinion on the special meaning which the-

ologians have found for this word, we must note that outside the New Testament, in the vernacular as well as in
classical Greek (see Grimm-Thayer), it never loses the sense
of *perpetuus*. It is a standing epithet of the emperor's
power." Webster's International Dictionary derives our
English word "perpetual," meaning "continuing forever,
everlasting, eternal, unceasing" (its own definition), from
this Latin word *perpetuus*. They give as an illustration of
the use of *aionios* the sentence, "I confess that I should
show myself grateful for your loving-kindness forever."
Their closing comment on *aionios* is, "In general, the word
depicts that of which the horizon is not in view, whether
the horizon be at an infinite distance, or whether it lies no
farther than the span of a Caesar's life."

Our next authority is *Biblico-Theological Lexicon of
New Testament Greek,* by Herman Cremer, D.D. He says
of *aion*: "In early Greek especially, and still also in Attic,
aion signifies the duration of human life as limited to a
certain space of time, hence the meanings, *the duration of
life, course of life, term of life, lifetime, life in its temporal
form.* From this original limitation of the conception to
human life, it may be explained how it sometimes denotes
the space of a human life, a human generation. Accordingly, the expansion of the conception of time unlimited was
easy, for it simply involved the abstraction of the idea of
limitation, and thus the word came to mean *unlimited duration.* Inasmuch, therefore, as *aion* may denote either the
duration of a definite space of time, or the (unending) duration of time in general, both future and past, according to
the context, it was the proper term for rendering the Hebrew *olam,*—for which the LXX (Greek translation of Old
Testament) used it constantly, the only distinction being
that the Hebrew word meant primarily, a remote, veiled,
undefined, and therefore, unlimited time, past or future,

and only secondarily, a definite (especially future) period whose limits must be ascertained by the context."

As to *aionios*, Cremer has but these brief words: "*Aionios* refers to time in its duration, constant, abiding, eternal."

We come now to the testimony of *A Greek-English Lexicon of the New Testament* by Joseph Henry Thayer, D.D. He gives as the first meaning of *aion, age, a human lifetime, life itself,* and for the second meaning, *an unbroken age, perpetuity of time, eternity*. His meanings of *aionios* are, first, *without beginning or end, that which has always been and always will be,* second, *without beginning,* third, *without end, never to cease, everlasting*. When comparing the synonyms, *aidios* and *aionios* he says, "*aidios* covers the complete philosophical idea—without beginning and without end; *also* either without beginning *or* without end, as respects the past; it is applied to what has existed *time out of mind. Aionios* (from Plato on) gives prominence to the immeasurableness of eternity (while such words as *suneches, continuous, unintermitted, diateles, perpetual, lasting to the end,* are not so applicable to an abstract term, like *aion*) ; *aionios* accordingly is especially adapted to supersensuous things."

Finally, we quote Liddell and Scott in their *Greek-English Lexicon* (classical) . *Aion* means *a space or period of time, a lifetime, life, an age, generation, an indefinitely long time, a space of time, eternity. Aionios* means *lasting, eternal*. Dr. E. B. Pusey* quotes J. Reddel, the best Greek Oxford scholar of his day as stating that *aionios* in classical Greek was used strictly of eternity, an eternal existence, such as shall be, when time shall be no more.

These authorities agree on the two meanings of *aion,* that of a limited space of time, and that of eternity, never

---

What is of Faith as to Everlasting Punishment?

ending, everlasting, the meaning to be used in any particular instance to be determined by the context in which it is found. They also agree upon the meaning of *aionios*, that it refers to time in its duration, constant, abiding, eternal, continuing forever, everlasting.

Our next step will be to show that in certain passages in the New Testament where *aion* appears, it cannot be used in its meaning of "a limited space of time," but can only mean "eternal." These passages have to do with the being of the Son of God, His reign, His glory, His throne, His priesthood, His post-resurrection life, none of which is of limited duration, for everything about God is of infinite proportions. These are Luke 1:33, 55; John 8:35 (second occurrence), 12:34; Romans 1:25, 9:5, 11:36, 16:27; II Corinthians 11:31; Galatians 1:5; Ephesians 3:11; Philippians 4:20; I Timothy 1:17; II Timothy 4:18; Hebrews 1:8; 5:6, 6:20, 7:17, 21, 24, 28; 13:8, 21; I Peter 4:11, 5:11; II Peter 3:18; Revelation 1:6, 18, 4:9, 10, 5:13, 7:12, 10:6, 11:15, 15:7. Instances where *aionios* is used, and where it can only mean "eternal," because its context speaks of the being of God, the glory of God, and the covenant of blood are Romans 16:26; Hebrews 9:14; 13:20, I Peter 5:10. This establishes the fact that the New Testament usage of *aion* and *aionios* includes their meaning of "eternal," whatever other meanings the former might have in other contexts such as those of "a limited period of time" (Colossians 1:26), or "an age as characterized by a certain system of evil" (Romans 12:2). As to *aionios*, the only places in the New Testament where it is translated by any other words than "eternal" or "everlasting" are Romans 16:25, II Timothy 1:9, and Titus 1:2 where it is rendered by the word "world." But even here it refers to "that which is anterior to the most remote period in the past conceivable by any imagination that man knows of" (*Expositor's Greek Testament*), namely, to the eternity before time began as we know it, time which runs concurrently with the created universe and the affairs of the human race. Thus, both *aion* and *aionios* are used in the New Testament in their meanings of "everlasting" and "eternal."

Now we come to the passages in the New Testament where *aionios* is used in connection with the life God gives the believer when He saves him. We have seen that this word is used in connection with the being of God, and that it can only mean "eternal" in this case. But the life which God gives the believer is Christ (Col. 3:4), which means that *aionios* when it describes the life given the believer, must mean "eternal," which agrees with the uniform meaning given by the four Greek authorities quoted. In all its occurrences in the New Testament, *aionios* never refers to a limited extent of time, but always to that which is eternal or everlasting. Even in Romans 16:25, II Timothy 1:9, and Titus 1:2, it refers to the eternity before time began. For the benefit of the student who does not have access to a Greek concordance, we list the passages where *aionios* is used in connection with the life given the believer; Mark 10:17, 30; Luke 10:25, 18:18, 30; John 3:15, 16, 36, 4:14, 36, 5:24, 39, 6:27, 40, 47, 54, 68, 10:28, 12:25, 50, 17:2, 3; Acts 13:46, 48; Romans 2:7, 5:21, 6:22, 23; II Corinthians 4:17, 18; 5:1; Galatians 6:8; I Timothy 1:16, 6:12; II Timothy 2:10; Titus 1:2, 3:7; Hebrews 5:9, 9:12; I Peter 5:10; I John 1:2, 2:25, 3:15, 5:11, 13, 20; Jude 21.

This brings us to the places where *aion* is used in connection with this same life, and because this life is eternal, *aion* must mean "eternal" here, not "an age"; Mark 10:17; John 4:14, 6:51, 58, 8:51, 52, 10:28, 11:26.

We have found that the life God gives the believer is described by two words, *aion* and *aionios*, both meaning "eternal." We notice now the statement of our Lord in Matthew

25:46, "These shall go away into (*aionios*) everlasting punishment: but the righteous into life (*aionios*) eternal." *Aionios* means "eternal" when used with the word "life." Does it mean "eternal" when used with the word "punishment"?

But now we will let Dr. E. B. Pusey speak,* as he quotes Augustine on this passage, and then adds his own comment. Augustine said of this text, "What a thing it is, to account eternal punishment to be a fire of long duration, and eternal life to be without end, since Christ comprised both in that very same place, in one and the same sentence, saying, 'These shall go into eternal punishment, but the righteous into life eternal.' If both are eternal, either both must be understood to be lasting with an end, or both perpetual without end. For like is related to like; on the one side, eternal punishment; on the other side, eternal life. But to say in one and the same sentence, life eternal shall be without end, punishment eternal shall have an end, were too absurd: whence, since the eternal life of the saints shall be without end, punishment eternal too shall doubtless have no end to those whose it shall be."

Dr. Pusey adds the following to Augustine's words: "The argument is not merely from language. It has a moral and religious aspect. Any ordinary writer who drew a contrast between two things, would, if he wished to be understood, use the self-same word in the self-same sense. He would avoid ambiguity. If he did not, we should count him ignorant of language, or if it were intentional, dishonest. I ask, 'In what matter of this world would you trust one who in any matter of this world, should use the self-same word in two distinct senses in the self-same sentence, without giving any hint that he was so doing?' In none. Find any case in which you would trust a man who did so in the things of

What is of Faith as to Everlasting Punishment?

men, and then ascribe it to your God in the things of God.
I could not trust man. I could not believe it of my God."

It remains for us to examine the New Testament passages
where *aion* and *aionios* are used of the future punishment
of the lost. We will look first at those passages which contain *aionios*. In Matthew 18:8 the phrase "everlasting fire"
is in the Greek "the fire which is everlasting." The use of
the definite article shows that this passage does not refer to
fire in general but to a particular fire (Rev. 20:10). This
fire will burn forever and is unquenchable (Mark 9:43).
Matthew 25:41 tells us that this everlasting fire is prepared
for the devil and his angels. The word "prepared" in the
Greek is in the perfect tense, which tense speaks of a past
complete action that has present results. The Lake of Fire
had been prepared before our Lord spoke these words, and
is now in existence. The fires of this lake are not purifying
but punitive. That is, their purpose is not to purify the
wicked dead in order that they might be brought to repentance and faith with the result that they will all be finally
saved, as those teach who advocate the universal restoration
of the entire human race. They are for the punishment of
Satan and his fallen angels, and for those of the human race
who enter eternity in a lost condition. Matthew 25:46 has
been dealt with above.

As to Mark 3:29, the best Greek texts have "sin" instead
of "damnation," which latter word appears in the A.V., as
the translation of a Greek word meaning "judgment," and
which is a rejected reading. The words "in danger of" are
from a Greek word which refers to anyone "held in anything so that he cannot escape." Thus the one who committed the sin referred to in this passage is in the grasp of
an eternal sin, the sin being eternal, not in the sense of
eternally repeating itself, but in that it is eternal in its guilt.
Such a sin demands eternal punishment. In II Thessalonians

1:9 we have "everlasting destruction." The Greek word translated "destruction" does not mean "annihilation." Moulton and Milligan define its first century Biblical usage as follows: "ruin, the loss of all that gives worth to existence." Thayer in his lexicon gives the meanings "ruin, destruction, death." The word comes from the verb meaning "to destroy." But to destroy something does not mean to put it out of existence, but to ruin it, to reduce it to such form that it loses all that gave worth to its existence. One may burn down a beautiful mansion. The materials which composed it are still in existence, a heap of ashes, but it is destroyed in that it cannot be used as a home any more. It is in such form that it has lost all that gave worth to its existence as a mansion. The eternal condition of the lost will be one of utter ruin, a condition in which the soul lives forever in a state devoid of all that makes existence worthwhile.

In Hebrews 6:2 we have "eternal judgment." The word "judgment" here is from a Greek word that refers to a condemnatory sentence, *aionios* being used to teach that this sentence is eternal in that the punishment it prescribes is unending. In Jude 7 we have lost human beings condemned to the same everlasting fire which has been prepared for Satan and the fallen angels, the latter in verse 6 being reserved for the Great White Throne judgment and the fire prepared for them (Matt. 25:41).

We come now to the passages in which *aion* is used. Because *aionios* describes the same future punishment which *aion* does, *aion* here cannot mean "a limited time," but "eternal," just as *aionios*. II Peter 2:17 tells us that "the mist of darkness" is reserved for those who reject the substitutionary atonement of the Lord Jesus. Jude 13 refers to those who like Cain refuse to place their faith in the blood of Jesus poured out on the Cross for sin, and who instead trust in their own good works. To these is reserved "the blackness of darkness forever." The expressions in Peter and Jude are from the same words in the Greek text, except that the best Greek manuscripts omit *aion* in the first passage. It however appears in the second which refers to the same darkness. The words "mist" and "blackness" come from one Greek word for "darkness," and the word "darkness" comes from another word meaning "darkness." Archbishop Trench in his *New Testament Synonyms* says this about the word translated "mist" and "blackness"; "The *zophos* (the former word) may be contemplated as a kind of emanation of *skotous* (the latter). It signifies in its first meaning the twilight gloom which broods over the regions of the setting sun, and constitutes so strong a contrast to the life and light of that Orient where the sun may be said to be daily new-born. . . . But it means more than this. There is a darkness darker still, that, namely, of the sunless underworld. . . . This too it further means, namely, that sunless world itself, though indeed this less often than the gloom which wraps it. . . . It will at once be perceived with what fitness the word in the New Testament is employed, being ever used to signify the darkness of that shadowy land where light is not, but only darkness visible." Such is the eternal fate of those who reject the precious blood of Jesus as the alone way of salvation from sin.

We come to Revelation 14:9-11 where the unsaved who worship the Wild Beast, namely, the Roman emperor who is Satan's regent in the revived Roman empire during the Great Tribulation, are said to be tormented, and where it is asserted that the smoke of their torment, that is, the smoke that issues from the cause of their torment, will ascend forever and forever, which means that their torment will be forever and forever. The Greek word translated "torment" was used in a secular document of the examina-

tion of slaves in the phrase "they under torture said."[*]
Thayer defines the word as follows, "to question by applying torture, to torture, to vex with grievous pains (of body
and mind), in the passive sense, to be harassed, distressed."
In Revelation 20:10, the eternal torment of Satan is spoken of. Thus, God's Word clearly teaches that the sufferings of the lost will be unending.

How this fact speaks to us of the infinite holiness, righteousness, and justice of God, and of the awfulness of sin.
But how it points us also to that Lonely Sufferer on Calvary's Cross, and brings to our ears the dreadful pathos of
that cry, "My God, my God, why hast thou forsaken me?"
What was it all for? The Lord Jesus suffered and died in
order that by satisfying the righteous demands of the law
which we violated, God might be able to offer us mercy
on the basis of justice satisfied. That mercy He offers you
now, unsaved reader, if you will accept it by faith in the
atoning work of His Son on the Cross. "For God so loved
the world, that He gave His Son, the only begotten one,
that whosoever believeth in Him might not perish but have
everlasting life." Put your trust in Him *now*, for tomorrow may be too late.

---

[*]*Moulton and Milligan.*

VI.

Hell, Hades, and Tartarus

THERE are three Greek words in the New Testament translated by the one English word "hell," which fact results in some confusion in our thinking.

One of these is "Gehenna." It is the Greek representative of the Hebrew "Ge-Hinnom," or Valley of Hinnom, a deep narrow valley to the south of Jerusalem, where, after the introduction of the worship of the fire-gods by Ahaz, the idolatrous Jews sacrificed their children to the god Molech. After the time of Josiah, when this practice was stopped, it became the common refuse-place of the city, where the bodies of criminals, carcasses of animals, and all sorts of filth were cast. From its depth and narrowness, and its fire and ascending smoke, it became the symbol of the place of the future punishment of the wicked. The word is used in Matthew 5:22 in the phrase "the hell of fire," (Greek), and thus refers to the final abode of the wicked dead which is called in Revelation 19:20 "the lake of fire burning with brimstone." This lake of fire is in existence now, for the word "prepared" in the Greek of Matthew 25:41 is in the perfect tense which refers to a past completed action having present results. Hell had been already prepared and was in existence when Jesus spoke these words. There is no one there now. The first occupants of that dreadful place will be the Beast and the false prophet, Satan following them 1000 years afterwards. Then at the

Great White Throne Judgment, which occurs at the close of the Millennium, all lost human beings, the fallen angels, and the demons will also be sent there for eternity. Our word "hell" is the correct rendering of the word "Gehenna," and should be so translated in the following passages, Matthew 5:22, 29, 30; 10:28; 18:9; 23:15, 33; Mark 9:43, 45, 47; Luke 12:5; James 3:6.

The second of these words is "Hades," which is a transliteration, not a translation, of the Greek word. When we transliterate a word we take the spelling of that word over into another language in the respective letter equivalents, whereas when we translate a word, we take the meaning over into that language. The word itself means "The Unseen." This was the technical Greek religious term used to designate the world of those who departed this life. The Septuagint, namely, the Greek translation of the Old Testament, uses this word to translate the Hebrew "Sheol," which has a similar general meaning. The "Hades" of the pagan Greeks was the invisible land, the realm of shadow, where all Greeks went, the virtuous, to that part called Elysium, the wicked, to the other part called Tartarus.

The difference between the pagan and Biblical conceptions of Hades is that the former conceives of Hades as the final abode of the dead, whereas the latter teaches that it is the temporary place of confinement until the Great White Throne Judgment in the case of the wicked dead, and until the resurrection of Christ, in the case of the righteous dead, the latter since that event going at once to heaven at death (Phil. 1:23).

As the pagan conception of Hades included two parts, so the Biblical idea divided it into two parts, the one called paradise (Luke 23:43, but not II Cor. 12:4, and Rev. 2:7), or Abraham's bosom (Luke 16:22), for the righteous dead, and the other part for the wicked dead having no specific designation except the general word "Hades" (Luke 16:23). This Greek word is found in the following passages, to be translated and interpreted generally as "Hades," the place of the departed dead, and for the reason that the translators of the Septuagint use this word to express in the Greek language what is meant in the Hebrew by the word "Sheol," the place of the departed dead.

In Matthew 11:23 and Luke 10:15, Capernaum is to be brought down to the realms of the dead, presumably here to that portion of Hades reserved for the wicked, because of its rejection of the attesting miracles of our Lord. In Luke 16:23, the rich man was in Hades, that part where the wicked dead are kept until the judgment of the Great White Throne. In Acts 2:27, 31, our Lord at His death went to Hades, the passage in Acts being quoted from Psalm 16:, where the Hebrew is "Sheol." His soul was not left in Hades, the "paradise" portion, nor did His body in Joseph's tomb see corruption, for He was raised from the dead on the third day. He as the Man Christ Jesus, possessing a human soul and spirit, as He possessed a human body, entered the abode of the righteous dead, having committed the keeping of His spirit to God the Father (Luke 23:46). The word "grave" in I Corinthians 15:55 is not from the word "Hades," for the best manuscripts have the word "death," while "Hades" is a rejected reading. The translation should read, "death."

In Revelation 6:8, Death and Hades follow in the wake of war and famine, Hades ready to receive the dead of the Great Tribulation period. In Revelation 20:13, 14, Death itself, and Hades with all the wicked dead are cast into the lake of fire.

There are just two places where this Greek word should be translated rather than transliterated. In Revelation 1:18, our Lord has the keys or control of The Unseen and of death. That is, He is master of the unseen world which in the Christian system includes Hades, Tartarus, and the kingdom of Satan in the atmosphere of this earth.

The other place is Matthew 16:18 where we translate "The Unseen." The word "prevail" in the Greek means "to be strong to another's detriment, to overpower." The word "gates" is an orientalism for the idea of centralized legal authority. Lot sat in the gate of Sodom. Boaz went to the gate of Bethlehem to settle a legal matter with reference to his proposed marriage to Ruth. The word refers to a council. The word "hades" is out of the question here as an adequate translation, because the wicked dead in that place have no power to overcome the Church, and the righteous dead there at the time our Lord spoke these words had neither the desire nor power. The holy angels in heaven would have no such desire. All that is left in the unseen world are Satan and his demons. These constitute the Council in the Unseen that desires to bring about the destruction of the Church.

The third word translated "hell" is in II Peter 2:4 where the Greek word is "Tartarus," the prison of the fallen angels that sinned at the time of the flood (Gen. 6:1-4; I Peter 3:19, 20; Jude 6).

This brief study contains all the passages where the word "hell" is used in the New Testament, and can be used as a guide to the correct translation in each case.

VII.

The Christian's "Thanatopsis"

ONE OF the passages in the English translation which
presents difficulties in interpretation is John 8:51, where
our Lord says, "Verily, verily, I say unto you, If a man keep
my saying, he shall never see death." We have called this
"Golden Nugget," "The Christian's 'Thanatopsis'." The
word "thanatopsis" comes from two Greek words which together mean "seeing death." Our Lord here presents the
Christian view of death.

The assertion in the Greek is very strong. The idea is,
"shall absolutely not see death." Then the statement is
made stronger by the addition of a phrase which in other
places in the New Testament is translated "forever." Thus,
"If any man keep my saying, he shall absolutely not see
death, never."

The key to the interpretation of the verse is found in the
meaning of the word "see." There are six words in the
Greek language which mean "to see." The first refers simply to the act of physical sight (Matt. 12:22). The second
refers to physical sight that is accompanied by mental discernment (I John 1:1, "have seen"). The third means "to
look upon, contemplate, view attentively," used, for instance, of a civilian watching a military parade (I John
1:1, "looked upon"). The fourth means "to scrutinize
with the purpose of bringing about the betterment of the

person so observed" (Hebrews 2:6, "visitest," Acts 20:28, "overseers"). The fifth word means "to fix one's eyes upon," metaph., "to fix one's mind upon one as an example" (Acts 3:4, "fastening his eyes upon him with John,"). Even Peter and John judged their beggars as to their worthiness to receive alms. The sixth word is the one used in John 8:51. It is used, primarily, not of an indifferent spectator, but of one who looks at a thing with interest and for a purpose. It expresses a fixed contemplation and a full acquaintance.

Now, the death spoken of here is physical death, for the Jews speak of Abraham as being dead, and our Lord does not correct them by saying that He was speaking of spiritual death. He therefore says that when a Christian is being put to sleep in Jesus (I Thess. 4:14, Greek), as he is dying, he will not look at Death with interest and for a purpose. He will be an indifferent spectator of Death, for he will have his eyes fixed on Jesus. The terrors of that awful thing called death, are not experienced by the one who puts his faith in the Lord Jesus. His attention will not be focused on death, nor will he feel its bitterness. This is what Paul means when he says (I Cor. 15:55), "O death, where is thy sting?" But those that go out of this life rejecting Him, have before them all the terrors of death. Oh, reader, are you sure that you are trusting in the precious blood of Jesus poured out in the substitutionary atonement on the Cross for you personally? We read in Hebrews 2:9 that Jesus tasted death for every man. That is, He not only died, but He experienced all the terror and bitterness of death in order that those who place their trust in Him as Saviour, will not experience the terror and bitterness of it all.

VIII.

A Pauline Paradox and Its Solution

THE Greek inscriptions show that many technical terms in pagan religions and in governmental circles of the first century A.D., are also found in the terminology of Christianity. For instance, the expression, "slave of the emperor," was in current use. There were imperial slaves all over the Roman world. This throws light upon Paul's claim to be a "bondslave of Jesus Christ" (Rom. 1:1), the word "servant" coming from a Greek word literally meaning "bondslave," the same Greek word being used in the inscriptions. Paul knew of this custom. The lord emperor was not only revered as a human ruler but also worshipped as a god. When Paul wrote these words to the Christians in the imperial city, he must have been conscious of the imperialistic challenge of Christianity proclaiming a Saviour whose bondslave he was, and who some day would come to displace the imperialism of Rome. Paul was some day to stand before Nero, not as a bondslave of the lord emperor, but as a bondslave of the King of kings, the One who came from the royal line of David.

Another such technical expression is found in I Corinthians 7:22, "the Lord's freeman." The title, "freedman of the emperor," is found frequently in the Greek inscriptions of the first century.

To be a bondslave of the emperor, was a position of servitude with a certain degree of honor attached to it, but to be the emperor's freeman, meant that the bondslave was liberated from that servitude and promoted to a position of a free man, which was a higher station. Paul in I Corinthians 7:22 says that the Christian is both the bondslave and the freeman of the Lord. How can he be both at the same time? The beautiful story can be told in three Greek words translated "bought" and "redeemed."

The first word means "to buy in the market place." It was used of the purchase of slaves. Sinners are bondslaves of Satan and sin (Rom. 6:17, 18; Eph. 2:2) We were purchased in the slave market, the price paid, the precious blood of Jesus. I Corinthians 6:20 uses this word. We were bondslaves of Satan, and we became bondslaves of Jesus Christ. A slave cannot say that he belongs to himself, but to his master. We belong to Christ. The word is also used in II Peter 2:1, where false teachers who deny the Lord who purchased them in the slave market, refuse to avail themselves of the high privilege of becoming His bondslaves. In Revelation 5:9, the saints in heaven are singing a song which speaks of the Lamb who bought them in the slave market to become His own bondslaves. Thus, Paul tells his readers that those who have put their trust in Jesus as Saviour, were purchased in the slave market, and are bondslaves of the coming King of kings (I Cor. 7:22, 23).

We are told in the same passage (I Cor. 7:22) that we are also the Lord's freemen. This brings us to the other words translated "redeemed." One means "to buy out of the market place." Galatians 3:13, which uses this word, tells us that we were purchased in the slave-market, but in such a way that while we are bondslaves of the purchaser, the Lord Jesus, we are never again to be put up for sale in any slave market. We have been bought out of the slave market. This means that we are bondslaves of the Lord Jesus forever. He will never sell us or permit us to be sold as slaves to anyone else. A bondslave of Jesus Christ never becomes a bondslave of Satan again.

The other word translated "redeemed" means "to release or liberate by payment of a ransom," and is used in I Peter 1:18; Titus 2:14. The noun having the same root means "ransom money used to liberate a slave." After our blessed Lord buys us in the slave market, the ransom money being His own precious blood, we become His private property. We are His bondslaves. Then He so arranges the details of the purchase that we will never be put up for sale in any slave market. He buys us out of the slave market. Then He sets us free. We are freemen, freed from the guilt, penalty, and power of sin, some day to be freed from the presence of sin. We are liberated from all that, so that we might realize in our lives that for which we were created, namely, to glorify God. It is the old story of the caged eagle, liberated to fly again in the pure air of the mountain tops. But how can we be His bondslaves and His freemen at the same time? After we have been purchased as His bondslaves, and have been liberated from our old master Satan, out of pure gratefulness of heart we say to our Lord, "Lord Jesus, we want to serve Thee as Thy bondslaves forever." Our position as His bondslaves is not one of compulsion, but of free will energized by an imparted divine nature and a supernaturally imparted love. Therefore, we are His bondslaves and His freemen at the same time, a thing impossible in the case of earthly slaves. Thus is solved one of the delightful paradoxes of Holy Scripture.

IX.

Paul the Scholar

SOMETIMES a very slight shade of meaning in a word may speak volumes. Paul in Acts 22, is presenting his defence before his fellow-countrymen. He states that he is a man, Jewish by race, born in Tarsus of Cilicia, yet brought up in Jerusalem at the feet of Gamaliel (22:3). Tarsus was a city outside of Palestine, Greek in its culture. The fact that Paul was born there would put him in an unfavorable light with the Jerusalem Jews. We see that prejudice of the Jews against their fellow-countrymen who had absorbed Greek culture and who read the Old Testament in the Greek Septuagint version rather than in their native Hebrew, manifested in the early church (Acts 6), where those responsible for the poor were neglecting the widows of men who were pure-blooded Jews, yet who had imbibed Greek culture, and therefore were called Grecians (6:1). But Paul was strictly honest in recounting his life. He said, "born in Tarsus, . . . yet brought up in this city." The word "yet" is from the milder of two adversative particles in the Greek, both meaning "but." He could have used the stronger adversative. Had he used the latter, he would have washed his hands of Tarsus and all Hellenistic culture. But he could not honestly do that. Saul of Tarsus had received training in the Greek language and literature. Indeed, he was well read in the latter, for in Acts 17:28 he quoted from two of the minor

Greek poets, Aratus and Cleanthes, and in Titus 1:12 from one of the Cretan poets. Anyone might have a smattering of Homer or Plato without being considered well trained, but to quote some minor writers, shows that Paul was a Jew of Hellenistic background. But that he also acquired a thorough training in the Hebrew Old Testament and in rabbinical lore, is seen clearly by another word he uses. He was educated at the feet of Gamaliel. He could have used either one of three prepositions each meaning "at." Had he used either of these, he would have had a position *before* the great teacher. But the preposition which he used means literally "beside, alongside," and carries with it the idea of close personal connection. Cannot you see the eager young man, Saul, seated close to his teacher, at his *side,* drinking in every word that fell from his lips? This may be a very small touch, but it speaks volumes. Paul was a scholar.

X.

Pauline Tactfulness

A N illustration of the tactfulness and delicacy of feeling of the apostle Paul is seen in his response to the gift which the Philippian saints sent to him, and which was the occasion for the letter. In 1:3-5 Paul says, "I thank my God . . . for your fellowship in the gospel from the first day until now." "Fellowship" is from a Greek word which means literally "to have in common with," and speaks here of the joint-participation of the Philippians with Paul in the gospel. The word "in" is from a preposition of motion, and thus speaks of progress. Thus Paul thanks God for the joint-participation of the Philippians in the progress of the gospel. The Philippian saints were joint-participants with Paul in the work of the gospel in that they helped supply his needs as he preached. They had been helping him from the first day when Lydia the purple dye seller had opened her home for the preaching of the gospel until that present moment when they had sent a gift to the great apostle who was in prison. In the Greek text the definite article "the" occurs before the adverb "now," which is a construction that we do not find in the English language. The definite article in Greek points out individual identity. It makes the thing referred to stand out in contrast to other things. Paul said that the Philippians had helped him in his missionary work from the first day until "the now." The word "now" refers to the time at which Paul wrote, but the article particularizes that time as being characterized by the receipt of the gift. "Now" is not a mere point in time, but a point in time whose character was marked by the receipt of the gift. The article is a delicate finger pointing to the gift without referring to it in so many words. Paul in the closing sentences of his letter (4:10-19) speaks of it in plain language, but he is so grateful for the gift that he cannot help but mention it at the very beginning. Yet with that rare tact and courtesy which was his, and which only our Lord can give, he thanked them for it without mentioning it by name. This joint participation of the Philippians in the progress of the gospel was the "good work" which God had begun in them. It was the grace of giving, and in this context, the grace of giving to missionary work.

XI.

Amalgamated Love

"SEEING ye have purified your souls in obeying the truth through the Spirit unto unfeigned love of the brethren, see that ye love one another with a pure heart fervently" (I Peter 1:22).

As one reads these words, the question arises as to why God exhorts saints who are already loving one another, to love one another. The answer to our question is found in the fact that the first word "love" comes from a Greek word referring to one kind of love, and the second word "love" is from another word speaking of a different kind of love.

The first word "love" is from a Greek word which speaks of that glow of the heart which is kindled by the perception of that in the object loved which affords one pleasure. Whatever in an object is adapted to give pleasure when perceived, tends to call out affection, and this affection is what this word expresses. The Greeks were very much occupied with the topic of friendship. This was an ideal word for the expression of this form of affection. The word is used in such expressions as, "to be in a friendly way at one's side," "to interest one's self in him in a friendly manner," "a man showed himself friendly to men by keeping open house." Thus this form of love is the response of the human spirit to what appeals to it as pleasurable. It speaks of a friendly affection.

This is the kind of love which these saints had for one another. This love was the result of their obedience to the truth through their dependence upon the Spirit. That is, their obedience to God's Word brought them all into right relationship to God in their personal lives, and into right relationship to one another in their fellowship with one another. This fellowship was a source of joy to them all, for the truth in the heart and life of each saint found its counterpart in and was attracted by the truth in the heart and life of the other saints. Each saint found in the heart of the other saint that which afforded him pleasure. He found a reflection of his own likes and dislikes, his own interests, his own thought-world in the life of his fellow-saint.

It is like the attraction which one artist has for another artist, or one musician, for another musician. This mutual attraction results in a mutual love awakened by the sense of pleasure one finds in the company of the other. So it was with these saints. They loved each other with a mutual reciprocal love because of the pleasure each had in the other's fellowship. It was a friendly love, a glow of the heart kindled by the perception of that in the other saint which afforded pleasure.

Now, this kind of love is a perfectly proper and legitimate love. But it is a love which is non-ethical. That is, it sets no standards of right and wrong. It does not include within its constituent elements, the idea of self-sacrifice in the interest of the one loved. It could therefore degenerate into something selfish and self-centered. One saint may find so much in another saint with which to gratify his desire for fellowship, that he does not think of the other person, but merely of himself and of his own welfare. Thus what started out as a mutual and friendly love, would become a selfish self-centered thing.

But God in His grace has provided a counter-balance which will make and keep this friendly love what it should be. The second use of the word "love" is from another Greek word. It speaks of that love which springs from an awakened sense of value in an object which causes one to prize the object loved. It expresses the love of approbation, of esteem, as over against the love of pure delight, which latter is our other word for love. It springs from an apprehension of the preciousness of the object loved. It derives its impulse more from the notion of prizing than of liking. It is a love which springs from the soul's sense of the value and preciousness of its object, and is the response of the heart to the recognized worth of the object loved.

Our first word is found frequently in the pagan Greek authors, but the second word is used very sparingly. This rather obscure word, used so infrequently in the pagan Greek writings, the New Testament writers as guided by the Holy Spirit select, and pour into it as into an empty receptacle, all the content of meaning we find in John 3:16 and I Corinthians 13, where it is used. It is the response of the heart of God to the preciousness of each lost human soul that results in the infinite love God shows at Calvary. Each human soul is precious, first, because it bears the image of its Maker, even though that image be marred by sin, and second, because, it is composed of material, if you please, which God can through redemption, conform to the very image of His beloved Son. Thus, this love is a love of self-sacrifice based upon the preciousness of the object loved.

God exhorts the saints who are already loving each other with a friendly love which is called out of their hearts because they find pleasure in each other's fellowship, to love each other also with a self-sacrificial love because of the preciousness of the saint who is loved, as precious to God as Christ is precious to Him. Thus, this friendly love is amalgamated with the love of self-sacrifice. The two are fused. The first is made a thing of heaven because it is purified, ennobled, elevated by the second.

Into this fellowship of the saints is introduced the love that sacrifices for the blessing of the other, the love that suffers long, the love that is kind, the love that does not envy, the love that does not vaunt itself and is not puffed up, the love that does not behave itself unseemly, the love that does not seek its own, the love that is not provoked, that thinks no evil, that does not rejoice in iniquity but rather in ,the truth, the love that bears, believes, hopes, and endures all things, the love that never fails.

This love is the love spoken of in Galatians 5:22, produced in the heart of the saint who is definitely subjected to the Holy Spirit, by the Holy Spirit Himself. This is the love that God is. This is the love that should saturate the friendly love which saints have for each other. Without it, the fellowship of the saints with one another becomes a selfish unsatisfactory thing, but amalgamated with it, this friendly love becomes a thing of heaven. The secret of the fullness of this divine love, is in the fullness of the Holy Spirit. And this is why God exhorts saints who are already loving one another, to be loving one another.

The translation reads as follows: "Wherefore, having purified your souls by means of your obedience to the truth, resulting in not an assumed but genuine love for the brethren, love that springs from your hearts by reason of the pleasure you take in them, from the heart love each other with an intense reciprocal love that springs from your hearts because of your estimation of the preciousness of your brethren, and which is self-sacrificial in its essence."

XII.

The Word "VISIT" in the New Testament

BY our English word "visit" we usually mean "the act of calling to see another, of paying a visit in the sense of a social call." Consequently we sometimes attach this meaning to the word when we find it in Scripture. But the Greek word of which it is the translation means something more than that.

The word "visit" is the translation of two closely related verbs which have the following meanings: first, "to look upon or after, to inspect, to examine with the eyes;" second, "to look upon in order to help or benefit, to look after, to have a care for, to provide for." The word "visit" is possibly the best single word translation of the Greek words, but the English reader can see that it does not adequately translate it. Take for instance, "Sick and in prison and ye visited me not" (Matt. 25:43). What a richer, fuller meaning we have when we go to the Greek text. It was no mere social call that would have met the need of the prisoner. Oriental prisons sometimes were cold and uncomfortable. Paul writes to Timothy from his prison in Rome, "The cloke that I left at Troas with Carpus, when thou comest, bring with thee" (II Tim. 4:13). What a prisoner needed was ministering care like the help which the Philippians sent to Paul by Epaphroditus. Truly, the latter's visit to Paul in his Roman prison is a good illustration of the meaning of the Greek word translated "visit" in Matthew 25:43.

Zacharias, at the birth of his son John the Baptist, know-ing that the latter would be the forerunner of the Messiah who would therefore shortly come, said, "Blessed be the Lord God of Israel; for He hath visited and redeemed His people" (Luke 1:68). When he used the word "visited," he really said "for He has looked upon His people in order to help and benefit them, and provide for them." Then in Luke 1:78 he said, "The day-spring from on high hath visited us." That Dayspring is none other than the Lord Jesus, who looked upon Israel and had a care for His chosen people so that He came to their aid. And when Israel re-fused the aid of its Messiah, He laments over Jerusalem and its inhabitants, and speaks of its destruction, closing with the words "Thou knewest not the day of thy visitation" (Luke 19:44). The word "visitation" is from a noun whose root is the same as the stem of our verb. Israel did not per-ceive that the coming of Jesus of Nazareth was the day when God was looking upon His people in order to help them. We have the same meaning in Luke 7:16.

The verb form is used of Moses in Acts 7:23 where Stephen speaks of him leaving the palace of Pharaoh to visit his Jewish brethren who were the slaves of the Egyptian king. "It came into his heart" to look after his brethren in order to help them. He had the consciousness that he was the God-ordained instrument to deliver Israel, and he was going to its aid.

In Acts 15:14 we have a very significant statement, "Sim-eon hath declared how God for the first time (in the house of Cornelius) did visit the Gentiles, to take out of them a people for His name." And so we could translate more fully "how God for the first time did look upon the Gentiles in order to help them and provide for them." After the first missionary journey, Paul said, "Let us go again and visit our brethren in every city where we have preached the word of the Lord, and see how they do" (Acts 15:36). Paul's use of the verb "visit" included a tour of inspection and the giving of spiritual aid where that was needed.

In Hebrews 2:6 we have, "What is man, that thou art mindful of him? or the son of man, that thou visitest him?" The words "son of man" are here a designation of the human race. The Psalmist exclaims at the wonder of it all, that considering the insignificance of man, God would look upon him in order to help him and give him aid. I Peter 2:12 speaks of the fact that the unsaved who have been attracted to the Lord Jesus by the beautiful lives of Christians, and have put their faith in Him, will "glorify God in the day of visitation." The word translated "visitation" is allied to our verb, and refers to the day when God looks after them and cares for their souls in salvation. In I Peter 2:25, the word "Bishop" is from another word closely allied to the same verb. Thus God becomes the Bishop of the souls of the saints in that He looks after their spiritual welfare and gives them aid. In James 1:27 we have, "Pure religion and undefiled before God and the Father is this, To visit the fatherless and widows in their affliction, and to keep himself unspotted from the world." Here again, the word "visit" does not refer to a social call, but to the act of looking after the fatherless and the widows in order to help them.

The noun forms of this word are found in the following places and are translated by the words "overseer or bishop;" Acts 20:28; Philippians 1:1; I Timothy 3:1, 2; Titus 1:7; I Peter 2:25; and Acts 1:20 where the word "bishopric" should be translated "overseership." The word has the following meanings, "an overseer, one charged with the duty of seeing that things to be done by others are done rightly, a guardian." In the case of a church officer called a "bishop," it means "one charged with the spiritual oversight and welfare of the local church, with the responsibility of giving spiritual help to the saints."

As a result of this study, the English reader can understand more clearly the passages where the word "visit" is found.

XIII.

Here and There in the New Testament

PAID IN FULL. Our Lord in Matthew 6:2 is speaking of hypocrites of His day who blew a trumpet in the synagogues and streets to call men's attention to the alms they were giving, doing this in order that they may be glorified by men. His comment on this procedure is "They have their reward." "Synagogue" is from a Greek word made up of a verb which means "to go," and a preposition which means "with" and signifies "fellowship." Thus the composite word refers to the action of people "going with one another," thus congregating in one place. The word became the name for the place of worship where the Jews congregated. The word "hypocrite" was used of an actor on the Greek stage, one who played the part of another. These who made a display of giving alms were hypocrites in the sense that they played the part of a generous person who out of a heart of love would give to the poor. But their motive in giving was to have men glorify them, not from a desire to help the needy. They were actors on the stage of this life. They received the applause of the audience. Jesus said, "They have their reward."

The word "have" is from the verb which means "to have," and a prefixed preposition which means "off" and implies separation. The combined idea is "to have off." It speaks of the possession of something which is a full and final payment. It came to mean "I have received in full." It was the

technical expression regularly used in drawing up a receipt.
Paul used it when he said (Phil. 4:18) "I have all." He
was acknowledging the gift of the Philippians brought by
Epaphroditus, and sending them a receipt for the same. The
Greek secular non-literary manuscripts give instances of its
use all over the Hellenistic world. Our Lord's words could
be translated "They have received their reward in full."
These hypocrites had been paid in full, and they had no
further claim for reward. So is it when we do Christian work
to be seen of men, when we exalt ourselves instead of the
Lord Jesus. We are paid in full on earth, our pay, the
plaudits of men. We have no reward awaiting us over
yonder.

PLAYING TRUANT. In II Thessalonians 3:11, Paul
speaks of certain Christian men in the local church who
were walking disorderly. The English word "disorderly"
means "confused, unmethodical, turbulent, unruly." But
none of these meanings exactly fits the Greek word of which
it is the translation. The use of the Greek word is clearly
seen in an early account of a father who apprenticed his son
to a weaver for one year. The contract provided for the
details of food and clothing for the period of apprenticeship. Then the contract stated that if there were any days
on which the boy *failed to attend* or *played truant,* the
father must see that the boy report for work an equivalent
number of days after the apprenticeship was over. The
word translated "disorderly" is the Greek word in the contract which means "to play truant." These Thessalonian
saints were playing truant from their daily employment.
The occasion for this is suggested in the context where Paul
says, "The Lord direct your hearts into the love of God,
and the patient waiting for Christ." The doctrine of the
immanent return of the Lord Jesus for His Church was
firmly believed in this church. The saints looked from day

to day for that event. Some argued, of course wrongly, that if the Lord might come the next day, that there was no need for earning one's daily bread. But Paul, who had taught them this great truth of the immanency of the Lord's return, and whose expectation was just as intense as that of the Thessalonian saints, calls their attention to the fact that he worked for his daily bread in order that he might not be obligated to anyone for support. His rule was that if anyone did not work, he should not eat. He defines what he means by "disorderly" in the words "working not at all." Thus, the context agrees with the first century usage of the word, "to play truant."

CALLED CHRISTIANS. It was at Antioch that the disciples were first called Christians (Acts 11:26). The name was coined by the pagans of the first century to identify the followers of the Christ from those who worshipped the Roman emperor who was called Caesar. The word "disciple" is the translation of a Greek word meaning "one who learns." The word does not include within its meaning the idea of salvation. Thus, the disciples of the Christ could be either saved or unsaved. They merely had to be followers of Him, those who were under His instruction and adhered to Him as a leader or teacher. Judas was the one disciple of the twelve who was not a true believer. In John 6:66 we have, "From that time many of his disciples went back and walked no more with him." They followed our Lord in His ethical teachings, but when He spoke of salvation through faith in a substitutionary blood sacrifice, they parted company with Him. Therefore, one must consult the context in which the word "disciple" is found, to find out whether the disciple mentioned is saved or unsaved.

Here we have the case of many people following the Lord who were known as His disciples. The pagan world called them "Christians." The Roman State was built around the Emperor not merely as the political but the religious head of the empire. Not only did the subjects of the empire render allegiance to the Caesar as the governing head, but they worshipped him as a god. Emperor worship, or as it is sometimes known, the Cult of the Caesar, bound together the empire's far-flung colonies and widely different peoples. These followers of the Caesar, members of the Cult of the Caesar, were called in the Greek language, *Kaisarianos,* followers of the *Kaisar* or Caesar.

Now appears a rival claimant to world worship and dominion, the Christ of Israel. There was a widespread consciousness in the Gentile portion of the race that some day there would appear in Israel, a great leader, called the Messiah. This was probably part of the knowledge which the Magi had when they came to worship the new-born King of the Jews (Matt. 2:1-11). While He was not well known during His life-time on earth, a fact which is attested by the meagre notice given Him by the historians of His day, yet when the Gospel of Grace was being preached throughout the Roman empire, and He was being proclaimed as the Christ, with all that that name involved, Rome took notice. The name "Christ" is the English spelling of the Greek word *Christos,* which in turn is the translation of the Hebrew word "Messiah." It was the Messiah who had died, and had risen again, who was described as the sinner's Saviour, and a king in His own right, coming from the famous line of Jewish kings, the Davidic. Here was a rival King and Priest, claiming the allegiance of the subjects of Rome. Those who put their faith in Him necessarily had to sever their allegiance to the ruling Caesar, so far as worshipping him was concerned. These who were once *Kaisarianos,* followers of the Caesar, now were known as *Christianos,* followers of the Christ.

Thus, the Roman world was divided into two rival cults, the Cult of the Caesar, and the Cult of the Christ.

Paul, speaking of the Christ (the definite article appears before "Christ" in the Greek, indicating that the term "Christ" was well-known) before Agrippa the Roman ruler, preached the gospel to him (Acts 26). Agrippa says to Paul, "Almost thou persuadest me to be a Christian." The literal Greek here is, "With but little persuasion thou wouldest fain make me a Christian." Agrippa scoffed at the idea of becoming a Christian. He was a proud *Kaisarianos,* a worshipper of the Caesar. He knew that he would lose his government position and his head also if he ever renounced his allegiance to Caesar in order to become a *Christianos.*

The name "Christian" was a term of reproach in the Roman world. It was the name of the members of that despised and hated sect which worshipped the Christ. Peter in his first epistle (4:16) says, "If any man suffer as a Christian (a *Christianos*), let him not be ashamed; but let him glorify God on this behalf." Thus, the persecution of the early Christians by Rome arose out of the antagonism of the empire against a rival supremacy, that of the Cult of the Christ.

The world coined the term, but the Holy Spirit in I Peter takes it up as one of the designations of a believer in the Lord Jesus. In the first century it designated those who worshipped the Christ and refused to worship the image of the emperor. How that reminds us of John's exhortation in his first epistle (5:21), "Little children, keep yourself from idols." That injunction applies to Christians today. An idol today is anything that a Christian might possess that is not in harmony with what the Lord Jesus is, anything that occupies a place in his life which has a tendency to exclude Christ. We have no Roman emperor today whom the State might direct us to worship. But let us keep a watchful eye open for the little idols that would keep us from the closest fellowship with and usefulness to our Lord.

In the Great Tribulation period, the Roman empire is again to rear its head. Emperor worship will be restored, and thus the Cult of the Caesar (Rev. 13). The Jewish remnant of 144,000 (Rev. 7:1-8) will proclaim the coming of the Christ, and the two rival supremacies will again be present in a revived Roman empire. There will be the *Kaisarianos* and the *Christianos,* the followers of Caesar and the followers of the Christ. But the personal advent of the Christ will displace the supremacy of the Caesars, and His Messianic rule will bring universal righteousness, peace, and prosperity to this earth.

REBUKE and REPROVE. These two words are the usual translations of two closely related words in the Greek text. When we keep in mind the distinction between these Greek words, a flood of light is thrown upon the passages in which they occur.

The word "rebuke" is the general translation of the word *epitimao.* This word is used when one rebukes another without bringing the one rebuked to a conviction of any fault on his part. It might be because the one rebuked was innocent of the charge, or that he was guilty but refused to acknowledge his guilt. Examples of the first are seen in the action of Peter rebuking the Lord Jesus (Matt. 16:23), the disciples rebuking the children for accepting the blessing of our Lord (Matt. 19:13), and the crowd rebuking the blind man for calling upon Jesus (Luke 18:39). Illustrations of the second are found in the case of the repentant robber rebuking his fellow malefactor (Luke 23:40), and Jesus rebuking the demon (Mark 9:25), neither rebuke having any effect upon the recipient.

The second word is *elegcho* and is usually translated by the word "reprove." This word speaks of a rebuke which results in the person's confession of his guilt, or if not his confession, his conviction of his sin. The word is used in Job 5:17 (Septuagint). "Behold, happy is the man whom God *correcteth*." It is God's reproof of His own that results in conviction of sin and their confession. "Reprove" in Proverbs 19:25 (Septuagint) is from *elegcho*. The person who has spiritual understanding will respond to a rebuke from God by acknowledging his guilt and confessing it.

Our Lord uses the word when He says, "Which of you *convinceth* me of sin?" (John 8:46). *Elegcho* is the correct word here, for it was used in the Greek law courts not merely of a reply to an opposing attorney, but of a refutation of his argument. No one could prove any charges of sin against our Lord. No one could bring charges against Him in such a way as to convince Him that He was guilty.

But what a flood of light is shed upon the great passage, "And when he (the Holy Spirit) is come, he will reprove the world of sin, and of righteousness, and of judgment" (John 16:8). What a commentary upon the work of the Holy Spirit in the case of the unsaved whom He brings to a saving faith in the Lord Jesus. Here *epitimao* would not do, for the unsaved are not guiltless nor do those whom the Holy Spirit reproves, refuse to acknowledge and confess their guilt. The word "world" here must be interpreted in a limited way because of *elegcho*. The word here refers to those of the unsaved who are brought by the Holy Spirit into the place of salvation. The reproof spoken of is an effectual one. The rest of the unsaved hate the light and do not come to the light, lest their deeds be proven to be evil and they be put under obligation to confess their guilt (John 3:20). With the help of these definitions and illustrations of *epitimao* and *elegcho*, the student of the English Bible is now prepared to study for himself the passages in which each is found.

Epitimao occurs in the following places and is translated in the A.V., by the words "rebuke" and "charge": Matthew 8:26, 12:16, 16:22, 17:18, 19:13, 20:31; Mark 1:25, 3:12, 4:39, 8:30, 32, 33, 9:25, 10:13, 48; Luke 4:35, 39, 41, 8:24, 9:21, 42, 55, 17:3, 18:15, 39, 19:39, 23:40; II Timothy 4:2; Jude 9.

Elegcho is found in the following places and is translated by the words "reprove, convict, tell a fault, convince": Matthew 18:15; Luke 3:19; John 3:20, 8:9, 46, 16:8; I Corinthians 14:24; Ephesians 5:11, 13; I Timothy 5:20; II Timothy 4:2; Titus 1:9, 13, 2:15; Hebrews 12:5; James 2:9; Revelation 3:19.

BASTAZO. This is one of the many colorful words in the Greek New Testament. It has a variety of meanings; *to take up with the hands, to bear what is burdensome, to bear away, to carry off, to pilfer*. Moulton and Milligan in their *Vocabulary of the Greek Testament* report the following uses of the word. The word appears in a secular manuscript of A.D. 117 in a formula about taxation, where it has the sense of "endure." It appears in the sentence "No one will endure your cheek." How this latter phrase has remained with us. The Ephesian church could not bear (bastazo) them that are evil (Rev. 2:2, 3). It could not endure them in the same sense that no one could endure the cheek, the insults, sarcasm, gainsaying, cutting words, rudeness, and abuse of the unknown person mentioned in that early manuscript.

A document of the third century speaks of the Emperor Trajan granting an audience to rival Greek and Jewish emissaries from Alexandria, "each bearing (*bastazo*) their own unique, private gods." How like in usage is this to the words in Acts 9:15, "He (Paul) is a chosen vessel unto me, to bear (*bastazo*) my name before the Gentiles, and kings, and the children of Israel." Closely allied to this usage of *bastazo* is that found in a papyrus manuscript which contains a spell in which the words occur, "I *carry* the corpse of Osiris . . . should so-and-so trouble me, I shall use it against him." Compare Galatians 6:17 where Paul says, "From henceforth let no man trouble me: for I bear *(bastazo)* in my body the marks of the Lord Jesus." The word "marks" is from the Greek *stigma,* which comes over into the English language in our word "stigma," and means, "a mark pricked in or branded upon the body." According to ancient oriental usage, slaves and soldiers bore the name or stamp of their master or commander branded or pricked into their bodies to indicate to what master or general they belonged, and there were even some devotees who stamped themselves in this way with the token of their gods.

Thus, Paul says that he bears branded on his body, the scars and marks left there by the perils, hardships, imprisonments, beatings and scourgings he endured for the Lord Jesus, and which proved him to be a faithful soldier of Jesus Christ. Thus he could exhort Timothy to endure hardness as a good soldier of Jesus Christ (II Tim. 2:3). In our Galatian passage, he says in effect that he has suffered enough from the Judaizers who dogged his footsteps for many long years, and that his body scarred as the result of suffering for his Lord, should be enough to cause them to let him alone in his declining years and give him a little time of peace and rest. So, as the bearing (bastazo) of a particular amulet associated with the god Osiris was used as a charm against an adversary, so the scarred body of the apostle should be enough to dissuade the Judaizers from their continued attacks upon him. And just as these Greek and Jewish emissaries bore their own unique private gods before Trajan in their dress, language, actions, and testimony, so Paul was to do the same before the Gentiles, kings, and children of Israel.

A common use of *bastazo* was "to pilfer," throwing a flood of light on John 12:6 where Judas is said to have "had the bag, and *bare* (pilfered *bastazo*) what was put therein." In Matthew 3:11, we have "whose shoes I am not worthy to bear." *Bastazo* was firmly established in its usage of "to take off someone's sandals," and it has this meaning here. Compare Mark 1:7. It was not a question of wearing Messiah's sandals, but of taking them off for Him, a slave's duty. What humility on the part of John.

The word also meant "to bear what is burdensome," and is used in that meaning in the following places: Matthew 8:17, 20:12; Mark 14:13; Luke 7:14, 14:27, 22:10; John 10:31, 16:12, 19:17, 20:15; Acts 3:2, 15:10, 21:35; Romans 15:1; Galatians 5:10, 6:2, 5, 17; Revelation 2:2, 3. There is another Greek word which is the simple unqualified word meaning "to bear." When *bastazo* is used, the writer wishes to add some detail to the simple idea of carrying something. One should always look for that additional idea. The reader should study these places listed for the additional light which the word *bastazo* sheds upon the meaning of the passage. It will paint many a vivid picture in his mind's eye.

DEITY and DIVINITY. There are two Greek words translated "Godhead" in the New Testament, occurring but once each, *theiotes* and *theotes*. The Greek words are not however identical in meaning.

Paul uses the first in Romans 1:20, where he speaks of the fact that mankind can see the *theiotes* of God as it looks at the created universe. Trench observes, "Paul is declaring how much of God may be known from the revelation of Himself which He has made in nature, from those vestiges of Himself which men may everywhere trace in the world around them. Yet it is not the personal God whom any man may learn to know by these aids: He can be known only by the revelation of Himself in His Son; but only His divine attributes, His majesty and glory . . . It is not to be doubted that St. Paul uses this vaguer, more abstract, and less personal word, just because he would affirm that men may know God's power and majesty . . . from His works, but would *not* imply that they may know Himself from these, or from anything short of the revelation of His eternal Word."

Peter in his second epistle (1:3) uses the word *theia* which is closely allied to *theiotes*, to describe God's power. The word is translated "divine" in the A.V. Paul uses *theion* in Acts 17:29 where it is translated "Godhead." In Romans 1:20 he is speaking of what may be known of God through nature. In his message to the Greek philosophers at Athens, he argues that the fact that we are the offspring of God by creation, gives us a picture, though inadequate, of what God is like. However, He cannot be known in a personal way through this means. Thus, in these passages, he is speaking of the divine aspects of Deity, but not of Deity as in itself absolute. The word *theiotes* was used in classical Greek to speak of something in which there was a manifestation of the divine, of some divine attributes, but never of absolute deity. The word was used when a human being was raised to the rank of a god. He was therefore divine. But absolute deity was never ascribed to him by this word. The word *theiotes* should therefore be translated in such a way as to bring out the thought of divinity, namely, that state of being in which the individual has divine characteristics. Paul in Romans 1:19 uses the Greek word *theos* which speaks of absolute deity, and then in the next verse says that the created universe shows His eternal power and divinity, using *theiotes*.

The other word *theotes* occurs in Colossians 2:9, where Paul says that "In him (the Lord Jesus) dwelleth all the fulness of the Godhead bodily." The Greek is very strong here. One could translate, "For in Him corporeally there is permanently at home all the fulness of the Godhead." That is, in our Lord Jesus in His incarnation and in the permanent possession of His human body now glorified, there resides by nature and permanently the fulness of the Godhead. The word "Godhead" is from our second word *theotes*. The word expresses Godhead in the absolute sense. *It is not merely divine attributes that are in mind now, but the possession of the essence of deity in an absolute sense.* The Greek Fathers never use *theiotes* but always *theotes* as alone adequately expressing the essential Godhead of the three several Persons in the Holy Trinity. The Latin Christian writers were not satisfied with *divinitas* which was in common use, but coined the word *deitas* as the only adequate representative of the Greek word *theotes*.

In these days when translators of the modernistic school will render the last sentence of John 1:1 "And the Word was divine," translating the word *theos* which means "absolute deity" by the word "divine," it behooves those who believe in the absolute deity of the Lord Jesus, to use the expression "deity of Jesus Christ," rather than "divinity of Jesus Christ." Paul never spoke of the divinity of Jesus Christ, always of His deity. Our Lord does have divine attributes, but He is also God the Son, possessing the same essence as God the Father, and is co-equal with the other two members of the Trinity in His deity.

BAPTIZE UNTO REPENTANCE. John the Baptist makes the statement, "I indeed baptize you with water unto repentance" (Matt. 3:11). Peter says, "Repent, and be baptized everyone of you in the name of Jesus Christ for the remission of sins" (Acts 2:38). The word "unto" signifies "result." For instance, "I am not ashamed of the gospel, for it is the power of God unto salvation" (Rom. 1:16). The word "for" in our second text has the same meaning.

Are we to understand that water baptism as administered by John the Baptist and Peter, resulted in the repentance of those who were the recipients of it, in the face of the fact that repentance is a work of the Holy Spirit in the heart of the unsaved, this repentance being "unto life," that is, resulting in life (Acts 11:18)?

The words "unto" and "for" in Matthew 3:11 and Acts 2:38 are from the Greek preposition *eis*. Dana and Mantey in their excellent treatment of Greek prepositions based upon the papyri findings, give as one of the uses of this word, "because of."* This usage is found in Matthew 12:41 where the men of Nineveh repented *at* or *because* of the preaching of Jonah, and in Romans 4:20, where Abraham did not stagger in unbelief, because of the promise of God. In the case of the men of Nineveh, Jonah's preaching was the cause of their repentance. In the case of Abraham, the reason why he did not stagger in unbelief, was because of the promise of God. The word "stagger" here is from a Greek word which means "to vacillate between two opinions." Thus it was the repentance of those who received John's message which was the cause of their baptism. The same was true of Peter's at Pentecost. John's words were, "I indeed baptize you with water because of repentance," and Peter's, "Repent, and be baptized everyone of you in the name of Jesus Christ because of the remission of sins." That this is the correct translation and interpretation of our texts is also seen from the testimony of Josephus to the effect that John the Baptist baptized people only after they had repented: "Who (John) was a good man, and commanded the Jews to exercise virtue, both as to righteousness towards one another and piety towards God, and so to come to baptism; for that the washing (with water) would be acceptable to him, if they made use of it, not in order to

Manual Grammar of the Greek New Testament.

the putting away of some sins, but for the purification of the body; supposing still that the soul was thoroughly purified beforehand by righteousness." John's words, "Bring forth therefore fruits meet for repentance" (Matt. 3:8), clearly show that he demanded some evidence of salvation before he would baptize a person.

Thus, we have the scriptural meaning of water baptism. It is the testimony of the person to the fact of his salvation. The only proper recipient of water baptism therefore is one who has received the Lord Jesus as his personal Saviour, and is trusting in His precious blood for salvation from sin.

The Greek text thus clears up a difficulty found in the English translation. Baptism is not the prerequisite of repentance, much less its cause, but the testimony of the one who has entered the door of salvation.

XIV.

An Exposition of the Greek Text of Romans VI

PAUL wrote chapter six of Romans in answer to two questions: "Shall we continue in sin, that grace may abound?" answering this question in verses 2-14; and "Shall we sin, because we are not under the law, but under grace?" replying to this question in verses 15-23. These questions were raised, not by the apostle himself, but by his hearers in the first century who did not understand grace, and thus arrived at false conclusions concerning it.

Paul answers the first question by showing that such a thing is impossible, since God's grace makes provision for an inward change in the believer the moment he receives the Lord Jesus as his Saviour, a change in which the power of indwelling sin is broken and the divine nature implanted. This results in the liberation of that person from the compelling power of the Adamic nature, and his acquisition of the desire and power to live a holy life. This, Paul argues, makes impossible a life of sin.

He replies to the second question by asserting that a Christian does not take advantage of divine grace, since he has ceased to be a bondslave of Satan and has become a bondslave of the Lord Jesus, having a nature whereby he hates sin and shuns the Devil, and loves to serve the Lord Jesus.

In answering these objections to his teaching of pure grace without any admixture of law as a means of controlling the saint and causing him to live a life pleasing to God, Paul deals with the mechanical impossibility of going on in sin. We are occupied in Romans VI, not with the question of *what kind* of a life the child of God should live, a subject which he presents in chapters 12-16, but with the question of *how* or *by what method* the believer is to live that life. The reason why so many children of God who are earnestly trying to live a Christian life which would glorify the Lord Jesus, fail in that endeavor, is because they do not understand the truth of this chapter. Their experience is like that of Paul, who before he came into the truth of Romans VI said, "I am carnal, sold under sin. For that which I do I do not understand: for what I would, that I do not; but what I hate, that do I" (7:15). Paul uses three words to designate the three spiritual classes of men, the natural man (I Cor. 2:14), namely, the unsaved person; the carnal man (I Cor. 3:1), the Christian who is not living the victorious life; and the spiritual man (I Cor. 2:15), the Christian who understands God's prescribed method for the saint which results in his living a holy life. Our exposition of the Greek text of this wonderful portion of God's Word should, under the blessing of God the Holy Spirit, solve the problem of some dear child of God who is not getting consistent victory over sin. It therefore should prove an intensely practical study.

The first question found its occasion in Paul's statement in 5:20, "where sin abounded, grace did much more abound." The words "much more abound" are from a word referring to a superabundance of something with an additional supply added to this superabundance. Paul's teaching here is that no matter how much sin there might be committed, there are always unlimited resources of grace in the great heart of God by which to extend mercy to the sinning individual. The reaction of the heart that does not understand grace is seen in the question asked, "What shall we say then? Shall we continue habitually to live in the sphere and grip of the sinful nature, in order that this grace may be increasingly lavished in superabundant outgoings?" The verb used, refers to habitual action. The word "sin" refers here not to acts of sin, but to the sinful nature, since Paul is dealing here with the mechanics of the Christian life, not the outward actions of the individual.

His first answer to this question is "God forbid." The literal Greek is, "May it not become." He dismisses the very thought as unthinkable. One could translate, "far be the thought."

His second answer is, "How shall we who are dead to sin, live any longer therein?" The word "how," leaves no room for the possibility of the continued habit of sin in the Christian life, for the Greek word means "how is it possible?" "We" is from a word that not only refers to the individuals concerned, but also to the quality or character of these individuals. The fuller translation is "such as we." "Are dead" is from a past tense verb, which tense also speaks of finality, and we translate "died once for all." "Sin" is in a construction in Greek which causes us to translate "with reference to sin." The verb "live" is from a word which speaks here of the life principle, not the actions of the person. The translation thus far reads, "What shall we say then? Shall we habitually abide under the control of sin in order that this grace previously mentioned may be increasingly lavished in superabundant outgoings? Far be the thought. Such as we who died once for all with reference to sin, how is it possible for us to exist in the grip of its motivating energy any longer?"

But let us look at the word "died." Death is not extinction of being, but a separation. In the case of physical death, it is the separation of the individual from his physical body. In the case of spiritual death, it is the separation of the person from the life of God. Here the word refers to the separation of the believer from the power of the sinful nature. Before salvation, he was compelled to obey its behests. Since salvation, its power over him is broken. We must be careful to note that Paul is not teaching what is called "the eradication of the sinful nature," namely, that that nature is taken away completely. The Bible teaches that this nature remains in the believer until he dies (Rom. 7:18, 21; I John 1:8), but the believer is not in it in the sense of being in its grip. Thus Paul answers the question as to whether a Christian should continue in habitual sin, by stating its impossibility, and on the ground that that nature which before salvation made him sin habitually, has had its power broken. It is a mechanical impossibility. We paraphrase the question: "Such as we who have been separated once for all from the power of the sinful nature, how is it possible for us to continue to exist in the grip of its motivating energy any longer?" Thus, when God justifies the believer, he also breaks the power of sin in the life. Grace does here what law never did. It not only forbids sin but also defeats its power in the person's life.

Then Paul proceeds to answer the question from another angle. In his first answer he showed the impossibility of habitual sin in a Christian's life by reason of the fact that the power of the sinful nature was broken when the believer was saved. Now he shows its impossibility in that the believer is made a partaker of the divine nature (II Peter 1:4). The life of God, surging through his being, causes him to hate sin and love holiness, and produces in him both the desire and the power to do God's will.

Paul speaks of this in Philippians 2:11, 12, where he says "Wherefore, my beloved, as ye have always obeyed, not as in my presence only, but now much more in my absence, carry to its ultimate goal your own salvation with fear and trembling, for God is the One who is constantly supplying you the impulse, giving you both the power to resolve and the strength to perform His good pleasure."

This truth Paul presents in verses 3 and 4 where we are taught that all believers were baptized into Jesus Christ and thus shared His death, in order that they also might share His resurrection life.

We look first at the phrase "baptized into Jesus Christ." It is set in a context of supernaturalism. In verse 2 we have the supernatural act of God breaking the power of indwelling sin for the believer. In verse 4 we have the supernatural act of God imparting divine life to the believer. Verse 3 reaches back to the action spoken of in verse 2 and forward to that spoken of in verse 4. We were baptized into Jesus Christ so that we might be baptized into His death on the Cross, in order that through our identification with Him in that death, we might die with reference to sin, that is, have the power of indwelling sin broken. We were also baptized into His death so that we might share His burial, and thus His resurrection, and in that way have His divine life imparted to us. Thus this baptism accomplished two things. It resulted in the power of sin being broken and the divine nature being implanted, which operation took place at the moment the believer placed his faith in the Lord Jesus. Therefore, since the results were operative in the believer the moment he was saved, the baptism into Jesus Christ in which that person shared His death, burial, and resurrection, must have taken place, potentially, previous

to his being saved, and actually, at the moment of salvation.
Our Lord died, was buried, and arose almost 2000 years
ago. In the mind and reckoning of God, each believer was
in Christ then, in order that he might when he believed,
participate in the benefits which His death, burial, and resurrection brought forth. Therefore, the baptism referred
to here is not water baptism, but the baptism by means of
the Holy Spirit (I Cor. 12:13). Let it be said in passing,
that the writer believes in the ordinance of water baptism
as obligatory upon all believers on the Lord Jesus Christ,
that it is their testimony to the fact of their salvation, and
he finds plenty of scriptural warrant for it elsewhere. No
ceremony of water baptism ever introduced a believing sinner into vital union with Jesus Christ. Furthermore, many
true children of God never have fulfilled their obligation
of testifying to their salvation in water baptism. And who
is prepared to deny that they have been united to Christ?
Paul is concerned here with the supernatural working of
God resulting in an inner change in the spiritual mechanics of the believer's life, and as a clear thinker who stays
within the compass of his subject, Paul does not introduce
the symbol where the supernatural alone is in view.

But how are we to understand the word "baptism"? This
word is the spelling in English letter equivalents of the
word *baptisma,* the verb of the same stem being *baptizo.*
The Greek word has two distinct uses, a mechanical one,
and a ritualistic one, to be determined by the context in
which it is found. Since the word "baptism" is only the
spelling of the Greek word *baptisma,* and not a word native
to the English language, it has no meaning of its own and
therefore must derive its meaning from the Greek word of
which it is the spelling. Furthermore, it must be interpreted and translated in its two meanings just as the Greek
word is. We will present usages of the Greek word as

found in classical Greek, and in the Koine Greek of secular documents, the Septuagint, and the New Testament.

For the following instances of the purely mechanical usage of *baptizo* in classical Greek, I am indebted to my honored and beloved teacher of Greek at Northwestern University, Professor John A. Scott, Ph.D., LL.D., classical Greek scholar who in the field of classical criticism has refuted the theory of Frederick August Wolf, who claimed that the Iliad and Odyssey were not written by the poet Homer but are a composite of the poetic expression of the Greek people, publishing the results of his findings in his book, *The Unity of Homer,* and who in the field of New Testament criticism has written the book, *We Would Know Jesus,* in which he demonstrates the historical accuracy of the four Gospels as confirmed by contemporary records, thereby rendering valuable assistance to the cause of evangelical Christianity in view of the destructive tendencies of that which passes for present day criticism of the New Testament: "The first use of *baptizo* is in the ninth book of the Odyssey, where the hissing of the burning eye of the Cyclops is compared to the sound of water where a smith dips, *baptizes,* a piece of iron, tempering it. In the Battle of the Frogs and Mice it is said that a mouse thrust a frog with a reed, and the frog leaped over the water, baptizing it with its blood. Euripides uses the word of a ship which goes down in the water and does not come back to the surface. Lucian dreams that he has seen a huge bird shot with a mighty arrow, and as it flies high in the air it baptizes the clouds with its blood. An ancient scholium to the Fifth Book of the Iliad makes a wounded soldier baptize the earth with his blood. It is the ordinary word for staining or dyeing, and words derived from it meaning "dyer" and "dyes" are common. The most common meaning is to plunge into a liquid, but it is so common in other meanings that in each case the meaning must be determined by the context." In Xenophon's *Anabasis* we have an instance where the word *baptizo* has both a mechanical and a ceremonial meaning. Before going to war, the Greek soldiers placed (*baptizo*) the points of their swords, and the barbarians the points of their spears in a bowl of blood.

In secular documents of the Koine period, Moulton and Milligan report the following usages: "a *submerged* boat, ceremonial *ablutions,* a person *overwhelmed* in calamities, a person *baptizo* upon the head."

We have in Leviticus 4:6 the words, "And the priest shall dip his finger in the blood, and sprinkle of the blood seven times before the Lord," where "dip" is from *baptizo* and "sprinkle" is from *rantizo* (Septuagint), the first referring to the action of introducing the finger into the blood, and the second, speaking of the ritualism of sprinkling that blood.

In the New Testament we find the word translated "washings" in Hebrews 9:10, speaking of the ablutions of Judaism; referring to ceremonial washing of cups, pots, brazen vessels, and of tables (Mark 7:4); and to the ceremony of water baptism (Matt. 3:7, 16; John 4:1; Acts 16:33; I Corinthians 1:14; I Peter 3:21). A purely mechanical usage is seen in Luke 16:24 where the rich man asks that Lazarus dip (baptize) his finger in water and cool his tongue.

The usage of the word as seen in the above examples, resolves itself into the following definition of the word *baptizo* in its mechanical meaning: "the introduction or placing of a person or thing into a new environment or into union with something else so as to alter its condition or its relationship to its previous environment or condition." And that is its usage in Romans VI. It refers to the act of God introducing a believing sinner into vital union with

Jesus Christ, in order that that believer might have the power of his sinful nature broken and the divine nature implanted through his identification with Christ in His death, burial, and resurrection, thus altering the condition and relationship of that sinner with regard to his previous state and environment, bringing him into a new environment, the kingdom of God. That is what Paul refers to when he says, "hath translated us into the kingdom of the Son of His love" (Col. 1:13). We have this same mechanical usage of *baptizo* in I Corinthians 12:13, "For by means of the instrumentality of one Spirit were we all baptized into one body," where Paul speaks of the act of the Holy Spirit placing or introducing the believing sinner into the body of Christ, as in our Roman text he refers to the same act, but speaks of the Head of the Body rather than the Body itself. The word "Spirit" is in the instrumental case, which case designates the means by which the action in the verb is accomplished. The Holy Spirit is the divine agent who Himself baptizes (introduces) the believer into vital union with the Lord Jesus. It should be clear from this that the baptism by means of the Spirit is not for power. Its sole purpose is to unite the believing sinner with his Saviour. Power for holy living and for service comes from the fullness of the Spirit. The baptism is an act which takes place at the moment the sinner believes, never to be repeated. The fullness is a moment by moment continuous state as the believer trusts the Lord Jesus for that fullness (John 7:37, 38).

We are now ready for the further examination of verses 3 and 4. The words "so many of us as" in the Greek, do not imply that some were not baptized, but designate all collectively. This is checked up by I Corinthians 12:13 in the statement "were we all baptized." This again points to the fact that Paul is speaking here of the baptism by the

Spirit, for all believers are in Christ, and yet all have not fulfilled their obligation of conforming to the ordinance of water baptism. The words "know ye not," in the original are literally "or are ye ignorant?", the Greek showing that the persons addressed were not ignorant of these facts, but conversant with them. The word "into" is from a Greek word which denotes an "inward union." The translation is as follows: "Or, are ye ignorant of the fact that all we who were baptized (introduced) into an inward union with Christ Jesus, into (a participation in) His death were baptized (introduced)?"

We now consider verse 4. The words "newness of life" do not refer to the new kind of life we are to live before the world. They do not refer to our Christian testimony as seen in our thoughts, words, and deeds. They speak of the new life implanted which is a motivating energy, providing both the desire and the power to live a Christian life. We are to walk, that is, conduct ourselves in the power of the new life which is imparted to us in regeneration. Whereas, before salvation, we walked in the power of the Adamic nature which gave us the desire and power to sin, we now are to walk in the energy of the new life God has imparted, which gives us both the desire and power to live a holy life. The translation is as follows: "Therefore, we were buried in company with Him through the intermediate instrumentality of this baptism (introduction) into His death, in order that even as Christ was raised out from among the dead through the glory of the Father, thus also we by means of a new life (imparted) should conduct ourselves," or, "thus also we from the power of a new life (imparted) should derive the motivating energy for our walk (thoughts, words, and deeds)."

To sum up verses 2-4: It is not possible for a saint to continue living a life of habitual sin, because the Holy

Spirit has baptized (introduced) him into vital union with Christ Jesus, this introduction having taken place potentially and in the mind and economy of God at the time our Lord died on the Cross, was buried in the tomb, and was raised from the dead, in order that the actual benefits of the believer's identification with Christ in these might be his at the moment he puts his faith in Jesus Christ as his Saviour, these benefits being the breaking of the power of indwelling sin and the impartation of the divine nature.

In verses 5-10 we have Paul's "in other words." He, master teacher that he is, seeks to make clearer his teaching in verses 2-4 by elaborating upon it in verses 5-10, and by presenting the same truth in a different way. We will look at verse 5. The word "if" in the Greek is not the conditional particle of an unfulfilled condition. It is a fulfilled condition here, its meaning being, "in view of the fact." "Planted" is from a compound word, one part of the word meaning, "to grow," and the other part implying close fellowship or participation on the part of two persons in a common action or state. The whole word speaks of an intimate and progressive union. The words "have been" are from a verb which speaks of entrance into a new state of existence. The verb is in the perfect tense, which tense in Greek speaks of an action completed in past time having present results. The word "likeness" speaks of a likeness which amounts well nigh to an identity. The translation so far is as follows: "For in view of the fact that we have become united with Him in the likeness of His death with the present result that we are identified with Him in His death." All believers from Adam's time to the time of the Great White Throne judgment were baptized (introduced into vital union) into the Lord Jesus when He died on the Cross. This vital union with Him resulted in our participating in His death, He dying a vicarious death in our behalf, we dying with reference to our sinful nature. In the case of our Lord, the result was that, having died once for all with reference to our sins, He will never die again (6:9). In the case of the believer, the result was that, having died once for all with reference to the sinful nature, he is forever delivered from its compelling power.

The words "we shall be," are "a future of logical result." They do not point to the future physical resurrection of the saint. Paul speaks of that in Romans 8:11. Here he is speaking of the spiritual resurrection of the believer which occurred potentially when Christ was raised out from among the dead, and actually, at the moment he believed. Thus, Paul argues that in view of the fact that believers have become united with Christ in the likeness of His death, the logical consequence of that identification with Christ in His death is identification with Him in His resurrection. The translation of verse 5 follows: "For, in view of the fact that we have become united with Him in the likeness of His death, with the present result that we are identified with Him in His death, certainly we also (as a necessary consequence) shall be in the likeness of His resurrection." As our Lord came out of the tomb in the same body in which He died, but with that body energized by a new life principle, (His precious blood having been poured out at Calvary, Levit. 17:11), and thus walked in newness of life, that is, walked in the energy of a new life, so the believer, identified with Him in His resurrection, leaves his old dead self in the tomb of his former life, and now walks in the energy of a new life principle surging through his being, the divine life imparted through his identification with Christ in His resurrection.

Paul now takes up this two-fold result in verses 6-10, the breaking of the power of the Adamic nature in verses 6-7, and the impartation of the divine nature in verses 8-10. We will look first at verses 6-7. The word "man" is not translated from the Greek word for "man" which refers to an individual male member of the human race, but from the word for "man" that is racial in its implications. It refers to the human race as contrasted to animals. Here it refers to the individual man or woman, boy or girl, seen as a human being, a personality.

There are two words in Greek which mean "old." One refers to that which is old in the sense of having existed from the beginning, the emphasis being upon the length of time it has been in existence. The other refers to that which is antiquated, out of date, belonging to a world of has-been, worn out. The second is used here. The expression, "our old man," refers therefore to the old unrenewed self, that person which we were before salvation did its work in our being, a human being dominated entirely by the Adamic nature, having a heart darkened by sin, totally depraved in its entire being. It is the person when looked at from this side of salvation that is antiquated, out of date, belonging to a world of has-been.

The words "is crucified" are more properly, "was crucified," coming from a past-tense verb in the Greek. When we died with Christ, that old unregenerate totally depraved person we were before salvation died. The words "of sin" are in a construction in the Greek called "the genitive of possession." The body here is the physical body possessed by the sinful nature in the sense that the latter dominates or controls it. The word "destroyed" is from a Greek word which means "to render idle or inoperative, to put an end to, to make inefficient." The words "serve sin" are from the verb whose stem is the same as the noun translated "bond-slave." It refers to habitual slavery to something. Our translation reads: "Knowing this, that our old self was crucified with Him, in order that the body (then) dominated by sin might be rendered inoperative (in that respect), and this for the purpose that we should no longer be habitually rendering a slave's obedience to sin." Thus God has put an end to the domination of the sinful nature over the believer, and has rendered the physical body idle, inoperative, in that respect.

Verse 7 is an illustration of the truth taught in verse 6. The words "is dead," are from a past tense in the Greek which speaks of the fact of a past action, the tense also speaking of finality, and should be translated "died once for all." The word "freed" is from the Greek word which is usually translated "righteous" in its noun form, and "justify" in its verb. As a man who has died physically is freed from bondage to sin in which he was held, so a person who has died to sin in a spiritual sense, is released from its bondage. Thus the human body is released from bondage to sin in that the crucifixion of the old self results in the body being liberated from the power of sin. The word "freed" is in the perfect tense, which tense is so often used when the writer is speaking of God's work of salvation in the believer, since this tense speaks of a past completed action having present, and in a context where salvation is spoken of, fixed and permanent results. Verse 7 therefore reads "For he who died once for all is in a permanent state of freedom from sin."

Having dealt with the breaking of the power of the Adamic nature in verses 6-7, Paul now turns to the matter of the impartation of the divine nature in verses 8-10. The first is the negative aspect of sanctification, where provision is made for the defeat of the sinful nature. The second is the positive side of sanctification, where provision is made for the introduction of a new life, Christ Jesus Himself (Col. 3:4), into the being and experience of the believer.

We look first at verse 8. The "if" refers to a fulfilled condition. There is no doubt about the fact that each believer died with Christ. "Be dead" is again from a past tense verb speaking of an accomplished fact. "Believe" is not to be taken here in the sense of "trust," which sense it has in contexts where the believer's faith in the Lord Jesus is referred to, but in the sense of a dogmatic belief. It is a belief that rests upon the logic of "since such and such a thing is true, it naturally follows that such and such will be the case." The future "shall" is not "a future of time," but of "logical result." The words "live with Him" do not refer to any fellowship in the sense of companionship which the believer may have with the Lord Jesus either in this life or in eternity. The preposition "with" is followed by the pronoun "Him" in the instrumental case. This case in Greek speaks of the means whereby the action or the state represented in the verb is accomplished. The word "live" here speaks of, not the experience of the believer, but the motivating energy which determines his conduct. That motivating energy is a Person, the Lord Jesus. He is the Life by means of which we live our new lives. He is our new existence. This is exactly what Paul means when he says, "For to me to live is Christ" (Phil. 1:21).

The Christian life is not primarily a system of ethics to be obeyed, for which obedience there is supplied both the desire and power. It is a Person living His life in and through another person, "Christ in you, the hope of glory" (Col. 1:27). That is what Paul means when he prays that Christ might be formed in the saints (Gal. 4:19). The Greek word "form" has no idea of physical shape, or of moulding some solid substance, or of creating or producing something. It refers to the action of an individual giving outward expression of his true inward nature. Paul prays that the lives of the saints may be so yielded to the Lord

Jesus, that He may be able to give outward expression of His own glorious Person in the thoughts, words, and deeds of the believer in whose heart He lives. Thus, the believer is not only alive in salvation by virtue of the fact that Christ is his life, but he lives his Christian life in dependence upon Him, or by means of Him. That is what Paul means by the words, "shall live with Him." The translation reads, "Now, since we died once for all with Christ, we believe that we shall also live by means of Him." Thus, as we died in company with Christ on the Cross, so also we shall live in company with Him, participating in the same life which He possesses. We offer the following paraphrase, "Now, since we died once for all with Christ, we believe that as a necessary consequence, we shall also derive our spiritual existence and the motivating impulse for our Christian experience from Him."

Verses 9 and 10 are presented as the basis for the above assertion, namely, that since we died with Christ we shall also live with Him; "Knowing that Christ having been raised out from among the dead, dies no more; death no longer has dominion over Him, for the death which He died, He died with reference to sin once for all: but the life He now lives, He lives with reference to God." Thus, the believer died with reference to his sinful nature once for all, resulting in his deliverance from its power. He now lives with respect to the life of God. His new life is Christ.

In verses 1-10, Paul has replied to the question "What shall we say then? Shall we continue habitually to live in the sphere and grip of the sinful nature, in order that this grace may be increasingly lavished in super-abundant outgoings?," by asserting that the mechanical set-up in the inner being of the believer is different from that in the unbeliever. In the latter, the sinful nature has supreme and absolute control. Nor does the unbeliever possess any goodness by nature which would combat the evil tendencies of the evil nature and produce goodness in his life. All one can expect from this mechanical set-up is a life of habitual sin. But, Paul asserts, in the case of the believer, this mechanical set-up has been changed. The new set-up which God installed is one in which the power of that sinful nature is broken, and one which includes the impartation of the divine nature, which latter combats the evil tendencies of the sinful nature (Gal. 5:17), and produces in the believer's life, the Christian graces (Gal. 5:22, 23). This makes impossible a life of habitual sin.

This new spiritual machinery operates in every child of God. But the degree of efficiency with which it works is dependent upon the care which the believer bestows upon it. An automobile engine under normal conditions will operate for a long time without any special attention. But if one expects the highest degree of efficiency from it, he finds it necessary to have a mechanic check over the various parts at frequent intervals and make the adjustments and repairs that are necessary.

A like situation obtains in the case of the mechanics of the Christian life. If the Christian desires the highest degree of efficiency from the salvation which God has given him, he must himself give special attention and care to his personal adjustment to this machinery. The Christian who is not informed as to the truth of Romans VI is in a position somewhat like the man who purchased a new automobile, but ignorant of the details of the mechanism, did not bestow the proper care upon it. Soon only three out of the six cylinders were operating. His car ran, but he was not getting the maximum of power from it. The engine stalled in traffic, became over-heated, and would not climb hills in high gear. After he had learned the details of the

mechanism and had the parts properly adjusted, the engine
gave him excellent service.

In the case of a Christian who does not understand Romans VI, the new spiritual mechanism which he received
when he was saved, operates, but not at its highest efficiency. When he understands what Paul is teaching in verses
1-10, and puts into practice the directions relative to his
adjustment to this new mechanism in verses 11-13, then he
will be obtaining the highest degree of efficiency from it.
And this is the explanation why some Christians are living such mediocre lives, while others are living Christlike
lives. It is not that the child of God does not want to live
the highest type of a Christian life. He does. If he fails,
it is because he does not know how. Listen to Paul again,
"To will is present with me; but how to perform that which
is good I find not" (Rom. 7:18). This personal adjustment
of the believer to his inner spiritual mechanism, Paul presents in verses 11-13.

The first responsibility of the believer is to reckon himself dead to sin. The word "reckon" is the translation of
a Greek word meaning "to count, compute, calculate, take
into account." That is, the believer is to live his Christian
life upon the basis of the fact that the power of the sinful nature is broken. He is to take these facts into his reckoning as he deals with temptations that confront him or
evil impulses that come from within. His attitude should
be that, in view of the fact that the power of the evil nature
is broken, he is under no obligation to obey its behests
(Rom. 8:12). He has been emancipated from sin, and the
proper procedure is to read God's emancipation proclamation to the insistent demands of the Adamic nature. The
believer must also realize that whereas before salvation, he
could not help it when he sinned, yet since God saved him,
should he sin, it is because of his free choice, since sin's

power has been broken. He is responsible for that sin. This should make him think twice before he contemplates an act of sin at the demand of the evil nature.

Then, he must also count upon the fact of his possession of the divine nature. This will keep him from depending upon himself and his own strength in his effort to live a life pleasing to the Lord Jesus, and will cause him to throw himself upon the resources of God. He will be trusting the Lord Jesus to fill him with the Holy Spirit (John 7:37, 38), with the result that the Holy Spirit will do two things for him. He will suppress the activities of the evil nature (Gal. 5:17) and He will produce in the believer a Christlike life (Gal. 5:22, 23). Paul says in Galations 5:16, 17, "This I say then, Walk in the Spirit, and ye shall not fulfill the crav- ings of the flesh, for the flesh has a strong desire to sup- press the Spirit, and the Spirit has a strong desire to sup- press the flesh, and these are entrenched in a permanent attitude of opposition to one another, so that ye should not do the things that ye would desire to be doing;" and in Galatians 5:22, 23, "The fruit of the Spirit is love, joy, peace, longsuffering, gentleness, goodness, faithfulness, meekness, self-control."

Contrast this adjustment of the intelligent Spirit-taught saint, with that of the believer who is not aware of the fact that God has broken the power of sin in his life, with the re- sult that he is more or less under its compelling power, try as he may to live free from sin. Since he is ignorant of the fact that God has placed within him His own nature, he de- pends upon himself and his own strength in an effort to defeat sin in his life and live a life pleasing to God. This believer is living a defeated life because he is not in proper adjustment to the new mechanical set-up in his spiritual being. When he learns of the facts which Paul presents in verses 1-10, he has in his possession a knowledge of the scriptural method of gaining victory over sin and the living of a life pleasing to God, and, acting upon instructions which he finds in verses 11-13 he has victory all along the line. The translation of verse 11 follows: "Thus also, as for you, constantly be taking into account the fact that you are those who are dead with respect to sin, and indeed those who are living ones with reference to God in Christ Jesus." A paraphrase may make things clearer yet. "Thus also, as for you, constantly be taking into account the fact that you are those who have had the power of sin broken in your lives and those who have had the divine nature implanted."

We come to verse 12. The words "let not sin reign," are in a construction in the Greek which forbids the continuation of an action already going on. The word "reign" is in the Greek "reign as king." The tense speaks of habitual action. "That ye should obey" is literally, "with a view to habitually obeying." The word "lusts" is literally "cravings." "Thereof" does not go back to "sin" but to "body." The gender of the pronoun requires this. "Lusts thereof" refers to the cravings of the human body, which cravings come from the sinful nature. The translation reads, "Therefore, stop allowing sin to reign habitually as king in your mortal bodies, with a view to your habitually obeying the cravings of that body." God is never unreasonable in His demands upon His own. What He asks of us is always within our ability to fulfill as we appropriate the divine resources of grace. Since the power of sin is broken and the divine nature is implanted, we are well able to keep sin from reigning in our lives.

In verse 13, Paul presents other exhortations to be obeyed upon the basis of what God has done for us as recorded in verse 11. "Yield" is from a Greek word which means "to put at the service of." Together with the word "neither," it forbids the continuance of an action already going on.

"Stop habitually putting your members at the service of,"
is the translation. Our members refer to our hands, feet,
tongue, eyes, mind, for instance. The word "instruments"
is in the Greek, "weapons of warfare." The second use of
the word "yield" is in a tense different from that used in the
first occurrence of the word. The first time it is used in this
verse, it refers to habitual action, the second time, to an
act performed once for all. The translation reads, "Neither
keep on putting your members habitually at the service of
sin as weapons of unrighteousness, but put yourselves once
for all at the service of God as those who are living ones out
from among the dead, and put your members once for all
at the service of God as weapons of righteousness."

The Christian therefore never acts alone. He either acts
in the energy imparted by the evil nature, or in that imparted by the divine nature. He makes the choice. He need
not choose to obey the evil nature, for its power over him
is broken. The inclination of his power of choice is on the
side of the divine nature. As a child of God, his choices
naturally gravitate towards the latter. His responsibility is
to see that he keeps his power of choice in that direction.
Gradually, just as a tree bends with the prevailing winds,
so the will of a child of God bends more and more habitually and even automatically towards the divine nature and
the doing of the right and away from the doing of what is
wrong. That is what Paul refers to when he speaks of "the
good fight of faith." It is a constant battle to keep our
choices in the direction of the right and our faith in the
Lord Jesus for the divine enablement by which we are able
to do the right.

When we do this, we have God's promise that then sin
shall not have dominion over us: for we are not under law
but under grace. There is no article before "law" in the
original. We saints are not under law as an unsaved person

is with the obligation to obey a commandment which gives neither the desire nor the power for obedience. We are under grace, which sweetly exhorts to a holy life, and gives both the desire and the power necessary to live that life.

We come now to the second question, "What then? shall we sin, because we are not under the law but under grace?" It is the reaction to Paul's statement in 6:14, "Ye are not under the law, but under grace." But there is a difference in the way these two questions are put. In the first, the Greek text tells us that a life of habitual sin is referred to. In the second, the Greek tense indicates that occasional, infrequent, single acts of sin are spoken of. The thought in the speaker's mind is, "Since your doctrine of superabundant grace teaches the impossibility of a life of habitual sin on the part of the Christian, will the fact that a Christian is not under the uncompromising rule of law but under the lenient sceptre of grace, allow for at least an act of sin once in awhile?" The idea that grace is lenient as over against the uncompromising rule of law, is an erroneous one. The Holy Spirit dwelling in the heart of a child of God, is infinitely more cognizant of sin in the life of the saint than any system of law ever could be. He is grieved at the slightest sin. In the first question, the desperately wicked heart offers an excuse for sinning in that a life of habitual sin gives God an opportunity to display His grace and thus glorify Himself, which is of course a perversion of the teaching of grace. In the second question, this same person seeks a loophole somewhere in God's plan of salvation whereby he might sin once in awhile, and thinks that he has found one in the fact that the Christian is beyond the reach of the law of God which could condemn him. Therefore, he argues that he can sin with impunity, and grace will always forgive.

One can see at once from what Paul tells us in 6:1-14, that the person who asks such a question as well as the one

in 6:1, is an unregenerate sinner. O child of God has no desire to go on in habitual sin nor yet to sin once in awhile.
A Christian is at time guilty of wilful sin. That is, he may
yield to temptation, knowing that it is sin. But to provide
for a planned life of infrequent acts of sin, is altogether
foreign to the nature of the saint. Paul answers this question as he did the first one, by the words "God forbid," "far
be the thought." Then he uses an illustration to show that
it is a mechanical impossibility for a Christian to desire to
sin even once in awhile. The question is "What then? shall
we commit occasional acts of sin (as opposed to a life of
habitual sin) because we are not under law but under
grace?" The definite article does not appear before "law"
in the original. Law as a method of divine dealing is referred to.

Paul's second answer is, "Do ye not know that to whom
ye keep presenting yourselves for service as bondslaves resulting in your obedience (to that person), bondslaves ye
are to the one whom ye are obeying, whether it be bondslaves of sin resulting in death, or bondslaves of obedience
resulting in righteousness?" The word "servants" in the
A. V. does not adequately translate the full content of the
Greek word which Paul used. His first century reader understood the various implications of the word and therefore understood Paul's argument better.

In the first place, there are various Greek words which
refer to a slave. One speaks of a slave captured in war. Another refers to a person born into slavery. The latter word
is used here. The sinner by his first birth comes into this
world with a totally depraved nature which he inherited
through this first birth. This makes him a bondslave of
Satan, for this fallen nature causes him to love sin. When
he is born from above through the supernatural work of
the Holy Spirit in answer to his faith in the Lord Jesus as

his Saviour, he is given the divine nature which causes him to love the things of God, and thus he becomes a bondslave of Jesus Christ. Paul argues that because the believer has had his slavery transferred from one master to another, in that he has been given a nature that causes him to forsake his former master Satan and cleave to his new Master, the Lord Jesus, that it is both unreasonable and impossible for him to desire to serve his old master any more, even on infrequent occasions.

Another implication which the word had in the first century was that the slave is one bound to his master. The Christian before salvation, was bound to Satan by the shackles of sin. In his identification with Christ in His death, these shackles were stricken off, and in his participation with Christ in His resurrection, he was bound to his new Master, Christ. It is the nature of a slave to serve the master to whom he is bound, Paul argues. Thus, it is the nature of the Christian to serve Jesus Christ.

The word spoke of the slave as one whose will is swallowed up in the will of his master. Before salvation wrought its work in the believer, his will was swallowed up in the will of Satan (Eph. 2:1-3). His totally depraved nature bent his will always in that direction. But since God in salvation broke the power of that evil nature and thus released the believer's will from the control of the evil nature, and gave the believer the divine nature which at once inclined that liberated will toward God, the Christian's will is swallowed up in the sweet will of God. How unreasonable it is, Paul argues, to think that a Christian would want to sin even occasionally.

Again, the word referred to a slave who is devoted to the interests of his master to the extent that he disregards his own interests. Before salvation, the believer served Satan recklessly, and to the disregard of his own interests. All he received for his slavery was death. But now his slavery has been transferred. He serves Jesus Christ, his new Master, not counting the cost to himself. Do you think, Paul argues, that a bondslave who loves his Lord and Master that much, would presume upon His grace, and desire to commit an occasional act of sin? Paul argues therefore in verse 16 that to suggest that a child of God desires to commit an occasional sin, would necessitate his becoming a slave of Satan again, which is an impossibility since that would involve a change of nature brought about by his loss of the divine nature and his acquisition of the Adamic nature again. Because the divine nature is the eternal possession of the believer, and the Adamic nature could only be his through natural generation, it is impossible, Paul answers, for a believer to become a slave of Satan again, and therefore it is not possible for him to make provision for occasional acts of sin in his life.

And so Paul says in view of all this, "But God be thanked that ye were (but are not now) by nature bondslaves of sin, but ye obeyed from your heart that type of teaching to which ye were delivered." The definite article does not appear before "servants" in verse 17. The absence of the article qualifies. Emphasis is upon character, quality, or nature. Thus we translated, "by nature bondslaves of sin." That is, the quality or nature of the person made him a bondslave of sin. Regarding the translation "that type of teaching to which ye were delivered," we might say that while Paul's teaching to which he here refers, was given the Christians and thus could be said to have been delivered to them, yet the Greek verb here is passive, and speaks of the believer being delivered to the teaching. That is, Christians are so constituted that they naturally desire to obey the Word of God. They have in salvation been handed over to its obedience. Therefore, a child of God does not make provision for occasional acts of sin, since he has ceased being a slave of Satan, and he has been so constituted inwardly by God that he renders obedience from the heart, willingly, to the Word of God. Paul adds this word of explanation to what he said in verse 17, "Having been set free from sin, ye became slaves of righteousness."

Now, after having explained that the thought of occasional sin in the life of a child of God is not to be entertained for a moment, because the believer's slavery has been transferred from one master, Satan, to another Master, even the Lord Jesus, and this, because the believer has had the power of the indwelling sinful nature broken and the divine nature implanted, Paul proceeds to show the attitude which the believer should be careful to maintain with reference to his change of masters. Paul apologizes for using such a human illustration as slavery to explain one's former relationship to Satan and one's present relationship to God. But he says that he finds it necessary to do so because of their defective spiritual insight which in turn is due to certain moral defects. The translation reads: "I am using a human term of speech because of the weakness of your flesh, for even as ye put your members as slaves at the service of uncleanness and lawlessness resulting in an abiding state of lawlessness, so now put your members once for all as slaves at the service of righteousness resulting in holiness."

One might ask at this point, why such an exhortation is necessary if the power of the evil nature has been broken and the divine nature implanted, resulting in a transfer of affection to another Master, even the Lord Jesus? Why is it necessary for Paul to exhort believers to put themselves at the service of Christ, when they have a nature that impels them to do so? The answer is that the will of the believer, even though it is inclined in regeneration towards Christ and the doing of good, still has a certain bent at times to the doing of evil, the result of the habitual and constant inclination it had towards evil before grace did its work. The habits formed by years of sin must be overcome. That moral twist must be unbent. *The only way to do this is to form new habits of the will by keeping our choices inclined towards obedience to our new Master, Christ. The divine nature is there to keep our choices in line with the Word of God as we yield to the ministry of the Holy Spirit and trust Him to work in us, but we must ever be on the alert lest those habits formed by years of choosing the wrong, lead us to render obedience to our old master, Satan. As we establish new habits of choice, gradually our renewed wills are bent more and more in the direction of the good, and it becomes increasingly easier to do the right and increasingly harder to do the wrong.*

Then Paul reminds the believer of the wasted years spent in sin, with their evil consequences. "For when ye were slaves of sin, ye were free with respect to righteousness." That is, in our unsaved state, there was no restraint put upon sin in our lives by any righteousness we might have had, for we had none. And because there was no check upon sin that would restrain evil in our lives, sin ran rampant. The apostle reminds the believer: "Therefore what fruit were ye constantly having at that time? of which things now ye are ashamed? for the end of those things is death." Thus another reason is presented why the believer does not want even to provide for an occasional sin in his life. He is ashamed of the years which he spent in sin, and of the corruption it bred. And so Paul concludes his argument with the words: "But now having been made free from sin and having become bondslaves of God, ye are having your fruit resulting in holiness, and the end, eternal life. For the pay which sin doles out is death, but the free gift of God is life eternal in Jesus Christ our Lord."

Thus Paul answers the second question: "What then? shall we sin occasionally because we are not under law but under grace?" by asserting that that cannot be the desire of a child of God and cannot be a fact in his life, and for the reason that he has had his slavery transferred from Satan to the Lord Jesus, this act of transference having been accomplished by the breaking of the power of the evil nature, which nature caused the person to love to serve the Devil, and by the impartation of the divine nature which impels the believer to serve the Lord Jesus.

Thus God's grace not only justifies the believer, that is, takes away the guilt and penalty of sin and bestows a positive righteousness, even the Lord Jesus Himself in whom the believer stands perfectly righteous for time and eternity, but it sanctifies him, in that it breaks the power of sin in his life, and produces in him a life which glorifies God.

Dear Christian reader, if you have not been obtaining consistent victory over sin, will you not let this study of Romans VI point the way to the victorious life? There is victory for you when you understand and follow God's directions with regard to the correct technique of how to gain this victory.

XV.

How To Be Hungry

PETER is speaking in his first epistle (2:1-3) of the divine imperative which must be obeyed if we as Christians expect to have a real hunger for God's Word. The words "laying aside" are in the Greek, not a command, but a past once-for-all action. The idea is, "having laid aside once for all." It is the God-expected action of every believer. Until he has made a complete break with all sin in his life, he cannot expect to have a hunger for the Word of God. The reason for this is that he has filled his heart with the husks of the world. This not only destroys his appetite but perverts his taste. Peter here gives us the reason why so many children of God have so little hunger for the Word.

The Greek word translated "guile" means "to catch with bait." We are not to be crafty, sly, underhanded persons, but above-board, open, sincere, accomplishing our purposes by fair means. "Hypocrisies" is from a Greek word used in the first century of one who impersonates another. How we saints sometimes play the part of something that we are not. Our faces should be open, free from deception, shining with the beauty of the Lord Jesus. A mask of deception hides Him. "Evil speakings" is literally, "speaking down" another person, that is, slandering him. The words "as new-born babes," describe the spiritual status of those to whom Peter is writing. The idea is, "as just-born babes, they should have an intense hunger for the Word of God."

The word "desire" is emphatic in the Greek, referring to an intense desire.

"Sincere" is from the Greek word for "guile," with the Greek letter Alpha prefixed, which negates its meaning. The idea is "unadulterated." God's Word is not like so many human teachings, adulterated with some ulterior motive, but pure, unadulterated, its only purpose that of blessing the one who puts his faith in it. The words "of the word" are from an adjective in the Greek, meaning literally "spiritual." "Grow" is literally, "be nourished up." The best Greek texts add to verse two the words, "and thus make progress in your salvation."

"If so be," does not imply a doubt but a fulfilled condition. These saints had found the Lord gracious. The word "gracious" is from a Greek word found also in Luke 5:39 where it is translated "better." Literally it means "excellent."

The translation reads: "Therefore, now that you have laid aside once for all every kind of wickedness and every kind of trickery, also hypocrisies, and envies, and all kinds of slanders, as just born infants, long for with an intense yearning the spiritual unadulterated milk, in order that by it you might be nourished up and thus make progress in your salvation, in view of the fact that you tasted for yourselves and have found that the Lord is excellent."

Sin in the life destroys one's appetite for the Word of God. When sin is put away, the normal thing is an intense hunger for the Word. The result is that we feed our souls upon it and thus make progress in our salvation.

XVI.

The Four-Fold Basis of Christian Unity

THE exhortations in the Pauline epistles grew out of the conditions found in the churches to which they were addressed. Because fallen human nature has not changed in two thousand years, conditions that obtained during Paul's time are existent in the churches of today.

There were minor divisions in the Philippian church, that church which in such a marked way helped in Paul's support as a missionary. Two of these divisions centered about two women in the church who were capable and prominent leaders in its work, especially taking leadership in supporting Paul. These women led two factions which were at variance with one another. To bring them together would be to heal the breach, not only between them, but between those who followed them.

The exhortation in Philippians 4:2, 3, is not abrupt. Paul had prepared the way by laying a groundwork for it in 2:1-4, where we have detailed exhortation, and 2:5-8, where we have the great Example portrayed who in His life exemplified the one outstanding thing that will heal all such divisions in the local church, namely, a Christlike humility. In 2:1, Paul presents four things which constitute the basis for unity among the saints. These demand careful treatment in the original.

First of all, the word "if" does not present a doubt as to whether there is any consolation in Christ. The word in the Greek presents a fulfilled condition, a fact, not a hypothetical case. For instance, a person says, "If it rains tomorrow, I shall carry an umbrella." That is, "It looks like it may rain. If it does, then I shall be prepared." This "if" introduces a guess, something possible in the future. But the "if" Paul uses is: "You say that he is preaching the gospel? Well, if he is doing that, the Lord will certainly bless him." The word could be translated, "since," or "in view of the fact." It represents a fulfilled condition. Paul is therefore exhorting to unity among the saints in the Philippian church in view of the fact that certain things are facts.

The first fact he presents is that there is a certain consolation in Christ. The word "any" in our translation is from a Greek word which is used with nouns of persons or things concerning which the writer cannot or will not speak particularly. The word "certain" is a good rendering. "Consolation" is from a word which does not mean "to console" in the sense of giving comfort. What these Philippian saints needed was not consolation, but exhortation. And "exhortation" is exactly what the word means. This exhortation to unity is found in Christ. His beautiful life is itself the exhortation to unity which these saints needed. His humility as spoken of in 2:5-8, is the very thing that would lead to unity, since the basis of these divisions was pride. His life therefore was the ground of appeal which Paul used. "In view of the fact that there is a certain ground of appeal in Christ which exhorts you, . . . be likeminded." If all the saints would keep their eyes on the Lord Jesus, and walk in His footsteps of humility, divisions in a local church would cease.

The second reason why there should be unity among the saints is that there is a "certain comfort of love." The word "comfort" comes from a Greek word made up of the words "beside," and "word," the entire word meaning "a word which comes to the side of one to stimulate or comfort." It speaks of persuasive address. It could be translated by the words, "incentive," or "encouragement." The word has the added element of tenderness in it.

The word "love" is from the Greek word for "divine love," the love that God is, the love which He produces in the heart of the saint wholly given over to the ministry of the Holy Spirit. The grammatical construction in the Greek makes it clear that this incentive to unity is produced by love. That is, the love which the Holy Spirit produces in the heart of the saint, causes and enables that saint to love his fellow-saint, and where divine love is, there is unity. Thus, love produces the incentive to unity. If the saints in a local church would love each other with the self-sacrificial love of John 3:16, and the love as analyzed for us in I Corinthians 13, divisions would cease, and unity would prevail. The secret of the possession of this love is found in a desire for the fullness of the Holy Spirit, and a trust in the Lord Jesus for that fullness (John 7:37, 38).

The third reason why unity should prevail among the saints is that there is a "certain fellowship of the Spirit." This does not mean that there is a fellowship between the saint and the Holy Spirit. The fellowship of the saint is with the Father and with His Son Jesus Christ (I John 1:3; Eph. 3:16, 17) made possible through the ministry of the Holy Spirit. The word "fellowship" is from a Greek word which refers to a relation between individuals which involves a common interest and a mutual, active participation in that interest. Here it refers to the ministry of the Spirit in the life of the saint, and the cooperation of the saint with the Spirit in His work of causing him to grow in grace, this cooperation consisting of the saint's yieldedness to the Spirit and the act of his free will in choosing the right and doing it. This ministry of the Spirit enables the saint to live in unity with his fellow-saints.

The fourth reason why the saints should be likeminded is that there are "certain bowels and mercies." In the orient, they speak of the heart, lungs, and liver as the seat of the tenderer affections. The word is translated "bowels." The Greek language has another word for the intestines. This word "bowels" is used in the east as we use the word "heart." "Mercies" is from a word which literally means "compassionate yearnings and actions." When brethren in the Lord are tenderhearted toward one another, and have compassion upon one another, divisions will cease and unity will prevail.

The four things therefore which will make for unity in a local church are, first, the exhortation which our Lord's life provides, namely, that of a Christlike humility, second, the incentive to unity which divine love provides as this love is produced in the heart of the saint by the Holy Spirit, third, the fact that each saint possesses the indwelling Holy Spirit who if yielded to will control that saint, and fourth, the fact that if saints show tenderheartedness to and compassion for each other, unity will prevail.

The fuller translation is as follows: In view of the fact therefore that there is a certain ground of appeal in Christ which exhorts, in view of the fact that there is a certain tender incentive which is produced by love, in view of the fact that there is a certain joint-participation with the Spirit in a common interest and activity, in view of the fact that there are certain tenderheartednesses and compassionate yearnings, fill full my joy by thinking the same thing, by having the same love, by being in heart-agreement, by thinking the one thing.

XVII.

The Meaning of "PERFECT" in the New Testament

THE Greek New Testament is the indispensable authority in cases where a wrong interpretation is put upon a word in a translation. The word "perfect" is frequently used in the meaning of "sinless." The easiest and most satisfactory way to settle the question of the meaning of this word when it is found in the New Testament, is to inquire into the usage of the Greek word of which it is the translation.

Moulton and Milligan in their *Vocabulary of the Greek Testament* which is based upon a study of the secular manuscripts using the same kind of Greek found in the New Testament, give the following uses of the word *teleios,* which is the word translated "perfect." It is found in the phrases "to her heirs being *of age;* all proving that women who have attained *maturity* are mistresses of their persons and can remain with their husbands or not as they choose; four *full-grown* cocks;" the italicised words being the translation of the Greek word *teleios.* From these illustrations of its use, we would define the word as meaning "full-grown mature." They report these instances also; "fourteen acacia trees in *good condition;* four cocks in *perfect condition;* a *complete* lampstand; in *good working order or condition;* one *perfect* Theban mill." In the case of the chickens it means "soundness, freedom from sickness and physical defect." In the case of the mill, it describes it as being in good working order and condition, that is, in such condition that the desired results would be obtained when it is operated. In the case of the lampstand, it speaks of the fact that all necessary parts are included. To summarize; the meaning of the word includes the ideas of "full-growth, maturity, workability, soundness, and completeness." In the pagan Greek mystery religions, the word referred to those devotees who were fully instructed as opposed to those who were novices.

Thayer in his *Lexicon of the Greek New Testament* gives the following meanings; *brought to its end, finished, wanting nothing necessary to completeness;* when used of men it means *full-grown, adult, of full age, mature.*

Now, we will look at some instances where Paul uses this Greek word in a context which defines it by contrast with another word. The words "full age" (Heb. 5:14) are from *teleios* which is set in contrast to the word "babe" (Heb. 5:13). The word "babe" is from *nepios,* a Greek word meaning "an infant, a little child, a minor, not of age," and in a metaphorical sense, "untaught, unskilled." The idea of immaturity is in the word, and according to the context in which it is found, it could refer to either mental or spiritual immaturity. Paul defines the word when he says that the person whom he calls a babe is "unskillful in the word of righteousness." Spiritual immaturity is referred to by the word "babe." Thus those spoken of as of full age are spiritually mature. The word *teleios* therefore when used of a Christian, describes him as spiritually mature.

Paul writes the Corinthians that he speaks wisdom among those who are perfect (I Cor. 2:6), and uses *teleios*. But he says that he could not speak to them as to spiritual Christians, but as to carnal ones, namely, babes in Christ (I Cor. 3:1). In passing, it might be well to note that the phrase "babes in Christ" as Paul uses it in the Greek, does not mean "young converts," but "Christians who have not attained to a mature Christian experience." It is a sad thing to see one who has been a Christian for many years and who is still a babe in Christ, immature. Here we have the same contrast which we found in the Hebrew passage, between *teleios* "perfect," that is, mature, and *nepios,* "babe," immature. Paul makes it clear that he is speaking of maturity and immaturity in spiritual things when he uses the word "spiritual" in 3:1 as describing the person in 2:6 who was spoken of as "perfect." Thus, the word "perfect" when used to describe a Christian means "spiritually mature."

In Ephesians 4:13, 14, we have the same contrast between a perfect (*teleios*) man and children (*nepios*). But *teleios* has an added shade of meaning here. Not only does it refer to spiritual maturity by its contrast to *nepios* which speaks of spiritual immaturity, but it speaks also of completeness. This latter shade of meaning comes from the words in the context, "the measure of the stature of the fulness of Christ." The word "completeness" speaks of a well-rounded Christian character, where the Christian graces are kept in proper balance. For instance, a Christian who has much zeal but little wisdom to guide that zeal into its proper channels and restrain it when necessary, is not a well balanced Christian, and not spiritually mature.

We come now to Paul's use of *teleios* and the verb of the same root *teleioo* in Philippians 3:12-15, which passage in the English translation (Authorized Version) involves a contradiction because the meaning of the tense of the verb could not be fully and clearly brought out in a translation such as the Authorized which is held down to a minimum of words. In 3:12, Paul states that he is not yet perfect. In 3:15, he urges those of the Philippian saints who are perfect to be "thus minded," namely, to account themselves as not yet perfect. How are we to understand this? Surely, the inspired Apostle does not ask them to deny the reality of something which they know to be a fact. The Greek solves the difficulty presented in the English.

The words "were already perfect" are from a word meaning "already" and the verb *teleioo* which means "to bring to the state of spiritual maturity." This verb is in the perfect tense which speaks of an action that was completed in past time, having results that exist in present time. The past completed action of this verb would refer to the process of sanctification, namely, the work of the Holy Spirit bringing the saint to that place of spiritual maturity in which the sanctifying process would have done its work so well that nothing needed to be added. In other words, the saint would be brought to a place of absolute spiritual maturity beyond which there is no room for growth. Furthermore, the results of this work would be permanent, and there would be no possibility of slipping back into a state of spiritual immaturity again. All this is involved in Paul's use of this tense. That Paul deliberately used this tense is clearly seen from the fact that the tense he used in the previous verb is the aorist, which is the customary tense used by the Greek when he desires merely to refer to a fact without referring to details. Whenever a Greek uses any other tense, he goes out of his way to do so. It is a sign that he wishes to refer to that fact in detail and for a certain purpose. When Paul says, "Not as though I . . . were already perfect," he means that the Holy Spirit had not yet brought him to the place in his Christian life where His sanctifying work was no longer needed, in other words, to the place of absolute spiritual maturity from which place there was no possibility of slipping back to a condition of spiritual immaturity, and beyond which there was no room for growth.

Then he exhorts those among the Philippian saints who were spiritually mature, to take the same attitude towards their own growth in grace. And here he uses the word *teleios* in a noun form, and in a relative sense. That is, a Christian is spiritually mature if he is not *nepios,* a babe. Just as an adult becomes more mature as he grows older and wiser, so a child of God grows in degrees of spiritual maturity. But he must ever realize that he will never be spiritually mature in an absolute sense, that is, come to the place where he cannot grow in the Christian life. He must always realize how far short he comes of absolute Christlikeness, what an infinite distance there is between the most Christlike saint and the Lord Jesus.

Thus, the contradiction in the English translation is cleared up by the Greek text. In 3:12, Paul is speaking of absolute spiritual maturity, in 3:15, of relative spiritual maturity. In 3:12, he is speaking of a process that had reached a state of completion. In 3:15, he refers to a process that was still going on. In 3:12, he denies having reached the place in his Christian life where there was no more improvement possible. In 3:15, he speaks of the constant need of growth in the Christian life. In 3:12 he denies being spiritually mature in an absolute sense. In 3:15, he asserts that as a spiritually mature Christian, he sees a need of more maturity in his spiritual experience.

It remains for us to trace briefly the use of *teleios* in the other passages where it occurs. In Matthew 5:48, the word implies growth into maturity of godliness on the part of the believer. The word when used here of God the Father does not refer to His sinlessness, but to His kindness, as the context points out, thus to His character. In Matthew 19:21, that spiritual maturity is meant which is the result and accompaniment of a self-sacrificial character. In Romans 12:2, it describes the will of God as a will that lacks nothing necessary to completeness. In I Corinthians 13:10, the word means "complete," and is contrasted to that which is incomplete. In I Corinthians 14:20, "be ye children," is from our word *nepios* which means "immaturity," while "men" is our word *teleios*, which here speaks of spiritual maturity. In Colossians 1:28, Paul's desire is to present the saints to whom he ministers as spiritually mature believers. Epaphras (Col. 4:12) prays that the Colossian saints might be spiritually mature believers. In Hebrews 9:11, the tabernacle of the New Testament in heaven is said to be more complete than the tabernacle which Moses built, for the latter lacked what the former has, the out-poured blood of Christ.

In James 1:4, 17, 25, *teleios* means "wanting nothing to completeness." In 3:2, it speaks of spiritual maturity. In I John 4:18 we have, "love that is wanting nothing necessary to completeness, casteth out fear." We have treated every occurrence of the word *teleios* in the New Testament. There are two places where *teleiotes* is used. In Colossians 3:12-14, the believer is exhorted to put on the Christian graces mentioned, as one puts on a garment. Then over all these he is put on charity (love, God's love supplied by the Holy Spirit, Gal. 5:22). The word "which" does not go back to "love," as the Greek indicates, but refers to the act of "putting on." That is, the act of putting on love as a garment over these other virtues, completes and keeps together all the rest, which, without it, are but the scattered elements of *teleiotes*, "perfectness" or "completeness." These other virtues are manifestations of love, but may be exhibited where love is absent. They are worthwhile only when permeated with divine love. Thus, this putting on of love makes for perfection in the sense of completeness of Christian character. Love is the binding factor which binds together our Christian garments as would a girdle. In Hebrews 6:1, this word refers to that which is complete, wanting nothing necessary to completeness, here the New Testament as contrasted to the incomplete First Testament consisting of animal sacrifices.

It remains for us to look at the places where the word "perfect" appears in the translation of the verb *teleioo*. In Luke 13:32, "today, tomorrow and the third day" is an expression used to designate a short while. "Perfected" here is used in the same sense as in Hebrews 2:10. In His death on the Cross, Jesus was made complete as the Saviour. In John 17:23 "made perfect" is to be understood in the sense of "brought to a state of completeness." The word "one" refers to the unity into which believers are brought by the fact that the Lord Jesus is in each saint. In being united together by the indwelling Christ, believers are in that state of completeness with reference to their salvation which would not be true of them if Christ were not in them. In II Corinthians 12:9, Paul's strength is brought to such a state by the power of the Holy Spirit that it is lacking nothing necessary to completeness. In Hebrews 2:10 and 5:9, the Lord Jesus through His death on the Cross was made perfect in that He was made complete as a Saviour; in 7:19 the Mosaic economy brought nothing to completeness in that it could not offer a sacrifice that could pay for sin. In Hebrews 9:9 and 10:1, we are told that the Levitical sacrifices could not make believers perfect, while in 10:14 and 12:23, we find that the New Testament sealed in Jesus' blood does.

In Hebrews 9:9, "make perfect as pertaining to the conscience," refers to the inability of the typical sacrifices themselves to bring the believer's conscience to a state of completeness in the sense that they could not "put his moral-religious consciousness in its inward feeling into a state of entire and joyful looking for of salvation so that his conscience should be an onward-waxing consciousness of perfect restoration, of entire clearing up, of total emancipation, of his relation to God" (Alford). The words "make perfect as pertaining to the conscience," therefore, refer to that work of God in salvation that is a complete work in the believer's conscience. "Abraham rejoiced to see my day," means that he rejoiced to see in the future of God's prophetic program, the death and resurrection of Messiah. The very fact of the constant repetition of the sacrifices showed him that sin had not yet been actually paid for. Thus believers under the First Testament sacrifices never had that sense of completeness in which there was nothing lacking that was necessary (Heb. 10:1). But our Lord on the Cross cried, "It stands completed," using the word *teleioo*, referring to His work of salvation wrought out on the Cross (John 19:30). Thus, believers today have that complete sense of forgiveness which was lacking in the Old Testament saints (Heb. 10:14). Abraham had righteousness reckoned to him, that is, put to his account. But he did not possess it as the believer does today. Therefore, he was not as complete in salvation as we are. He received that righteousness actually in his identification with Christ in His resurrection.

In Hebrews 12:23 we have "the spirits of just men made perfect." The Greek shows that it is the men who are made perfect. These are saints in heaven, made perfect in the sense that they have been brought to that spiritual maturity which is the result of sufferings, trials, of having run and ended their race. "All is accomplished, their probation, their righteousness, God's purposes respecting them." There is a completeness about them that is lacking in the saints yet on earth.

In James 2:22, Abraham's works made his faith perfect in the sense that it made that faith a complete faith. There is an intellectual assent which is not a complete saving faith (James 2:19). But in order for faith to issue in good works, it must be a faith that is the heart's submission to God. Abraham's obedience to God in preparing to sacrifice his son Isaac, drew out of his heart a faith that submitted to God's will. Thus his faith was made complete, lacking nothing necessary to a state of completeness. In I John 2:5 we have "in him verily is the love of God brought to a state of completeness." The word has the same meaning in 4:12, 17. In 4:18 we translate, "He that feareth is not brought to the state of spiritual maturity in the sphere of love."

XVIII.

About Anointing

THERE are two Greek words, both meaning "to anoint," and as used in the New Testament, referring to different kinds of anointing, and for different purposes. These are translated by the one English word "anoint." In order to arrive at a full-orbed accurate interpretation of the passages in which the word "anoint" occurs, it is necessary to know what Greek word lies back of the English translation.

One word is *aleipho*. The non-literary manuscripts of the early centuries give us some instances of its use as seen in the following examples: "which you will carefully grease," spoken of a yoke-band; a man whose wife had gone away, writes to her that since they had bathed together a month before, he had never bathed or anointed himself; an inscription in honor of a gymnasiarch, namely, the head of a gymnasium, does him honor as the "much-honored anointer." In the first case, the word is used of the action of applying grease to the yoke-band, the purpose of which was to keep it from chafing the ox. In the other two instances, it referred to the practice, common in the orient, of giving the body an olive-oil massage. Olive-oil was used in the east for medicinal and remedial purposes in the case of illness. It provided an excellent rub-down for the tired athlete after exercise. It prevented skin dryness in the hot dry climate of the orient.

We see this use of the word *aleipho* in Mark 6:13 and James 5:14, where the word is used of the application of oil for medicinal purposes. Thus we find in the latter text, the two God-appointed resources in the case of illness, prayer and medical help. It is also used of the application of ointment. A passage in Xenophon speaks of the greater suitableness of oil for the men and of ointment for women, saying that the latter are better pleased that the men should savour of the manly oil than the effeminate ointment. The ointment had oil for its base, but differed from the common oil in that it was highly scented. We can better understand the words of our Lord to the discourteous Pharisee (Luke 7:46), "My head with oil thou didst not anoint: but this woman hath anointed my feet with ointment." It was as if He said, "Thou withheldest from Me cheap and ordinary courtesies; while she bestowed upon Me costly and rare homages" (Trench). The Pharisee withheld from our Lord the courtesy of common oil for His head, that same anointing oil which the hypocrites denied themselves (Matt. 6:17). The woman anointed His tired, parched feet with the expensive, highly fragrant ointment which she as a woman naturally possessed, rather than with the anointing oil used commonly by men. The same precious ointment was used by Mary of Bethany (John 11:2, 12:3), and by the women at the tomb (Mark 16:1). How the fragrance of that ointment which permeated the room, spoke of the heavenly fragrance of the one Man among all men who combined in His wonderful Person and in most delicate balance, the gentleness of womanhood and the strength and virility of manhood, without either one detracting from the other. In the Septuagint, the Greek translation of the Old Testament, *aleipho* is the usual word for anointing with oil for either of the above purposes, although the other word for "anoint" is used in Amos 6:6. It is used in Ruth 3:3; II Samuel 12:20, 14:2; Daniel 10:3; Micah 6:15. *Aleipho* is the only word used for anointing with oil in the New Testament, there being no exceptions to this.

The other word used in the New Testament is *chrio*. It is never used here in connection with oil, but uniformly of the anointing with the Holy Spirit, although in the secular documents it had the same meaning as *aleipho*. *Chrio* is used in "The Spirit of the Lord is upon me, for he hath anointed me" (Luke 4:18), a quotation from Isaiah 61:1, where the same Greek word appears in the Septuagint translation. It is used in Acts 4:27, 10:38, of the anointing of our Lord with the Holy Spirit. In II Corinthians 1:21 the word is used in connection with the anointing of the believer with the Spirit. Hebrews 1:9 presents a seeming deviation of the rule that *chrio* is never used in the New Testament in connection with the anointing with oil. We have "God hath anointed thee (the Lord Jesus) with the oil of gladness," and *chrio* is used. How true the inspired writer was to the genius of the two words as they are used in the New Testament, for the word "oil" here does not refer to literal oil, but is symbolic of the Holy Spirit. In I John 2:20, 27, "unction" and "anointing" are from the noun form that comes from *chrio,* and refer to the anointing of the believer with the Holy Spirit.

Chrio is the usual word in the Septuagint of the anointing of the priests and kings at their induction into office. The anointing is with oil, but this oil is symbolic of the anointing of the Spirit, not for medicinal purposes. *Aleipho* is used in Exodus 40:15, which speaks of the anointing of the priest, and its usage here is an exception to the usual practice. The priest was anointed once only, at the time of his induction into the priest's office, the anointing being symbolic of a reality, the anointing with the Holy Spirit who by His presence with him, equipped the priest for his service. Believers in this Christian era are priests in the

New Testament sense. They are anointed with the Holy Spirit once and once only, at the moment they are saved. This anointing is the coming of the Spirit to take up His permanent residence in their hearts, thus providing the potential equipment for their service as priests. The baptism by the Spirit is for the introduction of the believer into the Body of Christ, the anointing with the Spirit is His coming to dwell in the Christian, and the fullness of the Spirit is for power for service.

XIX.

Two Kinds of Testings

THERE are two words in the Greek New Testament both meaning "to test." It is important in the interests of accurate interpretation, to distinguish between them, since they refer to different kinds of testings.

One is *dokimazo*. We will look at some instances of its use in the early manuscripts. These are of great help in the forming of an accurate judgment as to the usages of New Testament words, since an illustration is often clearer than a definition. The word is used in a manuscript of A.D. 140 which contains a plea for the exemption of physicians, and especially of those who have passed the examination. The words, "passed the examination" are the translation of *dokimazo*. From this we arrive at the definition. The word refers to the act of testing someone or something for the purpose of approving it. These physicians had passed their examinations for the degree of Doctor of Medicine. In the inscriptions, the word is almost a technical term for passing as fit for a public office. It is found in the sentence, "Whichever way, then, you also *approve* of, so it shall be," and in the phrase, "To instruct, if you will, the strategus or any other magistrate whom you may *sanction*."* The words "approve" and "sanction" are the translations of *dokimazo*.

The word has in it the idea of proving a thing whether it be worthy to be received or not. In classical Greek, it is

_____
Moulton and Milligan.

the technical word for putting money to the test. In the New Testament almost always it implies that the proof is victoriously surmounted. The word further implies that the trial itself was made in the expectation and hope that the issue would be such. At all events, there was no contrary hope or expectation.

The other word is *peirazo*. The word meant in the first place "to pierce, search, attempt." Then it came to mean "to try or test intentionally, and with the purpose of discovering what good or evil, what power or weakness, was in a person or thing." But the fact that men so often break down under this test, gave *peirazo* a predominant sense of putting to the proof with the intention and the hope that the one put to the test may break down under the test. Thus the word is used constantly of the solicitations and suggestions of Satan.

Dokimazo is used generally of God, but never of Satan, for Satan never puts to the test in order that he may approve. *Peirazo* is used at times of God, but only in the sense of testing in order to discover what evil or good may be in a person.

The English reader can see from this study that it is important that one recognize the difference in these words which both mean "to test," especially when one learns that they have the same translation in some parts of the New Testament. For instance, *dokimazo* occurs in Luke 14:19 and *peirazo* in John 6:6, and yet the one English word "prove" is the translation. The man who bought the oxen went to examine them, not for the purpose of discovering what their good points might be or whether they had any defects. He bought them for sound, healthy stock, and fully expecting that they were what the seller represented them to be, he merely went to put his approval upon what he had bought. That is *dokimazo*. When our Lord propounded the question to Philip, "Whence shall we buy bread, that these may eat?" He was testing him to discover what faith or lack of faith, what clear spiritual insight or lack of it, what natural or supernatural view, that apostle might have. The test brought out what was in Philip's thinking. He was reasoning along a naturalistic plane. That is *peirazo*. These two words are translated by the one English word "try" in Revelation 2:2 and I Corinthians 3:13. At the Judgment Seat of Christ, the believer's service will be tested, not for the purpose of finding out what good or evil there was in it, but to put God's approval upon that part of it which was the work of the Holy Spirit. A "Well done thou good and faithful servant . . . enter thou into the joy of thy Lord" (Matt. 25:23), and a reward in addition to those blessed words, are awaiting every believer in the Lord Jesus, for God will put His approval upon the Spirit-wrought works of the saints and reward them. It is precious to note that *dokimazo* is used here, not *peirazo*. The believer's works are not up for judgment with a penalty attached for those works not done in the power of the Holy Spirit. These latter works will be burned up, and the believer will lose the reward he would have received had they been done in the power of the Spirit. The Judgment Seat of Christ is not for the judgment of the believer himself, and certainly not for his retention or loss of salvation. It is not *peirazo*, to discover what evil or good there may be. It is *dokimazo*, to examine in order to approve. God expects to find that in the service of the saint upon which He can put His approval, for the Holy Spirit produces good works in all the saints (Eph. 2:10), more in those who are definitely subjected to His control.

In the case of the Church at Ephesus (Rev. 2:2) "trying" those who came to it representing themselves as apostles, we have *peirazo*. The Church was suspicious of these strangers. It had no reason to believe that it would find in these men that upon which it could put its approval. Thus *dokimazo* is not used here. The Church put these men to the test, that is, examined them to see what good or evil there was in them, intending to accept them if good, but to reject them if evil. They found them to be liars.

Both words are translated "examine" in I Corinthians 11:28 and II Corinthians 13:5. In the former passage, it is expected that the believer partake of the bread and wine at the Lord's table only when he can approve his life after having examined himself. If he finds nothing between him and his Saviour, then he is in an approved state, eligible to observe the Lord's Supper. This is *dokimazo*. In the second passage, the members of the Corinthian assembly are exhorted to examine themselves to see whether they are true believers or not. This is in accord with the meaning of *peirazo*, namely, that of finding out what there is of good or evil in a person. If the examination showed that they were true believers *peirazo*, then they could "prove" themselves, that is, put their approval upon that fact, the word "prove" being the translation of *dokimazo*. We will now list the places where each word is found, and study a few representative passages, leaving for the reader the delightful task of looking into the other instances of their use in the light of the distinctive meanings of each word.

Dokimazo is found in the following places and is translated by the words "discern, prove, did like, approve, try, examine, allow;" Luke 12:56, 14:19; Romans 1:28; 2:18, 12:2, 14:22; I Corinthians 3:13, 11:28, 16:3; II Corinhtians 8:8, 22, 13:5 ("prove"), Galatians 6:4; Ephesians 5:10; Philippians 1:10; I Thessalonians 2:4, 5:21; I Timothy 3:10; Hebrews 3:9; I Peter 1:7; I John 4:1. In Luke 12:56, the hypocrites could examine the weather conditions and put their approval upon them, but they were unable to understand the propitious character of the coming of Messiah to Israel, and then put their approval upon it. In Romans 1:28, lost humanity after scanning Deity for the purpose of putting its approval upon Him, did not find anything in or about Him that met with its approval, a sad commentary upon the total depravity of the human heart. In Romans 14:22 we have, "Spiritually prosperous is he who does not condemn himself in the thing which after having examined, he has put his approval upon." In I Thessalonians 2:4, Paul says that after God examined him, He put His approval upon him as one worthy to be entrusted with the gospel, the words "allowed" and "trieth" being from *dokimazo*. The other occurrences of *dokimazo* are translated by the words "prove, try, and examine," and the English reader should have no difficulty with them.

We come now to the places where *peirazo* is used, and where it is translated by the words "tempt, try, hath gone about, assayed." The word is found in Matthew 4:1, 3, 7, 16:1, 19:3, 22:18, 35; Mark 1:13, 8:11, 10:2, 12:15; Luke 4:2, 11:16, 20:23; John 6:6, 8:6; Acts 5:9, 15:10; 16:7, 24:6; I Corinthians 7:5, 10:9, 13; II Corinthians 13:5; Galatians 6:1; I Thessalonians 3:5; Hebrews 2:18, 3:9, 4:15, 11:17, 37; James 1:13, 14; Revelation 2:2, 10, 3:10. We will look at some representative passages. In Matthew 4:1, our Lord was led by the Holy Spirit into the wilderness to be tested by the Devil, the test being in the form of solicitations to do evil. In Matthew 4:7 our Lord said to Satan, "It stands written, Thou shalt not put the Lord thy God to the test" (to see what good or evil there may be in Him) The word does not mean here "to solicit to do evil." In Matthew 22:18, our Lord asks the hypocrites why they are putting Him to the test. Such an action on the part of man with relation to God always shows a state of unbelief. The words "hath gone about" in Acts 24:6 are from *peirazo*.

Paul was charged with bringing Greeks into the temple at Jerusalem, making a test-case of his action, possibly to show that Gentiles in this Age of Grace were not only admitted into salvation along with Israel, and were members of the same Body, but that they also had equal access to the Jewish temple along with the Jews. The charges of course were false, but they show the Jewish attitude towards Paul's ministry to the Gentiles. In I Corinthians 10:13, the word "tempted" refers to any test which Satan may put before us, the purpose of which is of course to bring out evil in our lives if he can, as in the case of Job, or a direct solicitation to do evil, as in the case of Israel as seen in the context. In Hebrews 11:17, Abraham when he was tried, that is, put to the test by God to see whether his faith would surmount the obstacle of the loss of his son, met the test, thus demonstrating his faith. The word *peirazo* is found in the Septuagint translation of the Old Testament passage reporting this incident, and is translated "tempted." In James 1:13, 14, the word "tempted" is to be understood as "solicit to do evil." God at times does test man in order to show man his sinfulness and develop his character (James 1:2, 12), but He never solicits man to do evil.

With the aid of this preliminary study, the student of the English Bible is equipped to study for himself in the light of the Greek text, all the texts in the New Testament using the words *dokimazo* and *peirazo*.

INDEX OF SCRIPTURE REFERENCES

INDEX OF SCRIPTURE REFERENCES—Continued

INDEX OF SCRIPTURE REFERENCES—Continued

Untranslatable Riches
From the Greek New Testament

DEDICATED

To John Adams Scott, Ph.D., LL.D., valiant
defender of the Faith once for all delivered to
the saints, my honored and beloved professor,
who during student days at Northwestern University introduced me to the study of this most
wonderful of all languages, and whose life,
scholarship, and encouraging letters have been
a constant source of inspiration all
down the years.

PREFACE

When one has read all the various translations, each of which brings out some different shade of meaning from the inexhaustible richness of the Greek text, there still remains a large untranslatable wealth of truth to which only a Greek student has access. The reason for this is that in a translation which keeps to a minimum of words, that is, where one English word for instance, is the translation of one Greek word, it is impossible for the translator to bring out all the shades of meaning of the Greek word. It sometimes requires ten or a dozen words to give a well-rounded, full-orbed concept of the Greek word.

For instance, the words "thankworthy" and "acceptable" in I Peter 2:19, 20 are the translation of a Greek word which means, "that which is beyond the ordinary course of what might be expected, and is therefore commendable." Here sixteen words are needed to bring out the total meaning of the one Greek word. What we have in our Authorized Version is an excellent "one-word" translation, and correct. But one misses some of the richness that lies hidden beneath the English word. Again, no translation can bring to the English reader the fact that this Greek word is the one translated "grace" when the writer is speaking of God's grace. And no translation can bring out the richness of meaning in the Greek word "grace" as it was used even in pagan Greece.

Or, take the case of the two words translated "love" in I Peter 1:22, the first one meaning "a love that is called out of one's heart by the pleasure one finds in the object loved, and which is non-ethical in its nature, an affection, a liking for someone or something," the second, meaning "a love called out of one's heart because of the preciousness of the object loved, and which is sacrificial in its nature, a love conferring blessings upon the object loved." In the first instance, it takes thirty-three words, most of which would appear in a translation that would do justice to the total meaning of the word, to translate the word adequately, and in the second case, thirty words. The single word "love" used to translate these two different Greek words, is a correct rendering and perfectly proper in the ordinary translation. But the English reader would never suspect that there was so much rich material still in the Greek text.

This is the justification for such a book as *Untranslatable Riches from the Greek New Testament for the English Reader* and its three companion volumes, *Golden Nuggets from the Greek New Testament for the English Reader*, *Bypaths in the Greek New Testament for the English Reader*, and *Treasures from the Greek New Testament for the English Reader*. Where a Greek word treated in this book is presented in a fuller or complete way or in its every occurrence in the New Testament in the other volumes, a footnote will direct the Bible student to the page or pages where the material can be found. Thus, the reader can make a further study of the word should he so desire.

The indexes of all four books are presented in one index in *Untranslatable Riches*, thus enabling the student of the English Bible to quickly find the material he wishes. The four volumes can thus be used as a reference work. The English reader with no knowledge of the Greek can obtain help from the Greek text in the case of approximately 1150 places treated in these books.

K. S. W.

CONTENTS

Chapter I

PAUL'S DOCTRINE OF VERBAL INSPIRATION

THE classic passage on this subject (I Cor. 2:9-16) was written to a racial group that stands out in history as the most intellectual of all peoples, the Greeks. They were a race of creative thinkers. The sole instrument which they used in their attempt to pierce through the mysteries of existence was human reason. This they sharpened to a keen edge. But it was inadequate to solve the great mysteries of origins, of the wherefore of human existence, of God, and of evil. Plato, one of their great philosophers, said, "We must lay hold of the best human opinion in order that borne by it as on a raft, we may sail over the dangerous sea of life, unless we can find a stronger boat, *or some sure word of God,* which will more surely and safely carry us." This great philosopher acknowledged that mere human reason was not sufficient to answer the riddles with which man is confronted, and that the only sure foundation for a system of religious truth was, not even the best of human opinion, but a revelation from God.

The man who wrote this passage, declaring to these intellectuals that the Bible has come, not from human reason, but by divine revelation, was himself trained in their schools. He was a native of Tarsus, a city where Greek culture predominated. The University of Tarsus was known all over the world. Strabo placed it ahead of the universities of Athens and Alexandria in its zeal for learning. Paul's people were Roman citizens, and also citizens of Tarsus, which latter fact tells us that his family was one of wealth and standing, for during the time of Paul, only people of wealth and standing in the community were allowed to possess Tarsian citizenship. This

13

explains Paul's statement, "I have suffered the loss of all things" (Phil. 3:8). The city was noted for its intense activity, its atmosphere of what we today call "drive." Paul was not reared in the lassitude and ease of an oriental city, but in an atmosphere of physical and mental achievement. That he had a thorough training in the University of Tarsus is evident from his words to the Corinthians: "And I having come to you, brethren, came, not having my message dominated by a transcendent rhetorical display or by philosophical subtlety . . . and my message and my preaching were not couched in specious words of philosophy" (I Cor. 2:1, 4). He could have used these had he wanted to. He was schooled in Greek rhetoric, philosophy, and sophistry, also in Greek literature. Thus in giving the Greeks his teaching of verbal inspiration, Paul was not looking at the subject from only one angle, that of a mystic who knew what fellowship with God was, and who had received communications from God, but he had had the other side of the problem in the Greek university, where he was brought into contact with human reason at its best.

He begins the treatment of his subject by telling the Greeks that neither scientific investigation nor human reason has ever been able to discover a sure foundation upon which a religious system could be built. He says, "Eye hath not seen, nor ear heard, . . . the things which God hath prepared for them that love him." The context makes it clear that these "things" consist of the revelation of truth, the holy Scriptures. But not only has scientific investigation never discovered this truth, but this truth has not been produced by the activity of man's reason, for he said, "neither have entered the heart of man." The Greek word translated "entered," does not refer to something entering the mind from the outside, but was used of things that come up in one's mind. We use the expression today, "It never entered my mind," meaning by that that the thing never occurred to us. Thus we have the statement of Paul that the truth of Scripture never arose in the consciousness of man, never found its source in the reason of man. Observe the bearing this has upon teaching that finds its basis in the theory of evolution, teaching to the effect that all that the human race knows is the result of divinity resident in man, and that therefore, all knowledge has come from within the race, none from without. After asserting the fact of the final inadequacy of reason in solving the riddle of existence, Paul proceeds to describe the three successive steps in the transmission of truth from the heart of God to the heart of man. These are, *revelation*, the act of God the Holy Spirit imparting to the Bible writers, truth incapable of being discovered by man's unaided reason (2:10-12): *inspiration*, the act of God the Holy Spirit enabling the Bible writers to write down in God-chosen words, infallibly, the truth revealed (2:13): and *illumination*, the act of God the Holy Spirit enabling believers to understand the truth given by *revelation* and written down by *inspiration* (2:14-16).

We will deal first with *revelation*. The first word in our English translation in verse nine, Authorized Version, is "but," and is the translation of the strong adversative particle in the Greek. But the first word in verse ten should not be "but," but "for," since the Greek word here is not adversative but explanatory. Paul explains that the Bible did not come by the way of scientific investigation and human reason, but that it came in another way, by revelation. Then he shows that the very fact that God gave this truth by revelation proves that in the nature of things it could not have been given in any other way, and proceeds in verse eleven to show that this is true. The word "revealed" is the translation of a Greek word which means "to uncover, to lay open what has been veiled or covered up." The word "us" refers to the Bible writers, for Paul is explaining to the Greeks his knowledge of the truth. The Holy Spirit who searches the deep things of God, uncovered this truth to the vision of these men.

Then Paul by the use of pure logic proves to these Greeks the impossibility of discovering God's Word through scientific investigation or human reason. The word "man" in the Greek is not the word which refers to an individual male member of the human race, but is the generic term for man, which includes individuals of both sexes. The second use of the word "man" is accompanied by the definite article which in Greek points out individuality. Thus, our translation is, "For who is there of men who knows the things of the (individual) man." That is, no individual knows the inner thoughts and heart-life of another person. Man is inscrutable to his fellowman.

The word "spirit" in the Greek refers here to the rational spirit, the power by which a human being feels, thinks, wills, and decides. Again, the word "man" in the phrase, "save the spirit of man," is preceded by the article. The Greek article originally came from the demonstrative pronoun, and it retains much of the demonstrative's force of pointing out. Therefore, we translate, "For who is there of men who knows the things of the (individual) man except the spirit of (that) man which is in him." Only the individual knows what is in his heart of hearts. To his fellow-man he is inscrutable.

Just so, Paul says, logic will lead us to the conclusion that if a man is inscrutable to his fellow-man, so God must be inscrutable to man. And just as only the individual person knows what is in *his* own heart, so only God knows what is in *His* own heart. Therefore, if man finds it impossible through scientific investigation and human reason to discover the inner secrets of his fellow-man, it is clear that he cannot find out the mind of God by the same methods. The only way in which a person can come to know the inner heart-life of another person is to have that person uncover the secrets of his inner life to him. It likewise follows that the only way in which a person can know the mind of God is to have God uncover His thoughts to man. Thus Paul has demonstrated to these Greeks the absolute need of a revelation from God if we are to know what is in His heart. The first step therefore, in the transmission of truth from the heart of God to the heart of the believer is *revelation*, the act of God the Holy Spirit uncovering the things in the heart of God to the Bible writers, thus imparting the truth of Scripture to them.

This brings us to the doctrine of verbal inspiration which Paul states in verse thirteen. After the Bible writers had been given the truth by means of the act of the Holy Spirit in uncovering it to them, the apostle says that they were not left to themselves to make a record of it. It is one thing to know a certain fact. It is quite another to find the exact words which will give someone else an adequate understanding of that fact. And right here is where the need of verbal inspiration comes in. Paul first makes the negative statement, "Which things we speak, not in words taught by human wisdom." That is, the words which the Bible writers used were not dictated by their human reason or wisdom.

Then the apostle makes the positive statement, "but in words taught by the Spirit." He says that the words which the Bible writers used were taught them by the Holy Spirit. That is, as they wrote the Scriptures, the Holy Spirit who had revealed the truth to them, now chooses the correct word out of the writer's vocabulary, whose content of meaning will give to the believer the exact truth God desires him to have. This however does not imply mechanical dictation nor the effacement of the writer's own personality. The Holy Spirit took the writers as He found them and used them infallibly. Luke's Greek is the purest and most beautiful. He was a native Greek. Paul's Greek is far more involved and difficult than John's, for Paul had a university training, while John's knowledge of Greek was that of the average man of the first century who knew Greek as his second language but never had any formal training in it. Professor John A. Scott in his excellent book, "We Would Know Jesus," speaks of "the superb control of the Greek language" which Luke everywhere showed, and of the "hard and crabbed Greek of Paul as shown in Romans," also of the flowing language of Paul's speeches recorded in the Acts, which quality is not due to Paul's delivery but Luke's literary excellence.

However, whether it is the pure Greek of Luke, the difficult Greek of Paul, or the simple Greek of John, it is all correct as to grammar and syntax. The Holy Spirit observed the rules of Greek grammar as they existed in the Koine Greek of that time. And the wonder of it all is seen in the fact that John brings to his readers just as precious, just as deep truth, in his simple Greek, as Paul does in his intricate constructions and involved sentences. God the Holy Spirit is above language. Thus we have in the original Hebrew and Greek texts of the Bible manuscripts, the very words that God taught the writers to use as they recorded the truth which they had received by reve lation. This is what is meant by verbal inspiration.

Then Paul in the words "comparing spiritual things with spirit ual," explains this process of choosing the right word in each case We will look carefully at the Greek word translated "comparing," for it throws a flood of light on Paul's teaching of verbal inspiration The word is a compound of the verb meaning "to judge," and a preposition meaning "with," thus "to judge with." It speaks of the action of judging something with something else. For instance, a milliner wishes to trim a red hat with ribbon of the same color. She takes the hat over to the spools of ribbon and "judges" the various shades of red ribbon "with" the hat. She compares the hat with ribbon after ribbon in an attempt to find one which will exactly match the color of the hat. She rejects one after another until she finally finds one ribbon that exactly matches the hat. And that is exactly what the word means, "to join fitly together, to combine, to compound." That is just the procedure which the Bible writers went through in writing their books. As led by the Holy Spirit, they searched their vocabularies for the exact word which would adequately express the truth they wished to record. By the process of comparing the word with the truth they wished to write down, they rejected all those words which the Holy Spirit showed them would not correctly express the thought, and finally chose the word to which the Holy Spirit had led them, and upon which the Holy Spirit had put His stamp of approval. Thus the Holy Spirit allowed the writers the free play of their personalities, vocabulary, and training, while at the same time guiding them to make an infallible record of truth infallibly revealed.

The words "spiritual things with spiritual," are from two adjectives in the Greek. The first word translated "spiritual" is in the accusative case, the direct object of the verb "comparing," and in the neuter gender. It refers to the spiritual truths already given the writers by revelation. The second use of the word "spiritual" is in the instrumental case, the instrumental of association. As to gender this word could be either masculine or neuter, for these two genders have the same form in the genitive through the dative cases. The English reader will please excuse these technicalities. We must look at the context to decide which gender is meant. The two things in the context which are compared and then combined, are the truth revealed and the words which would correctly convey this truth. The words "spiritual things" refers to this truth. Therefore the word "spiritual" in its second use in verse thirteen refers to the words. The gender is therefore masculine since the word "words" in this verse is masculine. Vincent translates this phrase, "combining spiritual things with spiritual words." *Expositor's Greek Testament* translates it, "wedding kindred speech to thought." Alford renders it, "putting together spiritual words to spiritual things."

We come now to the doctrine of *illumination*, namely, the act of God the Holy Spirit enabling the believer to understand the truth given by *revelation*, and by *inspiration* written down. Paul says, "the natural man receiveth not the things of the Spirit of God." The word "natural" is the translation of a Greek word which Paul uses to describe to the Corinthian Greeks the unregenerate man at his best, the man whom Greek philosophy commended, the man actuated by the higher thoughts and aims of the natural life. The word used here is not the Greek word which speaks of the sensual man. It is the word coined by Aristotle to distinguish the pleasures of the soul, such as ambition and the desire for knowledge, from those of the body. The natural man here spoken of is the educated man at the height of his intellectual powers, but devoid of the Spirit of God. The word translated "receiveth" does not imply an active appropriation, but a certain attitude of passive acceptance when favorable, and of rejection if unfavorable. This man, whose powers of apprehension are limited to the exercise of his reason, does not admit these spiritual things into his heart. The reason for this rejection is that they are foolishness to him.

Then Paul states the impossibility of his knowing them, and its reason, because they are spiritually discerned. The Greek word translated "discern" means "to investigate, inquire into, scrutinize, sift, question." Thus the investigation of, inquiry into, scrutinizing, and sifting of scripture truth is done in the energy of the Holy Spirit who illuminates the sacred page of Scripture to the believer. It is "he that is spiritual" that judgeth all things. The word "judgeth" is the translation of the same Greek word rendered "discerneth." The Spirit-controlled Christian investigates, inquires into, and scrutinizes the Bible and comes to an appreciation and understanding of its contents.

The fuller translation of this important passage is as follows: "But just as it stands written; The things which eye did not see and ear did not hear, and which did not arise within the heart of man, as many things as God prepared for those that love Him. For, to us God uncovered them through the agency of His Spirit. For the Spirit explores all things, yes, the deep things of God. For who is there of men who knows the things of the (individual) man, unless it be the spirit of (that) man which is in him. Even so also the things of God no one knows, but the Spirit of God (knows the things of God). But as for us, not the spirit which animates the world did we receive, but the Spirit who proceeds from God, in order that we might know the things which by God have been freely given to us; which things we speak, not in words taught by human wisdom, but in words taught by the Spirit, matching spiritual things with Spirit-taught words. But the man whose powers of apprehension are limited to the exercise of his reason, rejects the things of God since they are foolishness to him. And he is powerless to know them, because they are investigated

rough the instrumentality of the Spirit. But the man equipped by
he Spirit, comes to an apprehension of all things, yet he himself is
omprehended by no one. For who knows the Lord's mind, that he
hould instruct Him? But as for us, we have the mind of Christ."

Chapter II

PAUL'S LAST WORDS TO TIMOTHY

THE last words of great men are always significant. It was so in the case of the great apostle. He was writing from his prison cell in Rome. It was his second imprisonment. His preliminary hearing before Nero was over, and he was expecting the final trial, and death.

His letter was written in Greek to a young preacher whose father was a Greek and his mother a Hebrew. Paul, a son of Hebrew parents had, besides his training under the Jewish scholar Gamaliel, a well rounded schooling in Hellenistic culture, the Greek language, Greek philosophy, rhetoric, logic, argumentation, and literature. Timothy knew both Hebrew and Greek. Paul chooses to write to him in the Greek language. It was the international language of the day. Greek was far more expressive than Hebrew. It could compress more ideas and their various shades of meaning into one word, than any other language of that day or since. It is because of this that access to the Greek text of Paul's letter is such a great privilege. If the English language had been in use, and Timothy had read a translation of his letter in that language, he would have missed a great deal that lies embedded in the intricate grammatical structure of the Greek, and which could not be brought over into a standard translation such as the Authorized Version. What he would have read, would have been correct. But much would have been left behind in Paul's Greek. This is the author's reason for offering to the English reader who is not equipped to read the Greek, these word studies and a translation using as many additional English words as are necessary to bring out the full meaning of the original.

How wonderful it is that this letter has been preserved for almost 2000 years just as it left the hands of the writer. While it was copied by hand for 1500 years, yet the science of textual criticism assures us of a correct text. And here are a few lines of that part of the letter which we are to study together (II Tim. 4:1-22), in the Greek in which it was written.

Διαμαρτύρομαι ἐνώπιον τοῦ Θεοῦ καὶ Χριστοῦ Ἰησοῦ, τοῦ μέλλοντος κρίνειν ζῶντας καὶ νεκρούς, καὶ τὴν ἐπιφάνειαν αὐτοῦ καὶ τὴν βασιλείαν αὐτοῦ· κήρυξον τὸν λόγον, ἐπίστηθι εὐκαίρως ἀκαίρως, ἔλεγξον, ἐπιτίμησον, παρακάλεσον, ἐν πάσῃ μακροθυμίᾳ καὶ διδαχῇ.

Of course you say, "It is all Greek to me." Everything looks most unintelligible to the English reader, part of a world far beyond and apart from his ordinary sphere of life. He is quite right in his judgment, for to handle the Greek language and produce a translation which is expressive and yet strictly true to the original, is no child's play. Such a thing is not flung off of one's coat sleeve. The subject is so vast that the longer one delves into it, the more he is impressed with the fact that he has but touched its fringes. A translator of the Greek New Testament should have a knowledge of Greek grammar and syntax, the possession of a vocabulary, the ability to break words apart, add together the meanings of the various words which go to make up that word, and then select a word or words in the English language which give an adequate picture of that word with all the lights and shadows it contains. One needs to know the historical background of the usage of the word in classical and Koine Greek. One needs to know the writer, the purpose he had in writing, the particular way in which he habitually used a word. A translator must study closely the context in which the word is found and select that particular meaning from the many shades of meaning which the word has, which best fits that context. All this, and more is involved in the adequate translation of a word. Over and above all this equipment, there must be a definite dependence upon the Holy Spirit, a comprehensive knowledge of the great scope of Scripture, an apprehension of the great dispensations, an understanding of prophecy, and a consuming desire that the Lord Jesus be glorified.

The work itself is of the most taxing kind. It requires patient, slow, careful research, the consultation of a representative number of Greek authorities, the tabulation of each one's material on each word, and a weighing of that material in such a way as to select the best where authorities differ. After one has fully treated each separate word, he is ready for his translation. With your English translation open before you (the writer is using the Authorized Version), let us study the more important Greek words together. When we have finished our word studies, we will offer the fuller translation.

Verse One. Paul says, "I charge thee therefore." Paul's final charge to the young pastor, Timothy, the one upon whose shoulders he is now placing the responsibility for the care of all the churches and the leadership in maintaining the Faith once for all delivered to the saints, is given in view of the spiritual declension and departure from true doctrine which had even then already set in, and which in the last days would come to a head. The Greek word translated "charge" is a very strong word. In pagan Greek it was used to call the gods and men to witness. It was used in such an expression as "I adjure thee." Timothy had splendid moral and spiritual qualities. But he lacked the dogged perseverance and tremendous moral courage of the great apostle. Hence this strong word. The word translated "before," is a compound of a number of Greek words which together mean, "one who is in sight." It was used in such expressions as, "the case will be drawn up against you in the court at Heracleopolis *in the presence of,*" "deliver *personally,*" "I gave notice in *person.*"[1] It is used of one who does or says something in the presence of someone else, and does it with the consciousness that that one has him in sight and mind. Paul delivered this solemn charge to Timothy, conscious of the fact that he was doing so in the sight of God, and he wished Timothy to ever so regard the charge.

---

1. *Moulton & Milligan Greek Vocabulary of the New Testament.*

The expression, "God, and the Lord Jesus Christ" is in a construction in Greek which requires us to understand that the word "God" and the names "Lord Jesus Christ" refer to the same person.[1] The translation should read, "our God, even Christ Jesus," the word "Lord" not appearing in the best Greek texts. This gives us an insight into the Pauline attitude towards the deity of the Lord Jesus. He emphasizes the fact here, and in a way in which to defend it against both the heresies of the day and the cult of the Caesar, both of which were opposed to the doctrine of the deity of our Lord. Thus, the departing apostle leaves with his young understudy an indelible impression of the basic and large place which the deity of our Lord should occupy in our Christian teaching and preaching.

The Lord Jesus is described as One "who shall judge the quick and the dead." "Shall" is literally, "to be about" to do something. The word is used of someone who is on the point of doing something, and in Scripture, of those things which will come to pass by fixed necessity or divine appointment. Paul was living in the expectation of the imminent return of the Lord. "Judge" is from a construction which speaks of action going on. Thus, the various judgments are in the apostle's mind, the judgment of the Church, of the Nations, and that of the Great White Throne, a series of judgments, not one judgment. The word "quick" has changed its meaning in the years since the Authorized Version was translated. Today it means "fast, swift." Then it meant "alive."

The words, "appearing" and "kingdom," are in a construction which shows the thing by which a person adjures another. For instance, Mark 5:7 has "I adjure thee by God." Paul solemnly charged Timothy by the appearing and the kingdom of the Lord Jesus. The Greek word translated "appearing" means "to appear or become visible." It was often used by the Greeks of a glorious manifestation of the gods, and especially of their advent to help. It is used of the first Advent in II Timothy 1:10, here of the second. Thus the aged apos-

---

1. *Treasures* pp. 31-33.

tle, expecting martyrdom, puts upon the shoulders of Timothy, the great responsibility which he himself has carried these many years, and solemnly charges him in the presence of God, even the Lord Jesus, and by His glorious appearing and kingdom.

Verse two. The charge is to preach the Word. The English word "preach" brings to our mind at once the picture of the ordained clergyman standing in his pulpit on the Lord's Day ministering the Word. But the Greek word here left quite a different impression with Timothy. At once it called to his mind the Imperial Herald, spokesman of the Emperor, proclaiming in a formal, grave, and authoritative manner which must be listened to, the message which the Emperor gave him to announce. It brought before him the picture of the town official who would make a proclamation in a public gathering. The word is in a construction which makes it a summary command to be obeyed at once. It is a sharp command as in military language. This should be the pattern for the preacher today. His preaching should be characterized by that dignity which comes from the consciousness of the fact that he is an official herald of the King of kings. It should be accompanied by that note of authority which will command the respect, careful attention, and proper reaction of the listeners. There is no place for clowning in the pulpit of Jesus Christ.

Timothy is to preach the Word. The word "Word" here refers to the whole body of revealed truth, as will be seen by comparing this passage with I Thessalonians 1:6 and Galatians 6:6. The preacher must present, not book reviews, not politics, not economics, not current topics of the day, not a philosophy of life denying the Bible and based upon unproven theories of science, but the Word. The preacher as a herald cannot choose his message. He is given a message to proclaim by his Sovereign. If he will not proclaim that, let him step down from his exalted position.

He is to be instant in season and out of season in this proclamation. The words, "be instant," are from a word which means "to stand by, be present, to be at hand, to be ready." The exhortation is for the preacher to hold himself in constant readiness to proclaim the Word. The words, "in season," are from a word which means "opportune," "out of season," from a word which means "inopportune." The preacher is to proclaim the Word when the time is auspicious, favorable, opportune, and also when the circumstances seem unfavorable. So few times are still available for preaching that the preacher must take every chance he has to preach the Word. There is no closed season for preaching.

In his preaching he is to include reproof and rebuke. The Greek word translated "reprove,"[1] speaks of a rebuke which results in the person's confession of his guilt, or if not his confession, in his conviction of sin. Thus, the preacher is to deal with sin either in the lives of his unsaved hearers or in those of the saints to whom he ministers, and he is to do it in no uncertain tones. The word "sin" is not enough in the vocabulary of our preaching today. And as he deals with the sin that confronts him as he preaches, he is to expect results, the salvation of the lost and the sanctification of the saints.

The word "rebuke"[2] in the Greek, refers to a rebuke which does not bring the one rebuked to a conviction of any fault on his part. It might be because the one rebuked is innocent of the charge, or that he is guilty but refuses to acknowledge his guilt. This word implies a sharp severe rebuke with possibly a suggestion in some cases of impending penalty. Even where the preacher has experienced failure after failure in bringing sinners or saints to forsake their sin, or where there seems little hope of so doing, yet he is to sharply rebuke sin. He has discharged his duty, and the responsibility is upon his hearers to deal with the sin in their lives.

Not only is he to speak in stern language against sin, but he is to exhort. The word has in it the ideas of "please, I beg of you, I urge you." Thus, there is to be a mingling of severity and gentleness in his preaching. He is to exhort with all longsuffering and doctrine. The word "longsuffering" speaks of that temper which does not easily succumb under suffering, of that self-restraint which does not hastily

1, 2. *Treasures* pr. 70-72.

retaliate a wrong. The word "doctrine" is in the Greek, literally, "teaching." It speaks of instruction. Vincent says in this connection: "Longsuffering is to be maintained against the temptations to anger presented by the obstinacy and perverseness of certain hearers; and such is to be met, not merely with rebuke, but also with sound and reasonable instruction in the truth." Calvin says: "Those who are strong only in fervor and sharpness, but are not fortified with solid doctrine, weary themselves in their vigorous efforts, make a great noise, rave, . . . make no headway because they build without a foundation." Or, as Vincent says, "Men will not be won to the truth by scolding," and then quotes another as saying, "They should understand what they hear, and learn to perceive why they are rebuked."

Verses three and four. The exhortation to proclaim the Word is given in view of the coming defection from the Faith once for all delivered to the saints. The word "endure" means literally "to hold one's self upright or firm against a person or thing." It is a perfect description of the Modernist and his following today. The Greek word translated "sound," has the idea of "healthy, wholesome." The word "doctrine" is preceded by the definite article. It is Paul's system of doctrine that is referred to, the Pauline theology. "After" is from a preposition whose root meaning is "down." It speaks of "domination." "Lusts" is in the Greek, "cravings." These who set themselves against Pauline theology are dominated by their own private, personal cravings. Those cravings consist of the desire for personal gratification. They, having itching ears, heap to themselves teachers. The Greek makes it clear that the itching ears belong to the people. The word "heap" means "to accumulate in piles." It speaks of the crowd electing teachers *en masse*, an indiscriminate multitude of teachers. These teachers give the people what they want, not what they need. The word "itch" in its active verb form means "to scratch, to tickle, to make to itch," in the passive, "to itch." It describes that person who desires to hear for mere gratification, like the Greeks at Athens who spent their time in nothing else but either to tell or to hear, not some new thing, but some *newer* thing (Acts 17:21).

The comparative form of the adjective is used here, not the positive. Ernest Gordon, commenting on this verse says: "Hardly has the latest novelty been toyed with, than it is cast aside as stale and frayed, and a newer is sought. One has here the volatile spirit of the Greek city, so in contrast with the gravity and poise of the Christian spirit, engaged with eternal things." Such is the spirit of Modernism with its teachings of the divinity of mankind, and the relativity of truth, its rejection of the doctrine of total depravity, the sacrificial atonement, the resurrection, and the need of the new birth, catering to the desires of a fallen race. It gratifies man's pride. It soothes his troubled conscience. The desire for the gratification of one's cravings is insatiable, and is increased or aggravated by having that desire satisfied. Hence the heaping to themselves of teachers.

The words "turn away," carry the idea of "averting." That is, those who follow these heretics, not only turn away their ears from the truth, but see to it that their ears are always in such a position that they will never come in contact with the truth, like a country windmill whose owner has turned its vanes so that they will not catch the wind. Notice the active voice of the verb "turn away," and the passive voice of the verb "shall be turned." The first named action is performed by the people themselves, while in the case of the second one, they are acted upon by an outside force. The second occurrence of the word "turn" is from a verb which means "to turn or twist out." In a medical sense it means, "to wrench out of its proper place," as of the limbs. It is used of a dislocated arm, for instance. When people avert their ears from the truth, they lay themselves open to every Satanic influence, and are easily turned aside to error. Instead of being in correct adjustment to the truth, namely that of seeking it for the purpose of appropriating it, these people have put themselves out of adjustment and have been consequently wrenched out of place. They have become dislocated, put out of joint. Like a dislocated arm which has no freedom of action, they have given themselves over to a delusion which incapacitates them for any independent thinking along religious lines which they might do for themselves. They are in much the same condition as those under the reign of the Beast who, because they refuse to receive the love of the truth, are the victims of a strong delusion (II Thess. 2:10, 11). The word "fable" is from a Greek word which refers to fiction as opposed to fact. And surely, the teachings of Modernism are fictional as to their nature, for they have a theoretical basis, the unproved hypotheses of science, naturalism and evolution.

Verse five. In view of this sad condition in the visible church, Timothy is exhorted by the great apostle to do four things in connection with his proclamation of the Word. First, he is to watch in all things. "Watch" is from a Greek word which has the following meanings, "to be in a sober mood, to be calm and collected in spirit, to be temperate, dispassionate, circumspect, alert." All these would pass through the mind of Timothy as he meditated upon Paul's Greek. Second, the pastor is to endure afflictions. "Afflictions" in the Greek is "evils, hardships, troubles." The verb "endure" is aorist imperative. It is a sharp command given with military snap and curtness. Timothy needed just that. He was not cast in a heroic mould. How we in the ministry of the Word need that injunction today. What "softies" we sometimes are, afraid to come out clearly in our proclamation of the truth and our stand as to false doctrine, fearing the ostracism of our fellows, the ecclesiastical displeasure of our superiors, or the cutting off of our immediate financial income. I would rather walk a lonely road with Jesus than be without His fellowship in the crowd, wouldn't you? I would rather live in a cottage and eat simple food, and have Him as Head of my home and the Unseen Guest at every meal, than to live in royal style in a mansion without Him.

Third, the pastor is to do the work of an evangelist. The latter word is the transliteration of a Greek word that means, "one who brings good news." Paul does not exhort the local pastor to engage in an itinerant ministry, going from place to place holding evangelistic meetings. That work is for those specially gifted men called evangelists (Eph. 4:11). But the local pastor should be evangelistic in his message and methods. He must ever be reaching out for the lost both in his teaching, preaching, and personal contacts.

Fourth, he must make full proof of his ministry. The words "make full proof," are the translation of a Greek word which means "to cause a thing to be shown to the full, to carry through to the end, to fully perform." "Ministry" is from a Greek word which speaks of Christian work in general, covering every mode of service. One of the chief temptations of the pastorate is laziness and neglect. Paul lived an intense and tremendously active life. The word "drive" characterizes him perfectly. As the saying goes: "It is better to wear out for the Lord than to rust out."

Verse six. In verses one to five, Paul is urging Timothy to take the initiative because he himself is being called from the field of action, and Timothy must carry on. He says, "I am now ready to be offered." The "I" is emphatic in the Greek text. It is, "as for myself," in contradistinction to Timothy and others. To translate literally, "As for myself, I am already being offered." What he is now offering is the beginning of the end. The process has already begun which shall shed his blood. What was a possibility in Philippians :23, written during his first imprisonment, is now a certainty in his second. The word "offered" is from a Greek word used in pagan worship to refer to the libation or drink-offering poured out to a god. Paul uses the same word in Philippians 2:17, where he looks upon himself as the libation poured out upon the sacrifice, namely the Philippian's service to the Lord Jesus, the lesser part of a sacrifice poured out upon the more important part. Only one who considered himself less than the least of all saints could write in such deep humility.

Paul had had his preliminary hearing before Nero, and was expecting the final one, and death. He knew it would not be crucifixion, for a citizen of the Roman Empire was not crucified. If the death penalty was demanded by the State, it would be decapitation, hence the figurative reference to a libation.

He writes, "the time of my departure is at hand." Someone has said, "The servant of the Lord is immortal until his work is done." Paul's work was over, or Nero could not have taken his life. The word translated "departure" is interesting. The simple meaning of the word is "to unloose, undo again, break up." It meant "to depart." It was a common expression for death. It was used in military circles of the taking down of a tent and the departure of an army, and in nautical language, of the hoisting of an anchor and the sailing of a ship. Paul uses the same word in Philippians 1:23. During his first imprisonment, he was kept a prisoner at the Praetorium, the military camp of the Emperor's bodyguard, but now in his second, it is thought that he writes from a cold damp Roman dungeon. In his first use of the word, it would seem that he used the figure of striking one's tent. He was in a military camp, he was a tent-maker by trade, and he spoke of the human body as a tent. If so, it is probable that he had the same figure of speech in mind here.

The words, "is at hand," are from a word which means "to stand by, to be on hand." It was as if death already stood there. Peter also had a premonition of approaching death (II Peter 1:14).

Verse seven. And now he casts a swift glance over his past life, and sums it up in three sentences, using the figures of a Greek wrestler, a Greek runner, and a Roman soldier. He says, using the first figure, "I have fought the good fight." The definite article appears before the word "fight" in the Greek. The use of the indefinite article in the English translation is unwarranted, and makes the expression appear egotistical. The word "fight" is the translation of a word used in Greek athletics of a contest in the Greek stadium where the games were held. The word "good" refers to external goodness as seen by the eye, that which is the expression of internal intrinsic goodness. It is a goodness that is not moral here but aesthetic, a beauty of action that would characterize either the Greek wrestler's efforts or the Christian's warfare against evil. The words "have fought," are in the perfect tense, speaking of an action completed in past time with present results. Paul fought his fight with sin to a finish, and was resting in a complete victory. What a happy ending to a strenuous, active, heroic life. He says in his colorful Greek, "The beautiful contest I, like a wrestler, have fought to the finish, and at present am resting in a complete victory."

"I have finished my course." The Greek word translated "course," refers to a race course, the cinder path of the present day college athletic field. The words "have finished," are also in the perfect tense. Like a Greek runner, he has crossed the finishing line and is now resting at the goal. His life's work is over.

"I have kept the faith." "The faith" here is the deposit of truth with which God had entrusted Paul. The word "kept" means "to keep by guarding." Again, the apostle uses the perfect tense. His work of safe-guarding that truth is now at an end. He has defended it against the attacks of the Gnostics, the Judaizers, and the philosophers of Athens. He has laid it down now at the feet of Timothy. He, like a soldier who has grown old in the service of his country, is awaiting his discharge. And so he writes to Timothy, "The desperate, straining, agonizing contest marked by its beauty of technique, I, like a wrestler, have fought to a finish, and at present am resting in its victory; my race, I, like a runner have finished, and at present am resting at the goal; the Faith committed to my care, I, like a soldier, have kept safely through everlasting vigilance." All this would surge through Timothy's mind as he read Paul's Greek. Much of this is lost to the English reader, this untranslatable richness of the Greek New Testament.

Verse eight. But his use of illustrations from Greek athletics is not finished. He likens himself to the Greek athlete, who, having won his race, is looking up at the judge's stand, and awaiting his laurel wreath of victory. He says, "Henceforth there is laid up for me a crown of righteousness." "Henceforth" is from a word that means literally "what remains." "Crown" is from the Greek word referring to the victor's crown, a garland of oak leaves or ivy, given to the winner in the Greek games.[1] The victor's crown of righteous-

---

1. *Bypaths* pp. 60-70.

ness is the crown which belongs to or is the due reward of right-eousness. The righteous Judge is the just Judge, the Umpire who makes no mistakes and who always plays fair. The words "right-eousness" and "just" are the two translations of the Greek word used here. The word "love" is perfect in tense, and is the Greek word for a love that is called out of one's heart because of the preciousness of the object loved. The Greek word translated "appearing" means literally "to become visible," and was used of the glorious manifestation of the gods, here of the glorious coming of the Lord Jesus into the air to catch out the Church. To those who have considered precious His appearing and therefore have loved it and as a result at the present time are still holding that attitude in their hearts, to those the Lord Jesus will also give the victor's garland of righteousness. The definite article is used in the Greek text. It is a particular crown reserved for these. The word "give" can be here translated "award." Thus Paul, the spiritual athlete, his victory won, is resting at the goal posts, awaiting the award which the judge's stand will give him.

Verse nine. After his swift glance down the years of his strenuous life, Paul turns to his present circumstances. He is a prisoner in a cold Roman dungeon, awaiting his second trial before Nero, and death. Great soul that he was, he yet needed and craved human fel-lowship and sympathy in his hour of trial. How this reminds us of the Man of Sorrows who needed the fellowship and sympathy of the inner circle, Peter, James and John, in His hour of trial in Gethsem-ane. How real a Man He was, yet all the time Very God. Paul writes to Timothy, "Do thy diligence to come shortly unto me." The words "do thy diligence," in the Greek have the idea of "making haste, exerting effort," and can be translated "do your best." Timo-thy was urged to do his best to come to Paul quickly. Timothy was at Ephesus, bearing a heavy burden of responsibility.

Verses ten to twelve. Paul's associates who were carrying on the work in Rome, had left. He writes, "Demas hath forsaken me, hav-

g loved this present world." The Greek word "forsaken" means
o abandon, desert, leave in straits, leave helpless, leave in the
rch, let one down." This tells us that Demas had not only left Paul
far as fellowship was concerned, but he had left him in the lurch
o, so far as the work of the Gospel was concerned. He had been
e of Paul's dependable and trusted helpers. Paul said that he let
n down. This latter expression, so often heard today, was in com-
on use in Paul's day. Our Lord used it while on the Cross (Matt.
:46), and Paul used it in Hebrews 13:5. The Greek word is how-
er stronger than the English words. It is made up of three words,
o leave," "down," and "in," that is, to forsake one who is in a set
circumstances that are against him. It was a cruel blow to Paul.
ght to the last, his intense nature impelled him to do what he could
the service of the Lord. He was awaiting the executioner's axe.
w, one whom he had trusted, had let him down. Paul was in prison,
freedom of action curtailed. Here was one who had his liberty,
d who deserted the Christian work for the world, that world which
ench defines as "that floating mass of thoughts, opinions, maxims,
eculations, hopes, impulses, aims, aspirations at any time current
the world, which it may be impossible to seize and accurately de-
e, but which constitutes a most real and effective power, being the
ral or immoral atmosphere which at every moment of our lives we
ale, again inevitably to exhale, the subtle informing spirit of the
rld of men who are living alienated and apart from God." Demas
ed all this. He prized it highly, and therefore set his affection
on it. The spirit of the age had gotten hold of him. What a
rning example to those of us who are teachers and preachers of
e Word. How careful we should be to obey the exhortation of
ul, "Set your affection on things above, not on things on the earth"
ol. 3:2).

Crescens and Titus, others of Paul's helpers, had set out on their
n initiative as appears from a small particle Paul uses in verse 12
ich is translated "and," but is adversative in its nature, and
ould be translated "but." He writes Timothy, "Only Luke is with

me." The "only" refers to Paul's fellow-laborers. He had ma
friends in Rome. How beautiful it is to see that the "beloved ph
sician" should feel that his place was beside Paul when the end w
approaching. How true to his medical instinct this was; not
depreciate the grace of God moving him in his heart to the sa
action. What a trophy of God's grace Luke is. Here is a Gre
doctor of medicine, leaving his medical practice to be the person
physician of an itinerant preacher, to share his hardships and priv
tions, his dangers, and toil. The great success of the apostle who
he attended in a medical way, is due in some measure at least,
the physician's watchful care over his patient who was the recipie
of stonings, scourgings, and beatings, a man whose physical streng
was always at the ragged edge of exhaustion because of his inc
sant and intense work and long difficult journeys. Luke knew a
the marks (*stigmata*) of the Lord Jesus (Gal. 6:17) on the body of tl
apostle, the scars left after the assaults upon his person. He ha
bathed and tended those wounds. Now, his patient, grown old befo
his time, was suffering the discomforts of a Roman cell. He had
be guarded against disease. "Only Luke is with me." What a co
fort he was to Paul. A Gentile and a Jew, one in Christ Jesus.

Paul writes to Timothy, "Take Mark and bring him with thee
"Take" is literally, "pick up." That is, "on your way to Rom
stop by Mark's home and pick him up."

The word "and" in the Greek text is adversative, and has the id
of "but." It distinguishes the going of Demas, Crescens, and Tit
from that of Tychicus. The latter had been sent by Paul to Ephesu
possibly to take Timothy's place there while the latter came to Rom
The "but" implies that Paul had not sent the others. Crescens a
Titus had gone to some other field of Christian work, leaving Pa
alone in Rome, and without helpers.

Verse thirteen. The apostle asks Timothy when he sets out,
bring his cloak along which he left behind at the home of Carp
who lived in Troas. That meant that Timothy would have to ta

a coast-wise sailing vessel from Ephesus to Troas before setting out westward toward Rome. The Greek word translated "cloak," is the name of a circular cape which fell down to the knees, with an opening for the head in the center. H. V. Morton, a student of Roman times, and a traveller in the regions of the Pauline journeys, speaks of this type of cloak in his excellent book, "In The Steps of St. Paul." He has seen these cloaks on shepherds in what in the Bible was called Cilicia. They are felt cloaks called *kepenikler*, and are impervious to wind and water. They are so stiff, he says, that the wearer can step out of them and leave them in an upright position. They are made of the tough Cilician goat's hair with which Paul was familiar in the making of tents. Such a coat must have been a great comfort to Paul on his long journeys. Now he needed it to keep out the cold and damp of his Roman cell.

Paul asks Timothy to carry along his books and the parchments. The word "books" is the translation of a Greek word meaning a "book," which in turn comes from a Greek word that refers to the pith of the papyrus plant that grew in the Nile River. This pith was cut in strips and laid in rows, over which other rows were laid crosswise, and the whole was pressed into a paper-like material called papyrus. The books Paul asked for were papyrus rolls. The parchment manuscripts were made from the skins of sheep, goats, or antelopes, or of vellum, which latter was made from the skins of young calves. Even at the approach of death, and in the midst of the discomforts of his dungeon, the aged apostle did not allow his normal strenuous life and his habits of study to grow less intense in their nature. What a rebuke this is to those who, charged with the responsibility of expounding the Word of God, are content with mere surface understanding, not willing to do the exhausting work of research which only will bring out the inexhaustible riches of the Bible. What a reprimand this is to those who have had training in Greek, and who have put aside their Greek New Testament. What an exalted privilege it is to be called of God to minister the Word. As Alexander Whyte says in his book, *The Walk, Conversa-*

tion, and Character of Jesus Christ our Lord, "That elect, and hon
orable, and enviable class of men that we call students of New Testa
ment exegesis. Surely they are the happiest and the most enviabl
of all men, who have been set apart to nothing else but to the under
standing and the opening up of the hid treasures of God's Wor
and God's Son."

Verses fourteen and fifteen. Paul warns Timothy against a certai
Alexander. The word "coppersmith" in the Greek text refers to an
craftsman in metal. He was a metal worker of Ephesus, probabl
engaged in the manufacture of silver shrines of Diana. Paul'
preaching of the Gospel was cutting into his trade in idols, an
that touched his pocket book, and he was out to get Paul. The wor
"did" is literally "showed," with the idea of, not only "evil words,
but "evil deeds." One could translate, "showed me much ill-trea
ment." The word "reward" does not in the Greek text express
wish or desire. It is a simple future, a statement of a future fac
The word is to be taken in the sense of "will requite." The apost
takes satisfaction in the future punishment of Alexander because
his opposition to Christianity. *Expositor's Greek Testament* has t
following to say on this attitude of Paul's: "Was the future punis
ment of Alexander which Paul considered equitable, a matter of mo
satisfaction than distress to Paul? Yes, and provided that no eleme
of personal spite intrudes, such a feeling cannot be condemned.
God is a moral governor; if sin is a reality; those who kno
themselves to be on God's side cannot help a feeling of joy in kno
ing that evil will not always triumph over good."

The word "beware" is from a Greek word meaning "to gua
one's self." It often implies assault from without. The wo
"withstood" in the original has the idea of "to set one's self agains
Alexander set himself against Christianity. It interfered with
business. How this reminds us of our Lord's words; "For what is
man profited, if he shall gain the whole world, and lose his o
soul? or what shall a man give in exchange for his soul?" (Ma
16:26).

Verse sixteen. Then Paul speaks of his trial at Nero's tribunal. It is possible that Nero himself was presiding in person. He speaks of his "first answer." The word "answer" is the translation of a Greek word which literally means, "to talk one's self off from." It was a technical word used in the Greek law courts, referring to a verbal defense in a judicial trial,[1] namely, talking one's self off from a charge preferred against one. Paul was offering his defense against the charges of his accusers. But he stood alone, for he says, "No man stood with me." The word "stood" is also a technical word used of one who appeared in a court of justice in behalf of the accused. No one appeared, to act as his advocate, to advise him as to legal forms, to testify to his character. The last persecution had been so severe, that those who lived through it, dared not appear in Paul's defense. Paul says, "All forsook me." He used the same word when he wrote, "Demas hath forsaken me." Those whom he had reason to suppose would come to his aid, left him in the lurch, left him helpless, let him down.

Verse seventeen. But the Lord did not let Paul down. He made good his promise to Paul, "I will never leave thee, nor forsake thee" (Heb. 13:5),[2] this Lord of his who on one awful day was let down by His Father (Matt. 27:46).[3] He says, "The Lord stood with me." "Stood" is from a Greek word used in Romans 16:2, where it is translated "assist." The Roman saints were to stand by Phoebe the deaconess in whatever she needed, that is, they were to make themselves responsible for all her needs. So the Lord Jesus took His stand by the side of His faithful apostle and made Himself responsible for all his needs. He strengthened Paul, that is, poured strength into him, clothed him with strength.

The strengthening of Paul resulted in the preaching being fully known. "Preaching" refers in the Greek to a public proclamation

---

1. *Nuggets* p. 93.
2. *Treasures* p. 25.
3. *Bypaths* pp. 87-91.

given by an official herald. Paul used the same word in verse one. As long as there had been no public proclamation of the Gospel by Paul himself in Rome, the function of a herald had not been completely fulfilled by him. Thus, Paul brought in a full declaration of the Gospel as he gave his teachings to the court. If Nero sat on the judge's bench, he heard the Gospel from the lips of the great apostle himself.

We now consider the significance of Paul's words, "And I was delivered out of the mouth of the lion." Paul did not mean that he was delivered from death, for he had just written, "my life-blood is already being poured out as a libation." He did not mean that he was delivered from Nero's power, for he was aware that a second trial was awaiting him, and that he would be executed. He was not referring to the lions of the arena, for this could not come to a Roman citizen.

The expression, "I was delivered out of the mouth of the lion," is an echo of our Lord's words in Psalm 22:21 where He while hanging on the Cross prays to be delivered from the lion's mouth, namely from death, His humiliation. Hebrews 5:7 (Greek text) makes it clear that our Lord was not praying to be saved from death, that is, saved from dying, but, out of death, that is, saved from the grip of death, namely, to be raised out from among the dead.[1] Paul's humiliation in these circumstances would be his defeat at the hands of Satan when all his friends had let him down, and he would fail to proclaim the Gospel from the pulpit of the universe.

Verse eighteen. The words, "And the Lord shall deliver me from every evil work," are vitally bound up with "I was delivered from the mouth of the lion." The word for "evil" here refers to evil that is in active opposition to the good. The word "work" in the Greek text has a subjective reference and thus speaks of an action that would be committed by Paul. Thus, the expression does not

---

1. *Nuggets* pp. 30, 31.

speak of deliverance from an external evil personality here, but from a possible evil deed of the apostle's own doing. This is in harmony with the context. Failure to proclaim publicly the Gospel on this tremendous occasion, would have been in Paul's opinion "an evil work."

The word "delivered" is from a very tender word in the Greek text. It means "to draw to one's self out of harm's way." Paul was standing alone before the great tribunal, yet not alone, for the unseen Christ, standing at his side, drew Paul to Himself out of harm's way.

This was the climax of Paul's testimony to the Faith once for all delivered to the saints. He had faithfully preached the Glad Tidings through a long life in which hardships, trials, opposition, illness, heartache, and tremendous responsibility had been the rule rather than the exception; and now, at its close, just before his martyrdom, had he failed in maintaining that testimony to his Lord before the Court of the Emperor, what an inglorious ending that would have been to a glorious life. But God's grace Paul found to be sufficient right to the end of his life. He could now go to a martyr's death in triumph. He had remained faithful to his Lord.

Here are his last words to Timothy, as Timothy read them in all the richness of the Greek: (1) *I solemnly charge you as one who is living in the presence of our God, even Christ Jesus, the One who is on the point of judging the living and the dead, I solemnly charge you is not only living in His presence but also by His appearing and His kingdom,* (2) *make a public proclamation of the Word with such formality, gravity, and authority as must be heeded. Hold yourself in readiness for this proclamation when opportunity presents self and when it does not; reprove so as to bring forth conviction and confession of guilt; rebuke sharply, severely, and with a suggestion of impending penalty. Pleadingly exhort, doing all this with that utmost self-restraint which does not hastily retaliate a wrong, and accompany this exhortation with the most painstaking instruc-*

tion; (3) for the time will come when they will not endure ou
wholesome doctrine, in that they will hold themselves firm again:
it, but, dominated by their own personal cravings, they having ear
that desire merely to be gratified, gather to themselves an accumula
tion of teachers. (4) In fact, from the truth they shall avert th
ear, and (as a result) they shall receive a moral twist which wi
cause them to believe that which is fictitious. (5) But as for yo
you be constantly in a sober mood, calm, collected, wakeful, ale
in all things. Endure hardships. Let your work be evangelistic i
character. Your work of ministering fully perform in every deta
(6) for my life's blood is already being poured out as a libatio
and the time of my departure is already present. (7) The desperat
straining, agonizing contest marked by its beauty of technique,
like a wrestler, have fought to a finish, and at present am restin
in its victory. My race, I, like a runner, have finished, and at prese
am resting at the goal. The Faith committed to my care, I, like
soldier, have kept safely through everlasting vigilance. (8) Henc
forth, there is reserved for me the victor's laurel wreath of righteou
ness, which the Lord will award me on that day, the just Umpir
and not only me but also to all those who have loved His appearin

(9)   Do your best to come to me quickly, (10) for Demas let n
down, having set a high value upon this present age and thus h
come to love it. And he set out for Thessalonica, Crescens, f
Galatia, Titus, for Dalmatia. (11) Luke alone is with me. Mar
pick up, and bring with you, for he is profitable for ministerir
work. (12) But Tychicus I sent off to Ephesus. (13) My clo
which I left behind in Troas at the home of Carpus, when you are co
ing, carry along, and my papyrus rolls, especially my parchmen
(14) Alexander, the metal worker, showed me many instances
ill-treatment. The Lord shall pay him off in accordance with I
evil works. (15) And you also, with reference to him, be constan
guarding yourself, for he in an extraordinary manner set hims
in opposition to our words.

(16) *During my self defense at the preliminary trial, not even* *e person appeared in court, taking his stand by my side as a* *iend of mine, but all let me down. May it not be put to their* *count.* (17) *But the Lord took His stand at my side to render all* *e assistance I needed, and clothed me with strength, in order that* *rough me the public proclamation might be heralded abroad in* *ll measure, and that all the Gentiles might hear. And I was drawn* *His side out of the lion's mouth.* (18) *And the Lord will draw* *e to Himself away from every evil work actively opposed to that* *hich is good, and will keep me safe and sound for His kingdom,* *e heavenly one, to whom be the glory forever and ever. Amen.*

(19) *Greet Prisca and Aquila, and the household of Onesiphorous.* *20) Erastus was remaining in Corinth, but Trophimus, being ill,* *left behind in Miletus.* (21) *Do your best to come before winter.* *here greet you Eubulus, and Pudens, and Linus, and Claudia, and* *'l the brethren.* (22) *The Lord be with your spirit. Grace be with* *ou.*

Chapter III

AN EXPOSITION OF THE GREEK TEXT OF HEBREWS VI

ANY attempt to deal in an adequate way with this difficult porti
of God's word must be based, not only upon a careful exege
of its text in the Greek, but also upon a study of the historic
background and analysis of the book of which it is an integral pa
All correct exegesis is based upon and checked up by analys
Analysis is to the exegete what a compass is to a mariner, or
radio beam to an aviator. The latter two individuals cannot ho
to arrive at their destination without the aid of their instrumen
Similarly, no expositor of Hebrews VI can hope to arrive at a co
rect exegesis of that passage without constantly checking his po
tion by the analysis of the book. Therefore, before attempting t
interpretation of the section of Hebrews under discussion, we mu
lay a comprehensive groundwork consisting of the historical bac
ground and analysis of the book. The reader can then check t
interpretation of any particular detail by consulting this analys
That interpretation which agrees with the analysis is correct, a
that which is not in such agreement is not correct. The matter
correct interpretation therefore is reduced to a science. This eli
inates all discussion as to one's theological background or person
views. The working out of the problems of exegesis upon the bas
of the laws of analysis and the rules of Greek grammar, becom
almost as sure a scientific procedure as the working out of a proble
in mathematics or an experiment in chemistry. The writers of t
Bible, led by the Holy Spirit, wrote within the limits imposed t
their context. No scripture statement is unrelated to the context
which it is found. We therefore approach the study of this batt

44

ground of expositors with the confidence that we are, to change the figure, playing the game according to the rules, not offering the reader an interpretation colored by whatever theological background or personal opinions the writer may have. It is just the scientific way of obeying the laws governing the experiment and tabulating the facts as one finds them.

The book was written before A.D. 70, but after the ascension of our Lord (Heb. 10:11, 12). The temple in Jerusalem was destroyed in A.D. 70, but at the time of the writing of Hebrews, priests were still offering sacrifices, this fact showing that it was still standing. Our Lord is seen, seated in heaven after His ascension. Thus the date was somewhere between A.D. 33 and A.D. 70.

The book was written to prove that a certain proposition was true. The writer states the proposition in the following words: "He (Christ) is the mediator of a better covenant, which was established upon better promises" (8:6); "By so much was Jesus made a surety of a better testament" (7:22); "For if that first covenant had been faultless, then should no place have been sought for the second. For finding fault with them, he saith, Behold, the days come, saith the Lord, when I will make a new covenant with the house of Israel and with the house of Judah" (8:7, 8); "He taketh away the first (covenant), that he may establish the second" (10:9). The proposition is therefore, "The New Testament in Jesus' blood is superior to and supplants the First Testament in animal blood."

We must be careful to note that the book is not an argument to prove that Christianity is superior to and takes the place of Judaism. The New Testament is the reality of which the First Testament was the type. The type consisted of a blood sacrifice which symbolically gave the offerer salvation, while in reality, his salvation came from the New Testament which necessarily is a sacrifice, even the Lord Jesus at Calvary. Christianity is not a sacrifice nor a means of salvation. Christianity is a result of what happened at the Cross, namely, the Christian Church made up of all believers from Pentecost to the Rapture, together with the doctrines and practices of the members of that Church. Furthermore, the New Testament is a covenant made with the Jewish nation. The latter must be distinguished from the Church. It is not a matter of a choice between Judaism and Christianity with which the writer is dealing, but between the type and the reality, between the Levitical sacrifices and the substitutionary atonement of the Lord Jesus.

Since the argument of the book has to do with the abrogation of the Levitical system of sacrifices at the Cross, called in this book the First Testament (9:18), and the supplanting of the same by the sacrifice of our Lord, called in this book the New Testament (9:15), the concern of the writer must therefore be with reference to the *unsaved Jew,* for the proposition which the writer wishes to prove has already been accepted as true by the believing Jew of the first century, for when putting his faith in Christ as High Priest, it became necessary for him to forsake any dependence he may have had upon the typical sacrifices, and recognize in Him their fulfillment.

To prove to him on the basis of his own Old Testament Scriptures that the New Testament has superseded the First, would result in that Jew going on to faith in Christ, if he is really sincere in wanting to be saved. The author proves the proposition he advances twice, and from two different standpoints. First, he compares the relative merits of the founders of the testaments, arguing that a superior workman turns out a superior product. This he does in 1:1-8:6 where he proves that Christ, the Founder of the New Testament is superior to the founders, under God, of the First Testament, who are the prophets (1:1-3), the angels (1:4-2:18), Moses (3:1-6), Joshua (3:7-4:13), and Aaron (4:14-8:6). After stating in 8:6 the proposition he has just shown to be true, he proves it again by comparing the relative merits of the testaments themselves in 8:7-10:39; first, the New Testament was prophesied to be better (8:7-13), second, it is actual, the First Testament typical (9:1-15), third, it is made effective with better blood (9:16-10:39). Then he proves in 11:1-12:2

hat faith, not works, is the way of salvation, and closes his letter
vith admonitions (12:3-13:25).

In addition to proving that the New Testament in Jesus' blood is
uperior to and takes the place of the First Testament in animal blood,
he writer warns those of his unsaved readers who have made a profession of Christ, against the act of renouncing their profession and
returning to the temple sacrifices which they had left, and urges them
o go on to faith in the New Testament sacrifice, the Messiah.

He warns them against letting the New Testament truth slip away
(2:1-4), against hardening the heart against the Holy Spirit (3:7-19),
against falling away (5:11-6:12), against committing the wilful sin
of treading underfoot the Son of God, counting His blood as common blood, and doing insult to the Holy Spirit (10:26-29), all this
being involved in his act of renouncing his professed faith in Christ
and returning to the Levitical sacrifices. These are not separate and
distinct sins, but one sin described in various ways, the sin of this
first century Jew renouncing his professed faith in Messiah as High
Priest and of returning to the abrogated sacrifices of the First
Testament.

He urges them to put their faith in Messiah as High Priest. He is
apprehensive lest there may be among his Jewish readers some who
have an unbelieving heart and who are standing aloof (Greek for
"departing") from the living God (3:12). He fears lest some should
come short of rest in Christ and die in their sins as the generation
that came out of Egypt came short of rest in Canaan and died a
physical death in the wilderness because they did not appropriate the
land by faith (4:1, 2). Therefore he appeals to them to go on to
faith in Messiah. He appeals to them to be followers of those who
through faith and patience inherit the promises (6:12). When one
exhorts someone to do something, it is clear evidence that the latter
is not doing that which is exhorted. These Jews, while making a
profession, had no faith, and under the pressure of persecution, were
in danger of renouncing the intellectual assent which they gave to

the New Testament and returning to the First Testament (10:23,
32-34). The writer urges them to place their faith in the New
Testament High Priest (10:19, 20), using First Testament typology.
Under the First Testament system, the Israelite would enter the
Tabernacle in the person of the priest who would procure salvation
for him through a blood sacrifice. The writer exhorts the first
century Jew to enter, not the Holy of Holies of the temple on earth,
but the Holy of Holies of heaven, and in the same way, in the
Person of the new High Priest, by a freshly slain (new) and living
way, and to do so in the faith which brings full assurance of salvation, a faith they did not have. He warns them against drawing
back from their profession of faith in Christ to perdition, and urges
them on to faith in this same Christ, with the result that their souls
will be saved (10:38, 39). Finally, he devotes chapter eleven to
an argument based upon Old Testament scripture, that faith is the
way of salvation, urging them to look off and away to Jesus in
faith, a thing they were not doing (12:1, 2).

Thus, the purpose of the writer was to reach the professing Jews
of that date who outwardly had left the temple sacrifices, and had
identified themselves with those groups of people who were gathering
around an unseen Messiah, the High Priest of the New Testament
system who had at the Cross fulfilled the First Testament system of
typical sacrifices. These unsaved Jews were under the stress of persecution, and in danger of renouncing their profession and returning
to the abrogated sacrifices of the Levitical system (10:32-34).

We are now ready to present the detailed outline of the book
which is based upon the foregoing historical background and analysis.

I. *The New Testament is better than and takes the place of the
   First Testament because its Founder, the Messiah, is better than*
   (1:1—8:6).

   1. *The prophets* (1:1-3), since Messiah is
      a. God the Son (vv. 1, 2)
      b. Heir of all things (v. 2)

c. Creator of the universe (v. 2)
d. Outshining of God's glory (v. 3)
e. The expression of the nature or essence of Deity (v. 3)
f. The sustainer of the universe He created (v. 3)
g. The Sacrifice that paid for sin (v. 3)

2. *The angels* (1:4—2:18), since He

a. Has a better name, Son (1:4, 5)
b. Is worshipped by angels (v. 6)
c. Is Creator and Master of angels (v. 7)
d. Has an eternal throne (v. 8)
e. Rules in righteousness (v. 8)
f. Is anointed with the Holy Spirit (v. 9)
g. Is unchangeable (vv. 10-12)
h. Is seated at God's right hand (v. 13)
i. Has ushered in a Testament which displaces theirs (2:1-4)

(1) Warning against letting New Testament truth slip away (v. 1)
(2) If rejection of First Testament truth was punished (v. 2) how much more will rejection of New Testament truth be punished (v. 3), which truth was spoken by the Lord who is superior to angels, and which was attested by miracles (vv. 3, 4).

j. Is to be Ruler over the Messianic kingdom (vv. 5-9)

(1) Angels, being servants, cannot rule (v. 5)
(2) Adam placed over earth, lost his dominion through sin (vv. 6-8)
(3) Our Lord has regained it for man, who will be associated with Him in His rule (v. 9)

k. Is the High Priest who has put away sin by the sacrifice of Himself (vv. 10-18)

(1) He becomes Saviour through His death on the cross (v. 10)
(2) This death made possible through His incarnation (vv. 11-16)
(3) As High Priest for human beings, it was necessary that He become incarnate (vv. 17, 18)

3. *Moses* (3:1-6), because

a. He is Creator of Israel, Moses only a member of that house (v. 3)
b. He is Son of God over Israel, Moses only a servant (v. 5)
c. He is the reality, Moses the type (v. 5)

4. *Joshua* (3:7—4:13), because He leads into a spiritual rest which is better than the temporal rest into which Joshua led Israel.

a. Warning against hardening their hearts toward the Holy Spirit as the wilderness wanderers hardened their hearts against God (3:7-9)
b. That generation did not enter Canaan rest (vv. 10, 11)

c. The evidence of the fact that the recipient is saved is that he r
tains his profession of faith in Christ under the stress of persecutio
not going back to the First Testament sacrifice (vv. 6, 14)

d. The recipient will die in his sins if he fails to put his faith in Chri
as High Priest, just as the wilderness wanderers died a physic
death because of unbelief (3:15—4:8). The name "Joshua" shoul
be in text rather than "Jesus" (v. 8)

e. Exhortation to enter rest in Christ, and warning against continue
unbelief (vv. 10-13)

5. *Aaron* (4:14—8:6), since He

a. Ascended through the heavens into the actual Holy of Holies
(4:14-16)

b. Was taken, not from among men, but from the Godhead (5:1)

c. Is sinless (v. 2)

d. Is an eternal High Priest (v. 6)

e. Becomes actual High Priest through His death and resurrectio
(vv. 7-10)

f. Is the reality as High Priest, which does away with the types of th
First Testament (5:11—6:12)

(1) The recipients hard to teach and dull as to spiritual pe
ception (5:11)

(2) They had been instructed in New Testament truth (v. 12)

(3) They were babes, that is, immature in their spiritual thinkin
(v. 13)

(4) They are exhorted to put away "the beginning word of th
Christ," namely, the Levitical ritual, and be borne along t
New Testament truth (6:1)

(5) They are exhorted not to lay down again a foundation o
First Testament doctrines (vv. 1, 2)

(6) They had been enlightened by the Holy Spirit as to New Te
tament truth (v. 4)

(7) They had tasted of that which constitutes salvation (v. 4)

(8) They had been willingly led along by the Holy Spirit in H
pre-salvation work, thus being a "partaker" (same Gree
word translated "partner" in Luke 5:7)

(9) They had tasted the Word (v. 5)

(10) They had seen the attesting miracles (v. 5)

(11) They had been led into repentance (v. 6)

(12) Now should they fall away from their profession of faith i
Christ and back to the sacrifices, it would be impossible t
renew them to repentance (vv. 6-8)

(13) The saved among the recipients would not apostasize (v
9, 10)

(14) The unsaved exhorted to follow in the steps of faith of th
saved (vv. 11, 12)

g. Is a High Priest who actually brings the believer into an eternal standing in grace (vv. 13-20)
  (1) Abraham, the man of faith who was rewarded, a precedent (vv. 13-15)
  (2) God's oath and promise guarantee the believer's eternal retention of salvation (vv. 16-18)
  (3) This salvation made possible by the presence of the High Priest in the heavenly Holy of Holies (vv. 19, 20)
h. A High Priest after the order of Melchisedec (7:1-3)
  (1) Melchisedec, a sinner saved by grace, had no recorded parents, no recorded date of birth or death
  (2) A type therefore of Jesus Christ in His eternal priesthood.
i. A High Priest in a superior order of priesthood (7:4-10)
  (1) The Aaronic priests received tithes (vv. 4, 5)
  (2) Melchisedec received tithes from Abraham, therefore was better than he (vv. 6, 7)
  (3) Melchisedec in type still receiving tithes, whereas Aaronic priests die (v. 8)
  (4) Aaron in Abraham paid tithes to Melchisedec, therefore latter is superior; therefore, our Lord is better than Aaron, being a priest in the order of Melchisedec (vv. 9, 10)
j. Is High Priest of a Testament that offered a sacrifice that put away sin (vv. 11-22)
  (1) The First Testament neither offered nor made anything complete (v. 11)
  (2) First Testament priests came from tribe of Levi, New Testament priest from Judah (vv. 12-17)
  (3) First Testament set aside in favor of a better Testament (vv. 18-22)
k. Lives forever: the Aaronic priests died (vv. 23-28)
  (1) Because mortal, there were many Aaronic priests (v. 23)
  (2) Our Lord because eternal, has a non-transferable priesthood (vv. 24, 25)
  (3) Thus able to save the believer forever (v. 25)
  (4) A better High Priest, because sinless (vv. 26-28)
l. Officiates in a better tabernacle (8:1-6)
  (1) His tabernacle the heavenly one, Aaron's merely the type (vv. 1-5)
  (2) His Testament therefore better than the one Aaron served under (v. 6)

II. *The New Testament is better than and takes the place of the First Testament* (8:7—10:39), *because*

1. *It was prophesied to be better* (8:7-13)
  a. The First Testament faulty in that it did not put away sin (v. 7)
  b. New Testament made with Israel and Judah (v. 8)

    c. First Testament dealt with Israel as with a minor (v. 9)

    d. New Testament through indwelling Spirit brings believers to adult sonship (v. 10)

    e. Under New Testament, all Israel in millennium will be saved (v. 11)

    f. Under New Testament, sins put away (v. 12)

    g. New Testament displaces First Testament (v. 13)

2. *It is actual, the First Testament only typical* (9:1-15)

    a. First Testament typical (vv. 1-10)

        (1) Its sanctuary on earth (v. 1)

        (2) Its appointments typical (vv. 2-5)

        (3) Its priesthood temporary (vv. 6-10)

    b. New Testament actual (vv. 11-15)

        (1) The reality better than the type (v. 11)

        (2) The sacrificial blood better (v. 12)

            (a) Animal blood cleanses from ceremonial defilement (v. 13)

            (b) Jesus' blood cleanses from actual sin (v. 14)

            (c) Therefore, He is the Priest of a better Testament (v. 15)

3. *It is made effective with better blood* (9:16—10-39)

    a. The heavenly Testator Himself dies (9:16-22)

        (1) A last will or testament operative only at testator's death (vv. 16-17)

        (2) First Testament made operative by death of animal (vv. 18-22)

        (3) New Testament made operative by death of Christ.

    b. The better tabernacle purified with better blood (vv. 23, 24)

        (1) Earthly tabernacle cleansed with animal blood (v. 23)

        (2) Heavenly tabernacle cleansed with Jesus' blood (v. 24)

    c. The once for all sacrifice of our Lord better than all the sacrifices of the First Testament (9:25—10:39)

        (1) He suffered once on the cross (9:26); He appears in heaven as High Priest now (v. 24); He will come in His second advent to Israel (v. 28)

        (2) Blood of animals cannot take away sin (10:1-4)

        (3) In view of that fact, our Lord volunteers to become the sacrifice (vv. 5-9)

        (4) In so doing He sets aside the First and establishes the Second Testament (vv. 9, 10)

        (5) Notwithstanding this, Aaronic priests still offered animal sacrifices (v. 11)

        (6) The New Testament Priest procured a finished salvation (vv. 12-14)

        (7) The Holy Ghost through Jeremiah bears witness to the New Testament (vv. 15-17)

(8) The Cross does away with the Levitical sacrifices (v. 18)

(9) The unsaved professing Hebrew exhorted to place his faith in the High Priest Himself (vv. 19-22)

(10) Exhorted to hold fast his profession and not waver between the desire to go on to faith in Christ or to go back to the sacrifices (v. 23)

(11) Exhorted to continue attendance upon the New Testament assembly (v. 25)

(12) Warned not to sin wilfully in renouncing his professed faith in Christ and going back to the sacrifices (v. 26)

(13) For the one who would go back, there remains only judgment (v. 27)

(14) The one who rejected the First Testament was punished (v. 28)

(15) The one committing this threefold sin against the three Persons of the Triune God would be punished more severely (vv. 29-31); the sin namely, of

    (a) Treading under foot the Son of God, a sin against God the Father who sent the Son

    (b) Counting Jesus' blood the same as ours, a sin against God the Son who shed His blood

    (c) Doing despite to the Holy Spirit in turning away from His further ministrations, a sin against God the Spirit who had led them into repentance

(16) The recipients are urged to remember the persecutions they endured for their testimony to Christ, and not let them go for naught by returning to the sacrifices (vv. 32-37)

(17) They are urged to obtain justification through placing their faith in Messiah and not to draw back to perdition (vv. 38, 39)

III. *Faith, not works, the way of salvation as proved by instances of First Testament saints* (11:1—12:2).

1. Faith defined (11:1-3)
2. Faith illustrated (11:4-40)
3. Faith exhorted (12:1-2)

IV. *Final Warnings and Exhortations* (12:3—13:25).

1. If these Jews remain under the chastening hand of God and do not seek to escape persecution by renouncing their professed faith in Messiah, that is an evidence that they are saved. But if they do the opposite, that shows they have never been saved (12:3-17)

2. When they come to New Testament truth, they come, not to the thunders of Sinai, but to the grace of Calvary (vv. 18-24)

3. They are warned not to refuse the Lord Jesus, for those who refused
   Moses were punished (vv. 25-29)
4. General Exhortations (13:1-17)
5. Closing words (vv. 18-25)

One thing more is necessary before we look at the exegesis of the
Greek text of our passage. We must indicate its analytical structure.
The analytical section we are studying starts at 5:11 and goes to 6:12.
It consists of a description of the spiritual status of the Jew whom the
writer wishes to reach, of a warning not to go back to the abrogated
sacrifices of the Levitical system, and of an exhortation to put a heart
faith in the New Testament sacrifice, the Messiah. It is one of the
passages found throughout the book containing a warning not to go
back to the type but to go on to faith in the reality.

This individual is described as hard to teach and dull of hearing
(5:11), one who ought to be able to teach but cannot (5:12), one
who is a babe (5:13), who was enlightened, who tasted of the heavenly gift and had been made a partaker of the Holy Ghost (6:4), as
one who had tasted the word of God and the powers of the age to
come (6:5), and who had been brought to repentance (6:6).

He is exhorted to put off once for all any dependence upon the
Levitical sacrifices and to go on to faith in the New Testament Sacrifice (6:1). The first part of this exhortation is strengthened by the
warning that should he fall away, that is, renounce his professed faith
in Messiah as the High Priest of the New Testament and return to the
abrogated sacrifices of the First Testament, he would be crucifying
the Son of God. This would be an act which would make it impossible to restore him again to that place of repentance to which he had
been brought (6:6). The second part of the exhortation is repeated
in the words, "that ye be not slothful but followers of them who
through faith and patience inherit the promises" (6:12), this second
exhortation to faith being strengthened by the example of the saved
among these Jews who showed by their lives that they really had exercised saving faith, the "beloved" of 6:9. We must be careful to note
that this letter to the Hebrews is written to the professing church
made up of saved and unsaved, but the concern of the writer is with

eference to the unsaved. We are now ready for an exegetical study
f the Greek text of the passage under discussion, based upon the an-
lysis of the entire epistle, the only scientific way of going about our
vork. We have spent quite a bit of time and space upon our founda-
ion, but as in the case of a building, the larger and deeper the foun-
lation, the more stable and secure is the superstructure.

Verse eleven. The words "of whom" of 5:11 are from a preposi-
ion and a relative pronoun, which latter is in a case form that indi-
ates either the masculine or neuter gender. The last named individu-
l to which a masculine pronoun could point, is Melchisedec. But the
vriter is not concerned with him in what he has to say in 5:11-6:12.
Therefore, the pronoun is neuter, referring to the teaching of the
Melchisedecan priesthood of Jesus Christ, a thing which these Jewish
readers who were still unsaved, needed to be convinced of, if they
were to leave the Aaronic priesthood and its system of Levitical sacrifices. The superiority of the New Testament sacrifice over the Levitical offerings is the very thing which the writer is seeking to prove.
He shows that Melchisedec is better than Aaron. Therefore, the sacrifice of Christ is better than the Levitical sacrifices. The words "hard
to be uttered" are literally "hard of interpretation to be speaking."
It is difficult to make this teaching intelligible to these unsaved Hebrews. The difficulty is experienced by the writer. However, it is not
found in any lack in the writer, but in the spiritual condition of the
subjects of this warning and exhortation. They are dull of hearing.

The word "dull" is from a Greek word meaning "slow, sluggish."
It is used of the numbed limbs of a sick lion, and the stupid hopes of
the wolf that heard the nurse threaten to throw the child to the
wolves. It is a combination of two Greek words, one meaning "no,"
the other "to push," hence, "no push," thus "slow, sluggish." These
Hebrews were slow, sluggish, stupid, numbed, in their apprehension
of the teaching of New Testament truth. This made it difficult to
teach them. The difficulty lay therefore not in the writer but in them.

But they had not always been in that condition, as is shown by the
word translated "are." The word means "to become." It is in the

perfect tense which tense speaks of a process completed in past tim
having present results. These Hebrews had at one time a spiritu
apprehension of New Testament truth sufficiently clear that they sa
that the New Testament Sacrifice displaced the First Testament o
ferings. The writer tells us that also in the words, "who were onc
enlightened" (6:4). The inability to apprehend was not a natura
inherent, and pardonable weakness, but a culpable incapacity whic
was the result of past neglect of and a gradual working away from
New Testament truth (2:1-3). It was the hardening of the hear
against the ministrations of the Holy Spirit (3:7, 8). It was a dete
rioration of spiritual apprehension on the part of these unsaved He
brews who had been the recipients of the pre-salvation ministry o
the Holy Spirit, who had been leading them on step by step towar
the act of faith in the New Testament sacrifice, the Messiah. The us
of the perfect tense here tells us that the process had gone on to th
point of completion, with finished results. Their neglect had done it
work, and they as a result were in a settled state of spiritual stupidity
so far as their ability to apprehend New Testament truth was con
cerned. The fuller translation of 5:11 is as follows: "Concerning
which (teaching, namely, that the Lord Jesus is a high priest afte
the order of Melchisedec) there is much that we can say; yet when i
comes to the saying of it, one finds it difficult to explain, because you
are become those who are in a settled state of sluggishness, yes, o
stupidity in your apprehension of the same."

Verse twelve. "Time" is from the Greek word speaking of time
contemplated merely as the succession of moments, not from the
word referring to a definite portion of time having limits. The word
is in a construction which refers to extension. Thus because of the
length of time in which these Hebrews had been under the instruction of teachers presenting New Testament truth, they ought to be
teaching the same. The "ought" is one of moral obligation. The
word is used of a necessity imposed either by law or duty, or by the
matter under consideration. "Again" is in an emphatic position in
the Greek and is to be construed with "need," not "teach." They

again have need that some one be teaching them, the word "teach" showing a continuous process. These Hebrews had grown so sluggish in their apprehension of New Testament truth that it would require many lessons to do anything with them.

"Principles" is from a Greek word which refers to rudimentary ideas. The word "first" in the Greek text refers to the first in a series, the very beginning of things. "Oracles" is from the Greek word used also in Romans 3:2, and Acts 7:38, and refers to divine utterances. Thus, these Hebrews again needed someone to be teaching them, and the start should be made with the very beginnings of the rudiments of the divine utterances in New Testament truth. "Meat" is from the Greek word meaning "food" in general. Today the word "meat" refers to the edible flesh of animals. When the Authorized Version was translated, it meant food in general. Our Lord said, "My food is to do the will of Him that sent Me and to finish His work" (John 4:34). "Are become" is perfect tense, speaking of a process finished in past time with present results. These Hebrews by their neglect of New Testament truth, and their gradual turning away from it because of the pressure of persecution which they were undergoing, had come to the place where they could only assimilate milk. The word "strong" is literally "solid." Thus, only a liquid diet, milk, the very beginning of the rudimentary teachings of the New Testament could be administered, not solid food, the deeper teachings of the Word. The fuller translation follows. "In fact, when at this time you are under moral obligation to be teaching by reason of the extent of time (you have been under instruction), again you are in need of someone to be teaching you the very beginning of the rudimentary things in the oracles of God, and are become such as have need of milk, and not of solid food."

Verse thirteen. The writer continues his explanation in the words, "For everyone that useth milk is unskillful in the word of righteousness; for he is a babe." "Useth" has the idea of "has for his share in ordinary feeding." It refers to an exclusive diet of milk. Adults drink milk, but it is not their exclusive diet. "Unskillful" is from a

Greek word that means "inexperienced." The word "babe" is not the translation of a Greek word meaning an "infant," such as is used in Luke 2:16, nor from a word translated "child" as in Luke 1:7, which latter word is related to the verb which means "to give birth to," and therefore speaks of a child in its birth relationship to its parents; but from a word which means "immature" as contrasted to "mature." Paul uses this word three times in contrast to a word which means "mature."[1] In I Corinthians 2:6 he says that he speaks wisdom among the perfect, that is, the spiritually mature. But the Corinthian saints were babes in Christ, immature Christians. He speaks of those who are perfect, that is, spiritually mature, in contrast to children, namely, immature Christians (Eph. 4:13, 14). Here he contrasts these Hebrews who are immature so far as their spiritual apprehension is concerned, with those of full age, namely spiritually mature.

We must be careful to note that the Greek word "babe" in itself carries with it no implication of salvation. The phrase, "babe in Christ," as used today, refers to a new convert. Paul's use of it in I Corinthians 3:1 is different. There he refers to immature Christians. One can be forty years old in the Faith and still be immature spiritually. Furthermore, the word "babe" needed the qualifying phrase "in Christ" to indicate that these Corinthian "babes" were saved. Therefore, the word "babe" in our Hebrew passage cannot be made to show that the person referred to is a saved individual. It has no birth relationship idea about it. The analysis of the book and the context in which the word is found require that we understand it to refer to these unsaved Hebrews who because of their neglect of New Testament truth and their turning away from it, have again become immature in their spiritual apprehension of the same.

These who are described as perfect or mature and thus able to partake of solid food (strong meat), are said to, "by reason of use, have their senses exercised to discern both good and evil." The word "use" is translated from a Greek word which refers to a habit of the

---

1. *Treasures* pp. 113-121.

body or mind. It speaks here of the habitual use of the perceptive faculties (senses) which are being vigorously exercised. This results in the ability to discriminate between good and evil, and in this context, good and evil teaching. But these Hebrews had abused their perceptive faculties in rejecting the new light given and turning again to the First Testament sacrifices. Light rejected, blinds.

The translation of 5:13, 14 is as follows: (13) "For everyone whose sole diet is milk, is inexperienced in a message which is righteous in quality, for he is a (spiritually) immature person. (14) But solid food belongs to those who are (spiritually) mature, to those who on account of long usage have their powers of perception exercised to the point where they are able to discriminate between both that which is good in character and that which is evil."

Verses one and two. We now come to a careful study of the two Greek words translated "leaving" and "let us go on." A correct understanding of these is absolutely essential to the proper exegesis of the passage we are treating. The word translated "leaving" is a verb meaning "to put or place," with a preposition prefixed which means "off" or "away." The preposition implies separation and is used with a case in Greek which implies separation. The case speaks not only of the literal removal of one object from the vicinity of another, but also of the departure from antecedent relations such as derivation, cause, origin, and the like. It contemplates an alteration in state from the viewpoint of the original situation. It comprehends an original situation from which the idea expressed is in some way removed. Thus, the basic idea in the verb is that of an action which causes a separation. The various meanings of the word are as follows: "to send away, to bid go away or depart, to let go, to send from one's self, to let alone, to let be, to disregard." It is used of teachers, writers, and speakers when presenting a topic, in the sense of "to leave, not to discuss." In manuscripts of the Koine period, we have as reported in Moulton and Milligan's *Vocabulary of the Greek Testament,* the sentence, "Let the pot drop," and the clause, "not to leave me to be neglected in a strange land;" also an appeal from a forsaken girl to her lover, "Oh, lord, do not leave me." In Matthew 13:36 and Mark 4:36 this word is used of the sending away of the multitudes. *Expositor's Greek Testament* translates it here, "Let us abandon." Alford explains it in the words, "Leaving as behind and done with in order to go on to another thing." To use the word "leaving" in the sense that a superstructure of a house leaves the foundation and yet builds on it, as is done by some expositors, is a case of English eisegesis (reading into the text what is not there). But such a usage will not stand the scrutiny of the Greek exegesis of this word (taking out of the text what is there), nor is it in accord with the historical background and the analysis of the book.

The word is an aorist participle. Greek grammar tells us that the action of the aorist participle precedes the action of the leading verb in the sentence, which in this case is "let us go on." The aorist tense speaks of a once for all action. We could translate, "Therefore, having abandoned once for all the principles of the doctrine of Christ, let us go on to perfection." The act of abandoning is the pre-requisite to that of going on. One cannot go on without first separating one's self from that to which one is attached. The word translated "let us go on" is first person plural subjunctive, which is used for hortatory purposes in Greek. That is, we have an exhortation here. Another way of exhorting one in Greek is to use the imperative mode. There is a classification of the participle in Greek which is designated, "the participle used as an imperative." Our word "abandoning" is an imperative participle. It gives a command.

We come now to the word translated "let us go on." The verb means "to carry or bear." *Moulton* and *Milligan* report its use as "bring" and "carry," in such sentences from early Greek manuscripts as: "Her tunic, the white one which you have, bring when you come, but the turquoise one do not bring," and "Return from where you are before someone fetches you," the words "bring" and "fetch" being the translations of this word. The word is in the passive voice, which means that the subject is passive or inactive itself and is being acted upon by some outside agent. Thus we could translate, "abandoning once for all . . . let us be carried along."

Now what does the writer exhort these Hebrews to abandon, and to what does he urge them to allow themselves to be borne along? Well, what does a mariner do when he is at a loss as to exactly where he is? He checks his position by his instruments. The aviator in a similar situation checks his course by the radio beam. An exegete in a similar situation will consult the historical background and analysis of the book. And that is exactly what we will do. We found that the writer proves twice over that the New Testament in Jesus' Blood is superior to and takes the place of the First Testament in animal blood. After proving this, he shows that faith is the only way of appropriating the salvation which the High Priest procured for sinners at the Cross. In the light of this demonstration, he warns them against falling away. He exhorts them to go on to faith in the New Testament Sacrifice. Having left the temple sacrifices, and having identified themselves with the visible Church, from what could they fall away but from their profession of Christ as High Priest, and to what could they fall back to but First Testament sacrifices?

Thus the words, "the principles of the doctrine of Christ," must refer to the First Testament sacrifices, for these Jews are exhorted to abandon them. Likewise, the word "perfection" must speak of the New Testament Sacrifice to which they are exhorted to allow themselves to be borne along. Our analysis has guided us to the correct interpretation.

A study of the Greek text here will substantiate this. The words, "the principles of the doctrine of Christ" are literally, "the word of the beginning of the Christ." The phrase "of the beginning" does not modify "Christ," for He had no beginning. It therefore modifies "word." The phrase, "the beginning word of the Christ" refers to that teaching concerning Him which is first presented in the Bible. And what is that but the truth concerning His Person and work found in the symbolism of the Levitical sacrifices. The tabernacle, priesthood, and offerings all speak of Him in His Person and work. And this interpretation is in exact accord with the argument of the book. All dependence upon the Levitical sacrifices is to be set aside in order that the Hebrews can go on to "perfection," as we have it here. That the word "perfection" speaks of the New Testament Sacrifice, the Lord Jesus, and the Testament He inaugurated by His work on the Cross, is seen from the use of the Greek word here, referring to that which is complete, and in 7:11 where the writer argues that if perfection (same Greek word) were under the Levitical priesthood, then there would be no further need of another priesthood. But since God has brought in a priestly line after the order of Melchisedec, it logically follows that completeness obtains under the New Testament which He brought in. He states in 7:19 that the law of Moses, namely the sacrificial law, made nothing perfect. That is, the Levitical offerings were not complete in that the blood of bulls and goats could not pay for sin. Neither was their completeness in what they could do for the offerer. But "this Man (the Lord Jesus), after He had offered one sacrifice for sins, sat down in perpetuity on the right hand of God" (10:12). His sacrifice was complete. Thus, the writer exhorts these Hebrews to abandon the type for the reality, that which is incomplete for that which is complete. Before leaving this point, the English reader should know that the expressions, "the first principles of the oracles of God" (5:12), and "the principles of the doctrine of Christ" (6:1), are quite different in the Greek. The word "principles" in these verses comes from two different Greek words. The expression in 5:12 refers to the elementary teachings in New Testament truth, and the one in 6:1, to the teaching of the First Testament where Christ was first spoken of.

But the question arises, if these Hebrews had left the First Testament sacrifices and had made a profession of Christ, why does the writer exhort them to abandon these? The answer is that the Holy Spirit had enlightened them (6:4) so that they saw that the sacrifices had been done away with at the Cross, and that the New Testament sacrifice was the only way of salvation. They had acted upon that and had abandoned their dependence upon these, and had made a profession of faith in the New Testament sacrifice. Their former dependence upon the sacrifices had not resulted in their salvation for either one of the following two reasons. In the case of those Hebrews

o lived before the Cross, that dependence was a mere intellectual
ent such as they were giving now to the New Testament. And in
e case of those who were born since the Cross, their dependence
on the sacrifices was of no avail since these had been set aside by
d at the Cross. But under stress of persecution (10:32-34) they
re absenting themselves from the New Testament assemblies
0:25), and were wavering (10:23), literally "leaning," that is,
·y were leaning toward the Levitical system again, and letting New
stament truth slip away (2:1). The result was that their spiritual
rceptions were dulled, had become sluggish (5:11), and they them-
ves had become immature in their thinking along spiritual lines.
is growing dependence upon First Testament sacrifices, they were
horted to abandon, and abandoning these, they would be in that
ıce where the Holy Spirit could carry them along in His pre-salva-
n work to the act of faith. We must be careful to note that these
·brews had not yet finally and irrevocably discarded New Testa-
nt truth. The tendency was that way. The writer was attempting to
ıch them before it was too late.

If they would go back to the First Testament sacrifices, they would
laying again the foundation of the First Testament, and building
on it again. This foundation is given us in 6:1, 2. "Repentance
·m dead works" is First Testament teaching, was preached by John
· Baptist, and is in contrast to New Testament teaching of repent-
ce toward God (Acts 20:21). "Faith toward God" is First Testa-
·nt teaching, and is contrasted to the New Testament teaching of
th in our Lord Jesus Christ (Acts 20:21). "The doctrine of bap-
ms" (same Greek word translated "washings" in 9:10) refers to
· ceremonial ablutions or washings of Judaism, and is typical of
· New Testament cleansing of the conscience from dead works to
·ve the living and true God by the washing of regeneration and
newing of the Holy Ghost (Titus 3:5). The "laying on of hands"
fers to the imposition of the offerer's hand upon the sacrificial offer-
g of the Levitical system (Levit. 1:4), and is typical of the act of a
aner today laying his hand of faith upon the sacred head of the
mb of God. "The resurrection of the dead," an Old Testament

doctrine, is more fully developed in the doctrine of the out-resurre
tion from among the dead (Phil. 3:11 Greek) which indicates th
there are two resurrections, one of the saints, the other of the lo
"Eternal judgment" of the old dispensation is in contrast to the "
judgment for the believer in Christ" of the new. Thus, these Hebrev
are exhorted not to return to First Testament teaching, but to go on
faith in the New Testament Sacrifice.

Verse three. But coupled with this exhortation is an ominous hin
as Vincent calls it. It is in the words, "And this will we do if God pe
mit." Here are his words: "An ominous hint is conveyed that th
spiritual dullness of the readers may prevent the writer from develo
ing his theme, and them from receiving his higher instruction. Th
issue is dependent on the power which God may impart to his teac
ing, but His efforts may be thwarted by the impossibility of repen
ance on their part. No such impossibility is imposed by God, but
may reside in a moral condition which precludes the efficient actic
of the agencies which work for repentance, so that God cannot pern
the desired consequence to follow the word of teaching." All of whi
goes to say that while there is such a thing as the sovereign grace
God, yet there is also such a thing as the free will of man. God nev
in the case of salvation violates man's free will. The choice mu
be made by these Hebrews between going back to the sacrifices
on to faith in Christ as High Priest. But their spiritual declensic
if persisted in, would result in their putting themselves beyond th
reach of the Holy Spirit. This is implied in 3:7, 8 where they a
warned that if they desire to hear the voice of the Holy Spirit, th
should not harden their hearts, the implication being clear that th
could harden their hearts to the extent that they would have no mo
desire to hear the voice of the Holy Spirit. This shows that th
"impossibility" of 6:4, 6 resides in the condition of their heart
not in the grace of God. The translation of 6:1-3 is as follow
"Therefore, having put away once for all the beginning instructic
concerning the Messiah, let us be borne along to that which is co
plete, not laying again a foundation of repentance from dead work

and of faith toward God, of instruction concerning washings, imposition of hands, the resurrection of the dead, and eternal judgment. And this will we do, if only God permits."

Verse four. And now the writer presents a most solemn warning to those among his readers who would persist in their leanings toward the First Testament and their abandonment of the New. It would be impossible to renew them again to repentance. The Greek word translated "impossible" cannot be diluted to mean "difficult." The same word is used in Hebrews 6:18; 10:4, and 11:6, where it can only mean "impossible." Likewise, the word "renew" must be taken in its full force. *Expositor's Greek Testament* says that it means that those who have once experienced a renewal cannot again have a like experience. The person described cannot again be brought to a life-changing repentance. Repentance is a work of the Holy Spirit on the heart of the one who is approaching the act of faith in Christ. It is usually involved in that act, but can also exist separate and apart from it, as is seen in the present instance. These Hebrews had allowed the Holy Spirit to carry them along to the place of repentance. Now should they refuse the proffered faith by which they could lay hold of the High Priest as their Saviour, and return to the abrogated sacrifices of the First Testament, it would be impossible to bring them back to the act of repentance again. And as we have seen, the impossibility would inhere in their own spiritual condition, not in the grace of God.

In connection with this solemn warning, the writer reminds these Hebrews of all that a loving God had done for them. They were once enlightened. The word translated "once" is literally "once for all," and is used of that which is so done as to be of perpetual validity, and never needs repetition. That means that as these Hebrews listened to the message of the New Testament, the Holy Spirit enlightened their minds and hearts to clearly understand it. The work of the Spirit with reference to their understanding of New Testament truth had been so thorough that it needed never to be repeated for the purpose of making the truth clear to them.

These Hebrews had understood these issues perfectly. The type was set aside for the reality, the First Testament for the New. They were enlightened as every sinner is enlightened who comes under the hearing of God's Word. But as the unsaved in an evangelistic meeting today clearly understand the message of salvation but sometimes refuse the light and turn back into the darkness of sin and continued unbelief, so these Hebrews were in danger of doing a like thing.

They had tasted of the heavenly gift, and in such a way as to give them a distinct impression of its character and quality, for the words "once for all" qualify this word also. These Hebrews were like the spies at Kadesh-Barnea who saw the land and had the very fruit in their hands, and yet turned back (4:1-13). One of the pre-salvation ministries of the Spirit is to enable the unsaved who come under the hearing of the gospel, to have a certain appreciation of the blessedness of salvation. He equips them with a spiritual sense of taste with reference to the things of God. Many a sinner has been buoyed up by the message of the evangelist, has had stirrings in his bosom, has had a pleasant reaction towards the truth, and yet when the decision time came has said, "The world is too much with us," and has turned back into sin.

They had been made partakers of the Holy Ghost. We must be careful to note that the Greek word translated "partakers" does not mean "possessors," in the sense that these Hebrews possessed the Holy Spirit as an indwelling Person who had come to take up His permanent abode in their hearts. The word is a compound of the Greek verb "to have or hold" and a preposition meaning "with," thus "to hold with." It is used in Luke 5:7 where it is translated "partners," signifying one who co-operates with another in a common task or undertaking. It is used in Hebrews 1:9 where the angels are "fellows" of our Lord, partners or associates with Him in the work of salvation. It is used in Hebrews 3:1 where the recipients of this letter are called associates of the heavenly calling, Hebrews who had left the earthly calling of the nation Israel and d identified themselves with the Church which has a heavenly lling. It is used in Hebrews 3:14, where it speaks of those who e partners or associates of Christ.

The word was so used in secular Greek. Moulton and Milligan ve examples of its usage in the following phrases: "We, Dionysius n of Socrates and the *associate* collectors;" "Pikos son of Pamon- es and his *colleagues,*" "the *joint-owner* of a holding," "I am able to *take part in* the cultivation," "Some do so because they are *rtners* in their misdeeds." Thus the word signifies, not a posses- r, but a partner, a colleague, an associate, one who takes part th another in some one activity. It is so used here. These Hebrews came partners or associates of the Holy Spirit in the sense that ey willingly co-operated with Him in receiving His pre-salvation inistry, that of leading them on step by step toward the act of ith. He had led them into the act of repentance. The next step uld be that of faith. Here they were in danger of turning their cks upon the Spirit and returning to the sacrifices. Peter in his st epistle (1:2), in the words "through sanctification of the Spirit to obedience," speaks of this work of the Holy Spirit on the un- ved, setting them apart from unbelief to faith.[1] This word does t at all imply that these Hebrews had been born of the Spirit, aled with the Spirit, indwelt by the Spirit, anointed with the Spirit, ptized by the Spirit into the Body of Christ, or filled with the irit. This work of the Holy Spirit in leading them on towards ith was a once for all work, so thoroughly done that it needed ver to be repeated. However, there was nothing permanent of elf in this work, for the work was only a means to an end. This shown by the aorist participle used, referring to the mere fact, t a perfect, speaking of a finished act having present results. The ct that the writer did not use the perfect tense here, which is a ecialized tense, but rather the aorist, which is the maid of all rk, points to the incompleteness of the work of the Spirit in the

---

1. *Bypaths* pp. 39-43.

case of these Hebrews. So far as the work had been done, it w‹ perfect, thorough. But it would not be complete until the Hebre‹ accepted the proffered faith from the Spirit. The incompletene of the work would be due therefore, not to the Spirit, but to the‹ unwillingness to go on as a partner or co-operator with the Spirit.

Verse five. They had tasted "the good word of God," which equivalent to "tasted of the heavenly gift," and "the powers of tl world to come." The word translated "powers" is used in the Gospe repeatedly to refer to miracles, and is translated by the words, "wo‹ derful works, mighty works, miracles, powers." The word "world is the word which in Romans 12:2; I Corinthians 1:20, 2:6;] Corinthians 4:4 refers to an age, that is, a period of time characte‹ ized by a certain type of life or economy of government or oth‹ social regulating agency. In the passages just mentioned it refers ‹ "all that floating mass of thoughts, opinions, maxims, speculation hopes, impulses, aims, aspirations, at any time current in the worl‹ which it may be impossible to seize and accurately define, but whic constitute a most real and effective power, being the moral or in moral atmosphere which at every moment of our lives we inhal‹ again inevitably to exhale, the subtle informing spirit of the worl of men who are living alienated and apart from God" (Trencl *Synonyms of the New Testament*). It is the "age," the "spirit c genius of the age." This is the present age in which we are livin‹ The age to come is the Millennial Age. What a change there wi be when God the Son reigns on earth personally, and His Chose People are saved. These Hebrews had seen attesting miracles pe‹ formed, the performance of which proved to them that the Ne Testament was from God. This was another factor which mad their guilt so enormous. It is interesting to note in passing tha attesting miracles will again be performed in the Millennial Ag when the Lord Jesus comes back to earth.

Verse six. We come now to a study of the Greek word translate "fall away." It is used only here in the New Testament. It is foun in the Greek translation of the Old Testament in Ezekiel 14:13, 15:8

where Israel is seen falling away from the true worship of Jehovah. The Greek word itself means "to fall beside a person or thing, to slip aside, hence to deviate from the right path, to turn aside, to wander." Moulton and Milligan give two occasions of its use in the Greek papyri which exactly correspond to its usage in Hebrews. The first is; "If the terms of it (the contract) should be broken or it in any other way rendered invalid," which usage is similar to that in the case of these Hebrews should they break their contract which they made with the Holy Spirit when they willingly became His associates in His pre-salvation work, breaking their contract by refusing His further ministrations and going back to the First Testament sacrifices. The other instance of its use is in a document which speaks of a person who falls back on his earlier interpretation of a verb. How like the act of this Hebrew, should he fall back to his earlier position with regard to the sacrifices. The words "fall away" are from a participle in the aorist tense, the time of action being past time, the classification being a conditional participle. The translation reads therefore, "if they fell away." Paul here presents a hypothetical case, warning these unsaved Hebrews from making such a thing a reality.

Now the writer gives the reason why these Hebrews cannot be brought back to the place of repentance, should they return to the First Testament sacrifices. They would crucify to themselves the Son of God and put Him to an open shame. The word "afresh" is not needed nor is it warranted from the Greek. It was included in the translation from a prefixed preposition to the verb meaning "to crucify." But *Expositor's Greek Testament* makes it clear that this preposition here means "up" and refers to the lifting up on the Cross, also that the compound verb was used and understood by the Hellenistic world to mean only "crucify." Besides, any "crucifying to themselves" would be a fresh crucifixion. The words "to themselves" have the idea, "so far as they are concerned." "The apostate crucifies Christ on his own account by virtually confirming the judgment of the actual crucifiers, declaring that he too has made trial of Jesus and found Him no true Messiah but a deceiver and therefore worthy of death" (Ex. Gk. Test.). "The greatness of the guilt is aggravated by the fact that they thus treat the Son of God" (Vincent).

The words "put to an open shame" are from a Greek word used also in Numbers 25:4 (Septuagint translation), where it implies exposing to ignominy or infamy, such as was effected in barbarous times by exposing the quarters of the executed criminal, or leaving him hanging in chains. Archilochus says Plutarch, rendered himself infamous by writing obscene verses. He put himself to open shame.

All this these Hebrews would be doing to the Son of God if they renounced their professed faith in Messiah and went back to the First Testament. Should they do this, they would render their hearts so hard that they would be impervious to the ministry of the Holy Spirit. They would be irrevocably lost. There would be no more hope for them. Of course, it should be plain that this sin cannot be committed today. There is no temple in Jerusalem, no sacrifices to leave and to return to, no attesting miracles being performed, no question as to the closing of the old dispensation and the opening of the new. This sin is not the same as the rejection of Christ by the sinner today. It is not only a rejection of Christ, bad as that is. This sin involves the relative merits of the First and New Testaments, the abandonment of the type for the reality, the sin of the crucifixion of Messiah by His own people.

Verses seven and eight. In these verses the writer presents an analogy in nature. The abundant and frequently renewed rain, represents the free and reiterated bestowal of spiritual enlightenment and impulse to these Hebrews. One piece of ground reacts by producing herbage good for food. This is the Hebrew who accepts the New Testament by faith. On the other hand, the ground that receives the same rain, but produces thorns and briers, is likened to the Hebrew who being the recipient of the pre-salvation work of the Spirit, yet turns his back on Him and goes back to the First Testament sacri-es, the apostate who can look for nothing but certain judgment 0:26-31).

The translation of 6:4-8 is as follows: (4) "For it is impossible the case of those who were once for all enlightened, and who th tasted once for all the heavenly gift and became associates ellows, partners) of the Holy Spirit, (5) and who tasted once for the good word of God and the miracles of the coming age, (6) they broke their contract (if they reverted to their former posion), to renew them to repentance, since they crucify the Son of od on their own account and put Him to an open shame. (7) For nd which drank in the rain that comes oft upon it and produces rbage meet for those on whose account it is tilled, partakes of a essing from God. (8) But if it brings forth thorns and thistles, is rejected and nigh unto a curse, and its end is burning."

Verses nine to twelve. We come now to the concluding section of is analytical unit. We will need to remind ourselves again of the istorical background and analysis of the book, and the purpose of e author in writing it. He was writing to the visible professing hurch made up of saved and unsaved. There is no greeting to the ints like we find in most of the epistles. The concern of the writer with those of his unsaved Jewish readers who under stress of ersecution were in danger of renouncing their professed faith in hrist and returning to the abrogated sacrifices of the First Testa-ent. These he repeatedly warns against this act, and repeatedly xhorts to go on to faith in the New Testament sacrifice, Messiah. he fact that he urges them on in faith, shows that they merely made a rofession and were not saved. After issuing this solemn warning in :11-6:8, he addresses the saved among his readers and uses them as n example to urge the unsaved on to the act of faith.

He addresses them as "beloved." The word occurs only here in is epistle. It is plural in number, and the word used is the one at speaks of God's love. One could translate, "divinely loved ones." t is clear that the writer is differentiating between the saved and nsaved among his readers in this section, because after holding up he "beloved ones" as examples, he says, "We desire that everyone

of you do shew the same diligence to the full assurance of hope un
the end, that ye be not slothful, but followers of them who throug
faith and patience inherit the promises." These words imply th
some of his readers were not of the class called "beloved" who
lives showed that they were saved. This group whom he exhor
here is made up of those whom he warns in 5:11-6:9. He urges the
to follow those who have exercised faith, implying that they ha
no faith.

He says that he is persuaded better things of these who are save
"Persuaded" in the Greek implies that the writer had felt misgivin
but had overcome them. His conviction was the result of proc
The perfect tense is used, "I have come to a settled conviction." I
assures them that he is persuaded better things of them than tho:
of falling away and crucifying the Son of God. He also is persuade
that things that accompany salvation are true to them. One of the:
he gives in verse 10. The work of the Holy Spirit spoken of i
verses 4-6 precedes salvation. The constant practice of these calle
"beloved," namely, that of ministering to the saints, shows that th
Holy Spirit had produced His fruit in their lives, and that they wei
truly born-again ones.

The writer then uses these as an example for his unsaved reade
to follow. Their lives showed evidence of faith, and the mere pr
fessing Hebrew should go on to that act. In verses 13-20, the gre
example of faith, Abraham, is introduced to strengthen the exho
tation.

The translation of 6:9-12 is as follows: (9) "But we have con
to a settled persuasion concerning you, divinely loved ones, the thing
which are better and which are attached to a saved condition of lif
even if we thus speak. (10) For God is not unjust to forget you
work and the divine love which you exhibited toward His name i
that you ministered to the saints and are continuing to ministe
(11) But we are strongly desirous that each one of you show th
same diligence which will develop your hope into full assuranc
until the end, (12) in order that you may become, not sluggish, bu

imitators of those who through faith and patient waiting are now inheriting the promises."

The sluggishness here refererd to is not sluggishness of apprehension as in 5:11, but a certain slowness and hesitancy about going on to faith in the New Testament sacrifice. Thus as *Expositor's Greek Testament* says: "The writer courteously implies that some already showed the zeal demanded, but he desires that each individual, even those whose condition prompted the foregoing warning, should bestir themselves. He desires that they show a corresponding perfectness of hope."

May we suggest in closing, that we have not touched the wonderful beauty of the Book of Hebrews, namely, the Person and work of our Lord Jesus as High Priest seen in the symbolism of the Old Testament priesthood and ritual. The analysis of the book should help to open up these glories to the humble Bible student. In other words, the sixth chapter is not the Book of Hebrews, but just a rather difficult part that needs careful and thorough treatment.

Chapter IV

LIGHT FROM THE GREEK ON THE MINISTRY OF THE HOLY SPIRIT

The Imperative Necessity of His Ministry

THE ministry of the Holy Spirit is an all-important factor in th life of the Christian. It makes all the difference in the world a to whether a Christian has an intelligent understanding of what th Holy Spirit is ready to do for him in his life and in his service, an what his adjustment to the Holy Spirit should be in order that H may fulfill His ministry in and through the saint in the most efficie way. The secret of a successful, God-glorifying, powerful, swee courageous, victorious Christian life is in this correct adjustment the Holy Spirit on the part of the Christian. The imperative nece sity of His ministry is seen in Galatians 4:19, which verse we wi look at carefully in the Greek text.

The words, "my little children" are more accurately, "my chi dren." The diminutive form of the word "child" is not used her These to whom Paul was writing, had been won to the Lord Jes under the ministry of the great apostle. He says that he is travailir in birth for them. That is, he is straining every nerve and exertir all his pent-up love for them in earnestly praying for them. He praying that Christ be again formed in them.

The word "formed" in the Greek means "to give outward expre sion of one's inward character." We use the English word "form in that sense in the sentence, "I went to a tennis match yesterday, ar the winning player's form was excellent." We mean by that, that t outward expression which he gave of his inward ability to pla tennis, was excellent. Thus we translate, "My children, of who I travail in birth again until Christ be outwardly expressed in you

The verb is in the passive voice. That means that the subject of the verb is passive, inactive, does not act himself, but is acted upon by an outside agent. That brings us to the truth that the Lord Jesus, indwelling the believer's heart, does not express Himself, does not manifest Himself, in and through the life of that Christian. He has given that ministry over to the Holy Spirit. He is the agent who takes of the things of Christ and manifests them to us and through us. Our Lord speaks of this same passive state in which He dwells within the Christian's heart, and the fact that the Holy Spirit manifests Him in His beauty through the life of the saint, in John 16:14. His words are, "He shall glorify me: for he shall receive of mine, and shall shew it unto you." There is a demonstrative pronoun in the Greek text which is not brought out in the English translation. "That One shall glorify Me." That is, our Lord says in effect; "I will not glorify Myself. That One (the Holy Spirit), shall glorify Me." The word "receive" refers, not to a passive acceptance, but to an active appropriation. The Holy Spirit's ministry is to take of the things of Christ and show them to the believer. In that way He expresses the Lord Jesus through the Christian. The Christian's life is a prism in which the Holy Spirit breaks up into its component graces, the beauty of our Lord. If the believer does not have an intelligent understanding of and subjection to the ministry of the Holy Spirit, there is little of the Lord Jesus seen in his life. The Holy Spirit does the best He can under the limitations imposed upon Him by the believer, but He cannot do much under the circumstances. The Lord Jesus will not glorify Himself by His own self-expression through the Christian, and if the Holy Spirit cannot, because prevented by the believer, then the life of the Christian has little in it of the sweet graces of the Son of God. Herein lies the imperative necessity of the ministry of the Holy Spirit to the believer. Dr. Max I. Reich put this beautifully when he said: "If we make room for the Holy Spirit, He will make room for the Lord Jesus." The converse is also true, that if we do not make room for the Holy Spirit, He cannot make room for the Lord Jesus.

Before going on in our exposition of this wonderful verse, may
we pick up a golden nugget along our path. The passive voice of
the verb "be formed," brings us to this tremendous truth. God the
Father keeps Himself in the background and puts forth His adorable
Son. God the Son keeps Himself in the background and gives the
ministry of glorifying Him to the Holy Spirit. God the Holy Spirit
keeps Himself in the background and manifests forth the Son.
Observe the infinite humility of the three Persons of the Godhead.
The only three Persons in the universe who have the prerogative of
putting themselves forward and of glorifying themselves, do not
do so. What contempt this pours upon our petty pride, our desire
for pre-eminence, our pouting when we are not put forward as we
think we ought to be or appreciated as we think we deserve to be.

But to get back to our main line of thought. Paul prays that
Christ might *again* be outwardly expressed in these Christians.
That means that at one time in their lives He was being outwardly
expressed. At that time these believers were in correct adjustment
to the Holy Spirit and were the subjects of His ministry. The fact
that the Lord Jesus was not then being expressed in their lives, shows
that they were not at that time the recipients of that ministry. What
had happened to deprive them of the working of the Holy Spirit in
their lives? The answer is found in Paul's words to them (Gal.
1:6, 7), "I marvel that you are so soon removed from him that
called you into the grace of Christ, to another message of good news
which is not only good news of a different kind, but good news that
is diametrically opposed to the good news I preached to you, which
good news is not a substitute message for the one I gave you."
These Galatian Christians had turned from Paul's message of grace
to the message of the Judaizers. These latter were nominal Christians
who accepted Jesus as Messiah, and as the Saviour of Israel only.
They taught that a Gentile could be saved only by entering Christianity through the gate of Judaism. One of the tendencies of the
first century was that of religious syncretism, namely, the blending
together of several religions. When a Greek accepted Christianity

the tendency was to interpret his new found faith in terms of Greek philosophy. When a Jew came over to Christianity, the tendency was to interpret it in terms of Judaism, his old system of religion. This is what the Judaizers were doing. This is what Paul fought against.

These Judaizers came to the Galatian Christians who were truly regenerated, Spirit-indwelt children of God, and taught that they were justified by the Mosaic law (5:4). Because there was no such thing under the law as an indwelling Holy Spirit who had come to take up His permanent residence in the believer's heart for His ministry of sanctification, this teaching deprived these Galatian Christians of their dependence upon the Spirit, and thus also of the Spirit's work of manifesting Christ in outward expression in their lives (Acts 19:2). This is what Paul means when he says, "ye are fallen from grace" (5:4). The apostle is not talking about their justification. The Holy Spirit had nothing to do with that. Justification is a purely legal matter. The entire context is that of sanctification and the work of the Spirit. He says, "We through the Spirit wait for the hope of righteousness by faith" (5:5). He offers the cure for the condition in which they found themselves, in the words, "Walk in the Spirit, and ye shall not fulfill the lusts of the flesh" (5:16), and then speaks of the result of walking in the Spirit in verses 22 and 23. These Galatian Christians had fallen from grace in the sense that they had deprived themselves of the ministry of the Holy Spirit in which He ministered grace to them, daily grace for daily living (II Cor. 12:9; Gal. 5:4).

The position of these Galatian Christians is the position of those children of God who are not conversant with the teaching regarding the Person and work of the Holy Spirit. They are like those converts of John the Baptist who when confronted with Paul's question, "Did ye receive the Spirit when ye believed?" (Acts 19:2), answered, "We have not so much as heard whether there be any Holy Ghost."[1] This is the explanation for the fact that there is so little of the beauty of the Lord Jesus in the lives of so many earnest Christians.

---

1. *Nuggets* pp. 96, 97.

These are doing their best to live a good Christian life, but their own strength is not equal to the task. The Holy Spirit does all He can for them under the circumstances. Their lives are certainly different from what they were before they were saved. There has been a right-about-face. There is a certain amount of victory over sin. They enjoy the things of God. But as for their lives radiating the Lord Jesus, there is very little of that. The Lord Jesus dwelling in their hearts, will not give outward expression of Himself in their lives. He has given that ministry over to the Holy Spirit. And if the Holy Spirit is not recognized and depended upon for this work, He simply cannot perform it, for, just as Jesus never saves a person until that person recognizes Him as Saviour and by an act of his own free will puts his trust in Him, so the Holy Spirit is waiting for the Christian to recognize His ministry, and by an act of his free will, trust Him to perform it. The Galatian Christians fell from that state of dependence upon the Holy Spirit. Most Christians have never been in that state, and therefore have not fallen from it, but because of their ignorance of this teaching, are not the recipients of His work. It would have been well if the one who introduced them to the Saviour had then introduced them as well to the Holy Spirit. But alas, too often the soul winner himself is not in possession of the teaching of and experience in the ministry of the Spirit to the saint.

The Anointing With the Holy Spirit

There are two Greek words, *aleipho* and *chrio,* used in the New Testament, translated by the one English word "anoint." The former is used exclusively in the New Testament of the anointing with oil for medicinal purposes or for the well-being and comfort of the body in the dry hot climate of the East, or in the case of the application of ointment, for the latter purpose, but with the addition of an element of luxury, as in the case of the woman who anointed the feet of Jesus.[1] The latter is used only of the anointing with the Holy Spirit in the New Testament. It is used in secular

---

1. *Treasures* pp. 122-125.

manuscripts, of the application of a lotion to a sick horse, and of the anointing of camels.[1] The two words for "anoint" therefore refer to the act of applying something to either man or beast, this application being for a certain purpose, and to meet a certain condition.

We will look at Peter's words, "God anointed Jesus of Nazareth with the Holy Ghost and with power" (Acts 10:38). The words "Holy Ghost" and "power" are in the instrumental case in Greek, and are in the classification of "the instrumental of means." This expresses impersonal means, and indicates the means whereby the action in the verb is performed. When the means is a person, another case is used in connection with a preposition. The only deviation from this latter rule is where the verb is in the passive voice, in which case the instrumental of means is used. An illustration of this is in Romans 8:14, "For as many as are led by the Spirit of God." Here the subject of the verb is passive, inactive, and is being acted upon. These are being led by means of the activity of the Holy Spirit. But in Acts 10:38, the verb is in the active voice. The subject, "God," does the acting, and the Holy Spirit, designated by the instrumental case, even though Himself a Person, is here looked upon as a means that is impersonal so far as any activity in the premises is concerned. That means that the element which God used in anointing the Man Christ Jesus was the Holy Spirit. The Holy Spirit did not do the anointing. He is that with which Jesus was anointed. We saw that both Greek words meaning "to anoint," referred to the application of something to a person. Thus the act of God in anointing Jesus with the Holy Spirit, referred to His act of sending the Holy Spirit to rest upon Him for the ministry which He as the Man Christ Jesus was to accomplish on earth. It is a case of "position upon." This is made clearer by our Lord's words from Isaiah 61:1, "The Spirit of the Lord is upon me, because he hath anointed me to preach the gospel to the poor;" (Luke 4:18). Luke quotes from the Septuagint, the Greek

---

1. *Treasures* pp. 122-125.

translation of the Old Testament. However, the same passage in the Authorized Version of the Old Testament reads, "The Spirit of the Lord is upon me; because the Lord hath anointed me to preach good tidings to the poor."[1] The repetition of the word "Lord" in Isaiah 61:1 makes it clear that the pronoun "he" in Luke's quotation refers to the Lord God and not to the Holy Spirit. The Holy Spirit does not anoint. He is the anointing Himself. Our Lord explains the position of the Holy Spirit upon Him by saying that God placed the Holy Spirit upon Him to equip Him for His ministry in preaching the gospel. Thus, in the case of our Lord, the anointing with the Spirit refers to the Person of the Holy Spirit coming upon Him, this position of the Holy Spirit providing the potential equipment for ministry of which our Lord was to avail Himself. The anointing with the Holy Spirit would only become a factor in our Lord's life resulting in the impartation of power for service as He depended upon the Spirit for His ministry to and through Him.

We come now to the anointing of the believer with the Holy Spirit in this Age of Grace. Paul says in II Corinthians 1:21, 22, "Now he which stablisheth us with you in Christ, and hath anointed us, is God, who hath also sealed us, and given the earnest of the Spirit in our hearts." In I John 2:27 we have the words, "But the anointing which ye have received of him abideth in you, and ye need not that any man teach you: but as his anointing teacheth you of all things, and is truth, and is no lie, and even as it hath taught you, ye shall abide in him," and in verse 20, "But ye have an unction from the Holy One, and ye all know." We have here the noun form of *chrio*, which is *chrisma*, and is translated "anointing." In the case of our Lord, the Holy Spirit rested *upon* Him, for that was the order in the dispensation of law (Num. 11:29). In the case of the believer during this Age of Grace, the Holy Spirit is placed *within* him

---

1. The difference is found in the fact that the Authorized Version was translated from the Massoretic text of the Hebrew Bible, which was the resultant text of the critical work of Hebrew scholars from the years A.D. 500-900, while the Septuagint is a translation made between 285—150 B.C. from other Hebrew manuscripts.

John 14:17). His ministry in the believer today is not only for service as was the case in Old Testament times, but also for sanctication. But His indwelling is only potential so far as His ministry concerned. His indwelling does not at all mean that His ministry performed in its fullest manifestation and in an automatic way. the believer must avail himself of that ministry through the avenue trust, just as he availed himself of the ministry of the Saviour rough trusting Him. Two of the Spirit's ministries are given here, is work of teaching the believer the Word, and His work of giving e believer an innate ability to know in an intuitive way, things iritual. The Greek word for "know" in this passage gives us this tter truth. A slight correction is offered in the words "ye all know," at "ye know all things." Thus the anointing with the Spirit in the se of the believer refers to the act of God the Father sending e Spirit to take up His abode in his heart, and this in answer to e prayer of God the Son (John 14:16).

We look now at James 4:5, which reads, "Do you think that the ripture saith in vain, The spirit that dwelleth in us lusteth to envy?" he verb "dwell" is not from the Greek word which means "to take one's residence," but from a closely allied verb meaning "to cause take up residence, to send or bring to an abode." How true to her scripture is the usage of this word. The Holy Spirit does not f Himself take up His residence in the heart of the believer. He is aused to do so. In the outworking of the plan of salvation, there subordination among the members of the Godhead. Here the oly Spirit, Very God Himself, the third Person of the Triune God, sent by God the Father, caused to take up His residence in our earts.

But that is not all. The simple verb means, "to cause to take up sidence." A preposition is prefixed to this verb which means literaly "down," and gives the idea of permanency. Thus the Holy pirit has been caused to take up His permanent residence in our earts. This agrees with I John 2:27 where the word translated abide" means "to abide" in the sense of "to remain." Thus, the

Holy Spirit never leaves the believer. This means that he is sav
forever. To pray such a prayer in this Age of Grace as David pray
(Psalm 51:11) is not in order. Inasmuch as in Old Testament tim
the Holy Spirit only came upon believers for the time of a speci
service, their salvation was not affected.

But what do the words, "lusteth to envy" mean. The wo
"lusteth" is the translation of a Greek word that means "to earnes
or passionately desire." The indwelling Holy Spirit possessing
the potential power and help a saint needs, has a passionate des
to the point of envy. Of what is He envious, and what does
passionately desire? The context makes this clear. James is spe
ing here of adulterers and adulteresses in a spiritual sense, Christia
who were not living in separation from the world and unto G
They had committed spiritual adultery in playing false to their Lo
and in fellowshipping with the world. They were allowing th
evil natures to control them, those evil natures from which th
had been delivered when God saved them. The Holy Spirit is envio
of any control which that fallen nature might have over the believ
and passionately desirous of Himself controlling his thoughts, wor
and deeds. He is desirous of having the believer depend upon H
for His ministry to him, in order that He might discharge F
responsibility to the One who sent Him, namely, that of causing t
believer to grow in his Christian life.

The anointing with the Spirit refers therefore, to the act of G
the Father causing the Spirit to take up His permanent residence
the believer. It takes place just once, at the time the sinner puts I
faith in the Saviour, and is never repeated. Paul said to the discip
of John the Baptist, "Did ye receive the Spirit when ye believed
The Levitical priests were anointed once with oil, at their inducti
into the priesthood (Ex. 29:7). The same applies to the N
Testament priests. It is therefore not scriptural to pray for a fre
anointing of the Spirit for a brother who is about to minister in t
Word. Let us pray that he might be filled with the Spirit as he m

ters. That is scriptural and proper. God expects us to pray in cordance with what is revealed.

The anointing with the Spirit forms the basis of all His ministry and in behalf of the believer. Let us remember that it is potential its nature. The mere indwelling of the Spirit does not guarantee e full efficacy of His work in us, since that indwelling is not atomatic in its nature. God's ideal for the indwelling of the Spirit found in the word translated "caused to take up His residence." s root is in the word "home." The Spirit was sent to the believer's eart to make His home there. That means that the Christian must ake Him feel at home. He can do that by giving the Holy Spirit solute liberty of action in his heart, the home in which He lives. his means that the believer is to yield himself, all of himself, to e Spirit's control, depend upon the Spirit for guidance, teaching, rength. Then will the potential power resident in the presence of e Spirit in the heart of the believer be operative in his life.

The Baptism by the Spirit

The purpose of this study is to examine the Greek text in order at we may come to some clear-cut, definite conclusion as to the eaning and purpose of the baptism that is related to the Holy Spirit. e go at once to the Greek word translated "baptize," setting aside e English word, and for the reason that the word "baptize" is not word native to the English language, and therefore has no mean- g of its own. The English word "baptize" is not the translation f the Greek word, but only its transliteration. In translation we ring the meaning of a word over into the second language, in ansliteration, the spelling. Whatever meaning it may rightfully ave in the Bible, must come from the Greek word of which it is e spelling in English letter equivalents. This procedure will do way with any misapprehensions that exist as to the meaning of e English word "baptize." Thus we are on solid ground, and are ansported, so to speak, to the ancient past, to the time during

which the Greek word was used in the writing of the New Testame
manuscripts.

The Greek word is used in the New Testament in two ways. Wh
man does the baptizing, a ceremony is in view. This is the cer
monial usage. When God does the baptizing, that which is in vie
is the exertion of God's power. This latter usage we call for wa
of a better name, the mechanical usage, namely, that usage in whi
a person is said to do something to something else through t
exercise of his own strength by means of instruments, whether l
means of his own members or with the assistance of some oth
thing. Since we are not considering here the ceremonial usage, ar
for the reason that we are dealing with the act of God the Ho
Spirit, we will look at the mechanical usage of the word.

In classical Greek, the word "baptize" is used first in the nin
book of the Odyssey, where the hissing of the burning eye of t
Cyclops is compared to the sound of water where a smith dip
"baptizes" a piece of iron, tempering it. Euripedes uses the wo
of a ship which goes down in the water and does not come back
the surface. In Xenophon's *Anabasis* we have an instance whe
the word "baptize" is used of the practice of Greek soldiers i
placing the points of their spears in a bowl of blood before goir
to war. We see in this last instance a ceremonial usage also. Th
was a ceremony they observed, its observance involving the mecha
ical meaning of the word 'baptize," that of "placing in."

In secular documents of the Koine period, which documents a
written in the same kind of Greek that is used in the New Testamen
Moulton and Milligan report the following mechanical usages:
submerged boat, a person *overwhelmed* in calamities.

In the Septuagint, the translation of the Old Testament writte
in Koine Greek, the same type of Greek that is found in the secula
documents and in the New Testament, we have in Leviticus 4:6, "An
the priest shall dip his finger in the blood, and sprinkle of th
blood seven times before the Lord," where "dip" is the translatio
of the Greek word "baptize," and "sprinkle" is the rendering c

another Greek word, the word "dip" referring to the action of placing the finger in the blood, a purely mechanical usage here, and the second word speaking of the ritualism of sprinkling the blood.

In the New Testament, a purely mechanical usage is seen where the rich man asks that Lazarus dip his finger in water and cool his tongue (Luke 16:24), also in the case where our Lord dips the sop (John 13:26), and again, where He wears a vesture dipped in blood (Rev. 19:13), the verb in these three instances being *bapto*, a related word to *baptizo*, the verb usually used in the New Testament and translated "baptize."

The mechanical usage of the word as seen from the above illustrations resolves itself into the following definition of the Greek word "baptize:" "The introduction or placing of a person or thing into a new environment or into union with something else so as to alter its condition or its relationship to its previous environment or condition." The translation is *"to place into,"* or *"to introduce into."* These ideas were in the mind of the Greek as he used the word in its mechanical usage.[1]

We are now ready to consider the meaning and purpose of the baptism by the Spirit. We will look at the Greek text of I Corinthians 12:13, "By one Spirit are we all baptized into one body." The body here is clearly the Mystical Body of Christ of which He is the Head and all believers from Pentecost to the Rapture, namely, from the time the Church was formed until the Church is taken up to Heaven at the descent of the Lord into the air, are members. The word "Spirit" is in the instrumental case in Greek. Personal agency is expressed occasionally by the instrumental case. At such times the verb is always in the passive or middle voice. The Greek construction here follows this rule of Greek grammar. The personal agent in this case who does the baptizing is the Holy Spirit. He places or introduces the believing sinner into the Body of which the Lord Jesus is the living Head. We could translate, "By means of the

---

1. *Treasures* pp. 83-87.

personal agency of one Spirit, we all were placed in one body." The
verb is in the past tense, referring to a past action, and is aorist,
referring to a once-for-all act. This occurred potentially to all believers of this Age of Grace at Pentecost. It is the fulfillment of our
Lord's words, "Ye shall be baptized with the Holy Ghost not many
days hence" (Acts 1:5). Thus, the meaning of the Greek word,
"*to place*" or "*introduce into*," gives us the purpose of the baptism
by means of the Spirit, namely, the introduction of a believing
sinner into the body of Christ. In Romans 6:3[1] and Galatians 3:27,
we have this same operation of the Spirit, but instead of speaking
of the introduction of the believing sinner into the Body, Paul speaks
of the placing of that believer into vital union with the Head of the
Body.

This brings us to a careful distinction which we must make. It is
not the baptism with the Spirit or of the Spirit, in the sense that
the Holy Spirit is the element which is applied to us. It is the baptism by the Spirit. This baptism does not bring the Spirit to us in
the sense that God places the Spirit upon or in us. Rather, this
baptism brings the believer into vital union with Jesus Christ. This
means that the baptism by the Spirit is not for power, for in this
baptism there is nothing applied to or given the believer. He, the
believer, is placed into the Body of Christ. It is the baptism with the
Spirit in the sense that God the Father does the baptizing through
His personal agent, the Holy Spirit.

We will study the passages where the expression "baptize with
the Holy Spirit" occurs. In Matthew 3:11 we have John the Baptist
saying, "I indeed baptize you with water because of repentance[2] . . .
He shall baptize you with the Holy Ghost, and with fire." The word
"with" is from a preposition which is used with the locative and
instrumental cases in Greek. The particular classification of the
locative here is "the locative of place." The limits here are spatial.

---

1. *Treasures* pp. 83-87.
2. *Treasures* pp. 76-78.

John said literally, "I place you in water." His introduction of the believer into water is because of his repentance. It is the believer's outward visible testimony of an inward fact, his repentance. Here we have the mechanical usage of the word. But the instrumental can also be seen in this construction, "the instrumental of means," showing the impersonal means whereby the action of the verb is performed. And here we have the ceremonial usage of the word "baptize." Not only did John place them in water, but this placing in water was a ceremony or a rite. He not only baptized them into the water, but he baptized them by means of or with the water. The water was the element with or by which the believer was baptized.

But when we come to the phrase, "baptized with the Spirit," we find that the Greek grammatical construction will not allow us to interpret it as meaning that the Holy Spirit is the element with which we are baptized, as water is the element with which the believer is baptized in the ceremony of water baptism. We have the same case here as in the phrase "baptize with water," the locative. But here the limits indicated by the locative case are not spatial but logical. That is, the locative case, the case which shows the location within the con-fines of which the action in the verb takes place, is not used here with reference to a certain location in space like the Jordan River. It has nothing to do here with any limits in space. The limits indi-cated are not spatial because the Holy Spirit is not a substance occu-pying space. They are logical because the Holy Spirit is a Person. Thus we have "the locative of sphere" which confines one idea within the bounds of another. An action is limited within the confines of an idea rather than within those of a place. Therefore, the classifi-cation, "locative of place" will not apply here, and since it does not apply in this case, the Holy Spirit is not the element into which and with which we are baptized. Therefore the phrase, "baptized with the Spirit" does not mean that in this baptism, the Holy Spirit is applied to the believer as water is applied in the case of water baptism. In other words, there is no application of the Holy Spirit to the believer. He is not given to the believer by virtue of this baptism. We saw that it was the anointing with the Spirit whit referred to the act of God the Father causing the Spirit to take His permanent residence in the believer. Since there is no applic tion of the Spirit in baptism, there is no power imparted in the a of baptizing with the Spirit. This baptism is only for the purpo of uniting the believing sinner with the Head of the Body, Chri Jesus, and thus making him a member of that Body.

The classification of the locative here is "the locative of sphere since the limits imposed are logical. It is the "confining of one ide within the bounds of another, thus indicating the sphere withi which the former idea is to be applied."[1] Examples of this class fication in the New Testament are, "Ye have become babes in hea ing" (Heb. 5:11), where the word "babes" is limited and thu defined by the qualifying phrase "in hearing." That is, they wer not babes in the physical or mental sense. But their hearing of th Word was like that of a child, immature: "He was made strong i faith" (Rom. 4:20), where the meaning is that he was made strong not here in body or mind, but with reference to his faith. Hi faith was made strong: "Blessed are the pure in heart," (Matt. 5:8) where our Lord is speaking, not of ceremonial purity such as th religious leaders of Israel were so punctilious about, but of purit of heart, pure in the sphere of the heart. One could render thes phrases, "babes in the sphere of hearing," "strong in the sphere o faith," and "pure in the sphere of the heart." Thus we have, "H shall baptize you in the sphere of the Spirit." Here the word "Spirit" sets a limit upon the act of baptism. John is drawing a contras between his baptism, and our Lord's. John's was into and by mean of water, a ceremony. Our Lord's was to be with reference to th Spirit. A baptism with reference to the Spirit is a baptism in whicl the Holy Spirit is the sole agent. This baptism is limited to Hi sphere of operations. It is a baptism effected by means of His work ing. The Spirit baptism to which John referred is the same one

---

1. Dana and Mantey, *Manual Grammar of the Greek New Testament*, pp 86-88.

which Paul mentions in I Corinthians 12:13. It is a baptism with the Spirit in the sense that it is connected, not with water, but with the Spirit who Himself does the baptizing. The other places where the word "baptize" is used with the phrase "with the Holy Spirit" and where exactly the same Greek construction is found are Luke 3:16; John 1:33; Acts 1:5, 11:16. Mark 1:8 has the same words in the English, and the construction is the locative case in Greek, but the preposition is left out, which latter fact does not affect the classification, "locative of place or sphere," as the case might be. While the preposition in the Greek here is used also with the instrumental case, and the case ending of the noun could also be instrumental, the classification "instrumental of means," could not be used here, since the rules of Greek grammar require a passive or middle voice verb in this construction where a personal agent is involved. This kind of a verb is not found in the passages quoted from Matthew to Acts, but is found in I Corinthians 12:13. Therefore our rendering "baptized by means of the Spirit," is correct for the Corinthians passage but not correct for the others commented upon.

The phrase "with the Spirit" therefore defines what baptism is referred to, and the words, "by means of the Spirit," speak of the fact that the Holy Spirit is the divine Agent who Himself baptizes, the purpose of which baptism is to place the believing sinner into vital union with Jesus Christ and thus make him a member of the Body of which Christ is the living Head.

The reader will observe that our study of the significance of Spirit baptism has been based upon a careful adherence to the rules of Greek grammar. This is a most scientific method of interpretation. It is a most sure method. A. T. Robertson quotes Dr. A. M. Fairbairn as saying, "He is no theologian who is not first a grammarian." All correct theology must pay careful attention to the grammer of the Greek text, for a person is correctly understood only when his hearer or reader applies the rules of grammar which the speaker or writer uses. The Holy Spirit adheres to the grammar rules and idioms of the Koine Greek of the time when the New Testament was written. It is for us to learn those rules and interpret the Greek text accordingly. Then an interpreter of Scripture is on perfectly solid ground. He is far less likely to make a mistake in interpretation when using the Greek than when using a translation.

The Spirit of Adoption

Paul tells us that we have received the Spirit of adoption (Rom. 8:15). It is clear that the Holy Spirit is referred to here. But what does the qualifying phrase, "of adoption" mean? We will look at the Greek text. The word "adoption" is a noun of action. It is in the genitive case. We have here a construction which is called "the subjective genitive," in which the noun of action bears the same relationship to the word defined as the verb of a sentence does to the subject. The word "Spirit" would in this instance be the subject, and the word "adoption," the verb. Thus, it is the Holy Spirit who performs the act of adopting. He is in that sense the Spirit of adoption.

The Greek word translated "adoption" is made of two words, a word meaning "to place," and the word "son," its total meaning being "to place as a son." *Expositor's Greek Testament* has the following to say about this word; "It is a term of *relation*, expressing our sonship in respect of *standing*. It appears to be taken from the Roman custom with which Paul could not fail to be acquainted. Among the Jews there were cases of informal adoption, as in the instance of Mordecai and Esther (Esther 2:7). But adoption in the sense of the legal transference of a child to a family to which it did not belong by birth had no place in the Jewish law. In Roman law, on the other hand, provision was made for the transaction known as *adoptio*, the taking of a child who was not one's child by birth, to be his son, and *arrogatio*, the transference of a son who was independent, as by the death of his proper father, to another father by solemn public act of the people. Thus among the Romans a citizen might receive a child who was not his own by birth into his family and give him his name, but he could do so only by a formal act, attested by witnesses, and the son thus adopted had in all its entirety the position of a child by birth, with all the rights and all the obligations pertaining to that. By 'adoption' therefore, Paul does not mean the bestowal of the full privileges of the family on those who are sons by nature, but the acceptance into the family of those who do not by nature belong to it, and the placing of those who are not sons originally and by right in the relation proper to those who are sons by birth. Hence *huiothesia* (adoption) is never affirmed of Christ; for He alone is Son of God by nature. So Paul regards our sonship, not as lying in the natural relation in which men stand to God as His children, but as implying a new relation of grace, founded on a covenant relation to God and on the work of Christ (Gal. 4:5). The word seems to distinguish those who are made sons by an act of grace from the only-begotten Son of God . . . But the act of grace is not one which makes only an outward difference in our position; it is accomplished in the giving of a spirit (the Holy Spirit) which creates in us a new nature . . . We have not only the status, but the heart of sons."

There are two words used in the Greek New Testament relative to the place of the believer in God's family. One is *teknon*, which comes from *tikto* which means "to bear, to give birth to." Its proper translation is "child" or "born one." It speaks of a child of God in his birth-relationship. The other word is *huios*, the word used in the Greek word "adoption." This word speaks of a child of God in his legal relationship to God in His family. Under Roman law, the only thing that stood in the way of a person adopting a child not his own, was the fact that the child did not come of his own flesh and blood. This obstacle was surmounted by the fact that the law gave him the right to make the child his own if he fulfilled the proper legal requirements. But under the divine government of the universe, there were two things that stood in God's way of making human beings His children, the fact that they were not His children by birth and the fact that they were law-breakers. The first could easily have been remedied by regeneration, but the thing that stood in the way of this act of mercy on God's part was the fact that human beings are sinners, and God's justice demands that sin be paid for before mercy can be righteously bestowed. This is clearly recognized in John 1:12 where the Greek word translated "power" was a technical expression used in the law courts for a legal right to be or do something. The word "sons" is not from our word *huios* here but from *teknon*, and should be translated "children." To those who received the Lord Jesus as their Saviour, as the One who died in their stead on the Cross, thus satisfying the justice of God in view of man's sin, God gave the legal right to become His children. Regeneration is therefore dependent upon justification, since an act of mercy in a law court can only be justly based upon the fact of the law being satisfied in the punishment of the crime committed. In human law courts this is impossible, for the prisoner cannot be punished and be set free at the same time. And the judge certainly will not step down from the bench and take upon himself the penalty which he justly imposed upon the prisoner. But praise be to the Lord, it happened in the law court of the universe. God the Judge stepped down from His judgment bench, and at Calvary paid the sinner's penalty, thus satisfying His justice, and procuring for sinful man a legal right to receive the mercy of God. Thus, nothing stands in the way of a just God regenerating a believing sinner and placing him as His son in His family. The Holy Spirit as the Spirit of adoption regenerates the believing sinner and places him as a child of God in a legal standing in God's family, having all the privileges and rights of God's only-begotten Son. Think of it, to occupy a place in God's family in which He loves us just as much as He loves His only-begotten Son. Think of it, to have a place in God's family just as eternal and secure as His only-begotten Son. Think of it, to have a place in God's family in which all the loveliness of God's Son is ours. The Spirit of adoption is therefore the legal representative of God, so to speak, imparting to us the divine nature and placing us in the family of God, doing all this in accordance with the eternal and unchanging laws of God.

The Sanctification by the Holy Spirit

In the work of sanctification, the Holy Spirit has a two-fold ministry, one to the unsaved, another to the saved. The first is called positional sanctification, and refers to the work of the Spirit in bringing a lost sinner to the act of faith in the Lord Jesus as Saviour. The second is called progressive sanctification, and speaks of the work of the Spirit causing the Christian to grow in the knowledge and likeness of the Lord Jesus.

We will look at positional sanctification first. In I Peter 1:2 we have the words, "Elect according to the foreknowledge of God the Father through sanctification of the Spirit unto obedience and sprinkling of the blood of Jesus Christ." The first step in the salvation of a sinner is his election by God the Father, this election, or selection, as the word can be translated, is dominated by the foreknowledge of God the Father. The word "sanctification" is in a grammatical classification in the Greek called the "locative of sphere." This choice of the sinner was therefore in the sphere of the sanctification of the Spirit. That is, the choice of the sinner was to the end that he might be included in the work of the Spirit in sanctification. The word "sanctify" in the Greek means "to set apart," and the word "sanctification" refers to the setting apart process. The words "sanctification of the Spirit" are in a construction in the Greek called the subjective genitive. The word "sanctification" is a noun of action, and the word "Spirit" is in what is called "the genitive case." The word "Spirit" bears the same relationship to the word "sanctification" as the subject of a sentence does to the verb. The person or thing designated as the subject produces the action spoken of in the verb. Thus, the Holy Spirit is the one who does the sanctifying, the setting apart.

This setting apart work of the Spirit is "unto obedience," that is, it results in the obedience of the sinner to the Faith. We have the expression in Acts 6:7, "a great company of the priests were obedient to the faith." This obedience in I Peter 1:2 is not that engendered

in the heart of the saint, but produced in the heart of the sinner, fo
it is followed by the work of God the Son in cleansing that sinne
in response to his obedience. We have here the divine order; Go
the Father elects the sinner to salvation, God the Spirit brings hi
to the act of faith, and God the Son cleanses him from sin. W
have the same truth brought out in II Thessalonians 2:13, "Go
from the beginning chose you for salvation in the sphere of th
sanctification of the Spirit and in the sphere of belief of the truth.
Peter's words are similar, "Peter, an ambassador of Jesus Chri
with a commission to selected out ones, . . . selected out by th
foreordination of God the Father to be recipients of the setting-apa
work of the Spirit which results in obedience (of faith) and spri
kling of the blood of Jesus Christ."[1] This is the pre-salvation wor
of the Holy Spirit in which He takes up His work of bringing th
sinner chosen before the foundation of the universe to the act o
faith in the Lord Jesus.

An instance of the pre-salvation work of the Holy Spirit is foun
in John 16:8, where our Lord speaks of the Holy Spirit reprovin
the world. The Greek word here refers to a rebuke which results i
the person's confession of his guilt, or if not his confession, hi
conviction of sin.[2] This He does through the Word of God. Thi
acknowledgment however on the part of the sinner is not the sam
as the act of placing faith in the Lord Jesus for salvation. It is th
result of one of the ministries of the Holy Spirit to the unsaved
and as such leads that person on towards the place where he exercise
saving faith. The Holy Spirit brings this person to new conviction
concerning sin, righteousness, and judgment. The word "of" is th
translation of a Greek word meaning "concerning." He comes to
see under the Holy Spirit's illumination that his unbelief is sin, tha
the exaltation of the Lord Jesus is a proof of His righteousness, an
therefore he cherishes new convictions concerning righteousness
And, seeing the distinction between sin and righteousness, he i

---

1. *Bypaths*, pp. 39-43.
2. *Treasures*, pp. 70-72.

le to understand that the world's rejection of Christ as seen
the Cross is the same as his rejection of Christ, and that if
persists in that rejection, he will share in the judgment that was
eted out to the "prince of this world," namely, Satan.

In Hebrews 6:4-6, we have more of the pre-salvation work of the
irit. Through the Word, He enlightens the unsaved, and enables
em to have a certain appreciation of the blessedness that salvation
ings to the one who receives Christ as Saviour. As the recipient
these ministries of the Spirit, this unsaved person is said to be a
artaker of the Holy Ghost. The word "partaker" is the translation
a Greek word that literally means "one who holds with another."
is translated "partner" in Luke 5:7. It does not imply that this
erson possesses the Holy Spirit as an indweller, but merely that
has willingly co-operated with Him in allowing Him to lead him
toward Christ. A further work of the Spirit for the unsaved is to
roduce repentance in his mind and heart. The word "repentance"
the translation of a Greek word which means in the verb, "to
ange one's mind," and in the noun, "a change of mind." When
e Spirit reproves the unsaved concerning sin, He causes that one
change his mind regarding it. Before, he loved it. Now, he
rns against it and desires the Lord Jesus to break its power in
is life. He desires to be done with it. He changes his mind regard-
g righteousness. Before, he hated it. Now, he wants it in his
fe. He changes his mind regarding judgment in that, instead of
emaining under the wrath of God, he takes refuge in His grace.
he final step in the Spirit's ministry to this unsaved person as He
ads him on to Christ is to impart to him the necessary faith to
ppropriate the Lord Jesus as Saviour. There is nothing in the
otally depraved sin-darkened heart of the unsaved that would cause
im to turn to the Saviour, turn away from his sin, and desire
oliness. The hand of faith must be motivated by the Spirit. In
phesians 2:8 we have, "By grace are ye saved through faith; and
hat not of yourselves: it is the gift of God." The word "that" can-
ot in the Greek be made to refer to "faith." It is in the neuter

gender whereas the word "faith" is in the feminine gender. It ref
to the general idea of salvation in the context. The meaning is t
we are saved by grace, and that salvation does not find its sou
in us. That salvation is the gift of God. But the fact that faith
embedded in this statement, makes it clear that it is included
the salvation which God provides.

This pre-salvation work of the Spirit is spoken of in Script
as the sanctification of the Spirit. It is the setting-apart work
the Spirit in that He sets the unsaved person apart from his unbel
to the act of faith, from his standing in the first Adam which broug
him sin and death, to a new standing in the Last Adam which brix
him righteousness and life. This we call positional sanctification.

We come now to progressive sanctification. This is spoken of
I Thessalonians 5:23, "And the very God of peace sanctify y
wholly; and I pray God your whole spirit and soul and body
preserved blameless unto the coming of our Lord Jesus Chris
Literally it is, "And the God of peace set you apart wholly." T
refers to the work of the Holy Spirit setting the believer apart fr
sin, which is His work of putting sin out of the believer's life a
keeping it out as that believer trusts Him to do that for him, a
His work of setting the believer apart to a holy life, which is F
work of producing His own fruit in the believer's life as the believ
trusts Him to do that for him. These two aspects of the Spiri
work for the believer will be taken up more fully under the headir
"The Fullness of the Spirit."

The Fellowship and Communion of the Spirit

In Philippians 2:2, Paul exhorts the saints to be likeminded,
have the same love, to be of one accord, of one mind. In verse o
he gives the reasons why such unity is expected of the saints, a
why it should naturally obtain. One of these is that there is "
certain fellowship of the Spirit." In II Corinthians 13:14 we ha
the apostolic benediction, "the grace of the Lord Jesus Christ, a

he love of God, and the communion of the Holy Ghost, be with
ou all. Amen." The question before us is, "What is meant by the
ellowship and communion of the Holy Ghost?"

We will put aside the two English words and proceed to solid
ground, the Greek text. Too often we interpret the Bible by putting
upon certain English words a meaning which is current usage with
us in our ordinary conversation, and we do that without even consulting a dictionary. The two words "fellowship" and "communion,"
are the translation of one Greek word which we will carefully study.
Moulton and Milligan in their *Vocabulary of the Greek Testament*
cite the following examples of its use in secular documents: It is
used in a marriage contract of the time of Augustus, in the phrase
"to a *joint-participation in* the necessaries of life;" "*Belonging in
common to;*" "My brother on my father's side with whom I have no
partnership." They quote the phrase, "aiming to have *fellowship
with Zeus*" as comparable with I John 1:6 "If we say that we have
fellowship with him, and walk in darkness, we lie, and do not the
truth." Zeus was the principal god of the Greeks.

Thayer in his *Greek-English Lexicon of the New Testament* gives
the following on this word; "association, community, joint-participation, intercourse, the share which one has in anything, participation."
Commenting on I John 1:3, 6 he says, "which fellowship consists in
the fact that Christians are partakers in common of the same mind
as God and Christ, and of the blessings arising therefrom."

Our next task will be to examine every place where this Greek
word is found in the New Testament and where it is translated by
the words "fellowship" and "communion," and look at its usage.
Paul thanks God for the fellowship of the Philippian saints in the
Gospel, namely, their joint-participation with him in the progress
of the Gospel (Phil. 1:3-5).[1] In Ephesians 3:1-12 he speaks of a
mystery which was hid in God's heart until it was revealed to Paul,
and through Paul was given to the Church. It was given him "to

---

1. *Treasures*, pp. 55, 56.

make all men see what is the fellowship of this mystery." That is, the mystery is not known only to God now, but He is sharing it with believers, the word "sharing" expressing what the word "fellowship" here means. In Philippians 3:7-10, Paul has suffered the loss of all things that he may know the fellowship of Christ's sufferings, that is, be associated with Christ in His sufferings, have joint-participation with Him in those sufferings.

In I John 1:3, the apostle writes to the Christians in the Church at large, that he has in his Gospel reported the things which he heard Jesus say and which he saw Jesus do, and this, in order that they might have fellowship with him, namely joint-participation with John in the knowledge of the things Jesus said and did. That is, John tells them that he wishes to share these things with them. When he says, "Truly, our fellowship is with the Father, and with his Son Jesus Christ," we repeat Thayer's words, "which fellowship consists in the fact that Christians are partakers in common of the same mind as God and Christ, and of the blessings arising therefrom." God and His child have things in common. Then "if we (who profess to be Christians) say that we have fellowship with him (have things in common with Him), and walk in darkness, we lie, and do not the truth" (I John 1:6). That is, the things possessed in common here are a like nature, and thus the same likes and dislikes. But to be a partaker of the divine nature, to love holiness and hate sin, makes impossible a life lived in the darkness of sin. "But if we walk in the light as he is in the light, we (God and the believer) have fellowship one with another." The thing possessed in common here by both God and the saint is light. In the case of God, He is as to His essence, light. In the case of the believer, he lives in the sphere of the light which God is (I John 1:7).

Paul says in I Corinthians 1:9, "God is faithful, by whom ye were called unto the fellowship of his Son Jesus Christ our Lord." The words "fellowship of his Son" do not here mean "a communion or partnership with His Son." It is the possessive genitive here, namely, "into a communion or joint-participation belonging to His

Son, and named after His Son, and of which He is the Founder"
(*Expositor's Greek Testament*). The Greek word here denotes a
collective participation. In this the saints partake "with all those
that call on the name of the Lord Jesus." This fellowship is a
sharing in common on the part of all the saints. Its content, namely,
that which all the saints share in, is sonship to God, for it is a communion of His Son, and this is with Christ, since He is the "firstborn among many brethren," and heirship with Christ, for the
saints are joint-heirs with Christ.

In Acts 2:42 we have, "And they continued steadfastly in the
apostle's doctrine and fellowship, and in breaking of bread, and
in prayers." Vincent comments on this verse by saying that the
Greek word we are considering refers to "a relation between individuals which involves a common interest and a mutual, active
participation in that interest and in each other." In Galatians 2:9
we have, "And when James, Cephas, and John, who seemed to be
pillars, perceived the grace that was given unto me, they gave to me
and Barnabas the right hand of fellowship; that we should go
unto the heathen, and they unto the circumcision." The word "fellowship" here refers to the common interest which all had in the
salvation of the lost, and a mutual, active participation in that
interest.

The Macedonian churches had given a liberal gift of money to
Paul for needy saints, and the apostle says, "Praying us with much
intreaty that we would receive the gift and take upon us the fellowship of the ministering to the saints" (II Cor. 8:4). Here the Macedonian Christians who gave the money for the saints, ask Paul to
become their partner in its distribution. Thus we have the idea of
sharing, a sharing in the work of supplying needy saints with money,
the Macedonians, the givers, Paul, the distributor.

We will now look at the passages where the word "communion"
is the translation of our Greek word. In I Corinthians 10:16 we
have, "The cup of blessing which we bless, is it not the communion

of the blood of Christ? The bread which we break, is it not the communion of the body of Christ?" *Expositor's Greek Testament* has this to say: "The Lord's Supper constitutes a 'communion centering in Christ, as the Jewish festal rites centered in 'the altar,' and as 'the demons,' the unseen objects of idolatrous worship, supply their basis of communion in idolatrous feasts. Such fellowship involves (1) *the ground of communion*, the sacred object celebrated in common; (2) *the association* established amongst celebrants separating them from all others: The word 'communion' denotes the fellowship of persons with persons in one and the same object.' Thus, in the Lord's Supper, believers participate together in Christ in the recognition of His atonement on their behalf, and in remembrance of His death until He comes.

In II Corinthians 6:14 we have, "What communion hath light with darkness?" One could translate, "What things does light have in common with darkness?" Is there any common interest or mutual activity in which they participate one with another?

We are now ready to consider the meaning of the words, "fellowship of the Spirit," and "communion of the Holy Ghost," in the light of the study which we have just made of the Greek word which is translated by the words "fellowship" and "communion." The word "Ghost" is the translation of the same Greek word which is in other places rendered "Spirit." The Greek word, we have found, has the following meanings; "joint-participation, belonging in common to, a partnership, association, intercourse, sharing, a relation between individuals which involves a common interest and a mutual, active participation in that interest and in each other."

Therefore, when Paul speaks of a certain fellowship of the Holy Spirit that obtains in the lives of the saints, he refers to that relationship between the Spirit and the saint which involves a common interest and a mutual, active participation in that interest. That is, as the result of the Spirit's work in regeneration and in His control over the saint as the saint is definitely subjected to Him, there has been brought about in the life of the saint, a joint-participation on the part of the believer with the Holy Spirit in an interest and a mutual and active participation in the things of God and the work of God in saving lost souls. It is a partnership, so to speak, between God and the believer. Paul speaks of this in the words, "We are laborers together with God" (I Cor. 3:9). Another interest held in common is the Christian life and testimony of the believer. The Holy Spirit is desirous of producing the highest type of Christian experience in the life of the believer, and the believer has the same interest, and shows it by maintaining an attitude of dependence upon and trust in the Holy Spirit to produce that life in him. This fellowship is a co-operation on the part of the saint with the Holy Spirit in His work of sanctification. When Paul in his apostolic benediction prays that the communion of the Holy Ghost be with all the saints, he is asking that this mutual interest and activity may continue and become more rich and effective in the lives of the saints.

We now come to a consideration of the English word "fellowship." In its current usage among the saints, it refers to the fellowship which saints have with one another, that is, the companionship and friendliness and sociability which is enjoyed when the saints get together in prayer-meeting or preaching service, or in other Christian society. Hence, there is a danger of thinking that the phrase "fellowship of the Spirit" means "companionship with the Spirit." Right here is where some leave the path of sound doctrine and practice. They seek the Holy Spirit and His fullness for His sake alone. They seek intercourse with Him as an end in itself. Thus they lay themselves open to the snares of Satan and the control of evil spirits. There is no such thing in Scripture as the believer's fellowship or companionship with the Spirit comparable to the believer's fellowship or companionship with the Lord Jesus. The Holy Spirit's ministry is to glorify the Son, and in doing that He always calls the believer's attention to the Lord Jesus, never to Himself. He keeps Himself in the background. The Lord Jesus must always be central in the life of the saint. He is the One with whom we have fellowship in the commonly accepted usage of the word today. The Holy Spirit makes this possible. Sir Robert Anderson's words are to the point here: "In proportion therefore as mind and heart are fixed on Christ, we may count on the Spirit's presence and power, but if we make the Holy Ghost Himself the object of our aspirations and worship, some false spirit may counterfeit the true and take us for a prey."

The association which the correctly instructed saint has with the Holy Spirit, is in the form of a moment-by-moment conscious dependence upon Him, a trust in Him for His guidance and strength, and a yielding to Him for His ministry of putting sin out of the life and keeping it out, and of radiating the beauty of the Lord Jesus through his every thought, word, and deed, this, together with a co-operation with Him which takes the form of a mutual interest and active participation in the things of God.

G. D. Watson in *Living Words* has put this very beautifully in the following words: "The Holy Spirit will put a strict watch over you with a jealous love, and will rebuke you for little words and feelings, or for wasting your time, which other Christians never seem distressed over. So make up your mind that God is an infinite Sovereign, and has a right to do as He pleases with His own. He may not explain to you a thousand things which puzzle your reason in His dealings with you, but if you absolutely sell yourself to be His love slave, He will wrap you up in a jealous love, and bestow upon you many blessings which come only to those who are in the inner circle.

"Settle it forever, then, that you are to deal directly with the Holy Spirit, and that He is to have the privilege of tying your tongue, or chaining your hand, or closing your eyes, in ways that He does not seem to use with others. Now when you are so possessed with the living God that you are, in your secret heart, pleased and delighted over this peculiar, personal, private, jealous guardianship and management of the Holy Spirit over your life, you will have found the vestibule of heaven."

The Fullness of the Spirit

Our first task will be to inquire as to the exact meaning of the word "fullness" when used in connection with the ministry of the Spirit. The phrases, "filled with the Holy Spirit" and "full of the Holy Spirit," are used in the Authorized Version. They are the translation of either one of two verbs and of a noun. The verb *pimplemi* is used in Luke 1:15, 41, 67; Acts 2:4, 4:8, 31, 13:9. An illustration of its use other than with the word "Spirit" is in the phrase, "were filled with fear" (Luke 5:26). Thayer in his Greek-English lexicon has this to say about the use of this verb here: "What wholly takes possession of the mind, is said to fill it." Thus, the expression, "filled with the Holy Spirit" speaks of the Spirit possessing the mind and heart of the believer. This possession implies His control over that mind and heart. Thus the words "full" and "filled" refer to the control which the Spirit exerts over the believer who is said to be filled with Him.

The other verb is *pleroo*, and is used in Acts 13:52 and Ephesians 5:18. An example of its use other than that in relation to the Spirit is in the sentence, "Sorrow hath filled your heart" (John 16:6). Thayer says of its usage here, "to pervade, take possession of." Thus, as sorrow possessed or controlled the hearts of the disciples, so the Holy Spirit possesses or controls the believer who is said to be filled with Him.

The noun *pleres* is used in Luke 4:1; Acts 6:3, 5, 7:55, 9:17, 11:24. In Acts 6:5 it is used in the phrase "full of faith." Thayer says of this use, "thoroughly permeated Stephen in the sense that it possessed or controlled him." Thus, the fullness of the Holy Spirit refers to His control over the believer who is said to be filled with Him.

But let us press the point still further by looking at the Greek grammar involved in these expressions. In the expression, "filled

with the Holy Spirit," we have the verb "filled" in the passive voic
the subject in this case being inactive and being acted upon by a
outside agent, and the noun "Spirit" in the genitive case, th
genitive of description, indicating what the "filling" consisted o
The "filling" in this case refers to a certain control exerted ove
the believer. The word "Spirit" thus indicates who is exerting th
control. The expression "full of the Holy Spirit" is from a nou
"full," and another noun "Spirit," the latter in the genitive cas
The noun "full," meaning here "control," is a noun of actio
We have here a Greek construction called the subjective genitiv
in which the noun in the genitive case, here "Spirit," produce
the action in the noun of action, "full." Thus, the Holy Spirit i
the One who exerts control over the believer said to be filled wit
Him.

There is just one instance in the New Testament where the word
"filled with the Spirit" are not followed by the genitive case. I
Ephesians 5:18 we have the verb followed by the instrumental case
which latter case designates that by means of which the action i
the verb is performed. The action in the verb here is a certain con
trol exerted over the believer. The Holy Spirit is the divine in
strument who exerts this control. One could translate, "Be con
trolled by the Spirit."

We must not think of the Holy Spirit filling our hearts as wate
fills a bottle, or air, a vacuum, or a bushel of oats, an empty bas
ket. The heart of a Christian is not a receptacle to be emptied i
order that the Holy Spirit might fill it. The Holy Spirit is not a
substance to fill an empty receptacle. He is a Person to contro
another person, the believer. He does not fill a Christian's life
with Himself. He controls that person.

The heart is a symbol used to refer to the will, the reason, and
the emotions. Thus, the Holy Spirit possesses or controls the voli
tional, rational, and emotional activities of the believer who is said
to be filled with Him. He brings all these into the place of obedience

ιd conformity to the Word of God. Therefore, when we speak
f a Christian filled with the Spirit, we are referring to the control
hich a divine Person, the Holy Spirit, has over a human being,
ιe believer.

The believer is exhorted, "Be filled with the Spirit" (Eph. 5:18),
r as we have translated it, "Be controlled by the Spirit." The
ndency of the unsaved person is seen in the words of the hymn, "I
as a wandering sheep, I did not love the fold, I did not love my
hepherd's voice, I would not be controlled." This tendency is
roken when a sinner is saved, in that God breaks the power of
ιe sinful nature, which nature had exerted absolute control over
im, and gives him His own divine nature. The believer is then
xhorted to be controlled by the Holy Spirit. The Holy Spirit's
ιinistry in the premises is to maintain in the actual experience of
ιe Christian, that which God did for him the moment He saved
im. The Holy Spirit suppresses the activities of the evil nature
hose power was broken, and produces His fruit in the life. The
ery fact that an individual is exhorted to do something, demands
s a logical accompaniment, that person's exercise of his will in
ιe doing of that thing. That is, the believer here is not automati-
ally controlled by the Spirit just because the Spirit indwells him.
he control which the Spirit exerts over the believer is dependent
pon the believer's active and correct adjustment to the Spirit. The
ιord Jesus did not save us until we recognized Him as the Saviour
nd put our trust in Him for salvation. Just so, the Holy Spirit
oes not control us in the sense of permeating our will, reason, and
motions, until we recognize Him as the One who has been sent by
he Father to sanctify our lives, and trust Him to perform His
ιinistry in and through us. There must be an ever present con-
cious dependence upon and definite subjection to the Holy Spirit,
 constant yielding to His ministry and leaning upon Him for
uidance and power, if He is to control the believer *in the most effici-
nt manner and with the largest and best results.* The Lord Jesus
vaited for you and me to recognize Him as Saviour before He

saved us. The Holy Spirit indwelling a believer is waiting to recognized as the One to come to that believer's aid. Salvation by faith from start to finish. It is a work of God for man. But G waits for man, unsaved or saved as the case might be, to avail hi self of the salvation he needs, by means of faith. One of the reaso why the Holy Spirit has so little control over many Christians because they think He works automatically in their hearts.

Our Lord in John 7:37, 38 lays down two simple requiremen for the fullness of the Spirit, a thirst for His control and a trust the Lord Jesus for the Spirit's control.

"If any man thirst" refers to a desire on the part of the believ that the Holy Spirit be the One to control his every thought, wor and deed. We do not take a drink of water unless we are thirst We do not appropriate the control of the Spirit unless we desire Hi to control us. A desire for His control will include among oth things, a desire that He cause us to judge sin in our lives, a desi that He put sin out of our lives and keep it out, a desire that I separate us from all the ties we might have with that system evil called the world, a desire that He dethrone our self-life a enthrone the Lord Jesus as absolute Lord and Master, a desire th He produce in us His own fruit, a desire that He make us Chris like, a desire that He lead us and teach us. Such a desire is serious thing. It involves crucifixion of self, and self dies har The Spirit-controlled life is a crucified life. The other requireme is trust. Our Lord said, "He that believeth on Me, out from his i most being shall flow rivers of living water." The trust here in th context is not only trust in Him as Saviour, but trust in Hi as the One who fills with the Spirit. *The Spirit-controlled life a matter of trust.* Salvation is by faith. We received our justific tion by faith. We are to receive our sanctification by faith. It this constant desire for the Spirit's control and a trust in the Lor Jesus for the Spirit's control that results in the Spirit-controlle life. When one faces a new day, it is well to include in our praye thanksgiving for the presence of the Holy Spirit in our hearts, th expression of our desire for His control, and a definite assertion of our trust in the Lord Jesus for the Spirit's control during that day. It is well at intervals during the day when we are faced with temptation, or when we have a definite piece of Christian service to perform, or are in need of instruction from the Word or of strength for some duty, to recognize quietly the ministry of the Spirit and depend upon Him for all needed guidance, wisdom, and strength. He is waiting for us to recognize Him and trust Him for His aid. He is there, the indwelling Spirit, always at the service of the believer. But the point is that He comes to our aid when we avail ourselves of His help. There are just two things therefore which the believer must do in order to be controlled by the Spirit, desire that control and trust the Lord Jesus for that control.

There is no Scripture for the practice of asking for the fullness of the Spirit for one's self. Our Lord in Luke 11:13 said to His disciples, "How much more shall your heavenly Father give the Holy Spirit to them that ask Him?" He invited the disciples to ask for the Person of the Spirit, not His fullness. This was before Pentecost, and the Spirit had not yet come. It appears that they did not ask the Father for Him, and so our Lord says "I will pray the Father, and he shall give you another Comforter" (John 14:16). The "I" is intensive. They had not asked, so He did. The result was Pentecost. Distinguish therefore between asking for the Person of the Holy Spirit and for His fullness or control. It is not maintained that a believer who asks for the fullness of the Spirit does not experience His control over his life. Sometimes he does and sometimes he does not. If he asks in faith believing and at the same time yields his whole life to His control, and desires to be done with sin, the control of the Spirit follows. *But too often such asking is accompanied by an unyielded life.* But a trust in the Lord Jesus for that control involves the heart's submission to the Spirit. It involves the entire moral and spiritual being of the Christian. Many a sinner fearing the dire consequences of sin, has asked the Lord Jesus to save him, but has not been willing to give up his sin. Many a saint has asked the Holy Spirit to fill him, desiring more power for service, but has been unwilling to make a clean sweep of things and be done with some little pet sin in his life. But a statement of trust in the Lord Jesus for that fullness, forces one to face the sin question and the lack of surrender, and to be done with both. Furthermore, asking for that control may not be accompanied by trust but unbelief. A simple, "Lord Jesus, I do desire that the Holy Spirit control my every thought, word, and deed, and I do trust Thee for that control of the Spirit over my life," is the scriptural way of appropriating the fullness of the Spirit. If one is disposed to say, "Why split hairs and be so technical about this," one could cite the exactness with which our Lord uses His words in reference to the Holy Spirit when He says, "For he dwelleth with you and shall be in you" (John 14:17), thus distinguishing between the presence of the Spirit *with* the believer in Old Testament times under the law, and the presence of the Spirit *in* the believer under grace.

There is no Scripture for the practice of tarrying for the fullness of the Spirit. Our Lord said to the disciples, "I send the promise of my Father upon you: but tarry ye in the city of Jerusalem until ye be endued with power from on high" (Luke 24:49). But let us note some careful distinctions here. He did not tell them to tarry for the fullness, but for the Person and the coming of the Spirit. The Holy Spirit was scheduled to come to earth fifty days after the resurrection, as Pentecost was fifty days after the Feast of First Fruits. The disciples were to wait in Jerusalem for ten more days and the Spirit would come. This announcement by our Lord was made at the close of His forty day post-resurrection ministry. The Holy Spirit came at Pentecost. The word "tarry" is the translation of a Greek word that means "to sit down, to sojourn." They were to sojourn in the city of Jerusalem for ten days until the Holy Spirit came from heaven. He is here. We need not wait for Him. He indwells the believer the moment that person puts his faith in the Lord Jesus, and He awaits that person's desire and trust that He control him.

One may be disposed to quote Acts 19:2, "Have ye received the Holy Ghost since ye believed?" arguing that the Holy Spirit does not come in to abide until the child of God has come to a certain stage in his Christian experience. But the correct rendering is, "Did ye receive the Spirit when ye believed?" Paul was surprised at the absence of spirituality in these believers. It turned out that they had followed the preaching of John the Baptist, and therefore had not come under the provision of the indwelling Spirit of the Age of Grace.[1]

Or, one might say, "I am a Christian, but I do not have the Holy Spirit because I do not speak in tongues," quoting Acts 2:4, 10:46, and 19:6. But let us be careful to note that Acts 2:4 refers to the languages of the individuals mentioned in Acts 2:8-11, that the speaking in tongues of Acts 10:46 was an evidence for that time given to the Jews, that the Gentiles had also received the Spirit, the need for which is now past, and that Acts 19:6 has to do with a special case where Jews had come into salvation under the Old Testament dispensation of law and now were receiving the added benefits of the Age of Grace, a case which cannot occur today.

But again, one may insist that a believer does not receive the Spirit except by the laying on of hands, quoting Acts 8:17 and 19:6. The act of laying on of hands always signifies identification. In the case of Acts 8:17, the Samaritans who did not recognize the temple at Jerusalem, needed to recognize the authority of the church at that place. Submission to the laying on of the apostles' hands thus healed the breach between those Samaritans and the Christian Jews, and identified the former with the Jerusalem church. In Acts 19:6 we have Jews coming over into a new dispensation and authority, and a similar situation holds true for them. We have no such conditions today, and therefore the laying on of hands is not needed for the reception of the Spirit. Thus a consciousness of the

---

1. *Nuggets*, pp. 96, 97.

personal presence of the Holy Spirit in the believer, a desire for His control, and a trust in the Lord Jesus for that control, is the scriptural way of appropriating the ministry of the Holy Spirit.

This condition of being filled with the Spirit must not be a spasmodic thing in the life of the Christian. One hears teaching to the effect that the Holy Spirit fills one only when he is engaged in some particular piece of Christian service. That idea comes from the Old Testament ministry of the Holy Spirit. Before Pentecost, He came upon believers in order to equip them for a certain work they were to do for God, and left them when that service was over. But in the Church Age, this procedure does not obtain. The command, "Be filled (controlled) with the Spirit" is in a grammatical construction in Greek which speaks of a continuous process or state, as the case might be. For those who know Greek, we might say that the imperative mode in the aorist tense speaks of the fact of an action, while that mode in the present tense speaks of a continuous process or state. Here we have the present imperative. The tense in Greek used when a writer speaks of the fact of an action, is the aorist. When he uses any other tense, he goes out of his way to do so, and for the purpose of adding details. Had the inspired writer used the aorist tense here, he would have referred to the fact of being filled with the Spirit. But since he uses the present tense, he desires his Greek reader to understand that the exhortation is for one to be constantly, moment by moment, filled with the Spirit. That is, God's plan for the normal Christian life is that it should be a life constantly, consciously, and definitely subjected to the Spirit, a life that has a consuming desire for His control over every thought, word, and deed, thus a life unceasingly controlled by the Holy Spirit. The Christian needs this constant control of the Spirit over his life if he is to gain constant victory over sin, if the Lord Jesus in His beauty and fragrance of character is to be radiated by the Spirit through the life of the saint, if the saint is to walk in the path of God's will for him, if he is to live a life of prayer, and if he expects to understand his Bible as he should. *One annot do with less than the Spirit's constant control.* Indeed, it is sin not to be filled constantly with the Spirit. The mode of the erb is imperative. That means, that the words "Be filled" are a ommand. Failure to obey any command of Scripture is sin.

One hears the expression, "One baptism, many fillings." The rst half of this expression is correct, but the second half is not in ccord with the scriptural ideal for a normal Christian life. Let s look at the words, "many fillings." They speak of the Spirit-lled life as one would speak of a motor-car and its need of gasoline. 'hat is, the filling-station attendant fills the tank. We drive off. 'he running motor consumes the gasoline and the tank becomes mpty, and must be filled again. This is the illustration of the eliever who is filled with the Spirit, engages in a piece of Christian 'ork, lives through certain experiences, and in doing so, uses up ae power which came from that filling with the Spirit. Then he aust come back to the Spirit for another supply of power. This rocess is repeated over and over again.

But the thing wrong with all this is that the Christian's heart is ot an empty receptacle to be filled with a substance as the tank of motor car is to be filled with gasoline, but is a symbol of the will, ae emotions, and the reason, all of which are to be constantly con-olled. Again, the Spirit is not a certain amount of power given the believer which he can use in his activities. He is a Person ho controls another person, the believer. It is not that the believer ses the power of God but that God's power uses him. Furthermore, ae only things that would deprive the Christian of this fullness f the Spirit are a lack of definite subjection on his part to the pirit, or the presence of known and cherished sin in his life. nstead of saying, "One baptism, and many fillings," one should say, One baptism, and His constant control."

But this desire for the control of the Holy Spirit, and this trust in ae Lord Jesus for that control, is but part of the believer's obliga-on in the premises. One cannot say, "Just to realize with joy the Spirit's passionate longing to control my thoughts, words, ar deeds for the glory of the Lord Jesus, and to rest quietly in H energizing and supervising ministry, is all that is necessary." *Th Christian life is not a mere "let go and let God" affair. It is a "ta hold with God" business.* It is not a mere rest in God, an existen somewhat like that of a jelly-fish floating in the warm currents the Gulf Stream. God is not developing jelly-fish Christians. Go wants to develop heroes, Christian men and women of moral stamir and spiritual power. In the physical realm, no one becomes stron by merely eating wholesome food and resting. Exercise is what needed to change the food-energy into bone and muscle. In lil manner, the Christian must exercise himself spiritually if he is grow strong in his Christian life. That demands the exercise of h free will, the making of choices, the deciding between right ar wrong, the saying of a point blank NO to temptation, the consta striving to improve one's spiritual life, grow in the Christian grac and in Christlikeness. It involves not only the desire to be lovin but the definite endeavor to be loving. It is not merely a trustf rest in the Holy Spirit to make us loving, but a positive exertic of our own will to be loving. It is like bending one's arm. Th strength to bend one's arm is in that member of the body, but th strength is only potential and not active unless the will power exerted which will cause that strength to function. Just so, the pow of the Holy Spirit is potentially resident in the saint by virtue His indwelling presence, but it is only operative in that believ when he is yielded to and dependent upon the ministry of th Spirit, and then steps out in faith in the performance of the actic contemplated. For instance, when the believer is confronted with temptation, it is not enough to rest in the Holy Spirit's ministr to overcome that temptation for us. We must by an act of our ow free will say a bold, positive, and fearless NO to it. The insta we move in that direction, the Spirit is there with His wonderf energizing power. Indeed, you will say, that the very start of th step taken in the direction of the act of saying NO to that tempt tion was motivated by the Spirit. And that is true. Yet it is als

rue that it is the free action of the believer's will, and is his responsibility. Right here lies that mysterious, incomprehensible, and not-
to-be-understood interaction and mutual response between the free-
will of man and the sovereign grace of God.

This necessary action of the will on the part of the believer, in
addition to the trust in and dependence upon the Holy Spirit which
he saint must have, is seen clearly in the expression, "a certain
fellowship of the Spirit" (Phil. 2:1) which we found referred to
a relation between individuals which involves a common interest
and a mutual active participation in that interest and in each other."
It is the obligation of the believer to be supremely interested in the
things of God, for the Spirit is constantly exploring the deep things
of God (I Cor. 2:10). The Christian who does not maintain a real
interest in and hunger for the Word of God, and satisfy both by a
constant study of that Word, is not co-operating with the Spirit,
and is not giving the Spirit an opportunity to work in his life and
cause him to grow in the Christian graces. The Spirit works through
the Word of God that we have stored in our hearts, and not apart
from it.

Likewise, the believer who does not actively participate in the
activity necessary to the saying of YES to the will of God and of
NO to sin, is not co-operating with the Spirit. And the Christian who
does not engage in a Holy Spirit directed ministry of some kind
in the work of furthering the knowledge of the Word of God, is not
co-operating with the Spirit. It is this ideal combination of a moment by moment trust in, submission to, and dependence upon the
ministry of the Holy Spirit, and the constant interest in and participation with the Holy Spirit in the things of God, that produces
the best results in the Christian's experience. This combination
develops Christian men and women with a sense of responsibility,
with moral courage and stamina of a high order, with a balance and
poise that weathers the severest storms, with a delicate sense of
tact that enables them to move among their fellowmen without riding

roughshod over their tender hearts, but rather in a loving way so
that their passing leaves a sense of the presence of the Lord Jesus.
It develops spiritual giants, men and women who can be trusted
in a time of crisis.

Inaccurate Statements

It seems rather singular that the only branch of Christian doctrine
in which we allow ourselves a certain looseness and inaccuracy of
statement is in regard to the Person and work of the Holy Spirit.
The plea is, "Why be so technical?   We all mean the same thing,
even though we may use different terms or expressions to convey
our thoughts." But do we allow ourselves a like looseness and inaccuracy of statement when we speak of the Person and work of the
Lord Jesus?   How carefully we guard the doctrine of His virgin
birth, and His deity, making a careful distinction between His
divinity and deity.[1] How meticulous we are in our choice of words
when we formulate the doctrine of His substitutionary death on the
Cross.   We distinguish between His coming into the air to catch
out the Church and His coming to the earth to set up the Millennial
Kingdom.   To be just a bit inaccurate in a statement regarding the
origin of our Lord's humanity, the meaning of His death on the
Cross, and the fact of His bodily resurrection, would brand one as
a heretic, in present day language, a Modernist. But to play fast
and loose with the plainly revealed truth regarding the Person and
work of the Holy Spirit, produces no protest in evangelical circles.

If an evangelist would be as inaccurate in his statements regarding the need of a lost sinner for a Saviour, the work of that Saviour
on the Cross, and the way a sinner must appropriate that salvation
as we allow ourselves to be when we teach the saints about the
ministry of the Spirit, how many souls would be saved?   It is the
clear, simple, accurate, true to the Word statements of the evangelist
which the Holy Spirit uses. And if lost souls would be kept from

---

1. *Treasures*, pp. 74-76.

salvation by a message which does not accurately explain the way of salvation, then saints are being deprived of the most efficient ministry of the Holy Spirit because of the obscurities and inaccuracies so prevalent in much of the teaching regarding His Person and work.   One of the chief reasons for the lack of power in the Church is that the Holy Spirit is not recognized as He should be by the individual Christian.   And much of this lack of understanding of the ministry of the Spirit on the part of the saint is due to the inaccurate presentation of that important truth.   Such a presentation not only misinforms but makes it harder, sometimes well-nigh impossible for the clear, simple truth to be taught successfully.

Two of the most serious and harmful of these loose and inaccurate statements are petitions addressed to the Spirit in which the believer asks Him to fall fresh upon him, and to descend upon his heart. Two of the plainest truths in Scripture are the coming of the Spirit at Pentecost to form the Church, and His coming into the heart of the believer at the moment he receives the Lord Jesus as his Saviour, to take up His permanent residence in his being.   To voice such petitions as those above, is to ignore and deny the plain teaching of Scripture.   It is to give the believer the impression that the Holy Spirit is a far away Helper who does not dwell permanently in the heart of the saint, but comes to his aid when he calls.   Thus, the believer does not have the consciousness of the indwelling Spirit. He does not see that his body is an inner sanctuary in which the Holy Spirit dwells.   It is to ask for a second Pentecost.   It is to ask for the coming of the Person of the Spirit when what the saint needs and possibly desires is the fullness of the Spirit.   In that case, where is the proper adjustment of the believer to the Spirit which would enable Him to exercise His most efficient control over him? How senseless to meet a friend, have that friend at one's side, and yet plead with him to come to one.   What would this friend think of us?   And what does the Holy Spirit think of such looseness in resenting the proper relationship of the Spirit to the believer? The fellowship of two human beings with one another is the most

delicate and intricate of all relationships, demanding the most p
fect mutual adjustment to and understanding of one another if th
fellowship is to be of a high order. The same thing is true of t
fellowship of the Spirit with respect to the believer. And if t
proper adjustment is not made on the part of the saint, then t
Spirit is prevented from performing His ministry in and for th
saint in an efficient way. When a believer is taught to ask t
Spirit to fall fresh on him and to descend upon his heart, he is taug
to ignore the truth concerning His indwelling. Furthermore, t
idea of the descending Spirit falling fresh upon him takes the pla
of the conception of the fullness or control of the Spirit over his li
and the believer does not put himself into His control. The res
is that the Spirit is prevented from doing His best for the believ
and the saint lives a powerless mediocre Christian life.

Another wrong conception concerning the adjustment of t
believer to the Holy Spirit is found in the idea that the believ
must empty his heart of sin and self and live a separated life
order that the Holy Spirit can fill his heart. This is based aga
upon the misapprehension that the Christian's heart is a receptac
and the Spirit a substance to fill the space otherwise unoccupie
The word "heart" as used here is just a figure of speech whi
speaks of the will, emotions, and reason of the individual, and t
Holy Spirit is a divine Person who seeks to control and use the
to the glory of God.

This puts the cart before the horse. A Christian who attemp
to clean up his life by ridding his life of all sin, in order that l
may be filled with the Spirit, will never be filled with the Spir
It is just as impossible for a *sinner* to rid his life of sin and live
life in obedience to God's Word in order to receive the Lord Jes
as Saviour, as it is for the *saint* to dethrone self and enthrone t
Lord Jesus, live a separated life, and put all sin out of his life
order to be filled with the Spirit. It takes the precious blood
Jesus and the omnipotent power of God to save a sinner. It tak

e omnipotent power of the Spirit to put sin out of a Christian's
e, to enthrone the Lord Jesus, and to cut the saint's mooring lines
th the world. The lost sinner comes to the Lord Jesus saying,
ust as I am without one plea, but that thy blood was shed for me."
e saint with sin in his life should come to the Holy Spirit just
he is, with all his spiritual problems, and judging the sin in his
e for what it is, namely sin, consciously exert his free will and
y NO to the temptation to continue in that sin, and trust the
oly Spirit to put it out of his life and keep it out, depending upon
im to give both the desire and power to keep from committing that
n again. The Holy Spirit is eager to come to the aid of a saint
ho is not getting victory over sin, and make actual in his life
at victory which the Lord Jesus procured for him at the Cross.
is the Holy Spirit who will clean up the believer's life as he
-operates with Him. He will enthrone the Lord Jesus as Lord
the life as the saint trusts Him to do this. He will cause the
liever to live a life in separation from the world and unto God.

Then there is the practice of referring to the Holy Spirit as "it."
t" is a neuter pronoun and is used to refer to things, never persons.
o use the pronoun "it" is to deny personality to that which is
ferred to. Observe what evils follow the practice of using this
ronoun when referring to the Holy Spirit. It deprives Him of
ersonality in the conception of the speaker and his uninformed
steners. That does away with the doctrine of His personal in-
welling of the believer. That in turn takes away the practical
aching of personal holiness in view of the fact that the physical
ody of the believer is a temple of the Holy Spirit. Again, by denying
ersonality to the Holy Spirit, the use of the pronoun "it" prevents
e saint from bringing himself into proper adjustment to the Spirit,
that He, a Person, can control the believer. There is no heart
bmission to the will of the Spirit, merely the attempted appropria-
on of some mysterious power which the believer feels he needs
nd can use, which again is a wrong conception, for it is not the
liever who uses the power of God but the power of God that

uses him. Such a conception as that of the Holy Spirit grievi
over the saint who has sin in his life, is also made impossible, a
this potent check upon sin in the life of a Christian is taken aw
(Eph. 4:30). To sum it up; the believer who merely conceives
the Holy Spirit as an impersonal force which he can use, kno
nothing either in doctrine or practice, concerning the fullness
the Spirit.

But in justification of the practice of using the neuter prono
when referring to the Holy Spirit, some one may call attention
the fact that the Authorized Version uses the pronoun "itself"
Romans 8:16, 26, and the neuter pronoun "which," in Roma
5:5; I Corinthians 6:19; II Timothy 1:14; I Peter 1:11, and
John 3:24, when referring to the Holy Spirit. And here is whe
we need to go to the Greek text for an explanation which shou
clear up this difficulty. It will be necessary to mention some Gre
grammar rules in doing this.

Nouns in Greek are in either one of three genders. They a
either masculine, feminine, or neuter. They have certain endin
which indicate to what gender they belong. The word "spirit" ha
pens to be in the neuter gender. But that does not mean that t
Greeks considered that which is designated by the word "spiri
as being an inanimate object and therefore impersonal. The Gre
word for "wine" is masculine. But that does not mean that th
ascribed personality to "wine." The Greek word "wisdom"
feminine. But that again does not mean that they thought of wi
dom in a personal way. The Greek word for "child" is neute
but they did not therefore think of a child as an inanimate thin
In English the neuter pronoun is used for inanimate objects, t
masculine, for a male individual, and the feminine for the female.

Because the Greek word for "spirit" is neuter, Greek gramm
requires that the pronoun used when referring to that which
designated by this Greek word, must be neuter. The translato
used the neuter pronoun "itself" in Romans 8:16, 26, because t

reek pronoun is neuter. But there is such a thing as idiom in a
nguage, namely, a construction or expression peculiar to that
nguage, and not found in other languages, which if brought over
terally into the second language, would give a wrong impression.
he business of a translator is to bring over into the second language,
e thought of the first. He is not bound to give a literal translation
f an idiom. His business is to find that expression in the second
nguage which will adequately translate the meaning which the
liom has in its own language. The teaching of Scripture shows
early that the Holy Spirit is a Person. In view of this, the
ronoun "Himself" should be the translation in Romans 8:16, 26.
ee how the personality of the Spirit is so clearly implied in the
xpression, "The Spirit Himself."

The same procedure applies in the case where the word "which"
used. In John 14:17, 26, the pronoun is in the neuter gender,
nd yet the translators use the word "whom." Why did they not
llow the same procedure in the cases where they used "which?"
a all these instances the pronoun is neuter in the Greek text. They
so offer "Him" as the translation of the neuter pronoun of the
ird person (John 14:17). In every instance the pronoun should
e "whom" not "which."

But again, in John 14:26, the word "he" is from a masculine pro-
oun in Greek. But the pronoun here is masculine because its ante-
edent "Comforter" is masculine. The masculine gender of this
ronoun does not teach the personality of the Spirit any more than
e pronoun in the neuter gender speaks of the Spirit as an imper-
onal force. The genders of the pronouns in the Greek text which
efer to the Holy Spirit are determined by the genders of their
ntecedents. Suppose for a moment that the Spirit was not a
erson, and that the word "spirit" was masculine. It would be
ust as wrong for a translator to use the masculine pronoun "he"
f a masculine were used in the Greek, as for a translator, knowing
hat the Holy Spirit is a Person, to use a neuter pronoun when a
euter pronoun is found in the Greek text. One word for "house"

in Greek is masculine. But you would not translate its masculine pronoun by the word "he." Another word for "house" is feminine. But you would not render its feminine pronoun by the word "she." The pronoun would be "it" in both cases. The word "he" in John 16:8 is from a masculine pronoun in Greek. But that pronoun is masculine because its antecedent "Comforter" is masculine. Thus, the masculine gender of the Greek text does not teach the personality of the Spirit, nor can one therefore erroneously infer that the Spirit is not a Person but only an impersonal force just because the word "spirit" is neuter and its pronoun is therefore neuter. In every case, the English pronoun referring to the Holy Spirit should be in the masculine gender, thus showing that He is a Person, since the teaching of Scripture is that He is a Person.

INDEX

Of Scripture References Covering Volumes I to IV of This Series

The student of the English Bible often wishes that he had access to the Greek New Testament in order that he might be able to know just what Greek words are back of the English words which he is studying, and thus come to a clearer understanding of the Word. The series of books of which this one is the fourth, has been written to help meet this need. But one has more than a lexicon in them. They not only give the meaning of the Greek word, but also its particular shade of meaning and interpretation in the context in which it is found. In addition to that, these books offer a concordant study of words such as "perfect, anoint, temptation, visit, love, crown," listing the places where they are found in the New Testament, commenting on representative instances of their use, and leaving the other places for the study of the English reader. The four books treat approximately 1150 scripture references. The index to these has been placed in this fourth book for the convenience of the student. When studying a portion of the English New Testament, he can easily consult the single index and see if the author has commented upon its Greek text. The four books are: *Golden Nuggets from the Greek New Testament for the English Reader; Bypaths in the Greek New Testament for the English Reader; Treasures from the Greek New Testament for the English Reader;* and *Untranslatable Riches from the Greek New Testament for the English Reader.* These will be listed in the index under the abbreviated titles; *Nuggets, Bypaths, Treasures,* and *Riches.*

A special concordance, listing each place where the word "love" occurs in the New Testament, will be found in *Bypaths,* together with the distinctive Greek word for "love" in each instance (there are three different Greek words used), and the definition of each, with comment on representative passages. To include these in this index would make it unduly long.

INDEX

Of Scripture References Covering Volumes I to IV of This Series

Studies in the Vocabulary of the Greek New Testament

DEDICATED

To Richard W. Oliver, who is now in the presence of his Lord, and Howard W. Ferrin, classmates of mine who, during student days at Northwestern University, instructed me in the Word, and directed me to The Moody Bible Institute for training in Christian service—for which I shall ever be grateful.

Preface

One who undertakes to study God's Word and to explain it to others, should be a student of words. To the extent that he understands the meaning of the words in the New Testament, to that extent is he able to understand its statements and make them clear to others.

While the words used in the English New Testament are for the most part simple and easy to understand, yet there are factors involved which make a knowledge of the Greek words very helpful in arriving at an accurate, full-orbed interpretation of the passage in question.

For instance, some English words have changed their meaning in the 300 years since the Authorized Version was translated. Since this version still remains the most widely used translation of the Scriptures, there is need of bringing that particular part of the translation up to date. Then again, a student of the English Bible often interprets a word according to its current usage in ordinary conversation instead of in its more specialized meaning. Again, in the case of synonyms, one English word may be the translation of four Greek words, each having a shade of meaning slightly different from the other. This added light is denied the student of the English Bible. Consequently, while he may not arrive at an erroneous interpretation of the passage where the particular word occurs, yet he does not have as accurate and clear an interpretation of it as he might have. Or again, a Greek word may have a very rich content of meaning which would demand a few sentences if not a paragraph to bring out. But in a translation like the A.V., where the translation is held down to a minimum of words, it is impossible to bring out this richness of meaning. A knowledge of the Greek word is of help here.

9

Then, there are some words dealing with the theology of th
N.T., or its doctrines, which are not understood by the En
lish reader, but where a knowledge of the Greek word and i
usage is of great help.

The purpose of this book is to make available to the Bib
student who does not know Greek, an English-Greek vocabul
ry of some of the words used in the New Testament. The pla
has been to give the English word, the Greek word of whic
it is the translation, in transliterated form, the various mea
ings of the Greek word, and where necessary, every pla
where the Greek word is found in the New Testament. Th
student of the English Bible can therefore obtain a cleare
more comprehensive view of the English word he is studyin
by understanding the Greek word of which it is the transl
tion.

Where no concordance is given of a word, the stude
should understand that the English word is in its every occu
rence, the uniform translation of the Greek word. Where
concordance is given, the reason for the same may be th
various English words are used to translate the one Gree
word, the variants being given in each case. Or, in the case
synonyms, a concordance is necessary, since two or more Gree
words are translated by the one English word. Again, a co
cordance is given at times so that the student can make
study of the word in its every occurrence in the New Test
ment. There are a few words that are treated only in part
cular passages, where the definitions of the Greek word wi
not hold in other places where this English word is used, an
for the reason that other Greek words are found in the tex
These will be marked "*Limited.*"

The author, in defining the Greek word, has tried to give
well-rounded and complete view of it. The classical usage
presented first, next, the Koine usage in secular documen
and then the New Testament usage. Before 332 B.C., Gree
was confined for the most part to Greece itself. The ter

classical" is used to speak of Greek as it was spoken by the Greeks themselves in their own country prior to this date. But when Alexander the Great conquered the Medo-Persian empire, his armies spread the knowledge of the Greek language over the then-known world. Remaining as armies of occupation, and settling amongst the conquered peoples, they popularized the language, simplifying its grammatical and syntactical structure. The language as spoken by them became what is called Koine Greek. The word Koine means "common," and refers to the fact that the mingling of the various Greek tribes and dialects in the great armies of Greece, produced a common language, a language held in common by all Greeks, whereas before, the country of Greece was divided into various Greek states, each having its own Greek dialect. This Greek is called Koine. This is the Greek that became the international language.

Classical Greek compared to Koine Greek is comparable to English used by the great writers of the past as the latter is compared to the English which the average person uses in ordinary conversation. The Greek translation of the Old Testament, the Septuagint, is in Koine Greek. The New Testament is written in the same style of Greek. The New Testament was therefore written in the language of the ordinary person, not in the language of the scholar.

The author has not only tried to give the reader a view of the word as it was used by the ancient Greeks, but also a conception of how it was used by the average person in the first century in his ordinary conversation. In addition to that, he has presented the usage of the word in the New Testament.

Thus, after the student has examined all the various uses of the word, he can form a better, more accurate, and full-orbed conception of that word. Of course, he will not use the purely classical meaning of the word when interpreting the New Testament, except where the author has indicated, or where the context clearly shows that the purely classical mean-

ing is used. The classical meaning is given so that the studen
may have some background against which he can obtain
better appreciation of the word as it is used in the Ne
Testament.

The student should first set before himself the goal of stud
ing and mastering the meanings of each word. He can the
use the book as a reference work when studying the Ne
Testament. He can either start at the beginning and wor
slowly through the book, or he can consult the index, choos
the particular word that suits his fancy, and check the wor
off after he has studied it. A study of a single word woul
mean that the student gain a comprehensive view of the Gree
word, and then study the passages in which it occurs. Tha
will give him a bird's-eye view of the word as it is used in th
New Testament. In case a concordance of the word is no
given, the student should consult a Cruden's Concordance.

The reader is cautioned against putting this book on th
shelf as a reference work merely. If he does that, he will d
prive himself of a great deal of valuable information tha
would stand him in good stead in his study of the New Test
ment. If he puts himself to the discipline of working throug
this book, he will have gained not only a more accurate know
edge of these New Testament words, but also much spiritu
truth. *This book is more than an English-Greek vocabular
It offers an intensive study of the words it treats as they ar
related to their context in the New Testament. Furthermor
the study of these words in their every occurrence in the Ne
Testament, will open up many new lines of truth, and affor
a new and clearer appreciation of the passages studied. Pasto
and other Christian workers will obtain fresh material an
new ideas for Bible messages.*

The English translation used is the Authorized Versio
The Greek authorities quoted are: Joseph H. Thayer, *Gree
English Lexicon of the New Testament;* Liddel and Scot
Greek-English Lexicon (classical); Archbishop Trench, *Syn*

yms of the New Testament; Marvin R. Vincent, *Word Studies in the New Testament;* Herman Cremer, *Biblico-Theological Lexicon of New Testament Greek;* James Hope Moulton and George Milligan, *Vocabulary of the Greek Testament,* the work of these scholars being based upon the papyri, the latter being contemporary secular documents written in Koine Greek.   **K. S. W.**

Studies in the Vocabulary of the Greek New Testament

ARCHBISHOP TRENCH,

On the Study of Synonyms

"The value of this study as a discipline for training the mind into close and accurate habits of thought, the amount of instruction which may be drawn from it, the increase of intellectual wealth which it may yield, all this has been implicitly recognized by well-nigh all great writers — for well-nigh all from time to time have paused, themselves to play the dividers and discerners of words — explicitly by not a few who have proclaimed the value which this study had in their eyes. And instructive as in any language it must be, it must be eminently so in the Greek — a language spoken by a people of the subtlest intellect; who saw distinctions, where others saw none; who divided out to different words what others often were content to huddle confusedly under a common term; who were themselves singularly alive to its value, diligently cultivating the art of synonymous distinction . . .; and who have bequeathed a multitude of fine and delicate observations on the right discrimination of their own words to the after world. . . .

"And while thus the characteristic excellences of the Greek language especially invite us to the investigation of the likenesses and differences between words, to the study of the words of the New Testament there are reasons additional inviting us. If by such investigations as these we become aware of delicate variations in an author's meaning, which otherwise we might have missed, where is it so desirable that we should miss nothing, that we should lose no finer intention of the writer, as in those words which are the vehicles of the very mind of God Himself? If thus the intellectual riches of the student are increased, can this anywhere be of so great importance as there, where the intellectual may, if rightly used, prove spiritual riches as well? If it encourage thoughtful meditation on the exact forces of words, both as they are in themselves, and in their relation to other words, or in any way unveil to us their marvel and their mystery, this can nowhere else have a worth in the least approaching that which it acquires when the words with which we have to do are, to those who receive them aright, words of eternal life; while in the dead carcasses of the same, if men suffer the spirit of life to depart from them, all manner of corruptions and heresies may be, as they have been, bred.

"The *words* of the New Testament are eminently the *stoicheia* (rudiments, elements) of Christian theology, and he who will not begin with a patient study of those, shall never make any considerable, least of all any secure, advances in this: for here, as everywhere else, sure disappointment awaits him who thinks to possess the whole without first possessing the parts of which that whole is composed."[1]

---

1. *Synonyms of the New Testament*, R. C. Trench.

VOCABULARY

1, 2, 3. *Limited*

---

4. *Limited*

Studies in the Vocabulary of the
Greek New Testament

PERFECT. There are four words translated by the one word *perfect*. These must be distinguished.

Telaios the adjective, and *teleioo* the verb. The adjective is used in the papyri, of heirs being of age, of women who have attained maturity, of full-grown cocks, of acacia trees in good condition, of a complete lampstand, of something in good working order or condition. To summarize; the meaning of the adjective includes the ideas of full-growth, maturity, workability, soundness, and completeness. The verb refers to the act of bringing the person or thing to any one of the afore-mentioned conditions. When applied to a Christian, the word refers to one that is spiritually mature, complete, well-rounded in his Christian character.

The word occurs in the following scriptures; the adjective and noun in *Mt.* 5:48, 19:21; *Lk.* 1:45 (performance); *Rom.* 12:2; I *Cor.* 2:6, 13:10, 14:20 (men); *Eph.* 4:13; *Phil.* 3:15; *Col.* 1:28, 3:14, 4:12; *Heb.* 5:14 (of full age), 7:11, 9:11; *Jas.* 1:4, 17, 25, 3:2; I *John* 4:18; *Col.* 3:14; *Heb.* 6:1, 12:2 (finisher); I *Pet.* 1:13 (to the end); the verb in *Lk.* 2:43 (*had fulfilled*) 13:32; *John* 4:34 (*finish*), 5:36 (*finish*), 17:4, (*have finished*) 17:23, 19:28 (*fulfilled*); *Acts* 20:24 (*finish*); II *Cor.* 7:1, 12:9; *Gal.* 3:3; *Phil.* 3:12; *Heb.* 2:10, 5:9, 7:19, 28 (*consecrated*), 9:9, 10:1, 14, 11:40, 12:23; *Jas.* 2:22; I *John* 2:5, 4:12, 17, 18. Study these passages in the light of the above definitions, select the one that agrees best with the context, and see what additional light is thrown upon the passage, and how much clearer it becomes.

Katartizo. This word has the following meanings: "to repair, to restore to a former good condition, to prepare, to fit out, to equip." It was used of reconciling factions, setting broken bones, putting a dislocated limb into place, mending nets. Paul used it metaphorically in the sense of setting a person to rights, of bringing him into line. Used of a Christian, it referred to his equipment for Christian service (Eph. 4:11, 12). The verb occurs in *Mt.* 4:21 (*mending*), 21:16; *Mk.* 1:19; *Lk.* 6:40, *Rom.* 9:22 (*fitted*); *I Cor.* 1:10 (*perfectly joined together*), *II Cor.* 13:11; *Gal.* 6:1 (*restore*); *I Thes.* 3:10; *Heb.* 10:5 (*prepared*), 11:3 (*framed*), 13:21; *I Pet.* 5:10; the noun in *II Cor.* 13:9; *Eph.* 4:12.

In contrasting these two words, we would say that *teleios* refers to Christian experience, *katartizo* to Christian service, *teleios* to maturity and completeness of Christian character, *katartizo* to equipment for service.

Akribes, meaning "exactly, accurately, diligently," is translated by the word *perfect* in *Acts* 18:26, 23:15, 20, 24:22. In *II Tim.* 3:17, *perfect* is from *artios,* meaning "fitted, complete."

BLESSED. There are two Greek words, each with its distinctive meaning, both translated by the one word *blessed.*

Makarios. Some classical writers used this word to describe the state of the Greek gods as distinct from that of men who were subject to poverty and death, denoting a state of being of the gods who were exalted above earthly suffering and the limitations of earthly life. It was also used of the dead. Another word, *eudaimon,* was used of human happiness. Other writers used *makarios* to describe the state of certain men as supremely blest, fortunate, prosperous, wealthy. *Makarios* was chosen by the Bible writers to describe the state of the man who is the recipient of the divine favor and blessing. The LXX[5] uses it in Psalm 1:1, "Oh, the happiness of,"

---

5. *The Greek translation of the Old Testament.*

where it is the Greek translation of a word that in Hebrew thought denotes a state of true well-being. Cremer says that "it is the gracious and saving effect of God's favor . . ., but is enjoyed only when there is a corresponding behavior towards God; so that it forms the hoped-for good of those who in this life are subject to oppression." He says that, "In the N.T., *makarios* is quite a religiously qualified conception, expressing the life-joy and satisfaction of the man who does or shall experience God's favor and salvation, his blessedness altogether apart from his outward condition . . . It always signifies a happiness produced by some experience of God's favor, and specially conditioned by the revelation of grace." In summing up the meaning of the word as used of the state or condition of the believer, we would say that it refers to the spiritually prosperous state of that person who is the recipient of the sanctifying work of the Holy Spirit, who is enabled to minister these blessings to him when the believer yields to Him for that ministry and cooperates with Him in it. For instance, those who are reproached for the name of Christ, are in a spiritually prosperous condition, for the Holy Spirit is ministering to them with refreshing power (I Peter 4:14). Or, "Spiritually prosperous are the meek, for they shall inherit the earth" (Mt. 5:5). See classical usage of *makarios* (fortunate) in Acts 26:2, also in I Tim. 1:11, 6:15 (the state of exaltation above humanity). The word occurs in *Mt.* 5:3-11, 11:6, 13:16, 16:17, 24:46; *Lk.* 1:45, 6:20, 21, 22, 7:23, 10:23, 11:27, 28, 12:37, 38, 43, 14:14, 15, 23:29; *John* 13:17 (*happy*), 20:29; *Acts* 20:35, 26:2 (*happy*); *Rom.* 4:7, 8, 14:22 (*happy*); *I Cor.* 7:40 (*happier*); *I Tim.* 1:11, 6:15; *Tit.* 2:13; *Jas.* 1:12, 25; *I Pet.* 3:14 (*happy*), 4:14 (*happy*); Rev. 1:3, 14:13, 16:15, 19:9, 20:6, 22:7, 14. The noun *makarismos* is found in *Rom.* 4:6, 9; *Gal.* 4:15.

Eulogeo the verb, *eulogetos* the adjective, and *eulogia*, the noun. In classical Greek, *eulogeo* meant "to speak well of, to praise." *Eulogia* meant "good speaking, good words." The

word is a compound of *eu* meaning "well, good" and *logeo*
related to *lego*, "to speak." Our words "eulogy" and "eulogize"
are derived from this Greek word. It was used in the pagan
religions, as when a person who was chastened for his sin by
the god, dedicates a monument to the god, and in doing so
eulogeo, speaks well of, praises the deity. An extract from the
Christian papyri gives us, "to the beloved brother who is also
well-spoken of."[6] *Eulogia* is used in the same literature in the
sense of a "good report," also in the sentence, "If you have anything to say in his favor, come with him and tell me."[7] In the
N.T., when man is said to bless God (Lk. 2:28), the word refers to the act of speaking well of God, of speaking in His favor,
of extolling Him for what He is and does, in these senses, of
the act of praising Him, of eulogizing Him. The word *aineo*
is translated by the word "praise." It means "to extol."
Eulogeo however, in its intrinsic meaning carries the idea
which *aineo* merely refers to. When God is said to bless man
(Eph. 1:3), *eulogeo* refers to the act of God in which He
elevates man, makes him great, gives him prosperity, confers
benefits upon him. When man blesses God, it is an exaltation
with words. When God blesses man, it is an exaltation by
act, that of conferring benefits upon him. When man is said
to bless his fellow man (Lk. 6:28), he confers benefits upon
him (Rom. 12:14-21), or speaks well of (Lk. 1:28) in the sense
of eulogizing. The word is also used in the sense of asking
God's blessing on a thing, praying Him to bless it to one's
use, as in Mt. 26:26; I Cor. 10:16. Another use of the word is
found in Eph. 1:3 where the noun "blessings" refers to the
benefits or favors themselves which are conferred upon man.
The verb is found in *Mt.* 5:44, 14:19, 21:9, 23:39, 25:34, 26:26;
Mk. 6:41, 8:7, 10:16, 11:9, 10, 14:22; *Lk.* 1:28, 42, 64 (*praised*),
2:28, 34, 6:28, 9:16, 13:35, 19:38, 24:30, 50, 51, 53; *John* 12:13;
Acts 3:26; *Rom.* 12:14; *I Cor.* 4:12, 10:16, 14:16; *Gal.* 3:9;
Eph. 1:3; *Heb.* 6:14, 7:1, 6, 7, 11:20, 21; *Jas.* 3:9; *I Pet.* 3:9; the

6, 7. *Moulton and Milligan, Vocabulary of the Greek Testament.*

adjective in *Mk.* 14:61; *Lk.* 1:68; *Rom.* 1:25, 9:5; *II Cor.* 1:3, 11:31; *Eph.* 1:3; *I Pet.* 1:3; the noun in *Rom.* 15:29, 16:18 (*fair speeches*); *I Cor.* 10:16; *II Cor.* 9:5, 6 (*bounty and bountiful*); *Gal.* 3:14; *Eph.* 1:3; *Heb.* 6:7, 12:17; *Jas.* 3:10; *I Pet.* 3:9; *Rev.* 5:12, 13, 7:12. Make a study of this word in these passages, and see how much light is thrown upon the English translation you are using.

DISCIPLE. From the Greek verb *manthano* which means "to learn, to be apprised of, to increase one's knowledge," there are derived the words *mathetes* which means "a learner, a pupil, one who follows the teaching of someone else," thus, a disciple; and *matheteuo* which means "to follow the precepts and instructions of another," thus to be his disciple; also, "to make a disciple, to teach, to instruct." We must be careful to note that the Greek word for "disciple" does not carry with it the idea that that person who is named a disciple is necessarily a saved person. The word does not contain any implications of salvation. A person may learn something from someone else and yet not put that knowledge into practice or make it a part of his life. See John 6:66 in its context for an example of an unsaved disciple, and Matthew 10:1, for an illustration of saved (the eleven) and unsaved (Judas) discipleship. The word merely refers to one who puts himself under the teaching of someone else and learns from him. For the noun, see your English concordance. The verb is found in Mt. 13:52 (*instructed*), 27:57, 28:19 (*teach*); Acts 14:21 (*taught*). In the case of the word "disciple" the context must rule as to whether the particular disciple mentioned, is saved or unsaved, not the word itself.

DISORDERLY. The verb meaning "to conduct one's self in a disorderly manner" is *atakteo*. It comes from the verb *tasso* which is a military term referring to the act of arranging soldiers in military order in the ranks. When the Greeks wanted to make a word mean the opposite to what it meant originally, they placed the letter Alpha as its first letter. Thus *atakteo* refers to soldiers marching out of order or quitting the ranks, thus being disorderly. The word therefore means "deviating from the prescribed order or rule." Its original meaning was that of riot or rebellion. The word is found only in the Thessalonian epistles, in its verb form in II Thes. 3:7, as an adjective in I Thes. 5:14 (unruly), and as an adverb in II Thes. 3:6, 11.

However, in the Thessalonian epistles, this word is not used in its military sense, but in a metaphorical one. There has been a question as to whether the word referred to actual moral wrongdoing, or to a certain remissness in daily work or routine. The latter meaning is now supported by almost contemporary evidence from the papyri. It appears in a contract dated in A.D. 66, in which a father apprenticed his son to a craftsman. The father enters into an agreement with the craftsman that if there are any days when his son "plays truant" or "fails to attend," he is afterward to make them good. In a manuscript of A.D. 183, a weaver's apprentice must appear for an equivalent number of days, if from idleness or ill-health or any other reason he exceeds the twenty day vacation he is allowed in the year.

The word in II Thessalonians 3:11 most certainly is used in the sense of "playing truant from one's employment," since it is defined by the words, "working not at all," the Greek word *ergazomai* meaning "to labor, do work, to trade, to make gains by trading," which usage is in accord with the meaning of the word at that time. The same is the case with 3:6, 7. Paul supported himself while preaching. The word appears also in I Thessalonians 5:14 (unruly) where it could refer to any deviation from the prescribed order or rule of the Christian life.

PARABLE. This word comes from the Greek *parabole,* which in turn comes from *ballo* "to throw" and *para, "along-side."* Therefore, a parable is an illustration thrown in along-side of a truth to make the latter easier to understand.

SYNAGOGUE. This word comes from *ago* "to go" and *sun* "with." Thus it refers to the act of a group of people "going with one another," thus congregating in one place. Finally, it came to refer to the place where they congregated. The word was used to designate the buildings other than the central Jewish temple where the Jews congregated for worship.

CHURCH. The word *ekklesia* appears in the Greek text where this word is found in the translations. *Ekklesia* comes from *kaleo* "to call," and *ek* "out from." The compound verb means "to call out from." In classical Greek *ekklesia* referred to an assembly of the citizens summoned by the town crier. It is used in Acts 19:32-41 in its purely classical meaning. The town clerk dismissed the citizens who had been gathered together by the craftsmen of Ephesus. In its every other occurrence, it is translated "church," the church being looked upon as a called-out body of people, called out of the world of unsaved humanity to become the people of God. The word refers either to the Mystical Body of Christ made up of saved individuals only (Ephesians), or to the local churches, as for instance Rom. 16:5; Gal. 1:2. The word "assembly" is a good one-word translation of *ekklesia.* The genius of the word points to the fact that in the mind of God, the Church of Jesus Christ is a called-out group of people, separated out from the world to be a people that should maintain their separation from the world out of which they have been called.

REPENT is the translation of *metanoeo* which in classical Greek meant "to change one's mind or purpose, to change one's opinion." The noun *metanoia* meant "a change of mind on reflection." These two words used in classical Greek signified a change of mind regarding anything, but when brought over into the New Testament, their usage is limited to a change of mind in the religious sphere. They refer there to a change of moral thought and reflection which follows moral delinquency. This includes not only the act of changing one's attitude towards and opinion of sin but also that of forsaking it. Sorrow and contrition with respect to sin, are included in the Bible idea of repentance, but these follow and are consequent upon the sinner's change of mind with respect to it. The word *metamelomai* is used in Mt. 21:29, 32, 27:3; II Cor. 7:8; Heb. 7:21, where it is translated "repent." *Metanoeo* is the fuller and nobler term, expressive of moral action and issues. It is the word used by N.T., writers to express the foregoing meaning. In the case of Judas, *metamelomai* means "remorse." In the case of Heb. 7:21 it means only to change one's mind. The act of repentance is based first of all and primarily upon an intellectual apprehension of the character of sin, man's guilt with respect to it, and man's duty to turn away from it. The emotional and volitional aspects of the act of repentance follow, and are the result of this intellectual process of a change of mind with respect to it. This means that the correct approach of the Christian worker to a sinner whom he wishes to lead to the Lord is that of clearly explaining the issues involved. When the unsaved person is made to clearly understand the significance of sin, the intellectual process of changing his mind with respect to it can follow, with the result that sorrow, contrition, and turning away from it will also follow. A mere emotional appeal to the sinner is not the correct one. The Greek word *metanoeo* tells us that the intellectual appeal must come first, since the act of repenting is basically a mental one at the start.

BELIEVE, FAITH, FAITHFULNESS. The verb is *pisteuo*, the noun *pistis*, the adjective *pistos*. In classical Greek *pisteuo* meant *to believe, trust, trust in, put faith in, rely upon* a person or thing. In the passive voice it meant *I am entrusted with a thing, have it committed to me. Pistis* meant *trust* in others, *faith. Pistos* meant *faithful, trusty, true,* used of persons one believes or trusts.

In the papyri,[8] we find the following illustrations of the use of these words; *Whom no one would trust even if they were willing to work;* (confidence in the person's character and motives) ; *I have trusted no one to take it to her,* (confidence in the ability of another to perform a certain task). *Pisteuo* in every instance is translated by the word "believe," except in the following places; *Lk.* 16:11; *John* 2:24; *Rom.* 3:2; *I Cor.* 9:17; *Gal.* 2:7; *I Thes.* 2:4; *I Tim.* 1:11; *Tit.* 1:3, where the idea is that either of entrusting one's self or something else into the custody and safe keeping of another. *Pistis* is translated in every case except the following by the word *faith;* Acts 17:31 (*assurance*), and Heb. 10:39, literally *to them who are of faith. Pistos* is translated by the words *faithful, believing* and *true.*

When these words refer to the faith which a lost sinner must place in the Lord Jesus in order to be saved, they include the following ideas; the act of considering the Lord Jesus worthy of trust as to His character and motives, the act of placing confidence in His ability to do just what He says He will do, the act of entrusting the salvation of his soul into the hands of the Lord Jesus, the act of committing the work of saving his soul to the care of the Lord. This means a definite taking of one's self out of one's own keeping and entrusting one's self into the keeping of the Lord Jesus.

In *Acts* 8:13, 26:27; *Jas.* 2:19, the word refers merely to an intellectual assent to certain facts, in *Acts* 15:11, to a dogmatic belief that such and such is the case.

---

8. *Moulton and Milligan.*

"The N.T. conception of faith includes three main elements, mutually connected and requisite, though according to circumstances sometimes one and sometimes another may be more prominent, viz., (1) a fully convinced acknowledgement of the revelation of grace; (2) a self-surrendering fellowship (adhesion); and (3) a fully assured and unswerving trust (and with this at the same time hope) in the God of salvation or in Christ. None of these elements is wholly ignored by any of the N.T. writers."[9] Thus, the word sometimes refers to an acknowledgment that a certain statement is true (Mt. 21:25), and sometimes to a definite commitment of one's soul into the keeping of another (John 5:24).

SANCTIFY, SAINT, HOLY, HALLOW. These and their related English words are all translations of the same Greek root. The religious terms of Christianity were taken from those in use in the pagan Greek religions, for the New Testament was written in the international Greek of the Roman world. The Bible writers could not coin new terms since they would not be understood, and were therefore forced to use those already in use. However, while the technical and root meanings of these pagan religious terms were taken over by the writers, yet by their use in the New Testament, their moral and spiritual characters were changed and elevated.

The classical Greek word meaning *to sanctify* is *hagizo* which means to *consecrate,* for instance, altars, sacrifices, *to set apart for the gods, to present, to offer.* The word used in the New Testament answering to *hagizo* is *hagiazo* which means "to place in a relation to God answering to His holiness."[10] Neither word means merely "to set apart," but in the case of the pagan word, "to set apart for the gods," and in the case of the Christian word "to set apart for God." The worshipper of the pagan god acquired the character of that pagan god

9. *Cremer, Biblico-Theological Lexicon of New Testament Greek.*
10. *Cremer.*

and the religious ceremonies connected with its worship. The Greek temple at Corinth housed a large number of harlots who were connected with the worship of the Greek god. Thus, the set-apartness of the Greek worshipper was in character licentious, totally depraved, and sinful. The believer in the Lord Jesus is set apart for God by the Holy Spirit, out of the First Adam with the latter's sin and condemnation, into the Last Adam with the latter's righteousness and life. Thus, the worshipper of the God of the Bible partakes of the character of the God for whom he is set apart. This is positional sanctification, an act of God performed at the moment a sinner puts his faith in the Lord Jesus (I Cor. 1:2). The work of the Holy Spirit in the yielded saint, in which He sets the believer apart for God in his experience, by eliminating sin from his life and producing His fruit, a process which goes on constantly throughout the believer's life, is called progressive sanctification (I Thes. 5:23). When our Lord sanctifies Himself, He sets Himself apart for God as the Sacrifice for sin (John 17:19; Heb. 10:7). When man sanctifies God, "the word denotes that manner of treatment on the part of man which corresponds with the holiness of God, and which springs from faith, trust, and fear" (I Pet. 3:15).[11] In the case where the unbelieving wife is sanctified by the believing husband, and the unbelieving husband is sanctified by the believing wife, it "clearly cannot signify the sanctification in its fulness which the N.T. divine and saving work produces; for a personal faith is required in the object of it, which is in this case denied. Still it is unmistakably intimated that by virtue of the marriage union, the unbelieving side in its measure participates in the saving work and fellowship with God experienced by the believing side."[12]

The word *saint* is the translation of *hagios*. This word is one of the five words the Greeks used to express the idea of holiness, insofar as they had any conception of that quality.

11, 12. *Cremer.*

It is the one used most rarely. It is the only Greek word used
in the Bible to express the idea of the biblical conception of
holiness. The biblical content of the word is not found in any
or all of the five Greek words for holiness, except the ideas
of "the consecrated, the sublime, the venerable." The main
elements such as morality, spirituality, purity, are entirely
wanting. Thus this pagan Greek word had to be filled with
an additional content of meaning and in that sense coined
afresh.

Hagios appears to have been specially used of temples or
places of worship, of those places consecrated to the gods
which claimed general reverence. *Hagios* was used to designate that which deserved and claimed moral and religious
reverence.

As to the biblical use of *hagios* as expressing the idea of
God's holiness, Cremer says, "God's holiness signifies His opposition to sin manifesting itself in atonement and redemption or in judgment. . . . Holiness is the perfect purity of God
which in and for itself excludes all fellowship with the world,
and can only establish a relationship of free electing love,
whereby it asserts itself in the sanctification of God's people,
their cleansing and redemption; there the purity of God manifesting itself in atonement and redemption, and correspond-
ingly in judgment." The word is used "of men and things
occupying the relation to God which is conditioned and
brought about by His holiness, whether it be that God has
chosen them for His service, as instruments of His work, or
that God's holiness has sanctified them and taken them into
the fellowship of the redeeming God, the God of salvation."[13]

This word *hagios* is used as a name for the Christian believer (Rom. 1:7). As such it refers to him as one set apart
for God, partaking of a holy standing before God in Christ
Jesus (I Cor. 1:30 *sanctification*), with the obligation of living
a holy life (I Pet. 1:15, 16).

---

13. *Cremer.*

FELLOWSHIP, COMMUNION. These two words are the translation of *koinonia*. This Greek word is used in a marriage contract where the husband and wife agree to a *joint-participation* in the necessaries of life. The key idea in the word is that of a partnership, a possessing things in common, a belonging in common to. For instance, "What things does light have in common with darkness?" (II Cor. 6:14), or, "These things write we unto you that ye also may have joint-participation with us" (in our knowledge of the life of our Lord) (I John 1:3), or, "Our joint-participation is with the Father and with His Son Jesus Christ" (I John 1:3), that is, the things in which Christians participate in salvation, they participate in jointly with God, a common nature, common likes and dislikes; or, "The cup of blessing which we bless, is it not a joint-participation (which we saints have in common) in the blood of Christ? The bread which we break, is it not a joint-participation (which we saints have in common) in the body of Christ" (broken for us) (I Cor. 10:16)? That is, the saints participate in common with one another in the salvation benefits that proceed from the out-poured blood and the broken body of the Lord Jesus. In the light of the usage of the word *koinonia,* make a study of the following places where the word occurs, *I Cor.* 1:9; *II Cor.* 6:14, 8:4, 13:14; *Gal.* 2:9; *Eph.* 3:9; *Phil.* 1:5, 2:1, 3:10; *I John* 1:3, 6, 7. In *Acts* 2:42 and *I John* 1:3, 6, 7, the usage of the word also approaches the common usage of today, that of fellowship in the sense of companionship. In *Phil.* 2:1 and *II Cor.* 13:14 the word refers to the joint-participation of the believer and the Holy Spirit in a common interest and activity in the things of God. Study the usage of the word in *Rom.* 15:26 (contribution); *II Cor.* 9:13 (distribution); *Phm.* 6 (communication); *Heb.* 13:16 (to communicate).

PREDESTINATE is the translation of *proorizo* which is made up of *horizo* "to divide or separate from as a border or boundary, to mark out boundaries, to mark out, to determine, appoint," and *pro* "before." Thus, the compound word means "to divide or separate from a border or boundary beforehand, to determine or appoint beforehand." The genius of the word is that of placing limitations upon someone or something beforehand, these limitations bringing that person or thing within the sphere of a certain future or destiny. These meanings are carried over into the New Testament usage of the word. Thus, the "chosen-out" ones, have had limitations put around them which bring them within the sphere of becoming God's children by adoption (Eph. 1:5), and of being conformed to the image of the Lord Jesus (Rom. 8:29). See the other occurrences of *proorizo* in Acts 4:28; I Cor. 2:7; Eph. 1:11.

CHOOSE is from *eklegomai* which is made up of *lego* "to choose" and *ek* "out from." Thus, the compound word means "to pick, single out, to choose out." The genius of the word has in it the idea of not merely choosing, but that of choosing out from a number. The adjective *eklektos* comes from *eklegomai* and is translated by the words "chosen" and "elect." The elect are "the chosen-out ones." Divine election refers therefore to the act of God in which He chooses out certain from among mankind for salvation. This election does not imply the rejection of the rest, but is the outcome of the love of God lavished upon those chosen-out. Cremer says that "it is unwarranted to give special prominence either to the element of *selection from among others,* or to that of *preference above others.* The main import is that of *appointment for a certain object or goal.*" See John 15:16, 19; Eph. 1:4.

FOREKNOWLEDGE is the translation of *prognosis* (the noun) (Acts 2:23; I Pet. 1:2). *Proginosko,* the verb, is translated *foreknow* (Rom. 8:29), *foreknew* (Rom. 11:2), and *foreordained* (I Pet. 1:20). *Proginosko* in classical Greek neant "to know, perceive, learn, or understand beforehand." t implied a previous knowledge of a thing. It is used in its purely classical sense in Acts 26:5 and II Peter 3:17. But both *prognosis* and *proginosko* in other places in the New Testament have by their use in relationship to God, acquired an additional content of meaning.

The first occurrence of either one, the usage of which determines the usage of both in other places in the New Testament is in Acts 2:23, where *prognosis* is used. These words, when used of God in the New Testament, signify more than merely the fact of knowing something beforehand. That is a self-evident attribute of the omniscient God. The Bible wastes no space on self-evident facts. The words *determinate counsel and foreknowledge of God* (Acts 2:23), are in a construction in Greek which shows that the word *foreknowledge* refers to the same act that the words *determinate counsel* refer to, and is a farther description of that act. The word *counsel* refers to the results of a consultation between individuals, the word *determinate* describing this consultation as one that had for its purpose the fixing of limits upon, thus determining the destiny of someone, here, that of the Lord Jesus. In the councils of the Trinity, it was decided that the Lord Jesus should be given over into the hands of wicked men. The word *prognosis* refers to the same act, and therefore includes in it the idea in the words *determinate counsel*. It adds, however the idea of the foreordination of the Person whose destiny was decided upon in the council referred to. This word did not have this meaning in classical Greek. It was inevitable that when words of a pagan people were brought over into the New Testament, they often acquired an additional content of meaning by reason of the advanced conceptions of Christianity and its supernatural character. The translators of the Authorized Version used the word *foreordained* in I Pet. 1:20. The translation should be *foreordination* in Acts 2:23 and I Pet. 1:2, and *foreordained* in Rom. 8:29, 11:2.

JUSTIFY. The words *justify, justification, righteous, right eousness, just, right, meet,* are all translations of the same Greek root. The verb *justify* is *dikaioo,* the noun *righteous ness, dikaiosune,* the adjective *righteous, dikaios.* This mean that all these words have a general meaning that is common to all of them, even though their individual meaning may differ slightly. This again means that there is a definite and vital connection between the act of justifying and the right eousness of the individual who has been justified. We will look first at the usage of these words in pagan Greek litera ture. "In pagan Greece the *dikaios* person is he who does no selfishly nor yet self-for-gettingly transgress the bounds fixed for him, and gives to everyone his own, yet still desires what is his, and does not in the least withdraw the assertion of hi own claims."[14] Paul uses *dikaios* in its purely classical sense in Rom. 5:7. In the biblical sense, *dikaios* is "what is right, con formable to right, answering to the claims of usage, custom, or right. . . . The fundamental idea is that of a state or condition conformable to order, apart from the consideration whether usage or custom or other factors determine the order or direction. Thus, *dikaios* is synonymous with *agathos* (good) only that *dikaios* is a conception of a relation and presuppose a norm, whereas the subject of *agathos* is its own norm."[15]

In understanding the words *justify* and *righteous,* as they are used in the New Testament, it should always be kept in mind that their meaning is not a *subjective* one but an *ob jective* one. That is, the content of meaning in these words is not to be determined by each individual Bible expositor If that were the case, what is righteous one day, may not be righteous the next. The content of meaning in that case would be dependent upon the fluctuating standards and ethics of men. With the present trend towards the teaching of the relativity of all truth, this method of interpretation be

---

14. *Cremer.*
15, 16. *Cremer.*

comes a most vicious thing. What is right one day may be wrong the next.

God is the objective standard which determines the content of meaning of *dikaios,* and at the same time keeps that content of meaning constant and unchanging, since He is the unchanging One. "Righteousness in the biblical sense is a condition of rightness the standard of which is God, which is estimated according to the divine standard, which shows itself in behavior conformable to God, and has to do above all things with its relation to God, and with the walk before Him. It is, and it is called *dikaiosune theou* (righteousness of God) (Rom. 3:21, 1:17), righteousness as it belongs to God, and is of value before Him, Godlike righteousness, see Eph. 4:24; with this righteousness thus defined, the gospel (Rom. 1:17) comes into the world of nations which had been wont to measure by a different standard. Righteousness in the Scripture sense is a thoroughly religious conception, designating the normal relation of men and their acts, etc., to God. Righteousness in the profane mind is a preponderatingly social virtue, only with a certain religious background."[16]

Justification in the Bible sense therefore is the act of God removing from the believing sinner, his guilt and the penalty incurred by that guilt, and bestowing a positive righteousness, Christ Jesus Himself in whom the believer stands, not only innocent and uncondemned, but actually righteous in point of law for time and for eternity. The words *justify, justification, righteous, righteousness,* as used of man in his relation to God, have a legal, judicial basis. God is the Judge, man the defendant. God is the standard of all righteousness. The white linen curtains of the court of the Tabernacle, symbolized the righteousness which God is, the righteousness which God demands of any human being who desires to fellowship with Him, and the righteousness which God provides on the basis of the acceptance on the sinner's part, of the Lord Jesus who perfectly satisfied the just demands of God's holy law which we broke. A just person therefore is one who has been thus declared righteous (Rom. 1:17). The word is used in its non legal sense in Phil. 1:7 and Lk. 12:57 for instance, where it speaks of conduct that is conformable to what is right.

PROPITIATION. In Rom. 3:25; I John 2:2, 4:10, our Lord is said to be the propitiation with reference to our sins. The word in Rom. 3:25 is *hilasterion,* and in I John 2:2, 4:10, *hilasmos.* These words were used in the Greek pagan religions, *hilasterion,* "an expiatory sacrifice," *hilasmos,* "a means of appeasing." The word *appeasing* strikes the keynote meaning of both words. The pagan offered a sacrifice as a means of appeasing the anger and displeasure of his god. Pope has a couplet, "Let fierce Achilles, dreadful in his rage. The god propitiate, and the pest assuage." The word *propitiate* here means "to appease and render favorable, to conciliate." That was the pagan usage of *hilasterion* and *hilasmos.* But the petty peevishness, irascibility, and petulant anger of a pagan deity is not to be brought over into the New Testament meaning of these words. The attitude of the God of the Bible towards sinners is not comparable to that of the imagined attitude of a pagan god towards his worshippers.

In its biblical usage, *hilasmos* means "an expiation." Our Lord is the *hilasmos* in that He became the Sacrifice on the Cross which perfectly met the demands of the broken law. The word is used in the LXX in Levit. 25:9 and Num. 5:8, and is in both cases translated by the word *atonement.* The word "expiation" means "to extinguish the guilt of by sufferance of penalty or some equivalent, to make satisfaction for, to atone for." The word *hilasterion* is used in the LXX in Levit. 16:14, of the golden cover of the Ark of the Covenant upon which was sprinkled the atoning blood. It is translated *mercy seat* in Heb. 9:5. *Hilasmos* is "that which propitiates," and *hilasterion* is "the place of propitiation." Our Lord is both. *In the biblical usage of these words, the thought is not that of placating the anger of a vengeful God, but that of satisfying the righteous demands of His justice so that His government might be maintained, and that mercy might be shown on the basis of justice duly satisfied.*

The verb *hilaskomai*, which has the same root as *hilasterion* and *hilasmos*, is used in Lk. 18:13 and Heb. 2:17. The word in classical Greek meant "to appease, to sooth, to make propitious to one, to reconcile one's self to another." In Homer, it was always used of gods, to make the gods propitious, to cause them to be reconciled, to worship them. The pagan usage of *hilaskomai* is in the last analysis a procedure by which something is to be made good. It is used, for instance, where someone had wronged a person and after the latter's death, had paid him divine honors as somehow making things right, appeasing the outraged feelings of the dead man. The act of appeasing a god indicates that goodwill was not conceived to be the original and natural condition of the gods, but something that must first be earned. The word was used where someone wished to gain the goodwill of Apollo so that he would feel inclined to deliver an oracle.

When *hilaskomai* is used in the New Testament, Cremer says that God is never the object of the action denoted in the verb. It never means "to conciliate God." The heathen, he says, believed the deity to be naturally alienated in feeling from man; and though the energetic manifestation of this feeling is specially excited by sin, man has to suffer for it. Thus, the purpose of the propitiatory sacrifices and prayers that were offered, was to effect a change in this feeling. The occasion for this offering could be after the person had sinned, or it could be at a time when there was no distinct consciousness of particular guilt, but simply for the purpose of securing the favor of the god. But in the Bible, the situation is different. God is not of Himself already alienated from man. God is as to His nature, love, and He loves the sinner. Witness the statement in John 3:16. His feelings with respect to the human race need not be changed. But the sin of man placed an obstacle in God's way when He in His infinite love desired to bless man with salvation, and that obstacle was the broken law and the guilt of man. The former cried out for justice to be satisfied, and the latter needed to be cleansed away. Thus, in order that it would not be necessary for Him to demand that the penalty be meted out upon guilty mankind so that He might satisfy the demands of His broken law, and in order that He might lavish His mercy upon man on the basis of justice satisfied, He Himself became the expiation demanded by His holiness and justice. There is no thought here of God placating Himself, or of rendering Himself conciliatory to Himself, or of appeasing His own anger. The thought would be ridiculous. It is a purely legal operation. The Judge takes upon Himself the penalty of the one whom He has adjudged guilty, and thus can show mercy. The judgment seat becomes a mercy seat. When the publican asked God to be merciful to him the sinner (Lk. 18:13), he really asked Him to offer that sacrifice for his sin which would put that sin away and thus allow a holy and a righteous God to bless him with salvation. The verb *hilaskomai* appears in the text. He was looking ahead to the accomplishment of the work of salvation at the Cross. His faith stretched out to that event and laid hold of it. It is neither scriptural nor is it good practice to ask a seeking sinner today to pray that prayer, either in the sense of the meaning of *hilaskomai* or in the sense of asking God to be merciful to him. He should be taught that God has paid the penalty for his sin, and God's mercy on that basis is extended to him, and that on the basis of what God has done at the Cross, he should by faith appropriate the salvation God offers him. The verb *hilaskomai* is found in Heb. 2:17, where it is translated "to make reconciliation for." We have noted all the places where these three words occur in the New Testament.

CONFESS. This word is the translation of *homologeo* vhich is rendered uniformly throughout the New Testament)y the word *confess* except in the following places; *Mt.* 7:23 (*profess*), 14:7 (*promised*); *I Tim.* 6:12; *Tit.* 1:16 (*profess*); *Ieb.* 13:15 (*giving thanks*). The related noun *homologia* is :ranslated in *II Cor.* 9:13, *I Tim.* 6:12, 13, *Heb.* 3:1, 4:14, 10: !3, either by *profession* or *confession*. *Homologeo* is made up)f the words *homos* (*same*), and *lego* (*to speak*). Thus, the vord means "to say the same thing" as another, hence, "to igree with, to assent to a thing." It had various uses in classi- :al Greek; "to speak or say together, to speak one language, to igree with, to make an agreement, to come to terms, the latter neaning used especially of persons surrendering in war, to igree to a thing, to allow, admit, confess, grant," the latter ound in the sentence *I grant you;* the noun means "an agree- nent, a compact; in war, terms of surrender; an assent, an idmission, a confession."

The papyri give examples of the Koine use of the word. There is an agreement between two individuals, a person ;ives his consent, another one acknowledges having found iomething. The noun is used of a contract, an agreement.

With these usages in mind, we will study a few representa- :ive places where the word is found. In I John 1:9, confession)f sin on the part of the Christian is not a mere admission of :he same to God. The act of confession includes the act of :he Christian in coming to terms with God in regard to his iin, of agreeing with God as to what He says about that sin ind what the Christian ought to do about it, the entering into ı contract or agreement with Him that if He will cleanse :hat Christian from the defilement of that sin, the latter will not be repeated. In Lk. 12:8, confession of Christ means the public acknowledgment of Him and all that He is and stands for. The act of confession implies that the one confessing the Lord Jesus, has come to agree with the Bible's estimate of Him. In I John 4:2, the word refers to a public acknowledg-

ment of the fact that one has come to the place where he is i
agreement with the facts revealed in Scripture concernin
Jesus Christ. In Mt. 7:23, it means "to say openly, not to kee
silence," in Mt. 14:7, "to concede, to engage, to promise.
In the latter case, Herod entered into contract with the daugl
ter of Herodias to give her whatever she asked.

In the word, there is the idea of a person agreeing wit
someone or something, of entering into a contract with som
one, of assenting to the statement of another, of coming t
terms with another. When interpreting the word in i
occurrences in the New Testament, search for the particula
shade of meaning demanded by the context.

GOSPEL. In every case, this word is the translation c
euaggelion. The verb is *euaggelizomai.* The word *eu* mean
in classical Greek, "well" in its kind, as opposed to the Gree
word *kakos* which meant "bad, evil, bad" in its kind, "ugl
hideous," and *aggello* which meant "to bear a message, brin
tidings or news, proclaim." Thus, the verb means "to brin
a message of good news," and the noun, "good news." Th
word "gospel" comes from the Saxon word *gode-spell,* th
word *gode* meaning *good,* and "spell" meaning *a story, a tale
The word *euaggelion* was in just as common use in the fir
century as our words *good news.* "Have you any good new
(*euaggelion*) for me today?" must have been a common que
tion. Our word *gospel* today has a definite religious connota
tion. In the ordinary conversation of the first century, it di
not have such a meaning. However, it was taken over int
the Cult of the Caesar where it acquired a religious signif
cance. The Cult of the Caesar was the state religion of th
Roman empire, in which the emperor was worshipped as
god. When the announcement of the emperor's birthda
was made, or the accession of a new Caesar proclaimed, th
account of either event was designated by the word *euaggelior*

Thus, when the Bible writers were announcing the goo
news of salvation, they used the word *euaggelion,* which wor

neant to the first century readers "good news." See how this
nelps one in the understanding of a verse like Heb. 4:2, "for
unto us (first-century Jews) was the good news (of salvation
n Christ) preached, as well as the good news (of a land
lowing with milk and honey) to them (the generation which
ame out of Egypt)." There is the good news of the kingdom
(Mt. 4:23) announced at the First Advent and rejected, to
>e announced at the Second Advent and accepted by Israel,
;ood news to the effect that the Lord Jesus is the High Priest
vho saves the believer, and also King of kings who will reign
is the world Sovereign. There is the good news of Jesus
Christ (I Cor. 9:12), which is good news concerning Jesus
Christ, namely, that He died on the Cross and thus becomes
he Saviour of the sinner who puts his faith in Him. There
s the good news of the grace of God (Acts 20:24), referring
o the same thing as the good news of Jesus Christ.

The verb *euaggelizomai* is uniformly translated "to preach
he gospel" except where it may be rendered "bring or show
;lad (good) tidings," or "hath declared." In the following
places it is translated by the word "preach," but since there is
a Greek word that means "to preach" in the sense of "to
announce," *kerusso*, the translation should be expanded to
include the idea of good news: *Lk.* 3:18, 4:43, 16:16; *Acts* 5:42,
3:4, 12, 35, 40, 10:36, 11:20, 14:7, 15:35, 17:18; I Cor. 15:1, 2;
Gal. 1:16, 23; *Eph.* 2:17, 3:8; *Heb.* 4:6; *Rev.* 14:6. Thus, one
should translate for instance, "The kingdom of God is
preached as glad tidings," or, "preaching the Word as good
news," or, "preaching the Lord Jesus as good tidings."

The word *evangelist* comes from the Greek *euaggelistes,* a
pringer of good tidings.

BOWELS. This word is the translation of *splagchnon*
which in classical Greek referred to the inward parts, especial-
y to the nobler parts of the inner organs, the heart, lungs, and
liver. It was the oriental metaphor for our "heart," the seat

of the feelings, affections. In the Greek poets, the bowels
were regarded as the seat of the more violent passions such as
anger and love, but by the Hebrews as the seat of the tenderer
affections, kindness, benevolence and compassion. In a manuscript of B.C. 5, it was used in the phrase "for pity's sake."[17]
In its metaphorical usage in the New Testament, it means
what we in the occident speak of as the heart. It refers to the
emotions of compassion, pity, the tenderer affections. As in
classical Greek, it is also used to refer to the literal parts of
the body. The only place in the N.T., where it is so used is in
Acts 1:18. In Lk. 1:78, the words *tender mercy* are in the
Greek *splagchna*, the word for *bowels*. Thus, the idea in the
word is that of the tender affections. In II Cor. 7:15, the word
is translated *inward affection*. In other places, it is translated
by the word *bowels*. It would be better to have translated
II Cor. 6:12, "Ye are compressed (cramped) in your own
affections." Paul had just told them, "Ye are not straitened
(compressed or cramped) in us;" that is, "ample space is
granted you in our heart." Then he says, "Ye are straitened
(compressed or cramped) in your own affections, so that there
is no room there for us;" that is, "you do not grant a place
in your heart for love to me." Paul in Phil. 1:8 longs after
the Philippians with the tender-heartednesses of Jesus Christ.
In Phil. 2:1 he speaks of tender-heartednesses and mercies.
In Col. 3:12, he exhorts the saints to have a heart of mercy
and kindness. In Phm. 7, Philemon's beautiful Christian life
refreshes the affectionate natures of the saints. Paul sends the
runaway slave Onesimus back to his master, and says, "whom
I have sent again, him, that is, my own bowels" (v. 12). The
great apostle who had led Onesimus to the Lord, had so come
to love him, that when he sent him back to Philemon, his
heart went with him. The word *receive* is not in the best
texts. He exhorts Philemon to refresh his heart, his tender
emotions (v. 20). In I John 3:17 *splagchnon* is translated

---

17. *Moulton and Milligan.*

"bowels of compassion." The idea is, the shutting up of one's compassionate heart.

In the Gospel statements concerning our Lord, such as "He was moved with compassion," the word is *splagchnizomai*, the same word translated "bowels," but in the verb form. The word in its root therefore refers to a heart of compassion, kindness, pity, mercy, to the tenderer affections as produced in the heart of the yielded believer by the Holy Spirit.

BEAST. There are two Greek words translated by the one word "beast" in the Book of The Revelation. These Greek words have different meanings. For a proper appreciation of the places where they are found, the English reader should know the distinctive meaning of each word, and where each word is found.

The word *zoon* in classical Greek meant "a living being, an animal." The Greek word for "life" is *zoe*. The word *zoon* therefore refers to a living organism, whether animal or human, the emphasis being upon the fact that it is alive as opposed to the state of death. It is found in the following places in The Revelation, 4:6, 7, 8, 9, 5:6, 8, 11, 14, 6:1, 3, 5, 6, 7, 7:11, 14:3, 15:7, 19:4. In each case, the translation should read "living creature." These living creatures are the Cherubim. They are first mentioned in Gen. 3:24. They were the guardians of the entrance to Eden. Golden figures of these cherubim were carved out of one piece of gold with the Mercy Seat (Ex. 25:10-22). Ezekiel speaks of cherubim in Ezek. 1. The other places where *zoon* is used are Heb. 13:11; II Pet. 2:12; Jude 10.

The other word is *therion*, which in classical Greek referred to a wild animal, a wild beast, a savage beast that is hunted, a poisonous animal, a reptile. This word is found in The Revelation in 6:8, 11:7, 13:1, 2, 3, 4, 11, 12, 14, 15, 17, 18, 14:9, 11, 15:2, 16:2, 10, 13, 17:3, 7, 8, 11, 12, 13, 16, 17, 19:19, 20, 20:4, 10. In every place except 6:8 where literal

wild beasts are referred to, and 13:11, where the false prophet
is mentioned, the word "beast" (*therion*) refers to the Antichrist, future head of the revived Roman empire. He is the
wild Beast. The other places where *therion* is used are *Mk*
1:13; *Acts* 10:12, 11:6; 28:4, 5; *Tit.* 1:12; *Heb.* 12:20; *Jas.* 3:7

TEMPLE. There are two Greek words which are both
translated by the one word "temple" in the A.V. Each has its
distinctive meaning and refers to a particular thing. It is obvious that if the English reader expects to arrive at a full
orbed interpretation of the passages where the word "temple"
is used, he must know which word is used in the Greek text
and the meaning of that distinctive word.

The first word we will study is *hieron*. It is taken from
classical Greek, coming from the adjective *hieros*. The latter
meant "belonging to or connected with the gods." It meant
"holy, hallowed, consecrated," and was used of earthly things
devoted or dedicated by man to a god or to the service of a
god. It was used sometimes in opposition to several Greek
words which meant "profane," that is, "secular," as opposed
to "sacred." Thus the building set apart and dedicated to the
worship and service of the god was called a *hieron*. This
word was taken over into the N.T., and used to designate the
temple at Jerusalem. It is the all-inclusive word signifying
the whole compass of the sacred enclosure, with its porticos,
courts, and other subordinate buildings.

The other word is *naos*, which referred to the temple itself,
composed of the Holy of Holies and the Holy Place.

When our Lord taught in the temple, He taught in the
hieron, in one of the temple porches. He expelled the money-
changers from the *hieron*, the court of the Gentiles. When
the veil of the temple was rent at the time of the death of our
Lord, it was the veil of the *naos*, the curtain separating the
Holy of Holies from the Holy Place. When Zacharias entered
the temple to burn incense, he entered the *naos*, the Holy

lace where the altar of incense stood. The people were
without," in the *hieron*. Our Lord spoke of the temple
naos) of His body. Paul speaks of the body of the Christian
s the temple (*naos*), the inner sanctuary of the Holy Spirit.
The word "temple" is a good translation of *hieron*, the
ords "inner sanctuary," of *naos*.

Hieron is found in the following places: *Mt.* 4:5, 12:5, 6,
1:12, 14, 15, 23, 24:1, 26:55; *Mk.* 11:11, 15, 16, 27, 12:35,
3:1, 3, 14:49; *Lk.* 2:27, 37, 46, 4:9, 18:10, 19:45, 47, 20:1, 21:5,
7, 38, 22:52, 53, 24:53; John 2:14, 15, 5:14, 7:14, 28, 8:2, 20,
9, 10:23, 11:56, 18:20; *Acts* 2:46, 3:1, 2, 3, 8, 10, 4:1, 5:20, 21,
4, 25, 42, 19:27, 21:26, 27, 28, 29, 30, 22:17, 24:6, 12, 18, 25:
, 26:21, *I Cor.* 9:13.

Naos is found in the following places: *Mt.* 23:16, 17, 21, 35,
6:61, 27:5, 40, 51; *Mk.* 14:58, 15:29, 38; *Lk.* 1:9, 21, 22, 23:45;
ohn 2:19, 20, 21; *Acts* 7:48, 17:24, 19:24; *I Cor.* 3:16, 17, 6:19;
I Cor. 6:16; *Eph.* 2:21; *II Thes.* 2:4; *Rev.* 3:12, 7:15, 11:1,
, 19, 14:15, 17, 15:5, 6, 8, 16:1, 17, 21:22.

Make a study of each place where the word "temple" is
ound in the N.T., interpreting the passage in the light of the
listinctive meaning of the particular Greek word, and see
vhat a flood of additional light is thrown upon the English
ranslation and the passage in question.

FORSAKEN. This word is the translation of *egkataleipo*,
vhich latter is made up of three words, *eg* meaning *in*, *kata*
neaning *down*, and *leipo* meaning *to leave*. The composite
word means literally *to leave down in*, and was used of a person who let another person down in a set of circumstances that
were against him. The word has various meanings: "to abandon, desert, leave in straits, leave helpless, leave destitute, leave
in the lurch, let one down." Study Mt. 27:46; Mk. 15:34, and
Psalm 22:1 (same Greek word used in LXX), and apply these
various meanings. See Acts 2:27 where the words *wilt leave* are
from *egkataleipo*, and the word *hell* is the translation of *haides*

which is brought over into English in the names Hades, which latter refers here to the place of the departed righteous dead called Abraham's bosom (Lk. 16:22) or paradise (Lk. 23:43) Study the use of the word in II Cor. 4:9. See what light the use of the word throws upon Demas in II Tim. 4:10, as to his status with respect to salvation, as to his relationship to the apostle Paul, as to his responsibility at the time when Paul was in prison. Visualize Paul's aloneness at his trial before the Roman emperor, in the use of *egkataleipo* in II Tim. 4:16 Relate the use of the word in Mt. 27:46 with that in Heb. 13:5 Choose the particular meaning of the word in Heb. 10:25 The word has a special use in Rom. 9:29 where it means "leave surviving."

HELL. There are three Greek words, each referring to a different place, all of which are translated by the one word *hell,* a fact that causes considerable confusion in interpreting the passages where they occur. These words are *geenna, haides,* and *tartaroo.* The first comes into English in the word *Gehenna,* the second, in the word *Hades,* and the third, in the word *Tartarus.*

Geenna refers to the final abode of the wicked dead, called The Lake of Fire in The Revelation (20:14, 15). Where this word occurs, the translation should be *hell.* It is found in *Mt.* 5:22, 29, 30, 10:28, 18:9, 23:15, 33; *Mk.* 9:43, 45, 47; *Lk.* 12:5; *Jas.* 3:6.

Haides refers to the temporary abode of the dead before the resurrection and ascension of the Lord Jesus, the part reserved for the wicked dead, called *haides* (Lk. 16:23), the other for the righteous dead, called Abraham's bosom (Lk. 16:22), paradise (Lk. 23:43),[18] *haides* (Acts 2:27, 31); and to the temporary abode of the wicked dead from those events until the Great White Throne judgment, the righteous dead going at once to be with the Lord (Phil. 1:23; II Cor. 5:8).

---

18. *But not II Cor.* 12:4, *which is heaven.*

The word *haides* is from the Greek stem *id* which means "to see," and the Greek letter Alpha prefixed which makes the composite word mean "not to see," the noun meaning "the unseen." The word itself in its noun form refers to the unseen world made up of all moral intelligences not possessing a physical body. These would include the holy angels, the fallen angels, the demons, the wicked dead, and the righteous dead. As to the inhabitants in the unseen world, the holy angels are in heaven, the fallen angels in Tartarus, the wicked dead in Hades, the righteous dead in heaven, and the demons in the atmosphere of the earth and in the bottomless pit. All these are included in the unseen world. The context should decide as to whether the Greek word *haides* should be transliterated or translated. Where the context deals with departed human beings and their place of abode in the unseen world, it would seem that the word should be transliterated, and the specific name "Hades" be given that place. These places are *Mt.* 11:23; *Lk.* 10:15, 16:23; *Acts* 2:27, 31; *Rev.* 6:8, 20:13, 14. Where the context refers to the unseen world as a whole, the word should be translated, as for instance: Mt. 16:18, "the gates (councils) of the Unseen," namely, the councils of Satan in the unseen world, shall not prevail against the church; or Rev. 1:18, "I have the keys of the Unseen and of death." Our Lord controls the entire unseen world.

Tartarosas is the word in II Pet. 2:4 "cast down to hell." The fallen angels were sent to their temporary prison house, *Tartarus*, until the Great White Throne judgment. Make a study of these places where the word "hell" occurs, in the light of the distinctive Greek word found in each place, and see how much better you understand these passages.

FORM. When this word is used as a noun in the N.T., the Greek word *morphe* appears in the text. *Morphe* is a Greek philosophical term which refers to the outward expression one gives of himself, that outward expression proceeding from and being truly representative of one's inward character and nature. We use the word "form" in that way in the sentence, "The tennis-player's form was excellent." We mean that the outward expression he gave of his inward ability to play tennis, was excellent. The verb is *morphoomai,* which word refers to the act of a person giving outward expression of his true inward character, that outward expression proceeding from and truly representing his true inward nature. *Mórphe* is used in Phil. 2:6, 7 in the expressions, "Who being in the form of God," and "took upon Him the form of a servant." The first refers to our Lord being in that state of being in which He gives outward expression of His inner intrinsic essence, that of deity, that outward expression proceeding from and truly representing His essential nature, that of deity. The second refers to Him in the period of His humiliation when He gave outward expression of His inmost nature, that of a bondservant serving others in all humility, that outward expression proceeding from and being truly representative of His inmost nature. Both outward expressions came from His inmost nature as God. The one had to be temporarily laid aside in order that the other could be manifested. The other place where *morphe* is found is in Mk. 16:12 where it is said that Jesus "appeared in another form." This was the occurrence on the road to Emmaus. The word "another" is from *heteros* meaning "another of a different kind." That is, our Lord's outward expression of Himself at that time was of a nature different from the one by which these disciples would have ordinarily known Him, this outward expression proceeding from and being truly representative of His inner nature. It was the glorified Christ clothed with the enswathement of glory that is native to His glorified body.

The verb *morphoomai* is used in Gal. 4:19 in the phrase "until Christ be formed in you." Using our definition of *morphe,* we could translate, "Until Christ be outwardly expressed in you, that outward expression proceeding from and being truly representative of Him." These Galatian saints had ceased to depend upon the Holy Spirit to express the Lord Jesus in their lives, and were depending upon self-effort to obey the Mosaic law. Thus, Christ Jesus was not being outwardly expressed in their lives.

The word *morphosis,* having the same root as *morphe,* is found in Rom. 2:20, and II Tim. 3:5. In the former passage, the religious but unsaved Jew has the form of knowledge and of the truth, in that the outward expression of both in his life and teaching is the mere outward expression of an intellectual but not a heart grasp of the same. Thus we would speak of it as a mere form, an empty pretense lacking reality so far as the saving work of God is concerned. In II Tim. 3:5, these having a form of godliness, exhibit in their lives an outward expression of godliness which proceeds from and is truly representative of an inner state of godliness, but a godliness that is not the genuine godliness associated with salvation, but an imitation one that denies the power of God to save.

TRANSFIGURED. This word occurs in Mt. 17:2; Mk. 9:2. The Greek word is *metamorphoomai.* The word *meta,* prefixed to *morphoomai* signifies a change. The sentence, "He was transfigured before them," in an expanded translation could read: "His outward expression was changed before them, which outward expression proceeded from and was truly representative of His inward being." Our Lord's usual expression of Himself during the days of His earthly life was that of the Man Christ Jesus, a Man of sorrows and acquainted with grief, the Servant come to serve (Phil. 2:7). Now, He gives outward expression of the glory of the essence of His deity, that glory shining right through His human body and nature, that expression proceeding from and being truly representative of His intrinsic deity which He possessed. As a result, His face shone as the sun, and His raiment was white as the light.

TRANSFORM. In Rom. 12:2 this word is the translation of *metamorphoomai,* the same word translated "transfigured" in Mt. 17:2 and Mk. 9:2. The exhortation to the saints is to change their outward expression which they had before they were saved, which outward expression proceeded from and was truly representative of their totally depraved natures, to an outward expression which proceeds from and is truly representative of their new divine natures.

The word "transform" is used also in II Cor. 11:13-15. But here it is the translation of a word that has the opposite meaning to *metamorphoomai.* The word is *metaschematizo* which means "to change one's outward expression by assuming from the outside an expression that does not proceed from nor is it representative of one's true inner nature." The word "masquerade" is an exact English translation. Satan was originally the holy angel Lucifer. As such he gave outward expression of his inner nature as an angel of light, which expression proceeded from and was truly representative of that nature. That was *morphoomai.* Then he sinned and became an angel of darkness, giving outward expression of that darkness. That was m*orphoomai.* Then he changed his outward expression from that of darkness to one of light by assuming from the outside, an expression of light, which outward expression did not come from nor was it representative of his inner nature as an angel of darkness. That is *metaschematizo.* The translation could read: "masquerading as the apostles of Christ;" "Satan masquerades as an angel of light;" "his ministers masquerade as the ministers of righteousness."

CONFORM. This word in Rom. 12:2 is the translation of *sunschematizo* which means "to assume an outward expression that is patterned after something else, which outward expression does not come from within and is not representative of one's inward nature, but which is assumed from without." Paul is exhorting the saints not to assume an outward expression which is patterned after the world, which is assumed from without, and which does not come from nor is it representative of their inner renewed heart-life. In short, he exhorts them not to masquerade in the garments of the world.

The word "conformed" in Rom. 8:29 is from *sunmorphoomai* which means "to bring to the same outward expression as something else, that outward expression proceeding from and being truly representative of one's true inward nature." The saints are predestined to be brought to the same outward expression as that which now is true of the Lord Jesus. He in His glorified humanity gives outward expression of His radiant beauty of character as the spotless, sinless, wonderful Son of God. The saints glorified will have an outward expression like that of the Lord Jesus, which expression proceeds from and is truly representative of their divine natures. The same word is used in Phil. 3:10 where it is translated "made conformable to." Paul's desire was that he would be brought to the place where he would become, both as to his inner heart life and also as to the outward expression of the same, like his Lord in His life of death to self and service to others.

GODHEAD. This word appears three times in the New Testament, Acts 17:29; Rom. 1:20; and Col. 2:9. The one word "Godhead" is the translation of two Greek words which have a real distinction between them, a distinction that grounds itself on their different derivations. In Rom. 1:20 we have the word *theiotes*. In this word, Trench says that "Paul is declaring how much of God may be known from the revelation of Himself which He has made in nature, from those vestiges of Himself which men may everywhere trace in the world around them. Yet it is not the personal God whom any man may learn to know by these aids: He can be known only by the revelation of Himself in His Son; but only His divine attributes, His majesty and glory. . . . . and it is not to be doubted that St. Paul uses this vaguer, more abstract, and less personal word, just because he would affirm that men may know God's power and majesty, His *theia dunamis* (divine power) (II Pet. 1:3), from His works; but would *not* imply that they may know Himself from these, or from anything short of the revelation of His eternal Word. Motives not dissimilar induce him to use *to theion* rather than *ho theos* in addressing the Athenians on Mars' Hill (Acts 17:29)."

In Rom. 1:20, Paul states that the invisible things of God, here, His eternal power and His *theiotes*, His divinity, namely, the fact that He is a Being having divine attributes, are clearly seen by man through the created universe. Man, reasoning upon the basis of the law of cause and effect, namely, that every effect demands an adequate cause, comes to the conclusion that the universe as an effect demands an adequate cause, and that adequate cause must be a Being having divine attributes. It was as the creator of the universe that fallen man knew God (v. 21). Perhaps the word "Godhead" is the best one-word translation of *theiotes* in Rom. 1:20. But the term must be explained as above for a proper exegesis of this passage. The same is true of Acts 17:29. When Paul speaks of all men as the offspring of God, he uses the word *theos* for "God," the word that implies full deity as Paul knows God. But when he speaks of the Greek's conception of God or of what they as pagans might conceive God to be, he uses *theiotes*, for the Greeks could, apart from the revelation of God in Christ, only know Him as a Being of divine attributes.

In Col. 2:9 *theotes* is used. Here Trench says, "Paul is declaring that in the Son there dwells all the fulness of absolute

Godhead; they were no mere rays of divine glory which gilded Him, lighting up His Person for a season and with splendor not His own; but He was, and is, absolute and perfect God; and the apostle uses *theotes* to express this essential and personal Godhead of the Son." Here the word "divinity" will not do, only the word "deity." It is well in these days of apostasy, to speak of the *deity* of the Lord Jesus, not using the word "divinity" when we are referring to the fact that He is Very God. Modernism believes in His divinity, but in a way different from the scriptural conception of the term. Modernism has the pantheistic conception of the deity permeating all things and every man. Thus divinity, it says, is resident in every human being. It was resident in Christ as in all men. The difference between the divinity of Christ and that of all other men, it says, is one of degree, not of kind. Paul never speaks of the divinity of Christ, only of His deity. Our Lord has divine attributes since He is deity, but that is quite another matter from the Modernistic conception.

WORLD. There are three Greek words in the New Testament translated by this one English word, *kosmos, aion,* and *oikoumene.* It should be obvious that if one is to arrive at a full-orbed interpretation of the passages where the word "world" is found, one must know which Greek word is used, and the distinctive meaning of that Greek word. A knowledge of how these words were used in classical Greek, will help us to better understand their use in the New Testament.

The basic meaning of *kosmos* was "order." It was used in such expressions as "to sit in order." It meant "good order, good behavior, decency, a set form or order." When used of state or national existence, it meant "order, government." It also meant "an ornament, decoration, dress," especially of women. It was used to refer to the universe from the fact of its perfect arrangement. It was used in this case as opposed to the Greek word *chaos* which was used by the Greeks of the

first state of existence, the rude, unformed mass out of which
the universe was made. It was used to signify also empty im
measurable space. The reader will note that the Greeks be
lieved that the original state of the universe was one of chaos
This is in line with the theory of evolution and the nebular
hypothesis, which latter theory has been exploded by scien
tists, and which former theory is still held to tenaciously by
the scientific world despite the fact that all branches of scien
tific investigation have been thoroughly probed, but no ade
quate cause for evolution has been found. The theory of
evolution found its inception in the thinking of the Greek
philosophers from the sixth to the fourth centuries B.C.
Aristotle being one of its outstanding exponents. *Kosmos*
also was used to refer to the inhabitants of the earth.

The papyri give us illustrations of the use of *kosmos* in the
ordinary conversation of the *koine* period. A manuscript of
9 B.C., refers to the birthday of Augustus the Roman em
peror, as the beginning of good news to the world (*kosmos*)
At the Isthmian games (A.D. 67), a proclamation of the free
dom of the Greeks was made, and the emperor Nero was
described as the ruler of all the world (*kosmos*). The word
is found in a reference to a bride's trousseau in the sense of
"adornment." In a manuscript of 113 B.C., there is a com
plaint against certain persons who "throwing off all restraint
(*kosmos*), knocked down a street door!"[19]

Aion which comes from *aio* "to breathe," means "a space
or period of time," especially "a lifetime, life." It is used of
one's time of life, age, the age of man, an age, a generation.
It also means "a long space of time, eternity, forever." Again,
it was used of space of time clearly defined and marked out,
an era, age, period of a dispensation.

As to *aion*, the papyri speak of a person led off to death,
the literal Greek being "led off from *aion* life."[20] A report
of a public meeting speaks of a cry that was uttered by the

___

19, 20 *Moulton and Milligan.*

crowd, namely, "The Emperors forever" *(aion)* .[21] It is also found in the sense of "a period of life."

Oikoumene, the third word, made up of the Greek word for "home" *(oikos)* and the verb "to remain" *(meno)*, referred in classical Greek to the inhabitated world, namely, that portion of the earth inhabited by the Greeks, as opposed to the rest of the inhabited earth where non-Greeks or barbarians lived. Later it was used to designate the entire Roman empire. At the accession of Nero, the proclamation referred to him in the words "and the expectation and hope of the world has been declared Emperor, the good genius of the world and source of all good things, Nero, has been declared Caesar."[22] It was thus a common designation of the Roman Empire in the papyri.

We come now to the New Testament usage of the words. Cremer has the following to say about *kosmos:* "Kosmos denotes the sum-total of what God has created (John 17:5, 21: 25; Acts 17:24; Rom. 1:20; I Cor. 4:9)." The expression "since the beginning of the world" (Mt. 24:21), Cremer says, "involves a reference to the fact that the world is the abode of man, or that order of things within which humanity moves, of which man is the center. . . . This leads us to the more precise definition of the conception, . . . As *kosmos* is regarded as that order of things whose center is man, attention is directed chiefly to him, and *kosmos* denotes mankind within that order of things, humanity as it manifests itself in and through such an order (Mt. 18:7). . . . The way would thus seem sufficiently prepared for the usage which by *kosmos* denotes that order of things which is alienated from God, as manifested in and by the human race, in which mankind exists; in other words, humanity as alienated from God, and acting in opposition to Him and to His revelation."

After taking up the classical meanings of *aion,* Cremer says of this word: "aion may denote either the duration of a defi-

---

21, 22. *Moulton and Milligan.*

nite space of time, or the (unending) duration of time in general."

Trench, contending for the use of the word "world" as the proper translation of *kosmos,* and "age" as the correct rendering of *aion* says: "One must regret that, by this or some other device, our translators did not mark the difference between *kosmos,* the world contemplated under aspects of space, and *aion,* the same contemplated under aspects of time."

Taking up the usage of *aion* he says: "Thus signifying time, it comes presently to signify all which exists in the world under conditions of time; . . . and then, more ethically, the course and current of this world's affairs. But this course and current being full of sin, it is nothing wonderful that 'this *aion*' set over against 'that *aion*' (Mt. 12:32) acquires, like *kosmos,* an unfavorable meaning." "This *aion*" refers to this age in which man lives, marked by its sin and corruption, "that *aion* to come," to the Millennial Age where the Lord Jesus will reign on earth and rule with a rod of iron. The expression does not have reference to this life as contrasted to the life after death, but to two different ages on the earth. He cites Gal. 1:4, "Who gave Himself for our sins, that He might deliver us from this present evil *aion.*" Trench says that *aion* means "the age, the spirit or genius of the age." He defines *aion* as "All that floating mass of thoughts, opinions, maxims, speculations, hopes, impulses, aims, aspirations, at any time current in the world, which it may be impossible to seize and accurately define, but which constitutes a most real and effective power, being the moral or immoral atmosphere which at every moment of our lives we inhale, again inevitably to exhale." He says "All this is included in the *aion,* which is, as Bengel has expressed it, the subtle informing spirit of the *kosmos,* or world of men who are living alienated and apart from God."

To summarize: The word *kosmos* is used to refer to the world system, wicked and alienated from God yet cultured, educated, powerful, outwardly moral at times, the system of which Satan is the head, the fallen angels and the demons are his servants, and all mankind other than the saved, are his subjects. This includes those people, pursuits, pleasures, purposes, and places where God is not wanted (Mt. 4:8; John 12:31; I John 2:15, 16, being examples). It refers also to the human race, fallen, totally depraved (John 3:16). It may have reference to the created universe (John 1:10 first and second mention). It may also refer simply to mankind without any particular reference to man's fallen and wicked condition (Gal. 4:3; Jas. 2:5). *Kosmos* is translated in every place by the word "world" except in I Pet. 3:3 where it is rendered "adornment." In interpreting the passages where *kosmos* is found, the student should study the context in order to determine which one of the above meanings is to be used in any particular passage.

Aion is translated "world" in the following places where the student would do better to translate it by the word "age," and apply the definition given above, interpreting the passage in the light of the context: Mt. 12:32, 13:22, 39, 40, 49, 24:3, 28:20; *Mk.* 4:19, 10:30; *Lk.* 1:70, 16:8, 18:30, 20:34, 35; *John* 9:32; *Acts* 3:21, 15:18; *Rom.* 12:2; *I Cor.* 1:20, 2:6, 7, 8, 3:18, 10:11; *II Cor.* 4:4; *Gal.* 1:4; *Eph.* 1:21, 2:2, 3:9, 3:21, 6:12; *I Tim.* 6:17; *II Tim.* 4:10; *Tit.* 2:12; *Heb.* 1:2, 6:5, 9:26, 11:3.

In *Luke* 1:70; *John* 9:32; *Acts* 3:21, 15:18; *Eph.* 3:9, 3:21, the word is used to specify time as such, and does not have its usual meaning of a period of time characterized by a certain spirit or way of life, for instance Luke 1:70, "which have been since time began" (lit., "from ever"). In Hebrews 1:2 and 11:3 the word refers to the created universe and the periods of time as administered by God. *Aion* is translated "course" in Ephesians 2:2 where "world" is from *kosmos*.

Oikoumene is found in *Mt.* 24:14; *Lk.* 2:1, 4:5, 21:26; *Acts* 11:28, 17:6, 31, 19:27, 24:5; *Rom.* 10:18; *Heb.* 1:6, 2:5; *Rev.* 3:10, 12:9, 16:14.

Kosmos occurs so often that we cannot list the places in a brief work like this. The student can check with the places where *aion* and *oikoumene* are found. If the scripture is not listed there, *kosmos* is in the Greek text of the passage under consideration.

WORD. The Lord Jesus is called THE WORD in John 1:1, 14; I John 1:1, 5:7; Rev. 19:13. In John 1:1 we have the preexistence of the Word, His fellowship with God the Father in His preincarnate state, and His absolute deity. In John 1:14 the incarnation of the Word is in view. I John 1:1 speaks of the things which the disciples heard and saw with reference to the earthly life of the Word. In I John 5:7, the name "The Word" is used as a designation of our Lord in connection with the names *Father* and *Spirit*. In Rev. 19:13 the descending Conqueror is called The Word.

The purpose of this study is to ascertain the meaning and usage of the Greek word *logos* which is translated *word* in these passages, and thus come to understand its significance when used as a name of our Lord.

In classical Greek *logos* meant "the word or outward form by which the inward thought is expressed and made known," or "the inward thought or reason itself." *Logos* never meant in classical Greek a word in the grammatical sense as the mere name of a thing, but rather the thing referred to, the material, not the formal part. It also referred to the power of the mind which is manifested in speech, also to the reason. For instance, it is found in the phrase, "agreeably to reason." It meant "examination by reason, reflection," as opposed to "thoughtlessness, rashness." It is used in the phrase "to allow himself reflection." It was used in the sense of the esteem or regard one may have for another. The word is found in the phrase, "to be of no account or repute with one;" also in the phrase, "to make one of account;" also in the phrase "to make account," that is, to put a value on a person or thing. These classical uses of *logos* provide us with a background and basis upon which to study its New Testament usage.

Cremer commences his discussion of *logos* by stating the fact that the Greek language has three words, *hrema, onoma,* and *epos* which designate a word in its grammatical sense, a function which *logos* does not have. He says that *logos* is used of the living spoken word, "the word not in its outward form, but with reference to the thought connected with the form, . . . in short, not the word of language, but of conversation, of discourse; not the word as a part of speech, but the word as part of what is uttered."

Cremer finds the Johannine usage of *logos* as a name of the Lord Jesus to be in "perfect accord with the progress of God's gracious revelation in the Old Testament," and that "John's use of the term is the appropriate culmination of the view presented in other parts of the N.T., of the word of God, denoting . . . the mystery of Christ." He says that the term "the word of the Lord" in the O.T., refers to the Lord Jesus in His preincarnate state. In Jer. 1:4, 5, we have, "Then the Word of the Lord came unto me, saying, Before I formed thee in the belly I knew thee." Two acts which clearly imply personality, *forming* and *knowing*, are predicated of the Word of the Lord. Cremer quotes Neuman on Jer. 1:2 as follows; "The word of God, the self-revelation of the eternal Godhead from eternity in the Word, is the source and principle of all prophetic words; therein they have their divine basis." He states that the Aramaic paraphrase of Numbers 7:89 according to the Targums is, "The Word spoke with him from off the mercy seat." Cremer says, "God Himself is the word insofar as the word is the medium of His revelation of Himself, and the word, though personality and hypostasis are not yet attributed to it, occupies a middle place between God and man. . . . That this representation was included in the Jewish idea of the Messiah, is clear from Gen. 49:18 where the Jerusalem Targum has, 'I have waited, not for liberation through Sampson or Gideon, but for salvation through Thy Word.' "

This O.T., foregleam of the Lord Jesus as The Word, comes to full expression in the *Logos* of John in the N.T. The Lord Jesus in John's writings is the *Logos* in that He is "the representative and expression of what God has to say to ,the world, in whom and by whom God's mind and purposes towards the world find their expression" (*Cremer*).

The word *logos* was already in use among the Greeks before John used it. It was used to denote the principle which maintains order in the world. In connection with the Greek word for "seed" in its adjective form, it was used to express the generative principle or creative force in nature. The term was familiar to Greek philosophy. The word thus being already in use, among the Hebrews in a biblical way, and among the Greeks in a speculative and rather hazy, undefined way, John now proceeds to unfold the true nature of the Logos, Jesus Christ. Vincent quotes Godet as saying in this connection, "To those Hellenists and Hellenistic Jews, on the one hand, who were vainly philosophizing on the relations of the finite and infinite; to those investigators of the letter of the Scriptures, on the other, who speculated about the theocratic revelations, John said, by giving this name Logos to Jesus: 'The unknown Mediator between God and the world, the knowledge of whom you are striving after, we have seen, heard, and touched. Your philosophical speculations and your scriptural subtleties will never raise you to Him. Believe as we do in Jesus, and you will possess in Him that divine Revealer who engages your thoughts'."

Vincent says, "As Logos has the double meaning of *thought* and *speech,* so Christ is related to God as the word to the idea, the word being not merely a *name* for the idea, but the idea itself expressed." He quotes the following from William Austin: "The name *Word* is most excellently given to our

Saviour; for it expresses His nature in one, more than in any others. Therefore St. John, when he names the Person in the Trinity (1 John 5:7), chooses rather to call Him *Word* than *Son;* for *word* is a phrase more communicable than *son*. *Son* hath only reference to the *Father* that begot Him; but *word* may refer to him that *conceives* it; to him that *speaks* it; to *that which is spoken by* it; to *the voice* that it is clad in; and to the effects it raises in him that hears it. So Christ, as He is *the Word,* not only refers to His Father that begot Him, and from whom He comes forth, but to all the creatures that were made by Him; to the flesh that He took to clothe Him; and to the doctrine He brought and taught, and which lives yet in the hearts of all them that obediently do hear it. He it is that is *this Word;* and any other, prophet or preacher, he is but *a voice* (Luke 3:4). *Word is an inward conception of the mind;* and *voice* is but *a sign of intention.* St. John was but a sign, a *voice;* not worthy to untie the shoe-latchet of this Word. Christ is the *inner conception* 'in the bosom of His Father;' and that is properly *the Word*. And yet the Word is the intention uttered forth, as well as conceived within; for Christ was no less the Word in the womb of the Virgin, or in the cradle of the manger, or on the altar of the cross, than He was in the beginning, 'in the bosom of His Father.' For as the intention departs not from the mind when the word is uttered, so Christ, proceeding from the Father by eternal generation, and after here by birth and incarnation, remains still in Him and with Him in essence; as the intention, which is conceived and born in the mind, remains still with it and in it, though the word be spoken. He is therefore rightly called *the Word,* both by His coming from, and yet remaining still in, the Father."

DWELL.[23] This word in John 1:14; Rev. 7:15, 21:3, is the translation in these places of *skenoo* which means "to live in

---

23. *Limited.*

a tent," the Greek word for "tent" being *skene*. In John 1:14, we have, "the Word *became* (*ginomai*) flesh, and lived in a tent among us." That tent was His physical body. Paul speaks of our present physical body as a *skene*, a tent (II Cor. 5:1). In Rev. 7:15, 21:3, the Lord Jesus is seen in the body of His glory, dwelling in the same tent He lived in while on earth, but in that tent glorified. God the Son will live in that tent, His glorified human body, all through eternity, with the saved of the human race, who like Him will live in their earthly tents glorified.

VILE.[24] This is the translation of *tapeinonis* (Phil. 3:21). The same Greek word is used in Lk. 1:48 where it is translated "low estate," in Acts 8:33 where it is rendered "humiliation," and in Jas. 1:10, where we have "is made low." Our present physical bodies have been humiliated, made low, brought to a low condition by the fall of Adam. They have the sin principle indwelling them. They are mortal bodies subject to sickness, weariness, and death.

ABIDE.[25] This is one of John's favorite words. The Greek word is *meno*. Its classical usage will throw light upon the way it is used in the N.T. It meant "to stay, stand fast, abide, to stay at home, stay where one is, not stir, to remain as one was, to remain as before." In the N.T., it means "to sojourn, to tarry, to dwell at one's own house, to tarry as a guest, to lodge, to maintain unbroken fellowship with one, to adhere to his party, to be constantly present to help one, to put forth constant influence upon one." "In the mystic phraseology of John, God is said to *meno* in Christ, i.e., to dwell as it were in Him, to be continually operative in Him by His divine influence and energy (John 14:10); Christians are said to *meno* in God, to be rooted as it were in Him, knit to Him by the Spirit they have received from Him (I John 2:6, 24, 27, 3:6);

24, 25. *Limited.*

hence one is said to *meno* in Christ or in God, and conversely, Christ or God is said to *meno* in one (John 6:56, 15:4) ."[26] Thayer quotes Ruckert in the use of *meno* in the words "Something has established itself permanently within my soul, and always exerts its power in me."

The word therefore has the ideas of "permanence of position, occupying a place as one's dwelling place, holding and maintaining unbroken communion and fellowship with another." John uses *meno* in the following places; in the Gospel, 1:32, 33, 38, 39, 2:12, 3:36, 4:40, 5:38, 6:27, 56, 7:9, 8:31, 35, 9:41, 10:40, 11:6, 12:24, 34, 12:46, 14:10, 16, 17, 25, 15:4, 5, 6, 7, 9, 10, 11, 16, 19:31, 21:22, 23; in the First Epistle, 2:6, 10, 14, 17, 19, 24, 27, 28, 3:6, 9, 14, 15, 17, 24, 4:12, 13, 15, 16; in the Second Epistle, 2, 9. The words "abide, dwell, tarry, continue, be present," are the various translations in the A.V. Study these places where the word occurs, and obtain a comprehensive view of its usage.

In John 15, the abiding of the Christian in Christ refers to his maintaining unbroken fellowship with Him. *He makes his spiritual home in Christ.* There is nothing between himself and his Saviour, no sin unjudged and not put away. He depends upon Him for spiritual life and vigor as the branch is dependent upon the vine. The abiding of Christ in the Christian is His permanent residence in Him and His supplying that Christian with the necessary spiritual energy to produce fruit in his life through the ministry of the Holy Spirit.

COMING.[27] This word is the translation of *parousia* which is made up of the word *para* meaning "beside" and the participial form of the verb "to be," the compound word meaning literally "being beside."

In classical Greek it meant "a being present, the presence of a person or a thing, especially the presence of a person for

---

26. *Thayer.*
27. *Limited.*

the purpose of assisting, the arrival of a person." It was use
of one's substance or property. From the papyri, Moulto
and Milligan report the following; "the repair of what ha
been swept away by the river requires my presence." The
report its usage in the quasi-technical force of "a 'visit' of
king, emperor, or other person of authority, the official cha:
acter of the 'visit' being further emphasized by the taxes c
payments that were exacted to make preparations for it.
They say that in popular usage it had the general sense c
"arrival" or "presence."

There is another word translated "coming" (*erchomai*)
which refers to the movement of a person from one place t
another, and means "to go or to come." This is used, fo
instance in Mt. 16:28 in the words "till they see the Son o
Man coming in His kingdom." Here the emphasis is, no
upon His arrival or personal presence, but upon His comin;
from heaven to earth. *Parousia* is used in the following scrip
tures: *Mt.* 24:3, 27, 37, 39; *I Cor.* 15:23, 16:17; *II Cor.* 7:6, 7
10:10; *Phil* 1:26, 2:12; *I Thes.* 2:19, 3:13, 4:15, 5:23; *II Thes*
2:1, 8, 9; *Jas.* 5:7, 8; *II Pet.* 1:16, 3:4, 12; *I John* 2:28. Whe:
the word is used of the Lord Jesus, it means "a royal visit,"
but when it refers to Paul for instance it merely refers to hi
personal presence.

CONVERSATION. There are three Greek words trans
lated by the one English word "conversation." Today thi
word means discourse between individuals. In 1611 A.D.
when the Authorized Version was translated, it meant wha
the Greek words mean of which it is the translation. We have
a two-fold purpose therefore in our study, first, to find ou
what these three words meant in general, and second, to in
quire into the shades of meaning between them so that we car
arrive at a clearer, more accurate understanding and inter
pretation of the passages where each occurs.

The first word we will study is *anastrophe* (the noun), and *anastrepho* (the verb). In classical Greek, the verb meant among other things "to turn one's self about, to turn back, round, or about, to dwell in a place," the noun, "a turning back or about, occupation in a thing, a mode of life, behaviour." One can see that the ideas of "a mode of life" and "one's behaviour" are derived from the fact of one's activity.

Thayer's note is helpful. He says that the verb means "to conduct or behave one's self, to walk," the latter meaning not referring here to the physical act of walking but to the act of determining our course of conduct and the carrying out of that determined course of action. The noun means "one's walk, manner of life, conduct." In the biblical use of the word, the moral and spiritual aspect of one's manner of life is in view. The noun *anastrophe* is found in *Gal.* 1:13; *Eph.* 4:22; *I Tim.* 4:12; *Heb.* 13:7; *Jas.* 3:13; *I Pet.* 1:15, 18, 2:12, 3:1, 2, 16; *II Pet.* 2:77, 3:11; the verb in *II Cor.* 1:12; *Eph.* 2:3.

The second word is *politeuomai* (the verb) (Phil. 1:27), and *politeuma* (the noun) (Phil. 3:20). The word occurs only here in the N.T. In classical Greek, the verb meant "to be a citizen or a freeman, to live in a free state, to be a free citizen, to live as a free citizen." The noun meant "citizenship, life as a citizen." Here are two words which Paul uses in their original classical meaning. Philippi was a Roman colony. Its citizens therefore were citizens of the Roman empire. Roman citizenship carried with it great privileges and honors, also great responsibilities.

Paul is speaking of the Christian lives of the Philippian saints, their manner of life and their behavior. He could have used the words *"anastrepho"* and *"anastrophe"* which we found so frequently in the N.T. But because the Philippian church was located in a city that was a Roman colony, he had the opportunity of using a more specialized word. The first two words refer to conduct as such. Our present two words refer to conduct as related to one's position as a citizen of a

commonwealth. The citizen of Philippi was not only obligate
to order his manner of life in the right manner. He was no
merely obligated to do what he thought was right. He wa
to govern his conduct so that it would conform to what Rom
would expect of him. He had responsibilities and dutie
which inhered in his position as a citizen of Rome. Thus, ou
second two words are an advance upon the first two in tha
while the former in their context speak of behaviour that i
good or bad as the case might be, the latter refer to conduc
that is measured by a standard. Paul uses the second word i
the Philippian epistle, to teach the Philippians that they wer
also citizens of heaven, and as such, their conduct must b
governed by a standard, that of heaven. They are to live
heavenly life, for they were a colony of heaven on earth.

The third word is *tropos*. It is translated just once in th
N.T., by the word "conversation" (Heb. 13:5). The wor
comes from *trepo* which means "to turn or guide towards
thing, to turn one's self, to direct one's attention to a thing
to be occupied with it." Thus *tropos* comes to mean "manne
of life, behavior."

HARPAZO. This is a Greek word which has various mean
ings. It is not translated by one uniform English word. The
meanings are as follows: "to seize, to carry off by force, to
claim for one's self eagerly, to snatch out or away." It wa
used proverbially in the sense of "to rescue from the dange
of destruction." It was used also of divine power transferring
a person marvellously and swiftly from one place to another

The word is used in *Mt.* 11:12, 13:19; *John* 6:15, 10:12, 28
29; *Acts* 8:39, 23:10; *II Cor.* 12:2, 4; *I Thes.* 4:17; *Jude* 23;
Rev. 12:5. The procedure in Greek exegesis when a word has
a number of meanings, is to use only those meanings which
are in accord with the context. For instance, in the case o
harpazo in its use in connection with the wolf (John 10:12)
it would not do to interpret it in the sense of rescuing from

the danger of destruction. It would mean here "to seize and carry off by force, to claim for one's self eagerly." Study these places where the word occurs, using as many meanings as agree with the context. Pay especial attention to I Thes. 4:17, and see how much new truth you obtain regarding the Rapture of the Church.

QUICKEN. We must not make the mistake of thinking that this word refers to the act of energizing something or someone already alive. The Greeks had a word for that. It is the word *energeo,* from which we get our words "energy," and "energize." The word *energeo* is used in Eph. 2:2 where demonic activity is said to be working in (*energeo*), energizing the unsaved. It is used in Phil. 2:13, where God is said to be energizing the saved. *Energeo* means "to be operative, to be at work, to put forth power." This activity put forth in an individual energizes him to the doing of certain things intended by the one who is doing the energizing.

The word translated "quicken" namely, *zoopoieo* does not mean "to energize." It is made up of one of the Greek words for life, *zoe,* which refers to the life principle in contradistinction to *bios* which refers to that which sustains life, and the word *poieo* which means "to make." This verb in classical Greek meant "to produce animals," used especially of worms and grubs. The noun meant " a making alive, a bringing to life," the adjective, "able to make alive, generating power." This is the genius of the word. It is so used in the N.T. Moulton and Milligan say that the word was used as a frequent attribute of the Trinity in the late papyri. They give an extract of the sixth century A.D., from which we offer the following translation; "in the name of the One who is holy and who makes alive and who is of the same substance, the Three, Father, Son, and Holy Spirit."

Study this word in the following scriptures: *John* 5:21, 6:63; *Rom.* 4:17, 8:11; *I Cor.* 15:22, 36, 45; *II Cor.* 3:6; *Gal.* 3:21;

I Tim. 6:13; *I Pet.* 3:18. In some places the word is translated "be made alive" etc. To make alive or to give life presupposes a state of death. For instance, Rom. 8:11 does not refer to the Holy Spirit energizing or animating the physical body of the saint during this life, but to the act of giving life to that body after it has died. The verse refers to the future resurrection of the saints. The word "quick" thus means "alive," as in Heb. 4:12, "The word of God is alive and powerful (*energes*)." Here we have the Greek word "alive" used in connection with the word which means "energy," demonstrating that the two words have a distinct meaning of their own.

BAPTIZE, BAPTISM. These two words are not native to the English language. Therefore, they do not have any intrinsic meaning of their own. The only rightful meaning they can have is the one that is derived from the Greek word of which they are the spelling. The verb is spelled *baptizo,* from which with a slight change in spelling we get our word "baptize." The noun is *baptisma,* and taking off the last letter, we have "baptism."

We will study these words first in their classical usage. The word *baptizo* is related to another Greek word *bapto.* The latter meant "to dip, dip under." It was used of the smith tempering the red-hot steel. It was used also in the sense of "to dip in dye, to colour, to steep." It was used of the act of dyeing the hair, and of glazing earthen vessels. It was used as a proverb in the sense of "steeping someone in crimson," that is, giving him a bloody coxcomb. It meant also "to fill by dipping in, to draw." It was used of a ship that dipped, that is, sank. *Baptizo,* the related word meant "to dip repeatedly." It was used of the act of sinking ships. It meant also "to bathe." It was used in the phrase "soaked in wine," where the word "soaked" is the meaning of *baptizo.* It is found in the phrase "overhead and ears in debt," where the words "overhead and ears" are the graphic picture of what the word meant. The word here means therefore "completely submerged." Our present day English equivalent would be "sunk." A *baptes* is one who dips or dyes. A *baptisis* is a dipping, bathing, a washing, a drawing of water. A *baptisma* is that which is dipped. A *baptisterion* is a bathing place, a swimming bath. A *baptistes* is one that dips, a dyer. *Baptos* means "dipped, dyed, bright colored, drawn like water."

Baptizo is used in the ninth book of the Odyssey, where the hissing of the burning eye of the Cyclops is compared to the sound of water where a smith dips (*baptizo*) a piece of iron, tempering it. In the Battle of the Frogs and Mice, it is said that a mouse thrust a frog with a reed, and the frog leaped over the water, (*baptizo*) dyeing it with his blood. Euripedes uses the word of a ship which goes down in the water and does not come back to the surface. Lucian dreams that he has seen a huge bird shot with a mighty arrow, and as it flies high in the air, it dyes (*baptizo*) the clouds with his blood. An ancient scholium to the Fifth Book of the Iliad makes a wounded soldier dye (*baptizo*) the earth with his blood. In Xenophon's Anabasis, we have the instance where the Greek soldiers placed (*baptizo*) the points of their spears in a bowl of blood.

We come now to the usage of these words in Koine Greek, giving examples from the papyri, the LXX, and the New Testament.

In secular documents of the Koine period, Moulton and Milligan report the following uses of *baptizo*, "a *submerged* boat, ceremonial *ablutions,* a person *flooded* or *overwhelmed* in calamities." They say that the word was used in its metaphorical sense even among uneducated people. A biblical example of this use is found in our Lord's speaking of His Passion as a "baptism" (Mk. 10:38). These scholars report the use of *bapto* as referring to fullers and dyers. The word is used of colored garments, and of wool to be dyed. The word *baptisma* is found in a question regarding a new baptism someone is reported to be preaching. This use of this noun is peculiar to the N.T., and to ecclesiastical writers.

In the LXX we have in Leviticus 4:6 the words, "And the priest shall dip (*bapto*) his finger in the blood, and sprinkle (*prosraino*) of the blood seven times before the Lord." Here the word *bapto* is found in juxtaposition to *prosraino*, a verb closely allied to *prosrantizo*, *bapto* meaning "to dip," the latter verb "to sprinkle."

In the N.T., we have the rich man asking that Lazarus dip (*bapto*) his finger in water and cool his tongue (Luke 16:24). In Heb. 9:10 *baptisma* is translated "washings" and refers to the ceremonial ablutions of Judaism. In Mk. 7:4 *baptisma* is used of the ceremonial washing of cups, pots, brazen vessels, and tables. *Baptisma* is used in Mt. 3:7, and *baptizo* in Mt. 3:16, and I Cor. 1:14, of the rite of water baptism. In Mk. 10:38 our Lord speaks of His sufferings on the Cross as the *baptisma* with which He is to be *baptizo*.

In these examples of the various uses of the words *bapto* and *baptizo* we discover three distinct usages, a *mechanical* one, a *ceremonial* one, and a *metaphorical* one.

The *mechanical* usage can be illustrated by the action of the smith dipping the hot iron in water, tempering it, or the dyer dipping the cloth in the dye for the purpose of dying it. These instances of the use of our Greek word, give us the following definition of the word in its mechanical usage. The word refers to the introduction or placing of a person or thing into a new environment or into union with something else so as to alter its condition or its relationship to its previous environment or condition. While the word, we found, had other uses, yet the one that predominated above the others was the above one. Observe how perfectly this meaning is in accord with the usage of the word in Romans 6:3, 4, where the believing sinner is baptized into vital union with Jesus Christ. The believing sinner is introduced or placed in Christ, thus coming into union with Him. By that action he is taken out of his old environment and condition in which he had lived, the First Adam, and is placed into a new environment and condition, the Last Adam. By this action his condition is changed from that of a lost sinner with a totally depraved nature to that of a saint with a divine nature. His relationship to the law of God is changed from that of a guilty sinner to that of a justified saint. All this is accomplished by the act of the Holy Spirit introducing or placing him into vital union with Jesus Christ. *No ceremony of water baptism ever did that.* The entire context is supernatural in its character. The Greek word here should not be transliterated but translated, and the translation should read; "As many as were introduced (placed) into Christ Jesus, into His death were introduced. Therefore we were buried with Him through the aforementioned introduction into His death." The same holds true of I Cor. 12:13 which should be translated, "For through the instrumentality of one Spirit were we all placed into one body." It is because we so often associate the English word "baptism" with the rite of water baptism, that we read that ceremony into Romans 6. A student is one of the writer's Greek classes who is a Greek himself, who learned to speak that language as his mother tongue and studied it in the schools of Greece, stated during a class discussion that the Greek reader would react to the Greek text of Romans and the word *baptizo* as the writer has. The purely mechanical usage of our word is seen in the following places: Mt. 3:11 (second occurrence); Mk. 1:8 (second); Luke 3:6 (second), 16:24; John 1:33 (second), 13:26; Acts 1:5 (second), 11:16 (second); Rom. 6:3, 4; I Cor. 12:13; Gal. 3:27; Eph. 4:5; Col. 2:12; Rev. 19:13.

Before listing the places where the word occurs in its ceremonial usage, we will trace the usage of *baptizo* back to Levitical washings. In the LXX (Lev. 14: 8, 9, 15:5, 6, 7, 8, 10, 11, 16, 18, 21, 22, 27, 17:15, 15:13, 16:4, 24, 28) the word "wash" is *louo*. This Greek word is found in Acts 22:16 in connection with the word *baptizo* in the expression, "Be baptized and wash away thy sins." According to Mk. 7:4 "washing of cups" (*baptizo*), Lk. 11:38, and Heb. 9:10, where *baptizo* is used, that word seems to have been the technical term at the time for these washings. Expressions like those in Isaiah 1:16, and the prophecies like those in Ezek. 36:25, 37:23, and Zech. 13:1 are connected with the Levitical washings. These washings and the prophecies are connected with the purification which followed the act of expiation or cleansing from sin (Ex. 19:14; Lev. 13:14; Heb. 10:22, 23). Thus that which the word *baptizo* stood for was not unknown to the Jews. While the ceremonial washings of Leviticus were performed by the person himself, with one exception, and that was where Moses in installing Aaron and his sons as priests, himself washed them (Lev. 8:6), John *baptizo* his converts himself.

Baptizo in the ministry of our Lord and John was, like the theocratic washings and purifications, a symbol whose design was to point to the purging away of sin on whom the rite was performed (Mt. 3:6; John 3:22-25). John's baptism was in response to the repentance of the individual (Mt. 3:11). It was connected with his message of an atonement for sin that was to be offered in the future, and the necessity of faith in that atonement (Acts 19:4).

John's baptism had looked ahead to a coming Saviour. Paul's baptism, or Christian baptism now looks back to a Saviour who has died and who has arisen again (Acts 19:5). That the rite of water baptism is the outward testimony of the inward fact of a person's salvation, and that it follows his act of receiving Christ as Saviour and is not a prerequisite to his receiving salvation, is seen in the use of the preposition *eis* in Mt. 3:11 where the translation should read, "I indeed baptize you with water because of repentance." While the act of Christian baptism is a testimony of the person that his

sins have been washed away, it also pictures and symbolizes
the fact of the believing sinner's identification with Christ
in His death, burial, and resurrection (Rom. 6:), for *baptizo*
means, "to dip, to immerse." It never means "to sprinkle."
The Greeks had a word for "sprinkle" namely, *rantizo*. The
two words, *baptizo* and *rantizo* are used in juxtaposition in
Lev. 4:6.

The following are the places where *baptizo* is used of the
baptism administered by John the Baptist and by the disciples
of our Lord under the dispensation of law. *Mt.* 3:6, 11:1 (first
mention), 13, 14, 16; *Mk.* 1:4, 5, 8 (first mention), 9; *Lk.* 3:7,
12, 16 (first mention), 21, 7:29, 30; *John* 1:25, 26, 28, 31, 33
(first mention), 3:22, 23, 26, 4:1, 2, 10:40; *Acts* 1:5, (first
mention) 11:16 (first mention), 19:4 (first mention). The
noun *baptisma* when it is used of the baptism in the dispensation of law is found in the following places: *Mt.* 3:7, 21:25;
Mk. 1:4, 11:30; *Lk.* 3:3, 7:29, 20:4; *Acts* 1:22, 10:37, 13:24,
18:25, 19:34.

The word *baptizo* is used of the ablutions of the Jews
which were extra-Biblical, and which were called the tradi-
tions of the elders (*Mt.* 15:2), in *Mk.* 7:4, *Lk.* 11:38. The
noun *baptismos* is used in connection with the same practices in Mt. 7:4; Mk. 7:8. It is used of the Levitical ablutions
in Heb. 6:2, 9:10.

Baptizo is used of Christian baptism in *Mt.* 28:19; *Acts* 2:38,
41, 8:12, 13, 16, 36, 38, 9:18, 10:47, 48, 16:15, 33, 18:8, 19:5,
22:16; *I Cor.* 1:13, 14, 15, 16, 17, 15:29. *Baptisma* is used in
I Pet. 3:21 of Christian baptism.

The metaphorical use of *baptizo* we find in Mt. 20:22, 23;
Mk. 10:38, 39; Lk. 12:50. A metaphor is the use of a word
or phrase literally denoting one kind of object or idea in
place of another by way of suggesting a likeness or analogy
between them, for example, "the ship *plows* the sea." In the
above passages, our Lord is speaking of His sufferings in connection with the Cross. He speaks of them as a baptism. The

words were uttered while He was on His way to Jerusalem t
be crucified. John the Baptist had announced His coming an
had baptized the multitudes. Our Lord's disciples had bee
baptizing during the three years of His ministry. The word
baptizo and *baptisma* which are used by Matthew, Mark, an
Luke had by that time become the technical and commo
Greek words used to describe the rite administered by Joh
and our Lord's disciples. Our Lord used the rite of baptisn
as a metaphor to speak of His coming sufferings. Just as
convert was plunged into the baptismal waters, He was abou
to be plunged into His sufferings. Just as the person woul
be immersed in the water, so He would be overwhelmed b
His sufferings. Just as the person would come up out of th
water, so He would be freed from His sufferings and aris
from the dead.

There is one passage in which *baptizo* is found that w
have not classified. It is I Cor. 10:2 "were all baptized unt
Moses." *Expositor's Greek Testament* has an illuminating
note on it. " 'The cloud' shading and guiding the Israelite
from above, and the 'sea' making a path for them throug
the midst and drowning their enemies behind them, wer
glorious signs to 'our fathers' of God's salvation; together the
formed a washing of regeneration (Tit. 3:5), inauguratin
the national life; as it trode the miraculous path betwee
upper and nether waters, Israel was born into its Divin
estate. Thus 'they all received their baptism *unto Moses* i
the cloud and in the sea' since in this act they committe
themselves to the guidance of Moses, entering through hin
into acknowledged fellowship with God."

AIR. The Greeks had two words which meant "air," *ae*
and *aither*. *Aer* was used to designate the lower air, the thick
air or haze that surrounds the earth. *Aither* was the name
given the pure, upper air as opposed to the thick lower air
The pure upper air started at the mountain tops for the

Greeks of the ancient world, since they had no way of exploring the regions above these.

The word *aer*, referring to the lower atmosphere, namely, that below the mountain tops, is used in the N.T. *Aither* is not used, although it must have been in common use in the first century. One can understand the use of this word as that which would naturally be expected in such scriptures as Acts 22:23; I Cor. 9:26, 14:9; Rev. 9:2, 16:17. But it gives one pause to see it used in Eph. 2:2 and I Thes. 4:17. Study these latter two scriptures in the light of the particular meaning of the word *aer*.

ADOPTION. This word is the translation of *huiothesia*, a word made up of *huios* "a son," and *thesia*, a form of the verb *tithemi* meaning "to place," the compound word meaning "to place as a son." The Greek word *teknon* which means "a child," comes from the verb *tikto* "to give birth to." It therefore has in it the idea of birth relationship. The word means "a born-one." The word *huios* does not have this implication. *Huios* is used in Gal. 3:26 of the believer under grace as opposed to the believer under law. The latter was under the schoolmaster (the *paidagogos*), a slave charged with the moral supervision of a child in its minority. The word *teknon* is used in Galatians (4:25, 27, 28, 31) of the believer under law. Thus a *teknon* is a believer in his minority, a *huios*, an adult son. Believers under the covenant of law were *teknon*, that is born children of God in their minority. Believers under grace, are both *teknon*, born children of God and *huios*, adult sons of God. This meaning of an adult son is to be used only where the word refers to a believer in this age of grace. The word is used also in the N.T., as a Hebrew idiom, where a person having a peculiar quality, or is subject to a peculiar evil, is called the son, (*huios*) of that quality (Lk. 10:6, Eph. 2:2, 5:6, 8). The word *huios* is also used to refer to the male issue or child.

The A.V., uniformly translates *teknon* by the word "child" except in the following places where it is rendered by the word "son," which is the proper translation of *huios*. *Mt.* 9:2, 21:28; *Mk.* 2:5, 13:12; *Lk.* 2:48, 15:31, 16:25; *John* 1:12; *I Cor.* 4:14, 17; *Phil.* 2:15, 22; *I Tim.* 1:2, 18; *II Tim.* 1:2, 2:1; *Tit.* 1:4; *Phm.* 10; *I John* 3:1, 2. Study these passages, using the word "child" in the translation, keeping in mind the idea of the birth-relationship existing, and see what clearer light is thrown upon them. For instance, Mary calls Jesus "child." He was only twelve years old at the time. Yet this child was confuting the learned Doctors (Lk. 2:48). Timothy was Paul's child and the latter was his spiritual father, for Paul had won Timothy to the Lord. In John 1:12, regeneration is in view. In I John 3:1, 2, the fact that we are born-children of God, is in view, having the nature of God. In Phil. 2:15, believers, being children of God, and possessing therefore the nature of God, are expected to reflect in their lives the holiness, love, and other qualities of God.

The word *huios* is uniformly translated "son" except in certain places, some of which rightfully use the word "children" where the plural refers to children of both sexes. But the following places should be translated by the word "son": *Mt.* 23:15; *Lk.* 6:35, 16:8, 20:34, 36; *John* 12:36; *Acts* 3:25, 13:10; *Rom.* 9:26; *Gal.* 3:26; *Eph.* 2:2, 5:6; *Col.* 3:6; *I Thes.* 5:5. It will be observed that in many of the above places the Hebrew idiom is used where a person having a peculiar quality or is subject to a peculiar evil, is called the son (*huios*) of that quality or evil. He partakes of the nature of that quality.

Coming now to the word "adoption" (*huiothesia*), we find that it was a term used in Roman legal practice. It referred to a legal action by which a person takes into his family a child not his own, with the purpose of treating him as and giving him all the privileges of an own son. The custom was not common among the Jews, but was so among the Romans, with whom an adopted child is legally entitled to all rights and privileges of a natural-born child. This custom, well-known in the Roman empire, is used in the N.T., as an illustration of the act of God giving a believing sinner, who is not His natural child, a position as His adult son in His family. This is a legal act and position, and not the same as regeneration and a place in the family as a born-child of God.

The word is found in *Rom.* 8:15, 23, 9:4; *Gal.* 4:5; *Eph.* 1:5. In Rom. 8:15 it is the Holy Spirit who places believing sinners in the family of God as adult sons. In Rom. 8:23, believers have already been placed in the family of God, and are led by the Spirit as the adult sons of God. But only when their mortal bodies have been glorified at the Rapture, will they possess all that sonship involves. In Rom. 9:4, the nation Israel is said to have been placed in the special relationship as the peculiar people of God, thus God's own by adoption. Gal. 4:5 and Eph. 1:5 refer to the same thing that Rom. 8:15 refers to.

ACCESS is the translation of *prosagoge*, a word made up of the verb *ago* which means "to go," and the preposition *pros* which means "toward, facing." The word is used in Rom. 5:2, Eph. 2:18, 3:12. In the papyri the word was used in the technical sense of "a landing stage." It is thought that it was used as a nautical term of the approach of a ship to a haven or harbor where it could land. Thus the total idea in the word would be access into and rest in a haven or harbor. In the case of Rom. 5:2, God's grace is there pictured as a haven for the soul. The word "have" is perfect tense in Greek. Thus the words "have access" speak of a permanent haven for the soul.

The verb *prosago*, which is the base of the word translated "access," means in its intransitive use, "approach, a drawing near." Thus our word speaks not only of a haven of rest and security, but of a drawing near to God. The word *prosago* means also "to bring into the presence of," thus "to present, to introduce." It is found in the sentence, "Cronion, who now happens to be in Alexandria, will bring them before his highness the high-priest."[28] It is our blessed Lord who Himself brings believing sinners into the presence of God, who presents and introduces them. The word was used in classical Greek especially of access to a king's presence. The French word *entree* is an excellent translation of *prosagoge*. Our Lord brings believers by virtue of His precious blood, not only into the presence of God the Father, but into His unlimited favor and His infinite grace. The verb *prosago* is used in I Peter 3:18 in the expression, "that He might bring us to God." The translation could read, "that He might provide for you an *entree* into the presence of God." The second, not the first person is found in the best texts.

COMFORT. There are three Greek words translated by the one word "comfort."

The first is *paregoria*, used only in Col. 4:11. The word in its verb form means "to address, exhort, to console, comfort, appease, soothe." There is a medicine called *Paregoric* which is given to infants as a sedative. It tends to soothe and quiet them. The manufacturers certainly chose the right Greek word to describe the medicinal effects of their product. How precious to think that while Paul was in prison, deprived of his liberty to preach, his fellow-workers by their activities in preaching the gospel, were a soothing, quieting influence to him. In that sense they were a comfort to him. The noun form means "comfort, solace, relief, alleviation, consolation." We Christians, filled with the Holy Spirit, can be all that to our sorely-tried fellow-saints. The word is found in a pagan letter of consolation on the occasion of a death.

The second word is *paramutheomai*, and is used in *John* 11:19, 31; *I Cor.* 14:13; *Phil.* 2:1; *I Thes.* 2:11, 5:14. The word means "to speak to or address one whether by way of admoni-

---

28. *Moulton and Milligan.*

tion and incentive, or to calm and console, hence to encourage, console."

The third word is *tharseo*. It is translated "Be of good cheer," or "Be of good comfort" in *Mt.* 9:2, 22, 14:27; *Mk.* 6:50, 10:49; *Lk.* 8:48; *John* 16:33; *Acts* 23:11. It means "be of good courage, be of good cheer." A related verb *tharreo* means "to be of good courage, to be hopeful, confident, to be bold." *Tharseo* is found in the papyri in the sentence "eye . . . of my soul, take courage."[29]

The fourth word is *parakaleo*. The word is made up of the verb *kaleo*, which means "to call," and the preposition *para* which means "beside." Hence the compound word means "to call alongside." In classical Greek writers it meant "to call to one's side, call for, summon," the context indicating the purpose of the summons. It meant also "to address, speak to, (call to, call on)," which may be done in the way of exhortation, entreaty, comfort, instruction. Hence, there results a variety of senses in which it is used. Then it came to mean "to beg, entreat, beseech." Finally, it comes to mean "to encourage, strengthen, to comfort." It combines the ideas of exhorting, comforting, and encouraging in Rom. 12:8; I Cor. 14:31; I Thes. 3:2. Moulton and Milligan in reporting this word in the papyri, do not list any place where it means "to comfort." Its chief meaning in the papyri was "to ask, beseech." It meant "please, I exhort, I urge." This is the way it is most frequently used in the N.T. It is translated by the word "comfort" in the following places: *Mt.* 2:18, 5:4; *Lk.* 16:25; *Acts* 16:40, 20:12; *I Cor.* 14:31; *II Cor.* 1:4, 6, 2:7, 7:6, 7, 13, 13:11; *Eph.* 6:22; *Col.* 2:2, 4:8; *I Thes.* 3:2, 7, 4:18; 5:11; *II Thes.* 2:17. *Parakaleo* is the word used most frequently to bring the idea of comfort. From its other uses, one can see that it is probably the strongest word of the four.

---

29. *Moulton and Milligan.*

COMFORTER. This word is the translation of *parakletos* which comes from the above word *parakaleo*. It is found in John 14:16, 26, 15:26, 16:7, where it is translated "comforter," and in I John 2:1, where it is rendered by the word "advocate." The verb *parakaleo* refers to the act of calling someone to one's side in order to help one. The noun *parakletos* refers to the one who is called upon to render aid. It was used in the law courts of one who pleads another's cause before a judge, a counsel for the defence, an advocate. In the widest sense it means "a helper, a succorer, one who aids another." In the three passages in the Gospel noted above, the Holy Spirit is the Comforter to the saint, not that He comforts him in the sense of consoling him merely, but that He is sent to be the One to come to the aid of the Christian in the sense of ministering to him in his spiritual life. In the first epistle of John (2:1), the Lord Jesus is the *parakletos* of the believer in the sense that He pleads our cause before our heavenly Father in relation to sin in the life of the Christian, praying us back into fellowship with God by the way of our confession and the cleansing blood.

TRANCE. This is the translation of the Greek word *ekstasis*. This word comes from the verb *existemi*. The simple verb *histemi* means "to stand," the prefixed preposition, "out," thus, the compound word means "to stand out." The noun *ekstasis* thus means "a standing out." A person in a trance is one who in a sense is standing out of himself. He is actually in his physical body, but his attention has been so engaged by something or someone else that his mind does not register the impressions given him by his senses. He might as well be out of his body so far as recognized sense sensations are concerned.

In the Greek classics, the word meant "any casting down of a thing from its proper place or state: a displacement, a throwing of the mind out of its normal state, an alienation of mind, whether such an alienation as will cause lunacy; or it may be that of a man who by some sudden emotion is transported as it were out of himself, so that in his rapt condition, although he is awake, his mind is so drawn off from all surrounding objects and wholly fixed on things divine that he sees and hears nothing but the forms and images lying within, and thinks that he perceives with his bodily eyes and ears realities shown him by God."[30] The word also meant "amazement," namely, the state of one who, either owing to the importance or the novelty of an event, is thrown into a state of blended fear and wonder. Our word "ecstacy" is derived from the Greek *ekstasis*.

The word is used in Acts 10:10, 11:5, where Peter was on the housetop. Literally, "a trance fell upon him." In order that the apostle might see that it was right for him to go to the home of Cornelius, God had to give him a vision. But in order for Peter to see the vision, God needed to have his entire attention. This was accomplished by the Holy Spirit so controlling his thinking, that his senses did not register their impressions upon his mind. A like thing happened to John on the island of Patmos (Rev. 1:10) where the Greek reads, "I became in the Spirit." That is, the Spirit-filled apostle entered into a state in which the absolute control of the Spirit obtained. This was for the purpose of giving John the visions in the Book of the Revelation. Paul experienced a like thing while he was in the Temple (Acts 22:17, 18). The Lord Jesus appeared to Paul in order to give him a most important command.

These three recorded instances of Spirit-wrought trances occurred before the revelation was closed. Such trances are not now in order, for the Holy Spirit works through the written word of God.

In Mk. 5:42, the word is used in its verb and noun form in the words, "They were astonished with a great astonish-

---

30. *Thayer, Greek English Lexicon.*

ment." This was the effect of the bringing back to life of the daughter of the ruler of the synagogue. One could render it, "They were beside themselves with great amazement." Such was the effect of the miracle upon those who saw it that their senses were not registering. All they could think about, to the exclusion of everything else, was the miracle. The word is used in Mk. 16:8. Such was the effect upon those who saw the empty sepulchre, that they were beside themselves with amazement. In Lk. 5:26 the healing of the paralytic produced a like result.

The verb *existemi* is found in the following places and is translated by the words "were amazed, is beside himself, were astonished, bewitched, wondered;" *Mt.* 12:23; *Mk.* 2:12, 3:21, 5:42, 6:51; *Lk.* 2:47, 8:56, 24:22; *Acts* 2:7, 12, 8:9, 11, 13, 9:21, 10:45, 12:16; *II Cor.* 5:13. One can see that the words "amazed, wondered, astonished" hold a larger content of meaning and are far stronger in their New Testament usage than in our ordinary conversation. In the case of Simon the sorcerer, the word carries more than the idea of causing profound amazement. It is that his power over the people of Samaria was such that they acted under his spell as people would do who were so controlled by someone else that their normal sense functions did not register. Simon stood them out of themselves, so to speak. As the Holy Spirit controlled Peter, John, and Paul with the result that they received visions, so the power of Satan controlled these Samaritans in their actions while they were under the spell of Simon.

IMPUTED, RECKONED, COUNTED, ACCOUNTED, are translations of the Greek word *logizomai*. The word in the classics meant "to count, reckon, calculate, compute, to set to one's account." We will study its use in Gal. 3:6 as an illustration of its use in other passages. The word is used in the papyri as a business term: for instance, "*put to one's account;* let my revenues be *placed on deposit* at the store-

ouse; *reckoning* the wine to him at 16 drachmae the mono-
hore; a single artabae *being reckoned* at 180 myriads of
denari; I now give orders generally with regard to all payments actually made or *credited* to the government."[31]

Thus Abraham believed God, and his act of faith was
placed to his account in value as righteousness. He believed
God and his act of faith was *placed on deposit for him and
evaluated* as righteousness. He believed God and his act of
faith was *computed as to its value, and there was placed to his
account,* righteousness. He believed God, and his act of faith
was credited to his account for righteousness. Finally, he believed God, and his act of faith *was credited to him,* resulting
in righteousness.

All this does not mean, however, that Abraham's act of
faith was looked upon as a meritorious action deserving of
reward. It was not viewed as a good work by God and rewarded by the bestowal of righteousness. That would be salvation by works. But the fact that Abraham cast off all dependence upon good works as a means of finding acceptance
with God, and accepted God's way of bestowing salvation, was
answered by God in giving him that salvation. *Abraham
simply put himself in the place where a righteous God could
offer him salvation upon the basis of justice satisfied, and in
pure grace. God therefore put righteousness to his account.
He evaluated Abraham's act of faith as that which made it
possible for Him to give him salvation.*

The word *logizomai* is translated "imputed" in Rom. 4:6,
8, 11, 22, 23, 24; II Cor. 5:19; Jas. 2:23. In Rom. 4:8, the man
is called blessed, to whose account no sin is charged. At the
Cross, his sin was charged to the account of the Lord Jesus.
In Rom. 4:6, the man to whose account righteousness is put,
is called blessed. This is imputation, the act of putting something to someone's account. In the case of the Lord Jesus,
the sin of the human race was charged to Him. In the case

---

31. *Moulton and Milligan.*

of the believing sinner, the righteousness of God, Christ Jesus Himself, is put to his account.

It is translated "counted" or "accounted" in the following scriptures; Rom. 2:26, 4:3, 5; Gal. 3:6. In Rom. 2:26 we have, "Shall not his uncircumcision be put to his account for circumcision?"

The scripture where "reckoned" is used is Rom. 4:9, 10. In II Tim. 4:16 we have an excellent illustration of the use of *logizomai* in the words, "I pray God that it may not be laid to their charge." The above treatment of *logizomai* is chiefly confined to its use in connection with the substitutionary atonement for sin. There are other uses which are not covered by the foregoing work.

TRUTH, TRUE. This is the translation of the Greek words *aletheia* and *alethes*. The words are a compound made up of *lanthano* which means "to escape notice, to be unknown, unseen, hidden, concealed," and the Greek letter Alpha prefixed. When a Greek wants to make a word mean the opposite to what it originally meant, he prefixes the Greek letter Alpha. For instance, *dikaios* means "righteous," *adikaios*, "unrighteous." Thus, *lanthano* means "hidden, concealed," and *alanthano* means "unhidden, unconcealed." The Greek idea of truth is therefore that which is unconcealed, unhidden, that which will bear scrutiny and investigation, that which is open to the light of day.

Thayer defines *aletheia* the noun (truth) as follows; "verity, truth, what is true in any matter under consideration." In reference to religion, the word denotes "what is true in things appertaining to God and the duties of man." When used of the body of truth in Christianity, it refers to the truth as taught therein respecting God and the execution of His purposes through Christ, and respecting the duties of man, opposed alike to the superstitions of the Gentiles, the inventions of the Jews, and the corrupt opinions and precepts of alse teachers. It is used also of that candor of mind which s free from affectation, pretence, simulation, falsehood, deceit. It is also used of sincerity of mind and integrity of character, also of a mode of life in harmony with divine truth. The noun *aletheia* (truth), the verb *aletheuo* (to speak the truth), and the adjective *alethes* (true), are all translated in the N.T., by the words "truth" or "true." There is another word *alethinos* which is also translated by the word "true," but which has an added content of meaning that throws further light upon the places where it is used.

The word *alethinos,* used twenty two times in John's writings and only five times in the rest of the N.T., means, "that which has not only the name and semblance, but the real nature corresponding to the name." It is particularly used to express that which is all that it pretends to be, for instance, pure gold as opposed to adulterated metal. In every respect it corresponds to the idea signified by the name. It is real and true, genuine. It is opposed to that which is fictitious, counterfeit, imaginary, simulated, and pretended. It is what we mean by the expression, "All wool and a yard wide." It contrasts realities with semblances. It is opposed to that which is imperfect, defective, frail, uncertain. The differences between *alethes,* and the word *alethinos* are covered up in the A.V., since both are translated by the one word "true."

For instance, in John 3:33 and Rom. 3:4, God is the *alethes* God in that He cannot lie (Tit. 1:2). He is the truth-speaking and the truth-loving God. But in I Thes. 1:9 and John 17:3, He is the *alethinos* God. He is not like idols and other false gods that are the product of the diseased fancy of man, but a God who in His completeness of Being has the real nature corresponding to the name. He is in His Being all that the term "God" implies. In every respect He corresponds to the idea which is signified by the term "God." In the words of the Nicene creed, the Lord Jesus is *very* God of *very* God. The Latin Vulgate distinguishes between the word *alethes* and *alethinos* by the use of *verax* for the former, and the word *verus* (very) for the latter. By the words "Very God of Very God" we mean therefore that the Lord Jesus is *alethinos* God. He is in His Being all that the term "God" implies. We have almost lost the word *verus* (very) as an adjective, retaining it only as an adverb. Thus the word "truth" must do duty for both words, with a consequent loss of part of the meaning of the second word. Wycliffe's translation of John 15:1 is, "I am the *verri* vine," that is, the *alethinos* vine, the vine that corresponds in all details to what one would expect of the Lord Jesus as a Vine. This does not deny that Israel also was God's vine (Ps. 80:8; Jer. 2:21). But it does imply that no vine except the Lord Jesus realized this name in the sense that He was all that the name implied, and that to the full.

Trench says that "it does not of necessity follow, that whatever may be contrasted with the *alethinos* must thereby be concluded to have no substantial existence, to be altogether false and fraudulent. Inferior and subordinate realizations, partial and imperfect anticipations of the truth, may be set over against the truth in its highest form, in its ripest and completest development; and then to this last alone the title *alethinos* will be vouchsafed."

The Lord Jesus is the *alethinos* light (John 1:9). But that does not deny that John the Baptist was also a "burning and a shining light" (John 5:35). It does mean that our Lord Jesus was in His glorious Person all that the term "light" demanded and implied, and that to the full, while John was not. Our Lord is the *alethinos* bread (John 6:32). This does not suggest that the bread which Moses gave Israel was not also "bread from heaven" (Ps. 105:40), but that the latter was bread in a secondary and inferior degree. It was not in the highest sense food, for it did not nourish man's spiritual nature. The word *alethinos* is found in the following places, and is translated by the word "true." *Lk.* 16:11; *John* 1:9, 4:23, 37, 6:32, 7:28, 15:1, 17:3, 19:35; *I Thes.* 1:9; *Heb.* 8:2,

9:24, 10:22; *I John* 2:8, 5:20; *Rev.* 3:7, 14, 6:10, 15:3, 16:7, 19:2, 9, 11, 21:5, 22:6. Make a study of these scriptures in the light of the additional meaning in the word *alethinos*. In all other places in the N.T., where the words "truth" or "true" occur, *aletheia, alethes* or *aletheuo* are found.

REGENERATION, RENEWING. These words have a vital relationship to one another, and so will be treated together. The word "regeneration" is found in Mt. 19:28 and Tit. 3:5, and is the translation of the Greek word *paliggenesia*. The word "renewing" is found in Rom. 12:2 and Tit. 3:5, and is the translation of *anakainosis*.

We will study the word *paliggenesia* first. Archbishop Trench says of this word; "*Paliggenesia* is one among the many words which the gospel found, and, so to speak, glorified; enlarged the borders of its meaning; lifted it up into a higher sphere; made it the expression of far deeper thoughts, of far mightier truths, than any of which it had been the vehicle before." He gives examples of its use before it was taken over into the New Testament where its content of meaning was enlarged. In some passages the word means revivification and only that. In the Pythagorean doctrine of the transmigration of souls, their reappearance in new bodies was called their *paliggenesia*. The Stoics used this word to speak of the periodic renovation of the earth in the spring-time when it budded and blossomed again, awaking from its winter sleep, and in a sense, revived from its winter death. It was used of recollection or reminiscence which the Greeks carefully distinguished from memory. Memory, they said, is instinctive and is common to beasts and men. But recollection and reminiscence are more than merely remembering things. They are "the reviving of faded impressions by a distinct act of the will, the reflux, at the bidding of the mind, of knowledge that has once ebbed."[32] *Paliggenesia,* Trench says,

---

32. *Trench, Synonyms of the New Testament.*

"which has thus in heathen and Jewish Greek the meaning of a recovery, a restoration, a revival, yet never reaches, or even approaches, there the depth of meaning which it has acquired in Christian language."

The word *paliggenesia* is made up of the Greek word *palin* and *genesis*. *Palin* is an adverb meaning "back, again, back again." *Genesis* is a noun used in the N.T., in the sense of "origin, race, birth." It is rendered "birth" in Mt. 1:18. It means "race, lineage." It is translated "generation" in Mt. 1:1. It comes from the verb *ginomai* which means "to become, to begin to be." Used of persons it means "to become, to be born." In John 8:58 we have, "Before Abraham came into existence (i.e., was born), I am." "Was" is the A.V., translation of *ginomai* here, the verb which means "to come into existence." In Rom. 1:3, the words referring to our Lord, "which was made of the seed of David according to the flesh," could read, "who with reference to the flesh (His humanity), was born of the seed of David." Another clear case of the usage of *ginomai* in the sense of "to be born" is in Gal. 4:4 where the Greek reads "having become out of a woman as a source." The participle is aorist, the classification ingressive. The participle for *ginomai* refers here therefore to entrance into a new state. It was His humanity into which our Lord entered. This entrance into human existence had its source in a woman, the preposition being ek (*out of*) and the case being ablative, thus, ablative of source. This entrance into human existence was effected by the virgin birth. Thus, while *ginomai* means fundamentally "to become, to begin to be," it is used at times in the sense of "to begin to be by being born." The word *paliggenesia* therefore means "to be born again."

In John 3:3, reference is made by our Lord to regeneration, but there both the adverb and the verb are different. The verb is *gennao*, which in its active voice means "to beget," and in the passive voice, "to be born." The adverb is *anothen* which means either "from above," or, "again." The first meaning is ruled out in John 3:3 by two things in the context, the fact that Nicodemus understood our Lord to speak of a repetition of a birth, and the fact that our Lord designated the truth about the new birth as, not heavenly but earthly in its nature. The adverb *anothen* therefore in John 3:3 speaks of a second or repeated birth.

Now, *palin* and *anothen* are synonyms. Both words refer to the repetition of an act, but *anothen* includes in that act a reference to the beginning, and the idea of a going back to the starting-point. It means a repetition of the beginning, again from the outset on. When *anothen* is used, the emphasis is more upon the return to the very beginning. Regeneration consists of the impartation of the life of God, eternal life, to a sinner who is spiritually dead. This is, according to the meaning of *anothen,* not only a repetition of an act of giving spiritual life to an individual, but a repetition that goes back to the beginning or starting point. The new-birth is therefore, not a second birth to physical birth, but to the act of God imparting spiritual life to Adam as recorded in Gen. 2:7. The human race is thus conceived of here as having had the divine life of God as it stood in Adam, as having lost that divine life in Adam's fall, and as needing a second impartation of divine life through the *paliggenesia,* the new-birth.

In Tit. 3:5, *paliggenesia* (regeneration) is said to be one of the means God used in saving us. The preposition "by" is the translation of *dia,* the preposition of intermediate agency.

Regeneration is described as a washing here. The word is *lutron,* which word means "a bath." We have the same word used in Eph. 5:26 where the bath of water (genitive of description), the water-bath cleanses the life of the believer. The Word of God is conceived of as a water-bath cleansing the life by putting out of it things that are sinful, and introducing into it, things that are right. In our present text, regeneration is spoken of as a bath in that the impartation of the divine nature results in the cleansing of the life by the fact that the new life from God provides the believer with both the desire and power to do the will of God and to refuse to fulfil the behests of the evil nature whose power has been broken by the identification of the believer with the Lord Jesus in His death on the Cross.

The other instance of the use of *paliggenesia* is in Mt. 19:28. Here it is used of the new-birth of the entire creation which will occur after the Millennial Kingdom, when the curse now resting upon the material creation because of sin will be removed, and the universe will be restored to its pristine glory. This is spoken of in Rom. 8:21-22; II Peter 3:7-13; Rev. 21:1. Paul includes in this great event, the glorification of the saints which takes place 1000 years before at the Rapture of the Church, but which is followed by the glorification of those saints who will live and die after the Rapture, which ties the whole matter of glorification up with the final restoration of the universe.

Commenting on the use of *paliggenesia* for the regeneration of the individual sinner and also of the universe, Trench has the following to say: "Is then *paliggenesia* used in two different senses, with no common bond binding the diverse uses of it together? By no means: all laws of language are violated by any such supposition. The fact is, rather, that the word by our Lord is used in a wider, by the apostle in a narrower meaning. They are two circles of meaning, one comprehending more than the other, but their center is the same. The *paliggenesia* which Scripture proclaims begins with the *mikrokosmos* (little world) of single souls; but it does not end with this; it does not cease its effectual working till it has embraced the whole *makrokosmos* (great world) of the universe. The primary seat of the *paliggenesia* is the soul of man; it is there, it extends in ever-widening circles; and, first, to him of this that St. Paul speaks; but, having established its center

)ody; the day of resurrection being the day of *paliggenesia*
or it."

Speaking of the use of *paliggenesia* in Mt. 19:28, Trench
ays: "Doubtless our Lord there implies, or presupposes, the
resurrection, but He also includes much more. Beyond the
lay of resurrection, . . . a day will come when all nature shall
)ut off its soiled work-day garments, and clothe itself in holy-
lay attire, 'the times of restitution of all things' (Acts 3:21);
. . . a day by St. Paul regarded as one in the labor-pangs of
which all creation is groaning and travailing until now (Rom.
3:21-23). Man is the present subject of the *paliggenesia*, and
)f the wondrous change which it implies; but in that day it
will have included within its limits that whole world of which
man is the central figure: and here is the reconciliation of the
two passages, in one of which it is contemplated as pertaining
to the single soul, in the other to the whole redeemed creation. These refer both to the same event, but at different
epochs and stages of its development."

We come now to our other word, *anakainosis*, found only
in the N.T., in Rom. 12:2 and Tit. 3:5, and translated in both
places by the word "renewing." Commenting on the relationship of *paliggenesia* and *anakainosis* in Tit. 3:5, Trench has
the following: "Our Collect for Christmas day expresses excellently well the relation in which the *paliggenesia* and the
anakainosis stand to each other; we pray, 'that we being re-
generate,' in other words, having been already made the subjects of the *paliggenesia*, 'may daily be renewed by the Holy
Spirit,' may continually know the renewing of the Holy
Spirit. In this Collect, uttering, as do so many, profound
theological truth in forms at once the simplest and the most
accurate, the new birth is contemplated as already past, as
having found place once for all, while the 'renewal' or 'renovation' is daily proceeding, being as it is that gradual restoration of the divine image, which is ever going forward
in him who, through the new birth, has come under the trans-

forming powers of the world to come. It is called 'the renew:
of the Holy Ghost' inasmuch as He is the efficient cause, b
whom alone this putting on of the new man, and the puttin
off the old, is brought about.

"These two then are bound by the closest ties to one ar
other; the second the following up, the consequence, the cor
summation of the first. The *paliggenesia* is that free act c
God's mercy and power, whereby He causes the sinner to pa:
out of the kingdom of darkness into that of light, out of deat
into life; it is the 'born again' of John 3:3, the 'born of Goc
of I John 5:4, ... the 'born of incorruptible seed' of I Pet. 1
23; in it that glorious word begins to be fulfilled, 'behold,
make all things new' (Rev. 21:5). In it,—not in the prepara
tion for it, but in the act itself, — the subject of it is passive
even as the child has nothing to do with its own birth. Wit
the *anakainosis* it is otherwise. This is the gradual conformin
of the man more and more to that new spiritual world int
which he has been introduced, and in which he now lives an
moves; the restoration of the divine image; and in all this, s
far from being passive, he must be a fellow-worker with God.

Rom. 12:2 in a fuller and expanded translation is as fo
lows; "Stop perpetually assuming an outward expressio:
which does not come from your inner being but is put o'
from the outside, an expression patterned after this age, bu
let your outward expression be changed, an outward expre
sion which comes from your inner being, this changed ou'
ward expression being the result of the renewing of your minc
with a view to your putting to the test for the purpose of af
proving what is the will of God, that will which is good an
well-pleasing and complete." Paul is exhorting the saint
here to stop masquerading in the habiliments of the worlc
and instead to yield themselves to the ministry of the Hol
Spirit who will gradually produce in them the mind of Chris
Thus, they will be giving outward expression of their tru
inner regenerated Spirit-filled beings. The act of regenera

tion made them partakers of the divine nature. This is the basis upon which the Holy Spirit works in the Christian's life. *He has in His hands now an individual who has both the desire and the power to do the will of God. He augments this by His control over the saint when that saint yields to Him and cooperates with Him.* The first is *paliggenesia*, the second, *anakainosis*, the first, regeneration, the second, renewing (Tit. 3:5).

SIN. There are nine different Greek words in the N.T., which present sin in its various aspects, *hamartia, hamartema, parakoe, anomia, paranomia, parabasis, paraptoma, agnoema*, and *hettema*.

The word used most frequently in the N.T., is *hamartia*. This word in classical Greek never approaches the depth of meaning it has in the Bible. The pagan Greeks used it of a warrior who hurls his spear and fails to strike his foe. It is used of one who misses his way. *Hamartia* is used of a poet who selects a subject which it is impossible to treat poetically, or who seeks to attain results which lie beyond the limits of his art. The *hamartia* is a fearful mistake. It sometimes is employed in an ethical sense where the ideas of right and wrong are discussed, but it does not have the full significance of the biblical content of the word. In the moral sphere, it had the idea of missing the right, of going wrong. In the classics, its predominating significance was that of the failure to attain in any field of endeavor. Brought over into the N.T., this idea of failing to attain an end, gives it the idea of missing the divinely appointed goal, a deviation from what is pleasing to God, doing what is opposed to God's will, perversion of what is upright, a misdeed. Thus the word *hamartia* means a missing of the goal conformable to and fixed by God. It is interesting to note that in Romans the word *dikaiosune* which means "conformity to the standard" appears as the opposite of *hamartia*, a missing of the standard set by God

(6:16-18). The noun *hamartia* is everywhere translated in the N.T., by the word "sin" except in II Cor. 11:7, where it is rendered "offence," since the context speaks of Paul's relations to the Corinthians. In Eph. 1:7, 2:5, Col. 2:13, the word "sins" is not *hamartia* but *paraptoma*. The verb of the same root is also translated by the word "sin" except in Mt. 18:15, Lk. 17:3, 4, (trespass); Acts 25:8 (offended), I Pet. 2:20 (for your faults, i.e., having sinned).

The second word is *hamartema*. This word differs from *hamartia* in that it "is never sin regarded as sinfulness, or as the act of sinning, but only sin contemplated in its separate outcomings and deeds of disobedience to a divine law."[33] It is found in Mk. 3:28, 4:12; Rom. 3:25; I Cor. 6:18.

The third word is *parakoe*. It means "a failing to hear, a hearing amiss," the idea of active disobedience which follows on this inattentive or careless hearing, being superinduced upon the word. The sin is regarded as already committed in the failing to listen when God is speaking. In the O.T., the act of refusing to listen to God is described as disobedience (Jer. 11:10, 35:17). In Acts 7:57 this is seen very clearly. *Parakoe* is found in Rom. 5:19; II Cor. 10:6, and Heb. 2:2, where it is translated by the word "disobedience" in each case. What a flood of light is thrown upon Adam's original sin. He was careless about listening to the commands of God, inattentive when God was speaking. Then followed the act of disobedience to the divine command. The lack of an earnest and honest attempt to know God's will in any instance, is sin. This carelessness or inattentiveness with respect to the will of God, has its roots in the desire to have one's own way, and to cover up that desire and the consequent wrongdoing by the excuse that one did not know His will in the particular instance.

The fourth word is *anomia*. The word is a compound of the word *nomos* (law) and the letter Alpha which makes the

---

33. *Trench.*

OF THE GREEK NEW TESTAMENT

whole word mean literally "no law." The word means "contempt or violation of law, lawlessness." It refers to the condition or deed of one who is acting contrary to the law. It is set over against the Greek word *dikaiosune* (righteousness) in II Cor. 6:14. That is, "what things does righteousness have in common with *anomia* (lawlessness)?" The word *dikaiosune* refers to a fixed and objective standard of life set up by God. Any deviation from that standard is an act contrary to law. The word is used in classical Greek writings, joined with *anarchia,* which is defined as "the state of a people without government, without lawful government, lawlessness, anarchy." The word is made up of *archos,* "a leader, a chief, a commander" and Alpha, the compound word meaning "without a leader or commander." Thus, anyone in a regularly constituted government who does not recognize and obey that government is *anarchos,* without law, an anarchist, thus, *anomia,* lawless. The word is used in the N.T., of one who acts contrary to law. The word *paranomia* refers to the act of one going beyond the limits which the law lays down. It is used only in II Pet. 2:16. *Anomia* is found in the following places where it is translated either "iniquity" or "the transgression of the law." *Mt.* 7:23, 13:41, 23:28, 24:12; *Rom.* 4:7, 6:19, *II Cor.* 6:14; *II Thes.* 2:7; *Tit.* 2:14; *Heb.* 1:9, 8:12, 10:17; *I John* 3:4.

The next word is *parabasis.* It comes from *parabaino* which means "to step on one side" thus, "to transgress, violate." It is translated by the word "transgression" in the N.T., except in Rom. 2:23 where the A.V., has "breaking" the law. Trench says of this word; "There must be something to transgress before there can be a transgression. There was sin between Adam and Moses, as was attested by the fact that there was death; but those between the law given in Paradise (Gen. 2:16, 17) and the law given from Sinai, sinning indeed, yet did not sin 'after the similitude of Adam's transgression' (*parabaseos* Rom. 5:14). With the law came for the first time the possibility of the transgression of law (Rom. 4:15). This word is found in Rom. 2:23, 4:15, 5:14; Gal. 3:19; I Tim 2:14; Heb. 2:2, 9:15.

Paraptoma is our next word. This word comes from *para pipto* which means "to fall beside" a person or thing. Thus *paraptoma* means "a fall beside, a lapse or deviation from truth and uprightness." Cremer defines the word as follows "a fault, a mistake, an offence, neglect, error." He says that "*Paraptoma* does not in Scripture as in profane Greek, imply palliation or excuse, . . . it denotes sin as a missing and viola tion of right . . . It may therefore be regarded as synonymous with *parabasis*, which designates sin as a transgression of known rule of life, and as involving guilt . . . Still the word is not quite as strong as *parabasis*, . . . See for instance Gal. 6: . . . where, though a sin involving guilt is clearly meant, missing of the mark, rather than a transgression of the law, is the form of sin referred to. We must accordingly affirm that *parabasis* denotes *sin objectively viewed*, as a violation of known rule of life, but that in *paraptoma* reference is special ly made to the subjective passivity and suffering of him who misses or falls short of the enjoined command; and the word has come to be used both of great and serious guilt, . . . and generally of all sin, even though unknown and unintentional (Ps. 19:13, Gal. 6:1), so far as this is simply a missing of the right, and involves but little guilt, therefore a *missing o failure* including the activity and passivity of the acting sub ject." In Gal. 6:1 we have the case of Christians who, having been the subjects of the ministry of the Holy Spirit, had in following the teaching of the Judaizers, put themselves there by under law, and thus had deprived themselves of the victory over sin which the Spirit had been giving them. They were trying their best in their own strength to live a life of victory over sin, and sin had taken them unawares. Sin had entered their experience before they knew it, for they were shorn o the victorious power which they previously had had. This is

paraptoma, a sin which was not on their part a conscious disobedience of the will of God, but an unintentional one committed through the inability to prevent it entering the life.
The word is found in the following places where it is translated "trespass, offence, fall, fault;" *Mt.* 6:14, 15, 18:35; *Mk.*
11:25, 26; *Rom.* 4:25, 5:15, 16, 17, 18, 20, 11:11, 12; *II Cor.*
5:19; *Gal.* 6:1; *Eph.* 1:7, 2:1, 5; *Col.* 2:13; *Jas.* 5:16.

The next word is *agnoema.* This word comes from *agnoeo,*
a verb meaning "to be ignorant, not to understand, to sin
through ignorance." Trench says of this word, "Sin is designated as an *agnoema* when it is desired to make excuses for it,
so far as there is room for such, to regard it in the mildest
possible light (see Acts 3:17). There is always an element of
ignorance in every human transgression, which constitutes
it human and not devilish; and which, while it does not take
away, yet so far mitigates the sinfulness of it, as to render
its forgiveness not indeed necessary, but possible. Thus compare the words of the Lord, 'Father, forgive them, for they
know not what they do' (Lk. 23:34), with those of St. Paul,
'I obtained mercy because I did it ignorantly, in unbelief'
(I Tim. 1:13)." Commenting on the usage of this word in
Heb. 10:26, the only place where it is used in the N.T., Trench
says, "There is therefore an eminent fitness in the employment of the word on the one occasion referred to already,
where it appears in the N.T. The *agnoemata,* or 'errors' of
the people, for which the High Priest offered sacrifice on the
great day of atonement, were not wilful transgressions, 'pre-
sumptious sins' (Ps. 19:13), committed against . . . conscience
and with a high hand against God; those who committed
such were cut off from the congregation; no provision having
been made in the Levitical constitution for the forgiveness of
such (Num. 15:30, 31), but they were sins growing out of the
weakness of the flesh, out of an imperfect insight into God's
law, out of heedlessness and lack of due circumspection (...

Lev. 4:13; compare 5:15-19; Num. 15:22-29), and afterwar(
looked back on with shame and regret."

Our last word is *hettema*. This word does not appear i
classical Greek. A briefer form of the word, *hetta* is used, an
is opposed to *nika* (victory). It means " a discomfiture,
worsting to victory." It is used twice in the N.T., in Ror
11:12 where it has the non-ethical sense of diminution, d
crease, and in I Cor. 6:7 where it has the ethical sense (
coming short of duty, a fault.

To summarize: Sin in the N.T., is regarded as the missir
of a mark or aim (*hamartia* or *hamartema*) ; the overpassir
or transgressing of a line (*parabasis*) ; the inattentiveness (
disobedience to a voice (*parakoe*) ; the falling alongside whe)
one should have stood upright (*paraptoma*) ; the doir
through ignorance of something wrong which one shoul
have known about (*agnoema*) ; the coming short of one's du
(*hettema*) ; and the non-observance of a law (*anomia*).

HUMILITY, MEEKNESS, GENTLENESS. We will tre:
these words together, for they are closely related to or
another.

The word "humility" is the translation of *tapeinophrosur*
which hereafter in this study will be designated by the abbr
viation *tap.,* because of its length. Trench says of this worc
"The work for which Christ's gospel came into the world w:
no less than to put down the mighty from their seat, and (
exalt the humble and meek. It was then only in accordan(
with this its mission that it should dethrone the heathe
virtue *megalopsuchia* (human magnanimity and great soule(
ness), and set up the despised Christian grace *tap.,* in i
room, stripping that of the honor it had unjustly assume(
delivering this from the dishonor which as unjustly had clu(
to it hitherto; and in this direction advancing so far that
Christian writer has called this last not merely a grace, bi
the casket or treasure house in which all other graces are co)

tained . . . And indeed not the grace only, but the very word *tap.*, is itself a fruit of the gospel; no Greek writer employed it before the Christian era, nor, apart from the influence of Christian writers, after."

The word usually used by pagan writers which is related to *tap.*, the New Testament word, was *tapeinos*. Speaking of the use of the latter by the Greek writers, Trench says: "The instances are few and exceptional in which *tapeinos* signifies anything for them which is not grovelling, slavish, and mean-spirited." He states that this word is associated in the Greek classics with such words as the following: *aneleutheros* (not free, illiberal, slavish, servile, niggardly, stingy), *agennes* (without illustrious birth, low-born, cowardly, mean), *katephes* (downcast). But he also shows that at times the word was used with a better meaning. It is linked by Plato with a word that speaks of certain ones who were honored. Demosthenes uses it to describe words that are also moderate, modest, and temperate. Xenophon sets it over against those who are described as holding themselves to be above others. Plutarch says that the purpose of divine punishment is that the soul may become wise, prudent (*tapeinos*), and fearful before the face of God. Following these latter examples of the good use of the word *tapeinos* in pagan literature, Trench has this to say: "Combined with these prophetic intimations of the honor which should one day be rendered even to the very words expressive of humility, it is very interesting to note that Aristotle himself has a vindication, and it only needs to receive its due extension to be a complete one, of the Christian *tap.* . . .

"Having confessed how hard it is for a man to be truly great-souled, for he will not allow any great-souledness which does not rest on corresponding realities of goodness and moral greatness, . . . he goes on to observe, though merely by the way and little conscious how far his words reach, that to think humbly of one's self, *where that humble estimate is the true*

one, cannot be imputed to any culpable meanness of spirit
it is rather the true *sophrosune* (good sense, prudence
sobriety, sensibleness). But if this be so (and who will deny
it?), then, seeing that for every man the humble estimate of
himself is the true one, Aristotle has herein unconsciously
vindicated *tap.,* as a grace in which every man ought to
abound; for that which he, even according to the standard
which he set up, confessed to be a *chalepon* (a difficult thing)
namely to be truly great-souled, the Christian, convinced by
the Spirit of God, and having in his Lord a standard of perfect righteousness before his eyes, knows to be not merely a
chalepon, but an *adunaton* (an impossibility). Such is the
Christian *tap.,* no mere modesty or absence of pretension
which is all that the heathen would at the very best have
found in it; nor yet a selfmade grace; and Chrysostom is in
fact bringing in pride again under the disguise of humility
when he characterizes it as a making of ourselves small, *when
we are great* . . . Far truer and deeper is St. Bernard's definition: 'the esteeming of ourselves small, inasmuch as we are
so; the thinking truly, and because truly, therefore lowlily, of
ourselves'.

"But it may be objected, how does this account of Christian *tap.,* as springing out of and resting on the sense of un-
worthiness, agree with the fact that the sinless Lord laid claim
to this grace, and said, 'I am meek and lowly in heart
(*tapeinos,* . . . Mt. 11:29)? The answer is, that for the sinner
tap., involves the confession of sin, inasmuch as it involves the
confession of his true condition; while yet for the unfallen
creature the grace itself as truly exists, involving for such the
acknowledgement not of *sinfulness,* which would be untrue,
but of *creatureliness,* of absolute dependence, of having
nothing, but receiving all things of God. And thus the grace
of humility belongs to the highest angel before the throne,
being as he is a creature, yea, even to the Lord of Glory Himself. In His human nature He must be the pattern of all

humility, of all creaturely dependence; and it is only *as a man* that Christ thus claims to be *tapeinos*: His human life was a constant living on the fulness of His Father's love; He evermore, as man, took the place which beseemed the creature in the presence of its Creator."

Cremer has a helpful note on *tapeinos*. "The word is used in profane Greek very often in a morally contemptible sense, namely, cringing, servile, low, common, . . . and it is a notable peculiarity of Scripture usage that the LXX., Apocrypha and N.T., know nothing of this import of the word, but rather, in connection with, deepen the conception, and raise the word to be the designation of the noblest and most necessary of all virtues, which in contrast with *hubris* (wanton violence arising from the pride of strength, insolence) in every form is still something quite different from the *sophrosune* (good sense, prudence, sobriety, sensibleness) which is opposed to *hubris* among the Greeks. It is the disposition of the man who esteems himself as small before God and men, takes a low estimate of himself, . . . a representation foreign to profane Greek, though a presentiment of this virtue is traceable there." Cremer says that the Greek expression for humility is found in the words *poiein ta dikaia sigei*. That translated would be, "to habitually do the just and righteous things in a quiet way unnoticed by others." Then he adds, "But it must not be overlooked that this subdued stillness of feeling was no more than *a part* of humility, and the expression by no means attained or sufficed for the biblical conception, especially as denoting humility manifested before God, which arises from the perception of sin, or is at least inseparably connected therewith (. . . Luke 18:14); of this the Greeks had no presentiment. Humility with the Greeks was in fact nothing higher than *modesty, unassuming diffidence.* . . . The Greek *tapeinos* is nothing more than an element of *sophrosune* (good sense, prudence, sobriety, sensibleness), and in direct contrast with the *tap.*, of Scripture, it is in no way opposed

to self-righteousness. But the other element in humility, Phil
2:3, "In lowliness of mind (*tap.*) let each esteem other better
than themselves," is opposed to the Greek conception of
dikaiosune (justice), which, while not self-seeking, is not the
least unselfish, but gives to everyone his own. Hence it is
clear why we find in the N.T., as a substantial designation of
humility, a new word, *tapeinophrosune*."

We have dwelt at considerable length upon the classical
use of the N.T., words which mean *humility*, in order to more
clearly define the content of meaning in the Christian use of
these words. We have used the classical usage as a dark background against which the N.T., usage shines more clearly.
We can well understand why the Greeks had no proper conception of humility. True humility is a product of the Holy
Spirit in the yielded believer. The only self-description that
ever fell from our Lord's lips was, "I am meek and lowly"
(*tapeinos* Mt. 11:29). Paul singles out this grace of humility
(*tap.*) as the keynote that explains the mind of Christ (Phil.
2:3). Peter speaks of humility (*tap.*) as that particular virtue
which makes all the other Christian graces what they should
be (I Pet. 5:5).

Thayer gives the following definition of *tap*: "the having
a humble opinion of one's self; a deep sense of one's (moral)
littleness; modesty, humility, lowliness of mind." For *tapeinos*
Thayer gives: "not rising far from the ground, lowly, of low
degree, lowly in spirit, humble."

The word *tapeinophrosune* occurs in Acts 20:19; Eph. 4:2;
Phil. 2:3; Col. 2:18, 23, 3:12; I Pet. 5:5, and is translated in
these places by the words "humility, lowliness of mind,
humbleness of mind." In Col. 2:18, 23, it is used of the
affected and ostentatious humility of the Gnostics. The word
tapeinos is found in *Mt.* 11:29; *Lk.* 1:52; *Rom.* 12:16; *II Cor.*
7:6, 10:1; *Jas.* 1:9, 4:6; *I Pet.* 5:5. It is translated "lowly, low
degree, low estate, cast down, base, humble." *Tapeinosis*, a
word of the same stem, occurs in *Lk.* 1:48; *Acts* 8:33, *Phil.*

:21; *Jas.* 1:10, where it is translated "low estate, humiliation, vile, made low." This word means "lowness, low estate," and is used metaphorically in the sense of spiritual abasement which leads one to perceive and lament his moral littleness and guilt, as in Jas. 1:10. The verb *tapeinoo* is found in *Mt.* 18:4, 23:12; *Lk.* 3:5, 14:11, 18:14; *II Cor.* 11:7, 12:21; *Phil.* 2:8, 4:12; *Jas.* 4:10; *I Pet.* 5:6. It means "to make low, bring low, to bring into a humble condition, to abase, to assign a lower rank or place to, to humble or abase one's self, to be ranked below others who are honored or rewarded, to have a modest opinion of one's self, to behave in an unassuming manner."

MEEKNESS. This word is the translation of *praotes.* Trench says of this Greek word: "The gospel of Christ did not rehabilitate *praotes* so entirely as it had done *tapeinophrosune,* but this, because the word did not need rehabilitation to the same extent. *Praotes* did not require to be transformed from a bad sense to a good, but only to be lifted up from a lower level of good to a higher. This indeed it did need; for no one can read Aristotle's portraiture of the *praos* and of *praotes* . . ., mentally comparing the heathen virtue with the Christian grace, and not feel that Revelation has given these words a depth, a richness, a fulness of significance which they were very far from possessing before. The great moralist of Greece set *praotes* as the *mesotes peri orges* (a mean or middle, a state between two extremes), between the two extremes, *orgilotes* (irascibility, the nature of a person who is easily provoked or inflamed to anger), and *aorgesia* (defective in the passion of anger, the nature of a person who lacks gall), with, however, so much leaning to the latter that it might very easily run into this defect; and he finds it worthy of praise, more because by it a man retains his own equanimity and composure, . . . than for any nobler reason. Neither does Plutarch's own graceful little essay, *"Peri*

Aorgesias" (Concerning Lack of Gall), rise anywhere to
loftier pitch than this, though we might have looked f
something higher from him. *Praotes* is opposed by Plato
agriotes (fierceness, cruelty) . . .; by Aristotle to *chalepot*
(roughness, ruggedness, harshness) . . .; by Plutarch or som
other under his name, to *apotomia* (severity) . . .; all indic
tions of a somewhat superficial meaning by them attached
the word.

"Those modern expositors who will not allow for the ne
forces at work in sacred Greek, who would fain restrict, fo
instance, the *praotes* of the N.T., to that sense which the wor
as employed by the best classical writers, would have born
deprive themselves and as many as accept their interpretatio
of much of the deeper teaching in Scripture. . . . The scriptura
praotes is not in a man's outward behavior only; nor yet i
his relations to his fellow-men; as little in his mere natura
disposition. Rather is it an inwrought grace of the soul; an
the exercises of it are first and chiefly towards God (Mt. 1
29; Jas. 1:21). It is that temper of spirit in which we accep
His dealings with us as good, and therefore without disputin
or resisting; and it is closely linked with *tapeinophrosune*
and follows directly upon it (Eph. 4:2; Col. 3:12; compar
Zeph. 3:12); because it is only the humble heart which is als
the meek; and which, as such, does not fight against God, an
more or less struggle and contend with Him.

"This meekness, however, being first of all a meekness be
fore God, is also such in the face of men, even of evil men
out of a sense that these, with the insults and injuries whic
they may inflict, are permitted and employed by Him for th
chastening and purifying of His elect. This was the root o
David's *praotes,* when Shimei cursed and flung stones at him—
the consideration, namely, that the Lord had bidden him (I
Sam. 16:11), that it was just for him to suffer these things
however unjustly the other might inflict them; and out o
like convictions all true Christian *praotes* must spring. H

that is meek indeed will know himself a sinner among sinners; — or, if there was One who could not know Himself such, yet He too bore the sinner's doom, and endured the contradiction of sinners (Lk. 9:35, 36; John 18:22, 23); and this knowledge of his own sin will teach him to endure meekly the provocations with which they may provoke him, and not to withdraw himself from the burdens which their sin may impose upon him (Gal. 6:1; II Tim. 2:25; Tit. 3:2).

"*Praotes,* then, or meekness, if more than mere gentleness of manner, if indeed the Christian grace of meekness of spirit, must rest on deeper foundations than its own, on those namely which *tapeinophrosune* has laid for it, and can only subsist while it continues to rest on these. It is a grace in advance of *tapeinophrosune,* not as more precious than it, but as presupposing it, and as being unable to exist without it."

Praotes is found in *I Cor.* 4:21; *II Cor.* 10:1; *Gal.* 5:23, 6:1; *Eph.* 4:2; *Col.* 3:12; *I Tim.* 6:11; *II Tim.* 2:25; *Tit.* 3:2. The adjective *praos* (meek) occurs in Mt. 11:29.

GENTLENESS. This is the translation of *epieikeia.* Trench has the following to say regarding this word: "*Tapeinophrosune* (humility) and e*pieikeia* (gentleness), though joined together by Clement of Rome . . ., are in their meanings too far apart to be fit subjects of synonymous discrimination; but *praotes* (meekness), which stands between, holds on to both. The attempt has just been made to seize its points of contact with *tapeinophrosune.* Without going over this ground anew, we may consider the relations to *epieikeia* in which it stands.

"The mere existence of such a word as *epieikeia* is itself a signal evidence of the high development of ethics among the Greeks. It expresses exactly that moderation which recognizes the impossibility cleaving to all formal law, of anticipating and providing for all cases that will emerge, and present themselves to it for decision; which, with this, recognizes

the danger that ever waits upon the assertion of *legal* right
lest they should be pushed into *moral* wrongs; . . . whicl
therefore, urges not its own rights to the uttermost, but, goin
back in part or in the whole from these, rectifies and redresse
the unjustices of justice. It is thus more truly just than stri
justice would have been . . . . He (Aristotle) sets th
akribodikaios (severely judging, extreme to mark whát
amiss), the man who stands up for the last tittle of his lega
rights, over against the *epieikes*. . . . This aspect of *epieikei*
namely, that it is a going back from the letter of right for th
better preserving of the spirit, must never be lost sight of . . .

"The archetype and pattern of this grace is found in Goo
All His goings back from the strictness of His rights as agains
men; all His allowance of their imperfect righteousness, an
giving of a value to that which, rigorously estimated, woul
have none; all His refusals to exact extreme penalties; . . . al
His keeping in mind whereof we are made, and measurin
His dealings with us thereby; all of these we may contemplat
as *epieikeia* upon His part; even as they demand in return th
same, one toward another, upon ours. Peter, when himsel
restored, must strengthen his brethren (Lk. 22:32). Th
greatly forgiven servant in the parable (Mt. 18:23), havin
known the *epieikeia* of his lord and king, is justly expectec
to show the same to his fellow servant. The word is ofter
joined with *philanthropia* (friendliness, humanity, benevo
lence, liberal conduct, liberality) ; . . . with *hemerotes* (gentle
ness, kindness) ; . . . with *makrothumia* (longsuffering, for
bearance) ; with *anexikakia* (forbearance) ; . . . often too witl
praotes."

The word *epieikeia* is defined by Thayer as follows: "mild
ness, gentleness, fairness, sweet reasonableness." It occurs ir
Acts 24:4 and II Cor. 10:1. *Epieikes*, a word of the same root
is defined by the same authority as follows: "seemly, suitable
equitable, fair, mild, gentle." It is found in *Phil.* 4:5; *I Tim*
3:3; *Tit.* 3:2; *Jas.* 3:17; *I Pet.* 2:18.

We now offer a brief summary of the treatment of the three words "humility," "meekness," and "gentleness," pointing out their meanings and the distinctions that exist between them.

Humility is not mere modesty or absence of pretension, nor is it a self-made grace such as making ourselves small when we are great, but it is the esteeming of ourselves small, inasmuch as we are so, the thinking truly, and because truly, therefore lowlily of ourselves.

Meekness is that temper of spirit in which we accept God's dealings with us as good, without disputing or resisting them. The meek man will not fight against God, and more or less struggle or contend with Him. Meekness is also shown towards our fellow-man who mistreats us, insults us, treats us with injustice, in that the one who is being injured endures patiently and without any spirit of retaliation the provocations that are imposed upon him. The meek man will not withdraw himself from the burdens which other men's sins may impose upon him.

Gentleness is that temper of spirit which expresses exactly that moderation which recognizes the impossibility cleaving to all formal law, of anticipating and providing for all cases that will emerge and present themselves for decision; which with this, recognizes the danger that ever waits upon the assertion of legal rights, lest they should be pushed into moral wrongs, which therefore urges not its own rights to the uttermost, but, going back in part or in the whole from these, rectifies and redresses the unjustices of justice. Gentleness exhibits itself in the act of treating others with mildness, fairness, and sweet reasonableness.

Humility has to do with one's estimate of one's self, *meekness* with one's attitude toward the dealings of God and man with respect to one's self, and *gentleness* with one's treatment of others.

ENVY. This is the translation of two Greek words, *zelos* and *phthonos*. Trench has the following to say about them: "These words are often joined together; they are so by St. Paul (Gal. 5:20, 21) (emulations *zelos*, envy *phthonos*); by Clement of Rome . . ., by Cyprian, . . . by classical writers as well, . . . and by others. Still, there are differences between them; and this first, that *zelos* is . . . used sometimes in a good (as John 2:17; Rom. 10:2; II Cor. 9:2), sometimes, and in Scripture oftener, in an evil sense (as Acts 5:17; Rom. 13:13; Gal. 5:20; Jas. 3:14), in which last place, to make quite clear what *zelos* is meant, it is qualified by the addition of *pikros* (bitter, harsh, virulent), and is linked with *eritheia* (a partisan and factious spirit which does not disdain low acts); while *phthonos*, incapable of good, is used always and only in an evil signification. When *zelos* is taken in good part, it signifies the honorable emulation, with the consequent imitation, of that which presents itself to the mind's eye as excellent. . . . South here, as always, expresses himself well: 'We ought by all means to note the difference between envy and emulation; which latter is a brave and a noble thing, and quite of another nature, as consisting only in a generous imitation of something excellent; and that such an imitation as scorns to fall short of its copy, but strives, if possible, to outdo it. The emulator is impatient of a superior, not by depressing or maligning another, but by perfecting himself, so that while that sottish thing envy sometimes fills the whole soul, as a great dull fog does the air; this, on the contrary, inspires it with new life and vigor, whets and stirs up all the powers of it to action. And surely that which does so (if we also abstract it from those heats and sharpnesses that sometimes by accident may attend it), must needs be in the same degree lawful and laudable too, that it is for a man to make himself as useful and accomplished as he can.' . . .

"By Aristotle *zelos* is employed exclusively in this nobler sense, as that active emulation which grieves, not that another as the good, but that itself has it not; and which, not pausing ere, seeks to supply the deficiencies which it finds in itself. From this point of view he contrasts it with envy . . . Compare the words of our English poet: 'Envy, to which the gnoble mind's a slave, is emulation in the learned and the brave.'

"But it is only too easy for this zeal and honorable rivalry o degenerate into a meaner passion; . . . those who *together* aim at the same object, who are thus competitors, being in danger of being enemies as well; . . . These degeneracies which wait so near upon emulation, and which sometimes cause the word itself to be used for that into which it degenerates ('pale and bloodless *emulation*,' Shakespeare), may assume two shapes: either that of the desire to make war upon the good which it beholds in another, and thus to trouble that good, and make it less; therefore we find *zelos* and *eris* (contention, strife, wrangling) continually joined together (Rom. 13:13; II Cor. 12:20; Gal. 5:20 . . .) . . . Where there is not vigor and energy enough to attempt the *making* of it less, there may be at least the *wishing* of it less; with such petty carping and fault-finding as it may dare to indulge in . . . *Phthonos* is the meaner sin, . . . being merely displeasure at another's good; . . . with the desire that this good or this felicity may be less; and this, quite apart from any hope that thereby its own will be more . . .; so that it is no wonder that Solomon long ago could describe it as 'the rottenness of the bones' (Prov. 14:30). He that is conscious of it is conscious of no impulse or longing to raise himself to the level of him whom he envies, but only to depress the envied to his own."

To summarize: Zelos in its good sense refers to that honorable emulation, with the consequent imitation, of that which presents itself to the mind's eye as excellent, an emulation which consists only in a generous imitation of something excellent, an imitation that scorns to fall short of its copy, but strives, if possible, to outdo it, the emulator being impatient of a superior, not by depressing or maligning another, but by perfecting himself, which inspires him with new life and vigor, and whets and stirs up all the powers of his being to action. Thayer gives the following meanings: "excitement of mind, ardor, fervor of spirit, zeal, ardor in embracing, pursuing, defending anything." *Zelos* is used in a good sense in *John* 2:17; *Rom.* 10:2; *II Cor.* 7:7, 11, 9:2, 11:2; *Phil.* 3:6; *Col.* 4:13; *Heb.* 10:27. The word is translated "zeal, fervent mind, jealousy, indignation."

Zelos in its evil sense refers to envy, the desire to make war upon the good which it beholds in another, and thus to trouble that good and make it less; or, where there is not vigor and energy enough to attempt the *making* of it less, there may be at least the *wishing* of it less; with such petty carping and fault-finding as it may dare to indulge. The word is used in its evil sense in Acts 5:17, 13:45; Rom. 13:13; I Cor. 3:3 12:20; Gal. 5:20; Jas. 3:14, 16. It is translated "indignation, envy, emulations."

Phthonos is displeasure at another's good, with the desire that this good or this felicity may be less, and this, quite apart from any hope that thereby its own will be more. It is used in *Mt.* 27:18; *Mk.* 15:10; *Rom.* 1:29; *Gal.* 5:21; *Phil.* 1:15; *I Tim.* 6:4; *Tit.* 3:3; *Jas.* 4:5; *I Pet.* 2:1. In each of these cases it is used in an evil sense except in Jas. 4:5, where the Holy Spirit who has been caused to take up His permanent abode in us, has a passionate desire to the point of envy (phthonos). The Holy Spirit is passionately desirous of controlling the believer so that He can perform His office-work of causing the saint to grow in the Christian life, and He is envious of any control which the evil nature may exert over the believer. He is displeased with the evil nature and the success it may have in controlling him, and passionately desires that this felicity of the evil nature may be less, and this, quite apart from any felicity He Himself might enjoy in controlling the Christian. Here is a divine envy entirely apart from sin, manifesting a holy hatred of sin, caring nothing for its own interests, but only that sin be put out of the believer's life.

REST. This is the single translation of two Greek words which speak of *rest* from two different points of view. These must be distinguished if the Bible student is to arrive at a full-orbed and clear interpretation of the passages in which each appears. Trench has the following on these words: "Our Version renders both these words by 'rest'; *anapausis* at Mt. 11:29, 12:43; and *anesis* at II Cor. 2:13, 7:5; II Thes. 1:7. No one can object to this; while yet, on a closer scrutiny, we perceive that they repose on different points of view. *Anapausis,* from *anapauo,* implies the pause or cessation from labor (Rev. 4:8); it is the constant word in the Septuagint for the rest of the Sabbath; thus Ex. 16:23, 31:15, 35:2, and often. *Anesis,* from *aniemi,* implies the relaxing or letting down of chords or strings, which have before been strained or drawn tight, its exact and literal antithesis being *epitasis* (a stretching) . . . thus Plato . . . 'in the tightening (*epitasis*) and slackening (*anesis*) of the strings! . . .' Plato has the same opposition between *anesin* and *spoude* (haste, speed); . . . while Plutarch sets *anesis* over against *stenochoria* (narrowness of space, a confined space), as a dwelling at large, instead of in a narrow and straight room; and St. Paul over against *thlipsis* (a pressure, oppression, affliction) (II Cor. 8:13), not willing that there should be 'ease' (*anesis*) to other Churches, and 'affliction' (*thlipsis*), that is from an excessive contribution, to the Corinthian. Used figuratively, it expresses what we, employing the same image, call the relaxation of morals (thus Athenaeus, 14:13: *akolasia* (licentiousness, intemperance, any excess or extravagance) *kai* (and) *anesis,* setting it over against *sophrosune* (good sense, sobriety, prudence).

"It will at once be perceived how excellently chosen *echein anesin* ("let him have liberty") at Acts 24:23 is, to express what St. Luke has in hand to record. Felix, taking now a more favorable view of Paul's case, commands the centurion who had him in charge, to *relax* the strictness of his imprisonment, to keep him rather under honorable arrest than in actual confinement; which partial *relaxation* of his bonds is exactly what this phrase implies. . . .

"The distinction, then, is obvious. When our Lord promises *anapausis* to the weary and heavy laden who come to Him (Mt. 11:18, 29), His promise is, that they shall cease from their toils; shall no longer spend their labor for that which satisfieth not. When St. Paul expresses his confidence that the Thessalonians, troubled now, should yet find *anesia* in the day of Christ (II Thes. 1:7), he anticipates for them, not so much cessation from labor, as relaxation of the chords of affliction, now so tightly drawn, strained and stretched to the uttermost. It is true that this promise and that at the heart are not two, but one; yet for all this they present the blessedness which Christ will impart to His own under different aspects, and by help of different images; and each word has its own fitness in the place where it is employed."

The noun *anapausis* is found in Mt. 11:29, 12:43; Lk. 11:24; Rev. 4:8, 14:11. The verb *anapauo,* which is of the same root, and which means, "to cause or permit one to cease from any movement or labor in order to recover and collect his strength, to give rest, refresh, to give one's self rest, to take rest," occurs in *Mt.* 11:28, 26:45; *Mk.* 6:31, 14:41; *Lk.* 12:19; *I Cor.* 16:18; *II Cor.* 7:13; *Phm.* 7, 20; *I Pet.* 4:14; *Rev.* 6:11, 14:13. There are illustrations of the use of these words in the papyri. Moulton and Milligan report the use of *anapausis* in the case of a man over 70 who pleads for "relief" (*anapausis*) from public duties; also in the case of veterans who have been released from military service for a five years' rest. They say that the essential idea of this word is that of a respite or *temporary* rest as a preparation for future toil. They report the use of the verb *anapauo* as a technical term of agriculture where a farmer rests his land by sowing light crops upon it.

The word *anesis* is found in Acts 24:23 (liberty); II Cor. 2:13, 7:5, 8:13; II Thes. 1:7.

CHASTENING, ADMONITION. These are the respective translations of *paideia* and *nouthesia*. Trench has the following to say about these two Greek words: "It is worth while to attempt a discrimination between these words, occurring as they do together at Eph. 6:14, and being often there either not distinguished at all, or distinguished erroneously.

"*Paideia* is one among the many words, into which revealed religion has put a deeper meaning than it knew of, till this took possession of it; the new wine by a wondrous process making new even the old vessel into which it was poured. For the Greek, *paideia* was simply 'education;' nor, in all the definitions of it which Plato gives, is there the slightest prophetic anticipation of the new force which it one day should obtain. But the deeper apprehension of those who learned that 'foolishness is bound in the heart' alike 'of a child' and of a man, while yet 'the rod of correction may drive it far from him' (Prov. 22:15), led them, in assuming the word, to bring into it a further thought. They felt and understood that all effectual instruction for the sinful children of men, includes and implies chastening, or, as we are accustomed to say, out of a sense of the same truth, 'correction.' There must be *epanorthosis* (a setting right, a correcting, a revisal, an improvement), or 'rectification' in it; which last word, occurring but once in the N.T., is there found in closest connection with *paideia* (II Tim. 3:16).

"Two definitions of *paideia* — the one by a great heathen philosopher, the other by a great Christian theologian, — may be profitably compared. This is Plato's: '*Paideia* is the drawing on and the leading towards the right word which has been spoken according to its usage' (author's translation). And this is that of Basil the Great: 'The *Paideia* is a certain help given to the soul, a painstaking, laborious oft repeated clearing out of the blemishes that come from wickedness" (author's translation)." It will be observed that the pagan Greek usage of *paideia* was limited to the education of the intellect, whereas when the word was taken over into the N.T., an additional content of meaning was poured into it, for in its Christian usage it refers to the education of the moral and spiritual part of the individual's life, and that, principally, in the eradication of sins, faults, and weaknesses present in the life.

Taking up the other word, *nouthesia,* Trench says; "*Nouthesia* . . . is more successfully rendered, 'admonition'; . . . It is the training by word — by the word of encouragement, when this is sufficient, but also by that of remonstrance, of reproof, of blame, where these may be required; as set over against the training by act and by discipline, which is *paideia.* . . . The distinctive feature of *nouthesia* is the training by word of mouth. . . .

"Relatively, then, and by comparison with *paideia, nouthesia* is the milder term; while yet its association with *paideia* teaches us that this too is a most needful element of Christian education; that the *paideia* without it would be very incomplete; even as, when years advance, and there is no longer a child, but a young man, to deal with, it must give place to, or rather be swallowed up in, the *nouthesia* altogether. And yet the *nouthesia* itself, where need is, will be earnest and severe enough; it is much more than a feeble Eli-remonstrance: 'Nay, my sons, for it is no good report that I hear (I Sam. 2:24)'; indeed, of Eli it is expressly recorded in respect of those sons *ouk enouthetei autous* (he did not admonish them) (3:13) ."

From Trench's discussion it is clear that the word *paideia,* translated "chastening" in the N.T., does not mean punishment. Nor does it mean merely instruction. Nor does it have for its primary purpose, growth in the Christian virtues. Its primary purpose is to rid the life of sins, faults, and weaknesses by corrective measures which God in His providence either sends or allows to come into the life.

Paideia is found in Eph. 6:4 in connection with *nouthesia*. Trench says that it should be rendered by the word "discipline" rather than by "nurture." The word "nurture" implies growth whereas *paideia* speaks of corrective measures designed to eliminate those things in the life that hinder growth. The same thing holds true in the case of II Tim. 3:16 where the word is rendered "instruction." In Heb. 12:5, 7, 8, 11, *paideia* is uniformly translated "chastening" and "chastisement."

The verb *paideuo* which has the same root as *paideia*, has its classical usage of "to chastise in the sense of punish" in Lk. 23:16, 22, and "to instruct" in Acts 7:22, 22:3, but in the following scriptures it refers to the corrective discipline of God's providential dealings with the believer, the purpose of which is to eliminate from the life those things which hinder Christian growth; *I Cor.* 11:32; *II Cor.* 6:9; *I Tim.* 1:20 (may learn); *Heb.* 12:6, 7, 10; *Rev.* 3:19. In *II Tim.* 2:25 and *Tit.* 2:12, *paideuo* refers to the discipline which the Word of God itself affords.

The word *nouthesia* is found only in I Cor. 10:11; Eph. 6:4, and Tit. 3:10, where it is rendered "admonition."

SERVANT. There are five Greeks word used in the N. T., that speak of one who renders service, the translation of which is not however uniformly given by the use of the single word "servant." They are *doulos, therapon, diakonos, oiketes,* and *huperetes.*

Doulos is the most common word. It designated one who was born into his condition of slavery, one bound to his master as his slave, one who was in a permanent relationship to his master, which relationship could only be broken by death, one whose will was swallowed up in the will of his master, one who served his master even to the extent that he disregarded his own interests. This word was used in the first

century world as a designation of a class of slaves that represented a most abject, servile condition. It is the word taken
over into the N.T., to designate a sinner as a slave (Rom.
6:17). It is also used to speak of a believer as a bondslave of
the Lord Jesus (Rom. 1:1). However, in this latter case the
servility and abjectness are not included in the meaning of
the word, but the fact that the Bible writers used it to describe
the Christian, shows that they desired to retain its connotation
of humbleness on the part of the slave. As bondslaves of the
Lord Jesus, we are to ever remember that we must serve Him
in all humility of mind. Using the various meanings of *doulos*,
the reader can see for himself how the classical usage of the
word is in exact accord with its doctrinal implications in the
N.T. For instance, a sinner is born into slavery to sin by his
physical birth, and into a loving servitude to the Lord Jesus
by his spiritual new-birth. *Doulos* is found in the following
places: *Mt.* 8:9, 10:24, 25, 13:27, 28, 18:23, 26, 27, 28, 32, 20:
27, 21:34, 35, 36, 22:3, 4, 6, 8, 10, 24:45, 46, 48, 50, 25:14, 19,
21, 23, 26, 30, 26:51; *Mk.* 10:44, 12:2, 4, 13:34; 14:47; *Lk.* 2:29,
7:2, 3, 8, 10, 12:37, 38, 43, 45, 46, 47, 14:17, 21, 22, 23, 15:22,
17:7, 9, 10, 19:13, 15, 17, 22, 20:10, 11, 22:50; *John* 4:51, 8:34,
35, 13:16, 15:15, 15:20, 18:10, 18, 26; *Acts* 2:18, 4:29, 16:
17; *Rom.* 1:1, 6:16, 17, 19, 20; *I Cor.* 7:21, 22, 23, 12:13; *II Cor.*
4:5; *Gal.* 1:10, 3:28, 4:1, 7; *Eph.* 6:5, 6, 8; *Phil.* 1:1, 2:7; *Col*
3:11, 22, 4:1, 12; *I Tim.* 6:1; *II Tim.* 2:24; *Tit.* 1:1, 2:9; *Phm.*
16, *Jas.* 1:1; *I Pet.* 2:16; *II Pet.* 1:1, 2:19; *Jude* 1; *Rev.* 1:1,
2:20, 6:15, 7:3, 10:7, 11:18, 13:16, 15:3, 19:2, 5, 18, 22:3, 6.
Doulos is translated in these passages by the words "servant,
bond, or bondman." The verb *douleuo* which has the same
root as *doulos*, having therefore the same implications, and
which means "to be a slave, to serve, to do service, to obey,
to submit to," in a good sense "to yield obedience to, to obey
one's commands and render to him the services due," is found
in *Acts* 7:6; *Rom.* 6:18, 22; *I Cor.* 7:15, 9:19; *Gal.* 4:3; *Tit.* 2:3;
II Pet. 2:19. It is translated either by the word "servant" or

"bondage," together with the accompanying verb, and in Tit. 2:3 by the word "given."

Our next word is *therapon*. Trench says of this word: "The *therapon* . . . is the performer of present services, with no respect to the fact whether as a freeman or slave he renders them; as bound by duty, or impelled by love; and thus, as will necessarily follow, there goes habitually with the word the sense of one whose services are tenderer, nobler, freer than those of the *doulos*. Thus Achilles styles Patroclus his *therapon* . . ., one whose service was not constrained, but the officious ministration of love; very much like that of the squire or page of the Middle Ages. In the verb *therapeuo* (to serve, do service, to heal, cure, restore to health), . . . as distinguished from *douleuo* . . ., the nobler and tenderer character of the service comes still more strongly out. It may be used of the physician's watchful tendance of the sick, man's service to God, and is beautifully applied by Xenophon . . . to the care which the gods have of men.

"It will follow that the author of the Epistle to the Hebrews, calling Moses a *therapon* in the house of God (3:5), implies that he occupied a more confidential position, that a freer service, a higher dignity was his, than that merely of a *doulos*, approaching more closely to that of an *oikonomos* (the manager of a household, a steward, a superintendent) in God's house; and, referring to Num. 12:6-8, we find, confirming this view, that an exceptional dignity is there ascribed to Moses, lifting him above other *doulos* of God . . . It would have been well if our Translators had seen some way to indicate the exceptional and more honorable title given to him who 'was faithful in all God's house'." *Therapon* occurs but once in the N.T., at Heb. 3:5.

The next word is *diakonos*. It is derived, Trench thinks, from the verb *dioko* meaning "to hasten after, to pursue." Trench in comparing this word with the two preceding, has the following to say; "The difference between *diakonos* on one side, and *doulos* and *therapon* on the other, is this—that *diakonos* represents the servant in his activity for the work; . . . not in his relation, either servile, as that of the *doulos,* or more voluntary, as in the case of the *therapon, to a person.* The attendants at a feast, and this with no respect to their condition as free or servile, are *diakonos* (John 2:5, Mt. 22: 13, compare John 12:2). The importance of preserving the distinction between *doulos* and *diakonos* may be illustrated from the parable of the Marriage Supper (Mt. 22:2-14). In our Version the king's 'servants' bring in the invited guests (v. 3, 4, 8, 10). and his 'servants' are bidden to cast out that guest who was without a wedding garment (v. 13); but in the Greek, those, the bringers-in of the guests, are *doulos*: these, the fulfillers of the king's sentence, are *diakonos*—this distinction being a most real one, and belonging to the essentials of the parable; the *doulos* being *men,* the ambassadors of Christ, who invite their fellowmen into His kingdom now, the *diakonos angels,* who in all the judgment acts at the end of the world evermore appear as the executors of the Lord's will."

Thus, *diakonos* represents the servant in his activity for the work he is to do. It speaks of one who executes the commands of another, especially of a master. The word is found in *Mt.* 20:26, 22:13, 23:11; *Mk.* 9:35, 10:43; *John* 2:5, 9, 12:26; *Rom.* 13:4, 15:8, 16:1; *I Cor.* 3:5; *II Cor.* 3:6, 6:4, 11:15, 23; *Gal.* 2:17; *Eph.* 3:7, 6:21; *Phil.* 1:1; *Col.* 1:7, 23, 25, 4:7; *I Thes.* 3:2; *I Tim.* 3:8, 12, 4:6.

Diakonos is translated in these places "minister, servant, deacon." The verb *diakoneo* which is from the same root and which means "to be a servant, attendant, domestic, to serve, to wait upon, to minister to one, to wait at table and offer food and drink to guests, to supply food and the necessaries of life, render ministering offices to, to minister a thing to one, to serve one with or by supplying anything," is found in *Mt.* 4:11, 8:15, 20:28, 25:44, 27:55; *Mk.* 1:13, 31, 10:45, 15:

41; *Lk.* 4:39, 8:3, 10:40, 12:37, 17:8, 22:26, 27; *John* 12:2, 26; *Acts* 6:2, 19:22; *Rom.* 15:25; *II Cor.* 3:3, 8:19, 20; *I Tim.* 3:10, 13; *II Tim.* 1:18; *Phm.* 13; *Heb.* 6:10; *I Pet.* 1:12, 4:10, 11. *Diakoneo* is translated in these places "minister, serve, administer."

The word *diakonia* which has the same root as *diakonos* and means "service, ministering," used especially of those who execute commands, is found in *Lk.* 10:40; *Acts* 1:17, 25, 6:1, 4, 11:29, 12:25, 20:24, 21:19; *Rom.* 11:13, 12:7, 15:31; *I Cor.* 12:5, 16:15; *II Cor.* 3:7, 8, 9, 4:1, 5:18, 6:3, 8:4, 9:1, 12, 13, 11:8; *Eph.* 4:12; *Col.* 4:17; *I Tim.* 1:12; *II Tim.* 4:5, 11; *Heb.* 1:14; *Rev.* 2:19. *Diakonia* is translated in these places "ministry, serving, ministration, office, administration, service."

Oiketes is the next word which we will treat. This word has the same root as the Greek word for "house" (*oikos*). It designates a house-servant, one holding closer relations to the family than other slaves. Trench says of this word; "*Oiketes* is often used as equivalent to *doulos*. It certainly is so in *I* Pet. 2:18; and hardly otherwise on the three remaining occasions on which it occurs in the N.T., (Lk. 16:13; Acts 10:7; Rom. 14:4); nor does the LXX (Ex. 21:27; Deut. 6:21; Prov. 17:2) appear to recognize any distinction between them; the Apocrypha as little (Eccl. 10:25). At the same time *oiketes* ('domesticus') does not bring out and emphasize the servile relation so strongly as *doulos* does; rather contemplates that relation from a point of view calculated to mitigate, and which actually did tend very much to mitigate, its extreme severity. He is one of the household, of the 'family', in the older sense of this word; not indeed necessarily one born in the house; *oikogenes* (born in the house, home-bred, said of a slave) is the word for this in the LXX (Gen. 14:14, Eccl. 2:7)."

Our last word is *huperetes*. Trench says of this word: "*Huperetes* . . . is a word drawn from military matters; he was originally a rower . . ., as distinguished from the soldier, on board a war-galley; then the performer of any strong and hard labor; then the subordinate official who waited to accomplish the behests of his superior, as the orderly who attends a commander in war . . .; the herald who carries solemn messages. . . . In this sense, as an inferior minister to perform certain defined functions for Paul and Barnabas, Mark was their *huperetes* (Acts 13:5) ; and in this official sense of lictor, apparitor, and the like, we find the word constantly, indeed predominantly used in the N.T. (Mt. 5:25; Lk. 4:20; John 7:32, 18:18; Acts 5:22). The mention by St. John of *doulos* and *huperetes* together (18:18) is alone sufficient to indicate that a difference is by him observed between them; from which difference it will follow that he who struck the Lord on the face (John 18:22) could not be, as some suggest, the same whose ear the Lord had just healed (Lk. 22:51), seeing that this was a *doulos,* that profane and petulant striker a *huperetes,* of the High Priest. The meanings of *diakonos* and *huperetes* are much more nearly allied; they do in fact continually run into one another, and there are innumerable occasions on which the words might be indifferently used; the more official character and functions of the *huperetes* is the point in which the distinction between them resides."

The word is found in the following places: *Mt.* 5:25, 26:58; *Mk.* 14:54, 65; *Lk.* 1:2, 4:20; *John* 7:32, 45, 46, 18:3, 12, 18, 22, 36, 19:6; *Acts* 5:22, 26, 13:5, 26:16; *I Cor.* 4:1. It is translated by the words "officer, servant, minister."

We will now place these words together in a brief summary, so that the reader can obtain a bird's-eye view of the same and thus see them more clearly by way of contrast.

Doulos, the most common word, and one that spoke of a slave in the most servile condition, is not a specialized word. The chief idea that it conveys is that the slave is bound to his master. He is in a condition of bondage. The word *doulos* comes from *deo* which means "to bind." A *doulos* was a person who was born into the condition of slavery, one who was in a permanent relationship to his master which only death could break, one whose will was swallowed up in the will of his master, one who served his master even to the extent that he disregarded his own interests.

Therapon lays the emphasis upon the fact that the person serving is a performer of present services, with no respect to the fact whether as a freeman or a slave he renders them, whether bound by duty or impelled by love. There goes habitually with the word the sense of one whose services are tenderer, nobler, freer than those of a *doulos*.

Diakonos speaks of the servant in his activity for the work, not in his relation, either servile, as that of a *doulos*, or more voluntary, as in the case of a *therapon*. The word speaks of one who executes the commands of another, especially, those of a master.

Oiketes designates a household slave, one holding closer relations to the family than other slaves. He is one of the household of the "family."

Huperetes emphasizes the official capacity of the servant. It designated the subordinate official who waited to accomplish the behests of his superior.

To narrow our definitions down even more, we could say that *doulos* is a slave in his servile relation to his master, *therapon*, a slave whose services are more tender, nobler, and freer, *diakonos*, a slave seen in his activity executing the commands of his master, *oiketes* a household slave, and *huperetes*, a slave holding a subordinate official position.

PROPHECY. This is the translation of the Greek word *propheteuo*. We cannot do better than quote Trench's comments on this word. His presentation is by way of contrast, showing the difference between *propheteuo* and *manteuomai*, both originally used in the pagan religions, the former taken over into the Christian system, the latter, because of its objectionable heathen features, rejected. Trench has the following to say: "*Propheteuo* is a word of constant occurrence in the N.T.; *manteuomai* occurs but once, namely at Acts 16:16; where, of the girl possessed with the 'spirit of divination,' or 'spirit of Apollo,' it is said that she 'brought her masters much gain by *soothsaying*' (*manteuomai*). The abstinence from the use of this word on all other occasions, and the use of it on this one, is very observable, furnishing a notable example of that religious instinct wherewith the inspired writers abstain from words, whose employment would tend to break down the distinction between heathenism and revealed religion. Thus *eudaimonia,* although from a heathen point of view a religious word, for it ascribes happiness to the favor of some deity, is yet never employed to express Christian blessedness; nor could it fitly have been employed, *daimon* (a god, goddess, used of individual gods), which supplies its base, involving polytheistic error. In like manner *arete* the standing word in heathen ethics for 'virtue,' is of very rarest occurrence in the N.T.; it is found but once in all the writings of St. Paul (Phil. 4:8); and where else (which is only in the Epistles of St. Peter), it is in quite different uses from those in which Aristotle employs it. In the same way *ethe*, which gives us 'ethics," occurs only on a single occasion, and, which indicates that its absence elsewhere is not accidental, this once is in a quotation from a heathen poet (I Cor. 15:33).

"In conformity with this same law of moral fitness in the admission and exclusion of words, we meet with *propheteuo* as the constant word in the N.T., to express the prophesying by the Spirit of God: while directly a sacred writer has need to make mention of the lying art of heathen divination, he employs this word no longer, but *manteuomai* (to divine, to deliver an oracle, to presage, forebode) in preference (cf. I Sam. 28:8; Deut. 18:10). What the essential difference between the two things, 'prophesying' and 'soothsaying,' . . . is, and why it was necessary to keep them distinct and apart by different terms used to designate the one and the other, we shall best understand when we have considered the etymology of one, at least, of the words. But first, it is almost needless at this day to warn against what was once a very common error, one in which many of the Fathers shared, . . . namely a taking of the *pro* in *propheteuo* and *prophetes* (prophet) as temporal, which it is not any more than in *prophasis* (a pretext), and finding as the primary meaning of the word, he who declares things *before* they come to pass. This *fore*telling or *fore*announcing may be, and often is, of the office of the prophet, but is not of the essence of that office; and this as little in sacred as in classical Greek. The *prophetes* (prophet) is the *out*speaker; he who speaks *out* the counsel of God with the clearness, energy and authority which spring from the consciousness of speaking in God's name, and having received a direct message from Him to deliver. Of course all this appears in weaker and indistincter form in classical Greek, the word never coming to its full rights until used of the prophets of the true God. . . . From signifying . . . the interpreter of the gods, or of God, the word abated a little of the dignity of its meaning, and *prophetes* (prophet) was no more than as interpreter in a more general sense; but still of the good and true. . . . But it needs not to follow further the history of the word, as it moves outside the circle of Revelation. Neither indeed does it fare otherwise within this circle. Of the *prophetes* (prophet) alike of the Old Testament and of the New we may with the same confidence affirm that he is not primarily, but only accidentally, one who foretells things future; being rather one who, having been taught of God, speaks out his will (Deut. 18:18; Isa. 1; Jer. 1; Ezek. 2; I Cor. 14:3).

"In *manteuomai* we are introduced into quite a different sphere of things. The word, connected with *mantis* (one who divines, a seer, a presager, a foreboder) is through it connected, as Plato has taught us, with *mania* (madness, frenzy) and *mainomai* (to rage, be furious, to be mad, to rave especially with anger). It will follow from this, that it contains a reference to the tumult of the mind, the *fury,* the temporary *madness,* under which those were, who were supposed to be possessed by the god, during the time that they delivered their oracles; this mantic fury of theirs displaying itself in the eyes rolling, the lips foaming, the hair flying, and in other tokens of a more than natural agitation. It is quite possible that these symptoms were sometimes produced, as no doubt they were often aggravated, in the seers, Pythonesses, Sibyls, and the like, by the inhalation of earth-vapours, or by other artificial excitements. . . . Yet no one who believes that real spiritual forces underlie all forms of idolatry, but will acknowledge that there was often much more in these manifestations than mere trickeries and frauds; no one with any insight into the awful mystery of the false religions of the world, but will see in these symptoms the result of an actual relation in which these persons stood to a spiritual world – a spiritual world, it is true, which was not above them, but beneath.

"Revelation, on the other hand, knows nothing of this mantic fury, except to condemn it. 'The spirits of the prophets are subject to the prophets' (I Cor. 14:32). But then he (namely, the prophet) is *lifted above,* not *set beside,* his everyday self. It is not discord and disorder, but a higher harmony and a diviner order, which are introduced into his soul; so that he is not as one overborne in the region of his lower life by forces stronger than his own, by an insurrection from beneath: but his spirit is lifted out of that region into a clearer atmosphere, a diviner day, than any in which at other times it is permitted him to breathe. All that he before had still remains his, only purged, exalted, quickened by a power higher than his own, but yet not alien to his own; for man is most truly man when he is most filled with the fulness of

God. Even within the sphere of heathenism itself, the superior dignity of the *prophetes* (prophet) to the *mantis* (one who divines, a seer, a presager, a foreboder) was recognized; and recognized on these very grounds. Thus there is a well-known passage in the Timaeus of Plato . . ., where exactly for this reason, that the *mantis* is one in whom all discourse of reason is suspended, who, as the word itself implies, more or less *rages*, the line is drawn broadly and distinctly between him and the *prophetes* (prophet), the former being subordinated to the latter, and his utterances only allowed to pass after they have received the seal and approbation of the other. . . . The truth which the best heathen philosophy had a glimpse of here, was permanently embodied by the Christian Church in the fact that, while it assumed the *propheteuo* (to prophecy) to itself, it relegated the *manteuomai* (to divine) to that heathenism which it was about to displace and overthrow."

The words "prophecy" (the noun), "prophecy" (the verb), and "prophet" are all the translations in the N.T., of the same Greek word which we have been studying, so that what is true of the verb *propheteuo* is true of the related nouns.

HEBREW (*Hebraios*), JEW (*Ioudaios*), ISRAELITE (*Israelites*). Trench offers a comparative study of these three titles which is most illuminating. He says: "All these names are used to designate members of the elect family and chosen race; but they are very capable, as they are very well worthy, of being discriminated.

"*Hebraios* (Hebrew) claims to be first considered. It brings us back to a period earlier than any when one, and very much earlier than any when the other, of the titles we compare with it, were, or could have been, in existence, . . . this title containing allusion to the *passing over* of Abraham from the other side of Euphrates; who was, therefore, in the language of the Phoenician tribes among whom he came, 'Abraham *the Hebrew,'* or *Ho perates* (the one who is from beyond) as it is well given in the Septuagint (Gen. 14:13), being from *beyond (peran)* the river. . . . The name, as thus explained, is not one by which the chosen people know themselves, but by which others know them; not one which they have taken, but which others have imposed on them; and we find the use of *Hebraios* through all the O.T., entirely consistent with this explanation of its origin. In every case it is either a title by which foreigners designate the chosen race (Gen. 39:14, 17; 41:12; Ex. 1:16, 19; I Sam. 4:6; 13:19; 29:3; Judith 12:11); or by which they designate themselves to foreigners (Gen. 40:15; Ex. 2:7; 3:18; 5:3; 9:1; Jon. 1:9); or by which they speak of themselves in tacit opposition to other nations (Gen. 43:32; Deut. 15:12; I Sam. 13:3; Jer. 34:9, 14); never, that is, without such national antagonism, either latent or expressed.

"When, however, the name *Ioudaios* (Jew) arose, as it did in the later periods of Jewish history (the precise epoch will be presently considered), *Hebraios* modified its meaning. Nothing is more frequent with words than to retire into narrower limits, occupying a part only of some domain whereof once they occupied the whole; when, through the coming up of some new term, they are no longer needed in all their former extent; and when at the same time, through the unfolding of some new relation, they may profitably lend themselves to the expressing of this new. It was exactly thus with *Hebraios*. In the N.T., that point of view external to the nation, which it once always implied, exists no longer; neither is every member of the chosen family an *Hebraios* now, but only those who, whether dwelling in Palestine or elsewhere, have retained the sacred Hebrew tongue as their native language; the true complement and antithesis to *Hebraios* being *Hellenistes,* a word first appearing in the N.T., . . . and there employed to designate a Jew of the Dispersion who has unlearned his proper language, and now speaks Greek, and reads or hears read in the synagogue the Scriptures in the Septuagint Version.

"This distinction first appears in Acts 6:1, and is probably intended in the two other passages, where *Hebraios* occurs (II Cor. 11:22; Phil. 3:5) ; as well as in the superscription, on whosoever authority it rests, of the Epistle to the Hebrews. It is important to keep in mind that in language, not in place of habitation, lay the point of difference between the 'Hebrew' and the 'Hellenist.' He was a 'Hebrew,' wherever domiciled, who retained the use of the language of his fathers. Thus St. Paul, though settled in Tarsus, a Greek city in Asia Minor, describes himself as a 'Hebrew,' and of 'Hebrew' parents, 'a Hebrew of Hebrews' (Phil. 3:5; cf. Acts 23:6) ; though it is certainly possible that by all this he may mean no more than in a general way to set an emphasis on his Judaism. Doubtless, the greater number of 'Hebrews' *were* resident in Palestine; yet not this fact, but the language they spoke, constituted them such.

"It will be well however to keep in mind that this distinction and opposition of *Hebraios* to *Hellenistes* as a distinction *within the nation,* and not between it and other nations (which is clear at Acts 6:1, and probably is intended at Phil. 3:5; II Cor. 11:22), is exclusively a Scriptural one, being hardly recognized by later Christian writers, not at all by Jewish and heathen. . . . Only this much of it is recognized, that *Hebraios,* though otherwise a much rarer word than *Ioudaios* (Jew), is always employed when it is intended to designate the people *on the side of their language.* This rule Jewish, heathen, and Christian writers alike observe, and we speak to the present day of the *Jewish* nation, but of the *Hebrew* tongue.

"This name *Ioudaios* (Jew) is of much later origin. It does not carry us back to the very birth and cradle of the chosen people, to the day when the Father of the faithful passed over the river, and entered on the land of inheritance; but keeps rather a lasting record of the period of national disruption and decline. It arose, and could only have arisen, with the separation of the tribes into the two rival kingdoms of Israel and Judah. Then, inasmuch as the ten tribes, though with worst right, . . . assumed Israel as a title to themselves, the two drew their designation from the more important of them, and of Judah came the name . . . *Ioudaios*. . . . We meet *Ioudaios*, or rather its Hebrew equivalent, in books of the sacred canon composed anterior to, or during, the Captivity, as a designation of those who pertained to the smaller section of the tribes, to the kingdom of Judah (II Kin. 16:6; Jer. 32:12; 34:9; 38:19); and not first in Ezra, Nehemiah, and Esther; however in these, and especially in Esther, it may be of far more frequent occurrence.

"It is easy to see how the name extended to the whole nation. When the ten tribes were carried into Assyria, and were absorbed and lost among the nations, that smaller section of the people which remained henceforth represented the whole; and thus it was only natural that *Ioudaios* should express, as it now came to do, not one of the kingdom of Judah as distinguished from that of Israel, but any member of the nation, a 'Jew' in this wider sense, as opposed to a Gentile. In fact, the word underwent a process exactly the converse of that which *Hebraios* had undergone. For *Hebraios*, belonging first to the whole nation, came afterwards to belong to a part only; while *Ioudaios*, designating at first only the member of a part, ended by designating the whole. It now, in its later, like *Hebraios* in its earlier, stage of meaning, was a a title by which the descendant of Abraham called himself, when he would bring out the national distinction between himself and other peoples (Rom. 2:9, 10); thus 'Jew and Gentile;' never '*Israelite* and Gentile:' or which others used about him, when they had in view this same fact; thus the Eastern Wise Men inquire, 'Where is He that is born King of the Jews' (Matt. 2:2)? testifying by the form of this question that they were themselves Gentiles, for they would certainly have asked for the King *of Israel*, had they meant to claim any nearer share in Him. So, too, the Roman soldiers and the Roman governor give to Jesus the mocking title, 'King of the Jews' (Matt. 27:29, 37), while his own countrymen, the high priests, challenge Him to prove by coming down from the cross that He is 'King *of Israel*' (Matt. 27:42).

"For indeed the absolute name, that which expressed the whole dignity and glory of a member of the theocratic nation, of the people in peculiar covenant with God, was *Israelites*. . . . This name was for the Jew his especial badge and title of honor. To be descendants of Abraham, this honor they must share with the Ishmaelites (Gen. 16:15); of Abraham and Isaac with the Edomites (Gen. 24:25); but none except themselves were the seed of Jacob, such as in this name of Israelite they were declared to be. Nor was this all, but more gloriously still, their descent was herein traced up to him, not as he was Jacob, but as he was Israel, who as a Prince had power with God and with men, and prevailed (Gen. 32:28). That this title was accounted the noblest, we have ample proof. Thus, as we have seen, when the ten tribes threw off their allegiance to the house of David, they claimed in their pride and pretension the name of 'the kingdom of *Israel*' for the new kingdom which they set up—the kingdom, as the name was intended to imply, in which the line of the promises, the true succession of the early patriarchs, ran. So, too, there is no nobler title with which the Lord can adorn Nathanael than that of 'an *Israelite* indeed' (John 1:47), one in whom all which that name involved might indeed be found. And when St. Peter, and again when St. Paul, would obtain a hearing from the men of their own nation, when therefore they address them with the name most welcome to their ears, *andres Israelitai* (men, Israelites) (Acts 2:22; 3:12; 13:16; cf. Rom. 9:4; Phil. 3:5; II Cor. 11:22) is still the language with which they seek to secure their good-will.

"When, then, we restrict ourselves to the employment in the N.T., of these three words, and to the distinctions proper to them there, we may say that *Hebraios* is a Hebrew-speaking as contrasted with a Greek-speaking, or Hellenizing, Jew (which last in our Version we have well called a 'Grecian,' as differenced from *Hellen,* a veritable 'Greek' or other Gentile) ; *Ioudaios* is a Jew in his national distinction from a Gentile; while *Israelites,* the augustest title of all, is a Jew as he is a member of the theocracy, and thus an heir of the promises. In the first is predominantly noted his language; in the second his nationality . . .; in the third his theocratic privileges and glorious vocation."

GRACE (*charis*), MERCY (*eleos*). Trench has the following to say about these important words; "There has often been occasion to observe the manner in which Greek words taken up into Christian use are glorified and transformed, seeming to have waited for this adoption of them, to come to their full rights, and to reveal all the depth and the riches of meaning which they contained, or might be made to contain. *Charis* is one of these. It is hardly too much to say that the Greek mind has in no word uttered itself and all that was at its heart more distinctly than in this; so that it will abundantly repay our pains to trace briefly the steps by which it came to its highest honors. *Charis* . . . is first of all that property in a thing which causes it to give joy to the hearers or beholders of it, . . . and then, seeing that to a Greek there was nothing so joy-inspiring as grace or beauty, it implied the presence of this. . . .

"But *charis* after a while came to signify not necessarily the grace or beauty of a thing, as a quality appertaining to it; but the gracious or beautiful thing, act, thought, speech, or person it might be, itself — the grace embodying and uttering itself, where there was room or call for this, in gracious out-comings toward such as might be its objects; not any longer 'favor' in the sense of beauty, but 'the favor'; for our word here a little helps us to trace the history of the Greek. . . . There is a further sense which the word obtained, namely the thankfulness which the favor calls out in return; this also frequent in the N.T., (Luke 17:9; Rom. 6:17; II Cor. 8:16; though with it, as we are only treating the word in its relations to *eleos*, (mercy) we have nothing to do. It is at that earlier point which we have just been fixing that *charis* waited for and obtained its highest consecration; not indeed to have its meaning changed, but to have that meaning ennobled, glorified, lifted up from the setting forth of an earthly to the setting forth of a heavenly benefit, from signifying the favor and grace and goodness of man to man, to setting forth the favor, grace and goodness of God to man, and thus, of necessity, of the worthy to the unworthy, of the holy to the sinful. . . . Such was a meaning to which it had never raised itself before, and this not even in the Greek Scriptures of the elder Covenant. . . .

"Already, it is true, if not there, yet in another quarter there were preparations for this glorification of meaning to which *charis* was destined. These lay in the fact that already in the ethical terminology of the Greek schools *charis* implied ever a favor freely done, without claim or expectation of return — the word being thus predisposed to receive its new emphasis, its religious, I may say its dogmatic, significance; to set forth the entire and absolute freeness of the lovingkindness of God to men. Thus Aristotle, defining *charis*, lays the whole stress on this very point, that it is conferred freely, with no expectation of return, and finding its only motive in the bounty and free-heartedness of the giver. . . . St. Paul sets *charis* and *erga* (works) over against one another in directest antithesis, showing that they mutually exclude one another, it being of the essence of whatever is owed to *charis* that it is unearned and unmerited. . . .

"But while *charis* has thus reference to the *sins* of men, and
is that glorious attribute of God which these sins call out and
display, his free *gift* in their forgiveness, *eleos* (mercy) has
special and immediate regard to the *misery* which is the con
sequence of these sins, being the tender sense of this misery
displaying itself in the effort, which only the continued per
verseness of man can hinder or defeat, to assuage and entirely
remove it. . . . Of *eleos* we have this definition in Aristotle
"Mercy is a certain grief at that which is seen to be evil
pernicious, and wretched, to meet with that which is un
worthy, that which he himself in fear expected that he might
suffer, or certain of his own" (author's translation). It will
be at once perceived that much will have here to be modified
and something removed, when we come to speak of the *eleos*
of God. Grief does not and cannot touch Him, in whose pres
ence is fulness of joy; He does not demand unworthy suffering, . . . which is the Stoic definition of *eleos* . . . to move
Him, seeing that absolutely unworthy suffering there is none
in a world of sinners; neither can He, who is lifted up above
all chance and change, contemplate, in beholding misery, the
possibility of being Himself involved in the same. . . . We
may say then that the *charis* of God, his free grace and gift,
displayed in the forgiveness of sins, is extended to men, as
they are *guilty*, his *eleos*, as they are *miserable*. The lower
creation may be, and is, the object of God's *eleos*, inasmuch
as the burden of man's curse has redounded also upon it (Job
38:41; Ps. 147:9; John 4:11; Rom. 8:20-23), but of his *charis*
man alone; he only needs, he only is capable of receiving it.

"In the Divine mind, and in the order of our salvation as
conceived therein, the *eleos* precedes the *charis*. God so *loved*
the world with a pitying love (herein was the *eleos*), that He
gave his only begotten Son (herein the *charis*), that the world
through Him might be saved (cf. Eph. 2:4; Luke 1:78, 79).
But in the order of the manifestation of God's purposes of
salvation the grace must go before the mercy, the *charis* must

go before and make way for the *eleos*. It is true that the same persons are the subjects of both, being at once the guilty and the miserable; yet the righteousness of God, which it is quite as necessary should be maintained as his love, demands that the guilt should be done away, before the misery can be assuaged; only the forgiven may be blessed. He must pardon, before He can heal; men must be justified before they can be sanctified. And as the righteousness of God absolutely and in itself requires this, so no less that righteousness as it has expressed itself in the moral constitution of man, linking as it there has done misery with guilt, and making the first the inseparable companion of the second. From this it follows that in each of the apostolic salutations where these words occur, *charis* precedes *eleos* (I Tim. 1:2; II Tim. 1:2; Tit. 1:4; II John 3) ; nor could this order have been reversed. *Charis* on the same grounds in the more usual Pauline salutations precedes *eirene* (peace) (I Cor. 1:3; II Cor. 1:2) ; and often."

The word *charis* is rendered by the word "grace" in its every occurrence in the N.T., except in the following places: It has its purely classical meaning of the thankfulness which a favor calls out, in *Lk.* 6:32, 33, 34, 17:9; *Rom.* 6:17; *I Cor.* 15:57; *II Cor.* 2:14, 8:16, 9:15; *I Tim.* 1:12; *II Tim.* 1:3 (thanks). In I Pet 2:19, 20 (thankworthy, acceptable) we have an interesting use of the word. It means there "an action which is beyond the ordinary course of what is expected, and is therefore commendable." What a descriptive characterization of Calvary. *Charis* is translated "favor" in Lk. 1:30, 2:52; Acts 7:10, 46. One of the classical usages of *charis* was that of the favor with which the Greek would regard anything that was beautiful. That feeling of favor which the Greek had for something beautiful, included the element of pleasure which he derived from its contemplation, of being pleasantly disposed to that thing, of having admiration for it. *Charis* is used again in its purely classical usage in Lk. 4:22, where it is translated "gracious," and where it speaks of words full of beauty, of the pleasing properties of the words of the Lord Jesus, words which excited wonder, admiration, joy. *Charis* is translated "pleasure" in Acts 24:27, 25:9, where it refers to what the Jews would have considered a gracious act toward them, one they did not deserve, an act beyond the ordinary course of what might be expected. The word *charis* is translated "liberality" in I Cor. 16:3, where it refers to the money gift which the Gentile Christians were sending to the Jewish Christians in Jerusalem. Surely, this gift from the natural standpoint was something beyond the ordinary course of what might be expected, and was therefore commendable. These Gentiles were former pagans with an antipathy towards the Jewish race. But the grace of God in them made them kindly disposed toward Jews whom they had never seen. *Charis* is translated "benefit" in II Cor. 1:15. Paul is speaking here about the spiritual benefits which the Corinthian Christians would receive from his teaching, should he come to them again. From the genius of the word *charis,* we would judge that the spiritual "benefit" they would receive, would be far in excess of what they deserved, and in character so rich that it would be received with great rejoicing. In Phm. 7, *charis* is translated "joy." Here we have another classical usage of the word. *Charis* is related to *chairo* which means "to rejoice, be glad, be delighted or pleased." Thus, the noun *charis* on occasion means "joy."

Cremer has some valuable material on *charis*. He says: "The import of this word has been in a peculiar manner determined and defined by the peculiar use of it in the N.T., and especially in the Pauline Epistles. We cannot affirm that its scriptural use seriously differs from or contradicts its meaning in the classics, for the elements of the conception expressed by it are only emphasized in a distinctive manner in Holy Scripture; but by this very means it has become quite a different word in N.T., Greek, so that we may say it depended upon Christianity to realize its full import, and to elevate it to its rightful sphere. It signifies in the N.T., what we designate *Gnade*, grace, a conception which was not expressed by *charis* in profane Greek, and which, indeed, the classics do not contain. It may be affirmed that this conception, to express which the Greek *charis* has been appropriated as a perfect synonym, — a conception in its distinctive compass quite different from the negative *to pardon, to remit,* — first appeared with, and was first introduced by, Christianity. . . . We may, perhaps, add that no language so fully and accurately presents a synonym for it as does Old High German 'ginada,' literally, 'a coming near,' or 'an inclining towards.' " . . . The English word *grace* corresponds fully with the German *Gnade.*

"Now *charis* . . . signifies a kind affectionate, pleasing nature, and inclining disposition either in person or thing. Objectively, and for the most part physically, it denotes personal gracefulness, a pleasing work, beauty of speech, . . . gracefulness, agreeableness. . . . Then subjectively it means an inclining towards, . . . courteous or gracious disposition, friendly willingness, both on the part of the giver and the receiver; in the former case, *kindness, favor;* in the latter, *thanks, respect,* homage; favor, kindness, inclination towards; the disposition as generally cherished and habitually manifested, and as shown in the bestowment of a favor or in a service of love to anyone. . . .

"But the word especially denotes God's grace and favor *towards mankind or to any individual,* which, as a free act, excludes merit, and is not hindered by guilt, but forgives sin; it thus stands out in contrast with *erga* (works), *nomos* (law), *hamartia* (sin). It is called grace as denoting the relation and conduct of God towards sinful man. . . .

"*Charis* has been distinctly appropriate in the N.T. to designate the relation and conduct of God towards sinful man as revealed in and through Christ, especially as an act of spontaneous favor, of favor wherein no mention can be made

of obligation. . . . This element of spontaneousness is no
prominent in the classical use of the word, though it is trace
able even here. . . . But in the N.T. this element is speciall
emphasized. . . . With the worthlessness of works in connectio
with grace we thus have the non-imputation and forgivenes
of sin, i.e., *apolutrosis* (a releasing effected by payment of a
ransom), and as a *third* element, the positive gift of *dikaiosi*
(righteousness), leading on to *zoe* (life). . . . Thus it mus
be recognized that the Greek word in its application attain
for the first time an application and sphere of use adequate
to its real meaning; previously it was like a worn-out coin. . . .

"It cannot be said, however, that the N.T. *charis* denotes
'a manifestation of grace' corresponding with the classical
signification, *an act of kindness or of favor.* The distinction
made between *charis* and *doron* (a gift) shows this, cf. Rom.
5:15, 'the grace of God and the gift by grace'. . . . So also
didonai charis (to give grace), in Scripture, must not be con-
founded with the same expression in profane Greek, where it
means *to perform an act of kindness;* in Scripture it signifies,
to give grace, to cause grace to be experienced. . . ."

Comparing *charis* with *eleos,* Cremer has the following:
"*Eleos,* though adopted into the N.T. treasury, leaves un-
touched an essential aspect of the scriptural or N.T. conception of grace, inasmuch as it is used to express *the divine
behavior towards wretchedness and misery, not towards sin.*
It is just this aspect — the relation of *grace* to sin — which
must not be overlooked; in this freeness of grace — the *spontaneous inclination* which does not lie in *eleos* — is for the
first time fully realized."

Charis is used in the N.T., of that spontaneous act of God
that came from the infinite love in His heart, in which He
stepped down from His judgment throne to take upon Himself the guilt and penalty of human sin, thus satisfying His
justice, maintaining His government, and making possible the
bestowal of salvation upon the sinner who receives it by faith

in the Lord Jesus Christ who became a Sin-offering for him on the Cross (Rom. 3:24).

Charis also refers to the salvation which God provides, which salvation includes justification, sanctification, and glorification (Tit. 2:11). In Rom. 3:24 it is justifying grace. In Eph. 1:2 it is sanctifying grace, the enabling grace of God in the operation of the Holy Spirit in the life of the yielded saint. See also II Cor. 12:9, 8:6, 7; Heb. 4:16, 12:28.

EMPTY (*kenos*), VAIN (*mataios*). Trench has the following on these words: "The first, *kenos*, is 'empty,' . . . the second, *mataios*, 'vain.' . . .In the first is characterized the hollowness, in the second the aimlessness, or, if we may use the word, the resultlessness, connected as it is with *maten* (in vain, idly, fruitlessly), of that to which this epithet is given. Thus *kenai elpides* are empty hopes, such as are built on no solid foundation; and in the N.T. *kenoi logoi* (Eph. 5:6; cf. Deut. 32:47; Ex. 5:9) are words which have no inner substance and kernel of truth, hollow sophistries and apologies for sin; *kenos kopos,* labor which yields no return (I Cor. 15:58); so *kenophoniai* (empty discussion, discussion of vain and empty matters) (I Tim. 6:20; II Tim. 2:16); . . . and *kenodoxia* (groundless self-esteem, empty pride) (Phil. 2:3). . . . St. Paul reminds the Thessalonians (I Thes. 2:1) that his entrance to them was not *kene* (empty, vain), not unaccompanied with the demonstration of Spirit and of power. When used not of things but of persons, *kenos* predicates not merely an absence and emptiness of good, but, since the moral nature of man endures no vacuum, the presence of evil. It is thus employed only once in the N.T., namely at Jas. 2:20, where the *kenos anthropos* (vain man) is one in whom the higher wisdom has found no entrance, but who is puffed up with a vain conceit of his own spiritual insight, *'aufgeblasen'* (puffed up), as Luther has it. . . .

"But if *kenos* thus expresses the emptiness of all which i
not filled with God, *mataios* (vain), as observed already, wil
express the aimlessness, the leading to no object or end, th
vanity, of all which has not Him, who is the only true objec
and end of any intelligent creature, for its scope. In thing
natural it is *mataios* (vain), as Gregory of Nyssa, in his firs
Homily on Ecclesiastes explains it, to build houses of sand o
the sea-shore, to chase the wind, to shoot at the stars, to pur
sue one's own shadow. . . . That toil is *mataios* (vain) which
can issue in nothing . . .; that grief is *mataios* (vain) fo
which no ground exists . . .; that is a *mataios euche* (a vair
prayer, entreaty, wish or vow) which in the very nature o
things cannot obtain its fulfilment . . .; the prophecies of the
false prophet, which God will not bring to pass, are *manteia
mataiai* (vain prophesyings) (Ezek. 13:6, 7, 8); so in the N.T
mataioi kai anopheleis zeteseis (Tit. 3:9) are idle and un
profitable questions whose discussion can lead to no advance
ment in true godliness; cf. *mataiologia* (I Tim. 1:6)
mataiologoi (Tit. 1:10), vain talkers, the talk of whose lip
can tend only to poverty, or to worse (Isa. 32:6:LXX)
mataioponia (Clement of Rome, 9), labor which in its very
nature is in vain.

"*Mataiotes* (what is devoid of truth and appropriateness
perverseness, depravity) is a word altogether strange to pro
fane Greek; one too to which the old heathen world, had i
possessed it, could never have imparted that depth of mean
ing which in Scripture it has obtained. For indeed that
heathen world was itself too deeply and hopelessly sunken in
'vanity' to be fully alive to the fact that it was sunken in it a
all; was committed so far as to have lost all power to pro
nounce that judgment upon itself which in this word is pro
nounced upon it. One must, in part at least, have been de
livered from the *mataiotes,* to be in a condition at all to
esteem it for what it truly is. When the Preacher exclaimed
'All is vanity' (Eccl. 1:2), it is clear that something in him

was *not* vanity, else he could never have arrived at this conclusion. . . . It is not too much to say that of one book in Scripture, I mean of course the book of The Preacher, it is the key-word. In that book *mataiotes,* or its Hebrew equivalent, . . . occurs nearly forty times; and this 'vanity,' after the preacher has counted and cast up the total good of man's life and labors apart from God, constitutes the zero at which the sum of all is rated by him. The false gods of heathendom are eminently *ta mataia* (the vain things) (Acts 14:15; cf. II Chron. 11:15; Jer. 10:15; John 2:8); the *mataiousthai* (the becoming vain) is ascribed to as many as become followers of these (Rom. 1:21; II Kin. 17:15; Jer. 2:5; 28:17, 18); inasmuch as they, following after vain things, become themselves *mataiophrones,* (3 Macc. 6:11), like the vain things which they follow (Wisd. 13:1; 14:21-31); their whole conversation vain (I Pet. 1:18), the *mataiotes* (the vanity) having reached to the very center and citadel of their moral being, to the *nous* (mind) itself (Eph. 4:17). Nor is this all; this *mataiotes,* or *douleia tes phthoras* (bondage of corruption) (Rom. 8: 21), for the phrases are convertible, of which the end is death, reaches to that entire creation which was made dependant on man; and which with a certain blind consciousness of this is ever reaching out after a deliverance, such as it is never able to grasp, seeing that the restitution of all other things can only follow on the previous restitution of man."

But let us look at this word *mataios* again. Our word "vain" today usually means pride. It is so used once in the N.T. Thayer gives us further light on this word. He says it means, "devoid of force, truth, success, result, useless, to no purpose." Moulton and Milligan quote a clause from the papyri which perfectly illustrates the use of the word *mataios*: "wherein he vainly relates that he was ignorant of the securities which had been given him." They gave an illustration of the use of *mataiotes*: "suggests either absence of purpose or failure to attain any true purpose." Thus, these words refer to an ineffectual effort to attain some end or to the inability of something to function with respect to the purpose for which it is in existence or is intended. A vain religion is one which fails to measure up to what that life should be.

Regarding the word *kenos*, Thayer says: "empty, vain, devoid of truth; used metaphorically of endeavors, labors, acts, which result in nothing, it means vain, fruitless, without effect." It means "in vain, to no purpose." Moulton and Milligan give examples of its use in the papyri: "having rifled the contents aforesaid he threw the empty box into my house." They say that when applied to men as in Jas. 2:20 it means "pretentious, hollow." They quote another clause illustrating its use, "so that you shall oblige me to no purpose."

The reader will observe that *kenos* and *mataios* are very close together in their meanings, and that sometimes they can be used indiscriminately. But at times the distinction which Trench makes, still holds, namely, that *kenos* expresses the emptiness of all which is not filled with God, whereas *mataios* expresses the aimlessness, the leading to no object or end, the "in-vain-ness" of all that has not Him for its scope.

Kenos is found in *Mk.* 12:3; *Lk.* 1:53, 20:10, 11; *Acts* 4:25; *I Cor.* 15:10, 14, 58; *II Cor.* 6:1; *Gal.* 2:2; *Eph.* 5:6; *Phil* 2:16; *Col.* 2:8; *I Thes.* 2:1, 3:5; *Jas.* 2:20. It is translated in these places by the words "empty, vain."

Mataios occurs in *Acts* 14:15; *I Cor.* 3:20, 15:17; *Tit.* 3:9; *Jas.* 1:26; *I Pet.* 1:18. *Mataiotes* is found in *Rom.* 8:20; *Eph.* 4:17; *II Pet.* 2:18. The words "vanity" and "vain" appear in the translation. *Maten* is found in Mt. 15:9; Mk. 7:7. The translation is "in vain."

ANOTHER. This is the translation of *allos* and *heteros*. Trench says; "*Allos* is the numerically distinct; thus Christ spoke we are told 'another' parable, and still 'another,' but each succeeding one being of the same character as those which He had spoken before (Matt. 13:23, 24, 31, 33), *allos*[34] therefore in every case. But *heteros*, . . . superadds the notion of qualitative difference. One is 'divers,' the other is 'diverse.' There are not a few passages in the N.T. whose right interpretation, or at any rate their full understanding, will depend on an accurate seizing of the distinction between these words. Thus Christ promises to his disciples that He will send, not *heteros*, but *allos*, *Parakleton* (John 14:16), 'another' Comforter therefore, similar to Himself. . . .

"But if in the *allos* there is a negation of identity, there is oftentimes much more in *heteros*, the negation namely, up to a certain point, of resemblance; the assertion not merely of distinctness but of difference. A few examples will illustrate this. Thus St. Paul says, 'I see another law' (*heteros nomos*), a law quite different from the law of the spirit of life, even a law of sin and death, 'working in my members' (Rom. 7:23). After Joseph's death 'another king arose' in Egypt (*heteros basileus*, Acts 7:18; cf. Ex. 1:8), one, it is generally supposed, of quite another dynasty, at all events of quite another spirit, from his who had invited the children of Israel into Egypt, and so hospitably entertained them there. The *heteros hodos* and *heteros kardia* which God promises that He will give to his people are a new way and a new heart (Jer. 39:39; cf. Deut. 29:22). It was not 'another spirit' only but a different (*heteros pneuma*) which was in Caleb, as distinguished from the other spies (Num. 14:24). In the parable of the Pounds the slothful servant is *heteros* (Luke 19:18). . . . The spirit that has been wandering through dry places, seeking rest in them in vain, takes 'seven other spirits' (*heteros pneuma*), worse than himself, of a deeper malignity, with whose aid to repossess the house which he has quitted for a while (Matt. 12:45). Those who are crucified with the Lord are *heteros*

---

34. The Greek student will observe that the writer has kept *allos* and *heteros* uniform without respect to their syntactical relations, for the benefit of the English reader.

duo, kakourgoi, 'two others, madefactors,' as it should be
pointed (Luke 23:32); it would be inconceivable and revolt-
ing so to confound Him and them as to speak of them as
allos duo. It is only too plain why St. Jude should speak of
heteros sarx (different kind of flesh v. 7), as that which the
wicked whom he is denouncing followed after (Gen. 19:5).
Christ appears to his disciples *en heteros morphe* (in a different form) (Mark 16:12), the word indicating the mighty
change which had passed upon Him at his resurrection, as by
anticipation at his Transfiguration, and there expressed in
the same way (Luke 9:29). It is *heteros cheilesin,* with altogether other and different lips, that God will speak to his
people in the New Covenant (I Cor. 14:21); even as the
tongues of Pentecost are *heteros glossai* (Acts 2:4), being
quite different in kind from any other speech of men. It
would be easy to multiply the passages where *heteros* could
not be exchanged at all, or could only be exchanged at a loss,
for *allos,* at Matt. 11:3; I Cor. 15:40; Gal. 1:6. Others too
there are where at first sight *allos* seems quite as fit or a fitter
word; where yet *heteros* retains its proper force. Thus at
Luke 22:65 the *heteros polla* are . . . blasphemous speeches
now of one kind, now of another; the Roman soldiers taunt-
ing the Lord now from their own point of view, as a pretender
to Caesar's throne; and now from the Jewish, as claiming to
be Son of God. At the same time it would be idle to look for
qualitative difference as intended in every case where *heteros*
is used; thus see Heb. 11:36, where it would be difficult to
trace anything of the kind. . . .

"What holds good of *heteros,* holds good also of the com-
pounds into which it enters, of which the N.T. contains three;
namely, *heteroglossos* (I Cor. 14:21), by which word the
Apostle intends to bring out the non-intelligibility of the
tongues to many in the Church; it is true indeed that we have
also *alloglossos* (Ezek. 3:6); *heterodidaskalein* (I Tim. 1:3),
to teach other things, and things alien to the faith; *hetero-*

zugein (II Cor. 6:14), to yoke with others, and those as little to be yoked with as the ox with the ass (Deut. 22:10). . . . So too we have in ecclesiastical Greek *heterodoxia*, which is not merely another opinion, but one which, in so far as it is another, is a worse, a departure from the faith. The same reappears in our own 'heterogeneous,' which is not merely of another kind, but of another and a worse kind. For this point deserves attention, and is illustrated by several of the examples already adduced; namely, that *heteros* is very constantly, not this other and different, *allos kai diaphoron*, only, but such with the farther subaudition, that whatever difference there is, it is for the worse. Thus Socrates is accused of introducing into Athens *heteros kaina daimonia* (different, evil, and new deities) ; *heteros daimon* is an evil or hostile deity; *heteros thusiai*, ill-omened sacrifices, such as bring back on their offerer not a blessing but a curse; *heteros demagogoi* are popular leaders not of a different only, but of a worse stamp and spirit than was Pericles. So too in the Septuagint other gods than the true are invariably *heteros theos* (Deut. 5:7; Judg. 10:13; Ezek. 42:18; and often). . . . A barbarous tongue is *heteros glossa* (Isa. 28:11) (a different kind of tongue) . . . .

"We may bring this distinction practically to bear on the interpretation of the N.T. There is only one way in which the fine distinction between *heteros* and *allos,* and the point which St. Paul makes as he sets the one over against the other at Gal. 1:6, 7, can be reproduced for the English reader. 'I marvel,' says the Apostle, 'that ye are so soon removed from them that called you into the grace of Christ unto *another* (*heteros*) Gospel, which is not *another*' (*allos*). Dean Alford for the first 'other' has substituted 'different'; for indeed that is what St. Paul intends to express, namely, his wonder that they should have so soon accepted a Gospel different in character and kind from that which they had already received, which therefore had no right to be called another Gospel, to assume this name, being in fact no Gospel at all; since there could not be two Gospels, varying the one from the other. . . .

"There are other passages in the N.T. where the student may profitably exercise himself with the enquiry why one of these words is used in preference to the other, or rather why both are used, the one alternating with, or giving partial place to, the other. Such are I Cor. 12:8-10; II Cor. 11:4; Acts 4:12."

In summing up the difference between these two words we offer the following: *Heteros* means "another of a different kind," *allos*, "another of the same kind." *Heteros* denotes qualitative difference, *allos*, numerical difference. *Heteros* distinguishes one of two. *Allos* adds one besides. Every *heteros* is an *allos*, but not every *allos* is a *heteros*. *Heteros* involves the idea of difference, while *allos* denotes simply distinction of individuals. *Heteros* sometimes refers not only to difference in kind but also speaks of the fact that the character of the thing is evil or bad. That is, the fact that something differs in kind from something else, makes that thing sometimes to be of an evil character.

As an illustration of the importance of noting the distinction between these words when studying the N.T., we note that *heteros* in Mt. 11:3 solves the problem as to why John the Baptist came to doubt the Messiahship of the Lord Jesus. His question was, "Art thou He that should come, or look we for another (Messiah) of a different kind?" The Messiahship of the Lord Jesus had been authenticated to John at the former's baptism in Jordan, when the Father's voice from heaven said, "This is my beloved Son, in whom I am well pleased" (Mt. 3:17). He had announced Him both as Messiah (Mt. 3:1-3), and as the Lamb of God (John 1:36), or, in other words, as the King of Israel and the Saviour. In his preaching, John had in addition to this announced Jesus as a Messiah of Judgment (Mt. 3:11-12). But our Lord's ministry until His final rejection by official Israel had been as a Messiah of mercy, one who healed the sick, raised the dead, and forgave sins. The Lord Jesus as Messiah did not fit the picture that John had painted. John knew that his message had come from God. And since Jesus did not fit that picture of a Messiah of judgment, he questioned His Messiahship, and asked if he should look for a Messiah of a different (*heteros*) kind. Had John been alive when Jesus gave Jerusalem and the nation Israel over to judgment, and turned from the city and nation that rejected Him, the picture he painted would have been realized.

Heteros is found in the following places: *Mt.* 6:24, 8:21, 11:3, 12:45, 15:30, 16:14; *Mk.* 16:12; *Lk.* 3:18, 4:43, 5:7, 6:6, 7:41, 8:3, 6, 7, 8, 9:29, 56, 59, 61, 10:1, 11:16, 26, 14:19, 20, 31, 16:7, 13, 18, 17:34, 35, 18:10, 19:20, 20:11, 22:58, 65, 23:32, 40; *John* 19:37; *Acts* 1:20, 2:4, 13, 40, 4:12, 7:18, 8:34, 12:17, 13:35, 15:35, 17:7, 21, 34, 19:39, 20:15, 23:6, 27:1, 3; *Rom.* 2:1, 21, 7:3, 4, 23, 8:39, 13:8, 9; *I Cor.* 3:4, 4:6, 6:1, 8:4, 10:24, 29, 12:9, 10, 14:17, 21, 15:40; *II Cor.* 8:8, 11:4; *Gal.* 1:6, 19, 6:4; *Eph.* 3:5; *Phil* 2:4; *I Tim.* 1:10; *II Tim.* 2:2; *Heb.* 5:6, 7:11, 13, 15, 11:36; *Jas.* 2:25, 4:12; *Jude* 7. It is translated by the words "other, another, some, altered, else, next, one, strange." For instance, in Lk. 8:6, it is, "some of a different kind fell upon a rock." In Acts 17:21, the Athenians spent their time in nothing else of a different nature, showing how obsessed they were with the quest for something newer (the comparative is used in the Greek text). The minute they learned something new, it was toyed with as a novelty for a short while, then flung over the shoulder, and the quest for something newer was commenced again. In Jude 7, the fallen angels went after strange flesh, that is, flesh of a different nature and order of being than theirs, human flesh. Study the other places listed, and see how much additional light is thrown upon the English text.

The other word *allos*, is found so often in the N.T., that we cannot list its occurrences here. The student can check with the list of places where *heteros* is found. If the scripture location is not found there, *allos* appears in the Greek text.

FIGHT. This and other English words to be noted later, is the translation of *agonizomai* and the noun of the same root *agon,* both of which speak of great intensity of purpose and effort.

Agonizomai was a term used in Greek athletics. It meant "to contend for victory in the public athletic games, to wrestle as in a prize contest, straining every nerve to the uttermost towards the goal." *Agon* is the noun which speaks of the conflict or contest itself. The first-century Roman world was acquainted with these Greek athletic terms, for the Greek stadium was a familiar sight, and the Greek athletic games were well known in the large cities of the Empire. The Bible writers seized upon these terms, and used them to illustrate in a most vivid manner, the intensity of purpose and activity that should characterize both Christian living and Christian service. The present day football game is a fair example of the terrific struggle for supremacy in the Greek athletic games that was commonly seen by the first-century stadium crowds. The point is that if we Christians would live our Christian lives and serve the Lord Jesus with the intensity of purpose and effort that is put forth in a football contest, what God-glorifying lives we would live.

Agonizomai is used in *Lk.* 13:24; *John* 18:36; *I Cor.* 9:25; *Col.* 1:29, 4:12; *I Tim.* 6:12; *II Tim.* 4:7. It is translated by the words "strive, fight, labor fervently." *Agon* is found in *Phil.* 1:30; *Col.* 2:1; *I Thes.* 2:2; *I Tim.* 6:12; *II Tim.* 4:7; *Heb.* 12:1. The English words do not give us any idea of the intensity of purpose and effort that is found in the Greek words. Study these passages in the light of the meaning of the Greek text.

The word *agonia* is used in Lk. 22:44 where we have the words, "And being in an agony He prayed more earnestly."

Agonia speaks of combat, giving prominence to the pain and labor of the conflict. It is used in classical Greek, of fear, the emotion of a wrestler before the contest begins. It is not the same as *phobos* (fear), but trembling and anxiety about the issue. It speaks not of the fear that shrinks and would flee, but the fear that trembles as to the issue, an emotion which spurs on to the uttermost. This agony of soul was our Lord's in Gethsemane.

Great Truths To Live By

Dedicated

To that noble band of men and women, members of the medical profession, who, sometimes at great personal risk, often with self-sacrifice, are faithfully ministering to our physical needs; with the hope that this volume will in some small measure minister to their spiritual needs. The author's particular gratitude is expressed to his physician, M. J. Latimer, M. D., his dentist, J. A. Larsen, D. D. S., and his oculist, J. W. Lowell, M. D., who through their ministrations have enabled him to serve the Lord Jesus in the ministry of the Word these many years. What would this poor, sick world do without its doctors and nurses?

PREFACE

We are living in tremendous times. The rapid succession of events and their character, are enough to strike terror into the heart of the bravest. It is to enable the individual today, to adjust himself to the present world situation, that this book has been written. In its pages, the reader will find truth to live by, truth that will enable him to move through the intricacies of present day life with the peace of God in his heart, and with a courage that will not flinch as the days grow darker, truth that will serve as an anchor of the soul, holding him steadfast amidst the wildest storms.   K. S. W.

CONTENTS

CONTENTS

JESUS OF NAZARETH — WHO IS HE?

You have heard various preachments on the subject. You have listened to the opinions of different individuals. Have you ever investigated the original sources yourself, and come to a definite conclusion about the matter?

Suppose you had access to first century Greek and Latin manuscripts, secular and sacred, which would inform you as to how the Roman world of that time regarded Jesus. Would you then care to do some personal investigation, and thus form your own judgment regarding His identity? There He stands astride the pages of human history, the unique individual of all time. In the following pages, the author has given you access to original sources. Will you accept his challenge and do some investigating for yourself?

1

Jesus of Nazareth — Who Is He?

A s to the fact that such a person as Jesus of Nazareth flourished in the first century A. D., there is hardly any dispute
today. Any person who takes the trouble to inquire into the
istorical sources, will experience no more strain upon his faith
that Jesus lived than that Julius Caesar did. One would expect,
rom our present standpoint of the tremendous impact Jesus has
ad upon almost 2000 years of history, that secular historians
f the first century would mention Him often in their writings.
But such is not the case. And we readily understand the reason for
his when we consider the following facts: He was born in an ob-
cure part of the Roman empire. The land of Palestine was far
istant from the hub of the universe, Rome, a province of the
Roman empire. Few secular historians would note the birth of a
rovincial, or details about his life. Again, He would not be, so
ar as the historians were concerned, a person of high birth, al-
hough His lineage was in the royal line of David. That dynasty
was not in power then, nor had it been for over 500 years. Why
hould an historian take note of a peasant of a province far remote
rom Rome? While His crucifixion marks Him out as a par-
icular individual today, yet from the standpoint of the first cen-
ury, it was a common event. The Roman roads were lined with
rosses upon which victims writhed in agony until death put an
nd to their struggles. Nor was His action of claiming deity for
Iimself, anything uncommon in the first century. The Roman
mperors claimed to be divine, and required their subjects to
worship them. Other officials (Herod, for example) deified them-
elves. Thus, the secular historians of the first century took little

notice of Jesus of Nazareth. We do have one Jewish historian an
some Roman historians who mention Him, however.

Josephus, the Jewish historian, born A. D. 37, whose worl
were accepted by the Imperial Library at Rome, has this to sa
about Him, writing in a context in which he mentions Pontiu
Pilate; "Now there was about this time, Jesus, a wise man, if
be lawful to call Him a man, for he was a doer of wonderful work
a teacher of such men as receive the truth with pleasure. He dre
over to him both many of the Jews and many of the Gentile
He was (the) Christ; and when Pilate, at the suggestion of th
principal men among us, had condemned him to the cross, thos
who loved him at the first did not forsake him, for he appeared t
them alive again the third day, as the divine prophets had foretol
these and ten thousand other wonderful things concerning him
and the tribe of Christians so named after him is not extinct a
this day" (*Antiquities of the Jews,* by Josephus, Book 18, chap
ter 3, paragraph 3).

Here we have testimony from a reliable historian of the fir
century, and a man who was not a Christian. He was a Jew
prejudiced against Christianity. His words, "The tribe of Chris
tians so named after him is not extinct at this day," are enoug
to stamp him as not belonging to the Christian community, fo
any Christian of the first century having the education an
standing of Josephus, would clearly have seen that Christianit
was indestructible. Nevertheless, Josephus, with the impartialit
and honesty of a true historian, reports things as he observe
them. He speaks of three supernatural facts about Jesus, Hi
deity, ("if it be lawful to call Him a man"), His miracles ("H
was a doer of marvellous works"), and His resurrection ("H
appeared to them alive again the third day"). It is perfectly pos
sible that Josephus believed these things to be true, and yet at th
same time rejected the claims of Jesus of Nazareth to his faith an
obedience. Or, rejecting the supernatural, he may have reporte
what in that day was generally believed about Him. It is a fac
that no first century historian ever denied the historicity of th
Gospel narratives. In addition to these things, Josephus reporte
the fact that Jesus was a wise man, a teacher, that His followin

as composed of individuals who welcomed the truth, that His isciples came from both the Jews and the Gentiles, that Pilate ondemned Him to the Cross, and that He was the Jewish Mesah (Christ). This last was quite an admission on the part of a ew in the first century who himself did not embrace the Chrisan Faith, for the Jewish nation was solidly opposed to the claims f Jesus to the Messiahship. It goes to show how impartially and onestly Josephus reported the facts of history. He speaks of the old Testament prophets predicting ten thousand things conerning Jesus of Nazareth, these prophecies proving that He was that He claimed to be, the Jewish Messiah, the Son of God, yes, od the Son, for the prophecies of the Old Testament were fulled in Him. A word needs to be said about the number of preictions in the Old Testament concerning Messiah. There are bout three hundred. The words "ten thousand" were used in the rst century to speak of a large number. Paul uses them twice, though ye have ten thousand instructors in Christ" (I Cor. :15), and "ten thousand words in an unknown tongue" (I Cor. 4:19).

In an attempt to break the force of this passage from Josephus, Liberalism claims that it was placed in his writings by the Chrisan Church to strengthen the argument for miracles. But as hakespeare says, "Aye, that would be scanned." Had such been he case, the Jewish nation would have been the first to accuse he Church with having done so. But nothing of the sort has appened. Professor Kirsopp Lake, D.D., Litt.D., a liberal of berals, of Harvard University, accepts this passage as authentic, hile rejecting other passages from Josephus. The late Professor ohn A. Scott, formerly of Northwestern University, quotes this assage in his book *We Would Know Jesus* as authentic. Proessor Scott received his Ph.D., from Johns Hopkins, his LL.D. rom Illinois College. He studied at Göttingen and Munich, Gerany, was instructor, assistant professor, and associate professor f Greek 1897-1901, professor 1901-1904, head professor 904-1923, and John C. Shaffer professor of Greek at Northvestern University from 1923 to his retirement some years ago. Ie was Councilor to the American School at Athens, Greece,

member of American Philological Society (ex-president), a
Classical Association Middle West and South (ex-president) a
Archaeological Institute of America. His book, *The Unity*
Homer, refuted once for all the higher critical theory that t
Homeric poems were the work of many authors. His book, *W*
Would Know Jesus, in which he states his belief in the inspirati
of the Bible, the virgin birth, deity, vicarious atonement, a
resurrection of Jesus of Nazareth, is written, not from the stan
point of a theologian, but from that of a classical Greek schola
The book demonstrates the fact that vast erudition can be coupl
with a simple faith in the Word of God and what it teaches. T
author of the present volume had the high privilege of studyi
under this intellectual giant in the classrooms of Northweste
University. He owes much to his character and influence.

Tacitus, a Roman historian, lived during the first century. H
high character as an historian is generally conceded. He wro
about Jesus of Nazareth in the following words, which are mo
informative concerning the attitude of the Roman empire towar
Jesus and Christianity. His words are: "But neither by hum
aid, nor by the costly largesses by which he attempted to pr
pitiate the gods, was the prince (Nero) able to remove from hi
self the infamy which had attached to him in the opinion of all, f
having ordered the conflagration. To suppress this rumour, ther
fore, Nero caused others to be accused, on whom he inflict
exquisite torments, who were already hated by the people for the
crimes, and were commonly called CHRISTIANS. This nan
they derived from CHRIST their leader, who in the reign
TIBERIUS was put to death as a criminal, while PONTIU
PILATE was procurator. This destructive superstition, repress
for a while, again broke out, and spread not only through Jud
where it originated, but reached this city also, into which flow a
things that are vile and abominable, and where they are e
couraged. At first, they only were seized who confessed that th
belonged to this sect, and afterwards, a vast multitude, by the i
formation of those who were condemned, not so much for t
crime of burning the city, as for hatred of the human race. Thes
clothed in the skins of wild beasts, were exposed to derison, a

were either torn to pieces by dogs, or were affixed to crosses; or
when the daylight was past, were set on fire, that they might serve
instead of lamps for the night."

Suetonius, another Roman historian who lived in the first century, but whose life extended into the second, and who is considered a well informed and correct historian, writes as follows:
"He (Claudius) banished the Jews from Rome who were continually raising disturbances, Christ (Chrestus) being their
leader." And in the life of Nero, he says, "Christians were punished, a sort of men of a new and magical religion."

Pliny the Younger, a distinguished philosopher, in a letter to
the emperor Trajan in the beginning of the second century, gives
us some pertinent facts concerning the wide influence of Jesus of
Nazareth. The letter is as follows: "Pliny, to the emperor Trajan,
wisheth health, etc. It is my custom, Sir, to refer all things to you
of which I entertain any doubt; for who can better direct me in
my hesitation or instruct my ignorance? I was never before present
at any of the trials of the Christians; so that I am ignorant both
of the matter to be inquired into, and of the nature of the punishment which should be inflicted, and to what length the investigation is to be extended. I have, moreover, been in great uncertainty
whether any difference ought to be made on account of age, between the young and tender, and the robust; also whether any
place should be allowed for repentance and pardon; or whether
those who have once been Christians should be punished, although
they have now ceased to be such, and whether punishment should
be inflicted merely on account of the name, where no crimes are
charged, or whether crimes connected with the name are the
proper object of punishment. This, however, is the method which
I have pursued in regard to those who were brought before me as
Christians. I interrogated them whether they were Christians;
and upon their confessing that they were, I put the question to
them a second, and a third time, threatening them with capital
punishment; and when they persisted in their confession, I ordered them to be led away to execution; for whatever might be the
nature of their crime, I could not doubt that perverseness and
inflexible obstinacy deserve to be punished. There were others,

addicted to the same insanity, whom, because they were Roman citizens, I have noted to be sent to the city. In a short space the crime diffusing itself, as is common, a great variety of cases have fallen under my cognizance. An anonymous libel was exhibited to me, containing the names of many persons who denied that they were Christians or ever had been: and as evidence of their sincerity, they joined me in an address to the gods, and to your image, which I had ordered to be brought along with the images of the gods for this very purpose. Moreover, they sacrificed with wine and frankincense, and blasphemed the name of Christ: none of which things can those who are really Christians be constrained to do. Therefore I judged it proper to dismiss them. Others, named by the informer, at first confessed themselves to be Christians, and afterwards denied it; and some asserted that although they had been Christians, they had ceased to be such for more than three years, and some as much as twenty years. All these worshipped your image and the statues of the gods, and execrated Christ. But they affirmed that this was the sum of their fault or error, that they were accustomed, on a stated day, to meet together before day, to sing a hymn to Christ in concert, as to a god, and to bind themselves by a solemn oath not to commit any wickedness — but on the contrary, to abstain from theft, robbery, and adultery — also, never to violate their promise, nor to deny a pledge committed to them. These things being performed, it was their custom to separate; and to meet again at a promiscuous, innocent meal; which however, they had omitted, from the time of the publication of my edict, by which according to your orders, I forbade assemblies of this sort. On receiving this account, I judged it to be more necessary to examine by torture, two females, who were called deaconesses. But I discovered nothing except a depraved and immoderate superstition. Whereupon, suspending further judicial proceedings, I have recourse to you for advice; for it has appeared to me that the subject is highly deserving of consideration, especially on account of the great number of persons whose lives are put into jeopardy. Many persons of all ages, sexes, and conditions are accused, and many more will be in the same situation; for the contagion of this superstition has not merely pervaded the cities, but also all villages and country places; yet it seems to me that it might be restrained and corrected. It is a matter of fact, that the temples which were almost deserted begin again to be frequented; and the sacred solemnities which had been long intermitted are again attended; and the victims for the altars are now readily sold, which, a while ago, were almost without purchasers. Whence it is easy to conjecture what a multitude of men might be reclaimed, if only the door to repentance was left open."

The reply of Trajan to Pliny is another testimony from a pagan source, to the tremendous influence of Jesus of Nazareth upon the life of the Roman empire. His letter reads: "Trajan to Pliny — Health and happiness. You have taken the right method, my Pliny, in dealing with those who have been brought before you as Christians; for it is impossible to establish any universal rule which will apply to all cases. They should not be sought after; but when they are brought before you and convicted, they must be punished. Nevertheless, if any one deny that he is a Christian, and confirm his assertion by his conduct; that is, by worshipping our gods, although he may be suspected of having been one in time past, let him obtain pardon on repentance. But in no case permit a libel against any one to be received, unless it be signed by the person who presents it, for that would be a dangerous precedent, and in no wise suitable to the present age."

We turn now from the pagan writers to the Greek manuscripts of the New Testament for further information concerning Jesus of Nazareth. These manuscripts are all dated, even by the critics themselves, in the first century. There was a time when the liberal school of criticism held that the New Testament manuscripts were written in the second century. But when an early fragment of the Gospel according to John was found, and experts proved by it that the New Testament was written in the first century, the critical school had to discard its theory. In our investigation into the character of Jesus of Nazareth, we are now using New Testament manuscripts, having treated the secular documents of the same date of writing. Since we regard the latter as dependable sources, is it too much to ask that we accord the same character to the former? Is there any reason that has to do with literary criticism, that would cause us to question their trustworthiness? Suppose we should find upon investigation that we have more reason to trust the authenticity of the New Testament records than those of classical Greece. Would that encourage you to accept these New Testament records at their face value?

Professor John A. Scott says in his book, *Luke, Greek Physician and Historian*, "There is one great advantage which the New Testament can claim over all the writings of classical Greece, and that is the age and excellent condition of its manuscripts. Homer probably lived not far from 1000 B.C., yet the oldest manuscripts now extant containing the Iliad and the Odyssey are hardly older than the tenth century of the Christian era. Hence we see that almost two thousand years intervene between Homer and the oldest complete manuscript of his works which we possess. Most of the poetry of Pindar, who died about 450 B.C., has been lost, but the oldest manuscript of the poetry which has survived was written very near the year 1150 A.D. In other words, there is an interval of about 1600 years between Pindar and the date of his oldest manuscript. Demosthenes died in 322 B.C., while the oldest manuscript of any complete oration which we have is hardly earlier than 900 A.D. Those selected are the ones of which we have especially old and reliable manuscripts. With the New Testament we are in another world, for we have two manuscripts which were certainly written before 340, perhaps as early as 325 A.D. The New Testament probably received its final form about 100 A.D. Hence we have manuscripts of the New Testament which are removed from the compilation of that book by little more than two centuries, while in the case of the greatest writers of Greece the average interval is more than eight times as great, or sixteen centuries. . . . Well-meaning Christians often say that we must take the Gospels on faith. It takes about as much faith for me to believe the Gospels as it does for me to believe the binomial theorem or the multiplication table. Where knowledge enters agnosticism flees. Indeed, the very word 'agnostic' is simple Greek for 'one who has no knowledge.' The word may be prophetic, or only an accident, but if an accident "tis an accident that heaven provides.' "

But we can push our research further back than this. In recent times, the Chester Beatty manuscripts have been discovered, which are dated between A.D., 200-300. The original manuscripts of the New Testament were still in existence A.D. 200, according to Tertullian, one of the Church Fathers. But we can go still further back and forge an unbroken chain to the original documents which left the pens of the Bible writers, in the Writings of the Apostolic and Church Fathers, which are commentaries based upon the New Testament manuscripts, and which contain the entire New Testament in quotations, with the exception of John 8:1-11 which was stricken out of some early texts because of a mistaken fear that its contents would encourage adultery. Thus, we have an unbroken link between our present day Greek printed texts and the original hand written manuscripts. The errors which crept in during 1500 years of copying by hand have been eliminated and a correct text formed, so that scholars tell us that 999 words out of every thousand in our present Greek text are the same as those of the original autographs, and that the thousandth word concerning which there may be some difference of opinion is of so little consequence, that it does not affect any historical fact or doctrine. We have as available source material 8,000 hand written copies of the Latin Vulgate, 2,000 manuscripts of the New Testament in other languages, and 4,000 Greek manuscripts of the New Testament, 14,000 available sources, as against a mere handful of manuscripts of the classical writers. With this preponderance of evidence for the historical trustworthiness and accuracy of the New Testament manuscripts, no informed person will doubt their authenticity upon the basis of literary criticism.

We shall begin with the testimony of John the Evangelist, and look first at the Gospel that bears his name. We shall confine ourselves to his Greek text, following the scientific procedure of basing our interpretations and translations upon the rules of Greek grammar and syntax, and governing our exegesis by the analysis and historical background of the passage in question.

John begins his testimony regarding Jesus of Nazareth with the statement, "In the beginning was the Word, and the Word was in fellowship with God, and the Word was as to its essence, deity" (John 1:1). John uses the Greek word *logos* as a designation of Jesus of Nazareth. *Logos* is from the root *leg,* appearing in *legō,* the primitive meaning of which is "to lay:" then, "to pick out, gather, pick up:" hence, "to gather or put words together," and so, "to speak." Hence *logos* is first of all, a collecting or collection both of things in the mind, and of words by which they are expressed. It therefore signifies both the outward form by which the inward thought is expressed, and the inward thought itself. As signifying the outward form, it is never used in the merely grammatical sense, as simply the name of a thing or act but means a word as the thing referred to, the material, not the formal part; a word as embodying a conception or idea. A *Logos* has the double meaning of thought and speech, so Jesus of Nazareth is related to God as the word to the idea, the word being not merely a name for the idea, but the idea itself expressed. The *Logos* of John is the real, personal God, the Word, who was originally before the creation with God, and was God, one in essence and nature, yet personally distinct; the revealer and interpreter of the hidden being of God; the reflection and visible image of God, and the organ of all His manifestations in the world. He made all things, proceeding personally from God for the accomplishment of the act of creation, and became man in the person of Jesus of Nazareth, accomplishing the redemption of the world (Vincent's Word Studies).

The writer to the Hebrews says, "God, who in many parts and in many ways spoke in time past to the fathers by means of the prophets, has in these last days spoken to us in the person of His Son" (1:1). In Old Testament times, God spoke through the prophets by means of spoken words. Now, He speaks to us in the person of His Son, Jesus of Nazareth, not only in the words He (Jesus) spoke, but in the kind of person He was, in the kind of life He lived on earth, in the vicarious death He died on the Cross, and in the victorious resurrection He Himself accomplished. Jesus of Nazareth is the Word of God in that He

deity told out. He said, "He that hath seen Me, hath seen the
ather" (John 14:9). That is, He is the visible revelation of
hat invisible deity is like. And only deity could clearly manifest
rth deity. This manifestation was through a human medium
order that it might be perceptible to human intelligences. And
at is the reason for the incarnation.

This Person, John says, was in the beginning. The context,
hich speaks of the act of creating the universe (v. 3), indicates
at this beginning refers to the beginning of the created universe.
he verb John uses, speaks of absolute existence as contrasted
an existence that has had a beginning in time. One is re-
inded of Jesus' statement, "Before Abraham came into exis-
nce, I am" (John 8:58). Since Jesus existed before all created
ings were brought into existence, He is uncreated. Since He
uncreated, He is eternal. Since He is eternal, He is God. He
the Person of the Godhead who is the revealer of what deity
like, God the Son proceeding by eternal generation from God
e Father in a birth that never took place because it always was.
hus, in John's first five words, we have the deity of Jesus of
azareth.

But that is not all. John goes on to say, "And the Word was
active communion with God." The definite article precedes
e word "God" here, pointing out the fact that it is God the
ather to whom reference is made. Here we have brought to
ur attention a fellowship which never had a beginning, which
as broken for those six awful hours in which Jesus hung on
e Cross, and which was resumed after the debt of human sin
as paid, never to be broken again. The picture in the Greek
ext is that of God the Son facing God the Father in a fellowship
etween two persons of the Godhead.

But John is not satisfied to let the matter of the deity of Jesus
f Nazareth rest there. He says, "And the Word was as to its
ssence, deity." The article is absent before the word "God" in
his instance. The absence of the article qualifies, shows nature,
ssence. Jesus of Nazareth possesses the same essence that God
e Father and God the Spirit possess, and that, eternally. He

is absolute God, Very God of Very God. Such is John's openin
testimony to the identity of Jesus of Nazareth.

After informing his readers who Jesus of Nazareth is, Joh
tells them what He did. He says, "All things through His inte
mediate agency came into existence, and without Him, the
came into existence not even one thing which stands existed
(1:3). The inspired writer teaches us three things here. Firs
matter is not eternal, but was brought into existence. Secon
Jesus of Nazareth was the intermediate agent in the Godhea
who brought matter into existence.   Third, matter is indestru
tible. John uses the aorist tense in his first two verbs, a tense
Greek which speaks merely of the fact of an action without refe
ring to details, but in his third use of the verb which speaks
matter coming into existence, he uses the perfect tense, whic
speaks of a past completed act having present results. That i
the existence of matter today, depends upon the original act
creation. The perfect tense often speaks of permanent result
It is so used in this instance. Jesus was the intermediate age
of creation. God the Father is the ultimate source, Jesus, th
Son, the Person of the Godhead charged with the work
bringing into existence a universe which had no existence befor

Not only is Jesus of Nazareth the Creator, John says, but "i
Him is life, and this life is the light of men" (1:4). The partic
ular Greek word used for life here is *zōē,* speaking of the lif
principle. Life begets life. All that has life in the univers
receives its life from one source, Jesus of Nazareth. But here i
life which had no antecedent source. It always was. When on
pushes the idea of an absolute, eternal God as far as a finit
mind can reach, one is staggered at the immensity of the though
The little boy asks, "Who made God?" One cannot hold one
mind very long on the thought of the eternal being of God. Her
is a wonderful Being, omnipotent, omnipresent, and omniscien
who always was. This God is Jesus of Nazareth. We are ac
customed to looking at Him as the Carpenter of Nazareth, th
Man Christ Jesus, the Teacher, the Healer, the travel-stained
weary, itinerant preacher. But that takes into consideration onl

3 years of His life on earth. He had an eternal existence before he shepherds found Him as a little helpless baby in a manger in Bethlehem. John, the Seer, is looking beyond that to His preincarnate work of creation.

This life, John says, "was the light of men. And the light is shining in the darkness, and the darkness did not overcome it" (1:4, 5). The light that Jesus is, was shining in the midst of the darkness of human sin. It is the pre-incarnate light of Jesus, seen through the created universe, to which John refers here. It is the light which God gave of Himself to man before the incarnation of deity in human flesh as seen in Jesus of Nazareth. The Authorized Version has: "And the darkness comprehended it not." That is, the human race, its reasoning faculties darkened by sin, did not comprehend or understand the revelation of God through the created universe. But that is far from the truth. The word John uses is *katalambanō*, made up of the verb *lambanō* "to take hold of so as to make one's own, to seize, to take possession of, to apprehend," and the prefixed preposition *kata,* the local meaning of which is "down," the compound verb therefore meaning, "to lay hold of and pull down," thus, "to overcome." The human race did comprehend the revelation of deity seen through the created universe, and, antagonistic to it, attempted to overcome it in the sense of barring it from its religious consciousness, substituting for it, gods of man's own creation.

Paul gives us this information in the words: "The wrath of God is revealed from heaven against all ungodliness and unrighteousness of men who are holding down (suppressing) the truth in unrighteousness, because that which may be known of God is plainly evident among them, for God made it clear to them, for the invisible things of Him since the creation of the universe, are clearly seen, being understood by means of the things which are made, namely, His eternal power and His divinity, resulting in their being without a defence, because knowing God, they did not glorify Him as God, neither were they thankful, but became futile in their reasonings, and their foolish heart was darkened. Professing themselves to be wise, they became fools, and exchanged the glory of the uncorruptible God for an image made

like corruptible man, and birds, and fourfooted beasts, a
creeping things" (Rom. 1:18-23). Paul says that man suppress
the truth. That means that the human race was in possession
the truth. The truth here is that of a divine Creator to who
worship and obedience should be given, this truth seen throu;
the created universe. Man, reasoning from the law of cause a
effect, which law requires an adequate cause for every effe
reasoned that such a tremendous and wonderful effect which tl
universe was, demanded a divine Being for its creator. This
the light which both John and Paul state, was shining in tl
midst of the darkness of human sin. John says that mankii
did not extinguish it. Paul says that the race suppressed it. Th
was the light of creation which pointed to Jesus of Nazareth, i
Creator.

After speaking of Jesus of Nazareth in His pre-existence wi
reference to the created universe and therefore His eternal exi
tence with the correlative of the possession of absolute deity, i
His act of speaking a universe into existence, and of the ligl
which that universe gave to the human race concerning H
eternal power and divinity, John enters upon a discussion (
His incarnation. He presents His forerunner, John the Baptis
As kings of the orient had heralds who preceded them as the
journeyed through their domains, so Jesus of Nazareth, a kir
from the royal line of David, had a herald who announced H
coming.

He introduces him in the words, "There came upon the scen
a man, sent as an ambassador from the presence of God, hi
name, John" (1:6). How is that for an example of simple, cor
cise, terse diction, written in eight words in this fisherman'
Greek! Where did he learn to write in such a succinct style? H
never saw the inside of a higher school of learning. After
brief education such as was given to Hebrew boys, he went int
business with his father, catching and selling fish. The onl
answer is that his literary style was given him by the Holy Spiri
as he was guided in the writing of the Gospel attributed to hin
First, John notes the historical manifestation, the emergenc
of the Baptist into the economy of the revelation of the light. I

as first, the light which the created universe gave concerning
ie creatorship and deity of Jesus of Nazareth. But now, a
ersonal revelation is to be made in the form of an incarnation,
eity taking upon itself through virgin birth, a human body and
utting itself under human limitations. But this coming of God
ie Son upon the human scene, was to be announced by a herald,
forerunner. The verb translated "sent" (A. V.) was used of
king sending a personal representative, an ambassador, on a
ommission to do something for him. John the Baptist was the
avoy of the King from heaven. He was sent literally "from
eside God," that is, from His presence. This gives the mes-
enger of Jesus more dignity and significance than if John had
ritten merely "sent by God." The Baptist came preaching to
srael from the presence of God. He was a rugged, heroic man's
aan. He had been living in the deserted regions about Jeru-
alem, alone with God, his food and clothing of the simplest kind.
Ie came from the presence of God with the touch of God upon
im, and the power of God in his message.

John states his mission in the words: "This one came as a
ritness, in order that he may bear testimony concerning the
ght, in order that all might believe through him. That one was
ot the light, but he came in order to bear testimony concerning
ie light."

Then John introduces the One concerning whom the Baptist
ears testimony, in the words: "He was the light, the genuine
ght which illuminates every man, as it comes into the world."
ohn's use of the word "genuine" indicates that whereas there
s a light that is genuine, namely, real, perfect, substantial, there
s also one that is counterfeit, false. Satan, a fallen angel, is an
ngel of light. He is a God-aping devil, copying everything that
iod is and does, within the reach of his ability. He has, Paul
ays, disguised himself as an angel of light, assuming a light
overing which does not come from nor does it represent what
ie is in his inner being. He thus masquerades as an angel of
ight, impersonating the absolute God against whom he has sin-
ied. Jesus of Nazareth was the genuine light previous to His
ncarnation, who through His creative work, illuminated every

man, as that light was shed abroad in the universe, teachin
every person that there was a God in heaven who created th
universe and who should be worshipped. John gives His positio
as such in the universe, in the words: "In the universe He wa<
and the universe through His intermediate agency came int
existence, and the world of lost humanity did not know Him.
The heathen know that there is a Supreme Being, and they knov
this by means of the light which the created universe affords
But they worship demons through fear, and do not know th
living God experientially. The Greek word John uses mean
just that.

But not only does the world of sinners fail to know the pre
incarnate *Logos* experientially, but it fails to receive Him whe
He becomes incarnate. John says: "He came into the midst o
His own things, and His own people did not take Him to thei
hearts" (1:11). Jesus of Nazareth, the omnipresent God in th
universe, yet centralized as to His throne and authority in heaven
is the performer of and the participant in a stupendous miracle
so stupendous that no human mind would naturally think of sucl
a thing or of its possibility. He wraps about Himself the physica
body of an infant and puts Himself under human limitations
He comes from outside of the universe, yet all the while immanent in it, and through the womb of a virgin, is born, and
then laid in a manger in the town of Bethlehem in Judaea. He
lives as a peasant in the town of Nazareth and works as a day-
laborer in the carpenter shop of Joseph, his legal, but not His
actual father. He has come to His own things, His own land of
Palestine, His own capital city, His own Davidic throne. He
offers Himself as Messiah to His own people, the Jews. And
His own people do not reach out and take Him to themselves. Instead, they reject Him, and hand Him over to the Roman authorities in order that He might be crucified.

"But" John says, "as many as did appropriate Him, He gave
to them a legal right to become born-ones of God, to those who
place their trust in His Name" (1:12). To appropriate Jesus of
Nazareth and to put one's trust in His Name, are one and the
same thing. The expression "The Name" is an Old Testament

expression speaking of all that God is in His majesty, glory, and power. "The Name" as it applies to Jesus of Nazareth includes all that He is in His glorious Person. He is absolute God and true Man who died on Calvary's Cross as a willing substitute for sinful man, paying for the human race the just penalty of human sin, thus allowing a righteous God to bestow mercy on the basis of justice satisfied, upon a sinner who puts his trust in Jesus. He is given a legal right to receive the mercy of God as he recognizes Jesus of Nazareth as the One who procured that legal right for him at the Cross. The sinner has no legal right to the mercy of God. The law which he broke is against him. But Jesus satisfied the just demands of that law which you and I violated, and thus makes it possible for us to receive God's mercy in salvation. One of these mercies, John mentions here, regeneration. The words "born-ones" are the translation of a Greek word whose root has in it the idea of birth. Justification, namely, the removal of the guilt and penalty of sin, and the bestowal of a positive righteousness, comes first. This is the legal right to which reference is made. Regeneration, or the impartation of divine life, is second in the economy of salvation. Thus, Jesus of Nazareth, is not only the Creator of the universe, but also the source of salvation.

And then John speaks of the incarnation again in the beautiful words, "And the Word became flesh and lived in a tent among us" (1:14). The A. V., has "The Word was made flesh." To make something is to take something and mold it into a new form, changing its shape. The first form disappears to have something that has a different form take its place. But nothing like that happened to Jesus of Nazareth. Absolute God in His pre-incarnate state, He remained such in His incarnation. He did not relinquish His deity upon becoming man. He was not *made* flesh. He *became* flesh. The Greek word is *ginomai,* and it is in a tense and a classification of that tense which speaks of entrance into a new condition. By becoming flesh John means that the invisible, eternal, omnipresent, omnipotent, and omniscient God added to Himself a human body and put Himself under human limitations, yet without human sin. While still deity and omnipresent, He became localized in a human body. While still deity and therefore omniscient, He lived the life of a human being on earth. He thought with a human brain. He became exhausted. He broke into tears. He needed food, clothing, and shelter. He gave us a picture of what Deity is like through the medium of a human life. He lived in a tent in the midst of humanity. That tent was His human body. Thus, Jesus of Nazareth is a Person having two natures. He is absolute deity. He is true Man. His deity did not add to His humanity. His humanity did not detract from His deity.

This combination of deity and humanity in one Person, Jesus of Nazareth, John speaks of again in the words: "Deity in its invisible essence no one has ever yet seen. God only begotten, the one who is constantly in the bosom of the Father, that One has fully explained God" (1:18). The words "God only begotten" refer to Jesus of Nazareth. He is God only begotten, proceeding by eternal generation as the Son of God from the Father in a birth that never took place because it always was This one, John says, fully explained Deity. The Greek word translated "fully explained" means literally "to lead out." Jesus in the incarnation led Deity out from back of the curtain of its invisibility, showing the human race in and through a human life, what God was like. Our word, "exegesis" is the transliteration of the Greek word here. The science of exegesis is that of fully explaining in detail the meaning of a passage of Scripture. In the incarnation, Jesus of Nazareth fully explained God so far as a human medium could explain the infinite, and human minds and hearts could receive that revelation. And He could do that only because He was God Himself. John has answered our question, "Jesus of Nazareth, Who is He?"

We turn to Paul for an answer to the same question. He calls Jesus of Nazareth "God" in Titus 2:13. The Authorized Version has, "The glorious appearing of the great God and our Saviour Jesus Christ." One could gather from this wording that Paul is speaking of two individuals, God and Jesus of Nazareth, and one could maintain that the former was deity and the latter a man. But an examination of the Greek text discloses the fact that we have the deity of our Lord brought out in the translation, "the appearing of the glory of our great God and Saviour Jesus Christ." The translator finds that the text follows a rule in Greek syntax called Granville Sharp's rule, which is stated as follows: "When the Greek word *kai* (and) connects two nouns of the same case, if the article precedes the first noun and is not repeated before the second noun, the latter always relates to the same person that is expressed or described by the first noun; i.e., it denotes a farther description of the first-named person" (Dana and Mantey, *A Manual Grammar of the Greek New Testament,* p. 147). The expression in the Greek text conforms to this rule. Here Paul, the scholar, educated in the foremost Greek university of his time, the University of Tarsus, where he received his Greek training, and in the theological school in Jerusalem headed up by Gamaliel, where he received his training in the Old Testament, teaches that Jesus of Nazareth is deity. Peter, the fisherman, in his second epistle (1:1) has the same expression in his Greek text, "through the righteousness of our God and Saviour Jesus Christ." It is clear that Jesus of Nazareth was worshipped as God by the first century Church. The use of the pronoun "our" is polemic. The citizens of the Roman empire looked upon Caesar as their god. There were two cults in the empire at that time, the Cult of the Caesar, which was the state religion of the Roman empire, in which the emperor was worshipped as a god, and the Cult of Christ, Christianity, in which Jesus of Nazareth was worshipped as God. The people of Syrian Antioch, who had a reputation for coining nicknames, gave the name "Christian" to the disciples of Jesus of Nazareth. It was a term of derision and contempt. They were proud worshippers of Caesar. Agrippa said to Paul, "With but little persuasion, you would make me a Christian" (Acts 26:28).

It was a common practice in the Roman world to deify rulers. But Jesus of Nazareth must have been something more than a man, and His followers must have been convinced of that fact, for they willingly suffered a horrible martyrdom for their testimony to His deity. Thousands upon thousands of people do not go to a violent death for something they know is a fraud. One

cannot explain the willing acceptance of Jesus of Nazareth a
Saviour by a sin-loving pagan who accepted with Him that which
he formerly hated, namely, righteousness, and by that forsool
his sin which he loved, knowing that by so doing he would be
liable to capital punishment for his act, except upon the basis o
a supernatural working in his heart, providing for the willing ac
ceptance of that which he formerly hated, righteousness. Jesu,
of Nazareth therefore stands as history's outstanding enigma
unless He is accorded the place which the Bible gives Him, Very
God of Very God. One cannot explain Him without this fact o
His deity. One can dismiss Him with an "I do not believe that,"
but that does not solve the problem nor blot Him from the page:
of history. He stands there, astride the world of mankind, a
unique individual, God and Man in one Person.

The great apostle in Colossians 2:9 recognizes these two natures, deity and humanity, residing in the Person of Jesus of
Nazareth. He says, "In Him dwelleth all the fullness of the Godhead bodily" (A.V.). The Greek word which Paul uses and
which is translated "Godhead," needs some study. The word
"Godhead" is found three times in the above mentioned version
Romans 1:20; Acts 17:29, and Colossians 2:9. But it is the
translation of two different words. In the first two instances,
Paul uses *theiotēs,* in the last named, *theotēs.* In *theiotēs,* Trench[1]
says that "Paul is declaring how much of God may be known
from the revelation of Himself which He has made in nature . .
yet it is not the personal God whom any man may learn to know
by these aids: He can only be known by the revelation of Himself in His Son; but only His divine attributes, His majesty and
glory." But when Paul is speaking of Jesus of Nazareth, he uses
theotēs. Here, Trench says, "Paul is declaring that in the Son
there dwells all the fullness of absolute Godhead: they were no
mere rays of divine glory which gilded Him, lighting up His
Person for a season and with splendor not His own: but He was,
and is, absolute and perfect God." Paul, speaking of Jesus of
Nazareth in His incarnation, says: "In Him there is at home,

---

1. *Synonyms of the New Testament* R. C. Trench

ermanently, all the fullness of absolute deity in bodily fashion."
hat is, in the human body of Jesus of Nazareth, there resided
ermanently at home, all that goes to make deity what it is. It
as absolute deity clothed with a human body.

Finally, we will look at Paul's great, classic Christological
assage in Philippians 2:5-11. The Greek text literally leaps
: one in the words: "Let this mind be in you which was also
 Christ Jesus, who subsisting permanently in that state of being
 which He gives outward expression of the essence of deity,
aat outward expression coming from and being truly representa-
ve of His inner being, did not consider it a prize to be clutched,
ie being on an equality with deity (in the expression of the
ivine essence), but emptied Himself, having taken the outward
xpression of a bondslave, that expression coming from and being
uly representative of His inner being, having become in the
keness of man. And having been found in outward guise as
ian, He humbled Himself, having become obedient to the extent
f death, even such a death as that upon a cross: on which ac-
ount also God supereminently exalted Him, and in grace gave
Iim THE NAME which is above every name, to the end that
 the NAME which Jesus possesses, every knee should bow, of
iose in heaven and those upon the earth, and those under the
arth, and that every tongue should openly confess that Jesus
'hrist is Lord to the glory of God the Father."

See the statements Paul makes here concerning Jesus of
Jazareth. Jesus gives outward expression in His preincarnate
tate of the essence of deity, that expression necessitating the pos-
ession of deity. He claims equality with deity in the expression
f the divine essence. He empties Himself of self, setting aside
Iis desire to be worshipped. the legitimate desire of deity, in
rder to come to earth, take upon Himself the outward expression
f a bondslave, and go to the Cross for guilty sinners, paying
he penalty for their sins, satisfying the just demands of God's
aw, thus making a way whereby a righteous God can bestow
Iis grace upon believing sinners, yet on the basis of justice
atisfied.

But that is not all. Not only did the followers of Jesus worsh
Him as absolute deity, but He Himself claimed deity for Hi
self. As such, He stands alone among all the founders of t
great religions, none of whom claimed deity for himself.

Mohammed never claimed deity for himself. He called hims
a prophet. Mohammedanism has now approximately 200,000,0
followers. One might argue from this that this religion must
of divine origin. But as we examine into the sources of its grow
we discover that they were all natural. The religion was fi
spread by force of arms. It is easy to understand that a sin-lovi
pagan would readily embrace a new religion to save his life.
was spread by fanaticism and an appeal to fallen human natu
Every Moslem was taught to believe that if he died fighting t
"infidels," he was translated immediately into Paradise, whe
he would enjoy all kinds of sensual rewards. "The sword
said Mohammed, "is the key to heaven and to hell. A drop
blood shed in the cause of Allah, a night spent in arms, is of mo
avail than two months of fasting and prayer. Whoever falls
battle, his sins are forgiven, and at the day of judgment, l
limbs shall be supplied by the wings of angels and cherubim
The religion required no regeneration. Its worship consisted
external rites. The conscience was not touched. The person w
allowed to go on in his sin, just as long as he observed certa
outward rules. Man is incurably religious.   He demands t
exercises of religion. Mohammedanism satisfies this longing a
at the same time, allows its devotees to go on in the way of li
which they love. The chief reason for the outstanding success
Mohammedanism is that it is a religion which gives people wh
they want, and which caters to their evil natures. But with
his successes, Mohammed never claimed deity for himself.

The founder of Buddhism was Gautama, an Indian prince wl
flourished in 552 B.C. He had become dissatisfied with tl
gross sensuality of the Hinduism surrounding him, and withdre
from the world to mystical contemplation, in an endeavor to e
cape from the pain and sorrow of life. He formulated eight wa
of deliverance: first, right belief — belief in the doctrines l
taught, second, right feelings — namely, absence of all feelir

vard everyone and everything, third, right speech — not to lie
as to be found out, fourth, right actions — negative rules of
straint of one's passions, fifth — right means of livelihood —
tting one's living by means of begging, sixth — right endeavor
mental labor only, seventh, right memory — thought about
ddha's doctrines, and eighth — right meditation — putting
e's mind in a trance in order to communicate with Buddha, or
annihilation of thought. Instead of a way of salvation, there
only a degrading and pessimistic laziness. The success of
ddhism is found in the fact that it presented a way of escape
m the cares of life through the opium of annihilation of all
sire, because of the political patronage of an Indian king, Asoka,
o popularized it, and because of its readiness to incorporate
elf with other religions. But notwithstanding the tremendous
ccess of Buddhism, its founder never claimed deity for himself.

Confucius, the founder of the system of belief that bears his
me, never claimed deity. Confucius saw the breakdown of
rality in China, and started out to counteract it by gathering
ether, studying, and teaching the wisdom of the past to all who
uld listen to him. The enormous success of his ethical system
seen in the fact that the Confucian Classics were the basis of
instruction of the young in the schools of China. In addition
that, all preferment in government positions was dependent
on a knowledge of the teachings of Confucius. But this Chinese
e never claimed deity for himself.

Jesus of Nazareth stands alone among all of the founders of
great religions in asserting that He was God, and in accepting
worship of individuals. The battle royal had been going on
forty days and forty nights, Jesus of Nazareth, put to the
t and solicited to do evil by the devil. Exhausted, emaciated,
d famished, He is the target of the final assaults by Satan who
s in his first temptation, "In view of the fact that you are
n of God by nature, command that these stones become loaves
bread" (Matt. 4:3). There was no "If thou be" (A.V.) in
devil's theology. It was not an unfulfilled, future, hypothetical
dition with him. It was not that Satan was not sure whether
us of Nazareth was the Son of God. The Greek has the con-

ditional particle of a fulfilled condition. The devil knew th
Jesus of Nazareth was the Son of God by nature. That is, b
subscribed to the doctrine which teaches that Jesus is Very Go
of Very God, proceeding by eternal generation from God th
Father. Jesus of Nazareth did not deny that fact. He, the on
Person who ever lived a sinless life on earth, against whom n
one has ever successfully pointed an accusing finger, would hav
acted a monstrous lie if He was not God. He accepted the title.

But that is not all. Satan tempted Him to assert His dei
by creating bread for Himself. Jesus of Nazareth, although Go
lived His life on earth as a Man, in dependence upon God th
Father for His sustenance. He could create bread and fish t
feed 5000 people, but He could not create a crumb for Himsel
There Satan again appeals to His deity. Jesus answered, "Ma
shall not live by bread alone, but by every word that proceed
out of the mouth of God" (Matt. 4:4), refusing to cast off H
human dependence upon God as the Man Christ Jesus, and a
sert His deity.

On another occasion He asserted His deity in forgiving
person's sins. Four men had carried a paralytic on a litter to Hi
for healing. Jesus went to the source of the trouble and forgav
his sins. The Jewish theologians sitting by said, "Why does th
man thus speak blasphemies? Who can forgive sins but Go
only?" (Luke 2:7). Jesus asserted His deity by healing th
paralytic, the miracle demonstrating that He was who He claime
to be, the God who forgave sins. He called Himself the So
of Man here, and He said that He as the Son of Man had th
authority on earth to forgive sins. But the point is that He de
rived this authority from the fact that He was also deity.

On the occasion of Peter's great confession, Jesus of Nazaret
again acknowledged deity. Peter said, "As for you, you are th
Christ, the Son of God, the living God" (Matt. 16:16). Jesu
answers, "Flesh and blood has not revealed this to you, but m
Father who is in heaven." Jesus here states that the fact tha
He is the Son of God, thus God the Son, was a revelation from
God the Father. The teaching to the effect that Jesus of Nazaret
is deity, did not therefore come from man, but from God.

We have in John 5:18, the words (A.V.) "Therefore the Jews ought the more to kill Him, because He not only had broken the Sabbath, but said also that God was His Father, making Himself equal with God." The Jews here are the Jewish religious leaders, well educated, learned in the Old Testament scriptures. They had heard Jesus claim that God was His Father. The pronoun "his" does not bring out the full force of the Greek here. This English word is the translation of the ordinary pronoun of the third person in the genitive case in Greek. It expresses the general idea of ownership. But this construction does not appear in the original here. The word is *idios,* which means "one's own private, unique, individual possession." That is, Jesus claimed to own God as His Father in a way different from the way in which believers have God as their Father. His relationship to God as His Son was different, uniquely different, from that relationship sustained by every other person who claims sonship. These astute theologians saw clearly that in making this claim, Jesus was making Himself equal with God. And any person equal with God, must be God. On another occasion, Jesus differentiated between the sonship of believers and that of Himself. He said to Mary, "Go to my brethren, and say to them, I ascend to my Father, and your Father, and to my God, and your God" (John 20:17).

On still another occasion, the Jewish theologians accused Jesus of being possessed by a demon (John 10:20). In the course of His defence, He said "I and My Father are One" (10:30). The record then continues, "Then the Jews took up stones again to stone Him. Jesus answered them, Many good works have I shown you from my Father; because of what kind of works among them are you stoning Me? The Jews answered Him, For a good work we are not stoning you, but concerning blasphemy, and because you, being a man, are making yourself God" (10:31-33). We have here the testimony again of the Jewish leaders to the effect that Jesus of Nazareth claimed deity for Himself. As theologians, they were well acquainted with the implications of Jesus' words. They rejected Him and His claims because of sin in their lives, and by reason of their entrenched ecclesiasticism

which would allow no interference with its position. It would be
well to remember that here the testimony to the effect that Jesus
claimed deity for Himself, did not come from His followers,
but from the ranks of the opposition.

In the upper room discourse, just before His sufferings on the
Cross, He said to His disciples, "You believe in God. Believe
also in Me" (John 14:1). For a mere human being to say a
thing like that, would be monstrous. Jesus here again 'placed
Himself on an equality with God, thus claiming deity for Himself

The opposition of the Hebrew theologians put Jesus on the
defensive, and He found it necessary time and again to assert
His deity. He said on another occasion, "Your father Abraham
rejoiced to see my day: and he saw it, and was glad." Then
the Jews said to Him, "You are not yet fifty years old, and have
you seen Abraham?" Jesus said to them, "Verily, verily, I say
to you, Before Abraham came into existence, I am" (John 8:56-
58). Jesus uses the verb which speaks of coming into existence
when speaking of Abraham, but when alluding to Himself, He
uses the verb of being, and in this instance, in such a way that
it is clear that He is speaking of eternal existence. And the Jews
understood Him to do so, for the record continues, "Then they
took up stones to cast at Him." Jesus here reminded His Jewish
hearers of the time when Moses asked the God of the Old Testament what answer he should give Israel when they ask him the
name of the God who sent him, and God's answer was, "I AM
THAT I AM" (Ex. 3:14).   Jesus claimed to be the I AM
THAT I AM of the Old Testament, the God of the Jews, the
Self-existent One.

Finally, we will look at the testimony of doubting Thomas.
This disciple refused to believe that Jesus had arisen from the
dead until he could see the marks of the nails in His hands, and
put his. finger into that mark and his hand into the mark left
by the spear in His side. Jesus appeared to the disciples when
Thomas was present, and invited him to satisfy his spirit of
investigation. What Thomas wanted was scientific proof of the
fact that Jesus had risen from the dead in the same body in which
He had died. Upon investigation, Thomas said, "My Lord and

my God." And Jesus did not deny the allegation. Had He not been God, He would have been guilty of acting a monstrous lie.

Thus, Jesus of Nazareth stands alone among all of the founders of the great religions, in claiming deity for Himself. And unless we accept His claim as true, He becomes the greatest enigma of history.

There He stands — Jesus of Nazareth, astride the ages, a figure in history with whom one must reckon. He cannot be ignored by any thinking person. He is either accepted or rejected. Paul, in his address to the Athenian Greeks, speaks of this Jesus of Nazareth as the Man whom God will use to judge the world. Here are his words: "He hath appointed a day, in the which He will judge the world in righteousness by that Man whom He hath ordained, whereof He hath given assurance unto all men, in that He hath raised Him from the dead" (Acts 17:31).

This Jesus of Nazareth today offers to become your Saviour if you will trust Him as such. But, rejected as Saviour, He becomes your Judge when the great assize is held. You must choose, gentle reader. Make Him your Saviour now. You will find the way of salvation further explained in the next chapter, "Jesus and Nicodemus." Read it with an open heart and mind. Give your undying soul a chance to be saved.

JESUS AND NICODEMUS

The question of Job, "How should man be just with God?" is a question that finds its echo in every heart. It has as its basis the consciousness that man is not right with God, since man has sinned. In the conversation between Jesus and Nicodemus, the answer is given. It is arm-chair reading for you, dear reader, giving you access to a first-century Greek manuscript which records that conversation.

II

Jesus and Nicodemus

W E ARE to study together the account of a conversation that took place almost two thousand years ago. It was held in Aramaic, a modified form of Hebrew spoken in the first century by the Jews. The inspired writer, John the Apostle, has recorded it for us in *koinē* Greek. The word *koinē* is a Greek word meaning "common." Previous to 330 B.C., the Greek language was confined for the most part to the little country of Greece. This country was divided into a number of different sections in which the people spoke different dialects. It was all Greek, but the various localities spoke a slightly modified language from that spoken in the neighboring section. These various dialects were merged into one common Greek language as a result of four things: Greek colonization around the shores of the Mediterranean, the conquests of Alexander the Great, the great national festivals of the Greeks held at the religious centers as Olympia, Delos, and Delphi, and the close political and commercial affiliations of the separate Greek tribes. This unified language was spoken all over the Roman Empire in the first century, a language of international exchange. Where a person knew more than one language, it was usually the case that he knew Greek as his second language. This is one of the factors that caused the tremendous and rapid spread of Christianity in the Roman world. The New Testament was written in this language.

For 1500 years, until the age of printing, the manuscripts of the New Testament were copied by hand. During this time mistakes crept in. But through the labors of textual critics, these mistakes have been eliminated, with the result that in the best

texts of the Greek New Testament in use today, scholars tell us
that 999 words out of every 1000 are the same as those in the
original manuscripts. The 1000th word over which there is some
dispute, is of so minor a consequence that it affects no historical
fact nor doctrine. These textual critics had a vast amount of
material with which to work, 4,000 Greek manuscripts, 8,000
copies of the Latin Vulgate, and 2,000 copies of the New Testament in other languages, 14,000 available sources from which to
reconstruct a correct text.   Furthermore, these Greek manuscripts go back to the third century in an unbroken succession,
and with the writings of the Apostolic and Church Fathers, which
are commentaries on the Greek New Testament, and which
quote the entire Greek text with the exception of the first eleven
verses of John Chapter 8, form a direct link with the original
manuscripts of the New Testament. Tertullian, an early Church
Father, tells us that the original manuscripts were still in existence A.D. 200. Thus the record of the conversation which we
are to study together, the reader in his easy chair, and the writer
at his study desk with his Greek New Testament before him, is
correct, and in its every word, it is the inspired Word of God.

The A.V., begins the account of this conversation with the
third chapter. One glance at the Greek text tells us that John
began the account in what we know as chapter two verse 23,
where he introduces the conversation. John writes, "Now there
was a man of the Pharisees." That word "now" which is not
handled by the A.V., sends us back to the previous verses where
we read, "Now, when He was in Jerusalem at the Passover, at
the feast, many believed on His name, viewing with a critical and
discerning eye the miracles which He was constantly doing. But
Jesus Himself was not entrusting Himself to them because He
was constantly knowing by experience all things, and because He
was not having need that anyone should bear testimony concerning the individual man, for He Himself was constantly knowing by experience what was in the individual man." The con
nection is as follows: Jesus knew what was in the heart of the
individual. John's purpose now is to show what Jesus found in
the heart of man, not by telling us in so many words, but by

ringing to the attention of the reader, various individuals who would be exhibits. John records what these people say. Because man speaks out of the abundance of his heart, the reader can see what is in the heart of man.

This gives us an insight into the plan of John's Gospel. John is primarily a theologian in his Gospel, whose main purpose is to demonstrate the deity of our Lord. But in connection with his theology, John has an evangelistic out-reach for lost souls. He tells the reader what is in man, and thus shows him what is wrong with man. Then he brings to his attention the divine cure for sin, namely, the Blood of the Lord Jesus.

Nicodemus is exhibit number one. We will look at his character. He belonged to the sect called the Pharisees. These were the religious ritualists of that day. The Judaism of the first century was no longer that supernaturally revealed system in which the Israelite was taught to look ahead in faith to a coming Sacrifice which God would offer for his sins, this Sacrifice being typified by the Tabernacle offerings and priesthood. It was merely an ethical cult, preaching a salvation-by-works message. Nicodemus subscribed to this system of teaching. His name is a Greek name. It was a custom at that time amongst the Jews, for the parents to give their boys two names, a Jewish and a Gentile name. It was so in the case of the great Apostle, his Jewish name being Saul, and his Gentile name, Paul. The name "Nicodemus" is made up of two words, a word which means "to conquer," and one which means "the common people." The total word means, "One who conquers the people." Evidently, this name was given the boy at his birth. The Pharisaic tradition at that time included this idea, namely, that of a subjugation of the common people. The Lord Jesus spoke of the burdens which the Pharisees were wont to put upon the backs of the people in the form of religious practices which were extra-biblical.

The fact that Nicodemus preferred to be known in Jerusalem by his Greek rather than his Hebrew name, indicates that he had a definite leaning towards Greek culture. It might even indicate that he was a Hellenist, namely, a Jew who read the Old Testament in the Greek translation called the Septuagint. He

was certainly learned in Greek. There was a sentiment in
Hebrew nation against Hellenism. This crept out even in
Christian Church, in the case where the Church neglected
widows of certain Jews who had been reading the Old Testam
in Greek (Acts 6:1). This sentiment certainly must have b
most intense at Jerusalem, the center of Jewish culture. T
would indicate that Nicodemus was a prominent man in Je
salem, and big enough to be able to maintain his position in s
of the antagonism which his leaning towards Greek cult
aroused.

But not only was Nicodemus a Greek scholar. He was a
learned in Hebrew lore. This is clear from the words of Jes
when, wondering at his spiritual obtuseness, He said to him, "
for you, are you the teacher of the Israel and do you not h
an experiential knowledge of these things?" (3:10) The A.
takes no note of the definite articles before the words "mast
and "Israel." The article points out Nicodemus as the teac
of the unique nation Israel. He was thus looked upon as an o
standing teacher of Israel. He is described by John as a ru
of the Jews. The word "ruler" in the Greek text has in it
idea of one who is first or preeminent among his associates. Th
the man to whom our Lord was talking, was one of the m
prominent in the nation of Israel at that time, a Pharisee, a me
ber of the Sanhedrin, the ecclesiastical council of the Jews,
Greek scholar, and a Hebrew theologian.

John says, "There was a man of the Pharisees." There
two words in Greek which mean "man," anēr, which refers t
male individual of the human race, and anthrōpos, which is
racial, generic term, and which has the general idea of "mankin
Some Greek scholars think that this latter word comes from
other one which means "that which walks erect," in cont
distinction to the animals which walk on all fours. John, in usi
the latter word, tells his reader that Nicodemus was a represen
tive man, an individual having racial characteristics. What v
in his heart is found in the heart of every man. Nicodemus,
though a religious, sincere, educated, cultured individual, v
yet unsaved, and spiritually blind. He needed to be born again

This man, John said, came to Jesus by night. The Greek has "in a night-time visit." The emphasis is upon the kind of time hich Nicodemus chose, not day time, but night time. It seems at this fact of a night-time visit was prominent in the thinking John, for in the two places where he mentions Nicodemus later ":50 and 19:39), he mentions the fact that he came by night. the latter scripture, John speaks of Nicodemus as coming *first* by night. Subsequent to his first visit, Nicodemus takes e part of Jesus in a meeting of the Sanhedrin, and after His ucifixion, brings myrrh and aloes for the preparation of the dy. All this indicates that the reason Nicodemus came by night as because he did not want anyone to know of his visit to Jesus.

He addresses him as Rabbi. The Hebrew name is one used the Jews as a term of respect for their teachers. It means, My great one, my honorable sir." Jesus was not an official bbi amongst the Jews, but His prominence as a religious acher gained him a certain respect even amongst his enemies, d they gave Him this title.

He says, "We know." The use of the first person plural points the fact that Nicodemus is including the members of the San- drin in the estimate of Jesus which he is about to give. It is ear from I Peter 2:7 that the official leaders of Israel investi- ted the claims of Jesus regarding His Messiahship. Peter fers to "the stone which the builders disallowed." The stone fers to our Lord, and the builders, to the religious leaders of rael. The word "disallowed" is the translation of a Greek word hich means "to put a person to the test for the purpose of ap- roving him should he be found to meet the requirements laid wn, and having found that he does not satisfy the prescribed quirements, to reject him." Israel was looking for its Messiah. he Lord Jesus announced Himself as such. But Israel wanted Messiah that would deliver it from the political domination of ome and not from the power of sin. Nicodemus came, it seems. a private investigator, to satisfy himself regarding the claims Jesus. To open the conversation, he makes a statement as to hat official Israel believed concerning this new claimant to e Messiahship. He says, "We know that from God you are

come a teacher." The particular Greek word John uses, refe
to absolute knowledge, knowledge that is so sure that it is beyor
question. It is a "peradventure beyond a doubt knowledge." I
using this word, John quotes Nicodemus as putting the Sanhedr
on record that this august body which later turned out to be th
group of ecclesiastical wolves who crucified the Lord of Glor
was absolutely sure that Jesus was a true teacher come from Go
The words "from God" are in an emphatic position in the Gre
text, the idea of Nicodemus being that Jesus was not a teach
who came from man, but from God.

Nicodemus says, "We know that from God you are come
teacher." In reporting this statement, John uses the perfect ten
which in Greek refers to an action completed in past time havir
present results. By the use of this tense, John is telling us th
Nicodemus not only spoke of the coming of Jesus as a teacher
Jerusalem, but that He had established Himself there as a teach
in the hearts of the people. He had taken root, so to speak,
their affections and respect. The Jewish leaders were losing th
crowds, and they were following the new Teacher who wa
causing such excitement in Jerusalem.

After stating the fact that the Sanhedrin was positive of th
fact that Jesus had come from God as a teacher, and that He ha
already established a reputation for Himself among the peopl
Nicodemus tells the Lord Jesus why the members of the Sar
hedrin had come to this conclusion. The reason was that the
were convinced that no one was able to keep on constantly pe
forming the miracles which Jesus was doing, unless God wa
with him. The Greek text here emphasizes the fact that it wa
the constant performance of miracles which proved to the Sar
hedrin that Jesus was from God, the idea being that, had I
performed one or a few miracles, there might have been a po
sibility that they were mere impositions and not true miracle
Thus, the proof for the divine source of Jesus' teaching was al
solute. Furthermore, Nicodemus testified to the fact that the
religious teachers of the Jews, were acquainted with the divir
economy of miracles in the first century, namely, that the
primary purpose was to prove that the person who performe

hem spoke or wrote from God. Miracles were the divine authentication of the spokesman of God. This is also taught us by he particular word John uses in speaking of the miracles. There are seven different Greek words used in the New Testament which speak of miracles. Each one describes a miracle from a different standpoint. The one the inspired writer uses here looks at a miracle from the viewpoint of its character of a divine authentication of the person who performed it.

Thus, we have the statement of the first century false teachers in Israel to the effect first, that Jesus was a teacher who came from God, second, that He performed so many miracles that there could be no imposition or deception practiced, and third, that the primary purpose of these miracles was to prove that the person who performed them spoke or wrote from God. This is enough to prove that Jesus was what He claimed to be, the Son of God, yes, God the Son, possessing co-eternally with the Father and the Spirit, the essence of deity, and that He came as the Messiah of the Jews, was crucified, thus becoming the atonement for sin, and being raised from the dead, He became the Saviour of the one who believes. This is testimony, not from believers, not from within the ranks of Christianity, but from the opposition in the first century.

The testimony to the fact of the miracles of the first century, is not confined to the writers of the four Gospels. Josephus, the Jewish historian of the first century who wrote the history of the Jewish nation, his works accepted by the Imperial Library at Rome, writing in his book *Antiquities of the Jews*, Book 18, Chapter 3, paragraph 3, testifies to three supernatural things about the Lord Jesus. In his words, "if it be lawful to call him a man," he testified to the fact that He was Deity. When he wrote that He was "a doer of wonderful works," he testified to the fact of His miracles. When he spoke of His crucifixion, and said that "he appeared to them alive again the third day," he was speaking of the resurrection of the Son of God. In an attempt to break the force of this passage, Modernism claims that it was placed in the writings of Josephus by the Christian Church to strengthen the argument for miracles. There are three considerations which

show that this paragraph is not an interpolation.   In the firs
place, the Jewish nation has never accused the Church of doing
so, and had such been the case, that nation would have been th
first to raise a cry against it. In the second place, Kirsopp Lake
D.D., Litt. D., of Harvard University, a Modernist, accepts thi
passage as authentic, while rejecting other passages from Josephus
In the third place, the late John A. Scott, Ph.D., LL.D., formerl
head of the classical language department at Northwestern Uni
versity, quotes this passage in his book, *We Would Know Jesus*
as authentic. Professor Scott was a Christian. Again, Suetonius
a first century Roman historian, records the fact that Christianit
was a magical religion, by the use of the term "magical," referring
to the miracles of Christianity. We have also the testimony o
three infidels, Celsus in the second, and Porphory in the thir
century, who were scholars writing against Christianity, but wh
testified to the fact of miracles, and Julian the Apostate, in th
fourth century, a Roman emporer, who also bore witness to hi
belief in the same. In addition to this, we have the testimony o
the thousands of martyrs in the early Church who with their live
testified to the fact of miracles. One could possibly conceive o
a few or a dozen individuals suffering a horrible death such a
crucifixion for their testimony to something they knew was false
but one cannot conceive of many thousands doing the same
Again, the secular historians of the early centuries do not con
tradict any fact of the Gospel records, including the fact o
miracles. Then, we must also consider the generation which lived
at the time the miracles were purported to have taken place. The
Synoptic Gospels were written during the generation which saw
the miracles take place. These were scattered among the people
none of whom rejected their contents as false.

One might be disposed to wonder at the lack of reference to
the Lord Jesus in the secular history of the early centuries. The
following four considerations explain this failure of the historians
to mention Him. First, He was born in an obscure remote land
far from the hub of the universe, Rome. Second, He came from
peasant stock in a nation that was hated and despised. Of course
we Christians recognize the fact that He came from the roya

amily of David, but so far as the Roman world was concerned, He was just a peasant in a remote country of the Roman Empire. Third, crucifixion was a common event in the world at that time. Fourth, it was a common practice of Roman rulers to deify themselves, and when Jesus went about Palestine claiming to be the unique Son of God, He was to the general populace, just another person claiming to be a king, who deified himself.

Again, the first century could not have been deceived either by reason of an optical illusion, an hallucination, or a human imposition, because the miracles were very numerous, were varied in character, extended over a period of years, were performed over a large extent of territory, took place in public, were observed by the learned who were too smart to be fooled, and by the ignorant who were too stupid to think of such a thing, were seen by the friends and the enemies of the gospel, were not performed for profit, and were worthy of the dignity and majesty of the Son of God. Included in all this testimony, we have a scholar and a theologian of the first century, outstanding in Israel, giving his testimony to the fact that the Sanhedrin which crucified our Lord, was positive to the extent of absolute knowledge, that the Lord Jesus was a teacher from God, that He performed so many miracles that the first century world could not be fooled, and that these miracles authenticated Him, His claims, and His teachings as divinely inspired. This constituted the introductory statement of Nicodemus as he came to Jesus.

To this statement of Nicodemus, Jesus answers, "Verily, verily, I say unto thee, Except a man be born again, he cannot see the kingdom of God." This reply shows that behind the cautious designation of Jesus as a teacher, there was in the mind of Nicodemus a suspicion that He might be the Messiah. Certainly, Nicodemus had listened to or heard of the preaching of John the Baptist, announcing Jesus of Nazareth as the Messiah. Jesus does not directly answer the exact words of Nicodemus, but speaks to the intention and mental attitude of the Jewish teacher. He sees what is in the background of his thinking, and directs His answer to that. Jesus spoke of the kingdom of God. This Pharisee was thinking of the Kingdom of Heaven as spoken of

in Matthew's Gospel. The term "Kingdom of God" is the al
inclusive term speaking of all moral intelligences willingly su
ject to God in any age or dispensation. The term, "Kingdom
Heaven" refers to the millennial reign of the Lord Jesus as Me
siah over Israel and King over all the earth. Nicodemus wa
looking for the latter. But Jesus in His use of the former term
is teaching him that the only one who can rightly look for th
Kingdom of Heaven is a saved Jew. That person must enter th
Kingdom of God first, that is, be saved, since the promises of Go
to Israel were made to a spiritual Israel, not an apostate natio
His answer, therefore, in effect is as follows: "Nicodemus, you ar
looking for Messiah and the earthly kingdom of Israel. But yo
are unsaved, and need to be born again. Only to a saved Je
is the Kingdom of Heaven promised." This is in line with ou
Lord's teaching in Matthew 5:3, "Blessed are the poor in spiri
for theirs is the kingdom of heaven."

Since Nicodemus was a representative man of the human rac
having in his heart that which is found in every other perso
since he needed to be born again, and since John was writin
for the Gentiles, it follows that every human being needs to b
born again.

Our question now is, "What does Jesus mean when He speak
of the necessity of a man being born again?" The answer lies i
the meaning of the Greek word here translated "again." Th
Greek word is *anōthen*. It has two meanings, "again" and "fro
above." When a Greek word has more than one meaning, th
context decides as to what meaning is to be used in any particula
instance. For example, this word is found in John 3:31, "H
that cometh from above is above all: he that is of the earth i
earthly, and speaketh of the earth: he that cometh from heave
is above all." The context here speaks of the earth as contraste
to heaven. Therefore, our word *anōthen,* means "from above
here. But in the verse we are now considering, it means "again
and for the reason that Nicodemus in his answer to Jesus, s
understands it. He speaks of a second birth.

But now we come to even a finer distinction. There are tw
words in the Greek New Testament which mean "again," *palin*

which refers to the repetition of an act, and *anothen*, which speaks of the repetition of an act, but adds additional detail. It speaks of the repetition of an act, that repetition having the same source as the first act. It goes back to the outset of the matter, to the original state. Therefore, this being born a second time, has no reference to one's physical birth as the first time one is born, and for the reason that the source of physical birth is natural generation, whereas, the source of the new birth is supernatural generation. When Jesus speaks of being born again in verse five, he speaks of being born of the Holy Spirit.

This consideration takes us back to the original impartation of spiritual life to the First Adam. Genesis 2:7 states, "And the Lord God formed man of the dust of the ground, and breathed into his nostrils the breath of life; and man became a living soul." Hebrew scholars tell us that the word "life" in the original is plural. It therefore speaks of the impartation of physical life and of spiritual life. The First Adam was the federal head of the human race, and when in his unfallen state the human race stood in him, it partook of the spiritual life which had been imparted to him. But Adam in his fall into sin, lost this spiritual life for the whole human race, and plunged its members into total depravity and a lost condition. Jesus, therefore, speaking to this theologian of the Old Testament scriptures, reminds him of all this, and tells him that since he lost this spiritual life as he stood in the First Adam, he needs a fresh impartation of spiritual life, and this is given him through his being placed in the Last Adam in answer to his faith in a coming sacrifice for sin, the Last Adam being that sacrifice. All this is implicit in the words of Jesus, and to a theologian such as Nicodemus, learned in the Old Testament scriptures, should have been, at least, intellectually clear. But Nicodemus, wrapped up in the Pharisaic tradition, was blind to all this. In the answer of Jesus, we have an anticipation of the Pauline doctrine of the First and Last Adam, sin, and death by the First Adam, righteousness and life by the Last Adam. Furthermore, John the Baptist had announced the necessity of the new birth also, and in anticipation of the ministry of the coming Messiah. He said to the Pharisees and Sadducees, "Think

not to say within yourselves, We have Abraham to our father
for I say unto you, that God is able of these stones to raise u
children unto Abraham" (Matt. 3:9). The doctrinal position c
these false teachers was that since they were the fleshly descend
ants of Abraham, they were also God's children. But John th
Baptist declares that they must be saved, and thus be born agai
in order to become children of God. The same necessity obtain
today. The individual as he is born into this world is not a chil
of God, and in order to become such, he must be born of God th
Holy Spirit. It is not a matter of trying to live a good life or o
attempting to keep the Ten Commandments. The sin questio
enters here, and in the Judicial Courts of the Universe, sin coul
only be dealt with by death, for the penalty of sin is death. I
was the death of the Son of God on Calvary's Cross that satisfie
the demands of divine justice, and thus made possible the bestowa
of mercy on the basis of justice satisfied, to the sinner who ac
cepts Jesus Christ as his Saviour. John tells us that "as man
as appropriated Him, He gave to them a legal right to becom
born-ones of God, to those who put their trust in His Name
(1:12). The legal right here refers to that privilege procured b
Jesus Christ on the Cross for the sinner in which he is throug
belief in that substitutionary sacrifice, given salvation, the contex
here speaking of the new birth or regeneration. Jesus therefor
says, "Verily, verily, I am saying to you, except a person be bor
again, that second birth having the same source as the first one
he is not able to see the kingdom of God." The expression, "t
see the kingdom of God," refers, not merely to the act of seein
that kingdom so far as an intellectual and spiritual insight i
concerned, but refers to actual participation in that kingdom
This usage, for instance, is found in Luke 2:26, where it is sai
that it was revealed to Simeon "that he should not see death
before he had seen the Lord's Christ." Thus, the Lord Jesu
teaches that the way to be saved and to become a child of Go
is by being born again, this new birth referring to the act of Go
the Holy Spirit in imparting to the believing sinner, spiritual life.

Nicodemus reacts to this statement of Jesus, by asking how
a man can be born again when he is old. By his second question

Nicodemus shows plainly that he does not understand Jesus to mean a second physical birth, for he says, "He is not able to enter the womb of his mother a second time and be born, is he?" The Greek text here includes a negative which the Greek includes in his question when he expects a negative answer. Nicodemus expected that kind of an answer from Jesus. The emphasis in his question is on the word "how." His question is not, "How can a man be born physically a second time?" but "*how* can a man be born again?" Nicodemus asks for a further explanation of Jesus' words regarding the new birth. This explanation is found in the words of Jesus, "Except a man be born of water and of the Spirit, he cannot enter into the kingdom of God."

There are various interpretations of this statement which we will consider. Some interpret the word "water" here as referring to human birth as coming in a sac of water, and this in contrast to the birth by the Spirit. But the question arises at once as to whether the Lord Jesus would waste words on such a self-evident truth to the effect that in order for a person to be born into the kingdom of God, he must first be brought into existence by being born physically. Furthermore, we learned that the particular Greek word used here by John, meaning "again," has no reference to the physical birth as being a predecessor of the spiritual birth.

Others interpret the word "water" as referring to the rite of water baptism. But we submit that this is pure eisegesis, reading into the text something that is not there. Surely, the word "water" in itself, does not include within its meaning the idea of baptism. Furthermore, the only proper recipient of water baptism is one who has already been born again, the new-birth preceding water baptism, not the rite preceding the new birth. Again, the question arises as to how such a supernatural change as regeneration produces, could be the result of a mere ceremony. This could not be a reference to the water baptism which John the Baptist preached. The Baptist refused water baptism to the Pharisees and Sadducees because they were unsaved. He said, "Bring forth therefore fruits meet for repentance, and think not to say within yourselves, We have Abraham to our father." He demanded of these individuals, evidences of their salvation before he would baptize them. Josephus, the Jewish historian, states that John the Baptist would not baptize any except those who manifested a true faith in God. This makes it clear that our Lord was not speaking of the water baptism administered by John the Baptist, as one of the pre-requisites together with the new-birth which would enable one to enter the kingdom of God.

Others interpret the word "water" here as referring to the Word of God, referring to Ephesians 5:26 where Paul speaks of the washing of water by the Word, and also to I Peter 1:23 where the apostle speaks of being born again by the Word of God. This is a possible interpretation, true in itself. But the question is, is that what Jesus meant here? If He did, would it not be more natural for Him to have used two symbols, namely, water and oil, or two actualities, namely, the Word and the Spirit.

One of the basic rules of interpretation is to ascertain just what the Word of God meant to the one who recorded it, and to the one who received it at the time it was written. Another rule of interpretation is to take into consideration the other uses of the same term in other places. Our Lord was talking to a man who was learned in the Old Testament scriptures. He would be expected to use Jewish phraseology in a case like this. In John 7:37, 38, He uses the word "water" as referring to the Holy Spirit. When speaking to the Samaritan woman who as a Samaritan was familiar at least with the Pentateuch, He uses the word "water" in such a way that we are led to believe that He referred to the Holy Spirit, because He speaks of the water which He will give, as a spring of water leaping up into life eternal. In neither place does He explain the symbol, John finding it necessary to do so in 7:39, and for the reason that he is writing for Gentile believers. Nicodemus, as a Jewish theologian, is supposed to have been familiar with Isaiah 44:3, where water is a type of the Holy Spirit, and also with Isaiah 55:1, where the prophet says, "Ho, every one that thirsteth, come ye to the waters." These considerations lead the writer to incline to the interpretation that the word "water" here was used by Jesus as a symbol of the Holy Spirit as He does in the case of the Samaritan woman and also when He spoke at the great day of the feast.

The Greek word translated "and" has other uses than merely that of a connective. It has an emphatic or ascensive use, and is at that time translated by the word "even." Thus, the translation here could read, "Except a man be born of water, even of the Spirit, he cannot enter into the kingdom of God." Another consideration pointing to this interpretation and translation is the fact that when Jesus recurs again to the new birth in verses 6 and 8, He does not refer to water at all, but only to the Spirit. Evidently seeing the blank look on the face of Nicodemus, our Lord adds the words "even of the Spirit," thus explaining the symbol to this theologian of the Old Testament who should have understood it.

After stating the fact in verse three that it is necessary for a person to be born again in order to participate in the kingdom of God, and explaining that new-birth in verse five by saying that it is the supernatural work of the Holy Spirit, Jesus in verse six presses home the teaching to this Jewish leader that the fact that he has descended from Abraham does not provide him with an entrance into the kingdom of God, but that it is necessary for him to be born spiritually rather than physically to enter that kingdom. The Pharisees and Sadducees maintained that they were members of the kingdom of God, by virtue of the fact that they had Abraham as their father (Matt. 3:9) Jesus assures Nicodemus that this is not a passport to heaven, and he does so in the following words which are an expanded translation of the Greek here: "That which has been born of the flesh is as a result flesh, is of a fleshly nature, and stays flesh." The word "flesh" here refers to the entire individual, body, soul, and spirit, motivated by the totally depraved nature. Jesus teaches that the product of human generation can only be a totally depraved individual, and even though this individual boasts of membership in the Jewish nation, and that he comes from Abraham, yet he is not a fit subject for entrance into the kingdom of God as such. The perfect tense is used here, which speaks of a past complete action with present results, and in certain contexts like this one, of permanent results. The teaching here is that man in his totally depraved condition cannot be improved. Reformation will not

change him into a fit subject for the kingdom of God. The flesh
is incurably wicked, and cannot by any process be changed so
as to produce a righteous life. What that person needs, Jesus
says, is a new nature, a spiritual nature which will produce a
life pleasing to God, and which will be a life fit for the kingdom
of God. This is what Jesus teaches in the following words: "And
that which has been born of the Spirit is as a result spirit, and
is spiritual in nature, and stays spirit." That is, the new birth
is a permanent thing, produces a permanent change in the life of
the individual, and makes him a fit subject for the kingdom of
God. The words of Paul in Galatians 5:19-24 will help us to
understand this better: "The works of the flesh are manifest
which are these; Adultery, fornication, uncleanness, lasciviousness,
idolatry, witchcraft, hatred, variance, emulations, wrath, strife,
seditions, heresies, envyings, murders, drunkenness, revellings,
and such like: of the which I tell you before, as I have also told
you in time past, that they which do such things shall not inherit
the kingdom of God. But the fruit of the Spirit is love, joy,
peace, longsuffering, gentleness, goodness, faithfulness, meekness,
self-control: against such there is no law. And they that are
Christ's, have crucified the flesh with the affections and lusts."

After speaking of the necessity of the new birth, explaining
that the new birth is produced by the supernatural work of the
Holy Spirit, and stating the fact that, not a fleshly birth, even
though it comes from Abraham, but a spiritual birth from God,
is the divine pre-requisite for entrance into the kingdom of God,
Jesus still sees a blank look upon the face of Nicodemus. But He
sees something else, as we are told in the words, "Do not begin
to marvel that I said to you, It is necessary in the nature of the
case for you all to be born again, that birth having the same
source as the first one." There are several things we must notice
in this statement of Jesus. The first is found in the words, "Do
not begin to marvel." Jesus was reading the features of Nicodemus, and He noticed there not only a blank look, showing Him
that this Old Testament scholar was not understanding His
teaching, but that there were signs of him starting to marvel at
the teaching. This conversation took place at night. In order to

ead the features of Nicodemus, Jesus must have plainly seen his
ace. That means that the conversation took place under light.
either natural or artificial. There is no record of our Lord ever
spending a night in Jerusalem. That apostate city was so hostile
to Him, that there was no door that would open to Him for a
night's lodging. After teaching, preaching, and healing all day
long, the tired Son of God would find His rest in either one of
two places, either in the hills around Jerusalem, or at the home
in Bethany where He always found a welcome from Lazarus.
Mary, and Martha. It is not probable that Nicodemus would be
able to find Jesus in the hills at night, but it was a matter of
common knowledge that He spent many nights in that haven of
rest at Bethany. It is the humble opinion of the writer that this
conversation took place in that home. He would not at all
dogmatize upon this matter. He only offers it for what it is
worth, his own opinion based upon the above facts.

The second thing we want to notice is the word "ye" in the
A.V. We submit that the average reader would not notice that
this is a plural pronoun, and therefore does not refer to Nicodemus alone. In the Greek, the fact that the pronoun is plural,
stands out very plainly. In using the pronoun of the plural
number, Jesus evidently had several things in mind. First, He
recognized the fact that Nicodemus belonged to the Sanhedrin
and represented the position of that body with reference to Himself. Second, He was making it plain to Nicodemus that not only
was it necessary for him to be born again, but that all his associates in that venerable body of men also needed to be regenerated. Third, there may also be an implication that Jesus
was suggesting to Nicodemus that he take this teaching back
to the Sanhedrin itself.

The third thing we wish to notice is the Greek word translated
"must" in the A.V. One might gather from the English word that
the necessity of the new birth was a divine fiat, or an arbitrary
imperative. But the Greek word means, "It is a necessity in the
nature of the case." The question therefore follows, as to just
what it was in the nature of the case that makes the new birth
a reasonable or rational necessity. The answer to this question

we have already given in detail, but it may be helpful to briefly summarize the points again. That which makes the new birth an imperative necessity is as follows: There are just two races of individuals in this world, those having the First Adam as their federal head, and those having the Last Adam as their federal head. This first race stood in the First Adam before he fell, and thus possessed spiritual life in him. But the First Adam fell into sin, lost this spiritual life for the human race, and plunged it into a totally depraved and lost condition, and under the wrath of God. The second race, composed of those who are in the Last Adam as their federal head, are members of the Kingdom of God. But to be a member of the Kingdom of God, means that the individual must have a nature that produces in him a righteous life which is fitting to those who are in the Kingdom of God. This constitutes the necessity in the nature of the case.

Then Jesus goes on to explain to Nicodemus the mysterious and invisible character of the supernatural work of the Holy Spirit in the new-birth. He says, "The wind is constantly blowing where it desires to blow, and its sound you are constantly hearing, and you do not know from where it is coming and where it is going. Thus is everyone who has been born of the Spirit." Socrates, one of the great philosophers of Greece, realized something that Nicodemus did not comprehend, for he writes as follows: "The thunder as it comes and goes is not seen; the winds also are invisible though their effects are manifest; the soul of man is itself unseen; therefore despise not the unseen but honor God." In the teaching of Jesus, there is a comparison between the invisible but mighty power of the wind and the unseen but powerful operation of the Holy Spirit in regeneration. One hears the sound of the wind, but he cannot see where it comes from nor where it is going. It is so in the operation of the Holy Spirit as He imparts spiritual life to the believing sinner. And like the wind which, though it cannot be seen yet produces results that are visible, so the Holy Spirit in regeneration imparts the divine nature which produces results in the life of the individual which can be seen.

To this explanation, Nicodemus answers, "How is it possible for these things to become?" That is, Nicodemus is not merely asking as to how these things could be, for he does not recognize their existence, but he asks how these things could come into existence.

Jesus' answer to this is, "As for you, are you the teacher of the Israel and do you not have an experiential knowledge of these things?" The particular word for "knowledge" that John uses here, refers not to absolute knowledge as in the case of the Sanhedrin's estimate of Jesus, but a knowledge gained by experience. Jesus not only expected this teacher of Israel to have an intellectual knowledge of the new-birth, but an experiential knowledge of the same. That is, it should be, not merely a head knowledge, but a heart knowledge. The teaching of the new-birth should not be accepted merely by an intellectual assent, but by a heart appropriation. There is just about eighteen inches between the heart and the head. Just so, there is just eighteen inches between the roads leading to heaven and hell. A mere intellectual assent to the teachings of the Bible, does not save a person. These teachings must be appropriated by the heart, which means the heart's submission to the same. This involves the determination to be done with sin and to receive a new life from God that will make one hate sin and love righteousness. Thus, a heart faith in the Lord Jesus as Saviour results in an experience, namely, that of the individual receiving the supernatural work of the Holy Spirit in his inner being imparting the divine nature.

From this point on, the dialogue ceases, and we have an unbroken utterance of the Lord Jesus. He starts with a certification of the truth which He had just given to Nicodemus. He says, "Truly, truly, I am saying to you, that which we know with absolute knowledge we are speaking, and that which we have seen with discernment, to that we are bearing testimony, and our testimony you all are not receiving. If, as is the case, I told you concerning the earthly things, and you are not believing, how is it possible that if I tell you concerning the heavenly things, you will believe? And no one has ascended into heaven except the one who out of heaven has come down, the Son of man."

The word "if" in the Greek text is a particle of a fulfilled condition, and we have translated it by the words, "if, as is the case." Jesus had told him concerning the earthly things. The latter expression in the Greek is literally, "the things upon the earth." The words do not refer to things of an earthly nature, nor to worldly affairs, nor to things sinful, but to things whose proper place is on earth. Our Lord had just been speaking of the new-birth. This, although supernatural in nature, is looked upon as an earthly thing in the sense that it has to do with people on earth. Jesus said that not only did Nicodemus not believe these things, but also the Sanhedrin. This is made clear by the use of the plural verb in the Greek.

The heavenly things are literally in the Greek, "the things upon the heavens." These refer, not to holy things as compared with sinful, nor spiritual things as compared to temporal, but to things which are in heaven, to the mysteries of redemption of which Jesus is to speak as He presents the gospel to Nicodemus in verses 1 and 15.

Jesus answers the "we know" of Nicodemus by the "we know" of verse 11. When Nicodemus used that expression, he was speaking for a certain class of individuals, namely, the Sanhedrin. When Jesus used the expression, He was also speaking for a certain class of people, namely, those who had experienced the new-birth, thus, identifying Himself with the recipients of His grace.

In preparing the mind of Nicodemus for the truth concerning the heavenly things, He refers to His incarnation, and in effect, tells him that the Son of man is qualified to speak concerning these things because He is the only one who has come down from heaven. The words, "which is in heaven," are not in the best texts, and so we have not included them in our translation. However, in themselves they are true, and point to a tremendous fact, namely, the omnipresence of the Son of man. To possess omnipresence, is to possess deity. Thus, the Son of man is also the Son of God, and therefore, God the Son. Jesus is now ready to preach the gospel to Nicodemus, and He does it in Jewish terminolgy. If Nicodemus is too blind to understand the necessity of the new-birth, it might be that he will be able to see his need of salvation from sin, from the standpoint of an atonement offered for him.

Jesus reminds him of the wilderness experience of the Jews who were on their way to the Promised Land. They had murmured against God, being dissatisfied with the manna which came from heaven. God had sent fiery serpents among them as a judgment, and they bit the people, and as a result, many died. The people acknowledged their sin, and asked that the Lord take away the serpents. Instead of doing that, God had Moses place a serpent of brass on a pole, and when a person was bitten, all he had to do to be cured of the snake-bite, was to look at the serpent of brass. Our Lord uses that incident as an illustration which would give the gospel to Nicodemus. He said, in effect, "Nicodemus, you have been bitten by the snake-bite of sin. Just as that brass serpent was elevated upon a pole, so must the Son of man be lifted up, that whoever puts his trust in Him, might be having life eternal."

The words "be lifted up" are used by John to speak of crucifixion. The Greek word for "must" is the same one used when Jesus said to Nicodemus, "Ye must be born again." The Greek word means, "It is necessary in the nature of the case." Notice, if you will, the two divine imperatives. The first one is, "Nicodemus, it is necessary in the nature of the case for you all to be born again." The second one is, "It is necessary in the nature of the case for the Son of man to be lifted up." The first imperative has to do with an obligation that man must fulfill. The second one has to do with an obligation which the Son of God must fulfill. There would be no reason for the crucifixion of the Lord Jesus if man were not a sinner. Since the atonement is a divine fact and not a farce, man is clearly seen to be a sinner.

In John 3:14, the Lord Jesus says, "even so must the Son of man be lifted up." In 12:32 He says, "And I, if I be lifted up from the earth, will draw all men unto Me." It is interesting to note that the preposition "from" is in the Greek text, "out from." Thus, our Lord was speaking not merely of being lifted up from the earth on a Roman cross, for in that case a preposition

would have been used which means "from the edge of," but H
was speaking of being lifted up out of the earth. That includes Hi
Cross, His death, burial, resurrection, and ascension. In 3:14
the Cross is only in view, and for the reason that only the atone
ment is mentioned there. But, in 12:32, the drawing power o
our Lord Jesus is spoken of. A dead Christ on a cross, can draw
no sinner to Himself. It takes a crucified, risen, ascended
glorified God-man in the Glory to draw sinners to Himself. Thu
does Jesus preach the gospel to Nicodemus. He speaks of Him
self as the Sacrifice for sin to which all the Old Testamen
sacrifices pointed. He tells Nicodemus by this that the Levitica
system will soon be set aside, in favor of the actual atonement fo
sin which God will offer, and that that atonement will be Himsel
dying on a Roman cross. He explains to this spiritually blind
Jewish teacher, that faith in Him as this substitutionary sacrifice
results in the salvation of the individual. This is exactly what the
sacrifices taught, all the way from Genesis 3:21 where the Lord
God made coats of skins and clothed Adam and Eve, through
the Levitical system up to the time when Jesus was speaking
these words, namely, that the sinner should look ahead to a sacri
fice that would be offered for him by God. Since the Judaism of
the first century was a mere ethical cult, having lost that supernatural revelation of a sacrifice for sin in its teachings, Nicodemus
was blind to all this. We have evidences of the fact that this
Jewish leader did later accept the gospel message and the Lord
Jesus as his Saviour. In John 7:51, he takes the part of Jesus
against his associates in the Sanhedrin, and in 19:39 he brings
a mixture of myrrh and aloes with which to prepare the body of
Jesus for burial. The latter instance is certainly conclusive evidence that Nicodemus was saved, for the Sanhedrin had crucified
the Lord of Glory and he was taking his stand with the friends of
Jesus.

The conversation between Jesus and Nicodemus, so far as the
record of John is concerned, closes with verse 15. Verses 16 to
21 constitute John's elaboration upon and explanation of the
conversation. This appears clear from the following considerations; first, the words of Jesus, "even so must the Son of man

be lifted up," speak of Jesus looking into the future to a sacrifice which was not at the time of the conversation consumated, whereas the words, "God so loved the world that He gave His only begotten Son," look back to a past act in which God gave His Son. It is not reasonable to suppose that our Lord would change tenses that way in the midst of a conversation. It is Jesus looking forward to the Cross, and John looking back to it. At the time of this conversation, God had not yet given His Son as a Sacrifice on the Cross. Again, verses 16-21 are explanatory rather than progressive. Verses 16 and 17 repeat the object of Christ's mission, which already has been stated. Verses 18 and 19 speak of the historic results in faith and unbelief, results which at the time of the conversation were not in evidence. Verses 20 and 21 exhibit the causes of faith and unbelief. Finally, the designation "only begotten Son" is not one of the names by which Jesus designates Himself, but is used by John.

It appears that after John recorded this conversation, remembering that the gospel was given in Jewish terminology, and that he was writing for the Gentile world, he saw the need of some explanatory material that would give the gospel to the Gentiles in terms which they could more easily understand. In the last analysis, so far as the divine source and inspiration of these succeeding words is concerned, it made no difference whether Jesus spoke them on earth, or whether through the Holy Spirit, He spoke them from heaven, through John.

John 3:16 starts with the little word "for." This word connects a statement of Jesus in verse 14 with a statement of John in verse 16. In verse 14 we have, "even so is it necessary in the nature of the case for the Son of man to be lifted up." In verse 16 we have "God so loved the world that He gave His only begotten Son." The connection is as follows: The question comes, "What was there in the nature of the case that made the crucifixion a necessity?" It was not the justice of God which required the Son to pay the penalty of sin. God, in perfect righteousness could have required sinful man to pay his own penalty for his wrong-doing. The broken law would have been satisfied, for the wages of sin is death. It was the love of God for a race of lost

sinners that was the necessity in the nature of the case which
required that a substitute be found to pay for man's sin. That
substitute is the Lord Jesus.

John wrote "God so loved the world." He was thinking in
his native language, Aramaic, but he was writing in Greek. He
was now faced with a problem, that of finding the exact word in
the Greek language that would speak of the love of God for a
lost race. Here was a love that loved, not only the unlovely, and
unlovable, but one's enemies even to the point of total self-
sacrifice, where the person gives all that he has for the benefit
of the one loved. But where was one to find such a word in a
pagan language like Greek?   Missionaries tell us that when
translating the Bible into native languages, they cannot find a
word which would adequately give the idea of God's love. It was
so in the case of the Apostle John.

There are four words in the Greek language which mean
"love." One is *eraō*, which refers to a love based upon passion,
either good or bad, according to the context. This would not
do here. Another is *stergō*, which speaks of a natural love, such
as love of parents for children. But the unsaved are not children
of God, and therefore this word would not do here. Then there
is the word *phileō*, which refers to a love called out of one's heart
by the pleasure one takes in the object loved. But God takes no
pleasure in the wicked, and therefore, this was not a fitting word.
The fourth word is *agapaō*.   This is a love called out of one's
heart by the preciousness of the object loved. The purely classical
meaning of this word is in line with the doctrine John wished to
teach here. God's love for a lost race was called out of His heart
by the preciousness of each lost soul, precious because He finds
in that lost soul His own image, though that image is marred by
sin, and precious, because that lost soul is made of material that
God through salvation can transform into the very image of
Christ.

Then, when John adds the words, "that He gave His only begotten Son," he pours into that pagan word a meaning that it
never had before, namely, that of a love that gives itself in total
sacrifice for the benefit of the person loved, that person being

unlovely and unlovable, and a bitter enemy. This kind of love was never known in pagan Greece. Paul had chosen this word in the writing of his Roman epistle, to speak of the love which the Holy Spirit sheds abroad in our hearts, and in his Galatian letter, of the fruit of the Spirit. In I Corinthians 13, he gives the divine analysis of this love. John had the writings of Paul before him, and added one more element to this love by the context in which he placed it in 3:16, that of a total self-sacrifice for the benefit of the person loved. The order of the words in the Greek text of 3:16 is beautiful. "For thus did God love the world, so that His Son, the only begotten One He gave, in order that every one who puts his trust in Him might not perish but might constantly be having life eternal." The giving of His Son is made clear in the context. Our Lord had just spoken of being lifted up on a cross. God the Father gave His Son as a substitutionary sacrifice for sin, thus satisfying His justice, maintaining his divine government, and opening the flood-gates of mercy to a hell-deserving race of sinners.

In the words, "should not perish, but have everlasting life," there is a radical change in tenses, from the aorist which speaks of a once-for-all act to the present subjunctive which speaks of a continuous state. The contrast is one between the final utter ruin and lost estate of the unbeliever, and the possession of eternal life as an enduring experience on the part of the believer. The entire verse taken straight from the Greek text is as follows "For in this manner God loved the world, so that His Son, the only begotten One He gave, in order that every one who places his trust in Him might not perish but might be constantly having life eternal."

After stating the purpose of Christ's death on the Cross, namely, that of saving those who would believe, John assures the reader that even though the Cross revealed man's sin in a clearer way than it had ever been revealed, and even though the Cross brings heavier judgment upon those who refuse the Saviour, yet, that was not God's purpose in sending His Son. The Jewish idea was that the Messiah would come to condemn the world. The ordinary Jewish Messianic expectation was limited, and mis-

represented the love of God. John says, "For God did not sen
off His Son into the world in order that He might judge th
world, but in order that the world might be saved through Him.

The A.V., translates by the word "condemned." The Gree
word is *krinō*. The word meant originally "to separate," then "t
distinguish, to pick out, to be of opinion," and finally, "to judge.
The act of judgment was therefore that of forming an accurat
and honest opinion of someone, thus, appraising his character
and placing him in a certain position with respect to the law c
God. The result of such a judgment is commonly condemnation
for the human race is a fallen race. We will translate by the wor
"judgment," and have in the background of our minds the ide
of condemnation so far as an appraisal of character is concerned
The Greek word for "condemnation" is *katakrinō*, the prefixe
preposition *kata* meaning in its local sense, "down," thus giving
the idea of condemnation to the verbal idea. This word is a
advance upon *krinō*, in that it speaks of the passing of sentenc
upon the one judged.

In verse 18, John elaborates upon his previous words. He in
forms his reader that God did not send His Son to judge but t
save, and that whoever accepts His Son as Saviour, is not judged
Then he takes up the case of the unbeliever, and says that tha
person stands judged already. He uses the perfect tense which
speaks of a past complete action having present results. The un
believer does not wait until a future trial to see whether he is t
be judged guilty or not guilty, for John declares that he has bee
already judged with the present result that he is looked upon b
God as under His judgment. That is, he stands convicted of hi
sin of unbelief. The sin of which he is guilty, John says, is tha
he has not believed in the name of the only begotten Son of God
with the present result that he is in a permanent attitude of un
belief. John again uses the perfect tense here. This is no snap
judgment on the part of the unbeliever, John says, but a deliberate
and confirmed attitude towards God's Son. This, John says,
does not merely disclose human infirmity and passion, but shows
a wickedness of man which he chooses and prefers in the presence
of the goodness of God which has been revealed in the Cross.

This is further explained by John in the words, "And this is he judgment, that the light has come into the world, with the present result that it is here, and men loved rather the darkness than the light." The light here is the Lord Jesus, and its coming into the world refers to the incarnation. The words of the A.V., "is come," are a good translation of the Greek perfect tense, which speaks of a past complete act having present results. It is not as if the Lord Jesus had flashed across the vision of sinful humanity like a meteor through the sky, and then was gone, but that He came and lived here for thirty-three years in full view of mankind, and since His ascension, lives in the hearts and lives of believers. The human race therefore cannot plead an unfair opportunity to see the light. It stands judged because it rejects the light which it has before itself constantly. The rejection of God's Son, therefore, is not the result of ignorance, but of deliberate choice and preference.

But John hastens to inform his reader that this rejection of the Saviour is not fundamentally an intellectual thing, but has its roots in a totally depraved nature, for he says that this preference of darkness to light is found in the fact that men's works were constantly evil. The word "evil" is *poneros* which means "evil in active opposition to the good."

John continues this thought in the words, "For every one who habitually practices evil, is hating the light and does not come to the light, in order that his works might not be convicted." The distinctive word for "evil" here is *phaulos* which means "that which is paltry, ugly, poor," and refers to a dull, senseless viciousness. Thus, John states that at the basis of all rejection of Christ, is a totally depraved nature, a love of sin, and a hatred of the good.   . . . .

On the other hand, John says, that the person who practices the truth, comes to the light in order that the character of his works might be openly shown. This he does because he realizes that his deeds have been wrought in God in the sense that God the Holy Spirit dwelling in him, produces the works.

Expanded Translation of John 3:1-21

Now, there was a man of the Pharisees, Nicodemus by name
a chief one among the Jews. This one came to Him in a night
time visit and said to Him, Rabbi, we know positively and beyon
a peradventure of a doubt, that from God you are come a teacher
for no one is able to keep on constantly doing these attestin
miracles which you are constantly performing, unless God be wit
him. Answered Jesus and said to him, Truly, truly, I am sayin
to you, unless a person is born again, that new-birth having th
same source as the first one, he is not able to see the kingdom o
God. Says to him Nicodemus, How is it possible for a man t
be able to be born, being old? He is not able to enter into th
womb of his mother a second time and be born, is he? Answere
Jesus, Truly, truly, I am saying to you, unless a person is bor
of water, even of the Spirit, he is not able to enter into the king
dom of God. That which has been born of the flesh is as a presen
result flesh, is fleshly in nature, and stays flesh. And that whic
has been born of the Spirit is as a present result spirit, is spiritua
in nature, and stays spirit. Do not begin to marvel that I said t
you, It is necessary in the nature of the case for you all to be bor
again, that new-birth having the same source as the first one. Th
wind constantly blows where it desires to blow, and its soun
you are hearing, but you do not know from where it is comin
and where it is going. Thus is everyone who has been born o
the Spirit. Answered Nicodemus and said to Him, How is i
possible for these things to be able to become? Answered Jesu
and said to him, As for you, are you the teacher of the Israel
and do you not have an experiential knowledge of these things
Truly, truly, I am saying to you, that which we know positivel
and beyond a peradventure of a doubt, we are speaking, and tha
which we have with discernment seen we are bearing witness to
and our witness you all are not receiving. If, as is the case, I tol
you concerning earthly things and you are not believing, how i
it possible if I should tell you of heavenly things, that you wil
believe? And no one has ascended into heaven except the on
who came down from heaven, the Son of Man. And, even a
Moses elevated the snake in the wilderness, thus is it necessar

in the nature of the case for the Son of man to be lifted up, in order that every one who places his trust in Him might be having life eternal. For in this manner God loved the world, so that His Son, the only begotten One He gave, in order that every one who places his trust in Him might not perish but might be having life eternal. For God did not send off His Son into the world in order that He might judge the world, but in order that the world might be saved through Him. The one who places his trust in Him is not being judged. The one who is not believing has already been judged, because he has not placed his trust in the name of the only begotten Son of God, with the result that his unbelief is a permanent attitude. And this is the judgment, that the light has come into the world with the present result that it is here, and men loved rather the darkness than the light, for their works were evil and in active opposition to the good; for every one who practices evil things, is hating the light and is not coming to the light, in order that his works might not be convicted. But the one who constantly is doing the truth, constantly comes to the light in order that his works might be openly manifested, because they have been wrought in God.

Dear Reader: *Are you born again? Have you at any definite time in the past, come to the conclusion that what God's Word says of you, is true, namely, that you are a sinner and lost? And have you understood and embraced with all your heart the fact that the Lord Jesus paid the penalty for your sins on the Cross? And then did you appropriate Him by an act of faith as your Saviour? And did you thank Him for saving you? If you have not, wont you do so now?*

THE BELIEVER AND THE ISOLATION
OF THE EVIL NATURE

Every individual has evil impulses. Heredity, environment, education, training, circumstances, all play a part
in one's behavior. The average individual does not allow too many of these evil impulses to run rampant
through his experience. But there are some impulses
over which he has no control. He has fought them with
all the will power he could muster, and with no success.

In the pages of the Bible, we find the way of deliverance.
It is found in one of the most profound, metaphysical
passages in all literature. Paul, the Hellenistic Jew,
trained in the University of Tarsus, the foremost Greek
school of learning of the time, and in the rabbinical
school of theology at Jerusalem, is the author. One must
read carefully, to follow him through the intricate mazes
of the inner workings of man's personality. Are you,
gentle reader, longing for victory over certain evil impulses? Then read Paul in the following pages.

III

The Believer and the Isolation of the Evil Nature

ONE reads in medical advertisements, of a certain remedy which attacks the common cold germ in four ways. God attacks the sin in the human race in three ways. *First,* He *justifies* the believing sinner, that is, He removes the guilt and penalty of the person's sin, and bestows a positive righteousness, even Jesus Christ Himself, in whom the believer stands guiltless and righteous before God's law for time and eternity. *Second,* He *sanctifies* the person in that He breaks the power of the indwelling sinful nature and imparts His divine nature, thus freeing the individual from the power of sin and enabling him to live a life pleasing to God, doing this at the moment the sinner puts his faith in the Lord Jesus as Saviour. This act is followed by a process which goes on during the believer's life as he yields himself to the ministry of the Holy Spirit, who eliminates sin from his life and produces a life in which the Christian virtues are present. *Third,* He *glorifies* the believer in that He transforms his physical body at the time when the Lord Jesus comes back to take out His Church, making that body immortal, perfect, and free from indwelling sin. It is concerning the second of these phases that we wish to speak now.

When the medical profession speaks of a disease germ that has not yet been isolated, it means that that germ has never been identified and thus isolated from those germs which are known. Since that germ has never been identified, medicine has not been able to discover a remedy for it. Once the germ has been isolated, a remedy can usually be found. It is so in the case of the believer. The Christian who has never isolated the evil nature, that is,

who has not discovered the truth of Romans VI where Go
through the apostle Paul describes the inner change which occur
at the moment he is saved, and also the Christian's adjustme
to this inner change, does not have consistent victory over
But when in the Christian's thinking, this matter is cleared u
and this nature isolated, he has the remedy which will enable hi
to gain consistent victory over sin in his life.

The Scriptures are very clear as to the identity of the ev
nature which indwells an individual as he is born into this worl
One only has to glance at such portions as the following, in ord
to appraise the character of this sinful nature: "And God saw th
the wickedness of man was great in the earth, and that ever
imagination of the thoughts of his heart was only evil continually
(Gen. 6:5): "There is none righteous, no, not one; there is nor
that understandeth, there is none that seeketh after God. The
are all gone out of the way, they are together become unprofi
able; there is none that doeth good, no, not one. Their throa
is an open sepulchre; with their tongues they have used decei
the poison of asps is under their lips; whose mouth is full
cursing and bitterness; their feet are swift to shed blood; de
struction and misery are in their ways; and the way of peace ha
they not known; there is no fear of God before their eyes" (Ron
3:9-18): "Now the works of the flesh are manifest, which ar
these; adultery, fornication, uncleanness, lasciviousness, idolatr
witchcraft, hatred, variance, emulations, wrath, strife, sedition
heresies, envyings, murders, drunkenness, revellings" (Gal. 5:19
21). The Bible has thus isolated the germ called sin, identifyin
it as the fallen nature received from Adam. This nature remain
in the individual even after God has saved him, as we learn fro
I John 1:8, "If we up and say that we are not constantly havin
sin (the evil nature), ourselves we are deceiving, and the trut
is not in us." God, in salvation breaks the power of this sinf
nature over the believer, but leaves it in him as a disciplinar
measure. When the believer refuses its behests, and says a poin
blank NO to it, he glorifies God, defeats Satan, and grows i
spiritual strength and stature.   If the believer expects to gai
consistent victory over this nature, he must know two things

first, what God has done in his inner being with regard to that nature; and second, what adjustments it is necessary for him to make in relation to it. These two things Paul takes up in Romans VI.

Paul's presentation consists of two questions and their answers. The two questions are as follows: "What therefore shall we say? Shall we who profess to be Christians, continue to sustain habitually the same relationship to the evil nature which we sustained before we were saved, in order that God's grace might abound in thus forgiving our sins?" (Rom. 6:1): "What then? Shall we commit occasional acts of sin because we are not under the uncompromising rule of law, but under the lenient sceptre of grace?" (Rom. 6:14). The above consists of translation plus paraphrase. Neither of these questions ever occurred to Paul, for he knew grace. They were asked him by some person who had listened to the great apostle preach on grace, a person who did not understand the implications of God's grace, but who lived under law. Paul answers the first question in verses 2-14, by showing that it is a mechanical impossibility for the believer to sustain the same relationship habitually to the evil nature which he sustained before he was saved. He answers the second question by showing that the believing sinner has changed masters, before salvation, having Satan as his master, and since grace has wrought an inward change, having God as his master.

The key to the understanding of Romans VI is in the definite article which precedes the word "sin" of verse one in the Greek text. A rule of Greek syntax refers the sin mentioned in this verse back to the sin mentioned in 5:21. In the latter verse, sin is looked upon as reigning as a king, and it is clear that the reference here is to the sinful nature, not to acts of sin. Thus, the sinful nature is spoken of in 6:1 and throughout the chapter where that word occurs. When Paul says, "What shall we say then?" he refers back to his statement in 5:20, "Where sin abounded, grace was in superabundance, and then some on top of that." Paul's questioner had listened to him preach on that text and had approached him as follows: "Paul, do you mean to say that God is willing to forgive sin as fast as a man commits it? If that

is the case, shall we who profess to be Christians, continue t
sustain the same relationship to the evil nature which we did be
fore we were saved, thus allowing acts of sin to enter our ex
perience, thus allowing God to forgive those sins and displa
His grace?" The question thus simmers down to the relationshi
of the sinful nature to the Christian.

Paul's first answer is, "God forbid, away with the though'
let not such a thing occur." His second answer is, "How is i
possible for such as we who have once for all been separated fror
the power of the sinful nature, to live any longer in its grip?
Paul speaks of the Christian as being dead to sin (A.V.) Deat'
is not extinction but separation. The Christian has died to sin i
the sense that God in supernatural grace, *while leaving the sinfv
nature in the believer,* has *separated* him from it. There has bee
a definite cleavage, a disengagement of the person from the ev
nature. The evil nature is a dethroned monarch. Before salvatio
it was the master of the individual. Since salvation, the believe
is its master. When the believer begins to see this truth, he ha
isolated the nature, identified it in its proper character, and ha
within his grasp the remedy for it. It is the unknown and unsee
enemy which is hard to fight. The Christian who has not isolate
the evil nature, fights sin in the dark, and ignorant of the fac
that the sinful nature is no longer his master, continues to obe
it more or less because he has no knowledge of how to gai
victory over it. We have here the emancipation proclamation is
sued by God in which the Christian has been released from slaver
to the evil nature, but like many slaves after the Civil War, wh
were ignorant of Abraham Lincoln's emancipation proclamatior
and who continued in the service of the slave-master, so Chris
tians who are ignorant of Romans VI continue to be slaves c
the indwelling sinful nature to the extent that they are not gain
ing consistent victory over sin.

Paul was in this very situation before he came to know th
truth of Romans VI. He says, "I am carnal, sold under sin, fo
that which I do, I do not understand, for what I would, that
do not, but what I hate, that I do" (Rom. 7:14, 15). Paul kne
he was saved, but he did not understand his Christian experienc

The very thing he wished to do, namely, good, he did not do, and the very thing he did not want to do, namely, sin, he did do. He was struggling in his own strength to keep from sinning and to do what was right. He found that human endeavor was not equal to the task. Many Christians are in a like situation. The truth in Romans VI enables the believer to gain consistent victory over the indwelling sinful nature. The first fact that Paul brings out is that the sinful nature has had its power over the believer broken. The believer before salvation was absolutely the slave of the evil nature. But since grace has separated him from its power, he does not need to obey it. When he learns this, he learns that he has the power to say a point blank NO to it. This is one great step in the battle which he wages against indwelling sin. And the beautiful thing about it all is that the more he says NO to it, the easier it is to withstand it, until it becomes a habit with him to say NO to its behests. Thus, it is a matter of breaking the bad habit of saying YES to the evil nature and forming the good habit of saying NO.

In addition to breaking the power of the evil nature, God imparts His own divine nature to us. We have this truth given us in Paul's words in verse 4, "Even so we also should order our behavior in the power of a new life imparted." This new nature gives the Christian both the desire and the power to do God's will, and the desire and the power to refuse to obey the evil nature. Paul gives us this precious truth again in Philippians 2:12, 13, "Wherefore, my beloved, as ye have always obeyed, not as in my presence only but now much more in my absence, carry to its ultimate conclusion your salvation with fear and trembling, for God is the One who is constantly putting forth energy in you, imparting to you both the willingness and the ability to do His good pleasure." Since the Christian does not have to obey the evil nature, and since he has the desire to obey God, Paul says it is a mechanical impossibility for him to sustain habitually the same relationship to the evil nature which he did before salvation. This means that he gains consistent victory over sin. And the beautiful thing about it all again is, that the more often the Christian says YES to the admonitions and commands of the divine nature, the easier it becomes to say YES, until it becomes a habit to do so. Thus, the Christian life is also a matter of forming the good habit of obeying the Word of God.

These two supernatural changes wrought in the inner being of the believing sinner at the moment he puts his faith in the Lord Jesus, namely, the breaking of the power of indwelling sin and the imparting of the divine nature, were accomplished, Paul tells us, by the believing sinner being baptized into Jesus Christ. The law of cause and effect requires that every effect must have an adequate cause. Since the breaking of the power of indwelling sin and the impartation of the divine nature are operations which only God can perform, this baptism must be, not water baptism, but Holy Spirit baptism. The word "baptize" is the English spelling of the Greek word, not its translation. The Greek word itself means "the introduction or placing of a person or thing into a new environment or into union with something else so as to alter its condition or its relationship to its previous environment or condition." It refers here to the act of the Holy Spirit introducing or placing the believing sinner into vital union with Jesus Christ in order to alter that person's condition and environment. Before salvation, the sinner stands in the First Adam as his federal head. In that position, he receives the position which the First Adam had as the result of the fall, namely, guilty before God's law, possessing a fallen nature, and unrighteous in his thoughts, words, and deeds. His physical body becomes subject to death. But all this is changed when the Holy Spirit takes him out of his first position, and places him in the Last Adam, Jesus Christ. The result is that this believing sinner stands in his new federal Head, absolutely righteous before God's law, the power of indwelling sin broken, and the divine nature imparted. What a contrast this environment and condition is to the previous one he occupied. This introduction into Jesus Christ occurred potentially in the mind and purpose of God at the time the Lord Jesus hung on the Cross of Calvary, the results of which become operative in the life of the believing sinner when he places his faith in Jesus as Saviour and the Holy Spirit in answer to his faith, places him in the Lord Jesus.

Paul has answered his hearer's question, namely, "Shall we who profess to be Christians, continually sustain the same relationship to the sinful nature which we had before we were saved?" He declares that to be an impossibility, and for the reason that the power of the sinful nature has been broken and the divine nature imparted. As a result of the first operation of God's supernatural power, the believing sinner is not compelled to obey the evil nature anymore. As a result of the second operation, he does not desire to obey that nature anymore. When a person does not have to do something that he does not want to do, he does not do it. Furthermore, the imparted divine nature makes the Christian hate sin and love righteousness, and gives him both the desire and the power to say NO to that nature which before salvation enslaved him. The divine nature also gives the Christian the impelling motive and the power to do God's will. Thus, it is mechanically impossible for a Christian to live a life of habitual sin as he did before he was saved.

We now offer an expanded translation plus paraphrase of Romans 6:1-4 which we have been treating. The reader should know that the author has left behind in his workshop, the intricate technicalities of Greek grammar and syntax, and has offered his reader the results of his study of the Greek text in a translation that uses more words than a standard translation in order to bring out more truth, and has added explanatory paraphrase, doing all this in an effort to bring out the truth most clearly and most simply.

Translation and paraphrase: *What therefore shall we say? Shall we who profess to be Christians, continue to sustain habitually the same relationship to the evil nature which we did before we were saved, in order that this aforementioned grace might abound? Let not such a thing take place. How is it possible for such as we who were once for all separated from the indwelling sinful nature, any longer to live in its grip? Or, are you ignorant that we who were introduced into vital union with Christ Jesus by the Holy Spirit, into a participation in his death were introduced? Therefore, we were entombed with Him through this aforementioned introduction into His death, in order that, just as*

there was raised up Christ out from among the dead through th
glory of the Father, thus also we in the energy of a new lif
imparted might order our behavior.

Paul is a master teacher. In verses 1-4 he has brought to th
reader two outstanding facts, namely, that the power of indwelling
sin was broken and the divine nature implanted in the believing
sinner at the moment God saved him, with the result that he i
free from the sinful nature and its power, with the obligation t
remain free from it, and that at the same time the divine natur
was implanted with the result that he was given both the desir
and the power to do God's will. These two propositions, the in
spired apostle repeats in slightly different language in verses 5-10
He says, "For in view of the fact that we are become those unite
with Him with respect to the likeness of His death, certainly als
we shall be those united with Him with respect to the likeness o
His resurrection." The future here is the future of logical result
Paul is not here speaking of the future physical resurrection o
the believer, but of his past spiritual resurrection when he place
his faith in the Saviour. The believing sinner's identification wit
Christ in His death, breaks the power of the indwelling sinful na
ture. His identification with the Lord Jesus in His resurrection
imparts the divine nature. This results in what Paul tells us ir
verse 6, the expanded translation and paraphrase of which is as
follows: *Knowing this, that our old, decrepit, outworn, useles*
self, that person we were before we were saved, was crucified with
Him, in order that the physical body which at that time wa
dominated by the sinful nature, might be rendered inoperative in
that respect, to the end that we are no longer rendering an
habitual slave's obedience to the sinful nature, for the one who
has been once for all separated from the sinful nature, stands in
a permanent relationship of freedom from it.

Let us use a rather simple and homely illustration to make this
clear. It is that of a machine shop, in which there is a turning
lathe operated by means of a belt which is attached to a revolving
wheel in the ceiling of the room. When the workman wishes to
render the lathe inoperative, in other words, wishes to stop it, he
takes a pole and slides the belt off from the wheel, thus disengaging

the turning lathe from the revolving wheel which heretofore had driven it. That turning lathe is like the human body of the sinner, and the revolving wheel in the ceiling, like the evil nature. As the wheel in the ceiling makes the turning lathe go round, so the sinful nature controls the body of the sinner. And as the machinist renders the lathe inoperative by slipping off the belt which connected it with the wheel, so God in salvation slips the belt, so to speak, off from the sinful nature which connected it with the physical body of the believer, thus rendering that body inoperative so far as any control which that nature might have over the believer, is concerned.

The Christian is exhorted to maintain that relationship of disconnection which God has brought about between him and the indwelling sinful nature. However, God has not taken away the Christian's free will, and does not treat him as a machine. It is possible for the Christian by an act of his will to slip the belt back on, connecting himself with the evil nature, thus bringing sin into his life. But, he is not able to do this habitually, and for various reasons. In the first place, it is not the Christian's nature to sin. He has been made a partaker of the divine nature which impels him to hate sin and to love holiness. In the second place, the minute a Christian sins, the Holy Spirit is grieved, and that makes the believer decidely uncomfortable, spiritually. God also sends suffering and chastening into his life as a curb to sin. All these things taken together, preclude any possibility of the Christian taking advantage of divine grace. Thus, Paul has answered his hearer's question again, namely, that the believing sinner's death with Christ has disengaged that person from any connection with his indwelling sinful nature, resulting in that person's body being rendered inoperative so far as any control which the evil nature might exercise over it, is concerned. And he finishes the demonstration by saying, *Now, since we died once for all with Christ, we believe that we will also live by means of Him, knowing that Christ, having been raised out from among the dead, no longer dies. Death over Him no longer exercises lordship, for the death which He died, to the aforementioned sin He died once for all, but the life which He lives, He lives with respect to God.*

Now, to return to our illustration. The better machine shops no longer operate their machinery by means of a ceiling wheel, but by an individual electric motor installed beneath each machine, thus introducing a new source of power. Just so, God, when He saves a sinner, installs a new source of power, the divine nature. Before salvation, the sinner lived his life in the energy of the evil nature. After salvation has wrought its work in him, he has had the power of that nature broken, and he has at his disposal a new source of energy, the divine nature. The evil nature produced sin in his life. The divine nature produces righteousness. But here our illustration breaks down. No illustration is ever expected to walk on all fours, for the material or human can never perfectly illustrate the spiritual. However, like a dog on three legs, it gets there just the same.

The owner of a machine shop, when installing the electric motor, removes the ceiling wheels and does not use them anymore. He has a superior and more economical arrangement. But God, when He imparts the divine nature, leaves the evil nature in the believer, however, with its power over the individual broken, and for the reasons mentioned above. Hence, the Christian, being a free moral agent, having his will set absolutely free, must choose between living his life in the energy of the evil nature or in the power of the divine nature. He is not a machine, geared to the divine nature in such a way that he must live his life in its energy whether he wills it or no. His will is poised between the two, and he has the responsibility of refusing the behests of the evil nature, and obeying the urgings of the divine nature. *The Christian never acts alone. He acts and speaks in the energy of the evil nature or in the power of the divine nature.* The responsibility of the Christian in relation to these two natures, Paul takes up in 6:11-14.

And now to use another illustration. Here is Mr. Nomechanic. He is no mechanic. He does not know the first thing about machinery. He purchases a fine automobile, receives instructions how to operate it, and drives off. After a few months, he notices that the engine becomes overheated easily, stalls in traffic, and misses as he climbs hills. He takes the car back to the dealer, complaining that it is not working well, although it is a new automobile. The dealer asks him how often he has the car serviced, and discovers that the owner has never had a mechanic adjust the engine, brakes, and other mechanical parts. The car ran, but the owner did not obtain the most efficient service from it because he did not have it oiled and greased at regular intervals.

When God installs the divine nature in the inner being of a believing sinner, that nature operates, and produces the Christian graces in the life of the person. There is always a change for the better in the life of the person who receives the Lord Jesus as Saviour. And that change can only be accounted for by the fact that God has imparted His divine nature to the individual, at the same time breaking the power of the indwelling sinful nature. This shows clearly that there is an actual change in the inner spiritual being of the sinner whom God saves. But the point is, that the divine nature does not work at its highest efficiency in the life of the believer unless that person adjusts himself to it, unless he does something about it. That new nature is not a perpetual motion machine grinding out a Christian life in the person, irrespective of what that individual does. Like the owner of the automobile, who obtained the best results from his car after he had it serviced regularly, so the Christian can only expect to have the divine nature operate at its peak efficiency when he is properly adjusted to it. It is concerning this adjustment that we will now speak.

The first adjustment, Paul says, the believer should make, is to reckon himself dead to sin and alive to God. That is, he is to reckon or count upon the fact that the power of the indwelling sinful nature is broken and the divine nature is implanted. The Greek word translated "reckon" is *logizomai*. We get our word "logic" from it. The word means "to reckon, compute, calculate, to take into account, to make account of." Now, to count upon the fact that the power of the sinful nature is broken and the divine nature implanted, does not make those things so. Those facts are true, whether the believer counts upon their actuality or not. But living one's life on the basis of or in consideration of those facts results in their beneficial results in the life. Likewise, when the believer does not take these facts into account, disastrous results follow.

Now, to use another homely illustration. There is a party game in which a blindfolded person is brought into the room, and made to stand on a table board which rests on some books on the floor. Two young men lift the board about a foot, and warn the young man not to bump his head against the ceiling. Thinking that he is near the ceiling, he loses his balance and falls off. He lost his balance and fell because he reckoned himself where he was not. Just so, a Christian who fails to count upon the fact that the power of the sinful nature is broken in his life, fails to get consistent victory over it, with the result that he lives a mediocre Christian life. He reckoned himself where he was not.

Another young man is blindfolded and stood on the board. He knows the game. When the board is lifted and he is warned not to bump his head against the ceiling, he remains perfectly straight and maintains his equilibrium, because he reckoned himself where he was. And so it is with a Christian who counts upon the fact that the power of the sinful nature is broken. He knows that he does not have to obey it, and that he has the power to say NO to it, and he turns his back on it and does what is right.

And so it is with the Christian who does not count upon the fact that the divine nature is implanted in his inner being. He goes on living his Christian life as best he can in the energy of his own strength, with the result that he exhibits an imitation Christian experience, not the genuine thing. But the believer who counts upon the fact that he is a possessor of the divine nature, ceases from his own struggles at living a Christian life, and avails himself of the power of God supplied in the divine nature. So the first adjustment the Christian should make is that of counting upon the fact that the power of the indwelling sinful nature is broken and the divine nature imparted, and order his life on that principle.

When he does this, he will be obeying Paul's instructions in verses 12 and 13. The first one is, "Stop allowing the sinful nature to reign as king in your mortal body, with a view to obeying its (the body's) cravings." We have offered the translation and paraphrase without troubling the reader with all the technicalities of the Greek grammar and syntax involved. Before salvation had wrought its inner work in the believer, he as an unsaved person, was the slave of his indwelling sinful nature. That nature reigned as king in his life. Now, Paul says, after the person is saved, he is to stop allowing this evil nature to lord it over him. The very fact that Paul commands such an action, tells us that the believer is able to obey it. The shackles which had heretofore bound him to it, have now been stricken off. The connecting belt has been shunted off. His will is absolutely free. He has the ability to say a point blank NO to this fallen nature. And, yielded to the divine nature, he has the desire and power to do so. His will in itself does not give him the desire nor power to refuse to obey the behests of that nature. His will is free, unshackled, and in a position to say NO to the sinful nature. But the desire to say NO, and the ability to put that NO into action, are derived from the divine nature. Therefore, the believer's responsibility is to keep himself living habitually in the control of the new nature. This involves a constant attitude of opposition to the evil nature and a constant dependence upon and yieldedness to the divine nature.

The Greek grammar involved makes it absolutely sure that the cravings (lusts) spoken of here refer to those of the human body, not those of the evil nature. While these cravings find their source in that nature, yet Paul refers them to the body, and for the following reason. The evil nature is an unseen, intangible thing, very real, but not visible. Consequently, to keep a sharp lookout for the cravings that issue from it would be like fighting an enemy in the dark. But to watch the cravings of the human body, is practical and has promise of success. For instance, the Christian should watch what his eyes look at, his ears hear, and his tongue speaks, where his feet carry him, and what his hands do. The cravings of the members of his body are the things to be carefully scrutinized and weighed. Those cravings which bear the stamp and impress of the evil nature are not to be satisfied. The technique is to count upon the fact that the power of the evil nature has been broken, that it is a dethroned king, and say a point blank NO to it. As the Christian makes a practice of this he finds how easy it really becomes to say NO, until it becomes so habitual that the action becomes automatic. It is like turning off the radio. The Christian has the same power over the evil nature that he has over his radio. When an undesirable program suddenly comes in, he can turn the radio off and say, "There you are. You are not my master. I am yours. You cannot bring that evil trash into my life." The believer can learn to treat the evil nature the same way. *One must treat it rough.* When the Christian comes to believe what God has said about the fact that the power of the evil nature over him is broken, and that instead of being his master, the believer is its master, he will act upon this truth, and find how easy it is to give the evil nature, in the language of today, the brush-off. He turns a cold shoulder to it. Our blessed Lord did not gain the victory over Satan in the wilderness by merely quoting Scripture to him. He gained the victory by having obeyed that Scripture He quoted all down the years of His life, so that when the temptation came, He had reserves of spiritual strength stored up in His inner spiritual being by means of which He said a point blank NO to the devil. The Christian life can become just that way. While never free from temptation nor the onslaught of Satan, yet the believer can move through life like a ship on an even keel, riding out the storms of temptation because he has reserves of power that will enable him to plow through heavy seas without being tossed about by them. What a gyroscope is to a ship, so these reserves of spiritual power are to a Christian.

When the believer counts upon the fact that the power of the indwelling sinful nature is broken, and operates his life on that principle, he stops allowing that nature to reign as a king in his life. But he does something else. He obeys Paul's admonition, "Stop putting your members as weapons of unrighteousness at the service of the sinful nature." He not only refuses obedience to its sinful behests, but he refuses to put his eyes, ears, tongue, mind, hands, and feet at its service, in order that the fallen nature might use these as weapons of unrighteousness in the battle of Satan against God. The Christian is in a warfare. Paul sees him as a soldier of Jesus Christ fighting in the armies of righteousness. When the Christian puts his members at the service of the sinful nature, he is guilty of high treason, fighting against his own Captain, the Lord Jesus.

Instead of putting his members at the service of the indwelling sinful nature, the believer is exhorted by Paul as follows: "But put yourselves once for all at the service of God, as those who are living ones out from among the dead, and your members, put them once for all at the service of God as weapons of righteousness." It is a matter of substitution. To keep from putting our members at the service of the sinful nature, we should refuse to do so, and at the same time put them at the service of God by yielding them by a once for all act to God. *When the second act becomes automatic, that is, when an habitual yielding to the divine nature becomes so ingrained in our being that it is easier for us to yield to it than to the evil nature, the Christian has come into what is called the victorious life.* And that is what Paul is talking about when he says, "For (then) the evil nature shall not lord it over you, for you are not under law but under grace." But why is this so? What is there in the fact that a Christian is not under law but under grace, that gives him victory over the evil nature? The answer is found in the following bit of verse.

> *"Do this and live, the law commands,*
> *But gives me neither feet nor hands.*
> *A better word the gospel brings,*
> *It bids me fly, and gives me wings."*

Law neither gives the desire nor the power to do God's will. Grace sweetly exhorts and gives both the desire and the power to do His good pleasure. The Christian therefore has God's guarantee that if he obeys the instructions for victory over sin and for the living of a Christian life found in Romans 6:1-13, the indwelling sinful nature will not exercise autocratic control over his life.

Paul has answered his listener's first question, namely, "Sha
we who profess to be Christians, continue habitually to sustai
the same relationship to the totally depraved nature that we di
before we were saved in order that grace may abound?" H
showed that it was a mechanical impossibility to do so, inasmuc
that God broke the power of the indwelling sinful nature an
implanted the divine nature. Since the power of the evil natur
is broken, the believer does not have to sin, and since the divin
nature is implanted, he does not want to sin, and has both th
desire and the power to live a life pleasing to God. Paul ha
shown his questioner that it is impossible for a Christian to live
life of habitual sin. Now, the person who asked the first question
asks another. It is this. "What then? Shall we sin once in awhile
since we are not under law but under grace?" That is, if grac
makes it impossible for a Christian to sin habitually as he di
before he was saved, will not grace permit him to sin once i
awhile? Of course, the person who asked this question did no
understand grace. Arthur S. Way, in his excellent translatio
of the Pauline epistles, has read this person's mind well. H
translates and paraphrases; "'Ah then', my opponents will cry
'we may safely sin, since we are not under the uncompromising
rule of the law, but under the lenient sceptre of grace.'" The
person was right in saying that law is uncompromising, but
wrong when he thinks that grace is lenient with a Christian, and
will allow a life of planned, occasional sin.

Grace is stricter than law ever was. When God abrogated the
Old Testament law, He brought in a far more efficient deterrent
to evil when He sent the Holy Spirit to indwell Christians. While
law can only take notice of general rules of human behavior, the
Holy Spirit notices the slightest sin and deals with the details
of particular sins in the believer's life. A few motorcycle police-
men with their motors tuned up, are a far better deterrent to
speeding than a placard placed along the road giving the speed
limit. The Holy Spirit is grieved at the slightest sin in the Christian's life, and turns from His work of causing that believer to
grow in grace to that of convicting that person of his sin. Grace

xpects the highest type of Christian life. It gives both the desire
ad the power for that life.   If it is not forthcoming, grace
aastens the Christian and makes it so uncomfortable for that
erson, that he forsakes his sin, confesses it, and is restored to
·llowship with his Lord and Saviour.

In answering the question, namely, "What then. Shall we who
rofess to be Christians, live a life of planned, occasional sin,
ecause we are not under the uncompromising rule of law but
nder the lenient scepter of grace?" Paul says: *Do you not know
:at to the one to whom you put yourselves at the service of as
!aves resulting in obedience, slaves you are to the one to whom
ou are rendering obedience, whether it be slaves of the evil
ature resulting in death, or obedient slaves resulting in righteous-
:ess? But thanks be to God, that whereas you were at one time
!aves of the evil nature, now you obeyed out from the heart a
ype of teaching to which you were handed over. And having
een liberated from the evil nature, you became slaves of right-
ousness. I am using human terminology because of the limitations
f your human nature, for, just as you put your members as slaves
t the service of uncleanness and lawlessness resulting in lawlessness, thus now, put your members once for all as slaves at the
ervice of righteousness resulting in holiness. For when you were
laves of the evil nature, you were those who were free with
espect to righteousness. Therefore, what fruit were you having
hen, of which now you are ashamed? For the consummation of
hose things is death. But now, having been set free from the
·vil nature, and having become slaves to God, you are having
jour fruit resulting in holiness, and the consummation, life eternal.
For the pay which the evil nature doles out is death. But the
jratuitous gift of God is life eternal which is in Christ Jesus
our Lord* (translation and paraphrase, Rom. 6:16-23).

The key to the understanding of Paul's answer is in the various
meanings of the Greek word translated "servants." The word is
doulos. We will follow Paul's argument as we look at these
meanings. The question he is answering is as to whether God's
grace allows for a life of planned, occasional sin.   The word

speaks of one who is born into a condition of slavery. The Greek
had a word for a free man captured in war and made a slave
But this word (*doulos*) refers to one who has by birth inherite
his position and condition of slavery. When Adam fell, he con
tracted an evil nature which has been passed on to the huma
race because he is its federal head. This fallen nature has bee
handed down by birth to every individual human being. That i
what David meant when he said, "In sin did my mother conceiv
me" (Psalm 51:5). Thus, by human birth a person receives
nature that makes him a sinful creature with sinful desires, in
capable of anything else except sinful acts. He loves sin becaus
he has a nature which causes him to do so. That is the conditio
of the unsaved person. But in the believer, the power of this ev
nature has been broken, and it is no longer the nature of tha
individual to love sin. Instead, he hates it. The divine nature ha
been implanted, which nature gives him the desire and the powe
to do God's will. He loves righteousness now. It is his natur
to do what is right. *The Christian has changed masters becaus
he has changed natures.* How ridiculous, Paul says, it is to as
such a question as to whether a Christian may live a life o
planned, occasional sin. In view of these tremendous inne
changes, he is not the slave of sin anymore, but the loving bond
slave of God. He does not have to sin anymore, and he does no
want to sin. It is his nature to do what is right.

The word refers to one who is bound to another in bands s
strong that only death can break them. Before salvation wrough
its supernatural work in the believer, he was bound to Satan in
a bond so strong that only death could break it. That bond wa
a common nature, totally depraved. He loved what the devi
loves, namely, sin, and hated what the devil hates, namely
righteousness. His identification with the Lord Jesus in His
death broke the bands which had bound him to Satan as hi
slave, and his identification with Him in His resurrection, resulted
in the impartation of the divine nature. Now it is the believer'
nature to hate sin and to do God's will. But to live a life of plan
ned, occasional sin demands that the believer possess the totally

depraved nature as his own nature, and that that nature reign as king in his life. But that is an impossibility, for he is now the willing love-slave of the Lord Jesus, possessing the divine nature as the governing nature in his inner being. And as such he is bound to his new Master in bands which only death can break. And since Christ is his life (Col. 3:4), and Christ never dies, he will never die and be separated from Christ, to lose his divine nature and receive again the evil nature, which latter nature could be the only thing that would give him the desire to live a life of planned, occasional sin.

The word *doulos* means "one whose will is swallowed up in the will of another." Before salvation, the individual's will is swallowed up in the will of Satan. After salvation, his will is swallowed up in the sweet will of God. Paul argues that since the believer's will is swallowed up in the sweet will of God, that that would preclude any life of planned, occasional sin.

The word means "one who serves another to the disregard of his own interests." Before salvation, the person serves the devil to the disregard of his own interests. He keeps on in sin no matter how grievous the consequences. After salvation, the properly taught, Spirit-filled believer, serves the Lord Jesus with an utter abandon that says, "Nothing matters about me, as long as the Lord Jesus is glorified." Do you think, Paul argues, that such a person who loves and serves the Lord Jesus that way, would ever think of living a life of planned, occasional sin?

And so, Paul has answered the person's second question, "Shall we who profess to be Christians, live a life of planned, occasional sin because we are not under law but under grace?" by showing that when the sinner is saved, he changes masters, and by reason of the fact that he has changed natures. *It is the nature which determines what master the individual serves.*

This finishes our discussion of the subject, "The Believer and the Isolation of the Evil Nature." There is one more thing to be said, however. The divine nature is not the only spiritual source of power indwelling the believer which he has at his disposal. In this Age of Grace, the Holy Spirit has come to take up His permanent residence in him for the purpose of causing him to grow in the Christian life, enabling him to gain consistent victory over sin and live a life pleasing to God. The reader is urged to add to his knowledge of the divine provision for living the victorious life, and thus come to live a life on the highest Christian plane, by studying the author's work on the ministry of the Holy Spirit, in *Untranslatable Riches from the Greek New Testament.*

JESUS AND THE BELIEVER TODAY

God has so created man that he never enjoys complete satisfaction and rest of heart until he finds it in a vital experience of companionship with his Creator. King Solomon, who had at his disposal all that wealth could give him, after thoroughly investigating its possibilities, cried, "Vanity of vanities, all is vanity." That, put into modern English is, "Emptiness of emptinesses, all is emptiness," or "Futility of futilities, all is futility." All that earth can offer is futile when it comes to giving a person complete soul satisfaction.

In the following pages, the Word of God gives us information as to how a person who has been brought into right relationship to God, might cultivate and maintain a comradeship with Him in which he will find final and lasting soul satisfaction and rest.

IV

Jesus and the Believer Today

I F SOMEONE today claimed that he was a constant companion of Julius Caesar, enjoyed his fellowship day by day, and knew him very well, what would your reaction be? You would say, "Julius Caesar is dead. No one can be an intimate companion of this man today." But, suppose for a moment that Julius Caesar were alive today and on some remote planet, and that there were some means of communication so that people on earth could converse with him. If ten thousand people all claimed to have him for a constant companion, what would you say? Your answer would be, "Julius Caesar could only have intelligent contact with one person at a time."

This very thing which is impossible in the case of Julius Caesar, is possible in the case of the Lord Jesus, because He is not only human but God, because He is alive, and because there is a supernatural means whereby tens of thousands of people may be in constant touch with Him at the same time, twenty-four hours a day. It is concerning this fellowship of the believer with the Lord Jesus, that we wish now to speak. We will approach our subject from the angle of what the believer must do to cultivate and maintain a day by day fellowship with this Jesus who lived on earth in the first century, who died and was raised from the dead, and who now, in His glorified body resides in heaven. He is, to be sure, localized in His human body as a man, but, as God He is ever omnipresent, and thus, as close to the believer as any human companion on earth could be.

The first thing the believer must do is to learn to know the Lord Jesus, not now as Saviour only, but as his Lord and his

constant Helper, Guide, and Friend. *First,* he must study th
account of His life in the four Gospels. Here, he will come t
know what the Lord Jesus is like. The Holy Spirit will paint th
portrait of the Lord Jesus in his mind's eye. Erasmus, the grea
Greek scholar and humanist, a contemporary of Martin Luther
said in the preface of his Greek Testament: "These holy page
will summon up the living image of His mind. They will giv
you Christ Himself, talking, healing, dying, rising, the whole
Christ in a word; They will give Him to you in an intimacy se
close that He would be less visible to you if He stood before you
eyes." Erasmus was an unsaved man, and if he could see some
of the beauties of the Lord Jesus in the pages of the New Testament, how much clearer is the portrait which the Holy Spiri
can paint for the believer as he meditates upon the story of Jesus
Second, in addition to the believer's study of the four Gospels
he should become well acquainted with the other parts of the
Scriptures also, for in these the Lord Jesus will talk to him
Thus, in the study of the Bible, the believer has a Spirit-drawr
portrait of the Lord Jesus before him, and the words of Jesus
spoken to him. *Third,* the believer should maintain a day by day
fellowship with Him in prayer, in realizing His nearness, in
living in His presence. This is that sweet, mystical communion of
the believer who is yielded to the Holy Spirit, with his Lord and
Master.

John, in his first epistle (Chapter 1:1-2:2), gives us four things
the believer must do to cultivate and maintain this fellowship of
which we are now to speak. The first thing John does is to refer
the believer to the account of the earthly life of the Saviour in
1:1-4, where he says that *the incarnation is a revelation of that
in which the believer participates, namely, Christ, who is the believer's life.* It is, therefore, only as a person has Christ as his
life, that he is able to have fellowship with Him.

John speaks in verse one of the record which he has given us
of the earthly life of our Lord, and which we know as the Gospel
according to John. He begins in the words, "That which was
from the beginning." In his Gospel, John starts with the words,
"In the beginning was the Word." There he reaches back into

e eternity before the universe was created, and tells his reader
at the Lord Jesus was eternally existent before that event.
[ere, he only reaches back to the time when God spoke the
Jord, and a perfect universe sprang into existence. In 1:1-10
: his Gospel, after speaking of the pre-existent Christ, John
peaks of Him as the Creator, and of the fact that not only was
[e transcendent above the universe but that He was immanent
1 it, and that He revealed Himself through the light which the
aterial world gave the human race.   This is what John has
ference to in the words, "That which was from the beginning."

When he says, "Which we have heard," he is speaking of
acarnation, the coming of our great God and Saviour Jesus Christ
1 this world, and His assumption of a human body and the
atting of Himself under human limitations. The "we" is the
litorial "we" of John. It might possibly also include the other
isciples as eye-witnesses. The verb is in the perfect tense, which
2nse in Greek refers to a past completed action having present
2sults. The expanded translation would be, "that which we have
eard with the present result that it is ringing in our ears." By
1e use of this tense, John is telling his reader that though he
7rote the Gospel which is attributed to him, about sixty years
fter the events recorded took place, yet as he was writing the
tory of Jesus, he could hear His words just as clearly as he did
7hile He was on earth during His ministry. In the first century,
ooks were few, and people remembered much. Today, books
re plentiful, and people remember little. This is one of the things
hat could account for the vivid memories which John had of our
_ord's earthly life. Again, that earthly life was so unusual, and
ohn's experiences so extra-ordinary, that they left an indelible
mpression upon his mind. Another thing that insured the ac-
uracy of John's account was the fact that when Jesus promised
o send the disciples the Holy Spirit, He said that the Spirit
vould bring all things to their remembrance, whatever He had
aid (John 14:26). Thus, in the event that John failed to remem-
ier certain things, the Holy Spirit would be sure to remind him
if them as he wrote his account of the life of our Lord. In ad-
lition to all this, the superintending care of the Holy Spirit as

John wrote, insured the absolute accuracy of the record. John therefore, uses the perfect tense in order to assure the reade that his record of the life of Jesus was one that could be trusted.

Then he says, "Which we have seen with our eyes." Again h uses the perfect tense, and a particular word which speaks of th act of seeing with discernment. The expanded translation woul read, "That which we have seen with discernment, and which a a present result is in our mind's eye." Thus he tells his reader that while writing the record of our Lord's life, he could close hi physical eyes and see his Lord in his mind's eye as He walked o earth. He claimed a perfect retention after sixty years, of tha which he had seen in the life of the Lord Jesus. The phrase, "wit our eyes," John included in order to combat false doctrine i the first century which was known as Doceticsm, namely, th teaching that our Lord only had a seeming body, not a trul human one.

In the words, "Which we have looked upon," he uses a dif ferent word for "seeing," and changes to the aorist tense. Th verb means, "to gaze upon with wonder." The two verbs which mean, "to see," which John uses here, could be illustrated a follows: A military parade is swinging down the boulevard. A general of the army, and a mountaineer on his first visit to th city, are watching the parade. The general looks at it with a critical, understanding, discerning eye. The mountaineer jus gazes at it with wonder and awe. The disciples watched the Lor Jesus through the three and one half years of His ministry wit a critical, understanding, discerning eye. No wonder that the then gazed upon Him with wonder and awe as they began t realize the wonderful Personage with whom they were privilege to fellowship. The reason why John changed from the perfect t the aorist tense is that after using two verbs in the perfect tense which fact assured the reader of the accuracy of his record, h felt no need of repeating the procedure, and thus used the tense which the Greeks commonly made use of when they did not wish to speak in detail.

Then he says, "And our hands have handled." The Greek verb John uses means, "To handle with a view to investigation." It is the same word that Luke uses when he reports our Lord's words in the upper room after the resurrection, "Behold my hands and my feet, that it is I myself; handle Me and see; for a spirit hath not flesh and bones as ye see Me have" (24:39). The resurrection of our Lord is not mentioned in John's first epistle except here, and here incidently. John has told the reader so far that the disciples obtained their information regarding the incarnation first hand, and through the mediums of sight, hearing, and feeling. The expanded translation of his introductory words are as follows: "That which was from the beginning, that which we have heard with the present result that it is ringing in our ears, that which we have seen with discernment with our eyes, with the present result that it is vivid in our mind's eye, that which we gazed upon with wonder and our hands handled with a view to investigation, concerning the Word of the life."

John uses the phrase, "The Word of the life." The life referred to is the life that God is in Himself. The word John uses which is translated "word" is *logos* which comes from *legō*. This latter word means "to speak." When one has spoken the sum total of his thoughts concerning something, he has given to his hearer a total concept of that thing. Thus the word *logos* means "a total concept" of anything. Jesus Christ is the total concept of God in the sense that He in His incarnation gave the human race through human terms a concept of what deity is like. In that sense He is the Word of God. John thus speaks of Him as the Word of the life in that He is the total concept of deity.

Then he says, "The light was manifested." The Greek word here means "to make visible." It was in the incarnation of the Son of God that He made visible the life that God is. John says that he has seen it, and is bearing witness and announcing to his readers the life, namely, the eternal life. Then he says, "Which was with the Father." The word "which" that John uses, has a qualitative aspect about it. The life was of such a nature as to have been with the Father. The word "with" in the Greek text has the idea of "facing." The life was facing God the Father, that is, having fellowship with the Father. But in order to have fellowship, a person must be predicated. Therefore, the life spoken of here must be a person, and that person is the Lord Jesus. Here John refers to that eternal fellowship which existed between the Father and the Son, a fellowship which never had a beginning, and was interrupted only once, during those dark hours when Jesus hung on the Cross and cried, "My God, my God, why hast thou forsaken Me?" This life, John says, was manifested to him, namely, made visible to him in and through our Lord's earthly life.

Now John declares to his readers the purpose he had in writing the Gospel attributed to him. He says that it was in order that his readers may have fellowship with him. The first Epistle of John was not written to any local church nor to any particular individuals, but to the church at large in the Roman Empire. Many thousands of his readers never saw John nor ever would. The word "fellowship" today usually means "comradeship, companionship, social intercourse." How are we to understand John's words here in view of this? A look at the Greek word tells us that it refers to a joint-participation of two or more individuals in a common interest or activity. And this is the way the word "fellowship" is used here. It is used this way in academic circles, where a graduate student has a fellowship in the teaching profession in the school where he is continuing his studies.

John therefore says that he wrote the Gospel in order that his readers might have joint-participation with him in his first-hand knowledge of the Lord Jesus. John reports what he saw, heard, and felt concerning the Lord Jesus in His earthly life. As the Spirit-taught believer reverently reads the Gospel, he looks through John's eyes and sees Jesus, listens through John's ears and hears Him speak, and with John's hand touches Him. Thus, he has a joint-participation with John in the latter's first-hand knowledge of the earthly life of our Lord.

Then John says, "Our fellowship is with the Father, and with his Son Jesus Christ." That is, John is saying that the believer and God participate jointly in a common nature, the divine nature. Of course, we are not to understand that this divine nature is inherent in the individual as he is born into this world. On the contrary, Pauline teaching is to the effect that the person has a

otally depraved nature at that time. But, in response to the
sinner's act of faith in the Lord Jesus as Saviour, God the Holy
Spirit imparts to him the divine nature (II Peter 1:4). This we
call regeneration. We must be careful to distinguish this from
the nature of deity which God alone possesses. When two persons
have like natures, they have the same likes and dislikes, the same
interests and activities.   For instance, a grave digger and an
artist have nothing basically in common. But, two artists have
the same likes and dislikes, the same interests and activities. Thus
it is with God and the believer. They both hate sin and love
righteousness. They are both interested in the things of God and
the work of God. Therefore, this new life which is imparted to
the believer is the life that God is. This joint-participation in a
common interest and activity, issues in what we call fellowship,
namely, comradeship, companionship.   In this double sense does
John use the word "fellowship." John says that his purpose therefore in giving his readers a first-hand knowledge of the earthly
life of our Lord, is that they may become intimately and intelli-
gently acquainted with Him, having joint-participation together
in common interests and activities, which in turn will issue in a
beautiful companionship that will bring fullness of joy. Therefore,
the first step in the believer's cultivation of an intimate comradeship with the Lord Jesus, is to reverently study His life as
portrayed in the Gospel accounts, and to meditate upon His words
as He speaks through His inspired writers in the letters to the
churches.

After telling his reader in verses one and two, that the incarnation is a revelation of the life in which the believer participates,
that Christ is that life, and that if he wishes to have an intimate
companionship with the Lord Jesus, he must study the Word of
God in order to become better acquainted with Him, John in
verses five to seven informs him *that there must naturally be an
evidence of this joint-participation in the life of God seen in the
life of the believer*. That is, if the believer participates in the
same nature that God possesses, he must show in his life that he
loves the things that God loves, righteousness, and hates the things
that God hates, namely, sin. If this evidence is not found in the

life of the individual, that shows that that person is only a professing Christian, not a possessing one.

First, John lays down his fundamental proposition to the effec
that "God is light, and in Him is no darkness at all." Withou
troubling the reader with the rule of Greek syntax which helps u
here, we offer the translation, "God as to His nature is light.
That is, God is a Person, not an inanimate thing like light. Hi
nature is that of holiness, righteousness, purity, and all the othe
qualities that go to make up a perfect character. Then John pu
the statement negatively, when he says, "Darkness in Him doe
not exist, not even one bit."

Upon the basis of this proposition, he has two statements t
make. First, he says that the person who claims to be a joint
participant with God in His nature as light, and yet walk
habitually in the darkness of sin, is a liar, and does not practic
the truth. A translation with paraphrase of John's Greek here i
as follows: "If we up and say that we are constantly having fel
lowship with Him in the sense of participating with Him in
common nature and in common likes and dislikes, and at th
same time are habitually ordering our behavior within the spher
of the darkness of sin, we are lying and are not practicing th
truth." This person is an unsaved person, and for the following
reasons. First, he is ordering his conduct within the sphere of sin
which means that there is nothing of the righteousness of Go
that enters through this circle of sin in which this person live
and acts. His entire conduct is ensphered by sin. In the secon
place, his conduct as such is habitual, as shown by the tense and
mood of the verb which is translated "walk." No saved perso
sins habitually like he did before he was saved. When God save
a sinner, he changes him inwardly in such a way that he hate
sin and practices righteousness. God gives him the power to say
"no" to sin and "yes" to the Lord Jesus. This person, therefore
who claims to have things in common with God, but in whose
life sin is king, is an unsaved person.

Then in verse seven, John tells us who does have fellowship
with God. He says that it is the person who walks in the light.
This verse in translation and paraphrase is as follows: "But if

in the sphere of the light that God is, we are habitually ordering our behavior as He Himself is in the sphere of the light, we, the believer and God, are having constant fellowship with one another, and the blood of Jesus His Son keeps on constantly cleansing us from every sin." By walking in the light, John means the habitual ordering of our conduct within the sphere of the precepts, admonitions, and commands of God's Word. The person who does that constantly, has things in common with God and thus has companionship with Him. That this companionship is not a one-sided affair, namely, from the standpoint of the believer alone, but is engaged in by both the believer and God, is told us in John's use of a reciprocal pronoun. Wonder of wonders, there is reciprocity in this fellowship. Not only does the believer have fellowship with the Lord Jesus, but the Lord Jesus has fellowship with one of His creatures. Humbling thought, that He should delight in the fellowship afforded Him by worms of the dust such as we are, sinners saved by grace. And while this wonderful walk in the light and fellowship with Jesus is going on, the blood of Jesus is constantly cleansing us from every sin.

But the question now arises, as to why the necessity of the cleansing blood when the believer is walking in the sphere of the light and in fellowship with the Lord Jesus. The answer is found in the fact that even when walking in the sphere of the light, the believer has sins in his life of which he knows nothing. Sin in the life is recognized by means of our knowledge of the Word of God. As we come to know and understand our Bibles better, we come to see more clearly what sin is. Things we are doing today which are sinful will in the future as we know God's Word better, appear in their true identity. These unknown sins would keep us from fellowship with the Lord Jesus if this divine provision was not in effect, namely, the constant cleansing of the life by the blood of Jesus.

Thus, John has told us that God as to His nature is light, and that darkness in Him does not exist, not even one bit. Then he says that the person who claims to have constant fellowship with Him, and at the same time is habitually conducting himself within the sphere of the darkness of sin, is a liar, and does not practise the truth. This person is an unsaved person. Finally, he informs us that the person who habitually orders his behavior within the sphere of the light that God is, is having constant fellowship with Him, and the blood of Jesus is as constantly cleansing him from every sin. Thus, John has established his proposition that there must be evidence in a person's life of his joint-participation with God in a common nature, and in common likes and dislikes. In other words, where there is life, there must be fruit.

John has given his readers two things which the believer must do in order to cultivate and maintain a day by day fellowship with the Lord Jesus. The *first* is as follows: He has told him that the incarnation is a revelation of the life of God in which the believer participates, and that in order to have an intimate acquaintanceship with the Lord Jesus, the believer must come to know Him through a study of the Word of God. *Second,* John has made plain the necessity of the evidence of this joint-participation in the life of God on the part of the believer, namely, a manifestation of the qualities such as purity, holiness, and righteousness which make up the character of God. Now he informs his readers as to the proper attitude towards sin on the part of the person who is a joint-participant with God in the light which God is.

In the first place, the believer must recognize that he still has the totally depraved nature in him, although he is not in it in the sense that he is not in its grip (v. 8). This is the way John puts it in his Greek: "If we up and say that sin we are not constantly having, ourselves we are deceiving, and the truth is not in us." The word "sin" here is without the definite article, and does not speak, therefore, of acts of sin but of the sinful nature. There were some in John's day as there are now, who assert that the evil nature is completely eradicated in the believer sometime in his Christian experience. John is combating this false teaching. Paul is clear in Romans VI to the effect that when God saves a person, He breaks the power of indwelling sin. But nowhere in Scripture is there any hint that this nature is removed during the earthly life of the believer. The danger and harm in this false teaching is that the believer is put off his guard as to the activities of this evil nature, and thus allows sin to enter his life, which latter he calls mistakes. To be forewarned as to the position of an enemy, is to be forearmed. John says that the believer who denies the fact of the indwelling sinful nature, only deceives himself, nobody else. Everybody else can see sin in that person's life. The truth as to the indwelling sinful nature is not in that believer.

The second attitude which the believer must have towards sin is that in case sin enters his experience, he agrees with God as to that fact, and puts that sin away (v. 9). John says, "If we confess our sins, He is faithful and just to forgive us our sins, and to cleanse us from all unrighteousness." The Greek word translated "confess" deserves careful study. It is made up of a word meaning "to speak," and another word which means "the same," the total meaning of the word being, "to speak the same" thing that someone else speaks, thus to agree with that person. Confession of sin on the part of the believer means that he agrees with God as to the implications of sin present in his life. God says, "That thing is sin." The believer says to God, "That thing in my life is sin." God says, "You should repent of that sin." The believer says to God, "I do repent of that sin." God says, "You should put that sin out of your life and resolve never to do that thing again." The believer says to God, "I right now put that thing out of my life and resolve never to do it again." All of this means that confession of sin on the part of the believer is not a mere admission of the fact of sin in his life, but includes all the implications noted above.

When the believer thus confesses his sin, God is faithful to His Son who by His sacrifice on the Cross paid the penalty of that sin, and just with His own law in that when He shows mercy to the sinning believer, He does so on the basis of justice satisfied, and cleanses that believer from that sin. It is interesting to note that the tense and mood of the word "cleanseth" in verse seven speaks of a continuous action, that of cleansing the believer constantly from unknown sin in his life, while the tense and mood of the word "cleanse" in verse nine indicates that it is a particular and separate act, and for the reason that the believer does not commit acts of sin habitually where sin is known. The presence of sin in the life of the believer which is known and cherished, breaks the fellowship between the believer and the Lord Jesus, not in the sense that the joint-participation in a common nature is affected, for it is not, nor in the sense that that person's standing in grace is affected, for that again is not changed, but in the sense that the companionship between the believer and the Lord Jesus is broken. Sin in a believer's life is a matter, not so much of the breaking of the law, for that aspect of sin was taken care of at the Cross. Sin in the believer's life is a matter of defilement, which defilement must be cleansed away before the Lord Jesus will again have fellowship with the believer. Confession restores this fellowship, and in the case of immediate confession of sin after the act of sin has been committed, fellowship is not broken. Therefore, if the believer desires to maintain an intimate, moment by moment fellowship with the Lord Jesus, he must see to it that sin is kept out of his life, and that in case it enters, he must confess it at once. No properly instructed believer desires to have sin in his life. When sin does enter, it is due to various causes, for instance, ignorance of the Bible teaching concerning the inward transformation which is effected in the inner being of the believer at the moment he is saved, namely, the breaking of the power of the sinful nature and the impartation of the divine nature, or ignorance concerning the sanctifying ministry of the Holy Spirit. Or, it might be lack of Bible study and prayer, or failure to keep ever on the alert lest sin enter the life.

The third attitude of which John speaks is that the believer must recognize the fact that he was born with a sinful nature in the first place, and as a present result, he must always be careful lest sin enter his experience. This John gives us in the words. "If we say that we have not sinned, we make Him a liar, and His word is not in us." The words "have sinned" are in the Greek text in the perfect tense, which tense speaks of a past completed action having present results. The very fact that we in times past have sinned, is a demonstration of the fact that we are members of a fallen race, and that, even though salvation has begun its work in us, there is still a possibility of sin entering the life of the believer.

Thus, John has given us the three attitudes of the believer towards sin: *first,* he is to recognize the fact that the sinful nature remains in the believer during his earthly life, although its power is broken; *second,* the believer must agree with God as to sin in his life in order that he might be cleansed from that sin and restored to fellowship with the Lord Jesus; and *third,* he must ever remember that he is a member of a fallen race, and that sin is ever liable to enter his experience as a believer.

After informing his readers concerning the three-fold attitude towards sin which the believer must maintain if he is to enjoy an intimate fellowship with the Lord Jesus, John brings to his attention the responsibility he has with regard to sin. The believer is forbidden to commit an act of sin. These are John's words, "My little children, these things I am writing to you in order that you may not commit an act of sin." The tense and mood of the verb which John uses, indicates that he looks upon sin in the Christian life, not as habitual conduct, but as an infrequent, out of the ordinary thing. Thus, John declares that sin is not necessary in the Christian life. However, in his next statement he acknowledges the fact that it is possible. He says, "And if any man sin, we have an advocate with the Father, Jesus Christ the righteous." Again, the word "sin" which John uses indicates that it is an act of sin, not habitual sin. The expanded translation would be, "If any man commits an act of sin." The Greek word translated "advocate" is one that deserves particular attention. It is made up of two words, one which means "to call" and another which means "alongside." It is used in the Greek law courts of an attorney who was retained by his client to plead his cause. The Lord Jesus in heaven is One called alongside of the believer to plead his cause when he commits an act of sin. As such, He prays for the believer that the Holy Spirit might bring him to confession of sin, and then He cleanses that believer in His precious blood, thus restoring the believer to fellowship with Himself.

He does this upon the basis of the fact that He is the propitiation for the believer's sins. The word "propitiation" has the idea of "placating the anger of, buying the favor of" some person.

That is the meaning which the Greek word had in classical Gree
But the Greek word as it is used in the New Testament mean
"that sacrifice which perfectly satisfies the just demands of God
laws which the human race broke." Thus, if the believer commi
an act of sin, he is ever to remember that he has One who plea
his cause up there facing the Father, who will restore him
fellowship as he depends upon Him.

To summarize: the four things which the believer must do
order to cultivate and maintain an intimate fellowship with tl
Lord Jesus are as follows: *first,* he must study the Word of Go
in order to obtain the portrait of the Lord Jesus which it present
and in order that the Lord Jesus may talk to him through tl
Word; *second,* he must show evidence in his life of the new
divine life imparted to him in salvation, this evidence consisti
of the purity, holiness, righteousness and other qualities whic
make up the character of God; *third,* he must maintain a thre
fold attitude towards sin, recognizing the fact that the total
depraved nature remains in him during his entire earthly lif
although its power is broken, in case sin enters his experienc
agreeing with God as to all the implications of that fact and fc
lowing these out into action, and recognizing the fact that he w
born with a sinful nature and that sin is liable to enter his e:
perience; and *fourth,* his responsibility with regard to sin is th
he must not commit an act of sin, but in case he does, he shou
count upon the fact that he has One who pleads his cause u
there in heaven in fellowship with the Father, who is ready
bring the sinning believer back into fellowship with Himself.

Expanded Translation

*That which was from the beginning, which we have heard ar
which is at present ringing in our ears, that which we have wii
our eyes seen with discernment and which is at present in or
mind's eye, that which we gazed upon with wonder and our han
handled with a view to investigation, concerning the Word of tl
life, — And the life was made visible, and we have seen with di
cernment and have at present in our mind's eye and are bearir
witness and announcing to you the life which is eternal, whic*

s of such a nature as to have been in fellowship with the Father
and was made visible to us. That which we have seen with discernment and at present have in our mind's eye, and that which
we have heard and at present is ringing in our ears, we are announcing also to you in order that you also might be having joint-
participation with us. And the fellowship indeed which is ours
is with the Father and with His Son Jesus Christ. And these
things we are writing in order that our joy having been filled full in
time past, might persist in that state of fullness in the present time.

And it is this message which we have heard from him and at
present have ringing in our ears and are announcing to you, that
God as to His nature is light, and darkness in Him does not exist,
not even one bit. If we up and say that we are having constant
fellowship with Him and in the sphere of the darkness are as
constantly ordering our behavior, we are lying and not practicing
the truth. But if in the sphere of the light we are habitually
ordering our behavior as He Himself is in the sphere of the light,
fellowship we are constantly having with one another, and the
blood of Jesus His Son keeps continually cleansing us from every
sin.

If we up and say that sin we are not constantly having, ourselves we are deceiving and the truth is not in us. If we come to
an habitual agreement regarding our sins, faithful is He and just
to put away for us our sins and to cleanse us from every unrighteousness. If we up and say that we have not sinned, a liar
we are making Him and His Word is not in us.

My little children, these things I am writing to you in order
that you may not commit an act of sin. And if any person commits an act of sin, One who pleads our cause we constantly have
facing the Father, Jesus Christ the righteous One. And He
Himself is that Sacrifice which perfectly satisfies the just demands
of God's law concerning our sins, and not concerning ours alone
but also concerning those of the whole world.

JESUS AND PETER

The person who has come into a right relationship to God, not only desires to enjoy Him and companionship with Him, but also desires to serve Him. It is of this service and its motivating power, that the following pages speak.

V

Jesus and Peter

A<small>S ONE</small> reads the Greek New Testament, he is impressed with the fact that it is not written in the highly-polished periods of the Authorized Version. The writers make no attempt at literary style. The language they use is the ordinary, everyday language of the average person. It is the language of the streets, the shops, and the homes. We are to study together, John's account of one of the greatest crises Jesus had to meet. It is recorded for us in what we know as the twenty-first chapter of the Gospel according to John.

John starts his account with the words: "After these things, Jesus showed Himself again to His disciples at the Sea of Tiberius. And in this manner He showed Himself. There were there Simon Peter, and Thomas, the one commonly called The Twin, and Nathanael, the one from Cana of Galilee, and the sons of Zebedee, and others of His disciples, two." The name "Didymus" is the English spelling of the Greek name, and this name means "a twin." In this terse, succinct language, John introduces this important occurrence.

After setting the scene, John plunges at once to the heart of the matter with Peter's announcement to his fellow-disciples, "I go a fishing" (A. V.). From the words of the translation, one would gather that Peter's intention was merely to throw a net into the sea for a brief fling at fishing until such time as Jesus would appear as He promised to do. But when we examine the Greek text, we find something very serious. The words, "I go" are the translation of *hupagō*, which is used to denote the final departure of one who ceases to be another's companion or attendant. This was Peter's formal announcement after the consultation which the disciples had, presumably in his home, to the effect that he was abandoning his preaching commission received from the Lord Jesus, breaking his relations with Him so far as any future service was concerned. The words "a fishing" are the translation of the present infinitive of the verb *halieuō*. The action is durative, progressive, action going on constantly. The tense refers to the habitual action of fishing. This also includes the fact of the character of the person performing the action, namely, that he is a fisherman by trade. Thus, by using this word, John reports Peter as announcing the fact that he is going back to his fishing business permanently. This drastic decision on the part of Peter, is hard to believe except for the following considerations: First, the above translation and interpretation is based upon a rigid adherence to the rules of Greek grammar and the exact meaning of the Greek words involved. Second, when we remember that this decision was made by such a one as the unpredictable, vacillating, impetuous Peter, one can understand the possibility of such a thing. Third, the man who made this decision was the one who said to Jesus, "Be it far from thee Lord; this shall not be unto thee," referring to the Cross. This was the man who denied that he knew Jesus, and called down a divine curse upon himself, and took an oath upon the veracity of his statement, to the effect that he did not know the Lord. The disciple who was such an easy tool of Satan in these two occurrences, could also easily be used of him in this post-resurrection crisis which faced our Lord.

And this is the crisis. Here was one of the chief apostles, not only deserting his preaching commission to go back to business, but leading six other disciples with him to do the same thing. It is reasonable to suppose that the others would follow suit. Our Lord had been training these men to preach the gospel and carry on the work of saving souls after He ascended to heaven. Should these disciples desert their great commission, God's work on earth would be stopped. These men had the gospel, and were trained to propagate it. Should they fail Jesus now, the entire plan of God for the future would be ruined. Upon such a slender thread did the future of Christianity and the Millennial Empire hang, yes.

and the consummation of all of God's purposes. This was a master-stroke of Satan. He could not keep the Lord from going to the Cross. He could not keep His body in the tomb. Salvation had been procured by the out-poured blood of Jesus. Now, if there was to be no preaching of the good news of salvation, Satan argued, the plan of redemption for lost sinners would fail. This constituted the post-resurrection crisis which our Lord had to meet.

John goes on with the narrative in these words. "They say to him, 'We are coming also with you.'" The Greek word translated "coming" does not refer merely to the act of going with someone, but in a context like this, also includes the idea of joining that person's party or activity.

From this point on John records the various steps which the glorified Lord Jesus takes in meeting this crisis, and in bringing back the ringleader and his associates to their great commission, that of preaching the gospel. John says in his matter-of-fact fisherman's language, "They went out and went on board the ship, and during that night they caught not even one thing." He uses two words in his account, each meaning a boat, *ploion* referring to a large ship, and *ploiarion* which speaks of the little rowboat attached to the large fishing boat. Here he uses the first word, speaking of a large fishing boat, and since the definite article appears before the word, we understand it to be Peter's own boat which he used before the Lord called him to be a fisher of men. In the words, "They caught not even one thing," we recognize a fisherman's language, and the utter disgust which a fisherman has at his failure to catch fish. *This represented our Lord's first step in bringing his renegade disciples back to their preaching responsibilities. He made them business failures.* These men had fished these waters for many years, were experts at their trade, and knew where the fish were. But a miraculous intervention prevented them from gathering even one fish in their nets.

Then John continues the narrative, presenting the second step which Jesus takes to bring His disciples back to Himself. He says, "Now, morning having already come, Jesus stood on the seashore. However, the disciples did not know that it was Jesus. Then

Jesus says to them, 'Children under instruction, you haven't caught any fish, have you?' They answered Him 'No.' And He said to them, Throw the net on the right side of the boat and you will find. Thereupon they threw it, and no longer were they strong enough to drag the net because of the great number of fish."

Jesus appears upon the scene to take personal charge of the proceedings. He calls across the stretch of water and says, "Little children under instruction." The Greek word John uses, refers to a child who is under a pedagogue. By using this term, Jesus reminds the disciples that they have much yet to learn. The A. V., reports Jesus as saying, "Have ye any meat?" The word "meat" in the Greek text is made up of two words, one which means "to eat," and the other which means "towards." The word therefore speaks of a person who has something to eat which he puts towards something else which he eats. That something else is usually bread, and the thing which is put towards the bread is fish. Thus the word came to be used for fish. Our Lord, therefore was asking the disciples whether they had any fish. In addition to this, the question in the original includes a Greek negative which indicates to the one questioned, that the person asking the question expects the answer "no." Our Lord, in this question, is pressing home the lesson which He hoped they had learned during the night. He is reminding them of a fact which they would like to forget, namely, that they had not caught a thing. The answer in concert across the water, was a point-blank "no."

At the request of a stranger on shore, these practiced fishermen get out their net and throw it into the sea again. One wonders why they would do such a thing, knowing that there were no fish to be caught at that time and in that place. The explanation is as follows. H. V. Morton, in his book *In the Steps of the Master,* states that while he was visiting Palestine, he observed that it was a custom of the fishermen to have someone stationed on shore who could point out to them the schools of fish which they could not see from the boat. This author is an experienced traveller in Palestine, and a student of its history. He says that this is a custom which has obtained since the first century. This custom would explain the otherwise irrational action of the disciples in obeying a stranger on shore under the circumstances in which they found themselves.

This was the second step Jesus took in bringing His renegade disciples back in line. He, by a supernatural exertion of power, put a school of fish right at the side of the boat at that strategic moment. The lesson He wished to teach them, was that whereas, out of His will, they were business failures, yet when obeying Him, they would have success and have all their needs supplied. Back of all this, probably, was the disciples' concern over their means of livelihood. Jesus, by this miracle, assures them that if they serve Him, He will supply all their needs.

The miraculous draught of fish aroused in John a train of memories. There flashed across his mind the time when the Lord Jesus had called him and his brother Peter to be disciples, the accompanying miracle being a miraculous draught of fish. The recognition of Jesus on the part of John led to a series of events which he records in the following words; "Then that disciple whom Jesus was loving says to Peter, The Lord it is. Then Simon Peter, having heard that it was the Lord, put about himself his fisherman's blouse, for he was only partially clad, and threw himself into the sea. But the other disciples came in the little boat, for they were not far from the land, but about three hundred feet, dragging the net full of fish."

The A. V., has it that Peter was naked. The Greek word is *gumnos,* and means at times, "partially clad," and at other times "naked." Peter, working on a large fishing boat in such a public place as the Sea of Galilee and close in shore, was clad in his oriental tunic or undergarment, and upon seeing Jesus, put on his fisherman's blouse. He, in his impetuous way, jumped into the sea and waded ashore to Jesus. The other disciples rowed to shore in the small row boat which was attached to the large fishing boat.

Now Jesus takes the third step in His endeavor to bring these runaway disciples back to their responsibility of carrying on the preaching of the gospel after He should leave this earth for heaven. He knew that He had a tired, cold, discouraged, guilty group of men with whom to deal. Great issues were at stake, and He had to feel His way carefully. Instead of broaching the subject of their desertion, and calling them to repentance and a return to their preaching mission at once, He first sees to it that their physical needs are supplied, that they are rested, warmed, and fed. It is the same technique employed by missions engaged in soul-winning among the so-called derelicts of society. It is soap, soup, and then salvation. The man is easier to reach if his physical needs are cared for, and his mind and heart are at rest.

John gives us this in the following words: "Then, when they got out on the land, they see a charcoal fire, and fish laid upon it and bread. Jesus says to them, Bring now some of the fish which you have caught. Simon Peter went up and dragged the net to the land, full of fish, great ones, one hundred fifty-three. And even though there were so many, the net was not torn. Jesus says to them, Come here, have breakfast. No one of the disciples was daring to ask Him, As for you, who are you? knowing that it was the Lord. Jesus comes and takes the bread and gives it to them, and the fish likewise. This already is a third time in which Jesus showed Himself to the disciples, having been raised from the dead."

The A. V., reports our Lord as saying, "Come and dine." The Greek word refers to the act of breaking one's fast in the morning, namely, having breakfast. This is just another illustration of the matter-of-fact language which the Bible writers used, and also of the unnatural polish which the A. V., puts upon the presentation of the inspired penmen.

Jesus now takes the fourth step in bringing the disciples back to Himself and to their preaching mission. He addresses Peter, the key-log in the jam, knowing that if He can dislodge him, the others will follow down-stream. He turns therefore to the ringleader, and deals with him at the camp-fire in the hearing of the other disciples. He says to him, "Simon, son of Jonas, lovest thou Me more than these?" Our Lord could have meant either one of the following three things, "Do you love Me more than these disciples?" "Do you love Me more than these disciples love Me?" or, "Do you love Me more than these fish?" *The context decides*. We have seen that it was Peter's purpose to break his relations with the Lord Jesus so far as his preaching commission was concerned, and to go back permanently to his fishing business. The Lord Jesus goes at once to the heart of the matter, and asks Peter whether he loves his fishing business better than his Lord. It simmers down to the question as to whether Peter loves fish or Jesus.

The word for "love" John uses to report the question of Jesus is *agapaō*. This brings us to the problem as to whether the two different Greek words used for "love" in the conversation between Jesus and Peter, are used interchangeably here without any difference in meaning, or whether each has its distinctive meaning each time it is used.

The Lord Jesus uses the word *agapaō* the first two times He questions Peter, and *phileō*, the last time he asks Peter whether he loves Him. Peter uses the word *phileō* each time he answers the Lord. The question before us therefore is, as to whether these words are used interchangeably by John in reporting the conversation between Jesus and Peter, or whether each word is used deliberately for a certain purpose in each place.

We understand, of course, that the conversation was held in Aramaic, the mother tongue of Jesus and Peter. It was John's responsibility to report it in the *koine* Greek of the first century. God's word teaches that the Bible writers were verbally inspired. By verbal inspiration we mean that the Holy Spirit guided the writers infallibly in the choice of each word in the Greek text of the original manuscript. As to whether these two Greek words had their exact equivalents in Aramaic or not, or whether the ideas in them were contained in several Aramaic words, is beside the point when we take into consideration the fact that the Greek text of the New Testament was verbally inspired. We therefore will confine ourselves in the following discussion to the Greek text of the New Testament.

It will be well at this point to present a brief sketch of each of these words. The writer is greatly indebted to two articles appearing in the Princeton Theological Review of January and April of 1918. They are entitled, *The Terminology of Love in the*

New Testament, and are written by Benjamin B. Warfield. This writer has done a thorough piece of work in presenting the uses of the Greek words for "love" in classical Greek, in the Septuagint, and in the New Testament.

Agapaō' is used in its various forms in the New Testament about three hundred and twenty times. It is a love called out of a person's heart by an awakened sense of value in an object which causes one to prize it. It expresses a love of approbation and esteem. Its impulse comes from the idea of prizing. It is a love that recognizes the worthiness of the object loved. Thus, this love consists of the soul's sense of the value and preciousness of its object, and its response to its recognized worth in admiring affection.

Phileō is used forty-five times in its various forms in the New Testament. This is an unimpassioned love, a friendly love. It is a love called out of one's heart as a response to the pleasure one takes in a person or object. It is based upon an inner community between the person loving and the person or object loved. That is, both have things in common with one another. The one loving finds a reflection of his own nature in the person or thing loved. It is a love of liking, an affection for some one or something that is the outgoing of one's heart in delight to that which affords pleasure. The Greeks made much of friendship, and this word was used by them to designate this form of mutual attraction. Whatever in an object that is adapted to give pleasure, tends to call out this affection. The words which best express this kind of love are "fondness, affection, liking." It shows the inclination which springs out of commerce with a person or is called out by qualities in an object which are agreeable to us. As an outgrowth of its meaning of fondness, it sometimes carries that sentiment over into an outward expression of the same, that of kissing.

In contrasting *phileō* and *agapaō,* we might say that the former is a love of pleasure, the latter a love of preciousness; the former a love of delight, the latter a love of esteem; the former a love called out of the heart by the apprehension of pleasurable qualities in the object loved, the latter a love called out of the heart by the apprehension of valuable qualities in the object loved; the former takes pleasure in, the latter ascribes value to; the former is a love of liking, the latter a love of prizing.

These two words for "love" were taken over into the New Testament by the inspired writers. *Agapaō*, a relatively empty word, not much in use by the classical writers, was chosen by the Bible writers as the distinctive word to be used when speaking of God as love, of the love which the Holy Spirit produces in the heart of the yielded believer, and the love with which God loves the world of unsaved humanity. We have seen that it was admirably fitted for use in John 3:16, where God loves each lost sinner with a love called out of His heart by the preciousness of that lost soul. In its context there, an added meaning which the word never had in classical Greek was poured into it, namely, a love which sacrifices itself for the benefit of the object loved, that object being both unlovely and unlovable, and a bitter enemy of the one who loves. Paul chose this word as the one that would adequately denote Christian love, and poured into it in I Corinthians 13:, its various elements. The word *phileō* is never used in any of the above connections, showing that the Bible writers made a keen distinction between the words, and used them advisedly. *Phileō* was used for instance, where the Pharisees were fond of being seen praying on the street, and fond of the chief seats at a banquet. It was used of our Lord's friendship for Lazarus (John 11:3). It was used of God's fondness for believers who were fond of Jesus (John 16:27). But when it comes to speaking of the divine love which God is, and which He produces in the heart of the yielded believer, *phileō* is never used. We gather, therefore, that *agapaō* is a love of devotion, while *phileō* is a love of emotion. There is another distinction we must be careful to note, and that is that *agapaō* is love that has ethical qualities about it, obligations, responsibilities, where *phileō* is a non-ethical love, making no ethical demands upon the person loving. As a rule, these distinctions are rigidly adhered to in the use of these words in the New Testament. John, writing somewhere between A. D., 85 to 90, had the usage of these two words before him as he was recording the conversation between Jesus and Peter. There are, however, a few places where they are used, or seem to be used, interchangeably. But this does not invalidate the keen distinction usually observed by the writers in the use of these words. Archbishop Trench in his valuable book *Synonyms in the New Testament,* has this to say: "It is plain that when we affirm two or more words to be synonyms, that is, alike, but also different, with a resemblance in the main, but also with partial difference, we by no means deny that there may be a hundred passages where it would be quite possible to use the one as the other. All that we affirm is that, granting this, there is a hundred and first, where one would be more appropriate and the other not, or where, at all events one would be *more* appropriate than the other." Granted, that *agapaō* and *phileō,* in some places are used interchangeably. But in the conversation between Jesus and Peter, one cannot but be impressed with the fact that John used the words with a studied carefulness and deliberateness. Jesus uses *agapaō* twice, then suddenly goes to *phileō.* Peter uses *phileō* throughout. Jesus asks Peter for a love of devotion. Peter offers Him a love of emotion. Had Peter had a love of devotion for his Lord, he would not have deserted Him at this important and strategic time, for such a love would have impelled him to remain true to his Master and to the preaching commission which he was given. Naturally, under the circumstances in which Peter found himself, caught in the act of desertion, Peter could only confess to a love of emotion, a fondness for Jesus as his Teacher, a liking for Him and His fellowship. What Peter offered Jesus here was a non-ethical affection. For a more extended study of the Greek words for "love" see the author's book, *Bypaths in the Greek New Testament.*

The question comes as to whether Peter could have exhibited an *agapaō* love for the Lord Jesus at this time in view of the fact that this kind of love, a divine love which impels the person to sacrifice himself for the object loved, is only produced in the heart of a saved person in whom the Holy Spirit has established His residence. The answer is found in John 20:22 where Jesus says to the disciples previous to His meeting them at the Sea of Galilee, "Receive ye the Holy Ghost." The verb "receive" is in the aorist imperative, which construction in Greek commands instant obedience. The word is *lambanō* which means "to receive" in the sense of personally appropriating the thing to be received. The language and construction of the original here, can only mean that the disciples at that time received the Holy Spirit as an indweller as He is received by a believing sinner in this Age of Grace. Our Lord at one time spoke to the disciples of the Holy Spirit who was *with* them and would be *in* them. Here is the fulfillment of that prediction. It is unthinkable that our Lord would demand of a follower of His, something which he was not equipped to do. It does seem that this divine provision at this time was for the very purpose of forestalling such a crisis as developed in the desertion of Peter and his fellow-disciples. But alas, the human element entered in and also the great arch-enemy of man, Satan.

Jesus now takes the fifth step in His attempt to bring this renegade disciple back to his preaching mission. He says, "Simon, son of Jonas, do you have a love for Me called out of your heart by my preciousness to you, a love which impels you to sacrifice yourself for Me? And with this love do you love me more than you love these?" There were the great fish which they had caught, possibly still in the net, showing intermittent signs of life. The question simmered down to this, "Peter, are these fish more precious to you or am I more precious? By your actions you tell me plainly that you regard your fishing business of more value than the preaching mission upon which I sent you." This seems a terrible indictment of Peter, but when one takes into consideration the fact that the totally depraved nature is still in the saved individual, also that Satan is running around loose, and that tremendous and eternal issues were at stake here, one can understand the possibility of such a thing. This was no ordinary preacher called to preach by God, who leaves his pulpit to go back into business. That has happened over and over again. The only solution to such an action is, that the man loved material things better than his Lord. In the case of Peter it was the love of material things. But even though he was one of the chosen Twelve, yet it was perfectly possible for him to thus desert his

Lord, in view of the tremendous factors involved. Again, how else could one understand the question of our Lord? He was at tempting to bring Peter back to his preaching mission, and H appealed to his love for his Master as the impelling motive fo service.

To this question Peter answered, "Yes, Lord, as for you, you know with positive assurance that I have a fondness for you." Peter knew very well that he was not exhibiting *agapaō* love fo the Lord Jesus in his role as a deserter, and he could only assure Him of an affection and a fondness. To this our Lord answers "Be feeding my lambs." The verb is in the imperative mode, which mode issues a command to be obeyed. One does not command a person to do something when he is already doing it. It is clear that this command of Jesus was addressed to one who was not at that time obeying it. Peter was not feeding the great Teacher's lambs. This was a clarion call to go back to his preaching mission which he had deserted. Jesus had failed to elicit a love of devotion from Peter, and thus not having that fulcrum with which to call him back to his responsibility, *commands* him to do so. Our Lord's words here made an indelible impression upon the apostle, for writing many years afterwards, he said, "The elders which are among you I exhort, I, who am your fellow-elder, and a witness to bear testimony of the sufferings of Christ, and also a partaker of the glory that shall be revealed; shepherd the flock of God which is among you, not by constraint, but willingly; not for filthy lucre, but of a ready mind" (I Pet. 5:1, 2).

Jesus says to Peter a second time, "Simon, son of Jonas, do you have a love for Me called out of your heart by my preciousness to you, a love which impels you to sacrifice yourself for Me?" He says to Him, "Yes, Lord, as for you, you know with positive assurance that I have a fondness for you." He says to him, "Be tending my sheep." Jesus says to him the third time, "Simon, son of Jonas, do you have a fondness for Me?" Jesus now takes Peter's word and in effect says, "Peter, I am beginning to believe that you do not even have a fondness for Me, judging from your actions of deserting Me and your preaching mission." John says that Peter was grieved that our Lord used the word *phileō* the third time He asked him whether he loved Him. The point is not that Peter was grieved that the Lord asked him three times whether he loved Him, but that Jesus used the word He did with the implications back of it.

Peter answers, "As for you, you know by experience that I have a fondness for you." Jesus says to him, "Be feeding my sheep."

Now comes what seems to be an abrupt change of subject matter in the conversation. Previous to this the matter of Peter's love for our Lord was discussed, but now in a most abrupt fashion, our Lord predicts the kind of death which Peter will die. He speaks of Peter being carried as an old man to a place where he does not want to go, and that he will at that time stretch forth his hands. John comments on this statement by saying that the Lord Jesus was speaking of Peter's death which would glorify God. This together with the tradition that Peter was crucified as a Christian martyr, clearly indicates that our Lord was speaking of the martyr death of Peter.

But what is the connection between the foregoing conversation which was limited to Peter's love for Jesus and his preaching mission, and the announcement of the kind of death Peter would die? Jesus had appealed to Peter for a love of devotion, a love that would impel him to sacrifice himself for Him. All that Peter offered Him at that time was a love of emotion, a fondness or affection that offered no restraint to Peter in his desertion of his Master, and no impelling motive to faithfulness to his commission. Our Lord says in effect, "Peter, I asked you for a love of devotion. You have given Me only a love of emotion. Nevertheless, some day you will have a love of devotion for Me, even such a love that will impel you to die a martyr's death on a Roman cross for Me." We submit, that unless we take note of the distinction between the two Greek words for "love" here, there is no logical connection between the previous conversation and the announcement of the death which Peter would die.

The Expanded Translation of John 21:1-19

After these things Jesus showed Himself again to His disciples at the Sea of Tiberias. And in this manner He showed Himself.

*There were there Simon Peter, and Thomas, the one commonly
called The Twin, and Nathanael, the one from Cana of Galilee,
and the sons of Zebedee, and others of His disciples, two. Simon
Peter says to them, I am going off, severing my previous relationship, to engage continually in fishing. They say to him, We
also are coming with you to join you in the same. They went out
and went on board the boat, and during that night they caught
not even one thing. And as it was already becoming morning,
Jesus stood on the seashore. Thereupon Jesus says to them, Little
children under instruction, you do not have any fish, do you?
They answered Him, No. And He said to them, Throw the net
on the right side of the boat, and you will find. They threw therefore, and no longer were they strong enough to drag the net
because of the great number of fish.   Thereupon, that disciple
whom Jesus was loving, says to Peter, The Lord it is. Then Simon
Peter, having heard that it was the Lord, put his fisherman's
blouse about himself, for he was only partially clad, and threw
himself into the sea. And the other disciples came in the little
boat, for they were not far from the land, but about three hundred feet, dragging the net of fish. Then, when they had stepped
off upon the land, they see a charcoal fire there, and fish lying
upon it and bread. Jesus says to them, Bring now some of the
fish which you caught. Simon Peter went up and drew the net
to the land, full of fish, great ones, one hundred fifty-three. And
even though there were so many, yet the net was not torn. Jesus
says to them, Come here, have breakfast. No one of the disciples
was daring to ask Him, As for you, who are you? knowing that it
was the Lord. Jesus comes and takes the bread and gives it to
them, and the fish likewise. This already is a third time in which
Jesus showed Himself to the disciples after He had been raised
from amongst the dead.*

*Then when they had breakfasted, Jesus says to Simon Peter,
Simon, son of Jonas, do you love Me more than these, with a love
called out of your heart by my preciousness to you, a love which
impels you to sacrifice yourself for Me? He says to Him, Yes,
Lord. As for you, you know with absolute assurance that I am
fond of you. He says to him, Be feeding my lambs. He says to*

*him again a second time, Simon, son of Jonas, do you have a love
for Me called out of your heart by my preciousness to you, a love
which impels you to sacrifice yourself for Me? He says to Him,
Yes, Lord. As for you, you know with positive assurance that I
am fond of you. He says to him, Be tending my sheep. He says
to him the third time, Simon, son of Jonas, do you have a fondness for Me? Peter was grieved because He said to him the third
time, Do you have a fondness for Me? And he said to Him, Lord,
as for you, all things you know with positive assurance. As for
you, you know by experience that I have a fondness for you. Jesus
says to him, Be feeding my sheep. Truly, truly, I am saying to
you, When you were young, you girded yourself and kept on
walking where you were desiring to be walking. But when you
become old, you will stretch out your hands, and another will
gird you and carry you where you are not willing to be carried.
And this He said, indicating by what kind of a death he should
glorify God.*

From the foregoing study, it is clear that the Christian has
two kinds of love for the Lord Jesus, a *phileō* love, that is, an
affection or fondness which is non-ethical in its nature, in that it
makes no demands upon the person loving so far as self-sacrifice
is concerned with a view to benefitting the one loved, and an
agapaō love, namely, a love that impels the one loving to sacrifice
himself for the benefit of the one loved, this latter kind of love
being of the highest ethical nature.

Every Christian is fond of the Lord Jesus, has an affection for
Him. This is a natural thing. It is based upon a community of
nature and interests. The Christian partakes of the same nature
which the Lord Jesus has, the divine nature. Thus, he finds in
the Lord Jesus a reflection of what God has put in him in the
divine nature, and therefore is fond of Him. But this kind of love
will never impel the Christian to serve Him and live a life of
obedience and self-denial for Him. It did not do that for Peter.
Nor will this kind of love keep a Christian from disobeying the
Lord. It did not keep Peter from deserting Him. *Phileō* love is a
perfectly proper thing in its place. But it must not be depended

upon to furnish the motive power for the living of a Christian life or for service in Jesus' Name.

It is the other kind of love, the *agapaō* kind which produces the incentive for holy living and sacrificial service. Our Lord used that word when appealing to Peter to go back to his preaching commission. Our Lord said, "If a man love Me (*agapaō*), he will keep my words" (John 14:23). It is to the degree in which we have this kind of love flooding our souls, that we will live holy lives of self denial in the service of the Lord Jesus. And the secret of the production of this love is in the supernatural operation of the Holy Spirit. And the degree of this operation of the Spirit is dependant upon the yieldedness of the Christian to the ministry of the Spirit. The fruit of the Spirit is love (*agapē*), Paul tells us (Gal. 5:23). He says again, "The love of God is shed abroad in our hearts by the Holy Spirit" (Rom. 5:5). The secret of Christian service that glorifies the Lord Jesus is in the love which the Holy Spirit produces in the heart of the Christian. The quality of that service is measured by the intensity of the love in the heart of that Christian. The intensity of that love is determined by the degree of yieldedness of that person to the Holy Spirit.

Peter, in his first letter (1:22), gives us a beautiful illustration of the possibility of the amalgamation of these two kinds of love in one personality. Writing to Christians, he says: "Seeing ye have purified your souls in obeying the truth, resulting in an unfeigned brotherly love, out of the heart love one another fervently."

Phileō is used first by Peter, and then *agapaō*. These Christians to whom the apostle was writing, had a fondness, an affection, for one another. It was one Christian heart responding to another Christian heart. They found the Lord Jesus in the heart of a fellow-Christian, and therefore they were fond of that Christian. This was a non-ethical love. Now, Peter exhorts them to saturate this *phileō* love with the Holy Spirit produced *agapaō* love, and make that fondness and affection a thing of heaven. It is the amalgamation of the two loves which will result in an ideal Christian experience. Just so, the believer must be careful to see that the *phileō* fondness he has for the Lord Jesus, is saturated with the *agapaō* love produced by the Holy Spirit, lest a lack of the latter will result in a Christian experience in which the believer exhibits a great fondness for the Lord Jesus, but manifests little love for Him by a life devoid of earnest obedience and service. Here lies the explanation of why some Christians can sing and pray and testify about their love for the Lord Jesus, and yet their lives do not show a rich, ripe, mature experience. These have much *phileō* love, little *agapaō*, and for the reason that they do not live Spirit-controlled lives. The ideal is an amalgamation of the two kinds of love.

JESUS OF NAZARETH —
HIS COMING FOR HIS CHURCH

A comprehensive knowledge of the contents of the Bible, indicates that the history of the human race previous to the eternal conditions, is rapidly drawing to a close. The next great event in God's prophetic calendar is the coming of Jesus of Nazareth for His Church.

VI

Jesus of Nazareth — His Coming for His Church

T HE NEXT great event in the prophetic calendar in the Bible,
is the coming of Jesus of Nazareth for His Church. The
event is imminent.   There are no prophecies unfulfilled which
would withhold His coming. Briefly, its purpose is to raise the
righteous dead from Adam to the time of this coming, and to
translate believers who are on earth at that time. This will involve
the bringing of the former with Him from heaven, the transforming of their dead bodies which have moldered into dust, into
perfect glorified bodies, the transformation of the bodies of believers then on earth into like perfect, glorified bodies, and the
transportation of both classes to heaven. This event is called in
theological circles, The Rapture of the Church, in that the Church
of Jesus Christ will be joined forever to her great Bridegroom,
Jesus of Nazareth.

Our Lord speaks of His coming for His own in John 14:1-3,
where He tells His disciples that He is going to His Father's
house to prepare a place for them, and that He will come again
and receive them to Himself. In other words, He is coming from
heaven into the atmosphere of this earth to take the Church with
Him back to heaven.   And this event may take place at any
moment. Believers will be taken to heaven, and unbelievers will
be left on earth to undergo the terrible times of the Great Tribulation period.

We will address ourselves to the question as to what is involved in this great event. First of all, where is heaven, how far
is it from the earth, how long will it take the Lord Jesus to traverse that distance, and just how close to the earth will He come?

As to the locality of heaven, Isaiah gives us some hints. He reports the words of Lucifer, the mightiest angel God created, who was His regent on the perfect earth of Genesis 1:1 (Isaiah 14:12-14). Lucifer said, "I will ascend into heaven." This means that he was not in heaven when he rebelled against God. "I will exalt my throne above the stars of God." This tells us that Lucifer had a throne below the stars of God, on this earth, and having a throne, he reigned over a pre-Adamic race of beings, directing their worship to the God of heaven. This last utterance also teaches that God's throne is beyond the stars of the universe. God's throne, the place of His centralized authority, is in heaven. Heaven is outside of the universe. Lucifer speaks again: "I will sit also upon the mount of the congregation, in the sides of the north." This localizes heaven as above the earth in a line with the axis of the earth, above the north pole, and in a place beyond the farthest star. Heaven is not above the earth in all directions. The inhabitants at the equator look up and see blue sky. But heaven is not above them as they look directly up from where they stand. The explorers of Antartica looked up and saw blue sky. But heaven was not above them. Heaven has a fixed location above the north pole, in a line with the axis of the earth.

But how far is heaven from the earth? By new and more powerful telescopes, astronomers have recently discovered stars that are 500,000,000 light years from the earth. That means that it has taken light from these stars, travelling at the speed of 186,000 miles per second, 500,000,000 years to reach this earth. But how far are these stars from the earth? Multiply 500,000,000 by 60 (seconds), that number by 60 (minutes), that number by 24 (hours), that number by 365 (days), and that number by 186,000, and you will have the number of miles which these stars are from the earth. The number is 2,932,848,000,000,000,000,000. Heaven is at least that many miles from the earth. These astronomers say that beyond these stars, there is a thinning out of stars, indicating either that the material universe ends here, or that there may be a relatively empty space, after which stars may again appear. Such figures stagger one's imagination. Think of the great God who could speak such a universe into existence by divine fiat.

He spoke the word, and a universe sprang into existence. Job (38:7) says that the sons of God (the angels) shouted for joy when they saw the universe come into existence. And we should be careful to note that they did not exclaim with joy over a chaos, but a kosmos, a perfect, ordered creation. The chaos came as the result of Lucifer's fall.

Our Lord then, when coming to take out His Church from the earth, will travel a distance of 2,932,848,000,000,000,000,000 miles. If He travelled through space at the speed of light, 186,000 miles per second, it would take Him 500,000,000 years to reach the earth. But a bird's eye view of Bible history and prophecy shows that the divine program for the human race on earth previous to the new creation is only 7,000 years, 6,000 of which have just about rolled around. No, this Jesus of Nazareth who is Very God of Very God, will come with the speed of thought from heaven, one moment in heaven, the next, in the atmosphere of this earth.

But just how close to the earth will He come? Paul, in his classic account of the Rapture (I Thess. 4:13-18) says that we will "meet the Lord in the air." The Greeks have two words for "air," *aēr*, referring to the lower, denser atmosphere, and *aithēr*, speaking of the rarefied, thinner atmosphere. A Greek would stand on the summit of Mt. Olympus which is 6,403 feet high, and pointing downward would say, *aēr*, and pointing upward, would say *aithēr*. Now, which word did Paul use? A glance at the Greek text shows *aēr*. All of which means that the Lord Jesus, when He comes for His Bride, the Church, will descend to a distance within 6,403 feet of the earth.

The great apostle was writing to the Thessalonian Christians who were sorrowing over the loss of loved ones who had died. He tells them not to sorrow as others who have no hope. The tombstones in the cemeteries of Thessalonica were inscribed with the words "No Hope." These pagan Greeks, striving to pierce the future through their philosophies, could never arrive at any positive assurance of a reunion with loved ones in the after life. They had no hope. To these Christian Greeks, Paul holds out the assured hope of reunion with loved ones who were believers, a reunion in the air, when Jesus comes for His Church. He says that since we believe that Jesus died and rose again, God will bring with Jesus from heaven, our loved ones who have fallen asleep (euphemism for death) in Jesus. He states that we who are alive when Jesus comes, will not prevent (old English for "precede") the dead in the order in which we will receive our glorified bodies. They will receive their new bodies first.

After receiving our new bodies, we who are alive when Jesus comes, will be caught up together with the dead who have been raised. We will be caught up in the clouds (A. V.). There is no definite article in the Greek text before the word "clouds." There should not be one in the translation. We shall be caught up in clouds, clouds of believers. That is, the great masses of glorified saints going up to heaven, will have the appearance of clouds. The Greek word for "clouds" here is used in Hebrews 12:1 in the clause, "Wherefore seeing we also are compassed about with so great a cloud of witnesses," the inspired writer visualizing a Greek stadium with its thousands of onlookers occupying the tiers upon tiers of seats. The same word is used in the Greek classics of a large army of foot soldiers.

Paul says that we will be caught up. The Greek word translated "caught up" has a number of meanings which give us some important information regarding the Rapture. The word is *harpazō*. It means "to carry off by force." And this gives us the reason why the Lord Jesus will descend to 6,403 feet above the earth. Satan and his kingdom of demons occupy this lower atmosphere. Paul speaks of him as "the prince of the power of the air" (Eph. 2:2), and uses the Greek word *aēr* which speaks of the lower, denser atmosphere in which we live. The demons inhabit this portion of the atmosphere around the earth in order that they may prey upon Christian believers. They attempt to disrupt the workings of the Church, spoil the testimony and service of Christians, and prevent the unsaved from receiving the Lord Jesus as Saviour. They are trying to insulate the Church from heaven. At the time of the Rapture, they will attempt to keep the Church from going up to heaven with the Lord Jesus. Jesus of Nazareth will exert His omnipotent power in taking the saints with Him to heaven through the kingdoms of Satan, and against his power and that of his demons.

The word *harpazō* also means "to rescue from the danger of destruction." That means that the Church will be caught up to heaven before the seven year period of great tribulation occurs on earth. By the Church here we do not mean the visible organized present-day church composed of believers and unbelievers, but only those in the visible church whose Christian profession will stand the test of actual possession of salvation. The nominal Christian, that person merely identified with the visible church by membership, and not possessing a living faith in the Lord Jesus as Saviour, will be left on earth to go through the terrible times of the Great Tribulation.

As to the pre-Tribulation Rapture of the Church, more might be said. The divine analysis of the Book of the Revelation "the things seen" (the Patmos vision of the Lord Jesus), chapter one; "the things that are" (the Church Age), chapters two and three; "the things which shall be after these things" (events happening after the Church Age), chapters four to twenty two, found in 1:19 of the Revelation, indicates that the Church will be caught up before the tribulation period begins. Chapters six to nineteen describe that period. These events take place after the Church Age. Again, the promise given the Missionary Church which is in existence today and which blends with the last age of Church history, the Laodicean, to the effect that God will keep that Church from the hour of "the testing" (Rev. 3:10), namely, the tribulation period, also indicates a pre-tribulation rapture.

Again, there is nothing in Scripture which indicates that the Church will either enter or pass through the tribulation. Israel is given many signs which will warn her of the near approach of that period (Matt. 24), but the Gospels and epistles are entirely devoid of any sign given to the Church. The epistles speak of the Day of Christ Jesus (Phil. 1:6), an expression not found in the Old Testament or the Gospels. This is a day to which the Church is to look forward with joy. It is the end of the pathway of the Christian Church. If this day does not occur before the tribulation, then there is no place for it in the prophetic calendar of events which will take place during or after that period.

The Great Tribulation period is a time when the divine wrath is to be visited upon earth-dwellers, particularly upon Israel. But the promise to the Church is that it has been delivered from the wrath to come (I Thess. 1:9, 10, 5:8; Rom. 5:9). The Bible expressly states who will be the objects of the divine wrath during the tribulation period, namely, Israel and the ungodly of the Gentile nations. If the Church were destined to suffer, surely, the Bible would make note of that fact along with the mention of the above two companies of individuals. The biblical attitude of the believer is one of waiting for the glorification of his body (Rom. 8:23), and of looking for the Saviour (Phil. 3:20, 21, I Thess. 1:9, 10). The language is clear that the believer is to expect Him at any moment, not look for Him in connection with some predicted event for which signs have been given to Israel and not to the Church.

To teach that the Church will go through the tribulation period, is to nullify the biblical teaching of the imminent coming of the Lord Jesus for the Church. Events on earth are not yet in readiness for the Great Tribulation. Indeed, at this writing (1951), that period cannot come for years yet. But the Lord may return for His Church at any moment. Paul (Phil. 4:5), Peter (I Pet. 1:13-15), and John (I John 3:2, 3) all make the imminent coming of the Lord for the Church a ground of appeal for holy living and diligent service.

Finally, Paul in II Thessalonians 2:1-12, states that the day of the Lord (the Great Tribulation), cannot come unless the departure of the Church from the earth comes first. There are four days in Scripture; the day of man ("man's judgment," I Cor. 4:3), today, when man has his day under the permissive will of God; the day of Christ (Phil. 1:6), when Christ has His day, the Rapture, when He comes for His Bride; the day of the Lord (II Thess. 2:2, best Greek texts, not day of Christ, but day of Lord), when the Lord has His day of judgment, the tribulation period and the Millennium; the day of God (II Peter 3:12), the Millennium merging into eternity. In our II Thessalonian passage,

Paul is speaking of the Great Tribulation. Someone had written a letter to the Thessalonian church, stating that the period of the Great Tribulation was then present, and had forged Paul's name to the document. The great apostle calms their fears by saying that that day cannot come until "a falling away" (A. V.) comes first. The Greek word translated "falling away" has as one of its meanings, "a departure." The definite article appears before it in the original text. This word is used in other places in the New Testament, and in these places the context indicates that from which the departure is made. But here there is no such information. It follows that this particular departure must have been in the teaching of Paul to the Thessalonian saints, and was known by them and him. Paul had taught them about the Rapture in I Thessalonians 4:13-18. The context speaks of the Holy Spirit, the One who restrains iniquity on earth through the Church, leaving the earth for heaven (2:7, "letteth," old English for "restrain"). When He takes His departure, the Church must go with Him, for He indwells the Church. The words "falling away" are an interpretation of the Greek word, not a translation. Furthermore, no apostasy would withhold the coming of Antichrist and the Great Tribulation, but on the other hand, would prepare for the coming of both. Thus, the departure of the Church precedes the Great Tribulation. The Church will thus be rescued from the danger of destruction.

The word *harpazō* is used of divine power transferring a person marvellously and swiftly from one place to another. It refers here to the act of the Lord Jesus taking with Him to heaven all believers from Adam's time to the Rapture. How long will it take the Church to traverse that immense distance between earth and heaven? If the Church travelled 186,000 miles per second, it would take 500,000,000 years to reach heaven. The only solution to the problem is that it will go to heaven with the speed of thought. If it went any slower, the time consumed would be enormous. Believers will have new powers of locomotion in eternity. A supernatural "carpet" will whisk them to any part of the universe in an instant of time.

Again, *harpazō* means "to claim for one's self eagerly." Here, the great Bridegroom of the Church, comes from heaven to claim His Bride, the Church, and take her to Himself. Finally, the word means "to snatch out and away." This tells us that the Rapture will occur so suddenly that it will take the Church by surprise.

Some day soon that great event will take place. How soon? It cannot be far off. Glance down Bible history for a moment. It is significant that God has been in the habit of doing some great thing with reference to salvation, at the turn of a millennium or of two millenniums. The date of Adam is approximately 4,000 B. C. The plan of salvation in which God the Judge was to step down from His judgment throne to take upon Himself the guilt and penalty of human sin in order that He might satisfy His justice, maintain His government, and at the same time open the flood-gates of mercy to lost sinners, was pre-figured in the sacrifices which He instituted when He made coats of skins and clothed Adam and Eve. The initial step in the fulfillment of this plan He took 2,000 B. C., when He called Abraham to be the progenitor of the Jewish nation from which would come the Saviour who would die and pay for sin. The next step He took in 1,000 B. C., when He started the dynasty of David, from which line of kings the Messiah and Saviour would come. The next step was taken in A. D. 1, when God, in the Person of His Son came to earth, became incarnate in the human race by virgin birth, and died on Calvary's Cross, the substitutionary atonement for sin. That was His first Advent. The second Advent of the Son of God is predicted in Scripture. All indications point to the fact that the second Advent is near at hand. The Church has been in existence almost two thousand years. It would seem logical that God would repeat His custom of doing something of great importance at or near the turn of these two millenniums, that is, within the next half-century or so. That would be His coming to earth a second time. But the Rapture must take place before the second Advent. All of which means that we are fast approaching the wind-up of things. The Rapture should occur within the next fifty years or so. It could occur at any moment.

Or, look at this matter from the standpoint of Church history. The second and third chapters of The Revelation, contain the history of the Church, divided into seven periods or ages. They are as follows: The Apostolic Church, A. D. 33-96; The Martyr Church, A. D. 96-316; The State Church, A. D. 316-500; The Papal Church, A. D., 500-; The Reformation Church, A. D., 1500-; The Missionary Church, A. D., 1793-; The Apostate Church, now. We are living in the seventh and last age of the Church history. The Rapture will close the Church Age. So near are we to that great event.

Gentle reader. Are you ready for the coming of the Lord Jesus to take His Church with Him to heaven? If you have never seen yourself as a lost sinner and Jesus Christ as the Saviour of sinners, and never by an act of heart-faith put your trust in Him as your Saviour from sin through His precious blood, you are not ready for His coming. Should He come while you are in that state, you will be left on earth to go through the terrible times of suffering and affliction. But you can be ready. The day of grace is not over yet. He will receive you if you come to Him in faith believing.

Perchance, the reader is a saved individual. Are you ready for His coming? Is there anything between yourself and the Lord Jesus that would prevent communion with Him? Are you in the center of His will, living a life of constant yieldedness to the Holy Spirit?

THE BELIEVER AND HIS PHYSICAL BODY
IN THE FUTURE LIFE

Greek philosophy tried in vain to pierce the unseen world, both that of the present and the future. The Bible, since it is God's Word, does for the human race that which the philosophers of Athens were not able to do. It pierces into the future life, and tells us what the believer's physical body will be like at that time.

VII

The Believer and His Physical Body
in the Future Life

S ALVATION has in it, not only a provision for the standing of a
person before God's holy law, and a provision for his present
life on earth in relation to sin and righteousness, but it provides
for his physical body after death. The first provision we know as
justification, the act of God removing the guilt and penalty of sin
from the believing sinner, and bestowing a positive righteousness
in which the Christian stands uncondemned, guiltless, and righteous before God's law for time and eternity. This is a judicial
matter. The second provision is known as sanctification, the act
of God breaking the power of indwelling sin and implanting the
divine nature, also giving the believer the Holy Spirit as a permanent indweller, which act is followed by a continuous process
in which sin is eliminated from the life of the Christian and
righteousness produced in its place by the Holy Spirit, as the believer cooperates with Him in this work. The third provision is
glorification, the act of God transforming the physical body of the
believer for the eternity which is to come. Of this we wish to
speak now.

There are four changes which will take place in the physical
body of the believer. The first has to do with the activities of the
body and of the person who possesses it. In I Corinthians 15:44
Paul informs us that our present body as constituted, is a natural
body, and the future body, a spiritual one. The Greek word translated "natural" is *psuchikos*. The word is defined by Souter in
his lexicon as "the principle of life and the basis of its emotional
aspect, animating the present body of flesh, in contrast to the

higher life." Moulton and Milligan in their *Vocabulary of the Greek Testament* give the usage of the word in a secular document in the phrase, "My human *natural* powers." The noun *psuchē* (soul) is defined by them as "the seat of the feelings and desires." They give examples of its use in the following: "He also persisted in vexing my soul about his slave Antilla;" "while my soul is tempest-tossed;" "I exhort you, my lord, not to put grief into your soul and ruin your fortunes." It is used in a letter of a Christian in a phrase which reflects the trichotomy of I Thessalonians 5:23 in the words, "to our God and gracious Saviour and to His beloved Son, that they all may succour our body, soul, and spirit;" also in the clause, "who changed her mind, left the mill, and departed, persuaded by her father." From the above one can construct his own definition of the word *psuchē*. It is that part of man that knows, reasons, wills, desires, and feels. It refers to the will, the emotions, and the reason. Thus, a physical body that is a natural (*psuchikos*) body is one which is adapted to a life in which the activities of the will, the emotions, and the reason predominate in the sense that these occupy the larger part of the person's world, the things of time and place, the things of human life as it is lived on this earth.

But the body the believer will have after death is a spiritual body. The Greek word is *pneumatikos*. Thayer defines this word as "that part of man which is akin to God, and serves as His instrument or organ." It is that part of man which gives him God-consciousness. In this sense the animal creation does not have a *pneuma* or spirit. With the physical body, man has world-consciousness, with the soul he has self-consciousness, and with the spirit he has God-consciousness. With the spirit, man has to do with the things of God. He worships God by means of his human spirit, that is, when that spirit is energized by the Holy Spirit. He serves God in the same way. The present body is so constituted that it is the efficient organ of the soul. The future physical body will be so adjusted that it will be the efficient organ of the spirit. In this present life most of our time and activity has to do with the things of time and space, making a living, with the creative arts, with recreation, with the material world. The human spirit, however, should be the determining factor as to the character of the soul life. Yet it is in active use but a small part of the time, when we worship God, study the Bible, pray, serve God in some distinctive service in which we are giving out the Word of God to those who do not know Him. But in the future life, conditions will be changed. Then the soul-life as we know it now, will be a thing of the past. We will be occupied entirely with God and His worship and service. Our bodies will then be adjusted to the new life. They will be changed so that they will be efficient instruments of the human spirit. Just what the nature of this change will be, the Bible does not say.

The second change which takes place in the physical body, is that it will be an incorruptible one, and thus, an immortal one. Paul says: "This corruptible must put on incorruption, and this mortal, must put on immortality" (I Cor. 15:53). This present body has death in it, disease, decay. It becomes tired and exhausted. It may have deformities. Parts of it may have been taken away through an accident or operation. The future physical body will have no death in it, no weakness, deformity, disease. The parts that have been removed, will be restored. What a blessed state that will be, to have a body which can never die, in which there will be no indwelling sinful nature, which will never become weary or exhausted, in which there will never be any pain.

The third change will have to do with the composition of the body. Our present body is made of flesh, blood, and bones. Its life principle is in the blood. Moses knew this latter fact and stated it over 3000 years before medical science discovered it. He said in Leviticus 17:11, "The life of the flesh is in the blood." In our future physical body there will be a different life principle. The body will be devoid of blood, a body of flesh and bones. Paul in Philippians 3:21 speaks of the Lord Jesus "Who shall change our vile body, that it may be fashioned like unto His glorious body, according to the working whereby He is able to subdue all things unto Himself" (A. V.) An expanded translation here would give us the following: "Who shall change our humiliated body (that is, humiliated by the presence of sin and death), conforming it as to its outward expression to the body of His glory, according to the energy whereby He is able to marshall all things under Himself." Our future body will be like that which our Lord possesses now. He tells something about His present physical body in His words in Luke 24:39. He said, "Behold my hands and my feet, that I am I myself. Handle me with a view to investigation and see; because a spirit does not have flesh and bones as you with critical, understanding sight see that I have."

Those words tell us some interesting things about our Lord's body. There were the marks of the nails of the crucifixion still in His hands and feet, left there, even though His resurrection body was perfect, for purposes of identification. The body our Lord had after His resurrection, was the same body He had previous to the Cross, and in which He died. We will possess the same body in the future life which we have now, except changed. Since that is true, we will have the same facial expression, however, with all the sin-wrinkles ironed out. Since that is true, we will know each other in the future life.

Second, our Lord's body was a solid, physical body. The disciples handled His body with their hands, depending upon what their sense of touch would tell them as to its reality and composition. John says in his first epistle, "That which we handled with a view to investigation" (1:1). He uses the same Greek word Luke uses to report our Lord's words. It was therefore a body that would respond to the sense of touch, a body made of solid material. Our bodies will be like that.

Third, it was a body made up of flesh and bones, but changed in composition. Our future bodies will be made of flesh and bones, the same flesh and bones we have now, but changed as to composition.

Fourth, it was a body without blood. If our Lord's resurrection body had had blood, He would have mentioned that fact when He spoke of flesh and bones. His precious blood had all run out from a heart pierced by the spear of the Roman soldier. It paid the penalty for your sins and mine. Peter tells us we Christians were redeemed with the precious blood of Christ. Since our Lord's resurrection body did not have any blood in it, it must have had a new life principle animating it. Our future bodies will have a new life principle in them.

Fifth, our Lord in His physical body of flesh and bones went through the stone wall of the building in which the disciples were meeting. The doors of the room were closed. We will be capable of the same thing also. He had new powers of locomotion. He could make Himself visible or invisible at will. He was here one minute and in another place, the next. So will it be with us in the future life.

Finally, our Lord's resurrection body needed no clothing for a covering, but had a covering which was produced from within. Our Lord's body after the resurrection was not covered with clothing. The only clothes He had at the time of His death, were taken away from Him. His grave clothes He left in the sepulchre of Joseph. He emerged through the stone walls of the resurrection tomb clad in a new covering for His body that was produced from within. All this is given us in the Greek word Paul uses in the above scripture, translated "fashioned." It is the word *morphē*, which refers to an outward expression which is not put on from without, but one that comes from within and which is a true representative of one's inner nature. This, in the case of our Lord, was a glory covering, an enswathement of glory which covered His resurrection body. On the Mount of Transfiguration, our Lord's face and clothing shone with a radiance that came from within. A radiance similar to this, was the covering of His body after the resurrection.

It has always been God's plan for His creatures to cover themselves with a covering produced from within. Adam and Eve covered their bodies with an enswathement of glory which was produced from within their beings. When they sinned, they lost the power to produce such a covering from within. To cover their naked bodies which now had sin and death in them, they made clothing for themselves. Birds cover themselves with beautiful plumage which is produced from within. Animals cover themselves with fur which is produced from within. Thus, in the life to come, believers will cover their bodies with an enswathement of glory, a light covering, which will be produced from within.

Now, to gather together our information regarding the future body of the believer. It will be a body adapted to a spiritual life in which all one's time and activity have to do with God, His worship and service. It will be a body which will be incorruptible and immortal. It will be a body of flesh and bones, but no blood. This body will have a new life principle animating it. It will be a body, the covering of which will be produced from within.